Becoming a Public Relations Writer

Becoming a Public Relations Writer

A Writing Process Workbook for the Profession

Third Edition

Ronald D. Smith

 Routledge
Taylor & Francis Group

NEW YORK AND LONDON

First edition published 1995 by HarperCollins
Second edition published 2003 by Lawrence Erlbaum Associates

This edition published 2008
by Routledge
270 Madison Ave, New York, NY 10016

Simultaneously published in the UK
by Routledge
2 Park Square, Milton Park, Abingdon, Oxon OX14 4RN

Routledge is an imprint of the Taylor & Francis Group, an informa business

Typeset in Abode Caslon and Times New Roman by
Florence Production Ltd, Stoodleigh, Devon
Printed and bound in the United States of America on acid-free paper by
Sheridan Books, Inc., MI

Library of Congress Cataloging in Publication Data
Smith, Ronald D., 1948–
    Becoming a public relations writer: a writing process workbook for
    the profession/by Ronald D. Smith. – 3rd ed.
        p.cm.
    Includes bibliographical references and index.
    1. Public relations.   2. Public relations – Authorship.   3. Publicity.
    I. Title.
HM1221.S768 2007
659.2–dc22   2007021602

ISBN10: 0–8058–6301–X (pbk)
ISBN10: 1–4106–1761–0 (ebk)

ISBN13: 978–0–8058–6301–7 (pbk)
ISBN13: 978–1–4106–1761–3 (ebk)

Brief Contents

Contents

Preface

Note to the Student

The one skill that employers consistently say they seek among candidates for public relations positions is an ability to write well. Other skills are important; good writing is crucial. If you develop your writing abilities now, you can look confidently toward a bright professional future.

Becoming a Public Relations Writer can help you develop that writing skill. As a student in a public relations class, your progress toward becoming an effective professional writer rests on four pillars: yourself, your classmates, your instructor and this book.

Your Role. As the student, you are expected to put forth your best efforts in this class. Work hard and open yourself to advice and constructive criticism. You will need to face head-on the challenges that this program of study will offer you.

Your Classmates. No student is alone in this learning process. You are part of a team, and your classmates will be learning along with you. They also will share their ideas about writing in general and about your writing in particular. They will expect you to share your honest thoughts and advice about their writing as well.

Your Instructor. Every team needs a coach, and that is a major role your instructor will play. Your instructor will get you started and give you feedback and correction. You will get help when you need it and receive praise when it is due. Don't expect your instructor to have all the answers. For some questions there may be no single right answer. Rather, look to your instructor as someone who has traveled this road before you, someone who can share the benefit of personal experience as a writer and who can help you draw on your own experience and insight as you seek to develop as a professional writer.

This Book. "Becoming a Public Relations Writer" has been written to help guide you through the writing process. It will lead you through the various steps and stages of writing and will help you explore many formats and styles necessary to public relations writers. Because this book grows out of the author's professional and teaching experience, it is limited to the insight of one person. Your own experiences and those of your instructor and colleagues are likely to add to the conclusions and the advice offered here.

There may be times when your instructor will disagree with something in this book. So, too, there probably will be times when future employers and colleagues also disagree with this book, and with each other, with your instructor, and probably with you. Celebrate this intellectual diversity. Revel in the flexibility that is part of the art of public relations. Your chosen profession is rich with nuance and alive to various interpretations.

Note to the Instructor

Becoming a Public Relations Writer is based on a process approach to writing, which builds into the class a significant interaction between the student and the instructor as well as among the students. With this in mind, the book presumes and encourages an interactive environment, and it has been written to make use of several course-related activities. The following activities are likely to be part of your experience as you use this book:

Classroom Writing. Because information necessary for students has been included in the book, the instructor can focus a majority of in-class time on practice writing rather than lecturing about writing. Each chapter has exercises designed to provide a basis for these in-class activities. On some occasions, students may write in the presence of the instructor, who provides direction and feedback. At other times, students may use class time for rewriting, an integral part of the writing process. In-class writing is meant to be critiqued but not necessarily graded.

Homework Assignments. Each chapter includes exercises that provide the basis for out-of-class writing assignments. When they receive homework assignments, students should leave the classroom knowing what needs to be done, perhaps having discussed in general terms how they will approach the assignment. An effective learning situation is to invite students, upon turning in these assignments, to discuss their experiences with the assignment, especially what worked and what didn't work. It has been my experience that this provides an opportunity to reinforce and/or clarify the concepts important to the assignment. Throughout the interactive classroom environment, students should be encouraged to share problems, successes and insights with their instructor and their classmates.

Discussion Topics. Many exercises in this book are designed for an interactive learning approach built on discussion among students who help each other develop their writing skills. Each chapter has certain exercises that call for students to gather their thoughts in freewriting and then to discuss particular topics. Such procedures are designed to encourage participation, foster shared learning, and build levels of trust that will support student writing groups. I have found that this is time well spent in the learning process.

Writing Models. This book provides models and samples of various kinds of public relations writing so students can see in them patterns and guides. These models are not meant to be copied but rather to stimulate ideas for students' own writing. Some of these models use actual and hypothetical scenarios developed by the author; others are provided by public relations practitioners using examples of their professional writing. Students also are encouraged to share with each other samples of their writing. Instructors may find it useful to share some of their own writing with students. Regardless of the source, these models should be considered helpful samples rather than perfect examples.

Writing Conferences. Ideally, this course will include one-on-one writing conferences between the student and the instructor. Such conferences can provide an opportunity for students to evaluate their own progress and to discuss their strengths and limitations about writing. Conferences also offer an occasion for seeking and giving advice about making the writing process easier and better.

Writing Groups. As students move from the introductory materials into writing projects based on various formats used in public relations writing, they are encouraged to participate in out-of-class writing groups with other students in the class. Such groups provide opportunities for students to share advice, learn from each other, and sharpen their editing and critiquing skills. They also provide a valuable support to each student moving through the coursework.

Acknowledgements

John Donne was right that no one is an island. Neither does an author write alone, but instead reflects in some way the insight of others in the field who write, teach and engage in the practice.

Becoming a Public Relations Writer enjoys the input of many people. As the author of this textbook, I take personal responsibility for any errors or omissions, but I'm confident that these are fewer because of the advice and assistance of many knowledgeable people who helped with this book.

Collectively, my students have been major contributors to this book. It is in the classroom that I have tested and refined the ideas contained herein. My students have prodded me to articulate my ideas and to bolster them with plenty of real-world examples.

My academic colleagues at Buffalo State emphasize practical, applied communication, and I have benefited from ongoing professional conversations with them. My colleagues within the public Relations Society of America have consistently helped me with their insight and constructive criticism.

My publishing team at Routledge/Taylor & Francis (formerly Lawrence Erlbaum Associates) has been helpful and supportive through the progress of this third edition. In particular my editor, Linda Bathgate, has piloted this craft through the publishing waters.

Authors appreciate the comments and criticism of their peers, and I am particularly grateful to the faculty across the country who have taken time from their busy teaching schedules to review this book and offer comments and suggestions.

Personal Dedication

Like the entirety of my life, this book is dedicated to my family. Though they don't realize it, my three sons have been an inspiration as I worked on this book. We would sometimes sit across the desk from each other, me working at my computer, one of them at theirs.

As he progressed through college and now into his doctoral studies at the University of Osaka, my son Josh has challenged me to explain public relations every time I suggested that he consider the insights of the discipline on his own work as a sociologist studying and participating in Japanese culture. My son Aaron graduated with a degree in public relations and is now starting his own career in the field, where he is putting to good use his excellent writing skills and his keen strategic sense. My youngest son Matt is still uncertain about his career plans, but I'm confident that his writing talent and artistic sensitivity will serve him well in whatever he does.

My greatest appreciation goes to my wife, Dawn Minier Smith. During the evolution of this book from conception to this third edition, Dawn has been my sounding board. A writing teacher herself, she has lent her ear as I tested ideas, tried out new ways to present lessons, and attempted to make sense of theories, cases and observations. Since she doesn't see any domestic value in a wife fawning over her husband, Dawn's constructive criticism has been always trustworthy and thus most valuable. I always take her suggestions seriously. Sometimes I've even had the good sense to follow them.

An Invitation

This book is the result of much dialogue with others, particularly feedback from my students. But reader reaction is inevitably useful. I invite all readers—students, teachers and practitioners—to share your thoughts with me. Send your comments and suggestions for future editions. Share your success stories and your frustrations with this book. I also invite you to use my Web site, where I have included an expanding number of pages and links related to public relations and other aspects of strategic communication.

Ron Smith
smithrd@buffalostate.edu
faculty.buffalostate.edu/smithrd

About the Author

Ronald D. Smith, APR, is a professor of public communication at Buffalo State College, the largest college within the State University of New York. He is also chair of the 530-student Communication Department and project director for the American Indian Policy and Media Initiative.

During his 18 years as an educator, Smith has taught public relations planning, writing, research, and related classes to undergraduate and graduate students. In this book, he also draws on considerable professional experience, including 10 years as a public relations director and eight years as a newspaper reporter and editor. He has also been a Navy journalist, as well as a consultant in public relations and strategic communications, assisting businesses and nonprofit organizations with planning, research, communication management and media training.

Smith holds a bachelor's degree in English education from Lock Haven (Pa.) State College, now Lock Haven University, and a master's degree in public relations from Syracuse University.

In addition to this textbook, he is the author of *Strategic Planning for Public Relations* (2nd edition 2005, Erlbaum) and co-author of *MediaWriting* (3rd edition in press, Routledge/Taylor & Francis). He also is author of *Introduction to Language and Communication: A Primer on Human and Media Communication* (2004 for the United Arab Emirates University) and co-editor of *Shoot the Indian: Media, Misperception and Native Truth* (2007, American Indian Policy and Media Initiative). He has been lead researcher in several studies focusing on media and American Indians.

Smith is an accredited member of the Public Relations Society of America and has served as president of PRSA's Buffalo/Niagara chapter and chair of the Northeast District. The Buffalo chapter has honored him as "Practitioner of the Year" and with several other awards and citations.

PRINCIPLES OF EFFECTIVE WRITING

You already are a writer! The issue before you now is: Do you want to become a public relations writer? Do you want to build skills to help you succeed in your career? With this book and a fair amount of work, you can succeed. Repeat that thought: *You can become a public relations writer!* You'll probably even find yourself carried to a higher level of enjoyment with your writing. As Desiderius Erasmus, the Dutch Renaissance-era scholar, observed: "The desire to write grows with writing." So sharpen your writing talents and begin what can be a pleasurable journey toward becoming a public relations writer.

Part 1 of this book deals with the basics of writing in professional contacts. It begins with an exploration of your attitudes toward writing and follows with a refresher course of writing principles. It also features an overview of communication theory and a methodical look at some practices basic to all kinds of public relations writing. Part 1 includes four chapters:

- Chapter 1: Writing . . . And What It Means to You
- Chapter 2: Effective Writing
- Chapter 3: Persuasive Communication
- Chapter 4: The Writing Process.

1

Writing . . . and What It Means to You

Writing. Textbooks list it as the most important professional skill for public relations practitioners. Employers complain that job candidates can't do it adequately. Teachers fret that today's students don't do it as well as their predecessors. And in moments of candor, most students admit they are unsure about it.

Throughout your academic career, you have been faced with a lot of ideas about writing. Perhaps you have become aware of some mixed messages. If you have, that's good, because there certainly are a lot of different thoughts about writing—what it is, how we learn to write well, how we can use writing personally and professionally, and whether we are any good at it.

This chapter will help you begin to sort through what you have learned about writing and what you have experienced through writing. It will help you identify your own relationship with writing. We'll start with a section on freewriting, then look at the creative and functional aspects of writing, and end with a discussion of how to become a better writer and your personal commitment to this outcome. Here are your objectives for Chapter 1:

- To learn and use the technique of freewriting
- To understand the relationship between creative and functional writing
- To explain the concept of writing to influence
- To learn that writers generally develop a process of drafting and revising
- To make a commitment about your expectations for this course

Freewriting

Before we proceed, you need to learn a writing technique that you will be using a lot in this program—freewriting. As prescriptions for better writing go, this one is pretty painless when taken in moderation. *Freewriting* is a kind of stream-of-consciousness writing without stopping and without self-editing for a period of time to get initial thoughts on paper. It is a simple and effective procedure that can help you in several ways:

- Getting started when you're not quite sure where you're going
- Organizing your thoughts
- Preparing to write more formally or to go public with your writing
- Overcoming writer's block.

How do you freewrite? Take pen in hand or hand to keyboard. Simply start writing. Keep writing for a period of time; five minutes is a good length. Much longer and freewriting becomes drafting, and then you're not freewriting anymore.

The method is simple: Force yourself to keep writing throughout the five minutes. Don't pause to ponder. Don't edit. Don't correct spelling or grammatical errors. Freewriting is very informal, and it's usually not meant for anyone else to read. Rather, it can serve as a very rough first draft. Here is one of the author's freewrites that helped set the stage for this chapter:

> Begin by talking about the fun of writing, and the fear. I can do it. That's what the reader should take home. How to get to that point? Probably by talking about ideas like why to write, how to get in the mood, what writing can accomplish. Things like purpose. Motivation. Fun. Challenge. Motivation is a major goal of the opening chapter. Too often we think we can't when really we could if only we know how. It's just a matter of learning something new, or a better way of doing it. I want my students to begin this course with the thought, the belief, that they can become better writers. Through it all, a course like this should be fun. Challenging, but fun too.

What do you think about writing? Like so much about the art of writing, this question has no right or wrong answers. Merely by considering the question you can begin to arrive at your own conclusions. Or perhaps you can simply become more comfortable in your ambiguity. But, as you consider your own perspectives on writing, you already are in the process of becoming a better writer.

Chinese philosopher Xi Zhi urged his students to practice self-examination every day: "If you find faults, correct them. When you find none, try even harder." Good advice! As you seek to become a better writer, take time to poke around the wrinkles of your mind. Probe your attitudes about writing. Consider your comfort level as a wordsmith. Think about what you think about writing, especially your own writing. Have you been told, for example, that you are a good writer? If so, has the affirmation come from somebody who knows what he or she is talking about? On the other hand, do you think of yourself as an inadequate writer? It's unlikely that strangers on the streets or little children in the park have pointed this out to you, so where did you get the notion? And what have you done to dismiss it as the exaggeration of a self-conscious ego, or perhaps to embrace it as a worthy opponent to be bested.

Exercise 1.1—Freewriting on Writing

 Part 1: Freewrite for five minutes on the following topic: *What do you think of writing? Do you like to write? Do you find it easy? Do you write just for the fun of it, or only when you have to? Do you think you are a good writer? Why do you want to improve as a writer? How might you improve?*

Part 2: Take a few minutes to review what you wrote in Part 1. Go back and underline what you think is the most important or most insightful sentence or phrase. Discuss this with other students in your class.

Writing: Creative or Functional?

Self-examination is the first step toward excellence. You already have begun to become a better writer just by completing the first exercise. Now let's tighten the margins a bit and look at two relationships within writing that are important to us as public relations writers: creative writing and functional writing.

Sometimes, students in public relations writing classes say they like creative writing but are unsure of themselves with the functional writing they expect to find in public relations. That's understandable. The formats we use for various public relations purposes—news releases, organizational reports and proposals, persuasive appeals and so on—often have a number of "rules" to follow. It can feel like a paint-by-numbers approach to writing. Where's the creativity? Where's the fun? At what point does skill become talent?

Exercise 1.2—Considering Creative and Functional Writing

Part 1: Look up the following words in your dictionary and note their similarities and differences: creative, artistic, artful, imaginative, innovative and aesthetic. Now do the same with another set of words: purpose, intention, function, rationale and objective.

Part 2: Freewrite for five minutes on the following topic: *How do creative and functional writing compare? How do these definitions come together to describe writing?* Discuss this with your classmates. ■

Creative Writing

All writing is creative and artistic. *Creative writing* emphasizes imaginative, artistic and sometimes innovative style. It is the result of one mind creating an idea and sharing it with someone else. The idea may take various forms—a science fiction adventure, a carefully researched historical novel, lyrical poetry, a corporate report, an informative news release, a compelling sales letter, and so on. Writing is creative when we use it to shape a thought—molding it, wrapping it in a particular writing format, and ultimately sharing it with another person.

Creative writing is not solely a product of the imagination, although it may begin there. But it could just as well begin in an interview or through skillful research. What fills writing with creativity is the insight and ownership a writer brings to the ideas and facts. A public relations writer will adopt the task at hand and, however fleetingly, will possess the ideas and thoughts surrounding the writing project. A good writer will caress a thought, coupling facts and ideas, giving birth to vignettes and parables, gaining insight and making observations.

All this to promote a supermarket opening? Ah, but that's where the art takes shape, as the writer weaves words and phrases, facts and ideas, putting them before the reader in a way that serves the original purpose. We write creatively when we take a thought, wherever it originated, and artfully share it with others.

Functional Writing

Functional writing is an approach to writing that emphasizes purpose, format and objective. It is writing that is trying to accomplish a mission. Think about this: We always write for some reason. We hope to accomplish something through our words, so we write with purpose—more often, with several purposes.

Recall the last writing assignment you completed for a class. What was your purpose in writing it? To satisfy your will to do the best work possible? To show your professor that you understand the subject matter? To get a good grade? To make your professor happy? To simply have something, anything, to turn in? These are all reasons for writing. Now consider: What was the purpose behind the last business letter you wrote? How about the last job application? Or the last e-mail home? You wrote each for a reason, too. Think about what you already know about the following purposes of any type of writing:

- To describe someone or something
- To explain or justify
- To provide information
- To express an opinion
- To persuade toward some feeling or action
- To entertain
- To inspire or motivate
- To express our inner thoughts.

F. Scott Fitzgerald reminded us about such purposeful writing: "You don't write because you want to say something, you write because you have something to say." The thought pre-exists, giving rise to the act of writing.

A novel may be written to entertain or to present a point of view. Or maybe it's written simply to sell a lot of copies and make a bundle of money for the author. Consider poetry. Its purpose may be to enlighten the mind of the reader, or enrage one to action or inspire the soul. Maybe it's simply a means for self-expression, or part of an elaborate seduction scheme aimed at your new boyfriend or girlfriend.

Likewise there is purpose and reason behind every kind of writing—short story, rap lyrics, parable, love letter, Web page, greeting card, prayer, essay, feature story, research report . . . and public relations writing. The purpose may be profound or practical, but it's your reason for writing.

In the profession of public relations, we find use for virtually every writing purpose (except, perhaps, self-expression). We write news releases to inform external audiences and newsletters to share information with internal ones. We write brochures to explain our products and services. We write letters and guest editorials to express opinions, and public service advertisements to persuade. We prepare scripts for speeches and television programs that we hope will influence our audiences, and we create Web pages to educate and motivate. These are just some of the purposes and some of the formats a public relations writer will use to communicate effectively.

Creativity and Functionality

In Exercise 1.2 you were asked to consider the relationship between creative and functional writing. Reconsider what you wrote there in light of this observation: Creativity and functionality *can* coexist in your writing.

You may not have considered this idea before. Instead of either/or, think both/and. You don't have to put writing into boxes—one labeled "creative writing," the other marked "functional writing." Writing actually can be both. It is more like a seesaw, one side balancing toward functional writing, the other pointing more toward the creative side. Both aspects of writing complement each other. It is a matter of looking at the balance between the two. Let's combine creativity and functionality in writing under the heading "Writing to influence." That's what public relations writing is all about.

Writing to Influence

Because there are so many different formats for public relations writing, it's useful to categorize them into different types. A common division is to group public relations writing as being either informational or persuasive. Each is said to have certain formats. For example, news releases and brochures are usually seen as formats for informational writing, while speeches and public service advertising are said to be formats for persuasive writing.

That's a neat distinction in some ways. It helps us understand that there are various writing formats and that their differences influence how and when they can be used. But there is a problem with such a distinction because it's an oversimplification. All public relations writing is an attempt to influence people in some way. If you aren't trying to make an impact on your readers, why write? Without intending to affect readers in some way, you're just wasting time.

So let's look for a more unified perspective. As a writer, you have a particular effect in mind when you write. You want to increase your public's knowledge and understanding about something, you want them to feel a certain way about this information, and you probably want them to respond to that information in a particular way.

In some journalism-oriented formats such as news releases, information is presented in an objective manner. But the writer can still attempt to persuade, using techniques such as persuasive message sources and appeals. On the other hand, some public relations writing is meant to enhance relationships and to communicate between an organization and its public in a quest for mutual benefits. Here too, however, the writer is trying to influence readers, seeking at least to motivate and empower them in their efforts to strengthen the relationship.

Exercise 1.3—Defining Public Relations

Background: Many people are confused about the meaning of public relations, and no uniform definition exists even among public relations practitioners. Also, some people are critical of what they presume public relations to be about. Nevertheless, some commonly held characteristics of public relations include two-way communication, research and strategic planning, accuracy and honesty, effective and ethical behavior, and mutual benefits for both an organization and its publics.

Scenario: A relative whom you respect is trying to dissuade you from entering public relations. This person says public relations practitioners are manipulators who rely on half-truths and hype on behalf of unworthy clients.

Part 1: Write a short letter to this relative, telling him or her what public relations means to you. Address this person's lack of support for your intended profession.

Part 2: After writing this letter, review your freewrite from Exercise 1.2 about creative and functional writing. Then, with this in mind, freewrite on the following topic: *How is my letter an attempt to provide information, and how is it an attempt to persuade the reader?* Discuss this with your classmates.

Becoming a Better Writer

Some college students have no problem with self-confidence. They often think they are better writers than they really are: "But I always got good grades in writing." If you are such a student, you may be troubled when your public relations instructor requires you to conform to higher writing standards than you are used to. You may find it difficult to make a transition from an anything-goes freewriting style into the type of logical, focused writing needed in most forms of public relations writing.

On the other hand, too many students express discomfort and lack of confidence with their writing abilities, often because they don't know if their writing is good or not. As a student, two factors work against your feeling good about yourself as a writer. For one thing, in your educational career you have been in class for thousands of days, tens of thousands of hours. You may have had someone telling you that your writing needs to be corrected . . . and here's how. You may have been told, try again, do it over. After a while, the message comes through: Your writing always needs to be improved, and you can't fix it by yourself.

In either scenario, the fact may be that perhaps you aren't an accomplished writer—yet. But in this course, you can change that. How?

- By having plenty of opportunities to break bad writing habits and build better ones
- By learning and applying the elements of good public relations writing
- By gaining some criteria for evaluating your own writing. Then you won't have to guess if it's good writing or not. You'll know when it is. You'll also know when it isn't, so you can fix it.

An Acquired Talent

Speaking is natural communication. Writing isn't. People are born with a natural ability and inclination to speak, but no one is born with a special ability to write well. Writing is a learned skill. In our society, we begin learning to write early in life and continue to develop as writers throughout our lifetimes.

Learning to write is a lot like learning to play the saxophone, cultivating a strong backhand for tennis, or becoming a good dancer. A dancer, for example, must have an element of natural talent, but that talent improves with practice. Not just casual or occasional practice, but intensive, conscious and passionate practice. That's why prima ballerinas go to class every morning to fine-tune their skills. Similarly, that's why world-class athletes spend hours every day in exercise, muscle training and nutritional eating. Excellence doesn't come cheaply, and quality is built not on dreams but on persistent effort.

When you learn to write, you need the ingredients:

- A bit of ability
- A good teacher and writing coach
- A sense of order and beauty
- Respect for precision and innovation
- Confidence
- Another dose of confidence.

Then you need the recipe for writing:

- Practice
- Practice
- And a bit more practice.

Encouragement for such consistency came from Publilius Syrus, a writer, philosopher and slave in classical Rome: "Practice is the best of all instructors." Twenty centuries later, Thomas Wolfe similarly suggested: "Write every day." Previous students in public relations writing classes have given similar advice: "The more you write, the better your writing becomes."

Critical Observation

When you read, do you ever stop and think, "Wow! I like the way the writer said that!" If you really want to become a better writer, train yourself to be a more critical observer of other people's writing. Take note of how a writer has used the language, how words and phrases have been woven together.

But remember that effective writing is a continuing process of writing and rewriting. As a reader who wants to write, you may have a significant disadvantage. Your entire background in reading has exposed you mainly to the finished work of other writers. From the stories of J.K. Rowling to Henry David Thoreau and Mark Twain, from the Bill of Rights to Sports Illustrated—you have seen mainly completed pieces of writing. Too bad, because you've been missing a lot of good stuff.

The acclaimed novelist Ernest Hemingway was characteristically blunt: "The first draft of anything is shit." Supreme Court Justice Louis Brandeis said it more elegantly: "There is no great writing, only great rewriting."

When we see only the final writing, we focus on the talent of the authors. We use words like "gifted" and "genius" to describe them. But finished products don't allow us to see the so-called great writers as wordsmiths, as technicians who have fashioned their works of art one word at a time. The playwright and novelist Oscar Wilde gave this wonderful anecdote into the attention that writers give to their use of language: "I was working on the proof of one of my poems all morning, and took out a comma. In the afternoon I put it back in."

Distinguished literature and powerful rhetoric seldom came by inspiration, delivered as a finished package. Rather, the great writers crafted their words with care, often with patience and fortitude.

What might you find if you compared the various drafts of the Gettysburg Address with its final version? You would find, for example, that the first version had one sentence of 82 words, with several grammatical errors. Abraham Lincoln revised his text through six versions. He changed some phrases. "It is rather for us, the living, to stand here" evolved into "It is for us the living, rather, to be dedicated here to the unfinished work which they who fought here have thus far so nobly advanced." Far more eloquent phrasing. Lincoln also added some phrases, most notably "under God" in his draft phrase ". . . that this nation under God shall have a new birth of freedom."

Do you think you could learn something about Hemingway by seeing what he added or deleted as he completed the final manuscript for *A Farewell to Arms*? Would it be interesting to compare the script revisions of reruns of "The Simpsons" or your favorite episodes of "The O.C."? You might take comfort in knowing that some successful writers have been less than proficient about the mechanics of writing. Presidents have speechwriters; corporate officers have assistants who help shape their writing.

Even respected literary figures get help sometimes. Theodore Dreiser, who is ranked among the best American novelists, reportedly had several rewriters who polished and smoothed out his prose. F. Scott Fitzgerald is said to have been such a dreadful speller that his writing bordered on illiteracy. But he had supportive editors, and Fitzgerald has come to be regarded as one of the great novelists of the Jazz Age of American literature.

In public relations, plan on producing several drafts of any piece of writing. You will find that each version gets better. Each becomes more effective for your purposes, until eventually you are satisfied that you have produced the best piece of writing you can (within limitations of time and resources, of course). This book will help you develop your written communication skills, strengthening what works and perhaps finding something that can work even better.

Throughout this book you will find many opportunities to develop your writing talents. Sometimes you will be given samples of writing at various stages of development. You may share preliminary versions with classmates, and you may make suggestions on how other students might improve their writing. You might also ask to see examples of how your instructor writes in various versions. You can gain confidence and competence in seeing how other writers work over the words to create a more perfect piece of writing.

Do you think you can convince anyone that writing is an art to be learned? A skill to be cultivated? Even more important, are you convinced yourself? Your answer is crucial to your success in this course. You've got to be convinced, beyond a reasonable doubt, of two things. One, that writing can be learned. Two, that *you* can learn to be a better writer. Give some thought to this as you work on the following exercise.

Exercise 1.4—Committing to Becoming a Better Writer

 Type a letter of commitment to your instructor. In this letter, express your goals for this course and affirm your confidence that you can make progress toward becoming a better writer. This letter should be about a page long.   ■

Making an Ongoing Commitment

To become more effective in your writing, you must be in it for the long haul. Good writing requires consistent effort. The following two exercises are continuing projects that will last through the entire semester or academic term. Both are designed to help you build a stronger habit of frequent writing. Select one as an extended assignment.

Exercise 1.5—Creating a Writing Journal

Too many people don't write unless they have to for school or work, and that lack of involvement with writing shows. This exercise gives you a lot of freedom, so have fun with your writing. Develop it as a leisure-time activity and become a better writer in the process.

Turn in to your instructor two pages each week on any topic and in any writing format that interests you. Your writing does not have to be related to the formats explored in this class. Rather, use this assignment to expand your writing horizons by picking topics and formats unrelated to any class you are taking this term. Here are some ideas for writing topics:

* Write a letter to a cousin you haven't seen in awhile, or to your grandmother
* Write a poem or song lyrics
* Set out your thoughts on politics, religion, or the state of affairs in the world
* Write a new ending for an episode of your favorite television show
* Review a book you recently read, or a concert you attended
* Reminisce about a place you once visited, or speculate about where you'd like to visit
* Write about a sports figure, entertainer or politician
* Discuss your hopes and dreams for the future or your problems of the present
* Meditate on the eternal agony in the fires of hell, which await the girl or guy who dumped you
* Write dirty limericks if you want to . . . just write! ■

Exercise 1.6—Developing a Journal of Professional Observations

In this exercise, you will begin to develop a critical eye into your intended profession. Test your insights in new areas; let your curiosity lead you to poke around previously unexplored nooks and crannies. Have fun with this assignment as you ponder the public relations aspects of all that you encounter. You'll be surprised how useful public relations is in making sense out of life around you. You'll also be surprised how the habit of keeping a professional journal can enhance your writing skills.

Write two pages each week about your observations of public relations activities in everyday life. Situations pregnant in public relations possibilities are all around you—a government official handling criticism, a charity raising money, a company fighting a corporate takeover, a Little League team seeking a sponsor, a sorority dealing with pledges, your boss handling new employees, a military spokesperson fielding press inquiries, a TupperWare hostess holding a party.

Your observations may come from books or periodicals, news media, events with which you are familiar, or situations in which you are personally involved. Your writing will be evaluated on the basis of insight into public relations thought and practice, cohesive and logical organization, creative thinking and problem solving, and of course, effective writing. ■

2

Effective Writing

Too often, people write under the false belief that fancy words and long sentences are impressive. In reality, this doesn't impress most people. It is harder to read, and less likely to be understood and remembered. Rather than trying to impress readers with fancy writing, public relations practitioners should attempt to make an impression on readers with the quality of their writing.

Aim for simple sentences, but remember that simple sentences do not have to be simplistic. Even the most lofty and complex ideas can be expressed using simple, everyday language. The goal is to make your writing accessible to your readers. This chapter will serve as a reminder of many rules and guidelines you previously have learned about how to make your writing more effective. Its suggestions and guidelines provide a foundation for all kinds of writing: organizational publications, releases for print and broadcast media, scripts for speeches, and text for Web sites, e-mail and other computer-based communication tools.

This chapter is subdivided into four sections: standard usage, simple language, meaningful language, and inclusive language. Here are your objectives for Chapter 2:

- To effectively use standard conventions of the English language
- To construct simple and understandable messages
- To enhance the meaning your words convey
- To use language ethically
- To avoid biased language.

Standard Usage

The aim of public relations writing is to communicate clearly with your target publics. A basic ingredient in clear communication is correct use of language. This section outlines some of the standard approaches to *syntax*—the part of grammar that deals with the orderly arrangement of words into sentences. Syntax is what makes a sentence make sense.

Exercise 2.1—Knowing the Rules of Standard English

 Freewrite on the following topic: *What does it matter if I follow the "rules" of standard English?* Discuss this with your classmates. ∎

Usage Tip 1: Rules and Guidelines

The ultimate rule of public relations writing is to write so the reader can understand. How can you do this? By following the standard and ordinary guidelines of language use, including the basic rules of good grammar, word choice and common spelling. Using proper English doesn't mean making your writing stilted or stale. Occasionally, writers are tempted to bend a rule of grammar in order to maintain the higher rule of understanding. A lofty goal, perhaps, but such bending should be done only with understanding and careful consideration, never out of ignorance of the rules. It is better simply to revise the offending passage so that it is both understandable and correct.

As a student, begin now to build up your writing resources. First, get an up-to-date dictionary; the Associated Press recommends two that are commonly used by reporters: Webster's New World College Dictionary and, for more complete information, Webster's Third New International Dictionary of the English Language. Buy a copy of The New Roget's Thesaurus and Merriam-Webster's Dictionary of Synonyms, and adopt a good contemporary grammar reference book such as the Prentice-Hall Handbook for Writers, Stunk and White's The Elements of Style, or Kessler and McDonald's When Words Collide. Also, have access to a current edition of The World Almanac and Book of Facts. Once you have accumulated this mini library, use these resources often.

Correct English requires accurate spelling. There really is little choice here. Poor spelling signals a writer who isn't careful, and that will throw suspicion on the accuracy of everything you write. William Shakespeare sometimes used different spellings for the same word. He even spelled his own name three different ways. But times have changed, and anyhow—you're not Shakespeare. Stick with the appropriate spelling. That's where a stylebook and a dictionary can help. If the dictionary lists two acceptable spellings, check the stylebook; one of the alternatives is likely preferred.

Another important practical detail of effective writing is consistency. The news media have adopted certain standards of language usage to provide consistency of style, particularly for writing. Public relations writers should be familiar with these stylebooks. It is helpful to adopt one and incorporate it into all of your writing. The Associated Press Stylebook is by far the most commonly used guide in the United States. Reuters Stylebook is often used in Canada and other English-speaking nations. Individual newspapers and magazines often have their own, usually based on the AP Stylebook.

Appendix A of this book, "Common Sense Stylebook for Public Relations Writers," provides the basics of writing style generally consistent with the Associated Press. It is useful with external materials such as news releases and other writing for newspapers, magazines and the electronic media. This stylebook also provides some variations for a house style that can be appropriate for organizational media such as Web sites, newsletters and other publications, as well as style adjustments for broadcast media.

Usage Tip 2: Grammatical Myths

Myths and legends about the proper use of English abound. *Shall* or *will*? *Who* or *whom*? *That* or *which*? Certainly you need to pay attention to rules, and there is no place in public relations for sloppy writing. But be aware that some rules are changing. Some rules weren't really rules at all, just denizens of a grammatical netherworld. Here are some of the most common:

- Sentence fragments have a purpose and a right to exist. Sometimes. Especially in speeches and broadcast scripts.
- *Shall* is close to being listed as an archaic future form of the verb *to be*, as its older brother *shalt* already is. Not many people use the word precisely. Besides, for some people the word carries negative connotations from grade school, writing "I shall not bite the teacher" (100 times). And don't even think of using its negative contraction, *shan't*.
- Sometimes infinitives (the word *to* plus a verb) can be split. Occasionally they need to be. It would be difficult to improve on Star Trek's "to boldly go" where no one had gone before. For 600 years English writers have been putting adverbs within an infinitive, precisely to call particular attention to the adverb. So split away, as long as you want to intentionally emphasize the adverb.
- Not all sentences need a stated subject before the verb. Understood? Of course.
- Some purisms such as *agendum*, *stadia* and *referenda* are falling into disuse. Others such as *datum* cause confusion and occasional fights. Your public relations writing is no place to show off arcane linguistic knowledge.
- Sentences can end in a preposition. Occasionally, it's something we have to put up with.
- A double negative may not work well in mathematics. But in language we call this a *litotes* ((LEYE-tuh-teez)), which is a negation of the contrary, and we use it for understatement. *I'm not unhappy* is a perfectly fine sentence. It is a negative statement with an attitude, and it doesn't mean quite the same as *I'm happy*. But use this form sparingly, and only when it clearly enhances your writing.

Usage Tip 3: Levels of Formality

Effective public relations writers are fluent in *operational English* (also known as *standard English*, or *network standard* because it is commonly used by television reporters). This is the version of English most appropriate for professional interaction, such as in business or education. It is the type of writing you learned in school, and the type you will most likely be expected to use in your career.

Good writers also know how and when to use some of the many other varieties of English, a language rich in diversity. English has a formal style, informal versions, and many geographic and cultural variations. Together, these provide much of the beauty and power of the English language. This variety can be very useful to public relations writers. Position statements and news releases, for example, generally call for the use of formal and objective language. Appeal letters lend themselves to more informal and personal language.

Some writing is meant to be heard rather than read, and this sometimes calls for a particular language form. Language drawn from a particular cultural variation like Cajun or urban hip-hop may be appropriate for the script of a public service announcement. For some writers, Creole, Pennsylvania Dutch or other flavorful regional variations or dialects may be a useful writing tool. The key is to use the style most appropriate to the particular writing project and the target public and to carefully pretest to make sure the writing is not offensive or condescending to your readers.

Usage Tip 4: Bulky Sentences

Strive for simplicity. A good sentence should carry only one thought, and its phrases and clauses should support that thought rather than introduce extraneous information. This is particularly true when you are preparing a speech or writing a script or release for the broadcast media, because the audiences will not be able to reread an awkward sentence. Keep the subject and verb close together, making it easier for the hearer to understand the sentence.

Usage Tip 5: Evolving Usage and Rules

The essayist E.B. White once wrote in The New Yorker magazine that "the living language is like a cowpath; it is the creation of the cows themselves who, having created it, follow it or depart from it according to their whim and their needs. From daily use, the path undergoes change." Great allusion!

English is indeed a living and changing language. Words come, words go. Some move in and out of common usage, while others find that their meanings have changed. For example, the dictionary says that *gay* means lively, brightly colored and happy, but if you proclaim yourself to be in a gay mood, people undoubtedly will assume something about your sexual preference rather than your current disposition. Similarly, once the word *propaganda* was an accepted synonym for promotion or publicity, but the word since has taken on a negative tone associated with deception and misleading information.

Usage Tip 6: Noun–Pronoun Agreement

A singular noun takes a singular pronoun, with the same logic applying to plural nouns. For example, *The girl reads her book. The girls read their books.* But not all nouns are singular or plural. Another category, *collective nouns*, are singular words with a plural meaning. These words represent individuals working together as a unit, and they sometimes can be confusing for writers.

Collective nouns, generally groups of people acting as one entity, are singular in construction, even though they imply something in the plural: *The board will hold its annual meeting.* We don't write *their annual meeting*, because the board is a singular noun. It may be a group of people, but when they become a board they act singularly, as one body. In public relations writing, most references to organizations involve singular pronouns. Company, management, corporation, committee, council . . . all of these call for *it* rather than *they*.

Usage Tip 7: Subject–Verb Agreement

Trust your ear, but first train it not to deceive you. If the subject is singular, use a singular verb. If the subject is plural, use a plural verb. What could be simpler? *The boy was happy* (singular noun, singular verb). *The boys were happy* (plural noun, plural verb). You wouldn't say *The boys was happy* because your ear tells you it is wrong. The best way to train your ear for good language usage is to read many writers: news and current affairs, novels, poetry, histories and biographies, textbooks. Learn to listen critically so your ear will be comfortable with correct phrasing, such as *the media are . . .* and *ethics is . . .* Be aware of some problem situations that can cloud the issue of subject–verb agreement:

- Collective nouns are singular: *The class wants to postpone the exam. The agency is pitching a new account.*
- When a phrase or clause comes between the subject and the verb, use the verb that goes with the subject: *Several editions of the company newsletter were illustrated by Bibi Johenger (editions were). The news release published in 15 daily newspapers was considered a success (release was).*

- Some pronouns take singular verbs: *Anyone, anybody, each, either, everyone, everybody, neither, no one, nobody, someone, somebody.* Examples of this usage: *Everyone is in her automobile. Nobody is taking his walk.*
- Some pronouns take plural verbs: *Both, few, many, several, some.* Examples: *Many are the problems. Several were available for comment.*
- Still other pronouns can take singular or plural verbs, depending on the context: *All, any, most, none, some.* Examples: *Some of the candy was gone. Some of the people were happy to see her.*
- Compound subjects joined by *and* always take a plural verb: *Edward Bernays and Ivy Lee are important figures in the development of public relations as a profession.*
- Singular compound subjects joined by *or* or *nor* take singular verbs: *Either Carl Jung or Sigmund Freud was Edward Bernays' uncle; I can't remember which.*
- Compound subjects involving both a singular noun and a plural noun joined by *or* or *nor* agree with the subject closest to the verb. Examples: *Either the editor or the copy editors were very observant. Neither the copy editors nor the editor was observant.*
- Some singular nouns end with the letter *s*, but that doesn't make them plural. *Public relations is an interesting career choice.* Don't rely too much on computer spellchecks, which often fail to recognize that terms such as *ethics* or *public relations* really are singular nouns, despite their endings.
- Plural nouns with irregular endings still take plural verbs, even though they don't end in an *s*: *The media are important to public relations practitioners. The alumni were supportive.*

Usage Tip 8: Simple Punctuation

In general, use simple punctuation—commas, periods, question marks and quotation marks. Be wary about using semicolons and exclamation points. A problem that sometimes plagues student writers involves punctuation for *appositives* (a word or grouping of words that defines, describes or renames the preceding noun). *John Wortman, the company's new vice president, will visit the plant next Wednesday.* You can remove the appositive phrase *the company's new vice president* and still have a decent sentence. Use commas at both the beginning and the end of such descriptive phrases.

Usage Tip 9: Proper Word Placement

Make sure the words you use fit appropriately into the sentence. Consider the different meanings that result from the placement of the modifier *only* in the following sentences:

The only producer for the video complained about her salary. (one producer)

The producer for the only video complained about her salary. (one video)

The producer for the video only complained about her salary. (complained, not threatened or whined)

The producer for the video complained only about her salary. (salary, not equipment or facilities)

The placement of modifying phrases also can affect the meaning of a sentence. Using common syntax, the noun or pronoun following a modifying phrase is the subject of the action.

Going to class, Bella met her former roommate. (Bella was going to class.) Violations of this order sometimes are instantly recognized because they evoke comical images in our minds.

Consider these confusing sentences:

While running laps, my grandmother waited for practice to end. (Grandma running laps?) A clearer way to say it might be *While I ran laps, my grandma waited for practice to end.*

As an artist, I need your opinion about how to illustrate this article. (Who is the artist, me or you?) How about writing this sentence with greater clarity? *I need your artistic opinion about how to illustrate this article.*

In these examples, the modifier may be misplaced. It certainly is in the example about grandma. A misplaced modifier can cause a *non sequitur* (a Latin phrase that means "it does not follow") because the main point of the sentences does not follow logically from the introductory phrase.

Here is an example of a non sequitur caused by awkward word placement: *The newsletter will include a story about your promotion next month.* The problem is with *next month.* Is it next month's promotion or next month's newsletter?

Here's another example: *The device emits a noise that annoys rodents up to 100 feet.* Those are big rodents! Who would even consider annoying the critters mentioned in this sentence from an actual newspaper advertisement? The problem is with the phrase *up to 100 feet*; the simple addition of the word *away* at the end of the sentence would clear things up nicely.

In a classic example from his nationally syndicated column on writing (reprinted in "FYI: On Proper Word Placement"), James Kilpatrick urges writers to listen to what they write.

Usage Tip 10: Parallel Structure

Parallel structure means repeating a grammatical pattern for elements that are part of a series or compound construction, such as a series of nouns, verb phrases, infinitives, clauses, and so on. Balance a noun with a noun, an adjective with an adjective, a gerund phrase (-ing verb) with a gerund phrase, and so on.

Make sure items presented in a series are used in parallel fashion. Good writing doesn't mix elements in a series or switch voice. For example, you wouldn't write *Since my last visit, the baby has learned to crawl, roll over, and eating with two hands* because the final element is not parallel with the first two (both infinitives, with the *to* implied with *roll over*). Rather, you would write *The baby has learned to crawl, roll over, and eat with two hands* (all infinitives). Or perhaps, *The baby has learned the skills of crawling, rolling over and eating with two hands* (all gerund phrases).

Sometimes, writers signal that a parallel structure is coming. For example, they use words such as *either, neither, both* and *not only*. The reader knows that two things are being introduced by these signals, and the writer knows to present them in parallel fashion: *We've decided that we are either seeing a movie or going to the mall* (two gerund phrases). *Both where to go and what to do there were decisions left to their dates* (two noun clauses). *Not only functionality but also creativity is part of public relations writing* (two nouns).

Another way writers signal parallel elements is by introducing a sequence or signaling an upcoming series. Here's a verb series: *First, mix in the egg whites and milk; second, knead*

Taken from The Writer's Art column by James J. Kilpatrick. Distributed by Universal Press Syndicate. Reprinted by permission. All rights reserved.

Mangles and bangles and dangles

WRITER'S ART
By James J. Kilpatrick

A reader in Denver just sent me the faded clipping of an ad that appeared in the Rocky Mountain News in June 1967. It was an ad for a three-piece set of Farberware mixing bowls: "Designed to please a cook with round bottom for efficient beating."

Now, the text of that ad must have gone across half a dozen desks before it wound up in print. How could everyone have missed the ad's appeal to cooks with round bottoms? The answer, I suppose, is that too often writers and editors read copy without listening to it. Listening is vital.

The more we listen to our prose, the more likely we are to catch the mangled syntax and the dangling phrase. An AP correspondent in South Africa wasn't listening in April when he wrote that fighting between rival factions "has left 100 persons dead a week." A gruesome thought.

Another AP writer passed along recommendations by public health officials for rodent control: "Do not sweep an area where there have been rodents with a broom." We should sweep the area where there have been rodents with vacuum cleaners instead.

Wandering antecedents can cause a heap of trouble. The San Antonio Express-News reported a manslaughter charge against a 13-year-old boy. "Defense attorney Roberto Maldonado said the boy, whose father left home when he was a toddler, deeply regrets the accident." (We remedy the confusion by writing, "whose father left home when Mark was a toddler.")

At the time ice skater Tonya Harding was in the news, the Daily Clintonian in Clinton, Ind., carried a photo caption: "Tonya Harding gets into her truck after running out from the apartment where she is staying to keep it from getting towed in Beaverton, Ore." Unless trucks are towing apartments in Beaverton, the writer had the wrong antecedent for "it."

A weekly paper in Colorado carried an interesting crime report: "Wearing a bad haircut with a blue rhinestone collar, a woman reported her missing poodle." Hard to say what to do with that sentence.

Here is a nice historical dangle from House Beautiful: "Designed in 1792 for $500 by James Hoban, an Irish architect, John Adams became the first U.S. president to reside at 1600 Pennsylvania Avenue."

This one, from the Washington Monthly last winter, defies successful editing: "McCummings' profession was mugging. While attempting to rob and strangle a 71-year-old in a subway station, a transit cop heard the victim's cries and found him on the station platform being throttled by McCummings." The best thing to do with that sentence is to shoot it.

Thinking of shooting: Reporters seem to have a serious problem with homicides. In Fort Collins, Colo., "Spinharney shot and killed 26-year-old Leonard Zuchel four times." In Rock Hill, S.C., "Both girls appeared to have been shot to death, probably several times."

Some mangles tend to stop readers dead in their tracks, possibly several times. In San Antonio, "Juvenile Court Master Irma Hernandez ordered the boy detained on charges of engaging in juvenile conduct." Well, that figures.

In South Bend, Ind., the conductor of the South Bend Chamber Singers had a thought for the day: "I think we all feel it's really important to perform contemporary music while the performers are alive."

In Portland, a father and his long-lost daughter were reunited after 22 years: "He shook, tears streaming down parts of his face that weren't there when she was born."

This isn't exactly a mangle, but it will serve as one more reminder to listen to what we write. It comes from "Business Briefs" in the Sumner (Wash.) Community Sun: "With more than 17 years of cutting and designing hair under his belt, Dave Brown has just opened Dave's Family Hair Care at 926 Main Street."

All right, let's hear it for Dave! And let's listen to the sense of the stuff we write.

Universal Press Syndicate

---

the dough; third, bake for one hour. Here's a gerund series: *This recipe has three steps: mixing the egg whites and the milk, kneading the dough, and baking for one hour.*

Often, parallel structure is accomplished by writing in threes: *I came; I saw; I conquered . . . government of the people, by the people, for the people . . .* Such parallelism carries with it a rhythm that can inspire the reader. Another structure for parallelism with a similar impact is the turnaround statement. Nearly 50 years later, people still are inspired by the invitation that President John F. Kennedy gave in his inaugural address: "And so, my fellow Americans: ask not what your country can do for you—ask what you can do for your country."

Exercise 2.2—Correcting Standard Usage Problems

Read each sentence and decide if there is an error in usage in any of the underlined parts of the sentence. If you find an error, note the letter printed under the wrong word or phrase and write the letter in the blank space. You do not need to write the correct word. If you do not find an error, write the letter "E." No sentence has more than one error. Answers are listed in the answer key at the end of this chapter.

1. _____ <u>Its</u> important to <u>her</u> to <u>build</u> good media contacts, <u>especially</u> with local
         A   B   C   D
   newspapers.

2. _____ A <u>stack</u> of <u>news releases</u> <u>are</u> being delivered <u>to</u> the mail room.
           A   B   C   D

3. _____ The <u>oldest</u> twin <u>was</u> hired <u>last</u> January to <u>be</u> promotions director for the hockey
             A   B   C   D
   team.

4. _____ There is <u>little</u> question <u>that</u> Garcia, Jacobowski and <u>him</u> <u>will be working</u>
               A   B   C   D
   together on the community relations project.

5. _____ Everyone <u>is</u> asking <u>themselves</u> who will be selected <u>as</u> the honorary national
             A   B   C
   spokesperson for the <u>upcoming</u> literary campaign.
                             D

6. _____ <u>Nobody</u> <u>is</u> less likely than <u>him</u> to be accepted <u>into</u> the PRSA chapter.
         A   B   C   D

7. _____ The <u>editorial conference</u> is being <u>rescheduled,</u> <u>as</u> the photographer <u>will be</u> on
              A   B   C   D
   a field assignment.

8. _____ <u>Whom</u> has been <u>recommended</u> for the practitioner <u>award</u> at this <u>year's</u> chapter
         A   B   C   D
   banquet meeting?

9. _____ <u>There, displayed prominently</u> on the wall, <u>is</u> <u>Nabih's</u> new accreditation
                       A   B C
   certificate.

10. _____ Everyone in <u>class</u> <u>has</u> to <u>bring</u> <u>their</u> project the next time we meet.
                A   B   C   D

11. _____ The teacher opened the door, <u>lay</u> the book on the desk, <u>and</u> began by asking
                                  A   B
    <u>each of us</u> to take a piece of paper <u>and</u> answer the question.
        C   D

12. _____ The <u>intern</u> noticed that either printing charges or postage <u>were</u> left out of the
             A   B
    budget, but she <u>didn't</u> know if she should <u>point this out</u>.
                 C   D

Simple Language

The novelist Ernest Hemingway said it well: "The first and most important thing of all, at least for writers today, is to strip language clean, to lay it bare down to the bone." What was true in 1952 for Hemingway is equally important for us today. The public relations writer should keep one central idea in mind: People are doing you a favor by reading what you write. Don't make them work too hard. They won't read your messages if your writing is difficult or uninteresting.

Language Tip 1: Writing Naturally

In general, write the way you talk. Sometimes people try too hard to affect a writing style that isn't natural for them or their audience. Your goal should be to write in a way that sounds real and genuine rather than artificial or strained. At the same time, writing for a print release often requires greater attention to grammatical detail than writing that will be presented orally.

As you are trying to master the art of writing naturally, try reading your words aloud. A well-written piece will work not only on paper but also on the ear. A poorly written piece will sound bad, which should prod you to work on it some more.

As you read, listen for the cadence of your words—the rise and fall of the voice, the tempo and meter of the words. In particular, listen for any rhyme or alliteration (several words beginning with the same letter or sound). Make sure your writing sounds natural and that it doesn't unwittingly usher in a rhyming or sing-song effect. Use rhyme or other techniques if you wish, but don't fall into them accidentally.

Language Tip 2: Wordy Phrases

Treat your writing as a butcher treats meat: Trim the fat. Empty phrases take up unnecessary space. Instead of writing *Will the committee make a recommendation to increase the price?* why not ask simply *Will the committee recommend a price increase?* It's cleaner, shorter and easier to understand. Writers continually have to make decisions on when to write simply and when to use decorative words and elaborate phrases.

Exercise 2.3—Trimming Wordy Phrases

Rewrite the following sentences by trimming away the unnecessary wordiness. Examples are listed at the end of this chapter.

1. It is necessary to remember to proofread carefully.
2. It has been learned that the university will extend library hours due to the fact that finals are next week.
3. At this point in time, our client is ready to begin the research project.
4. There are five students who have outstanding records.
5. It is an accepted fact that the building was purchased in 1923.
6. The reason for the team's loss is because there were several key players who were sick.
7. The program will be beginning next month.

Language Tip 3: Simple Words

Abjure sesquipedalian obfuscatory terminology. If you understand this advice, follow it. If you don't know what it means, you're probably better off; you won't be tempted to use unnecessarily fancy words. Translation: Swear off big, confusing words. *Keep It Simple* could be a motto for the effective public relations writer.

Readability research shows that simpler, more common words make it easier for readers to understand a text. Messages averaging 1½ syllables a word have been found to be easiest to read. Some states have adopted the 1½-syllable formula as a standard for consumer-oriented legal documents for warranties, loans and contracts. The U.S. Army requires its training manuals be written at a 6th-grade level so every enlisted person can easily understand them.

Some of the world's most profound ideas have been presented in easy-to-read sentences accessible to virtually any audience. The Gettysburg Address, written by President Abraham Lincoln, for example, averages 1.3 syllables a word. Of 271 words, 202 have only one syllable. Yet is has many powerful and memorable phrases: "Four score and seven years ago our fathers brought forth on this continent, a new nation, conceived in Liberty, and dedicated to the proposition that all men are created equal." Indeed, the message Lincoln expressed nearly 150 years ago is still considered one of the most eloquent in the entire American experience. Fifty years after it was delivered, Lord George Curzon, a British statesman and orator, judged the address one of the three greatest speeches in the English language, calling it "a marvelous piece of English composition . . . a pure well of English undefiled. The more closely the address is analyzed, the more one must confess astonishment at his choice of words, the precision of its thought, its simplicity, directness and effectiveness." FYI, the other Top 2 on Lord Curzon's list were Lincoln's second inaugural address ("with malice toward none, with charity for all") and William Pitt's victory toast after the English defeated Napoleon at the Battle of Trafalgar ("England has saved herself by her exertions, and will, I trust, save Europe by her example").

Obviously there are times when the writer needs to use complex terms and phrases. But ask yourself these questions: What works best in this particular writing situation? Can I eliminate the technical words and still convey the meaning using examples or analogies? If I need the technical words, can I describe them in simple terms? Are there appropriate synonyms I should consider? Can I use one word instead of two? Can I use two or three simple words instead of one complicated word?

Language Tip 4: Short Sentences

Strive for simplicity in your writing, but avoid monotony. Not every sentence needs to begin with a subject; phrases and clauses can introduce variety and enhance readability. Compound and complex sentences are also useful writing tools.

Studies on readability show that shorter sentences are easier to understand. These studies suggest that general audiences have the best comprehension with sentences of about 16 words. That's an average. Some will be longer. Some shorter. As the writer, you will want to give variety and a rhythm to your text.

The *Gunning Readability Formula*, also known as the *Fog Index*, is a good tool for the public relations writer. This widely used tool is a simple way to measure the level of reading difficulty for any piece of writing. As described in "Tips for Better Writing: Fog Index," it does not determine directly if the writing is too basic or too advanced for the audience. It simply reflects the equivalent of a grade level. As the writer, you will decide what is appropriate for your intended readers.

Another popular readability tool is the Flesch–Kincaid grade-level scale. Some computer word-processing programs automatically calculate grade level as well as the percentage of passive sentences, providing some guidance for writers in revising their work.

Tips for Better Writing *Fog Index*

The Fog Index is simple to calculate:

1. Select a 100-word passage. For a lengthy piece of writing, select several different 100-word passages and average the Fog Index.

2. Count the number of sentences. If the passage does not end on a sentence break, calculate a percentage of the final sentence in the passage and add this to the count.

3. Divide the number of sentences into 100 to determine the average sentence length.

4. Count the number of long words in the passage. These are words of three or more syllables. However do not count proper nouns, words in which *er*, *es* or *ed* form the third and final syllable, hyphenated words like *state-of-the-art*, or compound words like *newspaper*.

5. Add the average sentence length and the number of long words (totals from Steps 3 and 4).

6. Multiply this total by 0.4. This number indicates the approximate grade level of the passage.

Remember that people can always understand writing that is less than their highest educational achievement without necessarily feeling that the writing is beneath them. Indeed, it's easier for us to read at less-than-challenging levels.

General-interest newspapers, for example, are usually written on about an eighth-grade level, and Associated Press wire copy is written at the level of an 11th-grade reader. The news media deal with some very sophisticated and complicated subjects in a style that makes their writing accessible to virtually all adults. As "FYI: Poison Pens" illustrates, sometimes high-level language can be quite confusing!

FYI *Poison Pens*

There is no evidence that this case actually appeared in court, but it is a classic example of the difference between writing to impress and writing to express.

A New York plumber of foreign extraction with a limited command of English wrote to the National Bureau of Standards. He said he had found that hydrochloric acid quickly opened drainage pipes when they got clogged. He asked if it was a good thing to use.

A Bureau scientist replied, "The efficacy of hydrochloric acid is indisputable, but the corrosive residue is incompatible with metallic permanence."

The plumber wrote back, thanking the bureau for telling him that the method was all right.

The scientist was a little disturbed and showed the correspondence to this boss, another scientist. The latter wrote the plumber:

"We cannot assume responsibility for the production of toxic and noxious residue with hydrochloric acid and suggest you use an alternative procedure."

The plumber wrote back that he agreed with the bureau—hydrochloric acid works fine.

The top scientist—boss of the first two—broke the impasse by tearing himself loose from technical terminology and writing this letter: "Don't use hydrochloric acid. It eats the hell out of pipes."

Reprinted with permission from "A case for clear writing," by C. Petrini and G.F. Shea in Training and Development 46, no. 1 (January 1992): 63–6.

Language Tip 5: Redundancies

Redundancies are phrases in which one or more of the words adds nothing to the meaning of the sentence. Like weeds in a garden, redundancies are words that take up space without adding anything useful. They compete for the reader's attention but offer nothing in return. For instance, what does *puppy dog* tell you that the single word *puppy* doesn't? Redundancies usually are adjectives, but don't dismiss all adjectives as being redundant. The problem with redundancies is that, as adjectives, they provide superfluous descriptions. In other words, they tell us what we already know.

Remember, however, that the repetition of words and phrases can be a useful tool in writing. What is to be avoided is not repetition for effect and comprehension but rather the redundant use of words that add no new meaning to the text.

Exercise 2.4—Eliminating Redundancies

Underline the redundant words that can be eliminated from the following sentences without losing any meaning. Examples are at the end of this chapter.

1. In the final outcome, we expect to see that important foreign imports will continue to maintain a positive current trend.

2. Local residents of this quiet little village will join together to do some advance planning for their annual family picnic on Easter Sunday, just as they have done previously each year.

3. Whether or not we are absolutely sure about Thelma's skill as an ice skater, we are convinced that she is a very unique personality who will be a positive asset to our team.

4. The study committee will refer back to its minutes to learn more about the past history of this important project to improve tourism for the city of Philadelphia.

5. The general consensus of opinion is that, at this point in time, the high school students should not protest against a school-night curfew.

6. The university recently produced two different versions of the report, giving close scrutiny to new techniques for growing crops in rice paddies and corn fields.

7. The Jewish rabbi met with the Episcopal priest and the Muslim imam. ■

Language Tip 6: Active Voice

Voice is the grammatical term that refers to the relationship between the subject and predicate of a sentence. *Active voice* means the subject is doing the action. *Passive voice* means the action is being done to the subject. Look at the following examples:

Active: *The president asked the community affairs director to coordinate an open house.* (12 words)
Passive: *It was requested by the president that an open house be coordinated by the community affairs director.* (17 words)

Active: *The director will study the report.* (6 words)
Passive: *The report will be studied by the director.* (8 words)

Active: *The editor accomplished little good when she attempted to revise the newsletter without conducting a reader-interest survey.* (17 words)
Passive: *Little good was accomplished when the editor attempted to revise the newsletter without conducting a reader-interest survey.* (17 words)

Active: *The company reported a 50 percent increase in its first-quarter profits.* (11 words)
Passive: *It was reported that the company had a 50 percent increase in its first-quarter profits.* (15 words)

Active: *After the wheel fell off the airplane, it hit the ground and bounced over the house.* (16 words)
Passive: *The house was bounced over by the wheel after it fell off the airplane and hit the ground.* (18 words)

Active: *All of the participants ran a fast race.* (8 words)
Passive: *A fast race was run by all of the participants.* (10 words)

Both active and passive voice offer something useful to the writer, whose job it is to decide which is more appropriate for each sentence. Here are some of the benefits of active voice:

- Eliminates unnecessary words. Active voice almost always is shorter. In the first set of the sentences above, note that the active version is 12 words to the passive version's 17, a saving of 30 percent.
- Gets to the point quickly. For example, in the second set of sentences above, the active version is quite straightforward. Readers learn quickly what the director will do.
- Increases readability. The Gunning Readability Formula and other similar tools are based on research showing that shorter sentences are easier to understand than longer ones.
- Provides more specific information. For example, in the sentences in the third set above, the active sentence informs the reader that the editor is a woman. In the fourth set, the reader learns that the company made the report. The passive versions lack that information.

Likewise, passive voice also has several benefits for writers:

- Emphasizes the receiver: *Miriam Yosaka has been given the Platinum Excalibur Award for excellence in public relations by the local chapter of PRSA.* This is a form often used in leads for news releases and newsletter articles because the news focus should be on the recipient of a promotion or award and not on the giver.
- Diverts attention from the doer: *Spaghetti sauce was spilled on the guest of honor.* The active alternative would be to call attention to the person who performed the action, such as *Donna spilled spaghetti sauce on the guest of honor.*
- Is useful when the doer is unknown or unimportant: *The banquet hall was repainted 15 years ago.*

Language Tip 7: Adjectives and Adverbs

A principle of effective public relations writing is to be judicious with adjectives and adverbs. Both can be helpful in explaining and qualifying, but they also can be overused. Mark Twain had some excellent advice about using adjectives: "When you catch an adjective, kill it. No, I don't mean utterly, but kill most of them—then the rest will be valuable. They weaken when they are close together. They give strength when they are wide apart."

An *adjective* modifies a noun or a word acting as a noun. *Limiting adjectives* qualify or limit meanings to a particular type or quantity, such as *The veteran firefighter ran through the side doorway carrying the year-old infant* (the limiting adjectives are *veteran*, *side* and *year-old*). Writers wanting to remain objective frequently use limiting adjectives, because these can add rich detail to the story.

Another type of adjective, the *descriptive adjective*, describes a quality of the object, as in *The exhausted firefighter ran through the fiery doorway carrying the frightened infant* (the descriptive adjectives are *exhausted*, *fiery* and *frightened*). While descriptive adjectives can enliven basic information, public relations writers try to limit their use of descriptive adjectives because they often ask the reader to trust the observations and conclusions of the writer. For example, it is an objective fact to report that a building is *40 stories high*, a limiting adjective. But using a descriptive adjective such as calling it a *tall building* asks the reader to accept the writer's interpretation of tall. For a reader in Manhattan, 40 stories isn't particularly tall; for someone in Flagstaff, Ariz., it might be considered quite tall. Let readers interpret objective information for themselves.

As adjectives modify nouns, *adverbs* do the same thing for verbs. They provide nuance and detail. For example, *The writer approached the task happily*. Or *fearfully*. Or *half-heartedly*. Adverbs should be used even more sparingly than adjectives, because so often they result from what the writer observed. Remember that good writers try not to ask a reader to accept their conclusions; rather, they provide details to allow readers to draw their own conclusions.

Meaningful Language

> "When I use a word," Humpty Dumpty said, in rather a scornful tone, "it means just what I choose it to mean—neither more nor less."
>
> "The question is," said Alice, "whether you can make words mean so many different things."

In *Through the Looking-Glass*, Lewis Carroll gives us that exchange. Humpty Dumpty can claim what he likes, but Alice's question is right on. Can writers expect a word to mean simply what they want? Or should we use words the way our readers will best understand them?

A public relations writer's greatest strength is the ability to share meaning and communicate accurate understandings between organizations and their publics. It's a matter of *diction*, the literary term associated with word choice, particularly the careful selection of words and phrases to best carry the meaning that the writer has in mind. Here are some tips on writing with more meaningful use of language.

Diction Tip 1: Word Pictures

A good writer is one who has learned how to weave such a richness into language that the reader not only grasps the meaning but feels an experience of the story. Here are several techniques for creating word pictures that can inspire the reader.

Description. Show, don't tell. That's common advice for public relations writers. Writing is most powerful when it demonstrates a fact and invites the reader to draw a conclusion, rather than when it interprets the situation for the reader. Effective writers provide information so their readers can properly interpret a situation for themselves. In the sentence *The little girl was happy to see her grandfather*, the reader must trust that the writer witnessed, understood and accurately represented some interchange between grandparent and child. More specific is *The little girl smiled, ran to her grandfather, and hugged him.* Now readers can "see" the happiness and draw their own conclusion rather than rely on the writer's interpretation.

Detail. An effective writer gives details. Instead of asking the reader to trust the writer's judgment and skill in observation, the writer simply presents the reader with evidence. Rather than reporting *The company lost a lot of money last year*, we provide much more meaning by stating *The company lost $1.5 million last year.* Likewise, try to use words that provide specific information rather than generalities. Here's an example of vague wording: *As soon as possible, we should complete this contract.* When is as soon as possible? And what does complete mean in this context? To write the contract? To reach agreement on the terms? To sign it?

Comparison. Analogies, metaphors and similes are types of figurative language that allow the writer to make lucid comparisons for the reader. Analogies are an effective way to show something in a way readers can understand. *Analogies* are comparisons that explain unfamiliar concepts by using familiar terms and imagery. For example, one student in a public relations writing class described cholesterol by creating a verbal image of gridlock on a busy city street where the flow of traffic was slowed by a truck that is double-parked. That is an analogy of how clogged arteries constrict the blood flow. It takes something readers already understand (traffic) and uses this image to explain something they may not understand (the effects of cholesterol). Effective public relations writers develop the ability to find common, everyday parallels for complex situations.

Using analogies requires systematic reasoning. As a student, you've been exposed to such reasoning on standardized tests: Puppy is to dog as (a) tabby is to cat, (b) sparrow is to bird, (c) flock is to duck, (d) fawn is to deer. Think logically about the relationships. You know that a puppy is a young dog. Consider the choices. Is a tabby a young cat? Is a sparrow a young bird? Is a flock a young duck? Is a fawn a young deer? Through this reasoning, it's clear that D is the correct answer.

Another useful literary technique is the *simile*, a direct comparison between two dissimilar concepts. Similes use the word *like* or *as* to make the comparison. For example, *The music of the orchestra was like the sound of birds chirping at daybreak.*

Still another figurative technique is the *metaphor*, which makes an indirect comparison and does not use the word *like* or *as*. For example, *The soccer team steamrolled over the competition.* Because of the poetic imagery used in metaphors, writers don't often use them in public relations writing.

Diction Tip 2: Precise Language

Mark Twain pointed out that the difference between the correct word and the almost correct word is the difference between lightning and a lightning bug. Good advice.

Some words seem alike but have significantly different meanings. Good writers don't necessarily avoid words with nuanced meanings, but they certainly make sure they use the correct word. *Disinterested* isn't the same as *uninterested*. *Comprise* is different from *include*. Likewise with *farther* and *further*, *imply* and *infer*, *less* and *fewer*. If you aren't sure of the differences among these sets of words, look them up in your dictionary and in The Associate Press Stylebook.

Also use the right combination of words. *Try to* is preferable to *try and*. *Different from* makes more sense than *different than*. *Neither* requires a *nor*, and *not only* must be followed by *but also*.

Sometimes meanings built into words makes them inappropriate for linking with certain other words, because doing so would lead to a contradiction. The term for this is *oxymoron* (from the Greek, "acutely foolish"). A writer may consciously use an oxymoron for creative effect, such as describing an audience reaction as *thunderous silence* or a committee's recommendation as a *definite maybe*. Occasionally, however, an unintended and unfortunate oxymoron creeps into a sentence, such as reference to an *uncrowned king*, *genuine imitation*, or *paid volunteer*.

Diction Tip 3: Strong Words

The way to avoid ambiguity is to use strong words, especially verbs. We noted earlier some of the problems associated with descriptive adjectives and adverbs. Amateur writers sometimes try to "dress up" their writing with too many of them, especially with flowery description.

There is a better way to improve your writing. Professional writers rely on the power of the verbs. For example, verbs based on *be*, *have*, *go*, and *make* provide basic information, but they don't communicate a rich meaning. Consider the difference between *The committee had meetings* and *The committee sponsored meetings* or *conducted meetings*. Compare the power of verbs in *The union had a vote* with *The union wanted a vote* or *called for*, *demanded*, or *threatened*.

Weak *is* and *go* verbs can be strengthened with more precise and meaningful verbs. *She has a new house* becomes stronger and more specific as *She lives in a new house* (or *leases* or *owns*). *He went to school* becomes much more meaningful if the reader learns *He ran to school*. Or *drove*. Or *walked*. Or *dashed*. Or *moseyed*.

"I love you," he said. That's nice, but notice how the meaning of this sentence becomes stronger with a more precise verb. *"I love you," he sobbed.* Or *muttered*. Or *shouted*. Or *snickered*. Or *announced*. Or *panted*. The effective writer should choose the specific verb based on the writing context, the norms and conventions associated with each particular writing format. For example, in a news release, the writer probably would stick with the word *said* because it is a neutral verb. Some of the more interpretive and descriptive verbs might be used in feature releases, appeal letters and other formats.

Diction Tip 4: Clichés and Journalese

Familiarity breeds contempt, or at least boredom. *Clichés* are familiar expressions overused to the point where they are now weary and stale. Clichés tell your reader where you are going before you get there. Avoid them.

Replace clichés with your own fresh expressions, and challenge common phrases that carry little information. For example, how long is it *until the cows come home*? And just where is *square one*? And is it really any sweeter to be *last but not least*?

Another note of caution: Avoid *journalese*, the kind of wording, especially for verbs, sometimes found in newspaper headlines. In the language of journalese, costs *skyrocket* and temperatures *soar*. Fires *rage* and rivers *rampage*. Projects are *kicked off*. Opponents *weigh in*. In journalese, people get a *go-ahead* and projects get a *green light*. While this might be appropriate for headlines, such writing can quickly become trite and overdone.

Exercise 2.5—Eliminating Clichés

Revise each of the following sentences by using original language in place of the cliché.

1. Let's run this idea up the flagpole and see who salutes.
2. After 9 p.m., taxis are few and far between.
3. It's time for journalists and public relations practitioners to bury the hatchet.
4. Get a ballpark estimate of how much it will cost to print the brochure.
5. It's time to bite the bullet and announce the layoffs.
6. John was green with envy when Lee was given the Oxford account.

Diction Tip 5: Loaded Words

Would you rather be called *fat* or *amply proportioned*? How about *corpulent*? *husky*? *pudgy*? *stout*? *big-boned*? It makes a difference, which is why dress makers have XL-Petite sizes and advertisers promote queen-size panty hose.

If you want to see the power of language—and the importance of avoiding loaded words—consider this: Will you get the same response if you tell your mother that she is *nagging* you than if you say she's being too *persistent*? Is calling someone *a colored person* the same as referring to *a person of color*? What's the difference among *indulgent, permissive* and *tolerant* parents? These can be loaded words, and it's best to avoid them.

The English language has many different, sometimes opposing, ways of expressing some ideas. Public relations writers take great care in choosing words with the appropriate denotation and connotation. *Denotation* is the basic dictionary definition of a word, its direct and explicit meaning. *Connotation* is the deeper meaning, the implicit suggestion or nuance that goes beyond the explicit meaning.

Often it is a matter of personal interpretation, giving rise to emotional associations. For example, *chat, chatter, prattle* and *babble* all denote the same thing—a loose and ready flow of inconsequential talk. But each connotes a different meaning—a light and friendly chat, aimless and rapid chatter, childish prattle and unintelligible babble.

Diction tip 6: Technical Language

One of the biggest contributions a good public relations writer can make to an organization is to translate its bureaucratic language into words and phrases that are meaningful to people new to or outside of the organization.

Technical language (also known as *jargon*) refers to words and phrases familiar within a particular group (such as an organization, industry, profession, hobby, and so on) but unfamiliar to people outside the group. Faced with technical language, or language that is unintelligible for a lay audience, you have several choices: translate it into more accessible English, explain it in simple terms, use it in obvious context, or delete the jargon altogether.

Faced with jargon, a writer may paraphrase. But don't simply put quotation marks around jargon. This merely calls attention to the technical language but does little to interpret it for readers.

Jargon is sometimes appropriate. Technical and "in" words can be used freely, as long as the readers are likely to understand them. Jargon might well be appropriate in pieces such as articles in industry newsletters, news releases to specific interest magazines or speeches before professional groups.

The use of jargon can raise ethical questions when it is meant to obscure the meaning for uninformed or uninitiated readers.

Exercise 2.6—Working with Technical Language

Part 1: Each of the following passages offers a medical explanation related to a type of cancer. Select either one of the medical explanations. Rewrite this explanation in lay terms so it is complete yet understandable to a first-year college student without a medical background.

Part 2: Add one or two paragraphs of additional information that you believe would be particularly relevant to readers as a way of encouraging them to adopt the habit of using the self-examination techniques that are associated with each disease. This might include information you find about people who have survived the disease and/or information about how the disease and detection techniques are particularly relevant to a college-age audience.

Resources: Use information you can find in general and medical encyclopedias, books, magazines and journals, interviews with medical professionals, and so on. You'll find accurate information from organizations such as the American Cancer Society or the National Institutes of Health. Use a search engine to find authoritative Web sites dealing with breast cancer or testicular cancer.

Breast Cancer. Highly treatable, carcinoma of the breast is most often curable when detected in early stages. Staging of breast cancer indicates the risk of metastasis; thus the need for early detection and treatment. Simultaneous bilateral breast cancer is uncommon; however, there is a progressive risk of recurrence.

Many breast cancers are initially discovered as lumps detected by the patient herself, with 80 percent of these being noncarcinomatous cysts or benign tumors. Physicians verify the suspicion of carcinoma through a series of examination procedures and imaging techniques, including palpation, aspiration, ultrasonography, thermography and diaphanography. Mammography is the most important screening modality for the early detection of breast cancer.

Clinical diagnosis of breast cancer is accomplished via biopsy. The most common primary treatment is surgery (including lumpectomy, segmented mastectomy, simple mastectomy, modified radical mastectomy, and radical mastectomy).

Adjuvant therapy includes radiation therapy, chemotherapy, and hormone therapy. Treatment also involves negating the patient's anxieties regarding appearance, self-esteem, and sexuality, as well as continuing risk factors regarding recurrence.

Lifelong follow-up is required to detect recurrences, which can occur as late as 30 years after the initial diagnosis. The risk of a primary cancer in the contralateral breast is significant, approximately 1 percent per year cumulatively. Therefore, patients should be instructed in breast self-examination and should have periodic examinations aimed at early detection, including routine mammograms after age 40.

Testicular Cancer.   Highly treatable and curable at an 80 to 95 percent rate depending on type, carcinoma of the testicle usually develops in men from post-pubescence through early middle-age (ages 15 to 34) and is the most prevalent carcinomatic variety for that age group. Testicular cancer can metastasize at a rapid rate; thus the need for early detection and treatment. Testicular cancer is seldom bilateral, and it carries only a slight rate of recurrence.

Most testicular cancers are initially discovered by the patient himself. Physicians verify the suspicion of carcinoma through a series of physical and radiologic examinations and testing procedures.

Diagnostic evaluation via imaging techniques includes computed tomography, intervenous pyelography, lymphangiography, and ultrasonography. Primary treatment of a testicular mass is accomplished via radical inguinal orchiectomy and microscopic examination. Adjuvant therapy includes radiation therapy or chemotherapy. Treatment also involves negating the patient's anxieties regarding sterility, impotency, and ejaculatory ability which are seldom the result of orchiectomy but which may be temporarily present due to therapeutic treatment.

Patients who have been cured of testicular cancer have a 5 percent cumulative risk of developing a cancer in the opposite testicle over the 25 years after initial diagnosis, though disease-free survival of three years is considered tantamount to a cure. Patients should be instructed in testicular self-examination and should have periodic examinations aimed at early detection. ∎

Diction Tip 7: New Words

Business and academic writers sometimes have to create new words, such as when dealing with an emerging field within science or high technology, for example. But writers who create new words are often simply seeking a short cut, which can confuse or alienate readers.

Two particular problem areas involve the use of the suffixes -*ify* and -*ize* to create a noun–verb hybrid. Some hybrids have crept into common usage, and we talk about *computerizing a classroom.*

But there are limits. Don't take a perfectly good noun, add a suffix, and expect people to appreciate a silly verblike structure, such as *Martin wants to CD-ROMify the office.* Sometimes parallel construction is not possible. We can *Latinize* a culture, but can we also *Paraguayify* it or *Kenyanize* it?

Meanwhile, adding -*ation* to the end of verbs can also lead to awkwardness, as in these words that unfortunately have been used in print: *conscienticization, Frenchification,* and *teacherization.*

Diction Tip 8: Foreign Words

Public relations writers generally try to avoid using non-English words and phrases that have not been adopted into the language. This is not about legitimate English words rooted in other languages—alcohol, alleluia, bona fide, restaurant, sushi and tobacco, for example.

Beware of truly foreign words and phrases: "ex post facto," "a priori," "poco a poco," "mano a mano." Don't use such terms with general audiences, who probably won't know what you mean. However, you might use them within specialized groups that understand the meaning. For example, classically trained musicians may appreciate subtle put-down in a theater review noting that *The applause began adagio and built to andante* ("adagio" means slow; "andante" isn't much faster) or *The audience left the theater prestissimo* ("prestissimo" means as fast as possible).

When you must use foreign words for a general audience, make sure you use them correctly. That B– you got in Spanish II may not be the best foundation for your writing. Use quotation marks around foreign words, and provide a translation: *The nursing supervisor noted with pride that Mercy Women's Health Center has been committed to the treatment of women "ab initio" (a Latin phrase meaning "from the beginning"), pointing out that the clinic was founded in 1842 as Sisters of Mercy Hospital for Women.*

Diction Tip 9: Pretentious Language

Pretentious language involves the use of words inflated to sound more impressive than they warrant. The car dealership advertises *experienced vehicles*. A government report refers to cows, pigs, and chickens collectively as *grain-consuming animal units*.

Often this is harmless, sometimes even silly. Bald people are called *follically impaired*, short people are *vertically challenged*, and senior citizens are *chronologically experienced*. Midriff bulge is called *personal insulation*. Cute! But senseless or nonsensical, pretentious language slows down the reader and sometimes is unclear in its meaning. Avoid it.

Diction Tip 10: Honest Language

Codes of ethics of the Public Relations Society of America, the Canadian Public Relations Society, the International Association of Business Communicators, and other professional organizations commit public relations writers to honesty and integrity, refraining from misleading information and correcting inaccuracies and misunderstandings.

The car dealership noted above sells *experienced vehicles*, the local thrift shop advertises *preworn jeans*, and a carpet store has *semi-antique rugs*. Interesting use of language and nobody gets hurt, so why fuss? Because sometimes people do get hurt. When pretentious language crosses the line, it loses its innocence and becomes dishonest. For example, when a marketer advertises rhinestones as *genuine artificial diamonds*, who gets hurt? Perhaps the new immigrant unfamiliar with the wiles of the marketplace. Maybe it's just the 10 year old looking for a present for Mother's Day, who ends up disappointed because he spent his paper-route money on junk.

The term *doublespeak* refers to language that intentionally obscures the real meaning behind the words. The use of doublespeak raises serious ethical questions for writers. It's a serious matter of misleading the public when the military reports the killing of civilian men, women and children as *collateral damage*, a term deliberately chosen to obscure reality and minimize opposition. The Army used the term frequently during the Vietnam War, with little public disapproval. But there was an outcry over that same military term when American terrorist Timothy McVeigh used it in reference to the children and adults killed when he bombed the Federal Building in Oklahoma City. It returned in Afghanistan, Iraq and Lebanon, but by then audiences had begun to understand it to mean civilian casualties; the phrase doesn't mask reality as much as it once did.

Similarly, it's outright deception when an annual report calls budget cuts *advanced downward adjustments* or when the Air Force says that civilians have been put on "nonduty, nonpay status." (As in fired?) Ethical writers know they should not use language that others will misunderstand.

A practical problem with doublespeak is that it often harms the reputation of the person or organization that engages in it. For example, after several months of clean-up following the 1989 Alaskan oil spill, officials of Exxon oil company said Prince William Sound was becoming "environmentally stabilized." But an Alaskan state official called this "an Exxon term. . . . As far as we're concerned, it's meaningless."

The National Council of Teachers of English, through its Committee on Public Doublespeak, has gone to battle with individuals and groups who do violence to the concept of meaningful language. The committee has criticized corporations for using doublespeak such as "initiate operations improvement," "employee repositioning," and "proactive down-sizing" when they lay off employees. It has identified deforestation projects that strip every tree and bush from hundreds of acres of forest, calling them instead "temporary meadows." It has criticized government reports that call death "failure to thrive" and medical reports that a patient "failed to fulfill his wellness potential" when he died.

The committee's outlook is global. It criticized a Russian report that a driver wasn't drunk, just in a "non-sober condition." It likewise criticized French police who said they don't kill but "neutralize" terrorists, and the Bosnian army officer who announced that "the only way to negotiate is to fight."

Each year the committee presents its Doublespeak Award. Since 1974, it has recognized individuals such as Palestinian leader Yasir Arafat (for saying that "it is precisely because we have been advocating coexistence that we have shed so much blood"), Army officer Oliver North (for his claim that he was "cleaning up the historical record" when, the committee said, he had "lied, destroyed official government documents, and created false documents"), and the first President Bush (for vetoing the Parental and Medical Leave bill amid assurances "that women do not have to worry about getting their jobs back after having a child or caring for a child during a serious illness"). The committee also has cited groups like the Department of Defense (for referring to a bombing mission as "visiting a site," and for calling human beings "soft targets" of such visits); the State Department (for referring to killing as "unlawful or arbitrary deprivation of life"); and the nuclear power industry (for inventing euphemisms around the Three Mile Island accident that referred to an explosion as "energetic disassembly," fire as "rapid oxidation," and an accident as an "event," an "abnormal evolution," and a "normal aberration").

The second Bush administration twice received the dubious award. The committee said George W. Bush "has set a high standard for his team by the inspired creation of the phrase 'weapons of mass destruction-related program activities' to describe what has yet to be seen." The committee also called former Defense Secretary Donald Rumsfeld's dismissive description of the Abu Ghraib prison torture as "brilliantly mind-befuddling." It also noted that the notorious "body bags" that carried dead soldiers home from the Vietnam War became "human remains pouches" during the Gulf War of Bush 1 and then morphed into "transfer tubes" during the Iraq and Afghanistan wars of Bush 2.

What are the practical consequences of doublespeak? Companies have faced personal injury lawsuits because their written instructions were considered jumbled and unclear. In Connecticut a few years ago, a judge said one company's contract wording was so murky it must have been made so on purpose, and the company had to pay a hefty fine. Try your hand at a situation ripe for doublespeak in "What Would You Do?: Avoiding Doublespeak."

What Would You Do? *Avoiding Doublespeak*

You are a public relations writer for City College. The academic dean wants you to write a news release because CC has recently been recertified by the National Council for Accreditation of Teacher Education. (NCATE certification is hard to come by, and makes a big difference when it comes to recruiting and fundraising.)

The dean wants you to write that CC is the only college with NCATE certification in the state, which is true, although two universities in the state also have the same certification. What would you do? How would you justify your decision?

Exercise 2.7—Freewriting on Language Ethics

Freewrite for five minutes on the following topic: *What is the difference between using language that misleads the reader and emphasizing the positive side of a situation?* Discuss this with your classmates.

■

Exercise 2.8—Decoding Doublespeak

Try your hand at deciphering the verbal chaos in this Doublespeak Quiz issued by the Committee on Public Doublespeak of the National Council of Teachers of English. Answers are listed at the end of this chapter.

1. ____   maximum incapacitation
2. ____   soft target
3. ____   detainee
4. ____   wildlife conservation program with some permanent facilities
5. ____   permanently remove from society
6. ____   employee repositioning
7. ____   impoverished agricultural worker
8. ____   sales credits
9. ____   pedestrian facilities
10. ___   multidimensional gaming with an entertainment complex
11. ___   thermal therapy
12. ___   visiting a site
13. ___   large, agricultural-based industry

14. ___   customer capital cost

15. ___   transportation counselor

16. ___   owner pretested

17. ___   forensic psychophysiological detection of deception

A. fired	**J.** kill
B. human beings in war zone	**K.** down payment
C. horse racing	**L.** bombing mission
D. bag of ice cubes	**M.** used
E. prisoner captured in war	**N.** sidewalks
F. peasant	**O.** death penalty
G. bribes and kickbacks	**P.** lie detector test
H. car salesperson	**Q.** casino
I. zoo	

Inclusive Language

Effective public relations writers are careful to use *inclusive language*—words and phrases that apply to all readers, without unnecessary exclusiveness. For example, *student* is an inclusive term for a kindergarten-through-graduate school audience; *schoolchildren* is more exclusive, biased in favor of people in the lower grades.

Why avoid bias in your writing? Not because it is the "nice" thing to do, and certainly not because it's "politically correct." For the public relations writer, the reason to avoid biased language is more self-serving: Using inclusive language makes you a more effective writer. If even one member of your audience feels excluded from what you are writing, you have created a barrier to communication. Notice the use of the word *feels*. It matters little if you meant to exclude. If any reader feels excluded, you are failing to communicate effectively. The fault is yours, however unintentional; the solution must also be yours.

Sometimes you may find people who don't find biased words offensive. Some women are comfortable with terms like *mankind*, and some women's organizations refer to their leaders as *chairmen*. Sometimes members of a minority group may use terms among themselves that would be insensitive coming from someone outside the group.

It doesn't really matter what most people would feel is appropriate; public relations is not focused on majority rule. Each individual in your audience decides if your writing is non-biased; each reader has a veto. You must care not only about the majority who may think *fireman* is OK but also about the minority of women firefighters who don't see themselves or their colleagues reflected in that term. Use words that include the man in a wheelchair who refuses to identify himself as handicapped because the term does not mirror his capabilities.

The problem with biased language of any kind is that it presumes one group sets the standard for the other. Usually the presumption is wrong, the result of arrogance, ignorance or insensitivity. Writers cannot afford such indiscretions. We must do everything in our power to make our publics and our audiences feel included in what we are writing about.

Let's look at some of the ways to eliminate bias based on gender, physical characteristics, and ethnicity, culture or lifestyle.

Bias Tip 1: Gender

Gender bias, sometimes called *sexist language*, results when the writer or speaker uses words that make someone feel left out because the reference seems to be only to the other gender. Almost always, the presumption is that men and masculine things are the norm; women and feminine things are seen in contrast to that norm. And that's bias. Here are a few ways of writing around such bias.

Avoid Masculine Pronouns. Avoid using masculine pronouns when you are referring to groups that can include both men and women. In the past, the pronoun *he* was used to refer to both sexes, but this is no longer accepted in many situations. Consider this sentence: *The professional artist should take great care of his brushes.* Here are several alternatives, each with a slightly difference nuance, giving the public relations writer many possibilities for avoiding pronoun bias:

- Use the plural form: *Professional artists should take great care of their brushes.* This may be the easiest way to handle the problem of exclusive language.
- Eliminate the possessive pronoun altogether: *The professional artist should take great care of brushes.*
- Use first or second person to make the reference more general: *As professional artists, we should take great care of our brushes.* Or, *As a professional artist, you should take great care of your brushes.*
- Use passive voice to eliminate the focus on the doer of the action: *For the professional artist, great care should be taken with brushes.*
- Use double pronouns: *The professional artist should take great care of his or her brushes.* Do this sparingly because it draws attention to its inclusiveness. Artificial forms such as *he/she* and *s/he* may be appropriate for business or internal writing formats but not for external publics.
- Use the word *one* for the pronoun, though this may sound stilted: *One should take great care of one's brushes.* Use it sparingly.

Avoid Masculine Nouns. Avoid using masculine words rooted in a generic sense. It is also important to avoid using feminine words generically, but this is seldom a problem. Find an alternative to *man* in the sense of *all people*.

Avoid Gender Stereotypes. Avoid using words that portray a gender stereotype. When possible, use words that are not gender specific to refer to both sexes. In a generic sense that does not identify particular individuals; words like *doctor*, *lawyer*, *actor* and *senator* include both women and men. Be careful not to create or perpetuate false stereotypes based on gender. Words commonly but falsely associated only with women—*secretary, nurse, kindergarten*

Exercise 2.9—Eliminating Gender Bias

 List generic alternatives for each of the following gender-specific words. Examples are listed at the end of this chapter.

Bellboy	Public relations man
Clergyman	Seaman
Deliveryman	Spokesman
Forefathers	Statesman
Foreman	Stewardess
Garbageman	Watchman
Housewife	

■

teacher—refer to both sexes. On the other hand, some words are inherently associated with only one gender—*nun, ballerina, husband*.

Use Inclusive Terms. Avoid words with feminine and masculine forms when an inclusive form can be used more effectively. Whenever possible, use the same word to refer to male and female members of the same group. In generic references, use terms like *business executive* rather than *businessman* or *businesswoman*, or *police officer* rather than *policeman* or *policewoman*, of course, gender-specific terms such as *chairwoman* or *fireman* are appropriate when you are referring to a particular woman or man.

Avoid archaic or dated feminine forms as well, such as *poetess, Jewess, aviatrix* and *priestess*. Even *actress* seems to be losing favor as the preferred term for many women television or movie performers, particularly those who seek out serious roles. Meanwhile, be careful with the Latin-based variants of *alumnus* (one man), *alumna* (one woman), *alumni* (several men, or a mixed group), and *alumnae* (several women) when referring to graduates of a college or university. Or simply call them *graduates*. Note also that, despite what some alumni offices mistakenly think, *alum* is not an acceptable short form. Outside the field of chemistry, it's not even a word.

Paraphrase Direct Quotations. In direct quotations, it may be necessary to paraphrase in order to avoid using exclusive language. Or, in your role as public relations adviser, you may ask the person you are quoting to reconsider a particular word or phrase.

Use Parallel Treatment. Treat women and men the same in similar situations. Don't use deferential, polite or honorary terms differently for men and women when referring in the same reference, such as *The movie starred Clooney, Diesel and Miss Lohan*.

Avoid Gender References. Avoid inappropriate references to the gender of a person involved in activities stereotypically associated with the other gender. It may be legitimate news that a woman has been elected president of the rod-and-gun club or that a man has received the hospital's Nurse of the Year award. Each case may represent the first occasion that someone of that gender has received the position or the award, and an insightful public relations writer will recognize the news value in such a first-of-a-kind situation and report it accordingly.

But not every situation deserves to have the spotlight shine on gender issues. Be smooth. Just because you think "Wow, that's a strange thing for a woman to be doing," you don't need to call inappropriate attention to it. Find an appropriate way of identifying a person or mentioning gender without calling undue attention. For example, instead of the sentence *The woman judge explained the charges to the jury, telling them not to discuss the case with anyone else*, you might write *When the judge explained the charges to the jury, she told them not to discuss the case with anyone else*. In both versions, it is clear to the reader that the judge is a woman, but the second version is smoother and more subtle.

Omit Unnecessary Personal Characteristics. Avoid unnecessary references to marital status, dress and other irrelevant personal characteristics. The key is significance. Writers always have more information than they use, and one of their responsibilities is to sort out the germane information from that which is immaterial.

When you are wondering about using a particular piece of information, the other-foot test might be helpful. Ask yourself: If the shoe were on the other foot, would I still want to write this? If you can honestly say that in your writing you would mention the occupation of the wife of one political candidate, then it's probably OK to write similarly about the husband of another. If you would mention what the male politician wore to the rally, then in fairness you can mention what the woman politician wore. But when you apply the other-foot test, often you realize that the information is really inappropriate and unnecessary.

If the fact that a person is single or divorced, married or partnered is significant to the story, then report it. But if it is superfluous information, don't use it.

Bias Tip 2: Physical Characteristics

In your writing, use discretion when you describe physical and other personal characteristics. If physical condition, age or other personal descriptions are relevant, provide the information in a nonbiased way. However, don't use such personal information without good reason. In the past, newspapers routinely described people by using their age, occupation, and addresses. Amid growing concerns about personal privacy, however, people in public communications need to question the relevance of such information. Does it matter that the new principal is 39?

Age bias can focus on words identified with youth or age. Avoid using phrases such as *old man* and referring to young women who work in an office as *the girls*.

Use appropriate terms to indicate physical conditions. Terms such as *dumb* or *crippled* no longer carry neutral connotations; instead, we might say someone is *unable to speak* or *uses a wheelchair to get around*. It's often a matter of putting the focus on the person rather than on the problem, such as writing about *people with handicaps* rather than *handicapped people* or *man with AIDS* rather than an *AIDS victim*. Likewise, consider the connotations for designations of mental or emotional conditions.

Don't confuse the distinction between diseases, injuries and physical conditions. For example, don't portray pregnancy, menopause or advanced age as illnesses or afflictions. These are physical conditions, but not negative ones.

Bias Tip 3: Ethnicity, Culture and Lifestyle

Avoid stereotypes based on supposed characteristics associated with race, national background, religion, lifestyle, politics, sexual orientation and other personal traits.

Avoid offensive, outdated and otherwise inappropriate terms. Obvious racial slurs seldom find their way into print anymore. But writers' sensitivities sometimes aren't fine-tuned about terms that are considered disrespectful by some groups. Words such as *mick*, *squaw*, and *canuck* carry negative connotations that make them inappropriate in many writing situations.

Use inclusive references. Consider this sentence: *The mayor met with representatives of various churches in the city.* This includes people who worship in churches, but where does it leave those who worship at the synagogue, temple, mosque, kiva or longhouse? The sentence might be more accurate if it reported *The mayor met with representatives of various religious groups in the city.*

Don't betray a Eurocentric bias, such as a survey that lists demographic categories as English, Irish, German, French, Italian, Spanish, Asian, Black and other.

It should be a basic principle of public relations writing that people deserve to be called by the names they prefer for themselves. Use those terms. For example, avoid using outdated terms such as *colored* or *Afro-American*. Today more accepted terms are *person of color* or *African-American*. Undoubtedly, new terms will emerge as English continues to evolve.

Likewise, be attentive to people in alternative lifestyles and nontraditional families. Many gay and lesbian couples consider themselves to be just as committed as legal spouses, and other people find that their identity as families is not bound by legal contracts and religious rituals. Whether you personally agree with such lifestyles is not the point. Rather, be aware in your professional writing that not everyone lives stereotypical lives.

Revisit the advice in the tip about not mentioning unnecessary gender information. Just as it's probably inappropriate to note that a surgeon is a woman or that the kindergarten teacher is a man, it's probably even less appropriate to write that he or she is gay, Hispanic, a Republican, Catholic, or a number of other descriptors that, while accurate, are irrelevant. If the information is part of the story, then by all means use it in context. But don't go out of your way to point out something that you personally may find odd or interesting unless it adds to the telling of the story.

Exercise 2.10—Eliminating Language Bias

Rewrite the following sentences as needed to eliminate any biased language. Answers are listed at the end of this chapter.

1. The medical report dealt with the birth process for monkeys, gorillas and man.

2. "Do something about your son," her neighbor's wife screamed out the back door.

3. According to union rules, policemen must be in proper uniform when they appear in public.

4. The highway gas station is manned at all times of the day and night for the convenience of travelers.

5. Mrs. Ramadera was elected chairman of the League of Women Voters.

6. Early immigrants to the country included Frenchmen, Germans, Swedes and Scotsmen.

7. The new chief of surgery is a woman doctor from Pittsburgh.

8. Five students in the class—three girls and two men—wrote the winning essays on malnutrition.

Answers to Chapter Exercises

Exercise 2.2

1-A, 2-C, 3-A, 4-C, 5-B, 6-C, 7-C, 8-A, 9-E, 10-D, 11-A, 12-B

Exercise 2.3

1. Remember to proofread carefully.
2. The university will extend library hours because finals are next week.
3. Now our client is ready to begin the research project.
4. Five students have outstanding records.
5. The building was purchased in 1923.
6. The team lost because several key players were sick.
7. The program will begin next month.

Exercise 2.4

1. In the <u>final</u> outcome, we expect to see that important <u>foreign</u> imports will continue <u>to maintain</u> a positive <u>current</u> trend.
2. <u>Local</u> residents of this quiet <u>little</u> village will join <u>together</u> to do some <u>advance</u> planning for their <u>annual</u> family picnic on Easter <u>Sunday</u>, just as they have done <u>previously</u> each year.
3. Whether <u>or not</u> we are <u>absolutely</u> sure about Thelma's skill as an ice skater, we are convinced that she is a <u>very</u> unique personality who will be a <u>positive</u> asset to our team.
4. The study committee will refer <u>back</u> to its minutes to learn more about the <u>past</u> history of this important project to improve tourism for <u>the city of</u> Philadelphia.
5. The <u>general</u> consensus <u>of opinion</u> is that, at this <u>point in time</u>, the high school students should not protest <u>against</u> a school-night <u>curfew</u>.
6. The university recently produced two <u>different</u> versions of the report, giving <u>close</u> scrutiny to new techniques for growing crops in <u>rice</u> paddies and corn fields.
7. The *Jewish* rabbi met with the Episcopal priest and the *Muslim* imam.

Exercise 2.8

1-O, 2-B, 3-E, 4-I, 5-J, 6-A, 7-F, 8-G, 9-N, 10-Q, 11-D, 12-L, 13-C, 14-K, 15-H, 16-M, 17-P

Exercise 2.9

Bellboy = bellhop, luggage attendant
Clergyman = rabbi, imam, roshi, priest, minister
Deliveryman = driver
Forefathers = ancestors
Foreman = supervisor
Garbageman = garbage collector
Housewife = homemaker
Public relations man = public relations practitioner
Seaman = sailor
Spokesman = spokesperson, company representative
Statesman = diplomat
Stewardess = flight attendant
Watchman = guard

Exercise 2.10

1. . . . birth process for monkeys, gorillas and humans.
2. . . . her neighbor screamed . . .
3. . . . police officers must be in proper uniform . . .
4. . . . is staffed at all times . . .
5. . . . elected to chair the League . . . (or elected head of the League).
6. . . . included people from France, Germany, Sweden and Scotland.
7. . . . is a doctor from Pittsburgh. (Indicate her gender in subsequent reference.)
8. . . . three girls and two boys . . . (or three women and two men, but don't indicate gender at all unless it is relevant to the story).

3

Persuasive Communication

It's a myth that research is tedious and theory is impractical. Research can be both interesting and illuminating, and theory can be a functional tool. For public relations writers, both are helpful approaches that provide guidelines and suggestions for creating messages that are meaningful and effective. In this chapter you will review the art and science of communication—what it is and what it isn't.

This chapter focuses on the rich base of theory and research, as well as the many guidelines and practical suggestions that flow from these. It looks specifically at persuasive communication and lessons drawn from research. It considers the persuasive factors associated with message sources and message content. Finally, the chapter provides an overview of propaganda, an unethical aspect of persuasive communication. Here are your objectives for Chapter 3:

- To understand the nature of communication
- To become familiar with various theories about communication
- To explain the role of persuasion in public relations writing
- To apply lessons from persuasion theory in your writing
- To explain the difference between persuasion and propaganda.

Theories of Public Communication

Researchers and theorists from many backgrounds have offered insights into the nature of *public communication*—the range of communication that extends beyond the purely personal interaction between people or small groups. The relevant research can be divided into three areas: the process of communication, the object of communication, and the effects of communication. Understanding each of these areas helps the public relations writer be more effective, because theory offers guidance and insight into what works, why it works and how it can work under different circumstances.

The Process of Communication

Sociologist Harold Lasswell gave a classic definition of communication: who says what in which channel to whom, with what effect. That was in 1948. More than half a century later, the question of what public communication is remains important to public relations writers.

Claude Shannon and Warren Weaver's *mathematical theory of communication*, better known as *information theory*, grew out of the field of telecommunications. Shannon and Weaver observe that an information source produces a message that is converted by a transmitter and sent via some channel to a receiver that reconstructs the message for the destination person. The clarity of this message can be reduced by *noise,* which is defined as something added to the signal not intended by the source. Noise can take many forms, including the linguistic clutter that the writing reminders in the previous chapter seek to help you avoid. One way of offsetting message disintegration caused by noise is by *redundancy*, the deliberate repetition of the message. What this means is that the more that noise causes the message to become distorted and misunderstood, the greater the need for repetition of the message. This is why public relations practitioners are seldom content to present a one-time-only message, but rather are continually seeking ways to repeat and reinforce the message.

The concept of *feedback* was drawn from *systems theory*, particularly Norbert Wiener's 1954 treatise on cybernetics, a field of study that deals with sensors and control mechanisms. With a better understanding of the role of feedback in the communication process, public relations writers try to create opportunities for organizations to talk with their publics rather than talking at them. Wilbur Schramm observed this instrumental approach to communication and outlined what has become a classic model: The message begins with the sender, who encodes it in some way and transmits it through a signal to a destination where it is decoded by the receiver.

The Object of Communication

It's perhaps the most famous koan of the Western world: If a tree falls in the forest and no one is nearby, does it make a sound? Let's give the question a communication twist: If you give a speech that no one hears, are you communicating? If you write a news release that doesn't get published, are you communicating?

A concept useful for public relations writing is that communication is a *receiver phenomenon*. Communication is not controlled by the sender but rather by the receiver. The speaker may be gifted, even eloquent, but if the speech is in Swahili and the audience does not understand Swahili, no real communication takes place. If the message is presented in sign language, Arabic script, Morse code, Japanese katakana, or any other system of language presentation that the audience does not understand, communication is thwarted.

The communication process can be blocked in many ways. As public relations writers, we should understand that our audiences will always be in control of the communication process. They will choose whether to pay attention to a message, their interests and abilities will determine if they understand the message, and eventually it will be their choice whether to act on it in any way.

For the public relations writer, meaning is a rich concept with many opportunities, some pitfalls and much room for effective creativity. Sven Windahl and Benno Signitzer, two contemporary European communication scholars, offer a model showing how meaning can take on different shapes during the communication process. They trace the evolution of the message as it was intended, sent, structured, received and perceived. If public relations writers are to communicate clearly, we should take into account factors such as interpretation, control, intermediaries, connotation and denotation.

One of the earliest theories to focus on the receiver in the communication process was the *uses-and-gratifications theory* associated with researchers Elihu Katz and Jay Blumler. They suggest that people make active choices in selecting media for particular purposes. Among those reasons are information, entertainment, value reassurance, social interaction and emotional release. Technologies such as interactive cable and information-on-demand rely on the validity of the uses-and-gratifications theory.

Martin Fishbein helped lay the groundwork for the related *expectancy-value theory*, which observes that people make media choices based on what they want, what they expect from the media, and how they evaluate the ability of the media to meet those expectations. Sandra Ball-Rokeach and Melvin DeFleur, meanwhile, developed the *dependency theory* that audiences, the media and society in general are in a three-way relationship.

Audiences use the media to the extent that the media provide information important to society and the people's role in it. The more relevant that information is, the more influential the media become.

The Effects of Communication

Throughout the latter half of the 20th century and into the 21st, social scientists have been researching the roles that media play in impacting on people's interests and attitudes, opinions and behaviors. The decades have seen the pendulum swing in both directions.

Powerful Effects. Theories from the first third of the 20th century presumed a *powerful effects model* for the mass media, in which researchers concluded that the media exert a direct, strong and predictable influence over people's attitudes, opinions and behavior. Terms such as *bullet theory* and *hypodermic needle theory* are associated with this cause-and-effect relationship between message and response. This model drew on *stimulus-response theory* or *conditioned reflex theory*, a simple approach typified by famous experiments by Ivan Pavlov, who conditioned dogs to anticipate food when they heard a particular sound. Closely associated with this approach is the *operant conditioning theory* of B.F. Skinner focusing on the role of reinforcement of behavior in creating attitude change.

The conditioning orientation of such theories does not translate well to public communication, however, because publics can be very complex. These learning-based theories suggest that certain information presented in a certain way causes people to arrive at a particular conclusion. Sometimes this works, especially when audiences have little personal interest in the issue at hand. But the more personally audiences are involved in an issue, the less useful these cognitive theories are to public relations writers.

Limited Effects. Around the middle of the last century, the powerful effects model gave way to a *limited effects model* that saw communication as being a weak influence over people. Educators Joseph Klapper and Hope Lunin Klapper argued that public communication ordinarily does not cause significant audience effects and has minimal consequence.

Closely associated with this model is the *two-step flow of communication theory.* Two social science researchers, Paul Lazarsfeld and Elihu Katz, studied communication and voting, identifying a predictable communication pattern. Instead of directly changing attitudes, they found, the media may influence opinion leaders, who then influence others through interpersonal means. Lazarsfeld eventually extended this idea into a *multistep flow of communication theory* which identifies several layers in the process.

Moderate-to-Powerful Effects. During the past several decades, the pendulum has swung back toward where it was a century ago. This stage of research is leading to a *moderate-to-powerful effects model*. Several researchers have shown that public media have strong, long-term effects on audiences and on public opinion, though these do not occur easily or predictably.

George Gerbner's *cultivation theory* reasons that exposure to public media cultivates a person's perceptions and expectations, with a major difference between heavy and light TV viewers. One primary cultivation effect Gerbner reports is that heavy viewers have a perception of a "mean world," with exaggerated fear, distrust and pessimism. Meanwhile, Elisabeth Noelle-Neumann's *spiral of silence theory* suggests that one media effect may actually be to hinder the communication process by giving people an exaggerated sense of isolation and a reluctance to express their opinions if they learn that their opinion is not shared by others. Psychologist Albert Bandura's *social learning theory* suggests that the media provide examples, or modeling, that become part of a personal reality to which audiences respond. Newer studies in the media's long-term effects on issues such as violence, sexuality and citizenship tend to boost the return to the powerful effects model.

In 1922, journalist Walter Lippmann identified an imagined pseudoenvironment constructed by the media that impacts public opinion. In 1972, journalism professors Donald Shaw and Maxwell McCombs extended this to the *agenda-setting theory* of the media, in which the media direct not what people think but rather what they think about. This observation has important implications for public relations practitioners, who try both to link organizational issues with those on the media agenda and to interest the media in organizational issues.

Associated with the agenda-setting theory are the related concepts of *priming*, how a news topic reminds media audiences of previous information, and *framing*, the way the news media treat a particular topic. If agenda-setting deals with what people think about, priming reminds them what they already know about the topic, and framing deals with how they think about the topic. Here is an example of framing: Many U.S. states are concerned with the issue of taxation or lack of taxation on Indian lands. Research from the American Indian Policy and Media Initiative at Buffalo State College points out that most mainstream news media unquestioningly adopt the framing language of state government, which often talks about "losing" money because of un-taxed sales on Indian lands. Seldom do reporters frame the story from the opposite frame: that because Indian lands are controlled by federal treaty and are not subject to state government, the states have no legal claim in the first place to the money they lament losing. Because framing offers a perspective on the news and presents a lens through which to make sense of the world, public relations writers often are quite concerned about how their message is framed by the media.

Exercise 3.1—Freewriting on Communication Theory

Freewrite for five minutes on the following topic: *How are theories about communication useful to a public relations writer?* Discuss this with your classmates. ∎

Communication and Persuasion

In Chapter 1 you were asked to view communication not as an either-or (either informational or promotional) but rather to understand that all public relations writing seeks to influence people in some way. Both-and is the operative metaphor. You may present information both in the neutral style of journalistic writing, and you may weave it into promotional formats. But whatever the format, you will use information to foster various effects. These are the objectives discussed in the previous section.

What is *persuasive communication?* The term means different things to people. A lot of conflicting connotations revolve around the notion of persuasion, with subtle differences in how people interpret it.

Persuasion Defined

Various perspectives about persuasion exist, but for our purposes as public relations writers, let's claim the following understanding: *Persuasion* is a process of communication that intends to influence people using ethical means that enhance a democratic society. We'll look more closely at each part of this definition.

Persuasion is a process of communication. Public relations writers focus on communication, so the role of messages and feedback is important to us. Further, understanding communication as a process helps us look at persuasion as an ongoing series of messages and responses, part of the cycle of interaction between an organization and its many publics.

Persuasion intends to influence people. If we are to profit by a deeper understanding of persuasion, we need to see it as being linked with people, our target publics. In public relations, we are trying to provide information that will influence our publics in some way or enhance our relationship with them.

Persuasion uses ethical means. For the public relations writer, any attempt at persuasion must be based on solid professional standards. If communication becomes misleading, deceptive or manipulative—by intention or through negligence—it has moved beyond the legitimate boundaries of persuasion. For some people, persuasion has a tarnished image because subversive communication techniques occasionally have been used to manipulate unknowing or gullible publics. For the public relations writer, however, persuasion is a noble concept because, by definition, it is not debased into misinformation or propaganda.

Persuasion enhances a democratic society. Philosophically and legally, organizations may try to persuade. In a democratic society, individuals and organizations enjoy the right of free speech that allows them to espouse a point of view, share it in the marketplace of ideas, and attempt to influence others to adopt that point of view. One of the basic roles of public relations people is to help organizations exercise this right. But people who receive an organization's messages must be seen as having the freedom not to be persuaded. Public relations practitioners must uphold a person's right to ignore or reject our messages.

Communication that doesn't meet these criteria should not be called persuasion. If communication makes no attempt to influence, by definition it is not trying to persuade. If communication is unethical or immoral, it instead should be called propaganda, not persuasive communication. And if the goal of communication is not to enhance relationships within an open society, then it is self-serving, nonresponsive and involved in something other than persuasion.

An Ancient Art

The art of persuasion is an ancient one, deeply rooted in classical civilization. More than 4,000 years ago, the philosopher Ptah-Hotep advised court speakers in Egypt to link their messages to the concern of the audiences. In the 5th century B.C.E. in the northern Mediterranean, the rhetorician Corax of Syracuse wrote a book about persuasive speaking. Meanwhile in Greece, Socrates of Athens and his student, Plato, studied and practiced *rhetoric*, the art of persuasive communication. Plato's student, Aristotle, later wrote "Rhetoric," a treatise discussing persuasion as the art of proving something to be true or false. In Rome, Marcus Tullius Cicero developed this rhetorical method for presenting persuasive arguments in public, and Marcus Fabius Quintilianus taught about the ethical content of persuasion.

Religion played a role in applying and handing on the rhetorical tradition. The early Christian Church preserved and enhanced the concepts of Greek and Roman rhetoric. In Roman Africa in the 4th and 5th centuries, Augustine of Hippo developed the art of preaching, insisting that truth is the ultimate goal of such public speaking. Later, in northern Europe during the 8th century, the Saxon theologian Alcuin reinterpreted Roman rhetorical teachings for the Emperor Charlemagne. For a time after the fall of Roman civilization, Aristotle was lost to much of the western world. Muslim scholars, Christian Arabs and Arabic-speaking Jews introduced Aristotle's teaching on rhetoric to the Islamic world during the 9th century. In the centuries that followed, Aristotle was reintroduced to the West, mainly via translations through Arabic and by the writings of both Arab and Jewish scholars. In the 14th century, the Christian philosopher-monk Thomas Aquinas revisited Aristotle to study the persuasive nature of religious communication.

Throughout the centuries, the various branches of the Christian Church developed the area of *apologetics*, the systematic attempt to assert the reasonableness of faith and to refute opposing arguments. Modern-day preachers and evangelists continue this tradition in persuasive communication for religious purposes. Following in their footsteps are the secular advocates of self-fulfillment who figure prominently in television infomercials that promote everything from financial independence to physical attractiveness or emotional fulfillment.

Persuasive communication has been at the heart of much of Western social and political development. It is a fundamental element of democracy that played a major role in the American Revolution, with examples such as Thomas Paine and Samuel Adams. The American movements for abolition, women's suffrage, civil rights and gay rights all have drawn heavily on the concepts and applications of persuasive communication, as has most war rhetoric in recent decades.

Just as persuasion is an ancient art, it also is becoming a contemporary science. This is true nowhere more than in the political arena. Recent political campaigns have become sophisticated strategic experiments with in-depth research, nuanced crafting of messages, careful and costly implementation, and ongoing evaluation. Meanwhile, throughout much of the last century, social scientists dealing with psychology, sociology and communication have given increasing scholarly attention to persuasive communication.

Attention to persuasive communication is primarily a product of Western, European-based civilization. Asian, African, Semitic and Native American traditions generally have put a lesser premium on influencing others. The philosophers and linguists of these cultures more often have focused on storytelling, the graceful use of language, the development of consensus, even the communicative value of silence. Don't interpret this observation as suggesting that persuasive communication is not a universal aspect of human interaction, or that certain cultures are incapable of being persuasive. It simply points out the priority in Western culture for a social assertiveness and a preference for the more functional aspects of language.

Research on Persuasion

Many theories about persuasive communication draw heavily on the field of social and personal psychology, since persuasion is seen as a personal phenomenon rather than simply an issue about the techniques and process of communication. Other theories deal more specifically with personality.

Social Psychology Research

One set of theories about persuasion revolves around the observation that people seek consistency between attitudes and information about those attitudes. The message source is an important factor in these consistency theories. The *balance theory* or *consonance theory* associated with Fritz Heider and the *symmetry theory* proposed by Theodore Newcomb suggest that people seek an attitude similar to that of their communication partners. They will agree or disagree with a person not only because of what that person says but also because of the relationship with the other person. The implications of this for public relations writers is that we can foster persuasion by building on good relationships between a source and our publics.

The *congruity theory* developed by psychologists Charles Osgood and Percy Tannenbaum suggests that people experience confusion when two attitudes are in conflict. Usually, this is resolved by the adoption of the easier attitude or by a blend of opposing attitudes. Similarly, the *cognitive dissonance theory* articulated by Leon Festinger focuses on the confusion that arises when information is out of step with a person's attitude. People will try to reduce the confusion, perhaps by changing the attitude but more likely by avoiding or ignoring the negative information, by seeking positive information to replace it, or simply by distorting or re-interpreting it to fit their attitudes. This theory helps explain why public relations writers are sometimes frustrated because our publics don't seem to act on information in the way we think they should. Closely related to cognitive dissonance are several concepts dealing with selectivity.

Through *selective exposure* and *selective avoidance*, people expose themselves to messages they think they will like and avoid what they expect not to like. These choices apparently are made because of personal interest rather than a deliberate avoidance of opposing viewpoints. Using *selective attention*, people pay attention to information that supports their attitudes and ignore information opposed to their attitudes. With both selective exposure and selective attention, we pay attention to what interests us. *Selective perception* leads people to interpret information based on how it fits their attitudes; we see what we want to see and what we expect to see. Similarly, using *selection retention* people remember information that is of interest and forget information that seems not to be relevant to them. Finally, via *selective recall*, people are more likely to remember information that supports their attitudes and conveniently forget conflicting information; we remember primarily what supports our beliefs.

Researchers Muzafer Sherif and Carl Hovland offered the *social judgment theory* which states that attitude change is more a change in a person's perception rather than a change in belief. From this theory, the writer may find it more useful to focus on presenting a new image about a client or organization rather than trying to change the beliefs and values of members of a target public.

Another area of theory into the process of persuasive communication returns to the threefold classical Greek emphasis articulated by Aristotle: *ethos* (source credibility), *pathos* (appeals to emotion or sentiment) and *logos* (appeals to logic or reason).

Theories from Personality Research

Two personality-based approaches are *psychological type theory*, stemming from Carl Jung and modified by Isabel Myers and Catherine Briggs, and *temperament theory*, a modification of the Myers-Briggs approach by David Keirsey and Marilyn Bates.

These related theories suggest that innate personality factors give each person a predisposition toward certain types of persuasive techniques. Some people are naturally more attracted to facts, figures and cause-and-effect examples. Others are persuaded more by nuance, a touching story, a poignant example or personal application. These theories offer much potential when public relations writers are able to match appropriate message styles with the personalities of their publics.

An outgrowth of personality theory is the field of *psychographics*, the study of consumer lifestyles. One model is VALS (Value and Lifestyles), a consumer segmentation system developed in 1978 by Arnold Mitchell and the Stanford Research Institute of Menlo Park, Calif. It was revised in 1989 as VALS2, incorporating newer lifestyle trends and providing greater application to strategic communication in areas such as marketing, advertising, promotions and public relations. In whatever form, VALS identifies categories of people such as need driven, outer directed and inner directed, with each category having several subcategories. Another categorization based on VALS groups people according to their orientation toward principles, status or action. Studies into psychographics can help persuaders better understand the motivation of various publics.

Another system with application to persuasive communication is *geodemographics*, which combines sociology, geography and demography to segment the country into neighborhood or residential types. This is based on the presumption that such segmentation identifies categories of people with similar lifestyles, values and consumer patterns. With this model, public relations practitioners can target messages to publics on the basis of where they can be reached and the types of people associated with particular environments. A prime application of geodemographics is the PRIZM classification developed by the Claritas Corporation of Alexandria, Va., which links Zip codes with sociographic and psychographic characteristics of residents. Other applications are GeoVALS, a blending of the traditional VALS segmentation with geodemographic data, and Strategic Mapping's ClusterPLUS, developed for marketing and customer-relationship purposes.

Exercise 3.2—Freewriting on Persuasion and Public Relations

Part 1: Look up each of the following words in your dictionary and write a brief definition: advocate, convince, entice, induce, influence, manipulate, persuade.

Part 2: Freewrite for five minutes on the following topic: *How does persuasion fit into the activities of a public relations writer?* Then discuss this with your classmates. ∎

Lessons from Research

So far, this chapter has dealt with many of the theories related to communication and persuasion. The value of a theory is its ability to help us develop guidelines and make predictions. The following guidelines are drawn from various researchers who have studied communication and persuasion over many years. Some guidelines are the result of several concurring studies; others are less conclusive, even speculative. They are offered here not as a list of dos and don'ts but rather as a series of tips and idea generators.

Message Sources

The source of a message, both the organization and the spokesperson, is important to any consideration of public relations writing. Some sources are better than others because they are more likely to be believed by a particular public. Carl Hovland was one of the first researchers to study the issue of *source credibility,* and his work still offers much insight into source effectiveness.

An effective communicator is a person or organization perceived by an audience as having the Three C's—credibility, charisma and control. In each category, note that the focus is on how the audience perceives a source, warranted or not. Let's look at the Three Cs of an effective communicator.

Credibility. A communicator with *credibility* is one who has expertise to speak about a particular subject, a recognized status or prestige, and a competence to communicate effectively, as well as apparent honesty, sincerity and lack of bias.

Credibility is particularly enhanced by *expertise*. The source of a message that has expert knowledge or experience regarding the subject is more credible; people are more likely to believe those who seem to know what they are talking about. The public relations writer can increase a communicator's credibility by emphasizing his or her education or personal experience. Likewise, audiences tend to put their faith in message sources with *status*, that is, with recognized social or organizational standing—also something the public relations writer can draw attention to. Credibility is also enhanced by a message source with *communication competence*, a speaker who is composed, articulate and, if not eloquent, at least pro ficient in oral communication. In addition, credibility is enhanced by *sincerity*, the character of trustworthiness. People are likely to believe someone who is reliable and honorable. Sources are especially credible when they appear to be *unbiased*. This is apparent when message sources speak apart from their expected positions, particularly when they speak against their own apparent self-interests or when they speak on behalf of organizations or causes other than their own.

Charisma. A *charismatic* communicator is one who is likable and who may be familiar to the audience, similar to the audience, and/or physically attractive.

Athletes and entertainers are sought after to endorse products and speak for causes because audiences tend to believe sources they admire and respect. This *likability* is an ambiguous characteristic that often differs even among various members of the same target public. Closely related is *familiarity*, the characteristic of being known by the audience. These two characteristics account for the frequent use of celebrity spokespeople, who audiences know (or think they know) and like.

Meanwhile, a source who shares characteristics with the audience may be more effective in persuasion than someone without those similarities. This *similarity* has many dimensions such as age, gender, race, ethnicity, occupation and affiliations. Shared attitudes are even stronger than demographic similarities. Audiences sometimes are more easily persuaded by *attractiveness*, that is, by someone whom the audience considers to be physically appealing, handsome, beautiful or sexy. This, however, is the least effective attribute of a persuasive source, and in some cases, the quality of physical attractiveness can work against a source's persuasive power by diminishing other, more important characteristics such as credibility.

Control. A communicator who exhibits the characteristic of *control* is one who has power or authority over the audience or who is in a position to examine and pass judgment over the audience. Audiences are more likely to be persuaded by someone in a position of *power* or *authority*. That is why employers, teachers and particularly parents are effective persuaders. Another aspect of control is *scrutiny*, the ability of a message source to investigate members of the audience, hold them accountable in some way, and pass judgment on them.

Tip for Better Writing *Effective Message Soures*

Use this checklist to make sure you have included each of the major elements of an effective message source.

- Credibility, based on one or more of the following elements:
  o Expertise, experience
  o Status, prestige
  o Communication competence
  o Honesty, sincerity, lack of bias

- Charisma, based on one or more of the following elements:
  o Likability
  o Familiarity to the audience
  o Similarity to the audience
  o Physical attractiveness

- Control, based on one or more of the following elements:
  o Power over the audience
  o Control over the audience
  o Ability to scrutinize or pass judgment on the audience.

The following applications can be made based on research dealing with sources of persuasive communication.

- Highly credible sources are more likely to be perceived as being fair and their conclusions viewed as justified. Some studies have reported attitude change 3½ times more often when the source is highly credible.
- A positive message from a stranger has more impact than the same message from a friend, probably because praise from a stranger seems more sincere than when it comes from a friend. Similarly, a negative message from a friend has more impact than criticism from a stranger, probably because it is seen as more sincere.
- The credibility of an original source is enhanced when the message is reiterated by an opinion leader.

- Likeable sources are perceived as more credible only when the audience has little personal involvement in the issue. With issues of higher personal involvement, likability is not a significant factor.
- Sources that are very attractive physically risk distracting audiences, who sometimes remember the source but not the message.
- Highly credible sources are especially effective in persuading audiences to change attitudes immediately after their presentation of the message. This effectiveness decreases over time.
- Attitude change produced by a noncredible source increases over time. This so-called *sleeper effect* suggests that at first people may consciously reject a message from a source they dislike or distrust, but that over time their memory of the source may fade while they remember the message. Some researchers argue that such a sleeper effect does not exist.

Public relations writers should remember that message sources are not only persons. Organizations also are seen as sources. Writers should consider that the way an organization is perceived, especially its visibility and reputation, has an impact on its effectiveness as a source in persuasive communication. Reputations for quality and responsibility helped both Johnson & Johnson's Tylenol survive the cyanide emergency and Pepsi-Cola deal with the syringe hoax. But obvious self-interest has rendered the tobacco industry unable to convince the public to disbelieve links between smoking and ill health. And Philip Morris tobacco company received a lot of criticism when it created a costly TV advertising campaign to congratulate itself on making a modest charitable contribution.

Many organizations enjoy a favorable perception or reputation with the public, but even this is very changeable. Polls show that big institutions—medicine, law, organized religion, higher education and the media—have lost some credibility. They have to work harder in their persuasive communication to remain effective communicators. Other institutions including government, politics and business traditionally have been viewed with significant skepticism, causing special difficulties for their public relations writers. "Tips for Better Writing: Effective Message Sources" contains all the elements that should be taken into consideration when choosing a message source.

Exercise 3.3—Effective Message Sources

You are a public relations writer for the local sheriff's department, assigned to develop a public service video aimed at high school students. The message is: Don't drink and drive on prom night. The sheriff has asked for your recommendations for a spokesperson for the video, which will be disseminated via television and over the Internet. Prepare the following information.

Part 1: Because the sheriff likes to have choices, identify three possible spokespersons to present your message. Analyze each as to their likely effectiveness as the source of persuasive communication, based on the Three Cs of an effective communicator, as noted above.

Part 2: Indicate your recommendation of the spokesperson you think would be most effective in persuading your target public. Justify this choice by discussing the particular elements of persuasive message sources that are evident in your choice.   ∎

Message Structure

Various research studies have found that the structure of a message can significantly affect the persuasion process. Specifically, researchers have looked at three elements of structure—the order of presentation, the value of drawing conclusions or making recommendations, and repetition within the message itself. Following are some of the lessons that can be drawn from this research.

- No significant difference exists between presenting arguments in order of least-to-most important or vice versa.
- Though research findings are not conclusive, many practitioners have found that it is usually best to sandwich the arguments. Present your own argument first, refute opposing arguments, and restate your own argument.
- The final word is the one most likely to be remembered by the audience, especially with less educated audiences or ones less personally involved in the issue.
- Presenting two sides of an argument is more effective than giving only one side, especially with sophisticated or educated audiences. This is especially important when the audience eventually is exposed to a contrary message.
- Presentation of only one side of an argument may cause temporary attitudinal change, but this can be wiped out if the audience later hears opposing arguments. Presentation of both sides of an argument results in an even larger attitude change than presentation of only one side, and this change is likely to remain high even if the audience later hears opposing arguments.
- Drawing a conclusion or making a recommendation is usually more persuasive than leaving it to the audience to draw the conclusion.
- Some evidence suggests that if an audience draws its own conclusion, it is more likely to resist changing that attitude in the future.
- Messages, especially those presented through the public media, are quickly forgotten if they are not at least moderately reinforced by repetition.
- Repetition is useful for keeping issues on the public agenda. It has also been shown to be helpful in increasing actions such as voter turnout.
- Too much repetition can cause the audience to tire of the message to the point of disagreeing with it.

Message Content

Research has looked at the content of messages, especially the relationship between emotion and logic, appeals to fear or guilt, and the use of humor and sex appeal. Here are some observations based on that research:

- A combination of factual and emotional appeals is more effective than either approach alone. By some criteria, two-thirds of the American population prefers factual presentations.
- Messages that are directed to the self-interests of the audience are more likely to gain audience awareness and interest.
- Appeals to fear, guilt and other negative emotions, as well as the presentations of threats to the audience, can cause the audience to avoid or distort the message.

- With moderate interest levels, low-to-moderate fear appeals can be more effective than strong fear appeals in producing attitude change.
- If the audience has a high interest level, strong fear appeals may be more effective in changing attitudes than weaker appeals. Fear appeals also are more persuasive when presented by sources with high credibility.
- Fear appeals are more effective when coupled with reassurances and specific recommendations for corrective action to reduce fears.
- A mix of advocacy and entertainment is more acceptable than advocacy alone.
- Fear appeals can affect acceptance and behavioral intentions without having subsequent impact on action. Specific instructions with fear appeals can affect action first without affecting either attitude or opinion.
- Three aspects make fear appeals persuasive: the degree of harm, the likelihood of harm, and the likelihood of an effective solution to eliminate the harm.
- Humor is more effective in increasing awareness and generating interest than in producing changes in attitude or action.
- Humor sometimes can generate a liking for the message source, but this can backfire if the audience thinks the use of humor is a manipulative device. The determining factor may be if the humor seems natural or contrived and whether it is appropriate to the subject.
- Humor sometimes causes audiences to evaluate a message not on its persuasive content but merely as an entertainment vehicle.
- Appeals based on humor quickly lose their persuasive effect with repetition.
- Appeals to sex, such as by using alluring models, can enhance the awareness and interest of audiences, especially younger ones.

Exercise 3.4—Effective Message Content

Part 1: Using the persuasive communicator you identified in Exercise 3.3, write a brief message (150–200 words) to high school students to persuade them not to drink and drive as they celebrate their prom and graduation.

Part 2: Write margin notes or footnotes to identify the persuasive tactics you use related to message structure and message content.

Media Factors in Persuasion

Research has looked at the media in relation to persuasion, to learn if some channels of communication are more effective in the persuasion process than other channels. Following are some of the insights stemming from this research.

- Face-to-face communication is more effective in changing attitudes than messages presented through any type of media.
- Speech produces less comprehension than a written message, but more acceptance.

- Little difference exists between intense oral exhortations and more subdued speaking. Both types of speech are more persuasive than written messages.
- Personal communication is more likely to be persuasive in all three categories of effects: awareness, acceptance and action.
- Public media are more useful in reinforcing existing attitudes than in changing attitudes.
- Public media may produce modification or minor attitude change but rarely can they convert audiences to the opposite point of view.
- Public media have more effect on weak or new attitudes than on established ones. The implication for public relations writers may be to use news and advertising media to reach neutrals and to seek early adoption of attitudes in new situations.
- A combination of public media and personal communication is more effective in changing attitudes than either type of communication alone.
- Print media produce greater attention and voluntary re-exposure than electronic media.
- Print media produce more comprehension, especially with complex issues, than broadcast media.
- Broadcast media produce more attention than print media.
- There is little difference in the persuasive effectiveness of mediated communication. In one study, a message was equally effective in written, audiotaped and videotaped formats.
- Televised or videotaped presentations heighten the impact of source factors.

Audience Factors in Persuasion

Much research also has been conducted with a focus on the audience receiving the persuasive message, leading to the following applications.

- Unsubstantiated messages produce more attitude change in people with low self-esteem than in people with higher self-esteem.
- People with high self-esteem are more likely to be persuaded by complex and well-substantiated messages. Those with low self-esteem are more likely to be persuaded by fear appeals.
- Audiences that make a commitment or personal decision are likely to resist subsequent pressures to change attitudes and opinions.
- The more involved the audience is in the persuasive situation, the more likely the persuasion will be effective. For example, low-involvement communication situations such as television viewing are less persuasive than high-involvement situations such as face-to-face communication.
- Audiences that participate actively in making decisions, such as role playing or assessing alternative solutions, retain attitude change over longer periods of time.
- A few studies have suggested that women may be more easily persuaded than men. But the conclusion here is weak and inconsistent.
- Some studies have shown that men are more persuasive as message sources than women are, regardless of the gender of the receiver. Other studies suggest that societal changes are eliminating any gender differences in persuasion.

Exercise 3.5—Persuasive Messages

Part 1: Write a brief essay (150–200 words) on one of the following two topics about recognized public relations pioneers, seeking to persuade your fellow classmates about the position you are taking. Use lessons from this chapter about message source, message structure, message content and audiences.

- Ivy Lee manipulated information and misled the public in his campaign to rehabilitate the image of John D. Rockefeller. Therefore, he should not be considered a model of ethical public relations because . . . *OR* Nevertheless, he can be considered a model of ethical public relations because . . .

- Edward Bernays exploited people and risked their health by encouraging women to smoke cigarettes in public. Therefore, he should not be considered a model of ethical public relations because . . . *OR* Nevertheless, he can be considered a model of ethical public relations because . . .

Part 2: After you have written this essay, write margin notes or footnotes to indicate the lessons in this section you used to design your persuasive message. ∎

Propaganda

Earlier in this chapter, we defined persuasion as a process of communication that intends to influence using ethical means which enhance a democratic society. Persuasion plays many important and useful roles in society. For example, organizations attempt to persuade people to drive defensively, avoid unhealthy diets, and reduce the risk of disease. Advertisers try to convince consumers to use a company's products or services. Charities solicit contributions from donors to achieve a social good. Groups lobby government officials or advocate in public forums to generate support for their causes or programs.

Each of these examples of persuasive communication seeks voluntary change. Each involves the skillful presentation of an argument in an attempt to convince someone about the rightness of a cause, the value of a service or the merit of an idea—all ethical and respectable goals. But a darker side to persuasive communication can be seen in activities such as false advertising, information campaigns that withhold important facts, and deliberate misrepresentations by public officials. This type of persuasion is *propaganda*—persuasive communication gone bad.

Propaganda did not always have a bad reputation. The word itself is related to "propagate," meaning "to grow" or "to publicize." As a synonym for persuasive communication, it grew out the name of the Catholic Church's 17th-century missionary activity, the Congregatio de Propaganda Fide (Congregation for the Propagation of the Faith). Until the early 1900s, the term was commonly used to mean information, promotion and persuasion. Even the founders of the public relations profession, such as Edward Bernays, used "propaganda" as a synonym for promotion and publicity. Gradually though, in the popular mind, the word came to be associated with deceptive communication efforts, stemming largely from the Nazi propaganda bureau of the 1930s, and more recently with disinformation campaigns of the 1950s and '60s

Cold War and even more recent governmental and political operations that have used news as a weapon to discredit and deceive.

The problem with propaganda, as the term now is understood, is not that it promotes ideological causes but that it does so dishonestly. Propaganda sneaks its message into an unsuspecting audience and indoctrinates people without their realizing what is happening. It is communication that conceals the identity of the source or the purpose of the message, and in doing so manipulates rather than persuades.

In 1925, when public relations was in its infancy, Ivy Lee warned of the dangers of propaganda and helped set an ethical tone for the emerging profession. Addressing the American Association of Teachers of Journalism, he explained that the "essential evil of propaganda is failure to disclose the source of information." Lee took a consumer approach. He advised editors to use good judgment when information reached their desks, and he urged the public to "exercise your right to demand knowledge as to the source of the information."

Persuasion versus Propaganda

Public relations writers should be careful with the following writing techniques, which easily can degenerate into oversimplification and deception. Here is a common listing for persuasive tactics that can also become tools of propaganda. Each tactic raises ethical issues for public relations writers. The first four tactics—plain folks, testimonial, bandwagon and transfer—are often used by public relations writers.

The technique of *plain folk appeals* tries to convince the audience that the message source is unsophisticated, average, just like you and me. It has been used by everybody from Abraham Lincoln to Adolph Hitler. The ethical public relations writer will be satisfied that the impression is accurate before using such an appeal.

Testimonials involve the supportive words or images of a well-known and supposed expert. Social causes use celebrities such as Jon Bon Jovi for newspaper reading and Magic Johnson on AIDS awareness, while corporations like Nike feature athletes such as Tiger Woods. The ethical public relations writer will ask several questions: Does the so-called expert really have a particular knowledge of the subject? Has the expert actually used the product or supported the cause? Is the testimony paid for? Is the testimony legitimate?

Parades are led by *bandwagons* that get the ambivalent crowds revved up and raring to go. As a communication technique, it presents the suggestion that "Everyone else is doing it, so why not you? Don't be the last kid on the block to buy this, wear that, smoke this, drink that." The ethical public relations writer will ask if the momentum is beneficial and warranted.

The *transfer* technique associates a respected symbol for something else. We wrap the nation's flag around an idea and then appeal to the public's patriotism, or we try to identify our cause with symbols of godliness or goodness, purity or political correctness. Conversely, we accuse political opponents of being unpatriotic or immoral. The ethical public relations writer will avoid associations that are questionable exaggerations.

The remaining techniques—name calling, card stacking, glittering generalities, stereotypes and repetition—are less frequently used for legitimate public relations purposes, because they carry with them ethical problems in most situations. Public relations writers often find they must expend energy and resources fighting against those techniques that have been turned against their organizations.

The technique of *name calling* is the opposite of the transfer technique. It involves creating scapegoats by associating opponents with unsavory people or ideas, rendering them equally reprehensible. The ethical public relations writer will let the facts speak for themselves without unfairly demeaning people on the other side of the argument.

Card stacking involves giving only one side of the story or deliberately misrepresenting the other side. The ethical public relations writer will try to make the case while admitting that the issue is a complex one with other legitimate points of view.

Glittering generalities are attempts to hide behind vague concepts that nobody could oppose. Politicians picture themselves as patriotic, clergy as godly, doctors as caring. Everyone is for peace, happiness and freedom. But often such generalities take the place of specifics. The ethical public relations writer will provide specific examples and details on which publics can make informed decisions.

Stereotypes are images people have about members of a particular social group. These highly simplified notions provide a convenient shorthand and often come into play in promotional writing, but an ethical public relations writer will avoid negative stereotypes that denigrate people.

Repetition is the presentation of the same information or official line over and over again. When it lacks an ethical base, it becomes "the big lie," an outrageous falsehood that some hearers accept when it is repeated often enough. Ethical public relations writers will not use the technique of repetition to provide a foundation for untruths.

Exercise 3.6—Writing Ethical Messages

You are a public relations writer for an organization seeking to interest college freshmen in one of the following:

- Fitness and exercise
- Gay and lesbian rights
- A local political issue.

Write four persuasive and ethical messages of about 25 words each for your organization. The first version of the message should use the plain folks technique; the second version should use the testimonial technique; the third, bandwagon; and the fourth, transfer. ■

Codes of Ethics

In each of the persuasive/propaganda techniques described above, adherence to ethical standards can offer guidance and direction to help the writer use these persuasive devices properly.

For example, the Member Code of Ethics of the Public Relations Society of America is clear. It advises the practitioner to:

- Serve the public interest
- Exemplify high standards of honesty and integrity
- Build mutual understanding and credibility
- Adhere to the highest standards of accuracy and truth

- Deal fairly with clients and employers, as well as with competitors and the media
- Respect all opinions and promote free expression and the free exchange of unprejudiced communication.

Meanwhile, the Canadian Public Relations Society highlights ethical conduct in its Declaration of Principles and its Code of Professional Standards:

- Obligations of a public trust are inherent in the practice of public relations
- Maintain high standards . . . so as to ensure that public relations shall be esteemed as an honourable profession
- The highest standards of honesty, accuracy and truth.

Similarly but more simply, the Code of Standards of the International Association of Business Communicators commits members to "the practice of honest, candid and timely communication." And the Code of Ethics of the International Public Relations Association calls upon professionals to "establish communications patterns and channels which [foster] the free flow of essential information" and to refrain from "circulating information which is not based on established and ascertainable facts" or "taking part in any venture or undertaking which is unethical or dishonest or capable of impairing human dignity and integrity."

See Appendix E, "Ethical Standards," for the complete text of codes of professional ethics.

What Would You Do?

You are a public relations writer for your college or university. Yesterday you sent a news release quoting the treasurer of your school that the operating budget will be short this year by $1,200,000. Today you learn that the figure was inflated; it did not include $400,000 already saved by energy improvements. What is your ethical judgment about how you should act? What do the professional codes advise?

You are preparing a newsletter for a friend who is one of several candidates for a local town council. The major opponent is a married man and father who has built a campaign championing family values. From two different sources, you have heard a rumor about this opponent: that he has a mistress. In addition, a friend of yours who is a police officer has told you confidentially that police once were called for apparent abuse of this woman, though she declined to press charges. What is your ethical judgement about how to act? What do the professional codes advise?

You are a public relations writer for a company that makes plumbing supplies. You are seeking a media placement in the trade press, a monthly magazine read by independent plumbing contractors. You know that buying an advertisement increases the likelihood of news coverage and positive editorial commentary. Such editorial and advertising packages seem to be common within this publication. You have a budget for advertising, to be used at your discretion. What is your ethical judgment about how to act? What do the professional codes advise?

4

The Writing Process

Like other writing genres, public relations writing involves making decisions about various important questions. Who are my publics? What do they know about my organization or client? What do they think about this? What information will be interesting and useful to them? How can I best reach them? How can I inform and persuade them? This chapter will help you with these considerations as you make the decisions that lead to effective writing.

Another ingredient in good writing is a focus on the process. Quality writing doesn't take shape instantly. It emerges slowly, one draft after another. Effective public relations writers have learned how to take time with their writing—building and shaping the words, molding, refining and caressing them.

This chapter will focus on identifying and analyzing your publics, setting your objectives, and developing a planning sheet for each writing task. It will also introduce you to communication research techniques and will present a nine-step writing process. Here are your objectives for Chapter 4:

- To develop effective objectives for your writing
- To organize a writing project using a planning sheet
- To conduct research for public relations writing
- To use media directories to identify contacts and disseminate information
- To use the nine-step process to prepare a publishable piece of writing.

The 'Public' in Public Relations

The heart of public relations planning is to focus on your *key publics,* the people who are the focus of the communication you are planning. These are the groups of people who can affect your organization and be affected by it. Public relations focuses on groups rather than on isolated individuals. If you call a group of people a public, define it as specifically as possible, remembering that a "general public" does not exist. For example, think not merely of "students" as a public but the more specific variations: graduate students, entering students, minority students, honor students, and so on.

One method of identifying publics is to conduct a *public relations audit* of the environment, a listing of all the possible publics important to your organization. The following audit outline borrows the concept of linkages from systems theory. Simply stated, *linkages* are associations. They are patterns outlining the relationship between two groups of people. For this public relations audit, linkages are based on the various kinds of consequences an organization can have with four types of publics: consumers, producers, enablers and limiters.

Consumers are publics comprising the people who use your product or service. Consumers exist in many forms, but consider the following organizations and their consumer publics: hospitals and patients, churches and parishioners, schools and students, television stations and viewers, sports teams and fans, merchants and customers. Each of these consumer publics could probably be subdivided to focus on their particular characteristics. Hospital consumers, for example, can include first-time patients, pediatric patients, underinsured patients, repeat patients, families of patients, and so on. An important part of public relations planning is to identify publics as narrowly as possible to be able to address their specific needs.

Producers are publics that provide the organization's service or product. They include employees and volunteers, as well as suppliers of goods, services and financial resources.

Enablers are publics that make it possible for the organization to operate and communicate. These may be professional colleagues, formal or informal regulators such as government agencies or trade associations, and the communication media.

Limiters are the opposite of enablers. These are publics that threaten or restrict the organization's performance, including formal competitors and other groups that seek to impede your organization.

Having identified all of the possible publics, it is easier to select the *key publics*—those few groups you want to communicate with for this particular writing project. To select key publics, look over the list of publics generated during the audit. Select those most closely aligned with the public relations situation.

Note that *Becoming a Public Relations Writer* uses the term "key publics" to identify those specific publics that you identify as being most important to your writing activity. Other books sometimes use the term "target public," though this seems to suggest that the public is more a bull's eye for the organization's darts rather than part of a reciprocal relationship.

Exercise 4.1—Identifying Publics

You are public relations director for one of the following organizations:

- A local neighborhood youth group, such as Boys and Girls Clubs of America. The public relations situation is a membership campaign.

- Talmiani Enterprises, a company that manufactures and distributes upholstery products to furniture stores and craft shops. The public relations situation is an effort to attract do-it-yourselfers as customers.

- Your college or university, as it prepares to recruit students for your department.

List several publics in each category (consumer, producer, enabler and limiter). Then indicate one or two key publics for your writing project.

Analysis of Key Publics

After you have selected your key publics, begin to analyze them. The more you can empathize with your audience, the more effective your writing will be.

In this analysis, get up close and personal. Delve into the gut-level motivations of your publics. What would interest them? What do they like and dislike? What do they need or think they need? Remember to keep the focus on the needs of your publics, not on what information you want to provide them. Think of WIN (wants, interests and needs): You will win your publics' support by addressing *their* wants, interests and needs rather than your own.

This stage may require some surveys, focus groups or other formal research, but it begins with common sense. In fact, existing information may be all that is needed for many writing projects. Draw on personal experience, perhaps coupled with informal interviews with friends and colleagues who can help shed some light on the interests and motivations of members of the key public.

Three approaches from the social sciences can help the public relations writer identify the wants, interests and needs of the key public. One approach comes from sociologist Harold Lasswell, who described eight motivations for people: power, respect, well-being, affection, wealth, skill, enlightenment, and vitality of mind and body. Another approach comes from Vance Packard, who identified eight compelling but hidden needs of consumers that can be addressed by would-be persuaders: emotional security, reassurance of self-worth, ego gratification, creative outlets, love objects, sense of power, sense of roots and immortality.

The third convenient starting point is the *hierarchy of needs* presented by psychologist Abraham Maslow. Four levels of needs are in the base of Maslow's pyramid:

- Health (physiological needs): food, water, shelter and other aspects of self-preservation
- Safety (security needs): safety, protection, freedom and future well-being
- Love (social needs): acceptance, belonging, friendship, peer approval, interpersonal relationships, and group identity, as well as giving and receiving love
- Esteem (personal needs): self-esteem, appreciation and respect.

Maslow's pyramid is crowned by a fifth level of needs in a category all their own:

- Fulfillment (self-actualization): beauty, meaning, living up to potential, developing talent, creativity, understanding and spiritual insight.

Maslow's hierarchy of needs sometimes is presented as a simple pyramid. However, the two-part pyramid in Exhibit 4.1 is a better image, because the fifth level of needs is significantly different from the others. Maslow pointed out that an element missing from the first four levels creates tension or a sense of yearning for an individual, while elements in the top level offer people opportunities to explore and add to their sense of accomplishment.

Maslow also observed that each level of needs must be satisfied before people are able to pay much attention to the next level. For example, a person who lacks food doesn't worry much about retirement benefits, and someone preoccupied with loneliness probably won't be interested in taking art lessons (unless you can position art lessons as a way to overcome loneliness).

Another category of human need important to public relations practitioners working in volunteerism, philanthropy and related areas is *altruism*, the need to help others. Much of human history has been shaped by the phenomenon of people helping each other. Charity and mercy are not only a basis of religious and moral codes but also are fundamental elements of human nature. The task of the public relations writer preparing organizational appeals is to give readers an opportunity both to help others and to exercise their own altruistic needs.

In analyzing key publics, public relations writers should consider both positive and negative perspectives. We are interested not only in what members of the key publics want, but also what they do not want. Our planning will be more effective if we also give thought to apprehension and resistance within the key publics. This can help us avoid messages that are likely to be resisted by our publics.

As part of your analysis of the publics, include a listing and analysis of the demographic and sociographic barriers to communication. Deal with matters such as ethnic differences between the organization and its publics, and the implied differences in language, culture, values, lifestyle and so on.

Another useful point of analysis for each public is drawn from Grunig's *situational theory* of publics, which identifies three factors in the evolution of publics: (1) the extent to which they are aware that a problem exists, thus knowing that they need information, (2) the extent to which they see themselves as either limited or free to act on the situation, and (3) the extent to which they recognize that they are involved or affected by the situation.

Communication Objectives for Public Relations

One of your tasks as a writer is to manage communication between an organization and its publics. This task involves setting *public relations objectives*—specific reasons why you are writing. Objectives enable you to envision exactly what you want to accomplish, and they help you stay focused on the task at hand.

Exhibit 4.1—MASLOW'S HIERARCHY OF NEEDS

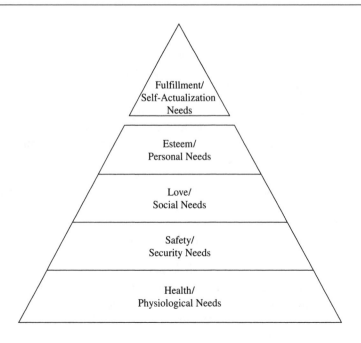

Characteristics of Public Relations Objectives

Objectives vary with each writing project and the many possibilities associated with it. Nevertheless, they have some common traits dealing with public, effect, clarity, measurement and timeframe.

Focus on Effects. Objectives focus on effects. Consider the phrasing of some of the typical objectives you may have seen attached to public relations situations:

- We want to promote recycling
- We want to teach people about heart disease.

These may sound like reasonable objectives. After all, each statement deals with public relations and each indicates what is being sought. But each is flawed because it fails to focus on the desired impact on a particular public. Objectives should tell us what we're aiming for. They should envision the impact we want to make on our publics, giving a glimpse of the end result. Specifically, we're interested in *effect objectives,* also called *impact objectives.* These focus not on the tools but rather on what we want to accomplish with our tools.

Consider another way to identify these objectives. These examples focus on the effects we hope to achieve:

- We are trying to educate people about recycling
- We want people to learn about heart disease.

Clarity and Specificity. Objectives are clear and specific. The effects oriented objectives above are better than the first set because they focus on the key publics. But they still are too broad. What does it mean "to educate"? In establishing objectives, avoid words and phrases that are ambiguous. Avoid verbs such as *educate, inform, enhance* and *publicize,* and adjectives such as *appropriate, reasonable* and *highest possible.*

Consider these objectives that are both effects oriented and clear:

- We want to increase awareness about the benefits of recycling
- We want to generate telephone inquiries on our 1–800 HeartSmart help line.

Measurement. A major component that remains missing in the previous set of objectives is the matter of measurement. We need to know what success will look like, and we need to measure that success. This measurement should be challenging but not so ambitious as to be unachievable. Consider how the following wording for objectives builds in this measurement:

- We want to increase the awareness of 50 percent of the students on campus about the benefits of recycling
- We want to generate 100 calls a week on our 1–800 HeartSmart help line.

Timeframe. The final characteristic of objectives is that they have an element of time. They establish a period of time for achieving success. Consider the following objectives:

- Throughout the next semester, we want to increase the awareness about the benefits of recycling among 50 percent of students living on campus
- We want to generate an average of 100 calls a week on our 1–800 HeartSmart help line during the first 12 weeks of the hotline promotion.

Usually, effect is achieved by degrees and according to an expected pattern. Awareness increases gradually; interest builds in stages that follow awareness; behaviors modify by steps after interest has been created. Objectives should reflect this. Seldom is it realistic to aim for 100 percent achievement of an intended effect. A more reasonable standard of performance should be sought, such as 60 percent awareness, understanding by three-quarters of the public, increasing from 40 to 60 percent. Where do we get these numbers? Be guided by your experience within the organization or with similar situations elsewhere. Keep up with relevant research in public relations, mass communication, marketing, advertising and related fields.

Good public relations objectives should be reasonable yet challenging. If your aim is too low, it can lead to the delusion that significant effect has been attained when in fact you have made only a modest impact. If your sights are unrealistically high, you are likely to be frustrated and embarrassed.

A Progression of Objectives

Note that the idea of "informing the public" is missing from the way these objectives have been written. This is not an oversight. Too often, public relations planners think in terms of informing, educating or publicizing. Such phrasing suggests that the act of informing automatically leads to preferred awareness, attitudes and actions. Don't be tempted to think in such simplistic terms, because communication is a complex process.

In public relations communication, we want to make sure that our message will reach our key publics, who will agree with this message and then will act on it accordingly. Note the three progressive levels of this process:

We want our message to reach our publics (awareness)
who will agree with it (acceptance)
and act or interact accordingly (action).

Awareness Objectives. The first level of objectives, *awareness objectives,* focuses on information, providing the *cognitive* component of the message. Awareness objectives specify what information you want your publics first to be exposed to and then to know, understand and remember. The public relations writer must be successful in presenting information to publics in ways that increase awareness, enhance comprehension and ensure retention. Consider the following scenario:

A promoter is trying to attract an audience for an upcoming concert. Marsha is a member of the key public for this message. Marsha is listening to her radio as she jogs through the park. She is tuned to the station that carries the announcement about the concert. Marsha hears the announcement. The awareness objective is achieved.

But suppose Marsha is so distracted by a dog that she isn't really paying attention to the announcement at all. In this case, the awareness objectives is not reached.

Another aspect of awareness objectives involves understanding. Marsha enjoys Chicano rock, and she is listening to a station broadcasting in Spanish, but she really doesn't understand the language so she pays no attention to announcements. Or if Marsha hears and understands but quickly forgets the message, the awareness objective is thwarted.

Acceptance Objectives. *Acceptance objectives* deal with the *affective*, or feeling, part of the message—how people respond emotionally to information they have received. They indicate the level of interest or the kind of attitude (positive or negative) an organization hopes to generate among its publics.

Attitudes are learned predispositions for or against a particular subject, usually reflecting one's deeper beliefs and often based on personal experience and on family and group influence as well as information. Personal communication, and to a lesser extent public communication, can affect a person's attitudes.

Information presented in the awareness level can affect the three kinds of attitudes: *compliance* (mere outward acceptance to avoid punishment or to gain reward), *identification* (imitation of an admired person or group), and *internalization* (adoption of the attitude as being consistent with one's beliefs or value system).

Back to Marsha and the concert announcement. Suppose the concert is for a group performing contemporary jazz, but we've already seen that Marsha is passionate about Chicano rock. Hates jazz. Because she accurately understands the nature of the concert, a negative attitude develops, defeating acceptance-level objectives.

Now suppose Marsha is dating Freddie, who has two great loves in his life: Marsha and jazz. So Marsha accepts jazz as a pragmatic way to get closer to Freddie and reap the benefits of a common, if feigned, interest. Or perhaps she identifies with Freddie's interests and decides to give jazz a try because she's learned to trust Freddie's guidance on other issues. Or perhaps Marsha is open to a new style of music, and the jazz she hears on the commercial really interests her. Each scenario means some kind of success for acceptance-level objectives.

Action Objectives. The third and final level of objectives is *action objectives*. When awareness and acceptance have been achieved, the next step deals with ways in which the receiver acts on the information. Specifically, this *conative* or behavioral component of the communication process offers two general types of action. One is *opinion* or *behavioral intention*, verbal action expressing acceptance of the message. The second type is *behavior*, physical action expressing that acceptance.

Logically, action should grow directly from a person's attitudes, and sometimes it does. But people don't always respond logically. We often fail to find easy solutions as we weave information into patterns that we hope are influential and persuasive.

Consider the rest of the Marsha scenario. She has decided, for whatever reason, that she will go to the jazz concert. She shares her opinion about this with her friend Joe, perhaps acting as an opinion leader for him. She then goes out and buys two tickets to the concert, her present to Freddie.

Throughout the process, the public relations writer who developed the concert promotion had several objectives. The information was presented through the first-level awareness objectives. It gained acceptance and eventually resulted in the desired behavior. But the writer also would understand that the process could have been halted at several points along the way—when another jogger, Max, paid more attention to the dog than to the announcement; when still another radio listener, Raj, didn't understand the message very well; when Josephine forgot all about the announcement by the time she got home; when Reggie paid a traffic fine instead of buying concert tickets. So many obstacles. When you think about all the places where the process could have stopped dead, it's a wonder anyone showed up at the concert.

Various writing styles fit into all three levels of objectives, and public relations writers usually develop objectives at each level. News releases are written not only to have an effect on awareness but also to gain acceptance and ultimately action. Additionally, each written piece may have several different objectives. For example, a newsletter article about the company president addressing the city council on highway improvement may have several objectives: to make employees aware of the company's civic-mindedness (awareness), to boost employee morale (acceptance), and to increase employee retention (action). A news release on the same issue may aim to have clients understand the company's interest in the community (awareness), to reinforce the company's image as being rooted in the community (acceptance), and to attract new clients (action). Exhibit 4.2 shows a road map from Hometown to Persuasion, with a route that takes you through several important locations.

Part of the challenge and the fun of public relations is dealing with possibilities rather than guaranteed outcomes. People have marvelously different ways of receiving information, processing it and acting on it.

Guidelines for Writing Public Relations Objectives

A well-written objective is a simple statement. It may sound a bit like a formula, but its power lies in its ability to specifically guide public relations activity. Consider the following seven steps in writing objectives:

Step 1: Public. Identify the specific public being addressed by the objective. Generally, only one public is addressed by each objective, unless several similar publics are to be treated in parallel fashion.

Step 2: Category. Indicate which of the three categories of objectives—awareness, acceptance or action—is being addressed in the objective. Note that each of the three categories will need to be addressed to each public, but this must be done separately to make it possible to measure the objective. Remember that objectives generally are presented in sets of the three categories.

Step 3: Direction. Objectives can move in several directions, creating something new or maintaining what exists, increasing or decreasing in intensity. Here is what the public relations writer can aim for:

- *Creating effects.* Objectives that create effects seek to establish something new. The focus is on that which did not exist before: a new awareness, a fresh attitude, a new behavior by the key public.
- *Maintaining effects.* Objectives that maintain effects involve continuing or reinforcing current situations. The focus is on what already exists: continuing the level of comprehension, keeping the present rate of participation.
- *Increasing effects.* Objectives that increase effects seek to bring about growth: increasing favorable attitudes, causing a larger retention rate, expanding awareness.
- *Decreasing effects.* Objectives that decrease effects, conversely, focus is on subtraction: lessening criticism, reducing disharmony, decreasing turnover, softening opposition.

Note what is not included in this outline: eliminating effects. We usually can't eliminate effects through public communication, though our message may include such an appeal. Realistically, however, our objective is to minimize a negative. For example, our publicly stated message may be to stop littering, but our objective would more realistically reflect a reduction in littering to a particular level.

Neither are we likely to change negative to positive (such as converting opponents). We may publicly state a desire that litterbugs become environmentalists, but realistically our

Exhibit 4.2—A ROAD MAP TO PERSUASION   This road map is based on a suggestion by Richard Fischer of the University of Memphis, who developed a map to explain to his students the route from Hometown to Persuasion.

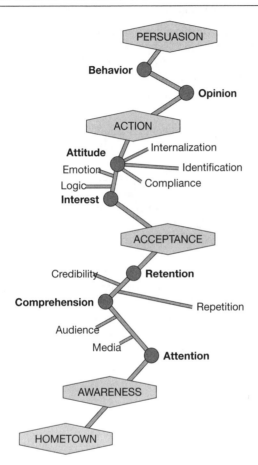

objective is to minimize littering behavior, and perhaps in a longer timeframe to interest them in environmental issues. Keep your eye on the possible, and don't be deluded by unapproachable visions of unreachable desires.

Step 4: Specific Effect. Each objective should indicate a specific effect related to the particular category being addressed. Awareness objectives can deal with attention to certain information, to comprehension or understanding of that information, and perhaps to retention, though the latter is often more a factor with advertising objectives than those for public relations writing. Acceptance objectives deal with interest levels or with positive or negative attitudes. Action objectives can lead to opinion statements or to behavior.

Step 5: Focus. Expand on the specific effect to clearly indicate the focus of this objective. This is where you can provide some detail to what you are seeking. But be careful not to move away from objectives and into either strategy or tactics. That comes elsewhere in your planning.

Step 6: Performance Measure. Well-written objectives include a desired level of achievement, presented in terms that are easily measurable. Usually these are written as raw numbers, as percentages, or as variations upon current conditions (200 new members, a 30 percent increase in contributions, double the amount of current inquiries.)

Step 7: Time Period. Conclude the objective statement with an indication of the timeframe in which the effects are to be observed. Exhibit 4.3 is a form for sketching out public relations objectives. Use it as a framework that calls attention to the level of each objective. Below are examples of objectives written following this framework, based on a promotion program by a radio station with a classical format for a key public of teenage musicians and teens who listen to music.

- Objective for students in music appreciation class: To have an effect on *awareness*, specifically by creating attention to the variety of styles within classical music (80 percent of students this semester).
- Objective for teen musicians: To have an effect on *awareness*, specifically by increasing their understanding that classical music provides many emotional styles (15 percent of musicians within three months).
- Objective for teen musicians: To have an effect on *acceptance*, specifically by creating interest in classical music as an alternative form of music (minimum 20 percent on an interest survey to be conducted at the end of the semester).
- Objective for teen-oriented music groups: To have an effect on *acceptance*, specifically by reinforcing their positive opinion that classical music provides training for contemporary musical styles (20 percent of recording groups next year)
- Objective for students in music appreciation class: To have an effect on *action*, specifically to generate teen listeners (10 percent of students listening one hour a week by the end of the semester).

"Tips for Better Writing: Public Relations Objectives" contains a checklist of the elements of a well-written objective.

Exhibit 4.3—HOW TO WRITE PUBLIC RELATIONS OBJECTIVES   Use this form as a guide for writing public relations objectives.

Writing Public Relations Objectives

Public	Objective for _____		
Category	To have an effect on	❏ Awareness	
		❏ Acceptance	
		❏ Action	
Direction	Specifically, to	❏ Create, Generate	
		❏ Increase, Maximize	
		❏ Maintain, Reinforce	
		❏ Decrease, Minimize	
Effect	(w/awareness category)	❏ Attention or	❏ Comprehension
	(w/acceptance category)	❏ Interest or	❏ ± Attitude
	(w/action category)	❏ Opinion or	❏ Behavior

Focus   About _____

Performance Measure_____

Time Period_____

Tips for Better Writing   *Public Relations Objectives*

Use this checklist to make sure you have included each of the major elements of a well-written objective:

- Specific public
- One of the three categories of objectives (awareness, acceptance or action)

- Direction for specific effect
- Specific effect
- "About statement to give focus
- Performance measure
- Time period.

Exercise 4.2—Writing Effective Public Relations Objectives

Write an objective in each of the three categories of public relations objectives for one of the following:

- Your college or university, with the focus on promoting its international exchange program to a key public of communication majors

- Your local county health agency, with the focus on promoting nutrition and a nutrition booklet for children. ∎

Planning Sheet

Good writing progresses logically. It emerges from the mind of the writer, based on careful and clear consideration of both the purpose for writing and the strategy for achieving this purpose. Good writing evolves from a plan. Planning takes time, but it is time well spent.

A *planning sheet* is a document that outlines what you need to think about to make your writing planning more effective. As you explore various elements of a planning sheet, keep this thought in mind: The planning sheet is meant to guide you toward an effective piece of writing. It is not for public consumption, so don't worry about crafting an eloquent statement. It is simply an outline of things to come. It is like an artist's sketchbook or an architect's drawing of the floor plans.

Note that the planning sheet is not the same as a public relations plan or a campaign book. The larger plan would deal with strategy, a variety of tactics, and administrative details such as budgets and timelines. The planning sheet, on the other hand, is an approach to a particular written tactic such as a news release, brochure, appeal letter, etc. It may pull elements such as key publics and objectives from the overall public relations plan, but it is part of the implementation of the tactics identified in such a plan.

The planning sheet consists of seven parts: public relations situation, key publics, benefit statement, tone of message, objectives, readability range, and evaluation methods. Let's look at each part of the planning sheet. See Exhibit 4.4 for an example of a completed planning sheet.

Public Relations Situation. Begin the planning sheet with a brief note on the general scope of this particular writing activity. In its brevity it will start you off on the right foot. Here are some examples:

- Membership in Hidden Valley Riding Club
- Promotion for a new Web site
- CEO's banquet for retired employees
- Search for a new vice principal
- Fundraising campaign for a new scholarship program
- Public education about a company's opposition to a highway-tax proposal.

Key Publics. List one or a few key publics that you will address in this piece of writing—probably no more than three publics. More than that, and you should consider preparing separate pieces for each. Then write a brief analysis of each of these publics, as noted in the first section in this chapter. Identify their major characteristics and note their wants, interests and needs.

Benefit Statement. The next step is to prepare a concise benefit statement for your eventual readers. What one thing do you want them to remember? Be clear in your own mind about what value your organization offers the key publics. Ideally, this will be the flip side of the analysis statement. It will provide a clear statement of how the organization can satisfy the public's wants, interests and needs.

Tone of Message. How do you want your message to feel? Consider if humor or fear appeals are appropriate. Weigh the pros and cons of a dispassionate and objective presentation, or the relative merits of emotions and logical approaches.

Public Relations Objectives. Clearly indicate the public relations objectives, using the process outlined in the previous chapter that focuses on the impact your organization wants to have on the key publics. Write at least one set of objectives (awareness, acceptance and action) for each public.

Readability Range. Indicate the grade-level range of members of your key public. This estimate will be useful later when you apply a readability rating such as the Fog Index or the Flesch Scale to your writing (see Chapter 2 for details about readability ratings).

Evaluation Methods. Even before you begin writing the first draft, give some thought to how you will evaluate the success of your effort. What methods will you use to measure its effectiveness in reaching the objectives you have set?

Exercise 4.3—Preparing a Planning Sheet

You have been hired as a public relations writer to draft the copy for a brochure or a direct-mail letter. Prepare a planning sheet only (not the actual brochure or letter copy) for one of the following:

- MacFarland Driving School, promoting a program to help senior citizens improve their driving skills
- Statewide Insurance Company, promoting renters' insurance for college roommates in off-campus apartments
- Upstate United, an advocacy group organizing a protest against plans to dam a local creek as a nonrecreational reservoir. ∎

Exhibit 4.4—SAMPLE PLANNING SHEET

Public Relations Situation
Promotional campaign to attract more customers for Teeny Tykes Day Care Center.

Analysis of Key Publics
- Families with no at-home parent(s):
  - Quality day care
  - Safety for child
  - Stimulating environment
  - Comfort of knowing that work schedule not detrimental to child's development
- Families with at-home parent:
  - Occasional time away from child
  - Opportunity for child to socialize with other children.

Benefit Statement
Teeny Tykes can assure members of the key public that it can provide quality day care for their children, with emphasis on safety, socialization, and emotional and intellectual development. Teeny Tykes can provide parents with certification reports and testimonials from other parents.

Tone of Message
Communication with potential new client families should be positive, encouraging. It should be child centered, demonstrating that although the parent will pay the bill, the center considers the child to be the primary customer.

Public Relations Objectives
- To have an effect on parents' awareness, specifically by increasing their understanding of the range of programs and services available at Teeny Tykes Day Care Center (affecting 85 percent of parents participating in an open house).
- To have an effect on parents' acceptance, specifically by instilling in them confidence that Teeny Tykes would be a good environment for their child (boosting confidence by 70 percent during a three-month campaign).
- To have an effect on parents' acceptance, specifically by creating in them the attitude that they will want their child to participate in the Teeny Tykes program (65 percent by the end of a three-month campaign).
- To have an effect on parents' action, specifically by having them enroll their child(ren) in Teeny Tykes, five days a week for families with two parents working outside the home, one or two days a week for families with an at-home parent (50 percent of parents who attended the open house by the end of a three-month campaign).

Readability Range
A grade level of 9–11 would make this information accessible to the key publics.

Evaluation Methods
Success will be determined as follows:
- By the amount of time parents at an open house engage the staff in discussion about the Center
- By the number of families who enroll their child in the Center.

Researching the Topic

Before you start to write, you may have to learn more about your topic. In other words, you might need to do *research,* which simply is a systematic way of gathering information about your topic. Good writers always know more about the topic than they actually write. You must gather enough information to make some reasonable judgments: what to put in, what to leave out; what to quote, what to paraphrase; what to attribute, what to let stand as common knowledge; what to stress, what to present with less emphasis.

Public relations writers don't always have the luxury of time. Some research must be accomplished in a very short time, and the effective public relations writer is the one who can both research and write under deadline pressure.

Research can be divided into three types: casual, secondary and primary. No hierarchy of importance is implied here. In some instances, it makes sense to begin with casual research, then proceed to secondary research. In other situations, secondary research often is the logical first step before an interview. Primary research is seldom necessary for a specific piece of writing, but it often is part of a wider public relations campaign. Let's take a look at each type.

Casual Research

Casual research is an informal process of finding out what already is known by the writer or the writer's organization or client. Think about the situation.

Informal Interviewing. Informal interviewing is the art of asking around. Adopt an attitude of being open to advice, and take every opportunity to find out what people are thinking. Pick the brains of your client and co-workers. Talk with people with experience and expertise.

Formal Interviewing. Interviews can also be more formal. For example, *intensive interviews* are those that use the same structure and ask the same questions to several different people.

Interviews remain one of the most important tools for a public relations writer. Whatever you are writing about, somebody someplace can give you needed information. Interviews may be conducted in person or by phone, mail, e-mail or video teleconferencing. In-person interviews generally are the most fruitful, because you can "read" body language and obtain some insights into the person being interviewed.

Effective public relations writers are sensitive to the comfort level of the person being interviewed. Some people are nervous about doing interviews, perhaps because they have been misquoted in the past. Remind them that you are on their side. Unlike a journalist who is sent out to obtain information for a particular story, you are collaborating with the interview subject. Let the person know that you recognize him or her as an expert who shares with you a common idea, cause or concern. You both want to present the information in its best light, in ways that will make it most easily understood, and in a manner that will support your organization's mission.

During the interview, take good notes. If the interview is done in person or by telephone, it's good practice to record the conversation, always with the knowledge and consent of the person you are interviewing. But even if you record the interview, taking some notes makes it easier to ask follow-up questions and saves you much embarrassment if the recorder doesn't work. "Tips for Better Writing: Improving Interviewing" offers several more tips for conducting an effective interview.

Unlike a journalist, a public relations writer will generally invite the subject of an interview to review the writing before it is released. Even if such approval isn't required, it is a good idea to invite the interviewee to review technical or sensitive matters.

The value of interviews often depends on who is being interviewed. The best advice: Get as close to the source as possible. For example, interviewing members of the sales department may be more productive than interviewing the CEO if you're working on a piece of product literature. The sales staff probably knows more about the competition, sales points to emphasize, possible objections, and so on.

Tips for Better Writing   *Improving Interviews*

Here are some suggestions for effective interviewing:

- *Write out your questions before the interview.* Begin with these questions, but remain flexible to follow the interviewee into areas you did not anticipate if it is relevant.

- *Establish rapport.* Show an interest in the person being interviewed and in the topic under discussion.

- *Explain the purpose of the interview.* Indicate how it can be an advantage for the interviewee to share information on an important topic.

- *Discuss the background research* you did in preparing for the interview. This will signal that you are prepared and will allow the interviewee to use this research as the basis for updating what you already know.

- *Distinguish between fact questions and opinion questions.* You need both kinds of information, so don't concentrate solely on obtaining simply factual information. Ask questions like: What does this mean? Why is this important? How will this help somebody? Enlist the interviewee's help in framing this information within the interests of your intended audience.

- *Conclude by inviting the interviewee to add anything else* that seems to be relevant to the topic or important for the key public to understand.

- *Rely more on open-ended questions* rather than simple yes/no questions.

Exercise 4.4—Preparing for an Interview

Prepare for an interview based on this scenario: Another student in your class has been chosen to participate in a three-week study tour to Moscow, Russia; Kiev, Ukraine; Warsaw, Poland; and Riga, Latvia. The tour is sponsored by the International Public Relations Education Committee. This student was selected in part because of faculty recommendations and in part because of an essay the student wrote about the role of public relations in the development of democracy in Eastern Europe.

Part 1: Develop a series of questions that you would ask the student if you were preparing a news release for IPREC.

Part 2: Using these questions, play the role of a public relations writer and "interview" another student, who will answer your questions without volunteering more information than the question seeks.

Part 3: Analyze the interview and evaluate each question's effectiveness. Suggest other questions that might have been useful.

Secondary Research

Secondary research is research conducted to find out what information is already available through existing sources. Writers have many possible sources of information about their topics. Your decision on how deeply to research the topic will be made on the basis of time and resources available, as well as on the importance of the writing project and your need for detailed information. Following is a look at some of these potential sources.

Organizational Files. The files held within an organization can provide a wealth of information, and many public relations practitioners develop files that may span decades of their organization's life. Develop the habit of clipping and saving pieces of information relevant to your organization or client.

Archives. Official archives are an organization's formal collection of documents, records, photographs, letters and sometimes memorabilia related to the organization. Often these are made available to outside researchers whose purpose serves the interests of the organization.

Libraries. Public, organizational and academic libraries have many resource materials to help a public relations writer. Public libraries have much useful and readily available information, and some organizations such as hospitals, associations and religious organizations often have specialized libraries with limited opportunities for public relations researchers. Public relations writers may also find that academic libraries have many specialized professional materials. The materials available in libraries can be categorized into *one-step resources* that provide information directly and *two-step resources* that direct the researcher to the information in other sources. Many of these resources are available both in published form and on CD-ROM computerized files. Increasingly, they are also becoming available online through the library Web site.

Encyclopedias are particularly helpful one-step resources as you begin to gather information about your topic. Look at comprehensive ones like Encyclopaedia Britannica and World Book Encyclopedia, as well as the many specialized publications that are available. Publications such as yearbooks, almanacs and fact books also are useful. Consider the credibility of the publisher, and particularly avoid online encyclopedias that rely on contributions from volunteer writers rather than on verified staff entries.

Among two-step resources are indexes to books available at the library. Periodical indexes are especially useful because they point to current information. General magazine indexes such as Readers' Guide to Periodical Literature are good beginning points. Public relations writers also should be familiar with the many specialized magazine indexes dealing with topics such as applied science, art, biological science, business, education, humanities, general science, law and social sciences. Newspapers are the focus of other indexes, such as The New York Times Index, Newspaper Source and Canada News Index. Other specialized indexes exist to point the researcher to television transcripts on commercial and public broadcasting programs in the United States and Canada. Online examples of two-step resources are LexisNexis, InfoTrak, and other services that point to and/or retrieve published articles.

Abstract services go beyond the information found in indexes. Abstracts provide brief summaries of the published material. Some of the more common abstract services deal with psychology, sociology, public administration, history, crime and communication.

As "FYI: Specialized Library Resources" points out, research on even specialized topics can result in a wealth of information.

FYI *Specialized Library Resources*

A world of information exists in many specialized areas. As just one example, consider the wealth of authoritative resources available to a public relations writer working in the field of religion. Such a writer should be familiar with magazine and newspaper indexes such as Religious and Theological Abstracts, Catholic Periodicals and Literature Index, Index to Jewish Periodicals, and Religion Index One: Periodicals.

Specialized encyclopedias include Encyclopedia of Religion, Encyclopedia of World Religions, Illustrated Encyclopedia of World Religions, Encyclopedia of American Religions, Encyclopedia of the American Religious Experience, Encyclopedia of Philosophy, Encyclopedia of Religion and Ethics, Encyclopedia of Religion in the South, Encyclopedia of Pentecostal and Charismatic Christianity, Encyclopedia of Fundamentalism, Encyclopedia of Unbelief, New Catholic Encyclopedia, Encyclopedia of Protestantism, Encyclopedia of Islam, Encyclopedia of Islam and the Muslim World, Islamic Encyclopedia, Encyclopedia of Judaism, Encyclopaedia Judaica, Encyclopedia of the Holocaust, Encyclopedia of Judaism and Christianity, Encyclopedia of Native American Religions, Encyclopedia of Cults and New Religions, Encyclopedia of Buddhism, Illustrated Encyclopedia of Zen Buddhism, Encyclopedia of Eastern Philosophy and Religion, Encyclopedia of Taoism, Concise Encyclopedia of Hinduism, Encyclopedia of Monasticism, Encyclopedia of Religion and Nature, Encyclopedia of Wicca and Witchcraft, Concise Encyclopedia of the Philosophy of Religion, Encyclopedia of Religion and Society, Encyclopedia of Religions in the United States, Encyclopedia of Religion and Social Justice, and Encyclopedia of Religion, Communication and Media.

Standard reference books include the Dictionary of Comparative Religion, Dictionary of Non-Christian Religions, Dictionary of Religion, Oxford Dictionary of World Religions, Dictionary of the Jewish Religion, Islamic Dictionary, Catholic Dictionary, Protestant Dictionary, Dictionary of Eastern Christianity, Dictionary of Western Churches, Dictionary of the Reformation, Illustrated Dictionary of Religions, Dictionary of Islam, Concise Dictionary of Religion, Dictionary of Apologetics and Philosophy of Religion, Dictionary of Methodism, and Dictionary of Cults, Sects, Religions and the Occult.

Annuals and directories include the American Jewish Yearbook, Catholic Almanac, Directory of Religious Organizations in the United States, Handbook of Denominations in the United States, Official Catholic Directory, World Religions Reference Library Almanac, and Yearbook of American Churches.

Exercise 4.5—Identifying Information Resources

Identify resource materials—specialized encyclopedias, dictionaries, directories, annuals and indexes—that should be familiar to a public relations writer specializing in one of the following areas: education, law, medicine, sports.

Government Materials. At every level of government, information is available that offers another important secondary information source for the public relations writer. Many public records are available in state and local government offices. Some of this information is also located in public and academic libraries. Yearbooks, census and data books, policy indexes, and government reports can be useful research sources. The federal government generates an abundance of information. Much of this is available directly from agencies or from the Library of Congress. Special indexes, yearbooks, and directories also can assist in searching for federal information, and some agencies have telephone research assistance. Increasingly government-generated information is available online through Web sites associated with the various government agencies.

Online Data Networks. On-site research in libraries and government offices can be time consuming, but the Internet provides a realistic alternative for public relations researchers. Data networks available via the Internet provide a great source of information available to public relations writers. Some online databases can be accessed through libraries or public services, others through private information companies. The information is updated frequently, as often as every hour. They can offer much the same information as the library-based services, editorial files of newspapers and magazines, as well as electronic clipping services and files of news releases. In addition, they provide access to specialized statistical information such as current marketing research and media audience data.

Online data networks are enhanced by search engines that can help the researcher identify reliable sources of relevant information. The cost for online data search networks varies. Some services offer a flat monthly rate; others charge on a per-piece basis.

The reliability of online information varies greatly. Services such as LexisNexis which offer the full text of newspaper and magazine articles, are very reliable. Information obtained directly from organizational Web sites is generally reliable, though it may be biased in favor of the organization posting the information. Be particularly wary of information posted by individuals, especially those without professional credentials.

Professional Materials. Many national organizations offer information useful for public relations writers. The Encyclopedia of Associations is an excellent source of information about such organizations and their services, including informational materials. Several specialized publications, such as Information Industry Directory (part of Gale Research), are helpful in tracking down professional materials.

Additionally, many local associations as well as businesses and agencies have professional libraries that may be used by researchers and writers. Hospitals, law offices, corporations, and religious and human service organizations may be willing to provide specialized information to public relations writers, especially when the writing project serves their organizational purposes.

Primary Research

Sometimes it may be necessary to conduct *primary research*—research that generates new data collected specifically for a particular project. Also known as *formal research*, primary research can include surveys, content analyses and focus groups. Usually, these will be part of a broad public relations campaign rather than an individual writing project. As important as formal research is, it is beyond the scope of this book. See the bibliography section for a listing of some books on formal research methodologies useful to public relations practitioners.

"Tips for Better Writing: Three Steps of Effective Research" suggests ways to conduct effective research of any type.

Media Directories

In addition to topical research, the public relations writer should develop a familiarity with another set of information resources, *media directories*. These include collections of data

---

Tips for Better Writing   *Three Steps of Effective Research*

Regardless of the method of research, any good program of information gathering will involve a three-step process of preparing for an interview:

1. Identify your information needs: what you want to know, specific bits of information you hope to locate.

2. Identify likely sources for this information: people to interview, books to review, data sources to investigate, encyclopedias to examine.

3. Identify the strategies needed to obtain the information from these sources: specific questions to be asked, files to be checked, entries to be searched, formal research methodologies to be undertaken.

---

related to newspapers and magazines, radio and television, telecommunications, advertising and other media-related areas. They are essential tools in helping writers identify media contacts, develop story ideas, and effectively disseminate information about a client or employer. Hundreds of media directories are published throughout North America in print, on CD-ROM and/or online. "FYI: Widely Used Media Directories" lists some of the most widely used. In addition to providing a directory of media, many of the companies also sell media mailing labels.

FYI   *Widely Used Media Directories*

Bacon's Directories (bacons.com): Newspaper directory for daily and weekly publications, news services, syndicates, publishers, columnists, Sunday supplements, and ethnic publications; magazine directory with market classifications; radio/television directory with stations, broadcast and cable networks, satellite systems, and syndicates.

Bowden Media Directory (bowden.com): Online database of 80,000 Canadian and U.S. media and related services.

Burrelles/Luce Media Database (burrellesluce.com): Called "Media Connect," with state-by-state listings for more than 40,000 media outlets including daily and nondaily newspapers, news services, syndicates, magazines (trade, professional and consumer), newsletters, radio and television stations, cable services and networks.

Editor and Publisher International Yearbook (editorandpublisher.com): Three-part directory of daily U.S. and Canadian newspapers; weekly, ethnic, special-interest papers; foreign newspapers; and news syndicates.

Gale Directory of Publications and Broadcast Media (gale.com): Print and online listings for thousands of daily, weekly, and special-interest newspapers; periodicals; radio; television; cable; networks and news syndicates.

Gebbie Press All-in-One Directory (gebbieinc.com): Print or CD one-volume directory of business, trade, financial, and consumer publications; news syndicates and daily and weekly newspapers; ethnic newspapers; television networks; television and radio stations.

Harrison's Guide to Top National TV and Talk Interview Shows (rtir.com/products.htm): Guide by Bradley Communications' Radio-TV Interview Report, with producer names and contacts, including pitching advice.

Matthews Media Directories (ccnmatthews.com): Directories specializing in Canadian print and electronic media.

Television and Cable Factbook and **Cable and TV Station Coverage Atlas** (warren-news.com): Commercial and public television stations, cable systems, instructional systems, low-power stations, foreign-language programming, media organizations, networks, satellite services, communication attorneys and engineers in the United States, Canada, Mexico and international markets.

Exercise 4.6—Obtaining Information from Media Directories

 Using media directories available to you, locate the asked-for information. For each question, choose either A, B, C or D.

1. To place a story with a topic related to travel, who would you contact at the daily newspaper in this city? (List name of newspaper and name of travel editor.)
   A. Burlington, Vt.
   B. New Orleans, La.
   C. Fresno, Calif.
   D. Seattle, Wash.

2. In what month is the annual special edition for senior citizens published in the daily newspaper in this city? (List name of newspaper, name of special section and month of publication.)
   A. Erie, Pa.
   B. Taylor, Texas
   C. Independence, Mo.
   D. Flint, Mich.

3. What is the CBS television affiliate in this city? (List call letters and channel number.)
   A. Miami, Fla.
   B. Tulsa, Okla.
   C. Raleigh, N.C.
   D. San Diego, Calif.

4. What city is the publication site of this newspaper? (List city and state.)
   A. San Juan Record
   B. Buffalo Tri City Register
   C. Cleveland Daily Banner
   D. Hartford News-Herald

5. An NBC television affiliate serves this city but is not located there. Who is the news director of the NBC television affiliate that serves this city? (List city in which the affiliate is located, station call letters, and news director.)
   A. Moline, Ill.
   B. Johnson City, Tenn.
   C. Wheeling, W.Va.
   D. Mount Vernon, Ill.

6. On what campus is the studio for the public television station in this city? (List station call letters and school.)
   A. Bloomington, Ill.
   B. Bozeman, Mont.
   C. Tampa, Fla.
   D. Fairbanks, Alaska

7. Based on the open, mid-week per-column-inch rate, how much would a 2-by-6-inch advertisement cost in the daily newspaper in this city? (List name of newspaper, per-column-inch rate and cost of 2-by-6-inch ad.)
   A. Los Alamos, N.M.
   B. St. Joseph, Mo.
   C. Alliance, Ohio
   D. Blackfoot, Idaho

8. What is the Hispanic or Spanish-language radio station serving this community? (List call letters and frequency.)
   A. Bakersfield, Calif.
   B. Hartford, Conn.
   C. Paterson, N.J.
   D. Greeley, Colo.

9. What two NBC television affiliates broadcast to this city? (List station call letters and cities of origin.)
   A. Michigan City, Ind.
   B. Hammond, La.
   C. Batavia, N.Y.
   D. Stockton, Calif.

10. What is the largest Sunday newspaper in this Canadian province? (List name of newspaper and circulation.)
    A. British Columbia
    B. Manitoba
    C. Alberta
    D. Quebec

11. What is the full name of this religious-oriented television network, its denominational base, and its headquarters city?
    A. JTN
    B. EWTN
    C. Bridges TV
    D. TBN

12. In what year was the community weekly newspaper founded in this town? (List name of newspaper and year.)
    A. Arapahoe, Neb.
    B. Marshall, Ark.
    C. Upper Marlboro, Md.
    D. Arab, Ala.

13. What is the name of the campus newspaper at each of these colleges or universities?
    A. Humboldt State University, Seton Hill College, Holmes Community College
    B. University of Rio Grande, Stonehill College, Foothill Community College
    C. Ocean County College, Eastern Arizona College, Contra Costa College
    D. Wichita State University, Valencia Community College, Durham College

14. What is the circulation of the largest daily newspaper in this city? (List name of newspaper and circulation.)
    A. Rome, Italy
    B. Munich, Germany
    C. Monterrey, Mexico
    D. Sydney, Australia

15. What is the television market ranking for this metropolitan area, and how many households does it serve? (List ranking number and number of households.)
    A. Denver, Colo.
    B. Knoxville, Tenn.
    C. Seattle-Tacoma, Wash.
    D. Reno, Nev.

Nine Steps to Effective Writing

Like any good process, writing progresses along a clearly marked path. The following approach is drawn from the experiences of many different writers. Use it for the remainder of this writing course. Adopt it as your own system for producing effective writing for any public relations purpose. The nine steps and their substeps are listed in "Tips for Better Writing: Nine Steps to Effective Writing," and each is discussed in more detail below.

Tips for Better Writing   *Nine Steps of Effective Writing*

1. Plan what you want to write:
   Indicate the writing project
   Identify and analyze key publics
   Note benefits
   Indicate tone
   Establish objectives
   Note dissemination means
   Estimate readability range
   Note evaluation methods

2. Research the needed information:
   Identify questions and issues
   Research topic
   Interview sources
   Organize content (themes and facts)

3. Organize your writing:
   Prepare a formal outline or use a graphic organizer

4. Write and print the first draft.

5. Review your planning sheet and revise the first draft:
   Review objectives and analysis of publics
   Revise for content
   Print a second draft

6. Polish the language in the second draft:
   Read aloud
   Review for language
   Rate for readability
   Print third draft

7. Proofread third draft for language mechanics:
    Correct for spelling
    Correct for punctuation
    Correct for style

8. Get the necessary approvals:
    Submit writing to reviewers
    Return to Step 5 for needed revisions

9. Present your writing in its final public or publishable form.

Step 1: Plan. The goal of the planning stage is to get yourself ready to present your message. The writing process begins as you prepare a planning sheet, focusing your attention on the task at hand. The decisions you make now will help you to carry on to the other steps in the writing process.

Step 2: Research. The goal of the research stage is to gather the necessary information so you can write your message. Gather information you want to communicate to your key publics. Identify issues and questions to be addressed. Check documentary sources (such as files and books) to obtain this information. Interview people familiar with the topic. Conduct formal research if necessary. After you have gathered all the information you need, organize it into appropriate themes and segments.

Step 3: Organize. The goal of the organizing stage is to develop a flexible outline for your writing. The traditional way of organizing your thoughts is to prepare a formal outline using categories and subcategories marked with capital letters, Arabic numerals, small letters, and Roman numerals. Such an outline can be very helpful because it requires clear thinking and careful planning before you actually begin writing.

An alternative way to organize your thoughts is by using *graphic organizers.* These are various visual tools that offer more flexibility than traditional outlines. Graphic organizers include charts, graphs and diagrams that represent ideas and information. They can help writers organize their thoughts and visualize the relationship between different concepts. Exhibit 4.5 shows a graphic organizer used as preparation for a news release.

Step 4: Draft. The goal of the drafting stage is to produce a starting point for your writing. Write the draft of your message. Let the words flow freely, and focus on the logical unfolding of your message rather than on the format or mechanics of your writing. Occasionally, a student will complain about writer's block, a situation in which the writer simply cannot think of how to start. If this happens, go back to the first step and review your ideas. Freewriting about the topic and your difficulties with it also can be a good way to unblock the mind. Usually, the planning sheet will help you overcome any confusion about how to approach the writing.

You don't need to start at the beginning as you write this first draft. It may be easier to begin simply by writing a quote, an example, or an easy-to-write explanation of some point. Then add detail, eventually returning to the beginning to write an introduction or lead.

Step 5: Revise. The goal of the revision stage is to make sure you are on target with what you set out to do during the planning stage. The computer becomes your most useful instrument, because the technology makes writing easy to revise. Some literary observers have suggested that the very nature of computers—with transient words on the screen—enhances this part of the writing process. Computers invite you to work with your words.

First, review your analysis of the key publics in your planning sheet, particularly their wants, interests and needs. Then review your stated objectives. Read your first draft to see if you left out any important information. Add what seems appropriate. Delete anything that seems to distract readers from your stated purpose. Reposition sentences and paragraphs so information is presented in a logical order.

In the revision stage, input from others can be particularly useful. As a student, incorporate the suggestions of your instructor and fellow students; in the field, consider the input of colleagues and co-workers. Collaboration and teamwork are important in the practice of public relations, and it is not uncommon for writing projects to reflect the work of several different writers and editors.

Step 6: Polish. The goal of the polishing stage is to smooth out your writing so it becomes more understandable and more interesting to read. This is a good time to take a break. If possible, put some distance between you and your writing. The most effective way to do this is to put your writing away and return to it the next day. This incubation time will make you fresh and ready to approach your writing objectively. If it isn't possible to set the writing aside for another day, give yourself a half-hour or so to step away from your writing. Even in a deadline situation, a brief respite to get a drink, make some phone calls, or walk around the block can do wonders for your writing.

Read the second draft out loud. Better yet, have someone read it to you. Hearing your words will help you notice mistakes and correct a variety of writing problems. Tune your ear for obstacles to good writing, such as poor or missing transitions, lack of sentence variety, and awkward phrases or sentences. Pay particular attention for the kind of grammatical errors that sometimes find their way into verbal messages, such as noun–pronoun disagreement. Apply a readability check to this draft, and decide if it needs to be rewritten at a level more appropriate for your reader.

Step 7: Proofread. The goal of the proofreading stage is to assure correctness in the mechanics of writing. You have already produced a version that both meets your objectives and uses language smoothly. Now turn your attention to the details of style, especially to punctuation and spelling. Edit your writing for these mechanical details. If any of these give you particular difficulty, read your draft one time through with only this problem in mind. For example, if you know that you often have errors with commas, read your draft once again and focus all of your concentration on the proper placement of commas. Make sure your writing conforms to appropriate stylebook standards. Here are some tips and a word of caution about the proofreading stage:

> **Tip 1:** A trick of book editors and newspaper copy editors is to read backwards—right to left, bottom to top. That way each word becomes the object of your attention, and you are likely to spot errors.

> **Tip 2:** Just as computers can be your friend, they also can deceive you. It is much easier to spot mistakes when you are proofreading a piece of paper rather than a computer monitor. At this stage of the writing process, print a hard copy of what you have written and proofread from this.

> **Tip 3:** Develop a list of your personal devils. You will find that over time you can identify your personal weaknesses. Make a list and keep it next to your computer as a quality control before you let anything go. For instance, maybe you often overlook *pubic* for *public* or consistently use *they* when you mean *it*. Use the "Find" function on your word processor to locate your personal devil.

And a word of caution: Like all tools, spelling and grammar checkers on computers are only as good as the person using them. Don't let yourself rely on these so much that you fail to copy read your writing. Some computers get confused by compound nouns such as *ethics* and *public relations*. Meanwhile, *its* and *it's*; *read* and *reed*; *right, write, rite* and *wright* all are words the computer will accept as being spelled correctly, and it may not distinguish their grammatical usage. But, as "FYI: Spellbound" illustrates, it takes a human being to know which word is appropriate for the writing context.

FYI *Spellbound*

I have a spelling checker
It came with my PC;
It plainly marks four my revue
Mistakes I cannot sea.

I've run this poem threw it,
I'm sure your please too no,
Its letter perfect in it's weigh,
My checker tolled me sew.

(Author unknown)

Step 8: Get Approvals. The goal of the approval stage is to obtain permission necessary to present the piece publicly. Often, public relations writers find themselves in the situation of needing to obtain approvals or sign-offs before they can publish or disseminate their writing. Junior members of a public relations department must submit their writing to their managers. Department managers themselves sometimes find that either discretion or organizational policy causes them to route their writing to executives above them in the chain of command or to other interested departments (such as the legal staff) for approval. Experienced practitioners who have built up a level of trust within the organization often find that such approvals are not necessary.

Agency writers always submit the writing to clients, who themselves may have an elaborate pecking order of approvals before the piece of writing is deemed appropriate for publication or distribution. It is not unusual for this approval process to add days, even weeks, to the production schedule, so writers should know the procedure and develop a schedule that allows for delays. Often, the approval process will throw the writer back to Step 5, revising the piece based on the input of the reviewers.

Step 9: Present. The goal of the presentation stage is to present your writing in its most professional version. Prepare the "publishable" version that you will share with members of your publics: the news release to be sent to editors, the brochure to be handed out, the appeal letter to be mailed, the Web page to be uploaded. Make this your writing at its finest and most complete.

Going through the Process

Following is an example of how a piece of writing developed from the idea stage represented by the planning sheet through the final version. The writing project is based on the planning sheet presented in Exhibit 4.4, part of a promotional campaign for a day care center. In the research step, the writer addressed the following questions: What does the program offer? How can parents use the service? What costs are involved? How can a parent sign up?

Exhibit 4.5 depicts a graphic organizer based on the information to be presented to the key public. Exhibit 4.6 shows the first draft of the writing project. Note that this is a very rough version. Marked on this draft is a major revision in which the writer has reviewed the

Exhibit 4.5—GRAPHIC ORGANIZER

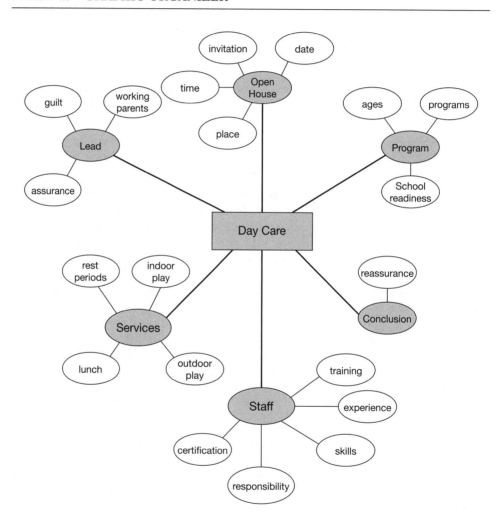

objectives, added some information not included in the first draft, and deleted other information that is less important. Exhibit 4.7 is the revised text. The writer has polished the draft by smoothing out the language; note the attention to transitions and sentence structure. The writer has also edited the piece, correcting spelling and punctuation. Exhibit 4.8 is the final presentation. The draft has been thoroughly revised, edited and finally prepared for public use.

Exhibit 4.6—EDITED FIRST DRAFT

It is tough enough being a parent, ~~in these troubled times~~ *today* without ~~having to~~ feeling guilty about leaving your child when you go ~~off~~ to work. The staff and management of Teeny Tykes ~~want to ease your burden~~ *offer you a re-assuring choice*

You ~~may be interested in attending~~ *are invited to* an Open House on Monday, July 13. ~~This Open House is free for parents and children. It is located~~ *at the Teeny Tykes Day Care Center* at 15 Kinderhausen Lane in Northfield. *Bring your family and see what Teeny Tykes can offer your child.*

Teeny Tykes is a full service day care center for children 2-5 years. ~~For the younger children~~ we provide supervised games, crafts, stories *and*, ~~and naptime~~. We also worked with the Northfield School District to provide a school-readyness program to help prepare our children for higher education after they graduate from Teeny Tykes. We ~~also~~ have nutritious lunches, *quiet rest periods,* ~~and snacks~~ and a ~~closed in~~ *supervised play in our* outdoor playground.

~~All~~ our staff have training in early childhood education and ~~emergency medical~~ *first aid.* *All of us are certified by the state. Most importantly,* ~~care.~~ We really care about children entrusted to us, and we take seriously our responsibility to you and your child. ~~At~~ Teeny Tykes ~~we~~ make your job ~~as~~ *Come see how can give you peace of mind and* ~~parents~~ *of parenting* a little bit easier.

Exhibit 4.7—REVISED DRAFT

It's tough being a parent today without feeling guilty about leaving your child when you go to work. The staff and management of Teeny Tykes offer you a reassuring choice.

] What You Need to Know [

You are invited to an Open House on Monday, July 13, at the Teeny Tykes Day Care Center at 15 Kinderhausen Lane in Northfield. Bring your family and see what Teeny Tykes can offer your child.

] About Day Care [

Teeny Tykes is a full service day care center for children aged 2 to 6 2-5 years. We provide supervized games, crafts and stories. We have nutritious lunches, quiet rest periods, and supervised play in our outdoor playground. We also worked with the Northfield School District to provide develop a school-readyness program to help prepare our children for higher education after they graduate from Teeny Tykes.

] For Your Child [

Our staff members have training in early childhood education and first aid. All of us are certified by the state. Most importantly, Even more, we really care about the children you entrusted to us, and we take seriously our responsibility to you and your child. Come see how Teen Tykes can give you peace of mind and make your job of parenting a little bit easier.

Teeny Tykes

] Putting the CARE in Day Care [Bodoni Bold Italic 36 pt   20 pt

Exhibit 4.8—FINAL PRESENTATION

It's tough being a parent today without feeling guilty about leaving your child when you go to work. The staff and management of Teen Tykes offer you a reassuring choice.

What You Need to Know

You are invited to an Open House on Monday, July 13, at the Teeny Tykes Day Care Center at 15 Kinderhausen Lane in Northfield. Bring your family. See what Teeny Tykes can offer your child.

About Day Care

Teeny Tykes is a full-service day care center for children aged 2 to 5. We provide games, crafts and stories. We have nutritious lunches, quiet rest periods, and supervised play in our outdoor playground. We worked with the Northfield School District to develop a school-readiness program to help prepare our children for "higher education" after they graduate from Teen Tykes.

For Your Child

All our staff members have training in early childhood education and first aid. All are certified by the state. Even more important, we really care about the children you entrust to us. Come see how Teen Tykes can give you peace of mind and make your job of parenting a little easier.

Teeny Tykes

Putting the CARE in Day Care

Exercise 4.7—Practicing the Writing Process

Part 1: Prepare a planning sheet for a letter to be sent to a key public of your choice as part of a campaign to increase membership in a neighborhood Scout troop or similar organization.

Part 2: Do whatever research is necessary to obtain information for this writing project. Then develop a graphic organizer to outline the various elements or sections you want to include in your writing.

Part 3: Type a draft of this letter. Aim for about 200 words. Then review your objectives and reconsider what you wrote in the first draft. Pay particular attention to your earlier analysis of the key public and the organization's objectives. Based on your review of the planning sheet, handwrite your revisions on your first draft. Read this draft aloud, and pay close attention to polishing the language. Handwrite your revisions for polishing the language. Then transfer the handwritten changes on your computer and print out a second draft.

Part 4: Mark copyediting changes on this draft as you edit it for details such as spelling, punctuation, grammar and AP style. Then make the handwritten polishing and editing changes on your computer or word processor and print out a final draft.

Reminder: You will turn in four pages for this assignment: a planning sheet, a graphic organizer, a first draft with handwritten revisions, and a second draft with handwritten polishing and copy editing. ∎

PUBLIC RELATIONS WRITING FOR JOURNALISTIC MEDIA

In the popular mind, public relations is closely linked with the news media. Indeed, for many people outside the profession, the specialty of media relations is the only aspect of public relations that is visible. The ranks of journalism have supplied more public relations practitioners than any other training ground, and many organizations have developed their public relations efforts along the lines of the public information model. This approach to public relations is based in the notion of news—a somewhat intangible quality that helps information take hold in the public imagination. Any writer interested in succeeding in public relations must develop an appreciation for the concept of news. It really is a concept based on respect for an organization's publics.

Public relations writers are not magicians. No sleight of hand can make insignificant information look like news. Neither are they like alchemists. Attempts to turn mere information into news are no more successful than efforts to turn lead into gold. Rather, effective public relations practitioners are like farmers and gardeners, who plant seeds, nurture crops, and sometimes graft different stocks to produce a more vibrant offspring. So, too, with public relations writers who help create, nurture and eventually harvest the newsworthy activities of their organizations.

The specialty of media relations provides the public relations writer with a window through which to expose the organization to its publics. This is an important component within an organization's comprehensive communication program. News releases are the most commonly used tools for media relations, but the field provides many other options for the innovative writer.

Part 2 of *Becoming a Public Relations Writer* deals with opportunities public relations writers have to maximize the newsworthy aspects of their organizations. It focuses on the nuance of writing for journalistic media. Part 2 includes six chapters:

- Chapter 5: News and the Public Relations Writer
- Chapter 6: News Releases
- Chapter 7: Working with the Media
- Chapter 8: Broadcast Media
- Chapter 9: Organizational Features
- Chapter 10: Advocacy and Opinion.

5

News and the Public
Relations Writer

News is often considered the prerogative of editors and reporters, but public relations practitioners also need to be oriented toward news. We must recognize news and respect it. Successful practitioners appreciate the power of news and the energy it can bring our organizations and clients.

This chapter will introduce you to various aspects of news—what makes events newsworthy, how to enhance on the news value of an organization's activities, and how public relations practitioners can work with journalists. It also will present the fact sheet format as an integral part of your professional repertoire.

This chapter will focus on what news is, how to recognize and generate it. It will also introduce simple formats for writing news and will address some of the legal aspects of public relations writing. Here are your objectives for Chapter 5:

- To develop an understanding of the elements of news
- To identify and generate newsworthy information about an organization
- To write in the simple news formats of fact sheet, factoid and event listing
- To explain the legal concept of defamation
- To explain the legal concept of privacy as it applies to communication.

Defining News

News is an elusive concept. Professional communicators analyze it, and everybody else talks about it knowingly. News is basically a matter of experience; veteran journalists and public relations people seem to just "know" what is newsworthy or how to make something more newsworthy. News is also a matter of preference—like politics, art, religion and computer platforms.

Dictionaries tell us what we already know: News is new information, something reported, something newsworthy. How wonderfully vague! Journalists and public relations practitioners, past and present, have tried to define news. Such a definition is important because it can help us develop a common understanding about what news is.

Having a common understanding about news is especially important to public relations writers, who are continually trying to anticipate what the gatekeeper will consider to be news. A *gatekeeper* is a person who controls the flow information. Gatekeepers may be the editor of a newspaper or newsletter, a radio or television news director, or a webmaster. Gatekeepers consider information available to them, then evaluate it in light of the needs and policies of their particular medium and the presumed interests of their audience. Then they decide whether the information has enough news value to be offered to the audience.

In the end, it all boils down to this: News is what the editor or news director says is news. The media call the shots. It doesn't matter if you and your boss or client think the information is important. If the media gatekeeper doesn't think it's news, it's not news. No appeals process.

The Venn diagram in Exhibit 5.1 graphically shows that news is the information in overlapping circles of interest for the media gatekeeper and public relations practitioners. Circle A indicates the interests of the news media, Circle B information about the organization, and Circle C the interests of a key public.

Exhibit 5.1—MODEL OF OVERLAPPING INTERESTS This model shows overlapping circles representing the various interests of the organization, the news media and the key public. Media relations focuses on the AB area (news), which represents the interests of the news media that coincide with information about the organization. Public relations writers, however, are particularly interested in the ABC area (strategic news), where the key public also is interested in the same issues as the news media. The BC area (direct news) represents the potential for the organization to take its message direct to its interested publics without using the news media.

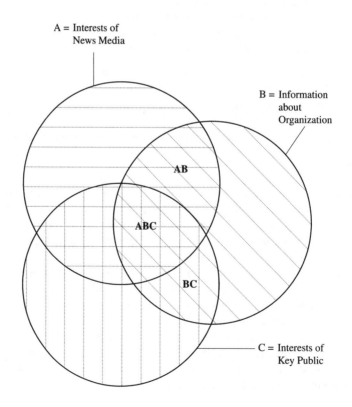

A = Interests of News Media

B = Information about Organization

C = Interests of Key Public

AB

ABC

BC

The AB area denotes newsworthy information about the organization that the media might be interested in reporting. The media gatekeeper is focused on the people who read the newspaper, listen to the radio newscast and view the television broadcast. Frankly, the gatekeeper doesn't care much about Circle B, though you and your boss care deeply about it. Your job, as public relations person, is to find out where Circle A overlaps Circle B. Then call this to the attention of the media gatekeeper. Remember that all of this is defined by the individual media. Circle A is much different for an employee newsletter than for a daily newspaper, different for a television station than for a special-interest radio station.

The ABC area represents news of interest not only to the news media but also to an organization's key public. This is the information of particular value to a public relations writer, because it is newsworthy information that the public will look for or at least will be attentive to.

Meanwhile, if you find that you have information in the BC area, look for ways to present it to your public through organizational or advertising media. Or reshape or enhance the information to make it of more interest to the news media.

Consider also the AC area, which indicates information not involving your organization that is of interest both to the media and to the key public. Look to these agendas for opportunities to insert their organizations into the news of the day.

You can see that there are many ways in which a deep understanding of news and its relationship to your organization can be of immense value to you as you try to work through the news media. However, we are in the midst of a monumental change, and public relations practitioners must deal with media evolution. Technology is reducing the influence of the gatekeepers, and increasingly the definition of news is being determined by the end user, our publics. The information-on-demand phenomenon is driving this change, giving our publics greater access to information they consider newsworthy and useful. The success of Internet e-zines, the growth of news distribution via e-mail, the proliferation of specialized cable TV channels, and the mushrooming readership of Web-based news releases all attest to this.

Over the next decade or so, the media landscape will look much different than it does today. Students in the classroom are sitting at the threshold of an era when direct-to-consumer news becomes the norm.

Exercise 5.1—Freewriting on News

Part 1: Look up the following words in your dictionary: information, facts, knowledge, news, truth, announcement.

Part 2: Freewrite for five minutes on the following topic: *What is news?* Then discuss this with your classmates. ∎

News Interest

Your job as a public relations writer is to know the mind of the gatekeeper, to understand media and anticipate audience interests. To accomplish this, you need a good working definition of news. The best method of approaching a definition of news is to look at the criteria for news or interest value that the gatekeepers use to determine the news value of information. News has certain observable characteristics, particular elements that, when present, transform information into news.

Journalists have identified the following elements of news, also known as *news value*: action, adventure, change, conflict, consequence, contest, controversy, drama, effect, fame, importance, interest, personality, popularity, prominence and proximity. The long list of descriptors offers clues about what editors and news directors are looking for when they judge the news value of any story.

For the public relations writer, we might look at a simpler listing. Four characteristics are especially important for the public relations writer: significance, localness, balance and timeliness. Adding these together provides us with a good working definition: *News* is information about *significant* and *local* interest, presented in a *balanced* and *timely* manner. These elements are basic to virtually all news releases that are used by the media. Two other elements of news value, *unusualness* and *fame*, are not crucial, but they can enhance the likelihood that information will be considered newsworthy. An easy way to remember these elements of news interest is to memorize the acronym *SiLoBaTi + UnFa,* made up from the first two letters of each of the elements. Let's look at each characteristic.

Significance. News interest involves information of significance. It has meaning for many people. If you were not a part of a particular organization and read a news release about it, would you ask, "So what?" If so, it probably is not news. For example, plans to add a dike along Water Street might be broadly significant to an entire community:

> SCARLET RIVER—The State University Center for Flood Control is reviewing proposals for an extension of the dike along Water Street. The plan calls for adding a 14-inch cap to hold back water during heavy flood stages to protect the city's downtown business section.

Or, something might be significant if it affects even only a few people but in a major way:

> SCARLET RIVER—The State University Center for Flood Control is warning residents of the dozen homes along Canal Street that they risk flood waters in their living rooms if Red Creek is relocated as proposed by the County Highway Administration.

Editors and news directors look for information that makes people talk. They look for the Wow! factor. News is something readers didn't know yesterday but want or need to know today. News is information of consequence to people who know it, something that helps them make informed decisions on topics of significance. A public relations writer should test every story idea against this standard: How much will the reader/viewer/listener care about this information?

Localness. News interest involves information about a local community, whatever that means to the particular medium. Newspaper editors say the lack of a local angle is the most common reason why they turn down news releases. Television news directors say the same thing about video news releases. Consider the following examples of the same event—in this case, a college graduation—prepared for two different media. The first version is intended for a metropolitan daily newspaper, the Martin City Express, which serves a two-county area in which the college is located. It serves the generalized interests of the newspaper and its readers.

> MARTIN CITY—Sen. Nancy Newcomer will receive an honorary degree during graduation ceremonies Friday at Oakwood College in Apache Center. The state senator, who chairs the Joint Legislative Education Task Force, will address the 430 graduates of the suburban college.
>   During the ceremony, about 75 students will receive awards . . .

A second version is meant for distribution to the Hillsvale Record and Sentinel, a small-town weekly newspaper serving a single community. The Hillsvale editor would find the first version to be of little local interest, but this second version would have much relevance to its readers:

> MARTIN CITY—Two Hillsvale residents are among the 50 honors graduates who will receive awards at commencement ceremonies Friday at Oakwood College. State Senator Nancy Newcomer will address the 430 graduates.
>   The local graduates, both alumni of Hillsvale Junior-Senior High School, include the following:
>
> • Jonathan Berman, who will receive the top academic award for chemistry majors. He is the son of Malcolm and Bertha Berman, of Main Street.
> • Sylvie Batherton, a dance major who will receive general academic honors. She is the daughter of Marian Armstrong, of Hillsvale R.D. 3 . . .

The concept of localness is not only defined geographically. The public relations writer might prepare a special version of the news release for El Tiempo, a newspaper serving the area's Hispanic community. In it, the writer might list those students who have identified themselves as part of the Hispanic community, or perhaps those graduates who are members of Adalante Hispanica, the student organization focusing on Hispanic issues.

Balance. News interest involves information presented in a balanced way. Just as good reporters strive to present all sides of an issue, good public relations writers also should write in a balanced manner. Obviously, as advocates for organizations and clients, we have an obligation to consider their interests, and we want them to be seen in the best possible light. But sometimes light reveals flaws and wrinkles. A good public relations person will acknowledge problems, perhaps even use them to the organization's advantage. Writing in a way that allows us to put our best foot forward generally means considering long-term interests, which are furthered when we earn respect for candor and honesty.

Consider this scenario. Simon Joyce is a candidate for city council in Haven Crest (population 75,000). You are a volunteer public relations writer helping his campaign. You are helping Joyce prepare a statement for tonight's electoral debate, which will be televised by the local cable station. You must decide how much information to provide. The following paragraph seems complete: "I like the outdoors and I think kids need more recreation opportunities, so of course I think the reservoir is a good idea. A very good idea! As a state project, this will not raise local taxes. But it will bring new jobs to our community, and we will have a better supply of water for our industries. We'll also have a nice picnic area for everybody to enjoy. How could anybody be against the project?"

Based on this statement, debate viewers and readers of tomorrow's news reports will find Joyce portrayed as a community-minded candidate. You've done a good job.

But perhaps there is something else to consider. In your concern about the long-term effect of information, you suggest that the candidate hit head-on one of the issues that may (or may not) arise. But because it's potentially embarrassing information, you counsel your client to add the following to his statement: "I should tell you that my cousin owns some of the land to be flooded by the project. Vinnie Joyce is going to make some money when the state buys this land. But I don't want anyone thinking I'm getting any financial benefit out of this. First off, everybody knows Vinnie is a tightwad who wouldn't share his profits with anybody, family or not. Second, right here and now I am asking Vinnie and all the folks who own land in the building area to contribute to a new fund. I'll make the first pledge of $500 myself. If we get this reservoir, I'd like to see the city buy some small sailboats so families can have some fun."

Imagine the effect of the first statement, unbalanced and incomplete. After an initial favorable news report, there could be embarrassing stories when the cousin's connection becomes known (as it inevitably would). Maybe the criticism would even come out during the debate itself. But by telling the full story, you have helped the candidate avoid embarrassment and turn a potentially negative response to his advantage.

Timeliness. News interest involves information that is timely. Facts are enhanced when they are connected with a current issue of public interest. Information today is better than yesterday. Information about tomorrow is even better. As a writer, you will determine what to release and when to release it. Consider the differences in the apparent news value of the following three leads:

> CENTERVILLE, Oct. 12—At a stockholders' meeting last week, the Jordan Shoe Company appointed Malcolm Tweedly to succeed Aston Dickerson as general manager.

> CENTERVILLE, Oct. 5—The Jordan Shoe Company today installed Malcolm Tweedly as the company's general manager, succeeding Aston Dickerson. The decision was made yesterday at the company's annual stockholders' meeting.

> CENTERVILLE, Oct. 4—Malcolm Tweedly will become general manager of the Jordan Shoe Company tomorrow afternoon in ceremonies in the plant cafeteria, succeeding Aston Dickerson. The promotion was announced today at the company's annual stockholders' meeting.

The first version is clearly dated. The other two take advance planning and quick turnaround on the part of the public relations staff, but the news value is enhanced. Version 2 is a responsible way of dealing with information, but Version 3 is an even more newsworthy way to make the announcement.

Be careful about what you try to announce ahead of time. Organizations trying to use advance news releases to generate early registrations often are thwarted by the timeliness factor. It simply isn't very newsworthy that your organization is planning an appreciation dinner in two months. Certainly you need advance registrations to determine how many dinners to order, but a news release isn't the way to go. Nonpublic media such as newsletters and direct mail, coupled perhaps with print advertising, can generate advance response.

Unusualness. News interest is enhanced when information deals with unusual incidents. Some people call it human interest; others see it as novelty. Human interest is like beauty—

difficult to define but obvious when you see it. The concept may be best understood through examples. Human interest is a report about the smallest infant born in your hospital, the oldest graduate of your continuing education program, the one-millionth unit manufactured at your suburban plant, the piano recital with "The Minute Waltz" played backward. Well, the latter is just bizarre, but if you are a music school, it just might gain some publicity for your recital.

Fame.   News interest is magnified when information deals with famous people. "Names make news" isn't just idle chatter. Information has greater news value when it involves well-known or important people. It is part of human nature to be interested in something that involves people we know, or know about. Maybe we respect them; maybe we despise them; or maybe we're just nosey. But people who are well known or in positions of prominence attract public attention, and that means news. Consider the news value in each of the following leads:

> MIDDLETON—The Chamber of Commerce will dedicate the new Downtown Sports Arena Wednesday afternoon.

> MIDDLETON—Gov. Jesse Glastenhoeven will speak to Little League players Wednesday afternoon as the Chamber of Commerce dedicates the new Downtown Sports Arena.

The dedication you are promoting as public relations director of the Middleton Chamber of Commerce may be just another ceremony that generates only a modest interest by the media. But if the governor is to participate, you've got a news story on your hands. Maybe the governor isn't coming after all, but good public relations planning might still help you play the fame game.

> MIDDLETON—One lucky Little League player participating in Wednesday's dedication of the new Downtown Sports Arena will take home a 1986 baseball card that Gov. Jesse Glastenhoeven donated from his personal collection. The card features José Canseco of the Oakland A's as Rookie of the Year.

Exercise 5.1—Noticing News

Clip four news stories from the metro or local section of your daily newspaper. For each, indicate the characteristics of news interest that you think are the major ingredients in your story idea: significance, localness, balance, timeliness, unusualness and fame. You probably will find that stories have more than one ingredient, so indicate all that are relevant but also note which one seems to be the strongest reason that the story was printed in the paper. ■

Categories of News

All news isn't the same, and journalists see variety within the concept of news. Consider the following categories of news: hard news, breaking news, soft news and specialized news.

Hard news is information with an edge to it. It deals with momentous events: accidents, crime, death, disaster, scandals, and activities with immediate results such as elections and trials. This often isn't news generated by public relations people, though we may well give organizational responses and background information as journalists cover hard news. Frequently, this deals with the negative news that public relations practitioners hope their organizations can avoid.

Breaking news is hard news that is happening even as the media are covering it. This presents a special problem for public relations writers, who may lack the time and facts to prepare a complete report. Instead, they often work with an ongoing series of updates on the basic facts. Breaking news may involve situations in which the outcome is yet unknown, such as sporting competitions or elections. Breaking news also may take public relations people into the area of crisis communication.

Soft news is lighter information. It deals with routine activities and programs, leisure, entertainment, events of human interest, developments without major consequences, and activities and trends with more distant results. Public relations writers often find that their accounts of upcoming events, new projects and programs, or personnel developments fall into this category of news.

Specialized news deals with information of importance to particular publics and particular segments of the media. This includes news about interest areas such as business, religion, sports, the arts, agriculture, science, health, family and home. This is an area of news that can be successfully mined by enterprising public relations writers. Successful practitioners are those who have learned to see beyond the general story to exploit information that may interest a particular public or media audience.

Finding News

Part of your responsibility as a public relations writer will be to take the initiative in finding newsworthy activities within your organization. Look carefully to see what is newsworthy. Some organizations have events that are routine occurrences within the organization but that may be of significance and interest to outsiders. Don't overlook this as a possible news activity.

There are two ways to consider a story's or activity's newsworthiness: the systems approach and the functional approach. Let's take a look at each.

Systems Approach

Review the planning process in Chapter 4 in which you considered all of an organization's publics. This format, using a *systems approach,* is based on the concept of linkages associated with systems theory. This can help us probe for news related to an organization's significant publics. As a case in point, consider a systems approach to identifying news for a private school:

Consumer publics include students. Is there something to report about honors lists? Science fairs? Student organizations? Essay contests? Scholarship winners? Parents also comprise a consumer public. Is anything happening with parent associations? Whole-family education?

Producer publics include teachers. What might you report about new faculty? In-service training? Advanced studies?

Enabling publics include the school board. Is newsworthy information coming from meetings? Elections? Enabling publics also include the state education department. Is anything happening regarding accreditation? Curricular regulations? New standards?

Limiting publics might be other schools. What might be happening in your school that would be of interest to private academies? School districts? Teacher unions, educational accreditation units, and governmental agencies also can be limiting publics.

Functional Approach

Sometimes public relations writers can benefit from a functional approach to finding news, in which we identify major activities of an organization and view each with an eye toward potential news stories. In this approach, we look at five categories: events, issues and trends, policies and governance, personnel, and relationships. The functional approach applied to a private school might identify the following potential news categories:

- *Events*: Assemblies, open houses, graduation, special observances
- *Issues/Trends*: Standardized test results, enrollment trends, curriculum changes
- *Policies/Governance*: Drug/Alcohol intervention, athletic eligibility, graduation requirements, progress reports to taxpayers
- *Personnel*: New administrators, the accomplishments of faculty and staff members
- *Relationships*: Neighborhood projects, service activities, lobbying efforts on behalf of educational standards, taxpayer bond campaigns.

Exercise 5.3—Identifying Newsworthy Activities

You are a public relations writer for one of the following organizations (try to select an organization with which you are personally familiar):

- A student organization such as club, team or sorority/fraternity
- A church, synagogue, mosque or other local religious congregation
- A community league for soccer, basketball or some other team sport.

Consider both the systems approach and the functional approach as ways to investigate your organization for newsworthy activities. Then identify at least 10 areas of potentially newsworthy activities for your organization.   ∎

Generating News

As a public relations writer you are not a magician. You can't create something from nothing, but you can orchestrate situations so they can become newsworthy. In fact, part of your usefulness to employers and clients, as well as much of your benefit to the media, lies in your ability to develop newsworthy activities.

There are four crucial points to effectively generating news for your organization:

- First, know the media, their news formats, and the elements of newsworthiness that they consider important.
- Second, know your organization or client, especially its mission and its goals. This information provides the framework for creating news opportunities that serve the needs of the media, the purposes of the organization, and the interests of the publics.
- Third, know your publics and ask yourself what is happening within the organization that may be of interest to your publics.

- Finally, pay attention to what is happening both in your community and around the world.

A key to generating news is to link your organization to a topic already on the public and/or media agenda. This is called creating a *news peg*. Think of a peg in your closet on which you hang your jeans. It's there; you just need to use it. The same is true with a news peg. It already exists as a topic of interest to the news media; you simply need to hang your organization's message on it. Where do you find a news peg? Read the newspaper. Follow television and radio news. Check out online news and even blogs related to your organization or client.

Following are 10 general activities that public relations practitioners can use to generate news for their clients and their organizations.

1. Awards. Organizations can draw attention to their values and important issues by giving an award to a person or group that exemplifies these standards. The monetary value of the award is less important than the prestige it seems to carry with both the organization giving it and the publics important to the recipient. For example, Citizens for a Clean Environment may give an award to a local auto-repair garage that allows customers to drop off used tires, which the garage then delivers to a recycling center. In fact, CCE might even make the first move by encouraging the garage to offer the service in the first place.

2. Contests. Everybody likes a good contest. Just as with giving awards, the news value is enhanced through a logical relationship between the sponsoring organization and the focus of the contest. A patriotic organization probably could hold a jump-rope contest, but when it sponsors an essay contest on the Bill of Rights, it is both increasing its level of news interest and advancing its own mission.

3. Personnel. Organizations seem to have no difficulty using this method to generate publicity. All organizations elect officers or hire managers, and these personnel selections are generally of interest to some media. Like the above examples, careful pairing between organizational objectives and these news pegs can be useful. For example, a school district concerned with truancy may announce the appointment of the vice principal to chair a special task force on school attendance.

4. Local Needs. Organizations with something to promote often find local examples of that cause to address. The news value is enhanced when you have something to say about the issue. For example, let's say stray dogs have been scaring children at the neighborhood park and stray cats have been using the sand pile as a litter box. As complaints mount at City Hall, the local Animal Protection League might step in with a timely reminder that it will take in animals that owners no longer can care for, or it might use the occasion to invite new volunteers to help its cause.

5. Reports. This is a complement to addressing a local need. When an organization wants to highlight an issue that is not yet on the public agenda, it can gather information and then issue a report. For example, the Sheriff's Department is concerned because many drivers do not use seat belts. The sheriff assigns a deputy on limited duty recovering from a gunshot wound to search the last year's files for information on traffic accidents, injury and seat-belt use. After a few days of digging, the deputy has the basis for a new Sheriff's Report on Seat-Belt Use.

You can also take a lesson in what works for other organizations. Because of the inherent news value of the State of the Nation and State of the State addresses by governmental leaders, other organizations are adopting a similar approach to draw attention to their annual progress. You may be able to generate interest among the media by using a State of the Corporation speech, State of the County presentation, State of the School District report, State of the Diocese address, or State of the University summary.

6. Localized Reports. Along a similar line, most organizations are connected to some extent with larger groups. Whenever the larger body issues a report, the local organization may be able to recast it in local terms and general local news interest. For example, if the state Small Business Administration reports that 75 percent of the small businesses hired additional employees last year, the local Chamber of Commerce may do a spot check to quickly survey local businesses to see if that pattern is represented locally, then report its findings.

7. Campaigns. When an organization launches a campaign, it's almost always newsworthy. But make the campaign appropriate to your organizational objectives. Let's revisit the Sheriff's Department and its concern about the use of seat belts. Let's say the department has observed that pregnant women often do not wear seat belts because they find them uncomfortable and they fear the belts may cause complications for their pregnancy. But the department knows that these are unfounded fears compared to the greater threat of being in a traffic accident while not wearing a seat belt. So the department announces a new program to have its deputies contact each obstetrician, midwife and childbirth educator in the county and each area hospital and birthing center, urging them to encourage their pregnant patients to wear seat belts. The news reports surrounding the announcement of the new program may reach many pregnant drivers even before the campaign begins.

8. Speeches. People in organizations often give speeches, which the public relations writer can use as the basis for news releases, letters to the editor, newsletter articles and other communication vehicles. It is potentially newsworthy when your CEO travels to the state capital to speak to a lawmaker about corporate taxation. There also may be news interest when your executive director addresses a local civic organization about the spirit of volunteerism in your community.

9. Celebrities. Names make news, and celebrities can draw attention to organizations and causes. For example, ask someone famous to give a speech to your organization. If you are working with a hunting-and-fishing organization, invite a like-minded member of the state legislature to address your members about the state's program for animal conservation. Or name a local community figure as honorary host for a charity event. Or write a letter of protest to the governor, and then give a copy to the local news media.

10. Public Issues. Good public relations practitioners will know the mission and goals of the organizations they serve, and they will take the initiative to tie into current issues and events in ways that can support that mission and further those goals. Here's an example: In a Northeastern city a few years ago, the local newspaper reported some strong anti-Catholic statements made by a traveling nondenominational preacher. The local Jewish Federation used this as a news peg, issuing a public statement that in essence said, "We know what prejudice feels like, and we abhor this." Religious tolerance was on the federation's agenda. Then some Protestant clergy issued similar statements, because their denominational agendas support inter-religious cooperation. The various religious groups involved themselves because it served their own self-interests to oppose religious intolerance and to maintain good relations among the local churches.

Another way of tying into external issues is to be aware of the many special events that may be taking place. Chases' Annual Events is an excellent source of ideas for tie-in stories. But don't just issue a comment; do something newsworthy. For example, if you are public relations director for an agency concerned with alcoholism, you might generate activity around the first weekend in April, observed as Alcohol Free Weekend. You might co-sponsor an alcohol-free dance with an area college, prepare a booklet about how to host alcohol-free social events, and try to interest the news media into reporting on the weekend and your agency's role in promoting it.

Read more about generating news in "Advice from a Pro: Joe Brennan on Generating News," then consider some of the ethical questions around news making in "What Would You Do?: Making News."

Advice From a Pro   *Joe Brennan on Generating News*

Joe Brennan, APR, is a former communications manager for the Research Institute on Addictions, a New York State agency that conducts research on aspects of alcoholism and other drug addictions. Part of Brennan's job was to make scientific findings understandable and interesting to nonscientific audiences. Working on a tight budget, he knew that his organization's message had greater impact when he could link it to an issue on the public agenda.

For example, when the governor addressed the topic of violence in his State of the State address, Brennan was quick to use this as a news peg. He gathered information about the role drugs play in violent crime. When a celebrity committed suicide, Brennan prepared a report that drew on the institute's studies of addiction and suicide. He also used the news peg of high-profile drug-related murders in letters he wrote to some of the state's larger newspapers.

What Would You Do?   *Making News*

Consider some of the ethical questions surrounding news making:

- What is the difference between legitimate news activities taking place within an organization and a publicity stunt?

- Do you find it ethical to create a publicity stunt to get attention for your organization?

- Does it matter if the action that gets attention is newsworthy or not?

- How strong must the news elements be to justify a publicity stunt?

- Are there any limits on the kind of stunts you might arrange for the organization?

Exercise 5.4—Creating Newsworthy Activities

You are the public relations director for one of the following organizations:

- Maurice Manufacturing Inc., a company that makes small kitchen appliances
- The Bertrand Center, a nonprofit agency advocating for people with physical disabilities
- The Pachysandra Alliance, an inner-city program offering free art classes to children, teens, and young adults.

Using the list of 10 ways to generate news, develop a brief, specific story idea (2–3 sentences) for each category. ∎

Writing in Simple News Formats

Public relations writers use many different formats to present news about their organizations. Some of the most basic are fact sheets, factoids and event listings. Let's look at each. (The most common news format, the news release, will be discussed in detail in the next chapter.)

Fact Sheets

Fact sheets provide information stripped down to the bare facts, making them the easiest and quickest way to disseminate information to the news media. Essentially, they are bits of strategic and newsworthy information that public relations writers give to reporters to provide a basis for stories the reporters will write. They answer the standard journalistic questions: Who, what, when, where, why and how? They might also provide background information, benefit statements, quotes and other information that the public relations writer thinks would be useful to the reporters.

Fact sheets can be included in a media kit along with a news release or disseminated to reporters in place of a release. Additionally, fact sheets have several uses beyond media relations, such as vehicles for providing information to employees or consumers.

For an organization with its public relations staff at the central headquarters and a number of outlying sites without public relations staffs, fact sheets can be especially useful. A school district, for example, may have a publicity contact at each school site prepare fact sheets for routine information to be distributed directly to the media or circulated "in house" among the various school buildings and administrative offices. These might provide information on things such as PTA meetings, scheduled athletic events, parent conferences and open houses.

In some business environments, fact sheets are preferred to news releases. Dentsu Public Relations, Japan's largest agency, notes that—for media relations in Japan—a news release that reads like a finished press story is viewed with annoyance and distrust. Japanese reporters "see their job to be that of putting the story together, and the best that the press release can do is to provide them with all the factual information they might need—and the phone number of someone they can contact in order to check further," according to Dentsu's guidebook for doing public relations in Japan. A fact sheet is probably the best vehicle for that.

Note that a defining characteristic of fact sheets, as the term is used here, is that they are event based, dealing with a specific activity. Event-based fact sheets are easy to prepare.

They require only minimum writing standards and little experience in writing for the news media, though they include essentially the same information that would be included in a more complex news format such as a news release. Despite their simple writing style, however, a graphic organizer can be useful in sorting out the proper information. Exhibit 5.2 shows the graphic organizer used to outline the fact sheet in Exhibit 5.3.

Exhibit 5.2—GRAPHIC ORGANIZER FOR NEWS FACT SHEET   This model graphically displays the various elements of the fact sheet depicted in Exhibit 5.3.

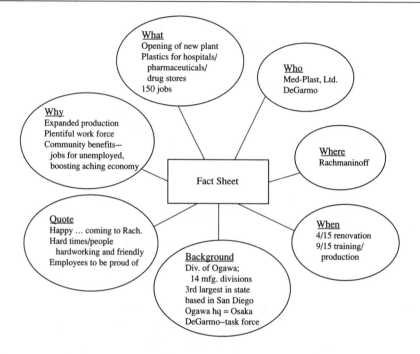

Exercise 5.5—Writing a Fact Sheet

Presume you were public relations director for one of the historic events listed below. Do a bit of research on the person and the invention or accomplishment, then prepare a fact sheet that could be given to reporters about the event in the scenario you select.

- You were public relations director for the Pharaoh Khufu/Cheops, announcing plans to build the Great Pyramid

- You were public relations account executive for a client, Vladimir Zworykin, announcing the invention of the television

- You were public relations consultant for Bartolommeo Christoforo, announcing the invention of the piano

- You were public relations director for God, announcing the creation of the world for the Angel Daily News.

Exhibit 5.3—FACT SHEET This fact sheet presents the same information displayed graphically in Exhibit 5.2. Note that, as a fact sheet, it focuses on a new event (the opening of a new plant).

MED-PLAST, LIMITED

A DIVISION OF OGAWA INDUSTRIES

123 MAIN STREET ⊡ CENTRAVILLE XX 12345
Regina VanDerPlanck ⊡ Vice President Corporate Communications ⊡ (123) 555-12345

Fact Sheet: New Textile Plant
Jan. 23, 2003

Who
Med-Plast, Limited (a division of Ogawa Industries)
John DeGarmo, president and CEO

What
Opening new plant
Manufacturing plastic materials for hospitals, pharmaceutical companies, drug stores
Hiring 150 production workers

Where
Rachmaninoff (Mathewson County), small town with 57 percent unemployment

When
Staggered hiring schedule
Renovation of former Central Rails plant begins April 15
Training and production begins Sept. 15

Why
Textiles Limited wishes to expand production
Seeks new plant in area with a plentiful work force
Prefers community that could benefit from this expansion

Benefits
New jobs for currently unemployed workers
Boost to ailing small-town economy

Quote
DeGarmo: "I'm happy about the prospect of coming to Rachmaninoff. The town has had some tough times, but the people here are hard working and friendly. They are the kind of employees any company would be proud to have."

Background on Textiles Limited
Based in Centraville
It is the state's third-largest producer of medical plastics
DeGarmo is a member of Manufacturer's Task Force on Depressed Communities

Background on Ogawa Industries
Based in San Diego
Nationwide company

Factoids

In addition to event-based fact sheets that serve as substitute news releases, a related communication tool can provide background on issues, programs or products. These *factoids* are brief bits of information about an organization and/or the programs or issues it deals with. Factoids, also called *breaker boxes*, simplify complex information, thus helping reporters and editorial writers, as well as readers, become familiar with topics of concern to an organization.

Fact sheets and factoids are similar in that both include a series of brief notes, often bulleted. But whereas fact sheets deal with events, factoids deal with issues. For example, a hospital preparing for a high-profile type of experimental heart surgery may prepare a factoid to explain to reporters the various surgical terms, techniques and equipment involved. Factoids may also provide an overview of the history of an organization or a program, or it may identify milestones in its development. Such factoids could be useful not only to reporters but also to many other publics.

Fact sheets and factoids can be complementary. A public relations writer may provide both to reporters—a fact sheet, for example, to provide information about the opening of a new treatment program for people found to have abused prescription medications, and a factoid to explain the novel treatment methods associated with the program.

Exercise 5.6—Writing a Factoid

 You are a public relations writer with one of the following organizations. Identify appropriate categories of information, then write a one-page factoid that provides background that can help reporters writing articles for special-interest magazines.

- A network of health care providers promoting self-examination for early detection of breast cancer or testicular cancer
- A travel agency promoting a particular type of vacation such as cruises, wilderness excursions, language immersion, or theater and museum tours
- An organization dealing with a technical or specialized topic with which you are familiar. ∎

Calendar Listings

Virtually all media provide opportunities for organizations to list *calendar listings*—brief announcements of upcoming activities in various types of community calendars or community bulletin boards.

Writers preparing event listings may approach this the way beginning journalists look at an assignment to write obituaries: dull formula writing. But these listings offer an important opportunity for the public relations writer to publicize the organization's message, and they deserve thoughtful preparation and attention to detail.

Begin with a plan that identifies and analyzes the key publics and then defines your objectives. Write a brief announcement consistent with examples from the relevant publication or broadcast media. Finally, send the announcement to the proper person. On many newspapers, the city desk does not handle the community events listings. If you send your announcement there, it may end up in the trash. Instead, send it to the calendar editor, events coordinator, or perhaps the public service director; check a media directory or the newspaper Web site, or telephone the newspaper switchboard to find out where to send your announcement. While it is usually unwise to send duplicate copies of a news release to different sections of a news-paper, a different rule applies to events listings. Most publications will use calendar listings, even if they supplement a news release used in a different section of the publication. Consider how the following media offer such opportunities:

Newspaper. Daily and weekly newspapers have special listings (perhaps even special sections) with calendars that announce events in the arts. If you are working with a museum, theater, dance troupe or art school, such listings should be part of your repertoire of com-munication channels. Likewise, some publications have similar listings for athletic events, which could be very useful to school districts, colleges and universities, community centers, and independent leagues. Other specialized listings may be focused on business, education, religion, and so on.

Magazine. Sometimes, specialized magazines and other periodicals have sections that list events and activities of interest to their readership.

Cable Television. Cable TV offers opportunities for organizations to use community bulletin boards that list everything from poetry readings to pancake breakfasts. Some of these are reserved for nonprofit organizations. Cable TV may also offer *crawls*, those messages that scroll across the bottom of the screen in which community organizations can promote their events.

Broadcast Television. Television stations, especially smaller ones, sometimes offer listing services similar to radio stations.

Radio. Some radio stations may provide listings of major events. Some stations that have community calendars accept written notices, often on postal cards. Others accept phone-in messages that are recorded for on-air playback.

Wire Service. For significant events with a high news value, wire services such as the Associated Press or PR Newswire may offer an outlet for your listings.

Computer. Increasingly, computer technology is being used by some news media to provide information of community interest through on-demand telephone services or online computer services. Newspapers and radio or television stations often complement their coverage of events with calendar listings at their Web sites.

FYI   *Public Relations Terms: A Mixed Bag*

Some of the terms surrounding public relations formats vary from place to place, and person to person. Here are the terms as used in this book:

News release is a pretty common term for a journalistic-based presentation of facts about a newsworthy activity. Alternative terms to be avoided include *press release* and *handout*.

Fact sheet is restricted to bulleted newsworthy information about an event or activity; it is used in place of or in addition to a news release.

Factoid refers to bulleted background information, often used to explain or accompany a news release. *Breaker box* is another term sometimes used. Some practitioners do not distinguish between fact sheets and factoids.

Calendar listing or *event listing* refers to a brief note about upcoming events and community activities. In some parts of the country, calendar listings are called *media alerts*, a term that in other places is reserved for news bulletins about crises or other sudden and major news. In this book, *media alert* is used as a synonym for the more common *media advisory*, which refers to a note or memo advising media gatekeepers about a crisis statement, news conference, photo opportunity or other upcoming newsworthy activity. More on these later.

All of which points out that terminology is fluid. So when you talk with public relations professionals, participate in an internship or interview for your first job, keep an open mind about the language of public relations.

Writing within the Law

Two areas of law can have a significant impact on the work of a public relations writer. These are defamation and privacy. Let's look at each.

Defamation

Anyone who wants to become a public relations writer should be familiar with the legal concept of defamation. Rooted in English common law, this concept has been consistently applied in the American legal system. The Supreme Court has seen defamation as communication that reasonable and average people in the community believe impugns "the honesty, virtue or reputation" of a person, who is thereby exposed "to public hatred, contempt and ridicule." Put another way, *defamation* is negative and harmful language that identifies a person and is published or communicated to a third party, the use of which involves some fault by the person or organization using the language. Defamation takes two forms: *slander* (oral defamation) and *libel* (written or broadcast defamation).

Simply using language that can harm a person's reputation does not make a writer guilty of defamation. Laws vary among states and between states and the federal government, but in general there are five elements that are involved in the legal understanding of defamation:

Defamation. Though it may sound simplistic, defamation defames somebody. That is, it holds someone up to public hatred, contempt or ridicule. It is language that reflects negatively on a person's morality or integrity or which discredits a person professionally. Courts have ruled that some words, because of their meanings or common interpretations, are libelous per se (Latin for "by itself"). These are words with a negative connotation that the courts have called "odious labels"—words such as *adulterer, blackmail, crook, deadbeat, drug addict, drunk, liar, pervert, poor credit risk, prostitute, retarded* and *suicide*. And, as "FYI: Allegedly,

There's No Need for This" points out, qualifying or hedging with such language won't absolve you of guilt. Note also that the law considers photos and drawings as extensions of words and thus as potentially defamatory forms of communication.

FYI *Allegedly, There's No Need for This*

Be aware that the use of a qualifier doesn't remove the risk of writing something libelous or disclosing something private.

Allegedly means "according to legal documents" or "according to claims made without proof." It is used only in specific reference to statements made in a police report, judicial brief, court filing or some other legal record—statements and claims which, though official, are not yet proven. The writer in effect is claiming the privilege of reporting that a document and the allegation contained within it in fact exist and are part of the public record.

Reportedly means an official report has been made, or at least a semi-official spoken account has been given to the writer. It does not in any way connote the accuracy of the report.

Generally, a public relations writer has no business using either of these words. Somebody writing on behalf of a client or an organization should be able to obtain the facts without having to rely on allegations, hearsay or outside reports.

Identification. Defamation identifies the person. Defamatory words probably are not libelous or slanderous if they do not clearly identify the person claiming to be injured. However, courts have ruled that the defamation does not need to be by name; innuendo and clues sufficient to identify a person may constitute defamation. Note that mistaken identification, whether from carelessness or because of an honest error, does not protect a writer from blame.

Publication. Defamation is information published or communicated to a third party. Written communication can involve many forms, including news releases, newsletters, memos, e-mail notices, and so on. Broadcast scripts and video presentations generally are considered parallel to other written forms of communication. It is not usually necessary to prove that a writer even knew that a third party had access to the information, only that is was communicated.

Fault. Defamation involves fault by the writer. The final ingredient of defamation is that the communication of the message involves some measure of carelessness or malice. The standards vary, depending on the status of the person making the claim. A private citizen generally has only to show that the person preparing the message was negligent. Malice has to be proved by public officials and public figures.

Harm. Compensation for defamation is based on personal harm. The four previous criteria can constitute defamation, but legal cases generally are reconciled on the basis of harm. The defamation must in some way have caused injury, such as causing the defamed person to become a social outcast, lose business revenues, or experience emotional problems. Juries determine first if defamation occurred and, if so, the extent of the harm caused and the amount of money needed to compensate the victim for the defamation.

There are three common defenses against defamation. One is truth—more specifically, *substantial truth* that can be proven in court. A second defense is that the communication is made in the public interest as a matter of *privilege*, such as a defamatory statement made during official or judicial proceedings or public meetings, or in news reports of such incidents. The third defense against defamation is *fair comment and criticism*, based on the right to critique and criticize in matters of public interest.

Three technicalities can also void claims of defamation: that the *statute of limitations* for filing a law suit has expired, that the person gave *consent* or invited the defamatory statement, and that the statement was made as part of a *broadcast by political candidates*.

The courts have been reluctant to uphold claims of defamation against groups. Companies can claim defamation only if they can prove that the language damaged the company itself, rather than individuals in it. Nonprofit organizations can claim defamation for language that hurts their ability to raise funds, and unincorporated associations can sue over language that prevents them from attracting members or support. The courts have not allowed defamation claims against social, political, religious and other types of groups on the grounds that individuals are not identified by hurtful language against groups. Basically, the larger the group, the more difficult it is to show that it was injured through defamation.

Public Relations Cases Involving Defamation. Increasingly, people are turning to the courts for protection of their rights and punishment of their perceived oppressors. In such an environment, every public relations writer should be especially careful to avoid even the possibility of a defamation suit. The competent writer will also have some understanding of the standards and values of the community in which the communication is made.

Several recent libel cases revolve around charges contained in news releases. A federal judge ruled that lawyers can be sued for defamatory statements they make in news releases about their cases. A Fort Lauderdale pharmaceutical company sued a Denver company that issued a news release claiming the Florida company had stolen its computer software. A computer software company sued a competitor for $1 billion, claiming its stock dropped because of false allegations in the competitor's news release. And a New Jersey humane association sued 15 former volunteers over their news release accusing the association of animal cruelty and false advertising.

A 1976 case has become a classic in the field of libel and public relations. The research director at a state mental hospital in Michigan, Dr. Ronald Hutchinson, sued Sen. William Proxmire for libel because the senator sent out news releases and published in a newsletter that the researcher was wasting public funds. The U.S. Supreme Court ruled that Hutchinson was not a public figure even in a limited sense, even though he had received a federal research grant. Thus he was entitled to protection as a private citizen. The court said that while the senator was privileged in making defamatory comments in Congress, he lost that privilege when he made those same comments in a news release and a constituent newsletter. The case eventually was settled out of court when Proxmire gave Hutchinson $10,000 and a public apology.

In another classic case, Marie Luisi filed a $20 million libel suit against the J. Walter Thompson advertising agency, which had fired her. The woman claimed she was libeled because an agency news release said she had been dismissed because of "improper activities" in the finances of her department. The state Supreme Court dismissed the case only because the woman failed to produce enough evidence to substantiate her claim that JWT had acted in a "grossly irresponsible" manner. The court did not dispute the role of the news release as the central and official corporate statement.

In Canada, meanwhile, a former Security Intelligence Service officer sued a member of parliament over her news release claiming he was a Soviet spy, and he received a formal apology from the legislator.

Exercise 5.7—Avoiding Defamatory Statements

You are public relations director for a major real estate firm, All County Realty. One of your agents, Chester Laredo, has been fired because of continuing poor sales.

The president of All County Realty, Marian Billadeau, told you confidentially that she has received repeated complaints from people trying to sell their houses and from people seeking to buy a house that Mr. Laredo was rude and late for appointments and that he frequently made offensive statements to clients. Ms. Billadeau said she warned Mr. Laredo several times but saw no improvement in his behavior. Mr. Laredo now has sued the agency for firing him without cause, and his case is pending before the local labor court. He has talked with business reporters at the local newspapers, claiming that he was treated unfairly and fired without cause. The reporters are asking your company for a statement.

In a memo to Ms. Billadeau, explore the implications of what might be said to the reporters and what should be avoided. ■

Privacy

Privacy involves the right to be left alone. Invasion of privacy is another legal area that can be hazardous in your chosen profession. As a public relations writer, you should hold the laws of privacy in high regard. Unlike laws against defamation that hinge on the accuracy of a claim, privacy laws focus on whether a person was singled out for attention without his or her consent, regardless of the accuracy of reports or statements.

In public relations, you may often find yourself writing about people and the things that happen to them: promotions, awards, retirements, and so on. All of these can be legitimate material for your writing. However, the legal right of privacy is evolving, with courts and legislatures expanding the concept, generally in favor of the individual. A relatively new area of law, the issue of privacy is an extension of constitutional provisions dealing with unreasonable search and government intrusion.

What does this mean to a public relations writer? Specifically, three aspects of law can affect the public relations writer: private facts, intrusion and misappropriation.

The legal concept of *private facts* refers to personal information that is intimate, offensive and not of legitimate public concern. Revealing private information such as facts about a person's finances, sexuality or health might be considered an invasion of privacy unless the information is clearly newsworthy or unless it has been presented with the person's knowledge and consent. A person fired after his arrest for public exposure couldn't sue his former employer for invasion of privacy, even if the employer had issued a public explanation for the firing, because the report was based on a police activity.

Intrusion involves gathering information secretly, such as by taping a private face-to-face or telephone conversation or interview without permission. It is permissible to tape public events and meetings without getting permission.

The area of privacy most frequently a problem for public relations people is *misappropriation*. This involves the use of a person's name or image for commercial purposes without permission, such as using someone's picture for promotional or advertising purposes. This includes the use of look-alikes and sound-alikes.

Though state laws vary, in general they are designed to protect people from being exposed unwillingly to the glare of publicity. Recall that truth is the ultimate defense against defamation. In charges of invasion of privacy, it is permission that offers legal protection. The key to privacy matters is *permission*, by which you can write whatever you think is appropriate, as long as you have approval from the person you are writing about. When in doubt, get permission or leave it out. As a public relations practitioner, you can protect yourself and your employer against lawsuits by making sure that the people you write about have given their consent, either implicitly or explicitly.

The concept of *explicit permission* is simple: The person gives you a written statement such as an individual consent release to allow the publication or other use of a photograph or video image. Another form of explicit permission is a *blanket consent release.* This is a signed statement, often part of an employee file or an employment policy release, which allows an organization to use information or photos for publicity or nonpaid promotional purposes. Blanket consent releases may be used with employees, volunteers, students, and other groups of internal publics. In general, these biographical information releases (also called *bio sheets*) cover only information related to the organization. It usually does not extend to unrelated personal information such as marital status, children, or political or religious affiliation.

Most organizational public relations offices maintain a bio sheet on employees and volunteers. Often these are reviewed and updated annually by each employee or volunteer. This provides the writer with ready access to accurate and current background information on people involved in potentially newsworthy activities. The information categories will be developed for the particular organization. A sample biographical information release is shown in Exhibit 5.4.

In addition to explicit permission, public relations writers sometimes find themselves dealing with *implicit permission*. This is based on the notion that any reasonable observer would see that the person is willingly participating in a situation. A person implies permission by participating in a news interview, a television program, or a posed photograph. In general, it is safe to consider implied consent for publicity about an employee in routine situations such as hiring, promotions, and awards. However, even when you make the judgment that you are dealing with implicit permission, it is best to check with the person you are writing about to verify permission.

The courts have applied the notion of implied consent even when intimate personal information is published. One classic example is the case of Oliver Sipple, a decorated Vietnam veteran who saved President Ford from being shot by deflecting Sarah Jane Moore's hand as she pointed a gun at the president during a visit to San Francisco in 1975. He became an instant hero, a national celebrity. Several news organizations subsequently identified Sipple

Exhibit 5.4—BIOGRAPHICAL INFORMATION RELEASE (SAMPLE)

I, _____, have provided the following information about myself, and I give permission for _____ to use this for noncommercial publicity and promotional purposes related to this organization. (Signed and dated)

Professional Information
Job title
Description of duties
Major accomplishments
Date of hiring
Previous positions held within this company
Professional achievements and awards

Occupational Information
Previous employment (name, location, highest position, inclusive dates)
Military service (branch, highest rank, inclusive dates, current status)

Educational Information
Colleges (name, location, degree, year)

Avocational Information
Relevant organizational memberships
Civic and community activities
Honors and awards

Personal Information (to be held confidential)
Home address
Date of birth
Family members

as a leader of the city's gay community. Sipple filed lawsuits claiming invasion of privacy because the reports identified him as a homosexual. He lost the lawsuits when a state appellate court ruled that Sipple's sexual life was not a private matter because he was, of his own free will, an activist for gay rights.

But in a similar case, the court ruled in favor of a California student who had undergone a sex-change operation years before her election as president of a university student council. The woman had gone to great lengths to conceal her former male identity, even legally changing her name. Thus, the court said her sexual history was a private matter protected by law and not a matter for news stories about her election to the council post.

There may be times when the public relations practitioner is restricted—by law or by organizational policy—to providing only the most basic information about a person. For example, information about current or former employees may be limited to verifying their employment and job title. One public relations manager found her hands tied when a former employee of her company became a whistleblower, telling both the government and the news media about allegedly illegal activity by the corporation. The fact that the employee may have been biased against the corporation could not be told by the public relations manager. Neither could she indicate that this employee had made similar accusations against two previous employers, accusations that had been found to be untrue. All she could do was verify the employment status of the whistleblower and endure the criticism of fellow employees who did not understand the legal constraints on her ability to publicly defend their company.

Public relations practitioners should work with organizational attorneys when dealing with possible intrusions into the privacy of current or former employees. Our role is not necessarily to blindly follow legal advice at the expense of our experience and instincts about helping the organization relate to its publics and provide public comment. But we should be familiar with legal implications as we counsel organizational management on the handling of delicate matters of public attention.

Public Relations Cases Involving Privacy. In the case of *Vassiliades v. Garfinckel's*, Mary Vassiliades was photographed before and after she had plastic surgery by Dr. Csaba Magassy. The surgeon later showed these photos at a promotional event for skin creams sponsored by the public relations department of Garfinckel's department store. A court in the District of Columbia said that, while the subject was newsworthy, use of Mrs. Vassiliades' photos without her consent for commercial purposes was a violation of her privacy. Because the store could show that the doctor told the company's public relations director that the patient had given her consent to use the photos, liability was placed on the doctor, not the store.

Exercise 5.8—Avoiding Invasion of Privacy Issues

You are director of public relations for the Acme Welding Company. An intern on your staff has written the following item for the next issue of the Welding Courier, the company's employee newsletter. Underline any problem areas within this article, and write a memo to your intern about any parts that carry the risk of invasion of privacy.

Michael Marakowski, a technician with the computer department, has been named Volunteer of the Year by the Abernathy Preschool Program, where his daughter Amanda is enrolled. Michael's ex-wife is a secretary with the Abernathy Program.

Michael, 35, who works on the night shift, has been with Acme Welding for more than six months. He just received his first performance evaluation and received a "Satisfactory-Plus" rating.

Acme Welding Personnel Director Martha Binetti said she is pleased that community-minded people such as Michael are working for this company.

Michael is also a volunteer peer counselor at the Alternative Men's Health Center in neighboring Indiana County, according to a co-worker. The health center is part of a system of clinics throughout the upstate area that have been active in fighting the spread of AIDS within high-risk populations.

6

News Releases

Communication historians report that the first news release was a graduation announcement issued in 1758 by King's College (now Columbia University). In the last 2½ centuries, the news release has become a mainstay of public relations writing, though that could be changing. Today, proportionally fewer people read newspapers than in previous generations; more than one-third of American households do not even subscribe to a newspaper. Television news attracts at most two-thirds of Americans aged 18 to 35. Many people, particularly younger and college-educated Americans, get their news through the Internet. Despite this fragmentation of media, however, public relations writers still count the news release as one of their most important tools.

Organizations in all kinds of situations use news releases to make announcements, encourage support, respond to critics, invite participation and report progress. Additionally, the same kind of writing associated with news releases is the basis for effective writing for organizational newsletters, Web sites and internal newspapers. Indeed, a new use for the news release is its posting on the organization's Web site.

For some practitioners, media relations will be the primary focus. For others, it may be less important, but the ability to write with a news approach remains a basic skill needed to succeed in the profession. In virtually every career opportunity in public relations, you will be expected to have mastered this type of writing. Job interviews often include an on-the-spot test of your ability to write a news release.

This chapter introduces you to the format and content of news releases. You will explore different types of releases and writing techniques associated with them. You will discover that news releases have many purposes and offer various benefits. They give information to reporters preparing stories for daily newspapers and provide facts to radio and television journalists who will follow up with interviews. They attract photographers to scheduled events and offer wire services information that can be boiled down into briefs and summaries. They serve as a prepackaged report that can be used by smaller newspapers and special-interest publications, and as material that organizations can post on their Web sites. Here are your objectives for this chapter:

- To write in appropriate news style
- To use the appropriate format for news releases
- To understand and apply the basics of news release writing
- To write different kinds of leads and news briefs

- To write news releases for local media
- To demonstrate competence in writing news releases for various purposes.

News-Style Writing

A *news release* is a communication format commonly used by organizations to provide information to the news media. It is a piece of news-based writing that has the look and feel of a news story written by a journalist. In essence, it is a news story written by a public relations person for journalistic use.

The news release may be one of the few truly egalitarian elements left in modern society. Whether written by a volunteer at a nonprofit organization, a highly paid public relations practitioner, or a college graduate just getting started, each news release has exactly the same chance of being used by an editor or news director. What determines acceptance or rejection is not where it comes from but how professionally the release is written.

Before we talk specifically about news releases, let's review some of the conventions of news-style writing that the effective public relations writer must observe. Drawn from print journalism, these are based on the need to be both objective and accessible to audiences. Most of what follows will be reminders, since you probably have learned these in previous classes or other writing activities; however, it is important material to review. Remember that the same news values and quality writing that make a good news story are needed to make a good news release.

Short Sentences

All public relations writing should strive for simplicity of style, but news writing especially cries out for this quality. Use short, simple words. Readability studies suggest using words averaging 1½ syllables. Sentences should be brief, with an average of 16 words when the writing is for general audiences. For visual appeal and readability, paragraphs should also be short, generally six lines maximum. When text is transferred into newspaper columns, a single typewritten line on 8½-by-11-inch paper will yield about 2½ or three lines of newspaper text. Thus six typed lines of news release type would yield about 15 lines in a newspaper—more than two inches of unbroken type. To ensure easier reading, newspapers need more frequent paragraph breaks.

Exercise 6.1—Simplifying Lengthy Sentences

Rewrite the following lengthy sentences in a shorter version that retains the same information as the original. Your revision probably will be longer than the original because it will include more than one sentence, but no individual sentence should be longer than 20 words.

1. Mitchell Aruba, vice president of research at Mountain Electronics, Ltd., has received the Medal of Distinction given by the Alumni Association of Southeastern University in recognition of his breakthrough invention of the robotic neonatal vascular pump that has become a frequently used tool in cardiac surgery on infants, tripling their chances of survival.

2. Explaining the Potawamiah County Bar Association's opposition to the bill proposed in the County Legislature by Commissioner Carl Frankelberger of Jasonville, association president Bertha Orczynski said the bill would limit the freedom of choice among senior citizens in selecting attorneys of their own choice in civil lawsuits.

3. The Metropolitan Academy for the Arts—a professional training ground for many local musicians and artists—has announced that its new director will be Octavio Diaz, currently managing producer of the Provincial Music Institute and a former professor of arts management at the University of Palos Verdes in your hometown.

4. The Health Advocacy Network of Apple County (HANAC) is creating a county-wide community task force of professionals drawn from the areas of health care, social work, education, religion, government, law enforcement, and business to focus on the growing problem of elder neglect and elder abuse, which HANAC claims is increasing at an alarming 25 percent a year, with the first meeting of the task force scheduled for next Monday at 7 p.m. in the County Building on Macintosh Road. ■

Simple Language

News releases have a few language idiosyncrasies that should be respected. Memorize and use them routinely. Here are some of the most common writing conventions for news releases:

- Use the basic word *said* rather than striving for more subjective alternatives such as *exclaimed, proclaimed, declared, related, asserted* and *remarked*.
- Make careful use of objective varieties such as *noted, added, pointed out, replied* and *declined to comment*.
- Use past tense *said* to report information that already has been provided or uttered.
- Avoid subjective superlatives such as *best, most useful* and *greatest*.
- Use great care with objective superlatives such as *biggest, first, unique* and *only*.
- Avoid hard-sell advertising-based terms such as *breakthrough* and *revolutionary*.
- Use simple verb tenses such as *will begin* rather than the progressive forms such as *will be beginning* that indicate an ongoing action.
- Prefer future forms of verbs such as *will attend* rather than *is planning to attend*.
- Prefer past perfect forms of verbs for past action of indeterminate timing: *The company has appointed a new director*.
- Use past tense only with specific times, and only when the time is relevant: *The company appointed a new director last week*.

Exercise 6.2—Using Simple Language

Circle the number of the correct answer in each set. Answers are listed at the end of this chapter.

1A. The plan will lead to 200 new jobs, promised the president.
1B. The plan will lead to 200 new jobs, noted the president.
1C. The plan will lead to 200 new jobs, said the president.

2A. The company will market a revolutionary new carpet.
2B. The company will market a carpet with many new features.
2C. The company will market a totally new kind of carpet.

3A. The captain said the ship usually is full.
3B. The captain says the ship usually is full.
3C. The captain says the ship is full more often than not.

4A. InterCity Bank will merge with State Bank.
4B. InterCity Bank has a plan to merge with State Bank.
4C. InterCity Bank announced plans to merge with State Bank.   ■

Titles of People

Public relations writers often find themselves writing about people in their relationship to organizations. We identify people by their occupations, job titles and functions.

- Formal titles denote authority, professional activity or academic achievement, such as President, Queen, Gen., Ensign, Bishop, Dr. These usually precede the name capitalized and with no commas. Follow stylebook rules for abbreviation.
- Short functional and occupational titles may precede the name with no commas and without capitalization.
- Longer functional titles may either precede or follow the name, set off by commas, without capitalization.

For a more complete review, see Appendix A in this book, "Common Sense Stylebook for Public Relations Writers," or consult a grammar and usage book or a media stylebook. Look at information dealing with appositives, titles and commas.

Exercise 6.3—Identifying People by Title

 Look at the following examples of titles. Circle the number of the correct choice(s) in each set of sentences. Answers are listed at the end of this chapter.

1A. President Martin Adamson will visit next Tuesday.
1B. Martin Adamson the president will visit next Tuesday.
1C. President Martin Adamson, will visit next Tuesday.

2A. The general manager Heidi Copeland will visit next Tuesday.
2B. The general manager, Heidi Copeland, will visit next Tuesday.
2C. The general manager Heidi Copeland, will visit next Tuesday.

3A. Prime Minister Claude Philippe Dubec, arrived.
3B. Prime Minister Claude Philippe Dubec arrived.
3C. Claude Philippe Dubec, prime minister, arrived.

4A. Hieronymus Kastenzakas the new ambassador, arrived from Greece.
4B. Hieronymus Kastenzakas, the new ambassador arrived from Greece.
4C. Hieronymus Kastenzakas, the new ambassador, arrived from Greece.

Attribution of Quotes

Often, public relations writers wish to present information and opinions that come from someone they have interviewed. Other times, the statements may emerge from printed materials. Or perhaps the public relations writer wants to suggest an appropriate comment by an organizational spokesperson.

In whatever context, statements made by people need to be attributed to them. The most common attribution involves the past-tense form of the verb *to say*, such as *she said* or *they said*. This attribution, also called a *speech tag,* is used not only with direct quotes but also with paraphrases. Conventional news-style writing has a few guidelines on how to use *quotations,* informally called *quotes,* within the format of a news release:

- A full-sentence quote (or the first sentence of a multisentence quote) should begin as a new paragraph.
- Attribution should follow (not precede) a brief full-sentence quote.
- Attribution may interrupt a longer full-sentence or multisentence quote.
- Attribution generally comes before partial quotes.
- Partial quotes cannot lead into a full-sentence quote.
- Paraphrases are appropriate substitutes for cumbersome or unimpressive quotes.
- When attributing quotes directly, use *said.* As for placement of the verb, natural word order would be to use the name of the speaker, then the verb, then the quote. But newswriting inverts the sentence to begin it with the quote. Use quote-*said*-speaker when the speaker is identified by a full name or long title. But use quote-speaker-*said* when the speaker is identified by only a pronoun or a short last name or reference.
- Attribution should be to people, not to organizations.

As a matter of strategy, public relations writers should observe four criteria in dealing with quotes. First, every quote requires the knowledge and permission of the person being quoted. Second, every quote should be strategic, furthering the objectives of the writing project. Third, every quote should sound natural. Read it out loud as a check to ensure that it does not sound contrived. Finally, every quote should be strong, with language that will evoke a response from the reader or that will remain in the reader's memory.

Remember that the quotation marks visually attract a reader's attention. Make sure that the information included within quotation marks is the most strategically effective language you can use. For example, in a newspaper story about prostitution and other vice crimes moving beyond the inner city, a police detective was quoted: "People have their heads in the sand about the suburbs. They still think it's Andy and Barney on patrol, peaceful and quiet. Well, it's not." That's the kind of quote that not only makes the point but stays with the reader for some time.

Exercise 6.4—Attributing Quotes Correctly

 Review your skills with the following examples of giving attribution. Circle the number of the correct choice(s) in each set of sentences. Answers are listed at the end of this chapter.

1A. Commissioner Frank Lee Jones said: "This can become a huge asset to our community."
1B. "This can become a huge asset to our community," said Commissioner Frank Lee Jones.
1C. "This can become a huge asset to our community," Commissioner Frank Lee Jones said.

2A. "We expect to see an increase in the number of applicants over the next six months," said the admissions director.
2B. The admissions director said: "We expect to see an increase in the number of applicants over the next six months."
2C. "We expect to see," the admissions director said, "an increase in the number of applicants over the next six months."

3A. Said the federation director: "When you consider the source of this funding and its exceptionally high standards—standards that can be met with only the greatest of difficulty by many organizations—we are especially pleased and honored to have been chosen to receive this prestigious award."
3B. "When you consider," said the federation director, "the source of this funding and its exceptionally high standards—standards that can be met with only the greatest of difficulty by many organizations—we are especially pleased and honored to have been chosen to receive this prestigious award."
3C. The director said she is especially pleased because the federation met the high standards of the foundation.

4A. "When TriChem renovated its plant, we hoped to see some environmental improvements. But we never expected to eliminate the pollution so quickly," said Dayananda.
4B. "When TriChem renovated its plant, we hoped to see some environmental improvements," said Dayananda. "But we never expected to eliminate the pollution so quickly."
4C. When TriChem renovated," said Dayananda, "its plant, we hoped to see some environmental improvements. But we never expected to eliminate the pollution so quickly." ∎

Writing Objectively

In news writing, readers should know they are obtaining facts, not the opinion, speculation, rants or editorial comments of the writer. As a public relations writer preparing news copy, you will need to observe this practice by writing objectively, avoiding commercial plugs, shunning condescending or condemnatory rhetoric, and eliminating flowery language and fawning reports.

Does this mean that a news piece includes no opinion? Absolutely not! A news release or any similar news-based writing can have plenty of opinion and comment. But the opinion must be presented with attribution; in other words, it should present the fact that so-and-so expressed an opinion. For example, it may be the writer's opinion that the annual fundraising effort is for a worthy cause, but the writer cannot include that as a matter of fact. However, the writer may report the fact that the mayor called the cause very worthy. The writer also may assemble evidence and include information about the positive community benefits provided through past fundraising efforts, allowing readers to conclude for themselves that the program is worthwhile.

As a public relations writer, you should report facts, attribute opinion, and make clear the difference between the two. Report facts because they provide information that is a matter of record or verification. Attribute opinions and document comments so they become factual records of what someone said, rather than the inappropriate opinions of the writer.

Exercise 6.5—Writing with Objectivity

With the following sets of sentences and paragraphs, circle the number of the preferred choice(s). Answers are listed at the end of this chapter.

1A. Some scientists say that the disappearance of the dinosaur was caused by a meteor hitting the earth.

1B. Scientists say that the disappearance of the dinosaur probably was caused by a meteor hitting the earth.

1C. The dinosaur disappeared because a meteor hit the earth.

2A. The ComText Corp. is pleased to announce that its Employee of the Year award will be presented to Manuella Cardamone of Charleston.

2B. The ComText Corp. announced that its Employee of the Year award will be presented to Manuella Cardamone of Charleston.

2C. The ComText Corp. will present its Employee of the Year award to Manuella Cardamone of Charleston.

3A. The Road King Tire Co., which manufactures the safest automobile tires on the road today, will build a quality control center in Moreno County. The new facility, which will employ 234 local workers, will inspect Road King tires before they are shipped to distribution centers throughout North America.

3B. The Road King Tire Co. will build a quality control center in Moreno County. The center will hire 234 local workers to inspect what Consumer's World magazine rates as the safest American-made automobile tire.

3C. The manufacturer of popular automobile tires, Road King Tire Co., is pleased to be opening a quality control center in Moreno County. At the new center, 234 local workers will guarantee the safety of the world's best automobile tires on the road today.

4A. Critics say Satomi's musical repertoire ranges from jazz to classical.

4B. Satomi's musical repertoire ranges from jazz to classical.

4C. An outstanding musician, Satomi has an amazingly broad repertoire, which easily ranges from jazz to classical.

Neutrality

A well-written piece of public relations writing will always be directed to a particular public. But if it takes a news format, the writer cannot appear to be writing personally to readers. Avoid *you* and *your* statements. Avoid telling readers what to do. Instead, write as if members of your key public were absent. Provide information but not directions.

Exercise 6.6—Writing with Neutrality

Circle the correct answer in each set. Answers are listed at the end of this chapter.

1A. If you are interested in attending the concert, you may obtain tickets by calling the box office at 123–4567.
1B. Tickets are available through the box office at 123–4567.
1C. Call the box office at 123–4567 for tickets.

2A. Interested students should register for the workshop before Jan. 15.
2B. The registration deadline is Jan. 15.
2C. You can register for the workshop before Jan. 15.

3A. Membership information is available at the museum office at 55 Greenfern Circle.
3B. Don't miss out on this opportunity. Sign up today for membership. Stop by at the museum office at 55 Greenfern Circle.
3C. The membership office at 55 Greenfern Circle will be happy to give out membership information. ∎

Accuracy

Accuracy is crucial. Check and double check all facts. Check spelling, punctuation and correct use of the stylebook. Pay particular attention to names and titles, and make sure there is a full first reference. Sometimes a result of rearranging, adding and deleting information as part of the revision process is that information is lost. Be careful that a stray surname or an unidentified person doesn't pop up within the story.

One way of checking for accuracy is to read your writing out loud. This will help you slow down and will prevent you from overlooking mistakes.

Newsworthy Information

News writing should not tell us what we already know or what we can easily conclude on our own. For example, don't write that *The CEO is proud of the company's success*. That's not news. Instead, cite reasons why the CEO is proud—because third-quarter profits were the highest ever or because this was the most accident-free year on record.

Neither is it news that *The employee said she is happy about her promotion* or *When the director asked the committee to meet, the committee chair said a meeting would be scheduled*.

Faced with nonnews statements such as these, you have two choices: eliminate the statement, which is probably what you'd do about the happy employee, or expand upon the statement, such as by noting more about the rescheduled meeting time and place.

News Release Format

Amateurs and professionals alike follow the same format for news releases. This format is so versatile that it lends itself to many writing purposes. Here are some guidelines about format to help you prepare a standard news release.

Physical Format

Use standard 8½-by-11-inch paper, preferably white or off-white. Use standard black ink. Avoid paper with decorative borders. Prepare the release on a computer or word processor, using line spacing of 1.5 or 2.

By definition, a news release is a beginning piece of information for an editor or news director. It should not look like a final copy but rather like a working draft that welcomes the editor to mark it for publication or air use. So justify the left margin and leave the right margin ragged. Don't hyphenate your text.

Use a clean, professional-looking type; 12-point Times Roman is the best choice, 11-point if you need to squeeze. Make sure you use a quality printer. Set margins at least one inch on each side, preferably 1½ inches. Indent paragraphs the standard five or six spaces, about a half inch. Don't use extra spacing between paragraphs.

When it is distributed, the release should be letter perfect in terms of accuracy and neatness. It should have no typeovers or hand corrections of any kind.

Components of a News Release

First impressions are important, and editors often make judgments about the credibility of a public relations writer (and his or her organization or client) when they first glance at the news release. Several standard components should be part of every news release, regardless of the type of organization preparing it. By including these components in your release, you signal to the editor that you know your craft. In addition to certain conventions of common usage presented below, you will find several optional items that writers sometimes include in their releases. An example of a properly formatted news release is shown in Exhibit 6.1.

Letterhead. Type your release on official organizational logo and letterhead, either the regular letterhead used for most of the organization's business correspondence or on special letterhead developed for news releases.

News Flag. A *news flag* simply is the word *news* printed in large type. This is an optional part of the release heading. Some writers use a news flag to make it absolutely clear to an editor that this is a news release rather than some other type of communication. Other writers feel that the news release format is obvious.

Organization Contact. This information may be part of the letterhead. It should feature the name and address of the sending organization. A general telephone number or perhaps a Web site might be included. Try to limit extraneous information and corporate tags such as affiliation with a parent company or a nonprofit funding source.

Exhibit 6.1—COMPONENTS OF A NEWS RELEASE   A properly formatted news release.

NEWS from

Organization's Name

Street Address
City, State, ZIP
Web Site (optional)

Public Relations Contact Person
Office Telephone Number
Out-of-Office Contact (Telephone/Pager)

FOR IMMEDIATE RELEASE
Sending Date

OPTIONAL HEADLINE, ALL-CAPS AND CENTERED

DATELINE CITY, State—Begin with the heading information, including the organization's name and address, and perhaps a main telephone number or Web site. Include the name and contact information for the public relations director or writer.

A news flag is an optional part of the heading. Note both the sending date and the release date, usually indicated by the phrase "For Immediate Release." Keep this heading as small as possible so as not to take up valuable space for the news release.

You may include a headline. If you do, use present tense and type it in all-capital letters and centered over the body of the news release.

Begin the body of the release immediately after the optional dateline, or after the date if you do not use a headline. Allow left and right margins of at least one inch. Type copy in line-spacing intervals of 1.5 or 2 to allow the editor to mark up the copy. Also, use an unjustified (ragged) right margin. Do not hyphenate words at the end of lines.

Keep paragraphs short, usually between two and five typed lines. Remember that one line of typed copy will equal about three lines of type in newspaper columns. Use standard paragraph indents of about one-half inch, with no extra spacing between paragraphs.

"The news release should look like a manuscript," said Ron Smith, the author of this textbook. "You want the editor to take out a pencil and begin marking up your news release for use in the paper. That's your immediate objective."

Make every effort to keep the release to a single page, and conclude the release with an end mark centered below the last line, said Smith.

If it is necessary to continue the news release to a second page, make the break on a paragraph. Never break in the middle of a paragraph. Include a more line at the bottom of the first page, and include a slugline at the top of the second page.

#####

Personal Contact. The heading also should identify the public relations contact person (usually the same person who prepared the news release). This information should include the name, as well as both day and evening/weekend telephone numbers; a fax number and e-mail address may also be appropriate. You may also include the Web address, particularly if you have developed a Web presence for reporters. There is no particular order for these various elements. Personal or organizational preference allows for flexible design, though a good design is one that takes up only a small amount of space.

Distribution Date. News releases need two dates. The first is the day the release is mailed, e-mailed, faxed, delivered or otherwise distributed. This is presented in the conventional manner for the editor or news director receiving the release: month, day and year (*June 26, 2007*) for North American media; day, month and year (*26 June 2007*) for releases prepared for media in other parts of the world or for military media, where such a format is more common. As "FYI: Publication Lead Time" explains, understanding lead time is an important part of determining when your news release should be sent.

FYI *Publication Lead Time*

The amount of time it takes reporters and other media professionals to gather and present their news is called *lead time*. This varies with both the type of medium and the kind of presentation that will be given.

The best way to know the lead time required by various media is to ask. Contact the city editor of a newspaper, the news director or assignment editor of a radio or television station, or the acquisitions editor or news editor of a magazine. Or ask an individual reporter or columnist. In general, however, typical lead times needed for various news media tactics are as follows:

Daily newspapers need about a week's notice for routine information, a day or several hours for important news, and less than an hour for major on-deadline news. Information for special sections such as travel, food and social events may have a longer lead time. News releases can be submitted at any time, but Sunday and Monday often find less competition for space because weekends traditionally are slow news days and are lightly staffed by most newspapers and have more pages because of increased advertising.

Nondaily newspapers need more lead time. Plan to provide information two to three publication dates before the relevant date of the information. For example, at least two weeks for a weekly newspaper, or a week-and-a-half for a twice-weekly newspaper.

Magazines published on a monthly basis require at least a two-month lead time for information to be published. Weekly news magazines have a much shorter lead time, but they seldom take information from public relations sources.

Radio stations should have about a week's notice for routine information and for upcoming events that reporters might cover, with important news being handled up to news time. Breaking news may be covered live. Other live coverage may be planned with a lead time of a week or longer. Talk shows and other programs with guests may require several weeks to schedule.

Television news operations should be given up to a week's notice for routine information and for events that reporters might cover, with important news being handled up to news time. Breaking news may be covered live. Talk shows and programs with guests may require several weeks to schedule.

Date of Intended Use. The second date indicates when the release may actually be used by the news media. Generally, this is handled with the phrase *For Immediate Release*, signifying that the release may be used as soon as the news media wishes to use it.

This phrase is standard in most parts of North America, so much so that journalists take it for granted that they may use a release as soon as they receive it. Some public relations practitioners have stopped using the phrase, prompted by journalists' observation that, in an era of instantaneous dissemination of news releases, *For Immediate Release* is becoming a holdover from an earlier era. Still, most practitioners continue to use the phrase on their releases.

An alternative to immediate release is to indicate an *embargo*, in which you ask that the release not be used before a specific time and day, such as *For release after 6 a.m., June 26,*

2007. Avoid asking for an embargo, because there is usually little need and dubious benefit. First, an embargo imposes no obligation on the news media, and it often causes conflict among various media if the embargo is not equally observed by each of them. Second, it seems to tease reporters with advance information they are asked not to use, especially inconsistent with the competitive environment in which many journalists work. With the current technology of rapid, even instantaneous transmission of news releases, the embargo is becoming a relic of the past.

However, organizations that deal with magazines and feature writers or with reporters on specialized publications continue to find embargoes helpful. They say that such reporters respect embargoes because they find it useful to maintain a practice that gives them extra time to prepare their stories. Because of printing schedules, often those publications could not use the information before the embargo date anyway. Veteran practitioners caution that writers dealing in international situations should take care, because the concept of embargo carries little or no significance in some cultures, risking that a story may be reported by a foreign source before domestic media report the information.

Some organizations use an embargo as a way to help reporters develop better stories. The Census Bureau, for example, posts embargoed news releases at its Web site (census.gov) and offers a password to reporters. The bureau explains that the embargo gives reporters time to reflect on the information and thus write more accurate stories.

Headline. The *headline* traditionally has been seen as an optional element for the news release. It signals for the editor or news director the content of the release, and thus may attract attention to its contents. But the headline is seldom published as written, and some writers would rather have the editor evaluate the newsworthiness of the release on the basis of the full lead paragraph rather than the shorter headline.

If a headline is used, it should have a prominent look, such as with the use of all-capital letters, underlining, boldface, and/or centering immediately above the text of the release. Headlines are written in the standard newspaper style, generally in the present tense. Alternately, some writers prefer to use a *title*, an indication of the topic of the release not presented in traditional headline style.

Electronic dissemination of news releases is causing the headline to make a comeback. Headlines are particularly useful with electronic archives. An agency, for example, may prepare several news releases in the same month for one of its clients. Let's call the client CompuTrim. Without headlines, all of the company's news releases for June would be archived under the same name, CompuTrim-USA. But with headlines, the news releases would be distinguishable in an archive such as LexisNexis. For example, *CompuTrim Names New CEO*, *CompuTrim Announces Record Third-Quarter Profits*, *CompuTrim Opening Branch in Seattle*.

Dateline. A *dateline* is an occasional element of a news release, featuring the name of the city or town where the release originates. Despite its name, the dateline does not include a date. The name stems from the early days of American journalism, when it could take several days, even weeks, to publish a story from a distant correspondent. With today's technology, all stories can be published the day they are written, so the date has disappeared from the dateline.

Though the dateline is not always needed, it is not optional. Use a dateline when the release is being sent beyond the local area of the sending organization. A dateline also is used to localize the release for the geographic location of one of an organization's branch sites.

When a dateline is used, the city name is typed in all-capital letters, followed by The Associated Press Stylebook state/province/country abbreviation in regular (both caps and lower-case) text. Some cities are well known nationally or regionally and may stand alone without the state/province/country designation. (Consult the AP Stylebook for a listing of these cities.) For datelines in regional releases, omit the state if it is not needed for clarity. For example: NEW YORK or LARAMIE, Wyo. or ST. PIE, Montreal, Canada. Use a dash to separate the dateline from the beginning text of the release.

End Mark. Place a final *end mark* at the conclusion of the release, centered following the last line. The most common version of this is a series of hatch marks (####). Alternatives are the word ((END)), often set off with double parentheses for greater emphasis, and the rather outdated printing notation, -30-.

More Line. Multipage news releases should contain a notation that signals to the editor or news director that the release is running more than a single page. This *more line* is typed at the bottom of the first page if the release is more than one page long. Common versions are ((more)) in double parentheses or ((more-more-more)). This notation can be used only after a complete paragraph. Never use it after a line of type that does not end the paragraph.

Slug Line. When text continues on a second page, use a *slug line* (usually in capital letters) at the top of the second page, repeating the first few words of the headline or offering a one- or two-word topic, and indicating the page number. For example, BANK PROMOTIONS— 2. Because the more line is used only after a full paragraph, the slug line will always be followed by a new paragraph of text.

Editor's Note. An optional feature that may follow the end mark is the *editor's note*, a message directed to editors and news directors and not meant for publication. An editor's note may verify an unusual spelling or give a street address for identification. Sometimes the note will offer special access to photographers, or it may offer interviews or additional information. The note is also a place to draw attention to a trademark or service mark or to provide background identification about the sending organization. The news release in Exhibit 6.3 includes a note to editors.

Basics of News Release Writing

Writing for public relations is not like a paint-by-numbers kit; you cannot simply fill in blanks on a news release template and prepare an effective release. Writing a good release takes talent, planning and experience. However, guidelines do exist to channel your talent and planning toward conventional news-style writing. What follows is not a formula but rather a pattern found in most effective news releases. Learn this model and adapt it to suit the needs of your particular writing project.

Most news releases follow a format similar to the basic news article, the well-known *inverted pyramid style*, in which the most important information is at the top, with information of lesser importance following. This provides for the most important information to be presented first. Exhibit 6.2 depicts the elements of a news release following the inverted pyramid style. But remember that no formula can dictate how a news release is written. Let the formula be your guide, but temper it with your own news judgment, writing skill and common sense.

Exhibit 6.2—ELEMENTS OF A NEWS RELEASE   The relationship between the various elements of a news brief and a news release.

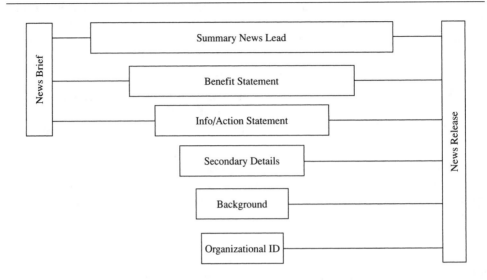

Lead

"Call me Ishmael."
"Now is the winter of our discontent made glorious summer by this sun of York."
"In the beginning God created the heavens and the earth."
"Yes, Virginia, there is a Santa Claus."
"You already are a writer!"

Beginnings are a big deal in all kinds of writing, and public relations writers take leads seriously. The *lead* (pronounced leed) is the first paragraph of a news release. Its purpose is to attract the attention of each member of your key public—first the media gatekeeper who will decide whether to use the release, then the reader, listener or viewer.

Because it serves as the gateway to the entire story, the lead is crucial to the success of a news release. The information in the lead is the basis for gatekeepers' decisions on whether to use the release. First impressions count, and few editors will waste time reading an entire release if the information in the lead does not grab their attention. Likewise, readers will decide whether to spend time with the story on the basis of whether the lead interests them. But a word of caution: A lead is strong not because of fancy writing but because it uses well-crafted writing to present significant information to readers.

The most common type of lead used by public relations writers is the *summary news lead*, which presents the most significant and interesting facts in the first one or two paragraphs. Too little information, and the lead is boring. Too much detail, and the reader becomes confused. As a writer, you will strive for an effective middle ground. You can accomplish this by drafting the basic facts, then sifting through additional information and using that which adds to the meaning without creating confusion. Focus on the main newsworthy elements of your story. Remember SiLoBaTi + UnFa from the previous chapter. News involves information that is *significant*, *local*, *balanced*, and *timely*, as well as information that is *unusual* and associated with *famous* people.

In general, the who/what/when/where/why/how approach is useful for writing leads, but don't try to include each element in a single sentence or even one paragraph. Weigh one element against another, and choose the strongest elements for the lead. Save other news elements for later in the story. Look at the example in "FYI: Developing a Lead" to see how a lead can be crafted as one bit of information is layered upon another. "Tips for Better Writing: Differences between Public Relations and Journalistic Writing" discusses the differences between the two fields as relates to lead writing. The most important advice about writing effective leads is to plan carefully, think clearly, and write to the point. Following are some additional reminders about writing a summary news lead.

News. Lead with the news. Don't begin with a minor detail, such as the attribution. Avoid the too-common mistake of leading with a focus on the organization, or worse, on the head of the organization. In other words, avoid this version:

> Torrance Lakeman, administrator of County Hospital, announced today that a cardiac care unit will be added next year to the hospital's services.

Instead of backing into the news, present it up front, then follow with the organizational link. In many cases, passive voice can be useful for this, because it places the important information (the object of the verb) at the beginning of the sentence.

> County Hospital will expand its services next year with the addition of a cardiac care unit, superintendent Torrance Lakeman said today.

FYI   *Developing a Lead*

Consider this scenario: Central University has received a $50,000 research grant from the State Council to Combat Drug Abuse. The purpose of this grant is to study persuasive communication, specifically the kind of messages that are effective in persuading teens and young adults to avoid illegal drug use. First we write the basic information:

> A researcher at Central University has received a grant.

Then we begin to add some details, weaving in some of the information that can make this a newsworthy statement.

> A communication researcher at Central University has received a $50,000 state grant to study drug abuse.

This version gives the reader a bit more to go on, but it's probably too generic to be considered a good lead. We want to be more specific by narrowing down the subject area, both to more accurately reflect the focus of the grant and to attract reader interest about the project.

> A communication researcher at Central University has received a $50,000 state grant to study ways to persuade college students not to abuse illegal drugs.

Now we have told the reader something about *who*, with more details to come. We've given several bits of information about *what*, and we've mentioned the *why* and the *where*. Certainly these are the major elements of the lead, to be expanded upon later. The *when* element is less important and can be dealt with later in the story. And the *how* will be explained in succeeding paragraphs.

Tips for Better Writing *Differences Between Public Relations and Jounalistic Writing*

A lead written by a public relations writer should be virtually the same as a reporter's lead. But some elements of news-release writing can differ from how a journalist might proceed.

Consider the situation of a writer in a college media relations or public affairs office, who tries to boost the prestige of the college by reporting on achievements of the faculty. The writer wants to show the organization in a positive light, but too often, in the hands of an inexperienced writer, the release can become sappy and promotional, looking something like this:

> Bison State University is proud to announce that Robert Johnson (Ph.D., Harmond University, 1988), associate professor of public communication in the University's Department of Communication, has accepted an invitation to present his breakthrough research findings at the annual conference of the Association for Education in Journalism and Mass Communication.
>
> The prestigious association, which represents communication academicians in colleges and universities throughout the United States and Canada, will convene June 27–31 in Montreal.
>
> Dr. Johnson's research presentation is entitled "Laff Trax: Toward a Socio-Rhetorical Approach to Subliminal Advertising as Embodied in Television Situation Comedies." His work is considered revolutionary by his peers.

A journalist is interested in news, not in helping the organization brag about itself and its people. The above release is pretentious and pompous, and thus of little value to the media. Most editors would toss it. Knowing this, a public relations writer has two choices: send it as written and hope that the reporter will rewrite the release instead of tossing it, or rewrite it yourself. Good public relations people prefer to do their own revision.

Here's how the above release might be revised by a writer knowledgeable of what the media wants and needs. This version is more balanced, and it thus has more chance of being used by the media:

> Advertising professor Robert Johnson of Bison State University's communication department will present his research on subliminal advertising to the Association for Education in Journalism and Mass Communication.
>
> The June 27–31 conference in Montreal will include communication educators from throughout North America. The text of Johnson's paper can be obtained at www.bisonstate.edu/communication/Johnson.

This version of the release eliminates some details such as the title of the presentation and it cuts through the fawning attention to Johnson and the college found in the earlier version. But it also presents appropriate information, such as the link to the communication department, the topic of the presentation, and the international status of the meeting—all important reputation builders for both the university and the department. More importantly, it's written in a style that has a far greater likelihood of being used than the previous version.

Context. News releases sometimes inefficiently begin with a focus on time, location or some other secondary detail at the expense of the real news. Here are two examples of poorly written leads that focus on the time and circumstance rather than on the news:

> At a morning news conference today, Mayor Michael Buckskin criticized the police department for failing to reduce the incidence of drunk driving.

> In a speech to her cabinet, district superintendent Dorothy Ernestine Miller said the salary issue will be resolved peacefully.

However, a more effective way to begin each news release would be to focus on the news first.

> Mayor Michael Buckskin criticized the police department for failing to reduce the incidence of drunk driving. The reproach was part of the mayor's news conference today.

> District superintendent Dorothy Ernestine Miller today assured her cabinet that the salary issue will be resolved peacefully.

Delayed Detail. The lead often gives general information, followed by details. For example, the final version of the lead for the Central University grant in "FYI: Developing a Lead" doesn't identify the professor who received the grant. That would go in the following paragraph. Look at the following example, which delays identification of the key person until the second paragraph.

> A Sullivan County pharmacist has been named vice president of the Tri-State Association of Hospital Pharmacists.
> Carolyn Teng, staff pharmacist at Sullivan-Memorial Hospital in Lake Point, was elected yesterday at the association's annual meeting in Lesterville.

Names. When should you use a name in a lead, and when should you make only a generic reference to an individual? In general, use the name only if most members of the audience would recognize it. For example, it's safe to identify by name the figure in the following release, because most readers could be expected to be familiar with the name.

> Gov. Elena Gutierrez will be the keynote speaker at the annual recognition luncheon Wednesday evening sponsored by the League of Community Volunteers.

But suppose the keynote speaker is the president of the local hospital, a person without strong name recognition. In that case, identify the speaker generically at first, then use the name of the president in the following sentence.

> The president of Midvale Hospital will be the keynote speaker at the annual recognition luncheon Wednesday evening sponsored by League of Community Volunteers.
> Dr. Laura Green will discuss the contributions volunteers have made to the quality of life in Midvale.

When the person is well known only in a narrow context, make sure the descriptive reference is dominant. For example, let's say that your college or university is announcing that its commencement speaker will be Richard Axel, the New York City biologist who received the 2004 Nobel Prize for medicine. Because Dr. Axel isn't a household name, you'd need to provide a descriptor.

> A recipient of the Nobel Prize for medicine will be the commencement speaker at Summerwood University next Saturday.
> Dr. Craig Mello, a biologist, will address 1,300 graduates at the school's Mercier Auditorium.

Another way to write this release would be to identify the person both by name and by credentials.

> Nobel Prize winner Craig Mello will be the commencement speaker at Summerwood University next Saturday. The University of Massachusetts biologist, who received the 2006 prize for medicine, will address 1,300 graduates at the school's Mercier Auditorium.

Reference. When providing identification in the paragraph following a generic reference, make sure the link is clear. Don't make the reader guess about whether the name refers to the generic reference. In the first version, the reference is unclear.

> Aethelwulf Public Relations has purchased controlling interest in a small agency begun by two Egbert College graduates.
> Baldwin Communications will specialize in public relations research.

In the sentence above, it is unclear that Baldwin Communications is the small agency referred to in the first paragraph. Rewriting can clear up that confusion.

> Aethelwulf Public Relations has purchased controlling interest in a small agency that two Egbert College graduates founded.
> The new subsidiary, Baldwin Communications, will specialize in public relations research.

Attribution. While attribution is needed for news releases, it does not have to be placed in the lead sentence. Instead, following sentences or paragraphs can provide lead attributing statements made in the lead.

> The Mid-State Turkey Hunters' Club will hold an open house from 6 to 9 p.m. Oct. 15, at the clubhouse on Squawker Road. The open house is part of the club's annual membership campaign, said club president Tony Phillips.

Details such as times, dates, addresses and fees are best left to follow-up paragraphs. One guideline is to consider if a common noun can be used instead of a proper noun in the lead. While a common noun lacks some of the detail of a proper noun, it also is more likely to provide relevant general information to a reader. Details then follow in subsequent sentences and paragraphs.

Topic. Avoid leads that report topics rather than provide information about the topic. For example, the reader learns little if the writer reports the following:

> The Employee Welfare committee met this morning to discuss items of concern to employees.

Rather, the writer might provide information that goes beyond simply identifying the subject matter.
> The Employee Welfare committee endorsed a new employee pension plan when it met this morning.

Historical Context. Avoid leads that begin with the background or historical context of a program or activity. By definition, history is not news. The following lead provides no newsworthy information until later in the story:

The After-School Child Care program began three years ago at Briggs Elementary School. More than 75 children in kindergarten through 5th grade participate in this program, which currently is beginning a membership drive for the upcoming school year. The program features . . .

Instead, jump right in with the news, then put the program in context.

Briggs Elementary School is accepting applicants for its After-School Child Care program, which currently includes more than 75 children in kindergarten through 5th grade. The program, which began three years ago, features . . .

Focus. Public relations writers often wish to give a particular strategic focus to a news release, particularly the lead. For example, we can talk of a *who* lead, a *what* lead, a *where* lead, and so on. The difference is subtle. Does the lead begin with the name of a person or with a reference to an event? Consider the delicate shift in focus for the following leads:

(Focus on who/organization)
Hill College will give an honorary doctor of letters degree to a Hillview physician because of his volunteer work with refugee children.

(Focus on who/recipient)
A Hillview physician will receive an honorary doctor of letters degree from Hill College because of his volunteer work with refugee children.

(Focus on what)
An honorary doctor of letters degree will be given by Hill College to a local physician because of his volunteer work with refugee children.

(Focus on when)
In commencement ceremonies Saturday morning, a Hillview physician will receive an honorary doctor of letters degree from Hill College because of his volunteer work with refugee children.

(Focus on where)
In the Hill College Amphitheater, a Hillview physician will receive an honorary doctor of letters degree from Hill College because of his volunteer work with refugee children.

(Focus on why)
In recognition of his volunteer work with refugee children, a Hillview physician will receive an honorary doctor of letters degree from Hill College.

It's up to the writer to decide which focus is most appropriate for a particular writing situation. The *who/organizational* focus is an approach that some writers would make, with the conscious or unconscious attempt to shine the spotlight on their organization. However, most newspaper editors would rewrite the lead, probably using the *who/recipient* or the *what* focus. They would rewrite the lead because a common newspaper policy is to focus on the recipient of an award or on the award itself rather than giver. So it becomes important for the writer to make a strategic decision about the lead.

The *when* focus is seldom justified strategically, because the time element is seldom most important. The *where* focus may be appropriate when the location is of particular relevance. For example, if the award ceremony were to be held in the rotunda of the state capitol, then it might be worth beginning with that fact.

As noted above, the *who* and *what* leads may be the most newsworthy from the media's perspective. Both allow the organization to highlight, in this case, the person and/or the award. However, the *why* focus presents a strategic opportunity for the public relations writer to highlight an explanation, sometimes in an attempt to forestall criticism. For example, if the college were concerned that other physicians, perhaps major benefactors, might feel slighted because of the award, the lead with the *why* focus could minimize some criticism. It also offers a subtle invitation to others to make the kind of social contributions being honored by the award.

Exercise 6.7—Writing Leads

You are a public relations writer for the Happy Pup Company, which manufactures and distributes dog food. Your company has given Dr. Aaron M. Jones a $300,000 grant to begin a series of support groups for persons who are afraid of animals. Dr. Jones is a psychologist at the college or university where this writing class is being offered. He specializes in human-animal interaction. He has written a best-selling popular book on pets called "Paws for a Moment." Happy Pup has given the grant as part of a community relations program that seeks to position the company as one that promotes responsible pet ownership for the mutual benefits of both people and animals.

Part 1: Write a *what* summary news lead focusing on your company's grant for the local newspaper.

Part 2: Write a *who* summary news lead focusing on Dr. Jones for the college newspaper.

Part 3: Write a *where* summary news lead focusing on your personal hometown (or another community of your choice) as one of the pilot communities where Dr. Jones will begin the support groups.

Part 4: Write a *why* lead focusing on your company's interest in giving the grant. Write this for the Happy Pup Times, an employee newsletter. As background, you are aware that some employees have been complaining that money spent on community relations programs could instead be used for salary increases.

Exercise 6.8—Simplifying Leads

You are a public relations writer for the Happy Pup Company, which manufactures and Each of the following leads has problems. Revise each to make it more appropriate for a news release. Possible revisions are listed at the end of this chapter.

1. The Eastern Cable Company is proud to appoint Euphrasia Gilhoolie as director of Customer Service and Maintenance, where she will direct a staff of 27 repairmen and women dedicated to customer satisfaction.

2. TOBY TYLER'S TOYOTA, known as the Friendliest Car Dealership in Town, happily invites everyone to his open house at the new showroom on James Pike next Monday all day long from 9–9. Free refreshments.

3. On Monday, June 15, at 9 a.m., the Haven High School Hamsters' starting line-up will begin a five-day basketball clinic for kids aged 6–10.

4. Aloysius Terrence O'Malley, president and chief executive officer of O'Malley Enterprises, has appointed as his senior vice president for corporate communications Melinda Hobermeyer.

5. The Department of Social Geography at Oceanview University will host urban planning specialists from Andorra, Liechtenstein, Luxembourg, Monaco, San Marino and Vatican City who are touring the United States to study examples of effective and innovative space usage by boundary-limited municipalities.

6. ADMIRALTY PARK, Ohio—The Peter Romanov Company, a long-time lock manufacturer located in this upscale community, announces that they have developed a revolutionary new security system for drivers to guarantee the security of their parked cars. ∎

Benefit Statement

A *benefit statement* is the biggest difference between how a public relations writer prepares a news release and how a journalist writes a news story with the same information. This statement clearly indicates the benefit you are offering the key public among the audience for this release, answering the question, "So what?" One of the smoothest ways to highlight the benefit statement is to develop it as a quote or narrative in which you implement your planning sheet ideas for explaining the advantage to your public.

Exercise 6.9—Writing Benefit Statements

Part 1: Using the *what* lead you wrote in Exercise 6.7 above, write a quote from the Happy Pup CEO as a follow-up paragraph that offers a benefit statement to readers.

Part 2: Using the *where* lead from Exercise 6.7, write a narrative or paraphrased follow-up paragraph that offers a benefit statement different from the one you wrote in Part 1. ∎

Info/Action Statement

The *info/action statement* provides a way to mobilize readers. It gives the key audience how-to instructions and ways to obtain more information. Often, the public relations writer will want to encourage a particular activity for the public, such as buying the concert tickets, visiting the museum, calling for more information, casting the vote, volunteering for the project or making the donation. One effective focus for an action statement is to direct readers to an organization's Web site. Try to include some invitation to action or opportunities for follow-up information in every news release.

Exercise 6.10—Writing Info/Action Statements

Using the *who* lead quote in Exercise 6.7, write a one-sentence action statement for a news release that invites the reader to get involved in the same way.   ■

Secondary Detail

Secondary details amplify information in the lead. Look back at each of the elements of the summary news lead: who, what, when, where and why. Also review the "So what?" information from the benefit statement. Consider how you might expand upon each of these elements to provide readers with relevant information.

Background Information

Background information provides a context for the report. This information often is an attempt to help address your objectives, perhaps by using quotes. This may include information on the history of a project or its wider setting. For example, when Med-Plast (see Chapter 5) prepared its fact sheet on the new plant, it included background information about the parent company. Likewise, if a local hospital were to announce plans for its annual fundraising campaign, readers would want to know the outcome of last year's appeal, both the amount of money raised and how it was used.

Organizational Identification

An optional part of the news release is an *organizational identification*. This is a paragraph with standard wording that routinely is dropped into a news release, usually at the end. For example:

> Apache is the oldest pharmaceutical company in the Southwest. It is a division of Worldwide Medical Products Inc., with offices and research laboratories in North and South America and in Europe.

Many news releases do not include an organizational ID. Such standard information is seldom published. But some writers find IDs useful for providing background on their organization, if not for media audiences, at least for editors and reporters. Some public relations writers who do use the drop-in paragraphs place them as the closing paragraphs of the release. Others use them as an explanatory note following the text. The final paragraph in the news release in Exhibit 6.4 is an example of an ID paragraph.

"Advice from a Pro: David Eisenstadt on News Release Writing" provides some well-heeded advice, while "Tips for Better Writing: News Releases" will help ensure that you have included all the right pieces.

Advice from a Pro   *David Eisenstadt on News Release Writing*

David Eisenstadt is president of The Communications Group Inc., a public relations agency in Toronto. He offers the following advice, based on his experience with various high-tech clients. By way of his credentials, consider that Mr. Eisenstadt, APR, is a fellow of both the Public Relations Association of America and the Canadian Public Relations Association.

"Market opportunities are missed when the high-technology news release fails to convey the real impact of the new product," he says, adding that the way to ensure news release success is to look at it with the eye of an editor. "It must sell itself to the non-technical decision-maker who will decide if it's worth investigating."

Eisenstadt offers the following suggestions for public relations writers preparing releases about high-tech products:

1. Avoid clichés such as "state of the art," "system" and "leading edge of technology."
2. Eliminate jargon. Instead of DBMS use database manager system and explain that term, unless you are sure the audience will understand the term.
3. Don't restructure the English language by toying with capitalization and normal spelling conventions that only confuse readers.
4. Make your "firsts" believable. High-tech industries are full of firsts that quickly become standard operating procedure. If your first solves a problem, deal with it in those terms and don't be overly boastful.
5. Pay attention to physical presentation. A fuzzy gray news release about a high-speed printer somehow rings off key. Make sure the editor is evaluating your news and not a clumsy presentation of it.
6. Leave out the sales pitch. Business is intensely competitive, but editors have little sympathy for quotes from the marketing manager about how well this little number will sell. Write about what readers want to know, and leave out the bell-ringing prose.
7. Leave out company histories. If it's newsworthy, include a separate brief company history. But don't waste the limited space in a new product release touting what is really irrelevant to the matter at hand.
8. Sell the sizzle, not the steak. Describe equipment in output terms. Readers care less about how the equipment came to be and more about what it can do for them.
9. Give the editor a place to call. Sometimes your new product fits an editorial package you haven't anticipated. Sometimes you've assumed knowledge the editor doesn't have. Always clearly indicate where more information is available.

Tips for Better Writing   *News Releases*

Use this checklist to make sure you have included or addressed each of the major elements of a well-written news release.

Planning Sheet
- Appropriate public(s)
- Analysis of key public(s)
- Benefit to key public(s)
- Writing objectives

Physical Format
- Heading and ending information
- Text (type, margins, spacing, indentation)

Writing
- Strong lead
- Benefit statement

- Action statement
- Information content
- Writing to objectives
- Relevance to public
- Impact of quotes
- Attribution of information
- Polished writing
- Factual accuracy

Writing Mechanics
- Spelling
- Stylebook
- Language usage
- Punctuation
- Professional appearance
- Readability level

Exhibit 6.3 shows the hypothetical example of a news release for local print media by a company we'll call InterGalactic Motors. The release includes the various elements outlined above. Notice that it begins with a news brief, the first two or three paragraphs that could stand alone and still present the essentials of the public relations message.

Exhibit 6.3—NEWS RELEASE WITH NEWS BRIEF

Kim Salvatore
Public Relations Director
(123) 987–6543 Ext. 21

InterGalactic Motors, Ltd.
Mid-State Division
123 Harrison Road
Centerville, Xx 12345

September 25, 2007
FOR IMMEDIATE RELEASE

The Mid-State Division of InterGalactic Motors will sponsor a Safe Driving Clinic Saturday, Oct. 13, at its Harrison Road Plant. The clinic is free for Marlon County Residents.

The clinic will provide both information and hands-on practice in driving safety. Participants also can earn extra points toward reduction of fines for traffic offenses, as well as credits toward discounts for auto insurance.

The Safe Driving Clinic will begin at 9 a.m. at the Employee Cafeteria, located in Building "G" at the plant. Area residents as well as nonresidents attending local colleges may register for the clinic by contacting the InterGalactic Employee Center at 987–6543.

The clinic will be led by InterGalactic Motors training and testing experts and by representatives of the Central Automobile Club of Centerville.

InterGalactic Motors is offering similar clinics at plants throughout the state. The public clinics were scheduled in the wake of testimony before Congress by Willam Newbauer, InterGalactic Motors president. Newbauer addressed the Joint Committee on Transportation and Safety in Washington last month (Aug. 15) on the need for auto manufacturers to take the lead in promoting driving safety.

#####

Note to Editors:
Willam is correct spelling.

Exhibit 6.4 shows another imaginary organization, St. Francis Hospital and Health Center, with this example of a news release for local print media. This one has the essential ingredients in a slightly different order. Note the use of the organizational identification paragraph.

Exhibit 6.4—NEWS RELEASE WITH NEWS BRIEF

**St. Francis Hospital
& Health Center**
12345 Main Street
Springfield, Xx 12345
www.sfhhc.org

Contact: Thomas Tyler
(123) 456-7890 - Office
(123) 654-3210 - Home

June 4, 2007
FOR IMMEDIATE RELEASE

Springfield banker Eli Holcomb has been elected to his second term as president of the board of directors of the St. Francis Hospital Foundation. Holcomb, vice president of the First Springfield Bank and Trust Co., has been a member of the foundation board for seven years.

Other newly elected officers include Marian Demerly, director of the Springfield County Library System, as vice president; Rabbi Steven Schneider of Beth Shalom Synagogue, as treasurer; and Sylvia Martain, associate director of the Native American Center, as secretary.

The hospital board also elected Michael Whitefeather, principle of Mission Academy, to serve a two-year term as a board trustee.

As the fund-raising arm of the hospital, the foundation sponsors the Springfield County Medical Appeal. That appeal annually provides more than $2 million for patient services at both St. Francis Hospital and its downtown family care center, St. Claire Clinic.

Details about the foundation, including audited statements of accountability, are available from the foundation office at (123) 456–7899 or at its Web site: www.sfhhc.org.

St. Francis Hospital and Health Center is a 436-bed facility with full medical services. It features special units for cardiac care, oncology, geriatrics and rehabilitation medicine, as well as emergency care. St. Claire Clinic is an extended-site facility providing a full range of family health services.

#####

Finally, Exhibit 6.5 depicts a news release for the hypothetical Capital Council for the Arts. This news release is recycled from a speech. Because of the nature of this story, there are few secondary details; most of the information presents an expanded benefit statement.

Note that each release includes a benefit statement and an action statement.

Exhibit 6.5—NEWS RELEASE FROM A SPEECH

---

capital council for the ARTS

5432 Charlemagne Boulevard
Capitol City, Xx 12345
(123) 555–5000
www.capitalarts.org

Francesca Brandi, Media Director
March 23, 2007
FOR IMMEDIATE RELEASE
Special to Buchanan County media

BUCHANAN TEACHER ASKS FUNDING FOR THE ARTS

CAPITOL CITY—Education in the arts is just as important as training in math and science, a Buchanan County teacher told Gov. Lucy Halloway this morning.

Joshua Melvert, supervising art instructor at Buchanan City Academy, testified before the state's Select Committee on Education at the invitation of Halloway. The governor was present when Smith argued for greater funding for arts education.

"There is no question that our students need a strong foundation in the sciences and technology so they can compete in the 21st century," Melvert told the committee. "But it is equally clear that culture, as the foundation of our civilization, also deserves to be encouraged in our schools."

The art teacher, an award-winning sculptor, told the committee that schools can give students an appreciation for art, music and other aspects of culture.

Melvert challenged the governor to affirm her campaign platform to make school curriculums more meaningful to students.

"Children are born to be creative and artistic," Melvert said in his testimony. "Even businesses need creative people. State policy should encourage the study of art to build self-esteem and to make young people feel good about themselves. We should help them express their feelings through music and art rather than through violence and drugs."

Melvert was one of nine teachers from throughout the state invited to address the session with the governor. Copies of his testimony to the committee are available from the Capital Council for the Arts at (555) 234–5678 or at the council's Web site: www.capitalarts.org.

#####

Note to Editors and News Directors:
Contact Melvert for interview at Buchanan City Academy, 555–5555

News Brief

One of the most important elements associated with news releases doesn't even have a well-known name. It is the part of the release that combines the lead and the benefit statement into a statement of interest to both the reader and the organization—part of the overlap areas of the medium's and the organization's circles of interest that we talked about in Chapter 5.

We will call this essential public relations message the *news brief,* with the caution that journalistic writers may think of a news brief as something different from a regular news release rather than the beginning of one. Nevertheless, the concept is a good one to learn. Look back at Exhibit 6.2, which shows the relationship between the various elements of a news brief and a news release.

Think of it this way: A news brief is a capsule of the information in the fuller release; it is clear and concise in serving the interests of the busy reader, who may not read any further. At the same time, a news brief is a well-crafted presentation of the organization's message; it summarizes the information, positioning it in terms that focus on the message's benefit to readers.

An effective public relations writer will approach every news release as an opportunity to provide such a brief, followed by additional information to add depth and detail.

Most public relations writers do not have the luxury of writing several different versions of each release. By beginning each release with a news brief, the writer serves the needs of newspapers, magazines, wire services and broadcast media that can use only a short report. Then, by continuing to build this report into a more in-depth news release, the public relations writer moves on to serve the needs of trade publications, community weeklies, special-interest newspaper sections and others who can use more than just the brief. The writer thus covers all the bases, producing a piece of writing that is likely to be effective because it has been prepared to satisfy the reader, the news media and the organization. Additionally, many organizations find that the news brief makes an excellent summary for a Web site, with a link to the fuller story for readers who want more information.

Exercise 6.11—Writing a Complete News Release

Prepare a planning sheet and then write a news release for one of the following scenarios. In the release, include the major elements: summary lead, benefit statement and action statement, along with secondary details and background as needed. Include a quote. Begin with the set of facts provided below. Make up any additional information you need for the release (something you would never do in real life, but permissible only for purposes of instruction in writing styles and formats). Use the proper news release format, including heading information about the sending organization. List yourself as the public relations contact person.

*   Your client is Sforzando Music Company. You are preparing a news release for parents, teachers and guidance counselors. The focus of this release is a new video about careers in music, such as teaching, performing, management, music therapy, publicity and journalism. Sforzando is a store with branches throughout two states. It sells music and instruments and provides music lessons.

- Your client is Vancouver Cruise. You are preparing a news release for travel media. The release will announce a new family-oriented cruise package through the Inside Passage between Vancouver, British Columbia, and Juneau, Alaska. Vancouver Cruise is a shipping line that specializes in Pacific vacation travel.

- Your client is a senator in your home state. You are preparing a news release about an upcoming public forum sponsored by the senator to obtain testimony about ways your state might assist cities in dealing with an increase in the number of homeless people. The forum will include invited experts, and it will be open to concerned citizens.

- Your client is the anthropology department at your college or university. You are preparing a news release announcing a spring break project to participate in an archeological dig in Puerto Rico's Montañas de Uroyan. The project is open to any student. The dig will be supervised by Dr. Rebecca Ruffin, an associate professor who chairs the department.

Exercise 6.12—Revising a News Release

You are public relations director of Starter Electronics in Albuquerque, N.M. A staff associate newly assigned to your department has given you the following draft of a news release. You realize it has several errors. Instead of returning it for revision, you decide to provide a lesson to your new colleague. Rewrite the following draft. Then explain to your associate why you made the various changes.

Starter Electronics of El Moreno County is proud to announce the appointment of a new superintendent of Starter's Plastics Division. Starter named employee Wesley L. Marlborough to the position. Mr. Marlborough will begin his new assignment at the end of the month.

"I am very happy to have been appointed to this important position," Mr. Marlborough said, barely able to contain his enthusiasm. "I am fortunate to have the opportunity to work for such a wonderful boss as Mrs. Quigley," he said. As superintendent of the Plastic Division, Mr. Marlborough will report to Anastasia Quigley who is in charge of the company's technology divisions.

Mr. Marlborough graduated from East Downhome High School in New Mexico, where he played basketball for the varsity team. After taking two years off to travel the Southwest, he went to college at Upper Pecos College at Fort Sumner. There he studied engineering technology and met his future wife, a dancer named Rita Brown.

He came to work for Starter Electronics six years ago, when he was hired to be a quality control worker. Before coming to Starter he held several odd jobs, and he was an electronics technician in the Navy.

Local News Releases

A story should be viewed in terms of what it means for people in various localities who may be affected by or interested in your organization. If your company earned a profit last year, how much was added to the local economy? If your foundation is distributing research grants, how many are going to organizations in a particular area of interest to local media? If your client, an entertainer, has won a national award, when is the next local concert scheduled?

Editors say the No. 1 reason they reject news releases is because there is no apparent or significant local information. This can't be said too strongly: If a story doesn't have a local angle, it's not news. One of your jobs as a public relations writer is to find the local angle, even to create a local angle. Then turn that local concern into the focus of the release.

Specials

Localized news releases are sometimes called *specials* because they are written especially for a particular publication (such as *Special to the Sacramento Bee*) or for a particular geographic area (such as *Special to Clinton County Media*). This signals to editors and news directors that the information is of special interest to their audiences. Consider the example of your college or university sports information office. The writer could prepare a general release to introduce a team's new season, such as the one below:

> TERESA, Anystate—The women's basketball team of Mount Teresa College will field a starting lineup of two seniors, two juniors, and a freshman, when the Tiger Ladies host the season opener against Carlton College.
>
> Marya Watts, who coached the Tiger Ladies in last year's undefeated season, announced the lineup for next Wednesday's game. The starters include:
> - Erica Fisher, freshman, a graduate of Hill Mall High School.
> - Lasheena Johnson, sophomore, a graduate of City Honors Academy in East City.
> - Marleena Beth Bradford, senior, a graduate of Bear Hollow High School. . . .

However, with this version, an editor would have to dig out information about local residents. To make the release more useful, the writer could have prepared special versions of the same story to highlight the information of local interest. Consider the following examples.

> Special to the Barry County Gazette—Erica Fisher, a graduate of Hill Mall High School, has been selected as a starter for the women's varsity basketball team at Mount Teresa College.
>
> Fisher, a freshman center for the Tiger Ladies, will play her first varsity game next Wednesday when Mount Teresa hosts Carlton College.
>
> Marya Watts, who coached the Tiger Ladies in last year's undefeated season, called Fisher "an outstanding player with the strength, determination and smarts to be a real winner, on and off the court."
>
> Special to the Cinnamon City Times—Lasheena Johnson, a graduate of City Honors Academy, has been selected as a starter . . .
>
> Special to the Evening News—Marleena Beth Bradford, a graduate of Bear Hollow High School, has been selected as a starter . . .

Another way to localize a release is to take a careful look at the bio sheet of a key figure in the release. Let's say you are writing a release to announce that the Sheffield Opera Board of Directors has named Francis Armbruster as its chairman. Armbruster is pastor of Visitation Episcopal Church in Sheffield. You note from the bio sheet that he holds a master of divinity degree from Zion Seminary, he graduated from Harriman Central High School, and he was formerly chaplain at Parkerville Hospital. Armed with this information, you might develop a series of specialized news releases with locally oriented leads for the daily newspapers in Sheffield, Harriman and Parkerville, and for newsletters and Web sites of Zion Seminary, Parkerville Hospital and the local Episcopal diocese.

Think about more than simple geography when you are localizing a news release. Think of other ways to tailor a news release for a particular audience. Consider how to address other demographic and sociographic factors of a particular audience: age, gender, ethnicity, education, economic status, occupation, religion and so on. For example, if one of the starting basketball players mentioned in the scenario above were Muslim, perhaps a tailored version of the release could be sent to the newspaper of the Islamic association. If another player were Hispanic, you'd consider writing a version for the local Hispanic newspaper.

The merge functions on computer software and data files make it easy to produce several different versions of a news release, allowing you to easily localize information for widespread dissemination.

Exercise 6.13—Writing a Localized News Release

You are a public relations consultant handling publicity for the following educational conference. You decide to use the election of a president to publicize the organization and its mission. Base your release on the following information. If you need additional information, interview another student who will play the role of the new president (or if your instructor allows, make up the needed information, remembering that fabricating information is never a possibility in the real world, only in the hypothesizing world of the classroom). You may suggest an appropriate quote for the new president. (All locations in the following scenario are actual places that can be found by using maps and media directories. The organization is fictitious.)

Part 1: Prepare a news release for general statewide use. Include a planning sheet.

Part 2: Using a media directory, identify four specific locations and print media (including daily and weekly newspapers and organizational newsletters) to receive localized releases focusing on the new president. Write only the leads for three of these four local media.

Part 3: Prepare a planning sheet and a full localized news release for one of these four local areas, using the following information:

• This morning, Marilyn Minsdorf was elected president of the Pennsylvania Association for Teachers of English and Language Arts, formerly the Pennsylvania Association of English Teachers. She will serve a two-year term.

- Minsdorf lives at 125 Elm Street, Jersey Shore, Pa.

- She is a 1982 graduate of Lock Haven State College in Pennsylvania, with a degree in secondary education and certification to teach English. The school's named changed in 1983 to Lock Haven University.

- She teaches 9th-grade Language Arts at Central Mountain High School in Mill Hall, Pa., part of the Keystone Central School District. She has taught there for seven years.

- She used to teach English at Lewisburg (Pa.) Junior High School.

- Her parents are Harvey Grampian and the late Lucinda Shemp Grampian of South Williamsport, Pa.

- She is married to David Minsdorf, president of R & D Construction in Jersey Shore. The couple has four children: Bridget, 15; Clancey, 14; Golda, 10; and Sadie, 3.

- She was the elected representative from PATELA's North Central District for the last two years.

- PATELA has 1,100 members, including high school teachers in public and nonpublic schools and college professors in teacher-education departments.

- The organization is concluding a three-day convention at the Commonwealth Convention Center in Harrisburg. An installation dinner will end the convention this evening.

- PATELA has two primary goals: to improve the status of language teachers, and to encourage quality in language instruction.

- The previous president is Arturo Todd, 10th-grade English teacher at Middletown (Pa.) High School. ∎

Types of News Releases

Public relations writers can produce all sorts of news releases, but some are more likely to be used by the media than others. Both announcement and follow-up releases offer the public relations writer a full range of possibilities.

Announcement Releases

News releases that provide information about a planned event are called announcement releases. They make up a large part of the releases most organizations disseminate. Announcement releases cover various subcategories: event releases, personnel releases, progress releases, program releases, product releases, bad-news releases, crisis releases and financial releases. Let's look briefly at each.

Event releases often have an obvious news value, because they present information about something of interest that will be happening soon. Editors and news directors appreciate this kind of information, especially when it is of significance to large segments of their audiences. "Tips for Better Writing: Event Release Model" provides more detail on writing event releases.

Personnel releases focusing on promotions and personnel changes often are judged to be newsworthy, especially when they involve management-level positions or people who are wellknown among the media's audiences. "Tips for Better Writing: Personnel Appointment Releases" provides more information on these documents.

Progress releases focus on developments within an organization. They have a moderate chance of being used by the media, especially when they are amplified by being significant to local audiences. Often these are periodic reports about the organization's progress as it relates to local interests.

Program releases offer organizations, especially nonprofit groups, the opportunity to announce new services of general interest. Or they may interest specialized media serving small portions of the organization's publics.

Product releases about new or existing products, equipment, capacities and facilities are the most difficult release to get used by the general media, because they so often suggest self-serving promotion. For corporate public relations writers, announcements of new products may be appropriate for very specialized trade publications, as well as trade or business sections within a general publication. This type of release can be tailored to specific media by focusing on product features or applications of particular interest to the media audience.

Bad-news releases deal with the reality that bad things sometimes happen to good organizations—plant closings, program cutbacks, product recalls, corporate takeovers. Painful as they are to an organization, these activities often warrant news releases, on the strategic notion that bad news is best told by the organization itself than by outside sources. Handled properly, bad-news releases can actually help an organization keep a proper balance amid the scrutiny of reporters and the suspicion of opponents.

Crisis releases are intended to deal directly, swiftly and accurately with a crisis, which is a major, unfortunate, sudden and unpredicted event that can seriously disrupt an organization's activity with potentially negative impact on its "bottom line" or mission.

Financial releases differ from other releases in that they often are meant for news venues and audiences with not only an interest in financial matters but also a special knowledge. In addition, financial releases often are bound by special requirements, such as those imposed by government agencies such as the Securities and Exchange Commission. "Advice from a Pro: Financial News Releases" outlines various types within the category.

Tips for Better Writing   *Event Release Model*

News releases can't be written as fill-in-the-blank formats, but they do offer a convenient pattern for presenting information. Following is a model for news releases that announce upcoming events.

1. Identify the event and the sponsoring organization.

2. Note the purpose of the event.

3. Indicate the benefit or advantage that the event offers the community or the specific audience.

4. Amplify this benefit with a quote by an organizational official.

5. Provide logistical details as to time and place, as well as any restrictions on participants.

6. Provide directions for readers on how to obtain additional information. Include the organizational Web site.

After you have written the draft, read it aloud. Pay attention to the flow of the language. Rearrange information to make it flow more smoothly.

Tips for Better Writing   *Personnel Appointment Releases*

One of the most frequently written types of release deals with personnel appointments. Here is a common format for this type of release:

1. Identify the newly appointed person by title or name, state the new position, and identify the organization. Amplify on the name later, if necessary.

2. Indicate the person's new responsibilities and the role that position plays in the organization. Focus on the benefit provided to the audience and/or community.

3. Attribute the announcement to an official of the organization. Indicate when the appointment becomes effective.

4. Briefly describe the work of the organization.

5. Note relevant professional information about the person: history with the organization, previous jobs, professional accreditation and awards.

6. Note the person's educational background, along with other noteworthy achievements.

7. Provide personal information only when it is clearly relevant to the position or of newsworthy interest to the audience.

8. If relevant, note the reason for the vacancy that led to the appointment, indicating the person being replaced or the reason that a new position was established.

9. Note an organizational Web site for additional information.

After you have written the release in this pattern, review it. Read it aloud. Rearrange information that seems out of place and eliminate information that is irrelevant.

Advice From a Pro   *Financial News Releases*

Laurel O'Brien, APR, is an expert in financial media relations with Nuveen Investments in Radnor, Pa.

Writing in The Public Relations Strategist (Winter 2001) about the new reality for news releases, O'Brien offers an overview of how the usefulness of the time-honored news release has broadened beyond the news media to include all of an organization's key publics. She suggests six categories of such releases that have value not only as information disseminated to the media but also as material to be archived at the organization's Web site for easy retrieval by other stakeholders.

The *investor release* is an attempt to foster corporate name reputation by generating as many news releases as possible with information for potential investors. People seeking financial information will pore through a company Web site as they make investment decisions.

The *disclosure release* satisfies the legal requirement for companies to provide material information to their investors. Many companies provide disclosure even beyond the minimum required by law, as a kind of insurance against any future lawsuit. They then can point to the release as proof that nothing was hidden. Even privately held companies and nonprofit organizations can use this approach as a way to forestall criticism.

The *marketing release* focuses on new products and services. Often the information in such releases is aimed at existing customers.

The *crisis release* is an opportunity for the organization to chronicle a crisis from its own point of view. Though the media undoubtedly will report on a developing crisis situation, the organization can use the crisis release to defend its reputation and shore up the support of its key publics.

The *vendors and alliances release* announces partnerships and vendor relationships, serving the interests of all parties in the alliance and providing potentially useful information to customers or investors. The general press probably won't be interested, but trade and business publications may pick up the information. Meanwhile, the company Web site is a good repository for this information.

The *vanity release* is prepared simply because an executive wants to see his or her pet project on the Web site. Such releases have a particular use for nonprofit and charitable organizations, as opportunities to thank donors and benefactors in a public environment. They are of little interest to news media.

Exercise 6.14—Determining News Release Patterns

Part 1: Obtain a copy of a metropolitan or community daily newspaper. In the metro or city section, identify articles or column items that seem to be based on news releases, such as one that announces a new program or that reports progress from an existing program or project.

Part 2: Analyze one of these articles. Identify a pattern (similar to the boxes related to events and personnel releases) that could be duplicated by public relations writers interested in preparing a program or progress news release. ■

Exercise 6.15—Writing Announcement News Releases

Write a news release for one of the following four scenarios. Use the set of facts provided. For additional information, interview another student who will play the role of the key figure. (Or once again, make up the information if your instructor permits, always mindful that fabricating information should never take place in the real world.) Include a planning sheet. Use the proper news release format, including heading information about the sending organization. List yourself as the contact person.

1. *Events/Activities.* The governor of your state will be the keynote speaker at your school's graduation ceremonies on the third Saturday of next May. The governor will also receive an honorary degree from your president. For additional information, "interview" the head of academic affairs or the commencement planning committee.

2. *Personnel activities.* You are public relations director of Canton Electronics located in your hometown. The 15-year-old company manufactures high-tech components for electronics systems in rockets. Most of your work is under contract with NASA. The company has 275 employees. Fill out a hypothetical bio sheet for Florindo Sanvincenzo, who has just been promoted to vice president for research and development, succeeding Milton Williams, who is retiring. Write a news release for Sanvincenzo's hometown newspaper.

3. *Programs/Services.* The Canada County YWCA is beginning a program, "Focus on Finance," to help women plan their personal finances. The focus will be on helping participants develop plans to overcome current financial problems. The program is free to county residents.

4. *Products.* Obtain a copy of a consumer-oriented publication that compares features among various brands of the same product. Use the information on the leading brand to prepare a news release introducing that product. ■

Follow-Up Releases

In addition to the previous category of announcement releases, another useful type of news release is the *follow-up release,* which involves responses to an event, an idea or an earlier report. Following are several types of follow-up releases: new-information releases, comment releases, position releases, public-interest tie-in releases, and speech releases. Here's an overview of each.

New-information releases offer an organization the opportunity to provide follow-up information to an earlier reported activity. This follow-up may repeat some information from an earlier release, because it is likely that some gatekeepers and many readers may be unfamiliar with the first release.

Comment releases give organizations an opportunity to set the record straight in response to an activity or news report in which they have been involved. For example, a report about mold found on sandwich rolls in an elementary school cafeteria may prompt a response by the bakery that made the rolls, explaining that they were clearly date-marked and that the school should have used them the previous week. The trick here would be to provide such information with risking its future business with the school district, perhaps by announcing a new service of an e-mail reminder for institutional clients of the expiration dates.

Position releases are those written to present an official opinion on an issue. For example, a political candidate may be approached by the media on a controversial public issue that relates to the candidate or her constituents. The release would provide accurate background information on the issue and then state the candidate's position on it.

Public interest tie-in releases allow organizations to be heard on current events that may not directly involve them but affect their work or in some other way impact their mission. For example, the City-County Council on Drug Abuse may issue a release in response to a series of arrests made by local police agencies, perhaps to applaud a cooperative effort in law enforcement or to point to a gap in preventative programs.

Speech releases are excellent ways to extend an organization's message by reporting what an official has said about a topic important to the organization and of interest to the media. Because they are reporting something that has recently happened, they are fact based as news releases should be, but they also offer the opportunity for organizations to present their opinions on subjects of public interest. Exhibit 6.5 on the Capital Council for the Arts is an example of a speech release.

Exercise 6.16—Writing Follow-Up News Releases

Write a news release for one of the following four scenarios. Use the set of facts provided. For additional information, interview another student who will play the role of the key figure. Include a planning sheet (or make up the information, again only with your instructor's permission). Use the proper news release format, including heading information about the sending organization. List yourself as the public relations contact person.

New information. Prepare a follow-up release to the events/activities release in the previous exercise, focused on the YWCA. Quote the director to indicate successful completion of the six-week workshop. Indicate the outcomes of the workshop.

Comment. Prepare a comment news release focusing on the president of your college or university as a follow-up to your announcement in Exercise 6.15—Events/Activities, responding to the following criticism. The county chairman of the political party opposing the governor has accused your school of "pandering to political opportunism" and "playing to the governor's baseless academic pretense." The critic opposes the granting of the honorary degree because the governor's new budget does not include a 15 percent increase in state scholarship aid for students in both public and private college; the critic was a leading supporter of increased scholarship aid. Just for kicks, let's say the critic is a major supporter of your school and an influential leader in the community; thus another balancing act for the media relations office.

Public issue tie-in. Prepare a release for the YWCA to tie into a published newspaper report indicating that most area law-enforcement agencies have noted an increase in shoplifting committed by single parents, often accompanied with the excuse that the shoplifting was a desperate attempt to make ends meet. Use the report to call attention to your "Focus on Finance" program, designed to help identify effective and legal means to handle financial difficulties.

Speech. Obtain a transcript of a speech or prepared testimony given recently in your state, provincial or federal capital. (A good source for this information is LexisNexis news; search news sources for "speech" or "prepared testimony" within the last three months.) Prepare a news release based on this speech. Write as if you a member of the public relations staff for the person giving the speech or testimony.

Answers to Chapter Exercises

Exercise 6.2
1C, 2B, 3A, 4A

Exercise 6.3
1A, 2B, 3B, 4C

Exercise 6.4
1B*, 2A, 3C, 4B
*1C also is grammatically correct, but because the identifier is lengthy (Commissioner Frank Lee Jones) it reads easier to place *said* before the identifier rather than after it.

Exercise 6.5
1A, 2C, 3B, 4B

Exercise 6.6
1B, 2B, 3A

Exercise 6.8

Following are examples of how the leads could be revised to streamline the language and conform to news-writing style.

1. Euphrasia Gilhoolie has been named director of customer service and maintenance at the Eastern Cable Company. She will direct a staff of 27.

2. Toby Tyler's Toyota will hold an open house at its new showroom on James Place from 9 a.m. to 9 p.m. Monday.

3. The starting players of the Haven High School Hamsters will hold a five-day basketball clinic for children aged 6 to 10 beginning at 9 a.m. Monday, June 15.

4. Melinda Hobermeyer has been named senior vice president for corporate communications at O'Malley Enterprises. Her appointment was announced by Aloysius T. O'Malley, president and CEO.

5. The department of social geography at Oceanview University will host urban planning specialists from six small land-locked countries in Europe. The urban planners are touring the United States to study examples of effective space usage by boundary-limited municipalities. [Later in the story: The planners are from Andorra, Liechtenstein, Luxembourg, Monaco, San Marino and Vatican City.]

6. The Peter Romanov Company of Admiralty Park has developed a new security system for parked cars.

Exercise 6.12

Major problems with the draft are:

- Focus in the lead on the company rather than the individual.
- Vague time reference for the date.
- First quote is without significance.
- Second quote is self-serving and of no interest to the public.
- Identification of supervisor is anti-climactic; two different spellings for her name.
- Some irrelevant and awkward information with the educational background.
- Vague information about previous work history.
- Missing information about the significance of the position.
- Missing information about the company.

Following is one way to rewrite the news release:

Wesley L. Marlborough has been appointed superintendent of the plastics division at Starter Electronics, according to Anastasia Quigley, Starter's vice president for production. The appointment will become effective November 30.

Marlborough will direct 30 employees in the division, overseeing production of Starter's line of fiber optics. Starter is a major supplier of fiber-optical materials for the Vegas Cable Television System at Albuquerque.

A native of East Downhome, Marlborough holds a bachelor's degree in engineering technology from Upper Pecos College at Fort Sumner. He was an electronics technician with the Navy before joining Starter in 1989.

7

Working with the Media

Public relations writers can foster good media relations by developing a respect for the women and men who work in the media and by showing a consistent pattern of professionalism. You will become a better public relations writer by gaining an understanding of what a journalist wants from you. You may not always be able to satisfy those wants, but you will be well served by a continual awareness of their interests and needs. Effective public relations practitioners consider news people to be allies in their work of managing communication between an organization and its publics.

This chapter explores the relationship between journalists and public relations writers. (The term *journalist* is used here to include reporters for both print and broadcast media, as well as media gatekeepers such as editors and news directors.) The chapter also looks at some of the ways news releases and other public relations vehicles can more effectively serve the needs of both the news media and the organization or client. Here are your objectives for Chapter 7:

- To appreciate the relationship between journalists and public relations writers
- To explain the various methods of distributing news releases
- To understand what journalists do with news releases
- To identify errors in news releases
- To promote publicity through memos and letters to journalists
- To write effective photo captions.

Journalists and Public Relations Writers

Symbiosis is the biological function of two organisms living together in a mutually beneficial relationship, helping each other to survive. It is nature's version of you-scratch-my-back-and-I'll-scratch-yours. Journalists and public relations practitioners have a symbiotic relationship. We need each other to do our jobs well. Consider the symbiotic elements of the following relationships.

Public relations writers need journalists to provide the vehicles to share our messages with our publics. We need the editors and news directors to accept our story ideas and to agree that our news releases have news value. We need reporters to interview our spokespeople. Some observers predict that, as audiences pay less attention to the news media, the media will be less useful for public relations practitioners. But for the foreseeable future, public relations writers will continue to rely on journalists.

Meanwhile, journalists need public relations practitioners, though some journalists are reluctant to admit it. We generate news for reporters by preparing releases, holding news conferences and providing story ideas. We help reporters with stories they initiate by arranging interviews, offering background information and answering questions. Some observers report that half of the stories in major newspapers and even more than that in smaller newspapers are based on such *information subsidies* from public relations practitioners.

These public relations materials help news organizations do their job, since it is impossible for reporters to be in all places and gather all the relevant information first hand. If the trend continues, with fewer reporters available to cover an increasing number of news sources, information subsidies from the public relations side will continue to increase, not only in volume but also in their value to the news media.

Some journalists harbor negative feelings toward our profession, devaluing news releases as mere "handouts." Some reporting textbooks caution journalists that "press releases" are advertisinglike ploys to "snare some publicity." Yet while journalists may be wary of public relations people as a group, they often give high marks to the individual practitioners with whom they work. Our performance seems to be better than our reputation; our individual professionalism is the key to the gradual enhancement of our standing as communication colleagues. "FYI: What's in a Name?" talks about another element of the relationship.

FYI *What's in a Name*

Note that the terms being used here are *news release* rather than press release and *news conference* instead of press conference. This is for two reasons:

First, a radio or television reporter is not, strictly speaking, a member of the press. Broadcast journalism deserves to be considered as something other than an electronic extension of newspapers. The public relations practitioner who understands the unique and complementary roles of broadcast and print journalism will be more effective.

Second, don't think of yourself as a press agent simply out to attract publicity. News releases report newsworthy activities. News conferences are forums to disseminate news to a wide representation of the media. Public relations professionals focus on news, and they don't waste reporters' time or risk their own credibility by trying to disguise uninteresting information as news.

Finally, never slip into using terms such as *handout* or *press piece* when you are referring to a news release.

Positive Practices

Reflect on these practices that can serve you well in the area of media relations. Do the following:

- Rely on news value alone to get your information used by the media.
- Become familiar with the media by knowing what they report as news of interest to their audiences.
- Get to know the gatekeepers.

- Look at your organization with a reporter's eye, asking yourself if people outside your organization might be interested in what is going on.
- Generate newsworthy activities for your organization and create opportunities to get your message out.
- Learn media deadlines and respect them. For example, contact morning newspapers in the afternoon, when staffs are generally available and less hurried than during the evening deadline times. Contact afternoon papers early in the morning, before their deadline crunch. Avoid radio newsrooms at the top of the hour when they are presenting news reports. Contact television news people early in the day when they are not pressured by approaching newscasts.
- Ask reporters how they prefer getting information from your organization or client. Some will want releases, which they may prefer to obtain by mail, fax or e-mail. Others may prefer fact sheets. A rare few may want phone calls. Do your best to accommodate the wishes of the reporters.

Counterproductive Practices

Some public relations practices are counterproductive and can give you a bad reputation with journalists, which will ruin the credibility of both you and your organization. Don't do the following:

- Don't spend a lot of time on attention-getting gimmicks, which usually don't work anyway.
- Don't beg or ask for a favor in having a story reported.
- Don't threaten to cancel your subscription if something isn't printed.
- Don't ask the publisher's friend or the editor's golf buddy for help in getting something printed.
- Don't ask to review a reporter's article before it is published.

Gray Areas

In the relationship between journalists and public relations writers, some gray areas exist in which *always* and *never* are inappropriate terms. Consider the following issues. In addition, "What Would You Do?: Giving Accurate Information" asks you to think about another gray area.

What Would You Do?   *Giving Accurate Information*

You are public relations director for your college or university. A reporter new to the local television station calls you and asks for information on an article she is preparing about enrollment trends. She needs background information, not an on-camera interview. You probably won't even be named.

You contact your registrar's office and learn the following information: New freshman admissions are 2,145 in regular categories, which compares to 2,255 last year, a decline of 110. But you have admitted 200 students under a special program for students who did not meet regular admission criteria but show promise;

last year only 70 such students were admitted. Under the state-sponsored program, the grades of these special-admit students are not considered when the education department calculates student progress, including grades.

In recent months, your president has been quoted several times predicting an increase in the number of students attending your school. You presume that most other colleges and universities in your area will be reporting increases in freshman attendance, and also that other schools also have special admission programs for some students.

The reporter is looking for a quick answer to her question: Is your freshmen admission higher or lower this year compared to last?

What do you tell the reporter? Do you put any qualifications on the information?

Information Limits. Setting limits on information you give a reporter should be done very carefully. It is best to consider that any information you provide may be reported freely. Remember that each reporter may interpret these terms differently, so make sure you are in agreement about the ground rules. Here are the common definitions of the terms you may encounter with a reporter. Use such conditions only when absolutely necessary.

Off the record means you are asking a reporter to agree not to print any information you provide, even if you are not identified as the source. Avoid this limitation. "Advice from a Pro: Al Rothstein on Going off the Record" delves further into this subject.

Deep background or *background only* means you are allowing a reporter to use information, without in any way identifying you as the source.

Not for attribution or *not for quote* means you are allowing a reporter to use information without giving specific attribution of the quotes to you as the source but with an indication of your credibility, such as by attributing the information to a company official or a high-ranking person in the administration.

It can't be stated too clearly: Be very careful about going off the record or setting other limits on how reporters may use information you give them. Most public relations practitioners never go off the record. Some note inherent ethical problems because they simply won't say anything that they wouldn't want to be quoted. Others see more practical problems: Off-the-record statements can embarrass the organization. The concept of going off the record should not be an issue for someone in an entry-level public relations position.

Favoritism. Don't play favorites among reporters. You will like some better than others, and you will think some do a better job in reporting on your organization (not necessarily the same ones). Perhaps some reporters are your neighbors or participate in the same organizations as you do. Certainly, you want to be friendly with reporters. But treat each journalist equally, and don't show on-the-job favoritism by giving information to one reporter or one medium ahead of others.

An *exclusive* is a written release or verbal information given to a particular reporter or medium but not to others. This is like skating on thin ice, and most public relations practitioners avoid providing information exclusively to one medium in a competitive market.

In cities with competing newspapers, try to schedule news conferences and other events so that they sometimes favor the schedule of the morning newspaper and other times accommodate the evening paper. Since radio and television reporters generally have similar

---

Advice from a Pro   *Al Rothstein on Going off the Record*

Al Rothstein is a media relations and spokesperson training specialist based in Atlanta and Jacksonville, Fla. Through his workshops and his consulting, he has worked with an impressive list of clients: bankers, social workers, accountants, dentists, and people in all aspects of law enforcement and the legal system.

The question often comes up: Should I go "off the record" to provide information to reporters?

Rothstein's advice is simple: The safest way to handle going off the record is not to. It's not a good place for public relations people to be. Most practitioners prefer to be as open as possible with reporters, and most reporters want it that way too. But Rothstein notes that some "media savvy" people have had success when going off the record. They were able to supply reporters with credible information without being quoted, and this helped them establish their own credibility among media representatives.

If you are considering going off the record, Rothstein advises in his seminars that you ask yourself the following questions:

1. Do you trust the reporter?

2. Do you want the information to be made public?

3. Do you have a clear understanding of what the reporter means by "off the record," and does the reporter have a clear understanding of what you mean? To some reporters, it might mean giving the reporter background that is not to be used in the story. To others, it could mean giving the reporter background to be used in the story but not attributed to you. Make sure you understand the ground rules as the reporter interprets them.

4. Did the reporter agree before you made your statement that you are off the record? You can't go there after you've already given the information.

5. Can you be sure your colleagues, competitors or people who read or see the story won't guess that you are the confidential source?

6. Will going off the record serve a purpose for you or your industry?

For more of Rothstein's advice, check out his Web site at rothsteinmedia.com.

---

deadlines and ongoing news reports, accommodating the schedules of broadcast media is easier.

Telephone Calls. Avoid routine follow-up telephone calls after you have sent out a news release. Do your best writing and let the delivery system work as it usually does. However, if you have disseminated what you believe is indisputably useful information to the media and find that it has not been used, a follow-up call may be appropriate. If your news judgment was wrong, you can learn a bit more about the interests and needs of the particular news media. If the release really was misplaced, you can send a duplicate.

Hospitality and Gifts. Use discretion about professional courtesies such as hospitality and gifts. The Member Code of Ethics of the Public Relations Society of America restricts any gifts to those that are "nominal, legal and infrequent." Codes of journalistic ethics similarly prohibit reporters from accepting gifts. The basis for the relationship between public relations writers and journalists always should be professional. Don't offer a reporter a gift without carefully considering how it might affect your professional relationship.

Thank-Yous. Consider the implications of a thank-you note to a reporter or editor. Keep the relationship on a professional tone. If a thank-you note might suggest that a reporter was doing you a particular favor by covering your story, avoid it. But it is always appropriate to let reporters and their bosses know that professionalism is appreciated and that fair and accurate reporting has had a positive impact on your organization.

Publicity Stunts. On the surface, *publicity stunts* are to be avoided. A publicity stunt is a gimmick planned mainly to gain publicity for something that has little news value. Avoid self-serving gimmicks, but don't dismiss the news value of legitimate special events. Sometimes a creative twist on a routine activity can elevate it into something of interest to the news media, if only perhaps because of its novel approach. Consider the concept of a *pseudoevent*, a newsworthy event created by a public relations person in order to attract media attention for his or her organization. To distinguish a legitimate special event from a publicity stunt, ask yourself: Even if the news media don't report this activity, would it still be worthwhile? If you can answer yes, then you are probably dealing with something more than a mere publicity stunt.

News Release Distribution

Once you have written your news release, you have to get it into the hands of the most appropriate journalist. The recipient may be the city editor or a section editor at a daily newspaper, the news director of a radio and television news department, or the acquisitions editor at a magazine. You can get the names of those people in any good media directory, or call the media outlet and ask. Many newspapers and radio or TV stations also have such information at their Web sites. When sending a release, always try to identify the recipient by name, and update your mailing lists frequently.

It is generally inappropriate to send a news release to more than one reporter at the same publication or station. Editors do not like to be embarrassed by using a release in two different parts of the same publication. However, it may be quite appropriate to send the same release to a reporter and a columnist at the same newspaper, or to a reporter and a talk show host at the same radio or television station. Here are three keys to handling multiple releases: (1) Establish in advance that more than one person at a media organization wants the release. (2) Make certain those involved know that you'll be distributing multiple releases. (3) Identify releases accordingly.

Following are several options for getting the release from Point A (your hands) to Point B (the hands of the media gatekeeper who will decide its fate).

Postal Delivery. Postal delivery is the most common method of delivering news releases to the media. First-class business-size envelopes get opened if you have sent them to the right person. Editors, news directors and reporters rightly resent it when they receive mail addressed to someone who no longer works in that capacity. Public relations practitioners sometimes use Express Mail or Priority Mail for out-of-town distribution.

In most medium and large cities, courier services are available as well. These commercial delivery services can be useful in getting a number of releases to several competitive media outlets at the same time.

Personal Delivery. The personal delivery of news releases seems to vary. Some public relations practitioners recommend it highly as a way of ensuring that a reporter or editor gets a news release. Others find that personal delivery is a thing of the past. Reporters usually are too busy to chat, and some newsrooms have policies against visits by outsiders (including public relations people). The best you can do is hand the release to a receptionist in the main lobby. If you do have the opportunity to deliver a release personally, keep the visit brief and businesslike.

Distribution Services. Distribution services are companies that handle the dissemination of news releases and other media information. Such services are sometimes used by organizations with large and frequent mailings. They distribute news releases either by mail or by fax. *Newswires* distribute information from corporations, financial institutions and other organizations with interests that extend over a wide geographic area. Public relations newswires operate similar to a journalistic newswire, providing news releases, backgrounders, position papers, advisories and related materials direct to the media. "FYI: Public Relations Wire Services" features a list of major public relations newswire services.

FYI   *Public Relations Wire Services*

Here are several public relations and business wire services. Most carry news releases, photos, and media alerts, and many also provide audio or video transmissions, offer information-on-demand downloads to news media and individuals, and/or offer broadcast fax and fax-on-demand services.

- *PR Newswire* (prnewswire.com) has offices in 25 U.S. cities and 9 foreign cities.

- *Hispanic PR Wire* (hispanicprwire.com) is a Miami-based company that includes both translation and bilingual placement services.

- *Black PR Wire* (blackprwire.com) is a partner with Hispanic PR Wire, providing news release distribution to specialized media, organizations, and community leaders. Both have a strategic alliance with Business Wire.

- *Business Wire* (businesswire.com) has bureaus in the United States, Europe and Asia, serving news organizations in 145 countries in 45 languages.

- *PR Web* (prwebdirect.com) distributes corporate news releases to newspapers, magazines, broadcast media, companies, and blog publishers.

- *Canada NewsWire* (newswire.ca), an affiliate of PR Newswire, has seven offices across the country with bilingual (English and French) services.

- *Market Wire* (marketwire.com) is a Canada-based distribution service for media internationally.

- *Press Release Network* (pressreleasenetwork.com) provides both newswire and online distribution to American and global media.

- *Eworld Wire* (eworldwire.com) distributes news releases and multimedia in various formats from offices in New York, Chicago, Los Angeles and London.

- *Bloomberg News* (bloomberg.com) is a global company that handles business and financial news and columns.

- *Dow Jones News Service* (dowjones.com) handles business and financial news.

- *India PR Wire* (indiaprwire.com) provides news from India-based clients to American and international media.

- *Kyodo News PR Wire* (prw.knodonews.jp/open/en) distributes news releases to Japanese and international media; includes a translation service.

- *Collegiate Presswire* (cpwire.com) distributes news releases to collegiate print and broadcast media.

- *Catholic PR Wire* (catholicprwire.com) is a special-interest bureau that distributes news releases from Catholic organizations to both news media and individuals.

- *Arab American Media Services* (aams.blogspot.com) provides news releases and features about Arab American and international events, posted online and made available to mainstream U.S. media.

Fax Distribution. The fax (short for facsimile) has become a common method to distribute written materials, including news releases. However, some editors say they prefer not to receive faxes if the release can be sent through the mail. Some states have passed laws limiting mass distribution of unsolicited faxes, a practice known as *bulk faxing* or *broadcast faxing.* Use discretion about faxes. Save them for information that is especially timely or for releases that an editor has asked for specifically.

Electronic Mail. *E-mail* is increasingly used to distribute news releases. Some reporters like it; some don't. On the plus side, electronic transmission of news releases can save reporters time, because the material is ready for editing and typesetting without the need for re-entering it into the publication's computer system. Also, they receive the information quicker, a benefit for reporters with pressing deadlines. On the minus side, some reporters simply don't like e-mail. They find that hard copy (that is, releases printed on paper) is easier to read and edit.

FYI *Journalists Prefer E-Mail*

How do journalists want to receive news releases and story leads? Fraser Seitel, a veteran communications consultant and teacher, tells readers of O'Dwyer's PR Services Report (July 2004) that e-mail is preferred by journalists for receiving news releases, and there are numbers to back that up. A prior study by the Columbia University Graduate School of Journalism reported that 76 percent of journalists prefer e-mail releases. Another study by Vocus, a provider of Web-based public relations software, found that 42 percent of journalists preferred e-mail with attachments and 41 percent wanted e-mail with links. Still another study found comparable percentages of 44 and 32 percent, with 8 percent wanting news in the body of an e-mail text.

All this leads to the conclusion that, while traditional delivery systems—mail, fax, phone, hand delivery—are not lost, they are less favored by journalists. And becoming more so by each passing week.

So the real question is: How does writing for e-mail distribution differ from writing for print distribution? Start with the same basic ingredients for any good news release, but remember that reporters want even crisper and cleaner information via e-mail. Provide links to the organization's Web site (not attachments) for ancillary information such as bios, photos, annual reports, fact sheets, calendars, program/product overviews, and news archives. Make reports and other lengthy files available in both HTML and PDF formats. Why not attachments? Because they take up too much e-mail space, slow things down, and are easy to ignore.

Use software that can tailor your distribution to a single "to" line rather than to a lengthy distribution list of reporters. Keep the subject line brief, perhaps beginning with a news flag, such as "News: MetroSport Names CEO". Here are some writing tips for e-mail news releases:

- Begin the text with a headline (caps and lowercase) of no more than 10 words.

- Use a summary news lead that incorporates the key elements of who-what-when-where-why and how.

- Then remember the standard rules: short paragraphs, bullets, lists—the kind of typographical devices that are scannable by your readers. Keep the entire release brief. Xpress Press, a news release distribution service, recommends 500 words or less organized into five short paragraphs.

- End with the typical contact information. Include not only e-mail and Web contacts but also telephone numbers and postal addresses.

When you provide photos, use high-resolution images in the universally recognized JPEG format that journalists can download. Images should be a minimum of 300 dpi. Because of the space photos consume, link this to your organization's Web site rather than sending them as e-mail attachments.

Meanwhile, even those journalists who want e-mail may have specific preferences. Some local news outlets want public relations practitioners to e-mail their releases directly, without going through a newswire service. Others prefer an e-mail query letter, giving them an opportunity to request the information. Before sending an e-mail news release, ask the editors, news directors and other gatekeepers how they want to receive information from your organization. Develop a personal relationship with your media contacts, and send them information in the format they prefer. The extra time you put into alternative distribution systems will pay off.

Web Dissemination. Many businesses and nonprofit organizations store current and past news releases, annual reports, backgrounders, speeches and other public documents on a computer network. A growing number of public relations practitioners are posting news releases on the Web, a relatively new practice that quickly has become routine. "FYI: News Distribution on Web Sites" lists some sites you might want to check out for an idea of how various organizations are using the Internet to provide news services to reporters and others looking for official information.

FYI *News Distribution on Web Sites*

Many organizations are posting their new releases on their Web sites, making newsworthy information available not only to reporters but also to consumers and other interested readers. Here are several examples of news posted at Web sites. Follow these links for news, pressroom, briefings, information, or similar locations within the Web site.

arthritis.org (National Arthritis Foundation)

att.com/news (AT&T)

cancer.org (American Cancer Society)

fbi.gov/pressroom.htm (Federal Bureau of Investigation)

grammy.org/press (National Academy of Recording Arts and Sciences)

littleleague.org/media (Little League Baseball)

madd.org/news (Mothers Against Drunk Driving)

nba.com/news (National Basketball Association)

nfl.com/news (National Football League)

nrahq.org (National Rifle Association)

un.org/news (United Nations)

united-church.ca/news (United Church of Canada)

vatican.va/news_services (Vatican)

whitehouse.gov (White House)

wnba.com/news (Women's National Basketball Association)

Some organizations use e-mail to notify journalists and others who have expressed an interest in receiving organizational information when new information is being uploaded to the organization's Web site. If you do post news materials on the Web, make certain they are carefully indexed so they can be easily accessed by users—not only reporters but also consumers, regulators, students and casual information-gatherers. Remember that your competitors and opponents will also have access to information on your Web site. Some organizations try to minimize providing information to unknown sources by asking journalists to register and receive a password, though many reporters and editors resist this practice.

FYI *Media Relations and the Web*

The Web offers several multimedia opportunities that can be very useful to an organization's media relations program. Many companies and nonprofit organizations have added "media rooms" (also called "press rooms" or "news rooms") to their Web sites where they provide a range of information and services to reporters. Some of these rooms are open to any Web visitor; others give access only to reporters via a pre-arranged password, though this can be annoying to journalists, particularly when they are writing on deadline and need some quick info about your organization.

Here are a few of the ways public relations practitioners can create journalist-friendly Web sites:

General Visibility. Don't bury your media room. Create a link from your homepage (second best, from your "about us" page). Make it easy for journalists (and other information seekers) both to find your news repository and to navigate around it.

Current News Release. The most useful and journalist-friendly feature of an organizational Web site is a menu of current news releases. Make the headline descriptive (but brief). File them chronologically, beginning with the most recent. If you have a lot of releases, consider grouping them into categories.

News Release Archive. Another common use of an organizational Web site for media relations purposes is to provide an archive of previous releases. These can be offered as both full-length articles and as news briefs. For ease of use, the archived releases can be filed topically, or they may be filed chronologically with a topical cross-listing. Make sure they can be easily retrieved by reporters and other interested readers.

General Archive. In addition to news releases, some organizations place a wide range of information on their Web sites: both short and longer versions of biographies and organization history, backgrounders, newsletters,

brochures, annual reports, FAQs and so on. Some organizations with an open-door policy on their news rooms even feature a section displaying articles that the media have written about them. A key to the usefulness of such information is that is must be easily accessible and must download quickly. If any of these are lengthy documents, consider making them available not only in HTML format but also as PDF files that retain their original formatting.

Online Photography. A Web site can feature high-quality color or black-and-white photographs that can be downloaded by the user. The most common format for online photos is JPEG (Joint Photographic Experts Group). As a second format, you might also have the same photos available as GIF (Graphics Interchange Format) files. File photos separately, or use a general thumbnail gallery that loads quickly. Make sure the photos are of high-quality, at least 300 dpi. Some visually focused organizations, such as museums and art galleries, also use their Web sites so journalists can order higher-resolution photos for professional publishing.

Audio or Video Clip. Radio and television stations can download audio actualities or video clips and B-rolls, recorded digitally by the organization sponsoring the Web site. Some organizations use their media pages to provide video clips of commercial or public service advertisements.

Tours and Models. Three-dimensional tours and models that can be downloaded can also be useful in giving reporters information about the organization and its products or services.

Contact Information. Your media page should include a complete directory of contact info: names, phone numbers, fax numbers, e-mail addresses, as well as mailing information.

Exercise 7.1—Freewriting on the Purpose of News Releases

 Before we continue, freewrite for five minutes on the following topic: *What should a news release accomplish for an organization or client?* Then discuss this with your classmates. ∎

How Journalists Handle News Releases

Ice cream melts in the summer. Rain falls down, not up. Editors rewrite news releases. It's almost a law of nature. Experienced public relations writers don't think of it as a reflection on their writing ability when their well-crafted news releases are rewritten. With experience, you will get used to this. Sometimes you won't notice any apparent improvement. Often you may conclude that the rewritten version fails to carry over important information from your original. Occasionally, you even may find that the rewrite has introduced ambiguity or error into the report. This, too, is part of reality for a public relations practitioner. Here are some points to consider about why editors rewrite and how to avoid the need for this work. "Advice from a Pro: Craig Miyamoto on Avoiding Rewrites" offers some tips on why editors rewrite and how to minimize the need for this work. Here are some other points to consider:

Advice from a Pro   *Craig Miyamoto on Avoiding Rewrites*

Craig Miyamoto APR, a fellow of the Public Relations Society of America, has a lot of experience in working with the news media. From his headquarters in Honolulu, he offers the following advice: "After you have sent a news release, be patient. It's almost impossible to predict how the news media will value (or discount completely) your submission. Whatever you do, don't call the reporter to find out why your story hasn't run."

Miyamoto says there are four most common explanations of why a news release isn't used:

1. It's not newsworthy. There is nothing you can do about that. It doesn't matter what you think; the editor's opinion is the only one that matters.

2. They ran out of space. Nothing you can do about that either.

3. They're holding it for publication at a later date.

4. They never got the story. (Actually, they probably did but they tossed it.)

Miyamoto's advice is that a good public relations writer never calls to ask why a story didn't run. That will only make editors angry, and you don't want to do that.

For more advice, check out Miyamoto's Web site at geocities.com/WallStreet/8925.

Poor Writing. Too often, reporters receive poorly written releases. Often these releases are sent by well-meaning but untrained amateurs who volunteer for schools, clubs and charities, or by untrained staff people in small business organizations. In addition, some organizations promote people into public relations positions without a formal background in the profession. Unskilled writers sometimes bury the news element in the second paragraph, or in the 22nd. Sometimes the release is more fluff than substance.

Poor writing also can happen when a public relations writer doesn't take the time to learn the interests of the editors or producers, such as by reading a recent edition of the publication or viewing a broadcast. A related problem is caused by an employer or client who insists on having releases written as they would like to see them published or broadcast, rather than as the media are most likely to use them. Since every rewrite risks introducing media-generated error or ambiguity, it is particularly important for a public relations writer to prepare the most professional and newsworthy material.

Because many releases arrive on their desks needing major revision, editors and news directors often get into the habit of rewriting every release. Journalists have learned that they need to revise most releases for style as well as for content. That is why journalists respect the work of public relations writers who show that they can produce news-based releases.

Policy. Weekly or community newspapers with small reporting staffs are likely to use the release "as is," but larger daily newspapers seldom do so. Often, this is due to a policy against using "handouts" as they are submitted in order to prevent the embarrassment of using a release identical to one used in another publication.

Starting Point. Reporters often need to expand upon the information provided, using the news release as a starting point. A fact sheet would function in the same way. A newspaper editor may assign a reporter to follow up on the release, contacting the organization and perhaps people on the other side of the issue. This often results in a more balanced story than the organization originally submitted.

Format. Sometimes releases are rewritten because they do not fit the medium's format. Some newspapers use only short items, so they have to rewrite lengthy releases that contain information they want to present to their readers. Meanwhile, electronic media generally use a release only as an idea-generator. A radio news director will want some recorded audio to go with the release. A television reporter may need on-camera interviews and other footage to support the story.

Despite the likelihood of being rewritten, the public relations writer should try to prepare the best news release possible. The more newsy and balanced the release is, the less need for revision.

One public relations director tells this story: He once found that a daily newspaper (one of two highly competitive papers in town) published his release word for word, with the byline of one of the paper's beat reporters. Apologetically, the reporter called to explain that an editor had seen the story on the computer screen before the reporter had a chance to edit it. But the editor liked what she read and added the reporter's byline on a well-written report that apparently grew out of the reporter's beat. (There's a compliment in there someplace for the public relations writer.) The lesson of this story? Good public relations writing is also good journalistic writing. "FYI: National Geographic Society News Release" presents a case study in how a news release gets reorganized once it is in the hands of editors.

FYI   *National Geographic Society News Release*

Veteran public relations practitioners expect to be rewritten. They write the best release they can, knowing that its biggest benefit may be to a journalist as material for a news report. That was the case with a release prepared by the National Geographic Society announcing the discovery of an ancient city in Mexico.

The manager of the Society's Public Affairs Office in Washington prepared the release as part of a media kit for a double news conference held simultaneously in Mexico City and in Washington, D.C. Striving for a balance, the writer reported the society's sponsorship in the fourth of 20 paragraphs.

Newspapers reporting the story took various approaches to the sponsorship as they rewrote the news release. The Los Angeles Times, for example, cited the society in the first paragraph of a 16-paragraph report. The Dallas Morning News did so in the fourth paragraph

of a 34-paragraph story. Other papers delayed mention of the society: the Atlanta Constitution to the eighth of 21 paragraphs, the New York Times to the sixth paragraph; the Boston Globe to the eighth; and the Washington Post to the 16th. Several newspapers published lengthy reports without mentioning the National Geographic connection at all.

Regardless of name placement, the NGS Public Affairs Office considered the release a success because it furthered the society's bottom line—furthering its mission to educate, foster geographic literacy, and encourage exploration. The release yielded reports in 75 American newspapers with a combined circulation of more than 15 million. The story also was carried in many foreign publications, and for several months the scientist who made the discovery gave interviews for print and broadcast media.

Common Errors in News Releases

Too often, the story ideas and news releases of public relations writers end up in the waste can next to an editor's desk. The reason? The journalist is looking for relevant news, but the public relations writer has offered something else. The result is a lot of wasted effort, frustration, and damage to an organization's reputation as a credible source of news. Following are excerpts from actual news releases sent to a metropolitan daily newspaper. The city editor has indicated the reason why each was rejected. Names and other identifying characteristics have been changed to avoid embarrassing the organization that sent the releases, but each retains its own style (errors and all).

Contest
This summer, the Local Lumberjacks baseball team, in conjunction with WWWW-AM, will participate in the XYZ Paint Company's "Winning Shoot Out Inning" contest.

   The contest gives fans the opportunity to win $1,000 cash if the Lumberjacks record three consecutive strike-outs—facing just three batters in a designated inning. If the Lumberjacks simply shut-out their opponent in the designated inning (no runs scored), contestants will win four box seats for an upcoming game. If they fail to shut-out the opposing team, contestants will still win a XYZ painters cap . . .

"Too commercial; too promotional," said the editor. It is also confusing. Lesson for public relations writers: Find alternatives to public news media for business promotions. Try advertising coupons, in-store promotions, direct mail and word-of-mouth.

Hospital
The Mammography Imaging Services of Memorial Hospital recently received a three-year accreditation from the American College of Radiology (ACR).

The Memorial Hospital Radiology Department's Mammography Unit was surveyed by the Committee on Mammography Accreditation of the ACR Commission on Standards and Accreditation. The ACR Mammography Accreditation Program offers radiologists the opportunity for peer review and evaluation of their facility's staff qualifications, equipment, quality control and quality assurance programs, image quality, breast dose, and processor quality control.

This voluntary program is directed by the ACR Committee on practice Accreditation of the Commission of Radiologic Practice . . .

The editor's verdict: "Not news." It is not even understandable. Lesson for public relations writers: Perhaps it could be newsworthy to a general-interest newspaper if the writer had dropped the jargon and focused on a short report about what accreditation means to patients.

Library

The Downtown Public Library is sponsoring its yearly summer reading program for children called "Telling Tales, Spinning Yarns." The primary aim of our program is to encourage children to continue to read for enjoyment through the summer months. To achieve this goal, the library provides incentive programming, crafts, games and prizes for children of all ages, ranging from three years olds through junior high . . .

This particular library is two states and 250 miles away. Asks the editor: "Why would anyone mail this to us?" Lesson for public relations writers: Keep a rein on your mailing list. Don't waste a good local release by distributing it beyond its interest area. Meanwhile, whose program is "our program" and what is "incentive programming"?

Competition

On Wednesday, May 19, from 9 a.m. to 11:30 a.m., students representing 37 high schools from across the State will be in the Convention Center of the State Capitol Plaza to discuss their projects in the annual Student Energy Research Competition. At noon, State Energy Development and Research Authority Chairman and State Energy Commissioner Walter Wattage III will preside at an award ceremony to announce top prize winners . . .

"Detail area winners and you'd hook me," said the editor. Lesson for public relations writers: An advance release may be too general. Instead, do a follow-up focusing on local news interests.

Training

_____ SFI, MTO, MFI, of _____, or _____ County, [in the original, the blanks were filled in by hand and the appropriate initials circled] successfully completed the 2005 State Fire Instructors Conference, a part of the new state fire training program offered at the Institute of Fire Science, Falling Rivers.

The Conference included workshops on PRINCIPLES OF CONSTRUCTION, FIRE DEPARTMENT OPERATIONS IN SPRINKLERED BUILDINGS, POSITIVE PRESSURE VENTILATION AND OSHA TRAINING.

Ugh! The editor kindly said this is "not newsworthy." Lesson for public relations writers: Fill in the blanks? Don't even think it.

Tree Planting

The Green Suburbs school district as well as several park and recreation areas will be the focal point for the planting of over one hundred trees in the Town of Green. This tree planting effort results from a committee that consists of industry, garden clubs, area government leaders, local schools, and a retirees group. This tree planting committee is responsible for a program called "Rooting For America" . . .

"No news. So what? No real hook," said the editor. Lesson for public relations writers: There must be a human angle in here someplace—involvement of a biology class from the local high school, students and senior citizens working together, something. A less boring telling of this story would improve it a lot.

<u>Voting Record</u>
Assemblywoman Billie Vohtgetter's (R, McElhatter) voting record on issues that affect the environment recently earned a strong rating from the Environmental Policy Lobby.

"The 1999 legislative session was an environment-oriented session which witnessed the passage of several pieces of legislation that will have lasting impacts on our society," said Vohtgetter, a member of the Legislative Environmental Conservation Committee. "Since many of the bills directly affected every resident of the 234th Legislative District, I always consider their full implications before casting my vote" . . .

The editor used a four-letter word for this boorish self-aggrandizement. No, not that word. He said: "PUFF!" Lesson to public relations writers: Some releases are better reserved for in-house distribution and for friendly gatherings where applause is appropriate. For news releases, stick with news.

<u>Scholarship</u>
Christopher B. Christopher, son of Mr. and Mrs. Clarence Christopher of Lindsey Avenue in South Suburbia, recently began studies as a freshman at Dakota College, a selective liberal arts college located in the Foothills plateau.

Christopher is a graduate of Central Suburbia High School where he was a member of the golf team and a recipient of the Governor's Scholarship and a Presidential Academic Fitness Award.

Dakota College celebrates its 175th anniversary this year . . .

This was one of six separate-but-similar releases received in one day from this college, located 200 miles away from the newspaper, in an adjacent state. The editor judged the release as non-news. "We don't use this. Not news. No room. Nobody cares." Lesson to public relations writers: Even hometown people pleasers must have some news value. If Christopher had made the dean's list, been elected to the student government, or graduated, there might be some interest. The college should have sent the release to the suburban weekly newspaper serving Christopher's neighborhood and to his high school alumni newsletter.

<u>Commentary</u>
Patrick Jones, a political scientist at Mount Martha University and an expert on the economics and politics of security issues in Western Europe, is in Paris next month and is available for commentary and analysis on European unification talks, which will take place Sept. 15.

"The possibility of unification is intriguing," Jones said from his office at the European Unification Research Center at the LaFrance Academy for Social Research, where he is a visiting scholar . . .

This college was located 400 miles away from the newspaper. "No local interest; no tie-in," said the editor. Interestingly, buried deep within the two-page story was information that a university in the newspaper's circulation area had published Jones' book on the subject. Lesson to public relations writers: Search your information carefully for information that can be highlighted for local interest. Then prepare a localized version.

<u>Awards</u>
Mark A. Tree won the Financial Administrator's Institute Competitive Award, it was announced at Jones University's Annual Honors Convocation.
   Tree, the son of Mr. and Mrs. Brewster Tree II of Hopachuchu, is a graduate of Hopachuchu Central High School . . .

Lucas G. Tree won the Faculty Award to the Outstanding Student in Finance, the Financial Administrator's Institute Recognition Award, the State Society of Certified Public Accountants Award, the Senior Honor Student Award in the College of Finance, and the Jackson Herkimer Memorial Scholarship, it was announced at Jones University's Annual Honors Convocation.
   Tree, the son of Mr. and Mrs. Brewster Tree II of Hopachuchu, is a graduate of Hopachuchu Central High School . . .

"Routine," the editor said about two separate releases that arrived separately on the same day. The editor had missed the apparent relationship between the two releases. Evidently, the public relations writer missed it also. Lesson to public relations writers: Don't overlook the obvious human interest factor that results from a coincidence of information. In this case, brothers receiving honors in the same field could be newsworthy.

Why So Many Poor Releases?

One reason explains the existence of such ineffective news releases: The writers forgot the needs of their customer—the media. In some cases, the task may have been given to an untrained person who, though perhaps a good writer of business-related materials or a well-meaning volunteer, has never learned the nuances of public relations writing. Some of this unprofessional writing will be your competition when you get a job in public relations. As you recognize some of the writing problems and how to avoid them, you are already moving ahead of that competition.

   In other cases, however, the problem may be that there are different ideas on what goes into a good news release. Organizational policy may be involved. A public relations intern working at a hospital noticed that the public relations office had an unusual way of preparing news releases, a way that was wrong according to what she remembered from class. She found that, regardless of news interest, every release prepared by the hospital began the same way: *Memorial Hospital of East Carbon Street in Southtown announces that . . .*

   The intern recognized that this was not the most effective way to begin a release, but that was the rule at this office. What should she do? First, her duty as an intern was to follow the organizational policy. Second, she should try to understand the policy. In this case, she discovered that the hospital was acting on the recommendation of a fundraising consultant who had observed, correctly, that the small hospital's side-street location meant that many residents did not know where it was located. The consultant had recommended that news releases emphasize the location and the connection with its geographic service area. So the policy had a logical basis, though this seems to be a too-rigid application of that logic. The student writer resolved to try to understand any such future policies so she could respond to their intent and adapt her writing to further the best interests of the organization.

Another student reported a similar problem. The practice at the bank where he was an intern was to conclude each news release with two long paragraphs of organizational identification. The first was a six-line paragraph that focused on the bank; the second was four lines that gave background on the holding company that owned the bank—altogether 10 lines, nearly a half page of every news release.

This student's most recent release was a one-page announcement of a new branch manager. The release featured a one-paragraph lead (four lines) about the appointment, two paragraphs (totaling six lines) about the new officer, and two paragraphs (10 lines) of standard organizational identification, which were used in every release by this company. Exactly half of the release was standard identification about the bank, information that had little chance of finding its way into a newspaper. The intern considered his options. He would continue to use the standard paragraphs as his internship supervisor required, but he would also track the releases to learn if the media used the standard paragraphs or any information they included. Then he would try to weave some of the information around more pertinent information in the release. Finally, if the opportunity presented itself, he would ask the supervisor about using a shorter version that had a better chance of being used.

Both students in the above real-life scenarios learned that office policy can get in the way of effective writing. In such situations, public relations writers may be most useful by offering advice that will benefit the organization.

Memos and Letters to the Media

Public relations writers find that business communiqués to editors of print media and to news directors or assignment editors of electronic media can generate coverage of their organizations. The five most common types of communication are media advisories, public advisories, story idea memos, pitch letters and query letters.

Media Advisory

Public relations writers occasionally find it useful to communicate directly with editors and news directors. *Media advisories,* also called *media alerts*, are straightforward memos notifying the media about an upcoming newsworthy activity related to the organization. Whereas a news release provides information about an event, a media advisory merely informs the media that something newsworthy will occur. For example, you may offer reporters advance access to a visiting celebrity willing to give an interview. Or you may notify photographers about a photo opportunity that emphasizes the visual aspects of an upcoming activity.

Advisories generally are written in memo form, addressed to a generic title, such as Editors and News Directors. Exhibit 7.1 is an example of an actual media advisory inviting reporters to a congressional hearing. Note that the writing is straightforward, allowing the information to speak for itself. Media advisories generally are not full of hype with particularly promotional styles of writing.

Some media advisories announce "good news" events. For example, if hockey legend Wayne Gretzky is coming to your college or university to present $1,000 scholarships to 30 boys and girls to attend summer hockey camp, your advisory would note this, along with information about place and time. But be careful with more significant news. If you are sending a media advisory to invite reporters to a news conference on a controversial topic, be very careful not to provide too much information about the content of the news conference. Just note the topic:

> Announcement of the results of a six-month investigation into allegations of financial mismanagement in City Hall.

Save the details for the news conference itself. If you give too much advance information, you'll read about the findings of your report in the morning edition of the newspaper on the day of the news conference.

Exhibit 7.1—MEDIA ADVISORY MEMO

FOR IMMEDIATE RELEASE
May 16, 2007

MEDIA ADVISORY—UPDATED
NOAA TO ANNOUNCE 2006 ATLANTIC HURRICANE SEASON OUTLOOK
Event Part of National Hurricane Preparedness Week: May 21–27

NOAA, alongside hurricane preparedness partner organizations, will release the 2006 Atlantic Hurricane Season Outlook as part of National Hurricane Preparedness Week.

WHAT: News conference to announce NOAA's 2006 Atlantic Hurricane Season Outlook.

WHEN: Monday, May 21, 2007, 11:00 a.m. EDT.

NOTE: Audio-only conference call feed will be available for USA and international media. Please call Theresa Eisenman at (301) 713–0622, for the respective phone numbers and pass codes.

WHERE: NOAA National Hurricane Center
11691 SW 17th Street
Miami, FL 33157
Main campus, Florida International University, corner of 117th Avenue and SW 17th Street.

LIVE SATELLITE FEED:
Satellite: IA5C/13
Downlink Frequency: 3960 Vertical, Audio: 6.2 / 6.8
Technical contact: (305) 341–4500 Globecast Miami.
NOTE: Satellite media tours will be available with NOAA National Hurricane Center personnel following the news conference. Booking for SMT: Theresa Eisenman at (301) 713–0622.

WHO: David A. Sampson, deputy secretary of commerce
Vice Admiral Conrad C. Lautenbacher, Jr., USN (Ret.), undersecretary of commerce for oceans and atmosphere and NOAA administrator
David Paulison, acting director of the Federal Emergency Management Agency and undersecretary of homeland security for emergency preparedness and response
Max Mayfield, director, NOAA National Hurricane Center.

Relevant Web Sites:
NOAA National Hurricane Center
NOAA National Hurricane Preparedness Week.

Media Contact:
Frank Lepore, NOAA National Hurricane Center, (305) 229–4404 or Theresa Eisenman, NOAA National Weather Service, (301) 713–0622.

Exercise 7.2—Writing a Media Advisory

 You are public information director for your college or university. Prepare a media advisory inviting reporters and news photographers to a news conference at which you will announce the appointment of a new president following a six-month search. It is public knowledge that four candidates who were interviewed in campus were among the finalists for the position. Provide hypothetical details as necessary.   ▪

Public Advisory

In emergency situations, organizations may wish to use news channels to communicate directly with media audiences on matters of public interest. For example, a law enforcement agency may report a scam artist preying on elderly homeowners, or a hospital may issue a warning about an outbreak of hepatitis. On these occasions, a *public advisory* is issued. This is a direct announcement in which an organization matter-of-factly warns media audiences of potential or imminent harm. Public advisories are brief, factual statements, often listing a telephone contact. Exhibit 7.2 is an example of a public advisory.

Exhibit 7.2—PUBLIC ADVISORY MEMO   This public advisory is written directly to the media audience as a warning from the organization.

PAKISTANI-AMERICAN FRIENDSHIP COMMITTEE

123 Park Lane ◉ Central City Xx 12345

To: Editors and News Directors
From: Hassan al-Haq
Date: December 12, 2007
Re: Public Advisory

   The Pakistani–American Friendship Committee is warning residents of Central City that people unrelated to the organization are misleadingly using its name to solicit money.

   A man and a woman have been reported going door-to-door asking for money, claiming to be raising funds for a relief effort for refugees in Central Asia. The Pakistani-American Friendship Committee does not collect money door-to-door, nor does it authorize anyone to do so on its behalf. Therefore, residents are advised not to give any money to these people.

   Both the Central City Police Department and the State Police have been notified.

#####

Exercise 7.3—Writing a Public Advisory

You are public information director for your college or university. Write a public advisory for campus and community media warning about the danger of salmonella food poisoning for anyone who ate football-shaped hors d'oeuvres at last night's reception honoring the retiring football coach. Mention the symptoms and potential severity of the illness (do your own online research on this), and indicate what people should do if they ate the contaminated food. ▪

Story Idea Memo

Except for community newspapers and trade publications, most news publications are reluctant to use feature stories written by public relations people. Editors prefer instead to assign their own reporters to write features. Nevertheless, public relations writers can use *story idea memos* (also called *tip sheets* or *interview opportunities*) as a means to invite editors and news directors to develop features about interesting people associated with their organization. Often the focus is on the interviewee's activities outside the organization. This kind of story idea memo lets journalists know that you are aware of them and their audiences, even if those stories you suggest have little direct involvement with your organization except for the possibility of being associated with interesting people. Exhibit 7.3 is an example of a typical story idea memo that directs the focus away from the organization.

Some public relations practitioners try to provide the media with these ideas on a regular basis. In doing so, they strengthen their own relationship with reporters and keep their organization's name before its publics. Here are some of the kinds of story ideas that might find their way into a story idea memo:

- The society matron who has spent 15 years volunteering at your soup kitchen
- The teacher at your school who each summer takes groups of children from single-parent families on backpacking trips
- The new guy in marketing who is training for the Olympics as a speed skater
- The graduate of your college who just won an Emmy for her work as a television writer.

Exercise 7.4—Writing a Story Idea Memo

You are a public relations writer with your college or university. Identify a person affiliated with your school such as a student, professor or staff person who is doing something of interest. Gather enough information to write a story idea memo about this person. Write the memo to assignment editors of area television stations. ▪

Exhibit 7.3—STORY IDEA MEMO   This story idea memo does not provide as much information as a news release because it is intended merely to pique the editor's interest in sending a reporter to do an interview and develop a feature story. Note that the company gets only a passing mention in this memo, as the focus of the eventual feature story would be on the person rather than the company.

One Franklin Park West
East Bay Xx, 12345
(123) 456-7890
www.comcorpr.com

ComCor Inc.
INNOVATIONS IN ELECTRONICS FOR THE NEW MILLENNIUM

To: Editors and News Directors
From: Rolf Pfennighauser, ComCor Inc.
Date: March 23, 2007
Re: Interview Opportunity

When Paul Walbrewster was playing center for his high school basketball team, his focus was to win regardless of the effort involved. The competitive spirit kept him going, and he would spend long hours training and practicing. This determination carried him and the East Bay Oysters to the state championships.

Today Paul is in a wheelchair, the legacy of an automobile accident. But don't call Paul a victim. "It's more like—I'm a survivor," he says. "I don't have time to feel victimized."

This 35-year-old maintains an active training schedule at O'Malley's Gym. He coaches a basketball team for boys and girls with physical handicaps at the East Side Community Center. And he is adjusting to his new promotion as senior sales representative for ComCor Electronics.

If you wish to interview Paul, you may contact him through the ComCor Communications Office at (123) 456–7890.

#####

Pitch Letter

Related to story idea memos, *pitch letters* are directed to media gatekeepers to entice them to do a story or interview on some aspect of an organization. The previously mentioned story idea memos are understated; they let the information content engage an editor. But there is nothing subtle about a pitch letter. It is unmistakably a sales letter, an attempt to attract the attention of an editor or news director.

An effective pitch letter tries to entice the editor, not with wild exaggerations but rather with enthusiasm and confidence about your program or product. It addresses the benefits to the media if they do the story rather than the advantage to the organization. And it provides a wrap-up, usually with a promise to follow the letter with a telephone call to see if the media has any interest in the issue. Exhibit 7.4 is an example of a pitch letter designed to get your client on a television talk show. With slight changes, it could easily be used to invite an interview or to ask for photo coverage of a speech.

A particular kind of pitch letter is a *query letter*, usually written by freelance writers. Queries propose a story idea to magazine editors or television producers and inquire about their interest in it. Public relations writers occasionally use query letters, or they may assist a freelance writer in querying an editor or producer.

Exhibit 7.4—PITCH LETTER: "MORNING WITH MARMADUKE"   This pitch letter is an enthusiastically written attempt to persuade an editor to invite someone to be a guest on a television talk show.

Cartier Communications

8033 Thyme Circle
Fort McKinley XX 12345
(123) 456-7890

Carlton Kleinhans
Producer
"Morning with Marmaduke"
WWWW-TV3

Dear Mr. Kleinhans:

Senator Veronica Collingsward is known as one of the "toughest cookies" in the State Senate. Admirers call her "tenacious" and "resourceful." What opponents call her can't be spoken on local television.

Sen. Collingsward has investigated dozens of cases of fraud against nursing home residents. Once, she went undercover, posing as an Alzheimer's patient. The information she gathered helped her colleagues in the Senate pass the Collingsward-O'Halleron bill to establish minimum standards for employees and volunteers at adult day-care facilities.

Without doubt, viewers of your "Morning with Marmaduke" program would be very interested in seeing Sen. Collingsward. Given the right promotion, her guest appearance could be one of your highest-watched segments.

I will contact you this week about arranging an appearance by Sen. Collingsward on "Morning with Marmaduke."

Sincerely,

Matilda Constantino
Cartier Communications

Exercise 7.5—Writing a Pitch Letter

You are the public information director with your college or university. You are trying to promote media attention toward one of the following people:

- A professor who teaches public relations has just returned from a three-week visit to Russia, where he or she helped Russian government workers learn about how public relations can make them more effective in their work.

- A professor who teaches public relations has completed a research project sponsored by the National Institutes of Health with recommendations for ways that local health agencies can use public relations techniques to more effectively encourage people to adopt better health practices.

Write a pitch letter to the producer of a talk show on a local radio station, encouraging that this professor be a guest on the program. ∎

Photo Caption

Photographs and the information that supports them can provide an important vehicle for an organization interested in communicating through the news media. Photos attract attention, and they can tell a story more quickly and with more impact than words alone. A *caption,* also called a *cutline,* is the written information that describes and explains the photograph. There are two types of captions: those that accompany a story, and those that stand alone.

Captions that accompany a story are generally one- or two-line identifications of the action or person portrayed in the photograph. A caption for a mug shot, for example, would include the name and perhaps the title of the person in the photo. A caption for an action shot, on the other hand, would present a brief description of the photograph. Because public relations writers do not know how an editor may use a photograph, some writers may provide both accompanying captions and stand-alone captions with each photo they distribute.

Occasionally, public relations writers may find that a photograph is strong enough to carry the organization's message without any story beyond the caption. These stand-alone captions generally include the following elements:

Dateline. A *dateline* for a caption is the same as for a news release. It features the name of the city or town where the photo originates. This location indicates where the photo was taken, not necessarily where the caption was written or where it is dispatched from. The dateline should be typed in capital letters.

Date. The date that the photo was made follows the dateline. This is important for newspapers and magazines, which often file photos for future use.

Legend. A *legend* or *overline* does for a caption what a headline does for a news release. It provides a title to attract reader interest. Overlines may be either brief headlines that summarize the news element of the photo, or *teasers* that attract the reader's attention.

Text. The text of a stand-alone caption includes the essentials of news—who, what, when, where, why, how—though in a more concise form than in a news release. The first sentence often explains or refers to the action apparent within the photo. The text also identifies every recognizable person pictured in the photo. The text of a photo caption is presented in a single paragraph.

Two elements are common to both stand-alone and accompanying captions: the photo credit and the organizational contact. The photo credit is a brief notation of the person who made the photograph. The organizational contact is the name and address of the organization providing the photo and caption, along with the name and telephone number of the public relations contact.

Writing Photo Captions

Public relations writers need to be just as careful in preparing captions as they are in writing news releases. Planning remains essential, with a strong awareness of the key public for this visual message and a clear understanding of the organization's objectives in providing the photo. The caption itself becomes a supplement to the photograph, an explanation of its content and an opportunity for the writer to focus on the interests of the audience. Following are some guidelines for writing effective captions.

Present Tense.   Generally, the text of a caption is written in the present tense. The logic behind this practice is that the reader/viewer is looking at the photo while reading the caption. Thus the photo depicts something that is perceived to be happening at that moment. A caption might read as follows:

> National Motors president Joan Gangnieri visits workers at the Midstate Uranus plant, where the first Z-54 of the new model year rolls off the assembly line.

Even though the visit took place three days ago, the photo shows it happening now, making it appropriate to use present tense for *visits* and *rolls off*.

Sometimes, however, the writer needs to provide additional information, and continuing in the present tense would be awkward. The caption may shift to the past tense after the opening sentence that describes the action in the photo.

> National Motors president Joan Gangnieri visits workers at the Midstate Uranus plant, where the first Z-54 of the new model year rolls off the assembly line. The company official was accompanied by State Senator Morris LeCatt, who guided legislation to provide tax incentives for Uranus to open its Midstate plant.

Active Voice. The caption should present information in the active voice rather than passively. Consider the passive voice in this caption for a photo depicting a woman and several children in a hospital setting:

> Cancer patients at St. Charles Lwanga Children's Hospital are visited by Dunnstown mayor Mary Elizabeth Jolin during an international meeting in Namasagali, Uganda, sponsored by the Cities and Partners project.

Using active voice puts more strength and presence into the words:

Dunnstown mayor Mary Elizabeth Jolin visits cancer patients at St. Charles Lwanga Children's Hospital in Namasagali, Uganda, during an international meeting sponsored by the Cities and Partners project.

Identification. If one person is clearly more prominent, you might highlight that person and then identify the others. But unless some faces are obscured or the photo depicts a large crowd, make it a practice to identify everyone in the photo. Always identify everyone in a photo in which people posed for the camera.

Determine where to place the identification by how many people need to be identified. With one or two people, usually the writer places the identification at the beginning of the caption. Identification for three or more people may be used later in the caption, though it is a good rule not to use photos that include more than five or six identifiable faces.

Sometimes captions identify people by their relative location in the photo. This is usually in a left-to-right order, though sometimes it is more appropriate to use a clockwise, top-to-bottom or some other sequence. Consider how the following caption identifies its photo depicting the queen and four schoolchildren:

Queen Elizabeth meets with students at the National School for Children on her visit to Montreal. Shown here are (left to right) Nicole LeBoeuf, Michel Beaver, the Queen, Kateri Buck and Martin St. Pierre.

Rather than location identification, a better version of the caption might identify people by their action in the photograph.

Queen Elizabeth meets with students at the National School for Children on her visit to Montreal. Nicole LeBoeuf and Michel Beaver present the Queen with a gift from the children, while Kateri Buck and Martin St. Pierre look on.

When referring to photographs and the action they portray, avoid phrases that point out the obvious. The following underlined phrases are unnecessary:

The above photo shows Sen. Daniel O'Shaunassey congratulating winners of the "Stand Up for America" essay contest . . .

Sen. Daniel O'Shaunassey, pictured above, congratulates winners of the "Stand Up for America" essay contest . . .

If possible, allow the action shown within the photo to be the source of identification. Sometimes identification is so obvious that the caption does not even need to mention it. Recognizable celebrities or characters like the Easter Bunny do not require locational identification in captions.

Balance. Just as with a news release, a public relations writer will use a photo caption to present the organization in a good light. But don't overplay this. Editors will judge a photo and caption on the basis of news interest. They will be attracted to a SiLoBaTi caption: significant, local, balanced and timely.

Exercise 7.7—Critiquing Photo Captions

Consider the following caption for a stand-alone photo depicting a man with three students. Make a list of its positive and negative qualities.

> CENTERVALE, Feb. 15—CITY ACCOUNTANT CONGRATULATES MATH WINNERS: Robert Dean, president and chief executive officer of Dean Associates, a local accounting firm, congratulates winners of the Dean Applied Math Challenge, sponsored by his company. The competition pits high school seniors against each other to solve math-related problems under time pressure and other distractions. Smith said he supports the competition because "as an accountant, I believe high school students should be encouraged and challenged to develop their math skills." The top three winners received prizes of $200 savings bonds. Pictured with Dean are the winning students—(left to right) Travis McGhee of Eastville High School, Maria Garcia-Oliveras of St. Elizabeth's Academy, and Roger Martinson of South Salem High School. The competition, held at Center Community College, drew 20 students from schools throughout Center County. (Photo by Michael Yu of Dean Associates)

Here is another version of the same caption. Evaluate this caption, again listing its positive and negative qualities.

> CENTERVALE, Feb. 15—ENDURANCE, SURVIVAL, AND MATH: As they worked on math problems, Travis McGhee endured ringing telephones, Maria Garcia-Oliveras had coffee spilled on her papers, and Roger Martinson was pestered by bagpipe music on a too-loud radio. But the three high school seniors overcame the distractions to win the Dean Applied Math Challenge. The event, with the distractions built in to test the student's ability to work under pressure, was held at Center Community College. It attracted 20 seniors from throughout Center County. Robert Dean says his accounting firm sponsors the annual event "to encourage and challenge students to develop their math skills." Dean presented $200 savings bonds to the winners—McGhee of Eastville High School, Garcia-Oliveras of St. Elizabeth's Academy, and Martinson of South Salem High School. (Photo by Michael Yu of Dean Associates) ∎

Distributing Photos and Captions

There generally are two ways that public relations practitioners disseminate photos and captions to journalists: printed photos with attached captions, and electronic photos and captions.

Many publications prefer the traditional format of printed photos, generally in standard sizes 5×7 inches or 8×10 inches. Additionally, some magazines and newspaper color sections (such as those dealing with travel, fashion or food) may prefer slide transparencies or negatives. These may be disseminated by delivering or mailing them to the publication. Here are some tips involving the dissemination of photos and captions:

- Print photos minimally 5×7, using photographic paper.
- Securely attach a caption to the photo, so there is no chance of the caption and photo becoming separated.
- Never use staples or paper clips to attach the caption to the photo. Instead use pressure-sensitive labels or use tape to secure the label to the back of the photo.
- Never write with pencil or pen on the back of a photo, because this can damage the photograph and make it unusable.

If you are a public relations practitioner with a large organization that distributes many photographs, you may wish to devise a numbering system for each photo sent out. This can help you quickly retrieve a photo or caption that a journalist may request or for which additional or follow-up information is needed. Note this ID number on the caption label. Following are examples of photo ID numbers:

- 070315C (07 refers to the year, 2007; 03 15 indicates the date as third month, 15th day, or March 15; C refers to the third photo sent that day)
- OP3-3/15/07rds (This indicates the third photo released to the Operations Department sent March 15, 2007 with a caption written by someone with the initials R.D.S.).

Exhibit 7.5—PHOTO CAPTION   Attach the caption to the back of the photo so the caption can wrap up over it.

Photo Caption Photo Caption
Photo Caption Photo Caption
Photo Caption Photo Caption
Photo Caption Photo Caption

Digital photos can be disseminated either on a CD or, more commonly, by directing journalists to the organization's Web site from which photos can be viewed, often as JPEG thumbnails, and then downloaded for media use. Make sure that the digital photos meet technical specifications for publication. The important technical factor is *dpi* (dots per inch, a measure for printed photos), similar to *ppi* (pixels per inch, a measure for on-screen images). These measures indicate the number of dots or pixels that fit side-by-side on a line that is one inch long. Most publications require that digital photos be provided minimally for 300 dpi, generally at 5×7 or 8×10 sizes. Web sites, on the other hand, need only 72 ppi for clear on-screen presentation, so don't presume that just because a photo looks good on your Web site it has any practical usefulness to print publications.

Another aspect of digital photography is the possibility of manipulating photos. Public relations practitioners must be meticulous in respecting ethical guidelines concerning photography. Avoid any manipulation of photos beyond the accepted practices of cropping and color balancing. Never add or remove objects or people from an image, and don't use vanity enhancements such as those that remove eye lines or gray hairs. The standards of accuracy and representation of reality that are expected in public relations are far higher than might be associated with advertising or fashion photography. In general, never apply any digital adjustments that provide a misleading impression of people, places or events.

Photo Consent Form

Written consent is not required for a photograph dealing with a public event and used for publicity purposes related to that event. This includes a news release or a caption for an organizational newsletter prepared by a public relations writer. In these instances, consent by participants is implied. Additionally, written permission is not required when a photo records a large number of people, such as a crowd scene.

Permission should be obtained when the photo will be used for promotional purposes detached from an actual report of a public event (such as in an annual report or a brochure) or when it may be used as a general file photo that is *evergreen*, which means it is filed and kept for possible future use. Stock consent forms are available at many stores that sell photo supplies or office supplies. They can also be prepared easily by the public relations office.

Most consent forms are rather simple statements. A typical consent form might be as follows: "The undersigned, having consented to being photographed, authorizes XYZ Organization to use and reproduce said photograph for publicity, promotional and other noncommercial purposes." Date and signature.

If the people depicted in the photograph are being paid and/or if the photo is to be used for advertising or other commercial purposes, a model release may be appropriate. These releases are more formal legal contracts that spell out the particular financial arrangement and how the photos may and may not be used.

8

Broadcast Media

In most ways, the broadcast news media are interested in the same thing as their print counterparts—news. But radio and television have some particular needs that go beyond what print journalists require. Radio, for example, needs access to interviews, and television seeks stories with strong visual elements. When public relations writers understand the needs of the broadcast media, they are better able to increase their effectiveness in using radio and television to communicate with their key publics. Here are your objectives for this chapter:

- To explain the difference between writing for print and for broadcast media
- To write in the concise style used by the broadcast media
- To use pronunciation guides accurately
- To prepare a news release including a radio actuality
- To outline the contents of a video news release
- To understand the use of B-roll packages
- To recognize the importance of nonbroadcast video opportunities.

Broadcast News Releases

When public relations writers turn their attention to radio and television, they find both opportunities and challenges. Because of the need for radio and television to present sound and visual action, the written word alone does not suffice. Unlike releases for the print media, broadcast news releases are not intended to be used verbatim but rather as idea generators and background resources for reporters.

Some public relations writers have found that it is not always necessary to provide separate releases to the broadcast media. A single news release or a single media kit may serve the purposes of radio and television, as well as newspapers and magazines. Nevertheless, there are times when specialized releases are appropriate for print and broadcast media. Important news conferences sometimes lend themselves to the preparation of releases in both versions. At other times, information may be released specifically to radio and television stations.

Some of the factors that must be taken into account when crafting news releases for broadcast media are the need to write for the ear, special stylistic considerations, and differences in leads.

The overall approach to preparing releases intended for broadcast use can be summed up easily: *Write for the ear.* The style should be conversational but not casual. It should reflect a professional rather than a familiar tone. As with any writing style, read your text aloud as you prepare it. This is the best way to recognize if the writing sounds both natural and appropriate. Here are some general guidelines about preparing broadcast news releases:

- Use short sentences
- Use active voice
- Use present tense of verbs, unless the time factor requires another tense
- Keep the subject and the verb close together
- Use strong verbs
- Limit your use of adverbs and adjectives
- Use contractions
- Avoid relative clauses (those introduced by *who*, *which*, *what* and *that*) at the beginning of a sentence
- Use generalities rather than specific explanatory details
- Repeat identifications on second reference
- Use "you" words
- Avoid alliterations and tongue twisters.

News writing shares the basics, whether the writer is preparing information for print or broadcast media. However, broadcast releases present a few special considerations for writers, and some of the usual stylebook guidelines for print media do not apply to writing releases for broadcast media. What follows are examples of some of these broadcast norms.

Names and Titles. Because it is meant for the ear, broadcast style calls for less precision and permits more generalization than would be appropriate with print media.

- Generally, don't use middle initials or middle names, unless the person is known by such use. For example, *Michael J. Fox* or *Sarah Jessica Parker*.
- Use titles before the name rather than after it. For example, write *BioTech president Marguerita Bench . . .* rather than *Marguerita Bench, BioTech president . . .* Alternatively, separate the title from the name, and use the title first, as in *The company president will visit the Bayville plant next month. Marguerita Bench is expected to arrive . . .*
- Simplify job titles. For example, instead of *Undersecretary of Defense for Public Affairs Melissa Freedman*, use *Defense official Melissa Freedman*.
- Use informal descriptors before the name instead of after. For example, *City Hall spokesman Joe Morrison* or *animal-rights activist Mary Chin*.
- Use an academic or medical title only when the person's credentials are important to the story, such as *Doctor Jack Kervorkian*, but not *Doctor Bill Cosby*. (Note that writing in broadcast style requires that the word "doctor" be spelled out rather than abbreviated.)

Numbers. Numbers are particularly difficult to comprehend by hearing alone. Broadcast style calls for numbers to be used as little as possible. When they are necessary, make them understandable.

- Spell out single-digit numbers (zero to nine) and eleven. Use numerals for numbers between 10 and 999. Use words or a combination of numerals and words for numbers of one thousand or more, such as *12 million*, *14 hundred* and *three billion*. Notice that no hyphen is used in such cases.

- If possible, use rounded numbers rather than specific numbers. For example, instead of *the $14,946,300 budget* (appropriate for releases to print media), write *the budget of nearly 15 million dollars* for releases to broadcast media. However, specific numbers may be needed for reporting votes, financial reports and other detailed pieces of information.
- Try to translate numbers into easy-to-understand human terms. For example, a *two-million-dollar tax increase for a city of 500,000 residents* can be made more understandable by writing about a *tax increase of four dollars for each city resident.*
- Write out terms associated with numbers, such as *55 dollars* and *78 percent.*
- If age is an important detail, use it before the noun, such as *the 50-year-old company* or *the seven-year-old child.*

Abbreviations. Broadcast copy frequently uses commonly understood abbreviations, in line with the notion of simplifying and making it easier for a listener to understand.

- Use abbreviations for well-known organizations, such as *F-B-I* for the Federal Bureau of Investigation or *U-N* for the United Nations.
- For acronyms of organizational names that are pronounced as words, such as *UNESCO* and *NASA,* write them in all-capital letters without periods.
- For organizational names that are pronounced as individual letters, write acronyms in all-capital letters separated by hyphens, such as *I-A-B-C* or *P-R-S-A.* Some acronyms need special treatment to represent the proper pronunciation, such as *N-C-Double-A* and *Triple A.*
- Use common abbreviations that would be familiar to listeners, but avoid unfamiliar or made-up ones. For example, *U-C-L-A* is an appropriate and understandable abbreviation for the University of California at Los Angeles, but *U-N-D* is not a commonly used abbreviation for the University of Notre Dame.

Punctuation. Writing for broadcast calls for a different use of punctuation than when writing for print. Hyphens are sometimes used in ways not called for by proper spelling, such as to facilitate pronunciation. For example, you would write *recreation* when referring to leisure activities but *re-creation* when referring to a second creation. Hyphens also are used to indicate abbreviations that are pronounced as letters rather than as words (see Abbreviations, above).

Quotations. Quotes pose special problems for writers of broadcast news releases, because the intended audience (the viewer or listener) will not be able to see quotation marks.

- Paraphrase the quotation. This is the easiest and best way to handle quotes. *The senator said the proposal was disrespectful to taxpayers. The report called the recommendation premature.*
- Signal the quotation. Use phrases like: *. . . the proposal was what she called "callous and ineffective," . . . which was, in her words, "unworkable and destined for failure"* or *The secretary's response was: "I'm not going to take the heat for this one."* Other clear indicators that a direct quote is being used: *As she put it . . ., To use his words . . ., The president's exact words were . . .*
- Provide an actuality for the reporter covering the story (more on this later in this chapter).

Copy Presentation. Make it as easy as possible for news reporters to understand and read your copy.

- Avoid using abbreviated forms of all words except *Mr., Ms.* and *Mrs.* Don't abbreviate words that normally would be abbreviated in print releases, such as *street*, *saint*, *doctor*, *company* and *incorporated*.
- Avoid splitting words from one line to the next. Turn off the hyphen option on your computer, because split words can be confusing for a broadcast reader.
- Capitalize and/or underline the word *not* in crucial situations to draw the attention of the broadcaster.
- To make reading easier, use hyphens for compound words that would not be hyphenated in a release for print media. For example, in broadcast copy include a hyphen in words such as semi-tropical and non-denominational.
- Type broadcast releases using double spacing. Traditionally, broadcast news scripts were typed in all-capital letters. Increasingly, however, broadcast reporters are using regular style (both capitals and lowercase letters) because this is easier to read. For broadcast news releases, use caps and lower case.

Exercise 8.1—Writing in Broadcast Style

Rewrite each of the following sentences in a style appropriate for broadcast news copy. Answers are listed at the end of this chapter.

1. The Acme Electronics President and CEO, Mrs. Gail J. Palecki, pointed out that 7 members of her management team will receive a performance bonus because the project was completed ahead of the June 30th schedule.
2. The city's $1,968,957 budget was approved 5–1 with 1 abstention when the City Council met last night. That means a $14.00 average increase in property taxes for every homeowner.
3. The president acknowledged that the new director, 32, is the youngest person ever to serve on the Corporate Leadership Team (CLT).
4. The LPGA contender will give an address before students being honored in the Scholar–Athlete Recognition Luncheon.
5. Only 9% of the funding will come from federal funds, with the remainder coming from state, county and municipal coffers.
6. Robert L. Jones, Democratic candidate for tax assessor in the Town of Armstrong, has announced the convening of a public forum to receive input from taxpayers.
7. "Comparisons with school districts in other states are inappropriate," said Dr. Janice Harrison, Superintendent of Schools for the Madison County School District.
8. The company promises to return generous dividends to investors, according to information from the Office of the Corporate Treasurer, headed by Treasurer June Dellivan.
9. In the words of Miriam Johansen, kindergarten teacher at Elmwood Elementary: "Kids today are spending entirely too much time with zombielike mind killers in front of their TVs and video games."

Broadcast Leads

The lead for a broadcast news release often differs from that of a print release because it is slower getting into the actual news. Print releases generally present the news right up front. Broadcast copywriters preparing reports of serious events, especially tragedies, use the same no-nonsense approach: factual, straightforward, crisp. But not all broadcast stories are major breaking news reports. Many, particularly those stories associated with news releases, often deal with softer news.

Radio listeners and television viewers often rely on the broadcaster to help set the stage before the news is presented. The lead for broadcast releases is where we set the stage. That is especially true for radio audiences, who frequently need to be "rounded up" for a news story because they pay only partial attention. They are often occupied with the commute to work or household chores, using the radio merely as background sound. In these instances, a report that jumps right into the news is likely to be missed. By the time the listener begins paying attention, the important details are past. We will discuss the various types of leads used in broadcast news releases: soft, setup, umbrella, background, question, statement and punch.

Soft Leads. The summary news lead associated with print releases focuses on the news—the stronger, the better. But for broadcast, a *soft lead* takes a gentler approach. This also has been called a *throw-away lead,* a *tune-in lead* and a *warm-up lead*. Whatever the name, it is an attention getter, a hook that pulls the casual audience into the story. The following lead might work for a print release:

> Harriet Tubman High School will begin a $4.5 million expansion project featuring a new library and online research center, an expansion of the athletic complex, and 14 new classrooms.

The lead for that same story might be written more softly for a broadcast release:

> A high-tech library, 14 more classrooms, and a bigger sports center highlight the 41/2-million-dollar expansion project at Tubman High.

Setup Leads. Instead of providing even generalized news, some broadcast leads try to set the stage for upcoming news. This is another response to the fact that many members of broadcast audiences, particularly radio listeners, are not giving the medium their full attention. The *setup lead* is a way of pulling them into the story. For example, in a print release presenting a summary news lead, you might write the following:

> The National Miss Beauty Pageant is adding college grades and volunteer experience to the list of what it takes to become a pageant winner . . .

The same information is presented differently in a broadcast release that uses a setup lead. Here's an example:

> Beauty pageants once focused on swimsuits and high heels. Now college grades and volunteer experience also play a role. This morning the National Miss pageant committee announced new standards for local beauty contests . . .

In the second version, the lead sentence doesn't give any news, but it serves to draw the listener into the report. So when the second sentence is given, the reader is now paying attention, ready to obtain more information about pageants.

A setup lead based on the information above about Harriet Tubman High School might read something like this:

> Big changes are in the works at Tubman High. A high-tech library, 14 more classrooms, and a bigger sports center highlight the 4½-million-dollar expansion project.

Umbrella Leads. When a story is a complicated one with several twists and turns, an *umbrella lead* can prepare the listener. Here's an example:

> Two different reactions are greeting the new graduation requirements announced by the state education department. Some parents like higher standards for graduates, but others fear the new policy will increase the drop-out rate.

Background Leads. It's generally not a good idea to begin a news story with a history lesson, but occasionally that's the best way to help the reader understand the context of the news. Here's an example of such a *background lead:*

> Six years ago, Kiowa College was reeling from financial scandal, enrollment drops and a nasty strike by faculty members. Today, two years after Louis Eagle became Kiowa president, the campus is calm and peaceful.

Question Leads. Sometimes a *question lead* can focus the listener's attention. Be careful not to overdo question leads, because they often seem to be teasing the audience with guessing games, something good reporters avoid doing. Worse, this can sound like advertisements. Nevertheless, a well-stated question may be the best way to get into a news report. Here is an example:

> How much will it cost your children to attend college? Senator Jon Montoya contacted every college in the state, and his projections are that . . .

Statement Leads. Another type of news opening, *statement leads*, begins with a compelling fact or opinion in the first sentence, then provides the attribution and context in the second. Here's an example of such a statement lead:

> More college students would volunteer to work with kids and senior citizens, but only if someone asks them personally. That's what public relations students found when they surveyed 400 sophomores at Oakwood University.

Punch Leads. Some leads are short sentences or even sentence fragments. Known as *punch leads*, they are just a bit more conversational than headlines, and they perform the same function. Here is an example:

> Six more weeks of winter, if you believe groundhogs and caterpillars. But forecasters at Weather Watch say the critters are wrong.

Exercise 8.2—Writing Broadcast Leads

Write a broadcast lead for each of the following stories. Make up additional details as needed.

- *Document discovery*. The head of the history department at your college or university is announcing the discovery of a 200-year-old document that gives Native Americans treaty rights to the land on which the college now stands.

- *Sports signing*. In a release to sports broadcasters, your college or university is announcing the signing of a hot new prospect (use your own name and background) as a starting player for a varsity sport of your choice.

- *Enrollment surge*. The dean of enrollment management at your college or university is explaining why enrollment suddenly surged by 15 percent after several years of steady enrollment. The reason is complicated, based on easier availability of student loans, more scholarship money given by alumni, a marketing "guarantee" that students can graduate in four years, the addition of several new majors dealing with business and computers, and tuition increases in several neighboring colleges.

- *Hate speech*. The dean of students at your college or university is announcing a new policy that will ban so-called hate speech on campus and will guarantee the safety of students living in dorms against harassment or violence based on national background, sexual orientation and religious beliefs. The school already has a policy of similar guarantees based on gender and race.

- *Branch campus*. The president of your college or university is making a statement explaining that the school is opening a branch location in a popular suburban mall. This announcement will undoubtedly lead to questions about the watering down of higher education as well as to your school's long-range intention about its present campus location. The branch location will be used for evening programs and professional development seminars. ∎

Pronouncers

One of the important needs of any writing is that it can be read clearly. When you are dealing with unfamiliar words, your writing can be more effective if you help the reader pronounce words properly. This is especially important with anything that is meant to be read aloud, such as a broadcast news release or a speech. But even something meant for silent reading can enhance the reader's understanding if assistance is provided for the pronunciation of difficult words.

The tool for this is the *pronouncer,* also called a *pronunciation guide.* The purpose of this simple phonetic spelling of hard-to-pronounce names, places and technical terms is to help readers give the proper pronunciation to words that may be unfamiliar to them.

Pronouncers are commonly used in broadcast news releases. Broadcasters' reputations lie, in part, in their ability to be perceived as expert and credible reporters. Mispronunciation hurts that credibility. You will find your reputation as a public relations writer enhanced among broadcast journalists if you can help them avoid the embarrassment of mispronouncing your copy. Speeches and scripts, fact sheets and brochures may also be enhanced by pronouncers when the subject material includes difficult or unusual words.

When using pronouncers, write each syllable separately, using all-caps for accented syllables: California ((kal-ih-FORN-yuh)), Tanzania ((tan-zuh-NEE-uh)). Following are some general phonetic guides:

CONSONANTS:

Use consonants as they are commonly pronounced, with the following exceptions:

S for soft C (city)
K for hard C (canal)
Z for hard S (disease)
G for hard G (grape)
J for soft G (gentle)
SH for soft CH (machine)
CH for hard CH or TCH (channel)

VOWELS:

AY (hate)
A (bat)
AH (father)
AW (awful)
AI (hair)
EE (retreat)
EH (bed)
EYE or Y (file)
IH (pretty)
OH (wrote)
OI (foil)
OO (tool)
OU (ground)
U (foot)
UH (putt)

An acceptable alternative to this phonetic guide is to use a common rhyme with a word, such as *James Rwytt ((sounds like "write")).* Generally, pronouncers are written following the word. Enclose them in double parentheses to prevent any confusion for the broadcaster reading your release and mistaking the pronouncer for part of the text. Write each syllable separately, connected by a hyphen. Use all-capital letters for the accented syllable. Don't use accent marks such as you might find in a dictionary. Likewise, don't underline or boldface the accented syllables.

> The Xiniel ((ZIN-ee-uhl)) Corporation of Java ((JAY-vuh)), New York, will host a Special Olympics competition next Wednesday at its headquarters on Pzrybsko ((PRIB-skoh)) Drive. State Senator Meiko Takai ((MAY-koh tah-KEYE)) will present trophies to each participating athlete.

The key to writing effective pronouncers is to use such simple and basic spellings that it becomes virtually impossible to mispronounce the word. Public relations writers find that pronunciation guides can be useful in various situations, especially when they are dealing with names of people or places.

Personal Names. Pronouncers are helpful with people's names. Many names have spellings that are not easy to pronounce. This is becoming more common as words from a variety of ethnic heritages are becoming popular and prominent. Careful public relations writers can help broadcast reporters pronounce these names accurately. Even the print media sometimes use pronouncers, as a metropolitan newspaper did when Edmund Przybyszewski was one of two winners of a $4.5 million state lottery. The paper told its readers that the name was pronounced SHIB-uh-CHEV-skee (probably not the pronunciation most readers would have come up with on their own). And many readers of newspapers and magazines had trouble when they encountered the name of the president of Iran, Mahmoud Ahmadinejad. Various print media have different rules for spelling names originally written in a non-Western alphabet. But the pronouncer can make things simpler: ((mah-MOOD ah-mah-dih-nee-ZHAHD)). Likewise, the senior senator from Hawaii, Daniel Inouye ((ee-NOH-way)), Venezuela's President Hugo Chavez ((OO-goh CHAH-vehs)), Ireland's President Mary McAleese ((MAH-ree MACK-uh-lees)). You'll find additional help at names.voa.gov, the Web site of the government-operated Voice of America radio network.

Place Names. Names of places often need pronunciation guides. In most parts of the United States and Canada, Native American words are frequently used in the names of rivers and lakes, towns and cities. In the Southwest and Southeast, Spanish place names also are common. French names are common in Louisiana, New England and elsewhere. Some of these names are so well known that they require no pronunciation guide. Public relations writers can presume that broadcasters will be able to properly pronounce Cincinnati, Dakota, Santa Fe and Massachusetts. But help is appropriate for some of California's offerings: Port Hueneme ((why-NEE-mee)), Marin ((mair-IN)), and Yucaipa ((you-KEYE-puh)). Or Pennsylvania's Monongahela ((muh-NON-guh-HEE-luh)) and Susquehanna ((suhs-kwuh-HAN-uh)) Rivers.

Some place names have regional pronunciations that are different from what might be expected. For example, the towns and villages of Berlin in a dozen states all pronounce their name as BUHR-lin. Or consider Buena Vista; it's pronounced BWAY-nuh Vista in California but BYOO-nuh Vista in Georgia, West Virginia, Colorado and Iowa.

Pronouncers also are often required for foreign place names. Consider how difficult it is to pronounce the following cities without the help of a pronunciation guide: the capital of North Korea, Pyongyang ((pee-young-YAHNG)); Japan's sacred shrine of Ise ((EE-say)); or the capital of Burkina Faso, Ouagadougou ((WAHG-uh-doo-goo)).

Exercise 8.3—Writing Pronouncers

Write pronouncers for the following words. If you are uncertain of the proper pronunciation, consult a dictionary, gazetteer, encyclopedia or pronunciation guidebook. Answers are listed at the end of this chapter.

Cairo (Ga.)	Pulaski (Ky.)
Coeur d'Alene (Idaho)	Pulaski (N.Y.)
Ethete (Wyo.)	Raquette Lake (N.Y.)
Lodi (Calif.)	Regina (Saskatchewan)
Louisville (Ky.)	Sacajaewea Peak (Ore.)
Louisville (Ala.)	St. Regis River (N.Y.)
Massillon (Ohio)	Trois Pistoles (Quebec)
Ocoee (Fla.)	Willammette River (Ore.)
Otsego (Mich.)	Worcester (Mass.)
Penetanguishene (Ontario)	Worcester (N.Y.)
Piscataquis River (Maine)	

Types of Broadcast Releases

As technology offers increasing prospects for packaging and transmitting messages, public relations practitioners have been quick to take advantage of the new opportunities. Actuality releases, audio and video news releases, B-rolls and new multimedia news releases are among the tools that public relations writers use when they wish to communicate with various publics.

Actuality Release

More sophisticated than the regular news release sent to the broadcast media is an *actuality release.* This is a news release that includes not only printed information but also a brief video- or audiotaped quote for use by the broadcast media. The recorded portion of the actuality is known as a *sound bite.* Increasingly, public relations writers are sending printed news releases to broadcast stations, in which they invite reporters to obtain recorded actualities from the organization's Web site or from a special telephone source.

The actuality release begins like any other broadcast release, with an appropriate lead (generally a soft lead). This is followed by one or several paragraphs of additional newsworthy information.

Then the writer uses a *lead-in* to provide the context of the actuality and the sound bite itself, used perhaps to give a benefit statement. This signal is sometimes called a *throw*, because it figuratively throws the report to another voice. The lead-in provides the transition from the reporter to the voice on tape. It also explains the context for the upcoming quote. One thing a lead-in should not do is steal the thunder from the upcoming quote. The lead-in must use different words and phrases than the listener will hear in the sound bite. It's best if the lead-in simply provides some background and signals that a taped voice is coming.

The *actuality* itself is the video- or audiotaped segment in which a person involved in the story presents first-hand information. *Factual actualities* offer eyewitness reports or explanations by experts. *Opinion actualities* give comments with an organization's viewpoints.

Actualities create a more interesting broadcast report, a plus for the journalist. They also help organizations by providing a richer message that includes not only the words but also the tone and emotion of the speaker, giving audiences a more realistic experience of the organization's message. A public relations writer preparing an actuality must carefully select a quote that meets two criteria: It is newsworthy enough to warrant its use by the media, and it is strategic enough to extend or support the organization's message.

In the release, the actuality should be clearly indicated, and the text of the relevant quote (or audio portion of a video segment) should be included. In typing the release, make the actuality look different from the rest of the release. The most common treatment is to type the actuality text in single spacing, with both right- and left-hand indents. Also indicate the length of the actuality, calculated in seconds.

Public relations writers give radio reporters a written news release with actualities presented on cassette tape or as a digital download file. The technology for producing taped actualities is relatively inexpensive. A high-quality recorder and a good unidirectional microphone are all the equipment needed.

For television reporters, public relations writers often accompany written news releases with *video B-rolls*, unedited videotaped pieces relevant to the story being presented. With technology bringing down the cost of broadcast-quality video cameras, many organizations are able to shoot their own footage. This can be a big advantage to television news teams, which are often short-staffed, especially when the newsworthy situation is in a location that is not easily accessible.

In preparing the actuality, the public relations writer acts as a reporter gathering news—interviewing people and recording presentations. With the tapes edited to feature a couple of brief sound bites, the writer weaves these into a news release. The actualities serve the same purpose as a quote in a news release for print media. Exhibit 8.1 shows how a broadcast release might use an actuality.

Exhibit 8.1—ACTUALITY RELEASE   Note how the actuality is presented in this release for the radio media. The sound bite is clearly indicated.

Pleasantville Academy

One Academy Place
Pleasantville, Any State, 12345

Moira McKinney
Public Information Officer
(123) 456-7890 ext. 111

March 23, 2007
FOR IMMEDIATE RELEASE

Because local college students are sharing their lunch money, Rwandan orphans will find a home off the streets.

For about two months, students at both Pleasantville Technical Institute and Tri-County Community College have been giving part of their lunch money to an Orphan's Fund destined for Rwanda. The students collected more than 15 thousand dollars for an African doctor who runs several orphanages in the capital city of Kigali.

Professor Raymond Ramashekhara ((ruh-MAH-shuh-KAH-ruh)) is a native of Rwanda and head of Pleasantville Tech's International Studies program. Last week, he carried the money to Doctor Luke Balyasindu ((BAH-lee-uh-SIN-doo)), who has received the Pan-African Peace Medal for his work with orphans and homeless people.

Doctor Luke tells how he will use the donation.

(SOUND BITE . . . 15 SECONDS)
We appreciate the generosity of the young people of Pleasantville, America. We will use your gift to provide a home for children who now live in the gutters. Through you, we will reflect the hope that they can grow up to be healthy and hard-working members of this nation, which itself has much hope for the future.

Doctor Luke says his new orphanage will house about 150 boys. Because of local custom, orphaned girls usually are cared for by relatives.

This isn't the first time the local colleges have joined to support worthy causes. They previously raised money for a school in Afghanistan and a clinic in Mexico.

Professor Ramashekhara and officials at both schools have praised the generosity of the local students. The professor says Pleasantville students prove that young Americans do care about the world around them, and he encourages other organizations to tap into the humanitarianism of young people.

Anyone wishing to contact Professor Ramashekhara can reach him at Pleasantville Tech.

#####

Exercise 8.4—Writing an Actuality Release for Radio

You are a public relations writer for your state chapter of the Association for Cancer Education and Prevention. Prepare a planning sheet and write an actuality release for radio stations. Base your release on the following information:

- ACEP is beginning a cancer-awareness campaign directed to college and university students in your part of the state. It is working with health centers at area schools and with local or regional organizations such as the Medical Society, the Guild of Nurses, and the Association of Health Educators.

- Underlying your release are the specific objectives of this campaign—to increase awareness among the key publics of issues related to breast cancer and testicular cancer, to create positive attitudes in young adults toward treating these diseases seriously, and to have young adults develop the habit of regular self-examination.

- The actuality releases will be distributed to commercial and campus radio stations serving your target publics. Identify the appropriate geographic area for distributing this release. The program will begin in one month, with an information rally at each campus and distribution of printed materials through the health centers. It will also be promoted through relevant courses in personal or public health, biology, and medicine.

- You, as public relations director for ACEP, are free to develop specific details related to this campaign. Enumerate the number of colleges or universities and the estimated total number of students affected by this regional campaign. Research the topic by obtaining information from general Web sites such as the American Cancer Society (cancer.org) or the National Cancer Institute (cancer.gov) or from specialized sites such as Testicular Cancer Online (tc-cancer.com), the Testicular Cancer Research Center (tcrc.acor.org), Breast Cancer Online (breastcancer.org) or the Susan G. Komen Breast Cancer Foundation (komen.org).

- Develop a quote appropriate to your key public. Use two or three sentences of this as an actuality, which would be provided as an audio cassette accompanying your news release.

Audio News Release

An extension of the actuality release is an *audio news release*, sometimes called a *radio news release*. Instead of a written release accompanied by a taped actuality, the ANR is packaged as a finished news segment providing both the announcer and the sound bite.

As ready-for-broadcast pieces, these packages can be dropped into a radio station's broadcast schedule. This is an appealing resource for short-staffed radio news teams. A study by Medialink, a company that produces and distributes ANRs, found that 84 percent of U.S. radio stations use ANRs, with most preferring a local angle. Another study by News/Broadcast Network found that 15 percent of radio stations use ANRs provided by satellite feed. The most common format is a 60-second spot aimed at morning drive-time audiences.

VNR-1 Communications of Arlington, Texas (vnr1.com), a company that produces a variety of electronic news releases, calls audio news releases "pound for pound the most cost-effective form of broadcast public relations." The company reports in its study that 83 percent of radio stations use ANRs, with 34 percent saying that printed materials accompanying the broadcast releases are used by radio news departments to localize the story. The company advises clients to have a local or regional tie-in and to use experts who are topical and easily understood. It also advises the time-proven caution: Avoid one-sided self-promotional pieces.

ANRs can be produced by public relations staffs with a modest amount of equipment: broadcast-quality recorders, microphones and a simple audio mixer are the main requirements. Additionally, several companies specialize in the production of audio news releases. Many of these companies not only produce the ANR but also make contact with news directors, sometimes making the news package available as an Internet download or feeding it via telephone to radio stations interested in broadcasting the piece.

Video News Release

Another communication vehicle for the public relations practitioner is the *video news release*, popularly called a VNR. This is a packaged public relations release for television. It includes a fully produced segment that can be dropped into a news report, including voice-overs by an announcer. It may also include a partly produced segment that can be dropped into a news report, with a local announcer reading from the script that accompanies the VNR and doing his or her own voice-overs.

When video news releases became popular in the 1980s, they were used mainly for product introductions. This marketing function made them suspect by many news people. Today, however, VNRs have many public relations purposes. Companies use them to deal in crisis situations, such as Pepsi-Cola's distribution of VNRs during its fight against a product-tampering hoax. Nonprofit organizations, meanwhile, use them to explain their work and support their cause, such as those produced by Mothers Against Drunk Driving or the Muscular Dystrophy Association.

Many smaller television stations and some larger ones use VNRs regularly. Nielsen Media Research reported that three out of four television stations use VNRs weekly. The practice is becoming more frequent as understaffed television news teams find they can rely on VNRs to provide them with accurate and honest video presentations. Additionally, VNRs can help stations fill the expanding news holes created by news segments on morning shows, Internet coverage, and early, midday and late news programming.

Television news operations are looking for new sources of information. The increasing use of VNRs parallels the use of nonlocal news feeds by underfinanced news programs. For example, the Project for Excellence in Journalism reported that material fed from and through television networks nearly doubled between 1998 and 2002, while reports by local correspondents fell from 62 to 43 percent. Many of the largest corporate feeders, such as CNN News and Fox News, pass along VNRs to their local affiliates.

Some broadcasters are concerned about the ethics of using video news releases, particularly when stations fail to let their viewers know that the footage has been provided as a public relations service; see the accompanying box, "FYI—Ethical Aspects of Video News Releases." Others are critical of the production quality, lack of local angles, and lack of subtlety with which some VNRs pitch a product or cause. Indeed, the two most common reasons for rejecting footage from public relations sources is that it isn't local or it is too commercial. So when broadcasters complain that some VNRs look like the handiwork of advertisers, public relations writers should listen.

Successful producers identify several criteria for VNRs: a strong current news peg, footage not otherwise available to news stations, concise and strategic interviews, and good supporting video. They also give witness to the fact that professional and newsworthy VNRs are used by television stations.

FYI   *Ethical Aspects of Video News Releases*

Most television stations use video news releases produced by corporations, nonprofit organizations and government agencies. Radio stations use similar audio materials. Nielsen Media Research reports that nearly all American television stations use at least some VNRs. Morning and early evening newscasts are the more likely times for this use. B-rolls are more likely to be aired than fully packaged VNRs. Various studies show that television stations seldom use fully packaged VNRs and instead edit information from B-rolls.

Public relations people liken B-rolls and both audio and video news releases to print releases, a time-honored way to provide information about the organizations in a format that newspapers can drop into their pages. ANRs and VNRs provide the same useful assistance to radio and television stations. B-rolls as well as audio and video releases are part of what sometimes is called *information subsidies*, newsworthy information packaged in a variety of formats that are provided to the media by public relations practitioners. Practically speaking, the media seem to welcome them, and those releases and other materials that are newsworthy and balanced and that serve audience interests sometimes get used.

But the issues surrounding such information subsidies have raised important ethical questions worth exploring here.

A 2004 statement by the Public Relations Society of America identifies three principals: (1) A VNR is the television equivalent of a press release and, as such, should always be truthful and represent the highest in ethical standards. (2) Producers and distributors of VNRs and the organizations they represent should clearly and plainly identify themselves. (3) Television stations airing VNRs should identify sources of the material. Ethical standards of the Radio-Television News Directors Association, meanwhile, similarly call for stations to inform their audiences about VNRs, when one is used and who produced it.

Additionally, the government has something to say about VNRs and related public relations materials. The Food and Drug Administration, for example, has special rules for VNRs dealing with medical topics. Both electronic news packages and unedited B-rolls must provide "fair balance," and the Federal Communication Commission requires that ANRs and VNRs tell viewers about risks and side effects and provide clear information about limitations of the drug. It also requires that information about recommended dosages be provided to journalists (though it cannot require journalists to use such details).

Meanwhile, the FCC has investigated the use of VNRs. In 2005, it told broadcasters to clearly identify the source of political or controversial material or information they are paid to air. And in the wake of disclosure that the Department of Health and Human Services produced VNRs and paid newspaper columnists and television commentators to support the White House plan for Medicare, the Government Accountability Office labeled the VNRs illegal government-funded "covert propaganda" and said the Bush White House had violated the law. Some members of Congress have taken up the issue, which may lead to stricter guidelines on the role that the federal government may play in such matters.

This is all part of the growing concern about *secured placement* of VNRs and *branded journalism*, both euphemisms for the practice of paying stations to run the pieces. The use of paid placements, particularly in newscasts and without identification, violates both the guidelines of public relations and journalistic ethical guidelines. Revelations in 2006 that the U.S. Defense Department was covertly paying Iraqi newspaper editors and reporters to print pro-U.S. stories caused a firestorm of ridicule and criticism against the Bush administration, which was left to defend a practice that violates journalistic practice and ethical principals.

But clearly there are ethical questions. Should news organizations use information supplied by public relations sources? Should audiences be told when such outside-produced footage is being used? Should the government step in to require disclosure of the use of

VNRs and ANRs? The answers for this book are "yes," "yes," and "probably not a good idea."

Yes, radio and television news departments should be able to use footage and material provided by public relations sources—if they want to. It should be their choice, the same as print reporters whether to use print news releases.

Yes, the media should disclose to its audiences when VNRs and ANRs are used. It goes to the credibility of their reporting, and public relations producers of VNRs should facilitate this disclosure. In the lead-in to the piece, notice can be given that footage (in the case of B-rolls), the actuality (for radio sound bites), or the entire report (for VNRs and ANRs) is provided courtesy of such-and-such company, organization or agency. Or an on-screen note about the origin of the footage may be provided. It remains the media's decision on how, or even if, to use the disclosure.

And finally, it doesn't seem necessary for the FCC to establish another set of regulations. Enforcement of existing regulations and a stronger sense of professional accountability to both publics and media audiences may be the answer.

Recently, blogs have raised questions about VNRs. The topic also is part of the standard fare for the Center for Media and Democracy, a group critical of most things concerning the public relations. According to its Web site (prwatch.org), the center "strengthens participatory democracy by investigating and exposing public relations spin and propaganda." In 2006, it released a study based on a very small sample (less than 1 percent of VNRs used by television stations) and concluded that all video news releases and satellite media tours are propagandistic and "fake news," a term similarly used by TV Guide in condemning the media's use of materials provided by public relations. The center urged the FCC to require disclosure about VNRs, specifically asking for a continuous on-screen notice such as "Footage provided by X" for both VNRs and B-rolls.

Though critics sometimes overreach when they see public relations as pernicious propaganda lurking around every corner, they do address the same legitimate questions that responsible members of the profession also are addressing. Embarrassing activities sometimes are done in the name of public relations, often by political and corporate operatives with little connection to the public relations profession. Public relations professionals are among the first to acknowledge when excesses occur or when ethical principals are violated. Thus when the White House or Congress uses taxpayer-funded VNRs, particularly for partisan purposes, a red flag should go up among public relations professionals. So, too, when the military uses public money to buy media placements, and when private corporations provide VNRs that mask the corporate sponsor.

Organizations also can extend the life of VNRs by posting them at their Web sites. It is accessible there not only to people already familiar with the organization and its Web site but also to information seekers who find the site through a search engine or linked news portal.

The difficulty many broadcast journalists have with video news releases is that they are virtually impossible to edit. As video packages, they are under the control of the public relations person who has produced them, which is why some journalists hesitate to use them. The most effective way to write a video news release is to provide enough flexibility so reporters can edit the release to fit the needs of the local television station. Often this means providing more than one version or some variation within the package. That is where B-rolls come in handy.

Providing flexibility for the news media to edit VNRs does not mean giving broadcast journalists only bland reports with little value to the organization that produces them. VNRs can be both subtle and persuasive. The task before the writer is to weave in pertinent information about the product, service or idea in such a way that it doesn't need to be edited out. Save the outright promotion for the advertising team, whose job it is to aggressively push the message. Your job as a public relations writer is to assist the news media in presenting an interesting and informative story that serves both their interests and yours.

What topics are useful for video news releases? Much of the general advice about generating news for an organization works with VNRs. Look for tie-ins with current issues, events and activities. News directors say VNRs that deal with business, consumer affairs and the economy get their attention, because those topics are of continuing interest to their audiences. Attention also is given to VNRs that deal with new technologies and medical research, as well as pieces strong in human interest. "Tips for Better Writing: Improving Chances a VNR Will Be Used" provides further advice for writing successful VNRs.

Tips for Better Writing   *Improving Chances a VNR Will Be Used*

Public relations writers can do several things to increase their chances that broadcasters will decide to use video news releases. Here are several ways to make a VNR more acceptable to reporters.

1. *Focus on the news value* of the information in the VNR. The piece should look and feel like news, because it should really *be* news. Keep the piece simple, resembling reports you see on the evening news instead of looking like a Hollywood production with dramatic lighting and special effects.

2. *Be clear that this is a news piece produced on behalf of the sponsoring organization*, which should be identified subtly and without promotionalism.

3. *Highlight the local content* of the VNR or help the broadcaster develop a local angle. For example, provide a list of local branches of the organization, area agencies dealing with the issue or local experts who might be used in interviews.

4. *Keep the piece short.* Between one and two minutes is best; longer than that, and your changes of having the piece air are very low. You might edit the VNR for several different lengths.

5. *Make the piece easy for the station to edit.* Keep the natural sound on a separate audio channel from your announcer so the station can edit in its own announcer with ease.

6. *Include a written advisory* to indicate the news value of the VNR and the unique aspects of the visuals. Include a brief fact sheet about the topic and a short biographical sketch about key people who appear in the VNR, as well as pronunciation guides for names.

7. *Include a script and a description of the B-rolls* featured in the VNR package. News directors often decide about using VNRs based on what they read in the advisory and script.

8. *Provide a point of contact* where reporters and editors can obtain additional information.

Exercise 8.5—Writing a Video News Release

You are public relations writer for the national office of RiverGuard, an environmental action group that lobbies federal, state and local government and advocates with the media and the public for strong laws and enforcement to reduce pollution in lakes, rivers and streams. Your headquarters are in Chicago. You are preparing a video news release for release in states that are affected by acid rain.

Part 1: Using environmental resources, identify states and regions affected by the problem of acid rain. Using media resources, identify the television markets in one of these areas.

Part 2: Identify at least six B-roll segments that could be used with the VNR.

Part 3: Write a basic outline or script for a VNR.

Part 4: Write a cover letter for television news directors in a single television market within one of the areas affected by acid rain. In this letter, highlight the newsworthiness of your VNR to station viewers, indicate that some of the footage is not available elsewhere, and suggest ways television stations might localize the VNR. ∎

B-Roll Packages

To accommodate reporters' concern for control over the news segment as it ultimately reaches the audience, public relations practitioners often provide *B-roll packages*. Unlike the actuality release, a B-roll package does not include a written news story. Rather, it provides background information through a series of different pieces of video footage. Unlike the video news release, the B-roll package remains unedited, providing a more flexible resource for the television journalist.

Despite reports that most television stations use VNRs, few use them as full packages. Most opt for the B-roll sound bites. In fact, that was all Pepsi-Cola provided for its announcement of a new policy on freshness dating on cans, which was used in 53 markets and was seen by 34 million viewers. On another occasion when it was fighting a hoax about product tampering, Pepsi produced two B-roll packages. One on the company's bottling process was seen by a reported 182 million viewers; the other showing someone tampering with a Pepsi can was seen by 95 million viewers. Surveys and interviews with station directors point to a common theme—broadcast reporters prefer B-rolls, which give the journalists access to information without giving up control over how that information is presented to their audiences.

Whereas fully produced VNRs can cost about $20,000, B-rolls are much less expensive. Both versions may be distributed to television stations on videocassettes, although increasingly they are being distributed via satellite. Some organizations have put VNRs and B-roll footage on Web sites so TV news directors can preview and download them. "Advice from a Pro: Tony Perri on Using B-Roll Packages" offers further tips.

Advice from a Pro   *Tony Perri on Using B-Roll Packages*

Executive producer Tony Perri recommends that organizations with newsworthy events present them to the media using B-rolls and natural sound rather than as a prepackaged VNR. Perri recommends including background footage, interviews and sound bites in the B-rolls.

Tony is president of Perri Productions, a video news service that is part of his Boulder Production Company (boulderproductioncompany.com) in Boulder, Colo. He has several other suggestions for increasing the likelihood that television news reporters will use footage supplied by public relations practitioners:

- Focus on lively feature-oriented stories.
- Use anecdotes to humanize the story.
- Keep the package short, because the stories will be given less than two minutes of air time.
- Avoid a strong marketing approach with a heavy emphasis on the organization or especially on its product or service. Remember that the value to reporters is that the footage presents news, not advertising.

As for production matters, Perri recommends not mixing voice-overs and sound bites but instead keeping each on a separate audio channel so local television stations can use their own announcers for voice-overs.

Multimedia News Release

The latest entry into the field of broadcast-style releases is called the *multimedia news release*. MNRs are packages that rework VNRs, B-rolls and related productions. This information can be customized and sent to key audiences, usually people already connected with the organization and/or who have asked to be kept informed about new developments.

MNRs not only can repackage and enhance information in VNRs, they also can offer links to Web sites, video FAQs, and extended or related interviews. MNRs can be disseminated through organizational Web sites, via e-mail, or on CD or DVD. They sometimes are distributed through specialized cable networks or through in-house video systems such as are found in hospitals and college dorms.

Nonbroadcast Video

Internet news releases are among the newest developments for public relations writing. Also called INRs, these are adaptations of the VNR. The difference is that the INR takes advantages of improvements in computer and video technology, such as the ability to incorporate streaming video into a Web site. Within a written news release, the viewer can download video images and audio bites. Public relations practitioners can use INRs proactively by sending journalists e-mail notices with links to the INR. They also can place the INRs at the organization's Web site for customers and others who visit the site.

A related public relations tool is a *webcast*, which is similar to a broadcast video but currently without the high quality and high-speed transmission of broadcast. Webcasts, whether live or prerecorded, are not sent to viewers. Rather, potential viewers are notified, usually by e-mail, and invited to view the webcast on the organization's Web site.

Beyond broadcast TV, *cable television* has opened up an entire new field for organizational videos. Programming opportunities in cable often make it possible for companies and nonprofit organizations to distribute not only short news segments but also entire programs. Some of these are produced professionally and distributed nationally, such as programs by educational, social service and religious organizations. Local productions often are produced at the cable company studios. Others are produced at in-house studios set up by businesses and nonprofit organizations or in the growing number of independent production centers available to organizations.

Video teleconferencing and *satellite media tours* also provide advantages for public relations practitioners. Organizations can purchase satellite time to distribute either a live presentation or a prerecorded video presentation as a kind of backgrounder. This is followed by live interaction between the audience and the presenter (in the case of a video teleconference) or by individual satellite-mediated interviews with journalists (in a satellite media tour). Writers involved in these situations help to prepare the background piece, and they often help to prepare participants for the interview.

Organizational video offers many opportunities to help organizations communicate with various publics. For example, colleges and universities produce video tours of their campuses for potential students. Hospitals make instructional videos both for patients and for staff. Nonprofit organizations use videos in fundraising campaigns with donors or to gain support for new programs. On the business side, corporations use video presentations to introduce new products and services to salespeople as well as customers.

Organizations can set up in-house post-production studios or editing facilities with relatively modest financial investments. Many companies and large nonprofit organizations have full-service corporate video centers. In some communities, networks of video production services have been set up by libraries, educational institutions, and other nonprofit organizations. All of these opportunities for organizational video call for the services of public relations writers familiar with both television production and instructional or promotional writing.

Answers to Chapter Exercises
Exercise 8.1

1. Rewards are in store for some Acme employees who completed the project ahead of schedule. President Gail Palecki will give a performance bonus to seven members of her management team.
2. City Council approved 5-to-1 a new budget of nearly two million dollars. That means an average 14-dollar increase in property taxes for every homeowner.
3. At age 32, the new director is the youngest person ever to serve on the corporate leadership team.
4. The L-P-G-A contender will be the main speaker at a Scholar-Athlete Recognition Luncheon.
5. Only nine percent of the funding will come from the federal government. Most of the budget will come from the state, county and local municipalities.
6. A tax-assessor candidate in the Town of Armstrong wants to hear from the voters. Robert Jones, a Democrat, says he will hold a public forum for taxpayer input.
7. Madison County school superintendent Janice Harrison says it's inappropriate to make comparisons with school districts in other states.
8. Corporate treasurer June Dellivan said the company expects investors to earn high dividends.
9. Miriam Johansen is a kindergarten teacher at Elmwood Elementary, where she observes a lot of young children. And she's critical of the amount of time they spend in front of TV and video games. She called these zombielike mind killers.

Exercise 8.3

Cairo ((KAY-roh))
Coeur d'Alene ((KOOR duh-LAYN))
Ethete ((EE-thuh-tee))
Lodi ((LOH-deye))
Louisville (Ky.) ((LOO-ee-vilh))
Louisville (Ala.) ((LOO-iss-vihl))
Massillon ((MASS-ih-lahn))
Ocoee ((oh-KOH-ee))
Otsego ((aht-SEE-goh))
Penetanguishene ((pehn-uh-tang-guh-SHEEN))
Piscataquis River ((pis-KAT-uh-kwis))

Pulaski (Ky.) ((puh-LASS-keye))
Pulaski (N.Y.) ((puh-LASS-kee))
Raquette Lake ((RACK-it))
Regina ((ruh-JEYE-nuh))
Sacajaewea Peak ((sak-uh-juh-WEE-uh))
St. Regis River ((REE-jis))
Trois Pistoles (Quebec)
   ((twah pee-STOHL))
Willammette ((wuh-LAM-et))
Worcester (Mass.) ((WUH-stuhr))
Worcester (N.Y.) ((WOO-stuhr))

9

Organizational Features

Feature writing is closely related to news writing. Related, but not the same. If news involves the hard-edged reports about fires and floods, trials and political scandals, then features are the reports that go behind the news and beyond it. They focus on the history of the building destroyed by fire, the plight of the families displaced by a flood, the heroism of paramedics. Features outline the development of the legal premise on which a trial revolves, and they call attention to the people whose lives are turned inside out by a political scandal. Hard news is the who, what, when and where. Features are the how and why.

News reports and feature stories complement each other. They round out the information and provide audiences with a fuller understanding than either writing style alone might do. At the same time, features provide a growing opportunity for public relations writers, because the mainstream news media are using less and less hard news and more feature material.

Public relations writers have found many opportunities to use features on behalf of their organizations and their clients. This chapter will introduce you to some of these opportunities, namely as they relate to features about people, organizations and issues. Here are your objectives for this chapter:

- To develop a proficiency with feature-style writing
- To show an understanding of the role feature writing plays in public relations
- To prepare and write features about people (such as biographical narratives, profiles and interviews)
- To prepare and write features about organizations (histories, profiles and back-grounders)
- To prepare and write features about issues (how-to articles, Q&As, case histories and information digests).

Features and Public Relations Writers

Public relations writers often find that they have opportunities to prepare feature releases rather than news releases. Each offers benefits and limitations. Each calls for different skills from the writer. As with any type of public relations writing, let your planning lead you to a particular format. Use the planning sheet. Identify your key publics and analyze their wants, interests and needs. Determine your objectives as they relate to the key publics. Then, if your planning and research lead you to conclude that a feature article would be an appropriate way to reach your objectives, begin to tackle the project.

Realize that each type of feature has particular strengths as well as some limitations. On the minus side, features are time consuming to write, and they may not be what an editor is seeking. But when they are appropriate, features offer the organization an opportunity to present its message in more depth, with more soul, and often with a greater level of reader interest than a news release, advisory or other tool of media relations. Also, feature articles have a role in other areas of public relations, such as with internal magazines, newsletters and similar publications, and with Web sites and other online opportunities.

Certain writing conventions are associated with features. Feature writing, for example, is not restricted to the inverted pyramid format. Instead, the writer has more flexibility in choosing a style that fits the particular topic. A biography or an organizational history may be chronological, for example, whereas a service article may present a start-to-finish series of action steps. But because effective features are less time bound in their approach, public relations writers like them. The story is written to allow its use next week, next month or the next time there is a news peg to give it relevance.

Perhaps the defining characteristic of feature writing is its use of what writers and editors call *color*. Color is information that makes the story come alive. It is an apt analogy or a particularly well-phrased metaphor, a revealing quote or an insightful narration. It is the level of description that helps readers "see" the event for themselves without the writer needing to interpret the event for them. Color goes beyond the basic story. Consider the following two passages about a boy and a dog. The first is a straightforward sentence, the kind that might be used in a news release. The second is a much more colorful version, which might be used in a feature story.

Version 1
The boy called his dog, which came running.

Version 2
"Come," said the oldest boy, a trace of apprehension in his voice. The three children waited in suspense. Then the youngest gave a cry of glee as the Dalmatian turned and bounded across the meadow toward them, leaping the few remaining mounds of late winter snow. For all its inexhaustible enthusiasm, the puppy was learning—finally—the training commands that the boys had practiced so faithfully.

All releases that result in published reports offer a follow-up opportunity, but none so much as the published feature article. *Feature reprints* can extend the life of the article and offer many secondary public relations uses over a considerable length of time. After an article has been printed, public relations practitioners often ask permission from the publication to reprint the article. These reprints are then distributed to important publics—especially consumers, producers and enablers.

Such reprints should be kept simple: the publication logo, publication date, and the article, perhaps with a contact address, phone number, and/or Web address for your organization. Don't dilute the value of the third-party endorsement of the article by repackaging it to look like a promotional piece orchestrated by your organization. Get permission from the publisher if you plan to use reprints beyond a small distribution within the organization.

Exercise 9.1—Freewriting about Features

Freewrite for five minutes on the following topic: *What is the role of feature writing in the practice of public relations?* Then discuss it with your classmates. ■

Writing about People

Much of what we write in the feature style will be about people involved with our organizations: managers and other bosses, guests and dignitaries, award winners, newcomers. Three different kinds of writing approaches lend themselves to writing about people. These are biographical narratives, personal profiles and personal interviews. Let's look at each type.

Biographical Narrative

Public relations writers often find it beneficial to prepare information about people important to an organization, cause or event. The most common way of presenting this information is in a *biographical narrative*, a straightforward account of a person's work history, accomplishments, education and so on. Biographical narratives serve the same purpose that file obituaries serve with news agencies and media organizations: They provide information that can be useful as supplements to news releases, advance information for speaking engagements, background for awards presentations and event fliers. Much of the factual basis for written biographies can be found in the bio sheets that most public relations offices keep on file.

A biographical narrative can be especially useful in presenting background information about a person involved in a news-related activity, such as with news releases about an upcoming speaker, a person hired by or promoted within an organization, or someone selected to lead an important activity or to receive a noteworthy honor. These narratives are often brief factual accounts. Some narratives are a chronological presentation of the person's accomplishments; others are sectionalized presentations dealing with significant aspects of the person's life, for example professional accomplishments, educational achievements, and family background. Exhibit 9.1 is an example of a narrative biography. Note that is provides essentially the same kind of information as the personal appointment news release outlined in Chapter 6, minus the news announcement.

Exhibit 9.1—BIOGRAPHICAL NARRATIVE   This hypothetical biographical narrative could be used as a sidebar story, or it could become part of a news release about the subject.

Epiphany Taylor—Biographical Sketch

Epiphany Taylor is the author of three award-winning books. *Unrelenting Pain* received the 1994 Elizabeth Gumme Award from the Midwestern Coalition Against Domestic Violence. *Lay the Blame Softly* was cited by the Library Association of the Southwest as the 1998 Best Read in the self-help category. *The Secret of the Enchanted Tulip* received the 2005 Alyssa Award for Children's Literature. Taylor currently is editing a book of poetry due to be published next January.

Prior to her career as a novelist, Taylor served as public education director for the Southwestern Alliance Against Domestic Violence. Her work received awards from the National Alliance Against Domestic Violence and the Public Relations Association of the Southwest.

She also worked as a reporter with the Deansville (Ariz.) Bugle. She received the 1988 award for investigative reporting from the Arizona Journalism Association and a citation from the Southwest Civil Rights League.

Taylor is a 1980 graduate of Oakview University, where she received a bachelor of arts degree in communication arts.

Personal Profile

A *personal profile* goes beyond the biographical narrative and provides information about a person, often an established figure such as a celebrity or an organizational executive, where interest lies more in the personality rather than in particular accomplishments. Whereas biographical narratives often are based on information provided by the person you are writing about, profiles are more likely to focus on what other people say about the subject. Half a dozen personal reminiscences might lay the foundation for a profile.

During the research stage of writing, the writer will identify likely information sources and develop probing questions to ask about the person being profiled. For example, suppose you were assigned to develop a personal profile about a professor at your college or university. Let's call him Gregor Alexander, a foreign-language professor who is receiving a President's Award for Distinguished Teaching. This could be a preliminary research program for your profile:

- First, you could interview some of his students: What is Dr. Alexander like in the classroom? What can you tell me about how he related to students? How has he helped you? What do you hear other students saying about Dr. Alexander?
- Next, you might interview some of the professor's colleagues: What is it like to teach in the same department as Dr. Alexander? What do you recall about the first time you met him? In what way is he the model of an effective teacher? What do you hear your students say about Dr. Alexander?
- Finally, you might try to interview some of Dr. Alexander's former students and members of organizations in which he is active, such as the Council for International Visitors and the Association of Modern Languages.

From all of these sources, you would weave together a profile, generously sprinkled with quotes and anecdotes from people who knew him. The profile would reveal various aspects of Dr. Alexander that even people who know him in one context may not have seen before.

Exhibit 9.2—BIOGRAPHICAL PROFILE   This hypothetical biographical profile provides more insight into its subject than a narrative offers. This might be the kind of profile that the subject's college alumni magazine would prepare.

Epiphany Taylor: Her Gentle Obsession

Most people are content to pursue one career. Epiphany Taylor has found success in three.

The 1980 graduate of the Oakview University was a soul in search of expression even as a student majoring in communication arts and working on the college newspaper. "The focal decor in my dorm room was this huge poster that said 'Express Yourself,'" recalls Taylor. "That's been a gentle obsession for me."

Her first job was as a police reporter with the Deansville (Ariz.) Bugle. Her triumph there came when she was assigned to cover a local bank robbery. Through a combination of investigative skill and what she readily admits is "a generous serving of luck," the Eppie Taylor byline received national attention when she reported that the bank robber was wanted by police in seven states for bombings against civil rights activists.

A clandestine interview reporting that the stolen money was intended to finance more bombings earned for Taylor the 1988 award for investigative reporting from the Arizona Journalism Association. It also brought a citation from the Southwest Civil Rights League. The awards were nice, but Taylor wanted to make a difference in people's lives in a way she could see.

"About that time, I reconnected with an old friend who, I learned, had become a victim of abuse. Her boyfriend beat her, and she felt like she had no choice but to put up with it," recalls Taylor. So she began investigating domestic violence. With what she learned, Taylor was able to help her friend end the abusive relationship.

"It felt really good to help save her life," says Taylor. "I wanted to do it again for others." So she became public education director with the Southwestern Alliance Against Domestic Violence. For the next five years, she directed an ambitious campaign in six states.

The alliance tracked Taylor's campaign as the reason that hundreds of women were able to free themselves from abuse. Once again the awards came, this time from the National Alliance Against Domestic Violence and the Public Relations Association of the Southwest. And once again awards only revealed an unfulfilled need.

"My grandmother had left me a country cottage and a small inheritance, so I decided to become what I had always wanted to be—a writer. Not just a journalist, a writer."

That was 10 years ago. Since then, Taylor has written three novels. Two of them deal with domestic violence. *Unrelenting Pain* received the 1994 Elizabeth Gumme Award from the Midwestern Coalition Against Domestic Violence. *Lay the Blame Softly* was cited by the Library Association of the Southwest as the 1998 Best Read in the self-help category. The third novel, *The Secret of the Enchanted Tulip*, received the 2005 Alyssa Award for Children's Literature.

Taylor currently is editing *Voices in Beyond the Abyss*, a book of poetry written by victims who have reclaimed their lives after abuse.

"I still have that old dorm poster," said Taylor. "The paper is wrinkled, but the message is still fresh. As long as we're alive, we've all got to find ways to express ourselves. That's why I'm still pursuing my gentle obsession."

Exercise 9.2—Writing Biographical Pieces

Select an adult member of your family. Presume that this person has been named to receive the Mayor's Community Service Medal in the community where he or she resides.

Part 1: Using the bio sheet outlined in Chapter 5 as a model, write a biographical narrative of this person (approximately 150 words) that could be used as a sidebar to a news release sent out by the mayor's office announcing several award recipients.

Part 2: Expanding on the information in Part 1, write a personal interview (approximately 500 words) that could be used in a newsletter published by the mayor's Community Service Office. Include quotes by the award recipient. Add an element of a profile with at least one quote from a person who knows him or her.

Personal Interview

Although profiles are useful for writing about who people are and what they have accomplished, interviews often are better tools for writing about what people know. Interviews go right to the source. In a *personal interview*, the writer asks a source to comment on what has, is or will be happening and to explain what the writer already has discovered in background research. Suppose that you are the writer with a public affairs department of your college or university. You are preparing a feature story about an associate professor in the nutrition department. We'll call her Dr. Mary Catherine Spraeger.

Should you do a profile or an interview? That depends on what you want to accomplish. If your goal is to provide information about Dr. Spraeger because she is being honored as "Science Educator of the Year," then a profile probably is the better vehicle. Her students and colleagues can provide much valuable information. On the other hand, if you wish to do a story about the research Dr. Spraeger has done on traditional ethnic recipes and cholesterol-controlling diets, then an interview would be a better approach. You want information mainly from Dr. Spraeger rather than her colleagues and students.

In preparing for an interview, begin with the planning sheet. Identify the key publics and their wants, interests and needs. Identify your objectives. Most especially, identify relevant questions to ask your interview subject. Follow this with research into the subject of the interview. Read the person's biography. Review any articles or books written by or about this person. Exhibit 9.2 is an example of an interview; compare it to the biographical narrative in Exhibit 9.1.

The use of quotes is an important aspect of the interview. Public relations writers have a certain degree of freedom to work with quotes. A disordered series of sentence fragments, interspersed with *ums* and *uhs*, several *y'knows*, and a poorly placed *whatchamacallit* or

---

Tips for Better Writing   *Interview Advice*

Sir David Frost is a veteran television interviewer; some say he's the father of TV news interviews. During his long career, he interviewed six British prime ministers, seven U.S. presidents, the Beatles, Prince Charles, and dozens of other celebrities. His interview with President Richard Nixon was taped for 28¾ hours over 12 days.

In 2006 he talked with CNN about the elements of a good interview. His advice: prepare for the interview, listen, create a relationship, and help the interviewee relax.

First, said Frost, "do your homework." He and his team had spent a full year preparing for the Nixon interview.

The second thing is to listen, he said. "Well, of course, you listen, because that's the fun of it, hearing what the person is going to say and following up. That's good fun. But in America, at that time, there were lots of talk show hosts who had a lot of prepared material that they were more concerned to get to than just doing the questioning and so on."

The third point is "just striking up some relationship with the guest, particularly in a longer interviewer and so on." Frost said the relationship may not be one of mutual respect; it might be more like mutual awareness. Frost suggested that eye contact with the person you're talking to is the best way to create the relationship.

"And if you relax the person, I mean, that's the other thing," Frost concluded. "Perhaps that's point number four. But if you relax the person, then you get the individual."

thingamajig may accurately recreate the interview, but it doesn't make for good reading. Because of that, it doesn't serve the interests of the reader, the writer or the person being interviewed.

Rather than presenting an unedited transcript, an effective writer works with the raw quotes to present the interviewee's ideas in a reasonably faithful-though-edited version. It's sort of like being a speech writer. Usually, the writer will let the interviewee see the final piece with the revised quotes to make sure the meaning remains intact. Accuracy, honesty, fairness and other ethical considerations are crucial in this editing/rewriting process.

Interviews can also provide public relations writers with the opportunity to share information and insights of one person with a host of readers. This information can be presented in two ways: as a narrative feature article or as interview notes.

A *narrative feature* is a story based on interviews, drawing on the feature-writing skills of the public relations practitioner. Feature writing is an art unto itself. Students interested in developing this would be well served to take a course or study a good book focused specifically on writing features or magazine articles.

Interview notes are near-verbatim transcripts in a question-and-answer format ("near" in the sense that the transcript should be edited for grammar and for easy flow of language). This style usually begins with either a brief narrative paragraph to set the stage or a biographical sketch of the person being interviewed. These transcripts of in-depth interviews allow reporters to build their stories as they see fit. Sometimes, the interviews are conducted by public relations writers; other times, they are conducted by reporters themselves. The online information resource CyberJournalist.net calls Web sites such as that of the Department of Defense (defenselink.mic/news) "a journalist's gold mine" because the DoD archives news releases, briefings and interview transcripts that, because they are part of the public record, can be used by other journalists as well as by all interested readers.

Increasingly, magazines and newspapers also are publishing transcripts of interviews by their own reporters, and radio and television news organizations are placing audio and/or video files of full interviews on their Web sites. Often this is seen as a way for the news organizations to better serve their audiences.

Sometimes, public relations practitioners tape journalistic interviews and provide online transcripts of them. This can provide interested readers with the whole story, or its purpose may be to set the record straight after a published or aired report that the organization feels may have left an incomplete or misunderstanding of the interview. For example, Denver Archbishop Charles Chaput felt that a New York Times reporter had missed some nuanced key points in a published report following an interview with the Catholic leader about the intersection of politics and church practice. The archdiocese, which had taped the interview, presented online the full transcript of the discussion between the archbishop and the reporter.

Writing about Organizations

Histories, profiles and backgrounders do for businesses and nonprofit groups what biographies, personal profiles and interviews do for people. These are the vehicles for writing about organizations. Public relations writers often find it useful to prepare articles that will help the news media understand their organizations and report accurately on their concerns and missions. These organizational stories often are prepared as feature releases. They also may be used for Web pages and may be useful for brochures and direct-mail pieces. Let's take a look at each type of organizational feature: history, profile and backgrounder.

Organizational History

Public relations writers often want to provide information about organizations. A common way to do this is with an organizational history, which presents a narrative on the beginnings and development of the organization, which often is important for a complete understanding of what the organization does or stands for. Often, an organization will team a history with a mission statement or vision statement. Those terms often are used interchangeably, though there is a difference. A mission statement indicates the purpose that the organization perceives for itself, while a vision statement deals with what the organization hopes to achieve.

Businesses, agencies, schools, associations and other organizations each have their own unique past and special purpose. A business founded as a family enterprise that grew into a national corporation has a special story to tell. A medical charity that first focused on polio and later changed its mission when that disease was brought under control also has a story. So does the city's first hospital, founded by nuns as a three-room clinic above a saloon.

As a public relations writer, you may want to research your organization's past and put it in a form that is interesting and useful to anyone trying to understand your organization. Such background information can be very helpful in increasing support for the organization today.

Historical articles should have a factual basis that offers names, dates and other specific pieces of the past. They also should put this into a framework that helps explain the organization's current mission, the contributions and achievements it has made, the problems and opportunities it faces, and perhaps the vision it holds of the future. Like personal biographies, organizational histories may be either chronological narratives or more colorful feature articles.

Remember that brevity is important for organizational histories. Bulleting key points such as milestones and achievements is a useful technique. Exhibit 9.3 is an example of a brief yet effective organizational history, along with brief mission and vision statements. "What Would You Do?: Writing an Organizational History" asks you to consider some ethical issues that might arise in the writing of an organization's history.

What Would You Do? *Writing an Organizational History*

Organizations often have something in their past that they are embarrassed about, or at least that they are reluctant to say much about. Suppose you are public relations director for one such organization, a chapter of the YMCA that was founded during the days of racial segregation. As a consequence, your organization was known for many years as the Black Y.

You know that this was not uncommon years ago. Many communities have a variety of such organizations: a Jewish country club because Jews weren't admitted to the other country club, a Catholic fraternity because once no other fraternity would accept Catholic students, a Hispanic congregation because Spanish-speaking worshippers didn't feel welcome in another parish, and so on.

What ethical considerations would factor into your decision on how to handle such historical information about your organization, the YMCA?

How would you determine if the issue is relevant today? How would you decide if it would be considered hurtful or divisive today (and whether this would matter in your decision about using such information)?

How would you balance your commitment to your client or boss with your commitment to the truth? And is historical information subject to the same level of commitment to truth as current information?

Organizational Profile

Sometimes, the history is expanded into an organizational profile. In addition to a look back at the organization, these profiles also provide an overview of the organization's mission or purpose, its operating practices and philosophy, and its achievements. *Organizational profiles*, also called *corporate backgrounders*, sometimes are written for readers with technical experience in the field. Others, meant for readers unfamiliar with the field, are written to untangle some of the technical terms and information.

Like other feature formats, profiles allow for flexible writing styles. To find a useful format for your writing, outline the topic. For example, a profile explaining the various departments and organizational components of a large corporation might begin with a section about the executive team, followed by paragraphs on each of the departments. A profile providing information summarizing a human service agency's annual report might begin with a mission statement, operating philosophy or credo, along with a description of each of the agency's programs, including statistics on costs and services provided. Exhibit 9.3 is an organizational profile that teams with an organizational history to provide a more complete overview of the professional organization Public Relations Society of America.

Exhibit 9.3—ORGANIZATIONAL PROFILE AND HISTORY The Public Relations Society of America offers a brief organizational profile and a longer historical overview of the organization. These can be found at the organization's Web site (prsa.org).

Organizational Profile
The Public Relations Society of America, based in New York City, is the world's largest organization for public relations professionals. The Society has more than 28,000 professional and student members. PRSA is organized into 112 Chapters nationwide, 19 Professional Interest Sections, along with Affinity Groups, which represent business and industry, counseling firms, independent practitioners, military, government, associations, hospitals, schools, professional services firms and nonprofit organizations. The Public Relations Student Society of America (PRSSA) has 255 Chapters at colleges and universities throughout the United States.

Organizational Overview and History
With the vision to unify, strengthen and advance the profession of public relations, the Public Relations Society of America (PRSA) has established itself as the pre-eminent organization that builds value, demand and global understanding for public relations.

PRSA is the world's largest organization for public relations professionals. Its nearly 20,000 members, organized into 112 Chapters, represent business and industry, technology, counseling firms, government, associations, hospitals, schools, professional services firms and nonprofit organizations.

Chartered in 1947, PRSA's primary objectives are to advance the standards of the public relations profession and to provide members with professional development opportunities through continuing education programs, information exchange forums and research projects conducted on the national and local levels.

PRSA builds the public relations profession and the public relations professional in three core areas:

Advancing the Profession. To attain the overall goal as the standard bearer for public relations, PRSA maintains and continually enhances all existing Professional Development programs using media opportunities at all levels (individual member, chapter, section and national) concentrating on Accreditation and the Code of Ethics.

Strengthening the Society. While constantly seeking new strategies to increase membership and enrich member services, the Society will strive to develop cohesion among the national staff, board and the local operating units of the society. The Society will continue to develop a governance structure well adapted to change and one which will constantly measure the effectiveness of its performance.

Establishing Global Leadership. In order to position PRSA as the acknowledged worldwide brand of public relations excellence, PRSA is dedicated to strengthening alliances with other public relations organizations throughout the world, internationally marketing its products and services, and continuing to extend Accreditation worldwide.

Exercise 9.3—Writing Organizational Profiles

 You are public relations writer for the academic department at your college or university that includes the public relations program. You are asked to prepare a backgrounder about the program that can be used for several purposes: to recruit prospective students, to recruit faculty, to raise money from alumni, and to build stronger relationships with public relations professionals around the state. List the section headings for the backgrounder and provide a brief explanation of the content of each section.   ■

Backgrounder

A *backgrounder* is a factual piece that provides a backdrop to a product or service associated with an organization or explains the context of a situation affecting the organization. It also may deal with technical information. In this way, a backgrounder is similar to the factoid, which was introduced in Chapter 5, though generally a backgrounder is more extensive.

As a writer of backgrounders, you will need to research particularly well so you can clearly understand the topic and its significance. You also will need to plan well, having a clear understanding of your key publics and the message to be conveyed to them. Because a backgrounder provides a written source for clear and objective information, it can be used by various people in several different ways:

- By reporters seeking information to help them prepare stories and reports
- By organizational spokespersons preparing to discuss issues with clients, reporters, colleagues and others
- By public relations writers preparing brochures, news releases, speeches, newsletter articles, Web pages, and other written materials
- By organizational representatives needing to respond to inquiries by colleagues, constituents, reporters, regulators and consumers
- By writers preparing grant applications and other funding requests.

Writers have much flexibility in choosing a format for backgrounders, as long as it effectively presents the factual information. Some appear as narratives with section subheads, others as chronologies. A graphic organizer can sometimes help make sense of the many different kinds of information that might go into a backgrounder. Many backgrounders are now being posted on organizational Web sites. Check out some of the following for examples of backgrounders, fact sheets, policy statements, and related information.

- Anti-Defamation League: adl.org
- National Council of Churches: ncccusa.org
- U.S. Conference of Catholic Bishops: nccbuscc.org/sdwp
- American Civil Liberties Union: aclu.org/news
- United Nations: un.org/news/facts
- Democratic National Committee: democrats.org/press.php
- Republican National Committee: rnc.org/news
- The White House: whitehouse.gov
- U.S. Department of Defense: defenselink.mic

Exercise 9.4—Writing Backgrounders

You are asked by your college or university to explain the relationship among public relations, advertising and marketing communication as part of its Web articles about your department. Prepare a backgrounder to be used with potential students and their parents. Include several section headings.

Writing about Issues

Some studies on the use of media releases suggest that articles taking a strong consumer approach have the greatest chance of being used by the media. They are full of the key ingredients of SiLoBaTi—information that is significant, local, balanced and timely. Consumer-interest releases are particularly significant to readers because they examine meaningful problems and suggest practical solutions. Anytime we can help the media do that for their audiences, the gatekeepers will pay attention.

Editors selecting releases for publication are attracted to various kinds of consumer-interest articles in which writers attribute information to their organizations matter-of-factly, without excessive or self-serving promotionalism. This kind of writing should clearly impart useful information and advice, but the writer needs to do this without overt commercialism. The desired tone can be achieved if the writer keeps the focus on user benefits rather than on the organization providing the goods and services. Public relations writers preparing consumer-interest articles have found the following general approaches to be useful:

- Write informally and personally to the reader. Use "you" words freely.
- Be a bit less free with "we" words to avoid sounding preachy or promotional.
- Emphasize what can be accomplished rather than what cannot.

- Consider source credibility. The most persuasive source is a person or organization similar to your key public that has successfully resolved this problem.
- Remember that you are writing for a reader who, though interested, may not have much background in dealing with this problem. Don't overestimate the reader's knowledge about the topic.

Four common approaches to consumer-interest releases are how-to articles, question-and-answer pieces, case studies, and information digests. These can be used as feature releases, or they may be placed on organizational Web sites. Additionally, they can be printed as brochures or as handouts and direct-mail pieces.

How-To Article

All public relations releases are attempts by a writer to address the wants, interests and needs of media audiences. But a *how-to article* (also called a *service article*) is more obvious than other writing formats in addressing such reader interest. It is a consumer-interest release that provides step-by-step instructions in addressing a problem or issue. A how-to article should be timely and significant to local readers. It should also be balanced, objective, and not obviously self-serving to the organizational preparing the release.

The how-to article often is overlooked by public relations writers, especially by those involved with corporate organizations. Nonprofit groups, on the other hand, have learned the value of such releases, perhaps because such organizations are program oriented and because their mission is to present information or advocate for a cause. Often, the shoestring budgets of nonprofit organizations have given their public relations writers experience in finding interesting angles that lead to publicity for their organizations. It would be a rare organization—corporate or nonprofit—that does not have some bit of advice to share with members of its publics. Consider the following examples:

- Psychiatric counseling center: Ways to reduce emotional stress during the holiday season
- Waste management firm: How homeowners can dispose of hazardous household garbage
- Private school: How parents can help their children prepare for college entrance exams
- Bank: Ways to encourage financial responsibility among young teens
- Law firm: How to save money when preparing wills
- Church, mosque or synagogue: How to select appropriate religious gifts for children
- AIDS treatment center: How to show compassion and support for families with a member who has HIV or AIDS
- Fitness center: Ways to exercise at home.

Following are several steps toward developing an effective how-to article, both for use as a feature for newspapers or magazines or for an internal publication or Web site. The ingredients are the same for both internal and external audiences:

Step 1: Problem. Address a problem of interest to your public. How-to articles grow out of the planning sheet. They are designed to help the reader solve a problem or achieve a desired result, in the process helping the organization achieve its objectives. As such, they begin with a clear statement of the problem. If you have carefully selected your topic, you should be able to identify a problem common to many members of your key public, and readers will easily see their own wants, interests and needs reflected in the article. This step in writing a service article also introduces the organization that serves as a model for how to address the problem.

Step 2: Cause. Note the cause and background of the problem. Having identified the problem, the writer goes on to explain how it has developed, both in general and with the model organization in particular. What caused it? How has it progressed to date?

Step 3: Significance. Now deal with where the problem is heading and with its significance. How will this affect the model organization or other organizations facing a similar problem? Try to set up a familiar situation with which the audience can identify.

Step 4: Solution. Explain the solution. The heart of the how-to article is a detailed explanation of how to fix the problem. What is the remedy? How did the model organization move toward a solution? How can the reader create that remedy? This part of the service article may unfold step by step as the writer outlines, often with great detail, how to achieve the desired solution. Or the article may list various possible solutions. Either way, try to help readers gain a sufficient understanding so they can recreate the solution for themselves.

Step 5: Conclusion. Wrap up the article for the reader. As a feature story, the how-to article usually has an obvious ending. Often this is a final motivational message or a well-chosen quote summing up the benefit to the model organization and potential imitators among the readers.

Exhibit 9.4 shows an example of a how-to or service article prepared by the Better Business Bureau of Alaska, Oregon and Western Washington, presenting its expert advice to readers.

Exhibit 9.4—HOW-TO ARTICLE   The Better Business Bureau of Alaska, Oregon and Western Washington posted this how-to article on its Web site (thebbb.org), to offer its expert advice on how readers can make charitable contributions without fear of being scammed. This is an example of a how-to article.

Better Business Bureau

Serving Alaska, Oregon & Western Washington

Where Ethics Never Go Out of Style

DuPont, WA—December 6, 2005—The Better Business bureau serving Alaska, Oregon, and Western Washington has partnered with over 350 local charities to provide extensive information to interested donors.

Better Business Bureau charity reports are designed to help consumers make informed giving decisions by examining promotional materials, annual reports and IRS filings of non-profit organizations. Reports summarize mission and purpose of charities, percentage spent on overhead, monetary benefit contributed to the cause, and compliance with 20 voluntary standards of charitable accountability. The evaluation also indicates whether donations made to the group are tax-deductible.

Local charity reports are available online at www.thebbb.org and in the BBB Yellow Pages, a free directory of BBB members and local charities available by request online or by calling 206.431.2227.

Find 329 national organizations available at www.give.org. A 2001 merger of the National Charities Information Bureau and the Philanthropic Advisory Service of the Council of Better Business Bureaus resulted in give.org.

BBB Basics for Giving:

- Do not give cash; always make contributions by check and make your check payable to the charity, not to the individual collecting the donation.

- Keep records of your donations (receipts, canceled checks, and bank statements) so you can document your charitable giving at tax time. Although the value of your time as a volunteer is not deductible, out-of-pocket expenses (including transportation costs) directly related to your volunteer service to a charity are deductible.

- Don't be fooled by names that look impressive or that closely resemble the name of a well-known organization.

- Check out the organization with the local charity registration office (usually a division of the state attorney general's office) and with your Better Business Bureau.

Exercise 9.5—Writing a How-To Article

In preparation for writing a service article, write a brief step-by-step explanation of how to accomplish one of the following tasks:

1. How to make a favorable and lasting impression on your professor in a class within your major (for an article directed to entering freshmen and transfer students).

2. How to apply for internships in your major (for an article on the department Web site directed to new majors).

3. How to gain practical work experience in the field of public relations (for an article directed toward first-year students at your college or university). ∎

Question-and-Answer Feature

An often-used writing format among public relations practitioners is the *question-and-answer piece*, informally called a *Q&A*. Writers associated with Web sites are likely to call this format *frequently asked questions*, or *FAQs*. Whatever its name, this format consists of a series of carefully selected questions that address relevant aspects of an issue, followed by short paragraphs responding to the questions.

The key to writing a good Q&A is to understand both the topic and the key public well enough to anticipate all of the important questions. Q&As may be used with internal or external audiences. They may be distributed as information sheets or news releases, or they can be used as the basis for brochures and newsletter articles as well as for Web pages. The process for preparing effective Q&As proceeds logically.

Step 1: Topic. Select a topic of interest. Every organization deals with information that interests someone. The writer for a Q&A should begin with a planning sheet that generates a clearly identified topic interesting members of one of the organization's publics. To qualify for a Q&A, the topic should be sufficiently new or complex to provide readers with useful information.

Step 2: Reader Interest. Every public relations writing activity begins with a planning sheet, and the Q&A is no exception. Focus here on the wants, interests and needs of the key public. Time spent at this research stage will make the writer more effective in the subsequent steps.

Step 3: Questions. The effectiveness of the finished Q&A rests on the appropriateness of the questions. These should be relevant to the topic and interesting to the key public. They should be presented in a logical order, with each question flowing gently and logically into the next. They also should include the full range of questions that will set the stage for presenting information that meets both the organization's objectives and the reader's interests. Content of the questions should lead both to basic facts as well as to the deeper significance underlying the facts. Readers are most likely to remain interested when the questions are phrased in personal terms: *What can I do? How will I know? What does this mean to me?* An effective way to test your presumptions is to ask a small group of members of your key public if this is the information they want to know.

Step 4: Responses. Having identified the appropriate questions, the writer provides a response to each of them. These answers should be brief. A lengthy answer often indicates that the question is overly complex and perhaps should be divided into several question-and-answer segments. The response is written in a style to complement the question. For example, a series of questions stated in "me" and "I" terms may be answered with a "you" tone. Such a style presents the organization as an expert adviser on the subject.

Step 5: Write. Having done the planning and preparation in the first four steps, write the Q&A feature article. The general format is to begin with an introductory section of a couple of paragraphs in which you state the topic, indicate the significance and benefits, and note the source of the information. It is a good idea to include a quote as part of this introduction. Then provide a series of short questions and concise responses. Q&A pieces often wrap up with a paragraph or two of general information about the organization or the issue.

The main thing to remember when writing a question-and-answer piece for media release is to keep it focused on the audience. A newspaper or magazine is unlikely to use a Q&A that is obviously promoting your organization. Rather, editors are more likely to select a piece that has a strong news peg and that highlights tips and advice for the audience. The same advice holds true for Q&As prepared for brochures or Web sites. Readers are unlikely to stick with a piece that is highly promotional rather than one that addresses their interests and obviously serves their needs.

Exercise 9.6—Writing Q&A Features

Your class has been asked by the local Association for Cancer Education and Prevention to prepare a question-and-answer piece about cancer. Some students have been asked to write about breast cancer, others on testicular cancer. They key public for both pieces is students entering area colleges and universities.

Part 1: Prepare a planning sheet to develop an approach for this writing assignment.

Part 2: Write a feature release in question-and-answer style. Include at least eight questions. Quote your instructor as Director of Public Education for the ACEP. For accurate and up-to-date information, check the online resources noted in Exercise 2.6 "Working with Technical Language," or use a search engine to find current and authoritative information about either breast cancer or testicular cancer as these relate to persons of college age. ∎

Case Study

The *case study* (sometimes called a *case history*) is often associated with product publicity, in which the writer provides a narrative of how the product has been used by a representative consumer. But this style of reporting also can be useful for service-oriented businesses and nonprofit organizations. In both instances, the writer profiles actual users of the service. This is source credibility at its best.

This type of consumer-interest feature tells the story of how a program, product or service has been used by an organization. It shows the program in action. A particular value of the case study is the heightened credibility of third-party endorsements. Instead of the company itself telling about the benefits of its product, the case study allows a real-life customer to explain the benefits to would-be consumers with similar problems.

Writers of case studies should get permission from the organization before they present the story, and they may need to get the customer's approval for the finished article as well. It is not too surprising that some organizations are reluctant to be identified through a case study. Often this is because either they are embarrassed by having the problem in the first place or because they prefer not to share their experience and its successful outcome with readers who may also be competitors. Despite these concerns, however, public relations opportunities abound. Many organizations readily agree to be the focus of a cast study, and trade magazines and other specialized publications generally welcome well-written case studies because they serve the interests of their readers.

Planning sheets are especially helpful to a writer preparing a case study. The focus for this type of writing must be clearly on the key public—the reader of the publication that will be asked to publish the case study. With careful writing, this reader will be able to identify with the organization in the case study that serves as an example and a model that has successfully used the product. Case studies generally have four major elements:

Step 1: Problem. Begin by identifying the problem. Based on the planning sheet, the writer begins by clearly indicating the problem being addressed in the study. The focus of the article is a particular organization, but the problem should be one that is shared by many organizations.

Step 2: Solution. Explain how the organization solved the problem. The writer should explain the decisions and actions that led to a favorable resolution.

Step 3: Benefits. Clearly show the benefits of the solution. The case study article ends with a clear indication of the value of the solution approach to any organization facing a similar problem. However, restraint is important. Don't let this conclusion become too commercialized. Hold down the fluff and excessive mention of the product or service.

Step 4: Illustration. If possible, include charts, tables and photographs to provide visual appeal for the case study. Use illustrations to help the reader identify with the problem and to better understand the proposed solution.

Exercise 9.7—Writing Case Studies

Select an organization and develop a feature article using the case study approach. Begin by identifying a problem associated with the organization, and then tell the story of how some person or organization solved such a problem.

Information Digest

Another vehicle for feature writing is the *information digest*, which takes heavy-duty material such as from research reports or technical accounts and "translates" is into accessible language for the average consumer. This type of writing is a kind of paraphrased reprint of the original material.

Writers need two special abilities to write information digests. First, they must be able to understand complex or technical information. Second, they must then be able to interpret this information for readers who, though interested in the topic, lack the experience, training or background to grasp the meaning of the original. Exhibit 9.5 "Research in Brief" is a good example of an information digest. The writer has taken a complex topic, in this case a medial research report in a scientific journal, and revised it as a digest that is easy for nonscientific readers to understand. "Research in Brief" is designed for particular publics such as policy makers, therapists, people in law enforcement, and medical researchers in other fields.

Exercise 9.8—Writing Information Digests

Go to an Internet search engine and look at the Web site of an organization associated with scientific or technical information. Topics might deal with some aspect of engineering, aerospace or oceanographic technology, medical research, environment, natural disasters, communications technology, or other areas. Using the information you find there, write an information digest that would be interesting and understandable to an average, nonscientific reader.

Exhibit 9.5—INFORMATION DIGEST   A public relations writer studied a technical medical report and interviewed the scientist before producing this easy-to-understand report for the nonscientific reader. Reprinted with permission of the Research Institute on Addictions.

RESEARCH INSTITUTE *on* ADDICTIONS   Howard T. Blane, Director

Research In Brief

Childhood Victimization May Lead to Alcohol Problems for Women

Nearly 90 percent of alcoholic women were physically or sexually abused as children, according to a study conducted at the Research Institute on Addictions (RIA) and published recently in the *Journal of Studies on Alcohol*.

Research scientists Brenda A. Miller, Ph.D., and William R. Downs, Ph.D., studied 472 women aged 18 to 45. The group included women receiving services for alcoholism, drinking and driving, partner violence, or mental health problems. It also included women in the general population who were recruited by a random phone survey.

High Rates of Abuse

Eighty-seven percent of the alcoholic women reported being sexually abused as a child or suffering severe violence at the hands of a parent, compared to 59 percent of women in the general population.

Sexual abuse includes any unwanted and forced sexual experiences before age 18, either with a relative or with a person who was not related. Severe parental violence includes choking, kicking, biting, hitting with a heavy object, badly beating a child, using a knife or a gun to threaten or attack her, or seriously threatening to kill her.

The table shows the rates of victimization for both groups. Compared to women in the general population, a

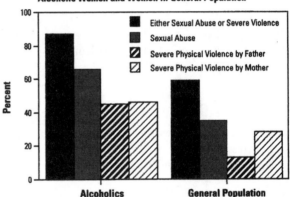

Rates of Childhood Victimization: Alcoholic Women and Women in General Population

- ■ Either Sexual Abuse or Severe Violence
- ■ Sexual Abuse
- ▨ Severe Physical Violence by Father
- ▨ Severe Physical Violence by Mother

Differences between the alcoholics and the general population were significant at $p \leq .001$, except severe violence by mother, which was significant at $p \leq .01$.

significantly higher percentage of the alcoholic women experienced physical or sexual abuse. This data suggests that childhood victimization may play a significant role in the development of women's alcohol problems.

The researchers explored the possibility that factors other than victimization may have contributed to the women's alcohol problems. Using statistical procedures, they controlled for the effects of parental alcoholism and demographic differences. The strong relationship between childhood victimization and alcohol problems

persisted even after these influences were held constant. This finding is important because it shows that parental alcoholism alone does not explain women's alcoholism. Victimization is independently linked to alcohol problems in women.

The investigators also tested the possibility that the high rates of childhood victimization among the women in alcoholism treatment are related not to their alcoholism but to their treatment-seeking. To test this, they compared women in alcoholism clinics to women in other treatment settings, such as

New York State Office of Alcoholism and Substance Abuse Services   Marguerite T. Saunders, Commissioner

10

Advocacy and Opinion

Previous chapters have presented writing formats in which blatant advocacy is inappropriate and opinion is suspect. When news is the rule, writers cannot openly advocate for an organizational point of view. Under the norm of objectivity, writers can present opinion only indirectly and subtly.

But advocacy and opinion are not always inappropriate for public relations writers. Sometimes they are just what the writer needs, especially when it is important to clearly state the organization's point of view and attempt to win support for that position. Just as objectivity is important in some writing formats, open and evident promotion can be a pillar of other forms of public relations writing.

Several formats are available to the writer to present openly persuasive forms of written communication. The focus of this chapter is on various ways an organization can present its opinions to its key publics, including position statements, letters to the editor, op-ed commentaries and guest editorials, issue advisories, proclamations and petitions. Here are your objectives for Chapter 10:

- To apply concepts of issues management in various writing activities
- To prepare and write advocacy pieces such as position statements, letters to the editor, op-ed commentaries and guest editorials, issue advisories, proclamations and petitions.

Issues Management

Part of the public relations research process is the monitoring of the environment in which the organization operates. This continual attention to how the organization is affected by social, legal, professional and economic trends—and the public opinion surrounding them—is known as *issues management*. The public relations practitioner will identify issues that may affect the organization, suggesting ways in which the organization might address these issues. Sometimes these issues emerge slowly; other times they burst on the scene. Foresight can pay off, giving the organization time to prepare a considered response instead of being put on the spot for an unexpected comment.

Exercise 10.1—Freewriting on Issues Management

 Freewrite for five minutes on the following topic: *In what ways do you think a public relations practitioner can help an organization identify and deal with issues affecting its success?* Then discuss this with your classmates.   ■

Identifying Issues

Management of issues important to an organization is an ongoing process of research, analysis and communication. Writing skills are called into play at each step, and the public relations writer who is aware of the strategic importance of issues management can be a valuable asset to any organization.

The public relations practitioner has two roles to play in the early stages of managing an issue: (1) identifying pending issues that can be expected to affect the organization, and (2) anticipating the likely and eventual emergence of issues. Both identification and prediction are based on the ongoing research conducted by the organization. This systematic analysis of an organization, its communication practices and its relationship with its publics is called a *public relations audit.*

A public relations audit may include several methods of gathering information, including environmental audits, performance/perception audits, literature reviews, interviews, focus groups, surveys and content analysis. Following is a look at the various methodologies useful in conducting a public relations audit.

- *Environmental audits* are procedures built into public relations planning. They can provide an early warning system for issues that might affect the organization. Recall that publics can be identified according to their linkages to organizations—consumers, producers, enablers and limiters. By conducting an environmental audit on a regular basis (at least once a year), you are likely to detect any emerging issues in time to deal with these publics.

- *Performance/Perception audits* are procedures that focus on the organization itself—the quality of its performance in providing products or services, its visibility among key publics, and especially its reputation. In public relations situations, perception is reality. What people think about an organization is just as important as how well it performs. One of your main concerns is to learn if your publics think about you in the same way you think about yourself.

- *Literature reviews* that cite references to an issue from newspapers and magazines, academic journals, government documents, authoritative Web sites and other information sources provide a current and often in-depth look that can point out trends and emerging issues. Each discipline or industry generates many articles, reports and other literature that offer an excellent insight into current issues within that discipline.

- *Interviews* are a type of informal research that can be conducted with key people such as top management, managers, community leaders, media leaders, governmental officials and significant consumers. You also might interview antagonists, outside experts and others willing to offer constructive criticism and suggestions about your organization.

- *Focus groups* are a form of research that gathers a small number of people who can represent your publics. During a structured group interview, these people can provide informal, anecdotal information about your organization.
- *Surveys* are a formal research technique that can be conducted to gather information from larger numbers of respondents. Surveys may focus on internal groups such as employees, volunteers and shareholders, or they may deal with external groups such as consumers and community or industry leaders.
- *Content analyses* are another formal research procedure that can alert you to changing trends in the levels of visibility, criticism and support. This research measures patterns in attitude and opinion found in texts such as letters to the editor, news reports, professional publications and incoming letters.

Analyzing Issues

After you have identified issues and trends that affect your organization, the next step is to assess these issues. This step may involve further research as you more fully investigate the particular issue. It also involves the continued monitoring of the issue to keep your response current and on track. In the analysis stage, you will look at the issue from two points of view:

- *From the organization's perspective*: What are the causes of the issue? What is the likely impact, especially the potential for harm? What are the options for dealing with the issue?
- *From the public's perspective*: Is this an issue of interest to people outside the organization? What is its likely impact on them?

During this stage you will begin writing about the issue. Present the background. Identify the pros and cons. Articulate the impact on both the organization and the various publics that are relevant to this issue. The formal position should grow out of such considerations.

Tips for Better Writing   *Issues Analysis Report*

Some public relations writers will find themselves in the interim step of preparing an issues analysis for the organization's manager. Typically, such an analysis would involve the issue background (issue, significance, history, current status and projection). The writer might then outline the various positions open to the organization, perhaps with a pro-and-con treatment of each possible position, which the organization's decision makers then would consider as they select their official position.

Communicating the Position

Public relations practitioners will define various levels of publics to be considered as they plan a communication program for issues management. Certainly, some publics should be notified before others. For example, you might inform stockholders by mail of a corporation's formal position at the same time the financial media are notified, thus communicating directly with stockholders rather than having them read the news in the financial media.

Organizations generally should present a new position to employees before it is communicated to consumers, especially if the position requires the cooperation of employees to implement. Such formal positions can be communicated through various media, including news releases, position statements, letters and other direct-mail pieces, lobbying materials, speeches and organizational advertising. Increasingly, organizations are finding that a combination of e-mail or Web sites provides the best opportunities to communicate with specialized internal audiences quickly, efficiently and either simultaneous to or just ahead of the release of the information to news media and other public audiences. All of this requires a carefully planned timetable to ensure the proper orchestration of the message.

Of course, once they are accepted, position statements should be posted prominently at the organization's Web site for public consumption. See how some organizations present their position statements online: American Dietetic Association (eatright.org), International Confederation of Principals (icponline.org), American Nuclear Society (ans.org/pi/ps/), Mothers Against Drunk Driving (madd.org/aboutus/4225).

Position Statement

Often, organizations want to give their opinion on matters of public or organizational interest. *Position statements* are presentations, usually in written form, reflecting the considered and official position of the organization. Increasingly, the position statement is becoming an important part of the basic toolbox of public relations practitioners. Position statements are an example of the contribution that public relations makes in a democratic society. When written with skill and with integrity, they contribute to the unobstructed flow of ideas that is vital in a free society.

Distribution of position statements may be either at the initiative of the organization or in response to requests for information, especially when the request comes from significant publics. Position statements may be given directly to members of external key publics such as legislators, donors, investors, colleagues, community leaders and so on, or they may be distributed to reporters and other media representatives. Additionally, position statements may be distributed to internal publics such as employees, volunteers and board members to help them understand the actions and policies of the organization.

Position statements vary in depth, intensity and length. A *position paper* (sometimes called a *white paper)* may be a lengthy and detailed presentation, perhaps 25 pages long, by an organization expressing the opinion of its executive board on a major issue of long-term significance. If it is lengthy, however, it should include an official summary. A *position paragraph* is a brief statement by an organization addressing a transitory or local issue.

Content analysis on effective opinion pieces shows that they generally position the issue within a wider context of interest to publics and readers. They summarize the issue and the opinion quickly, with details and follow-up arguments. They use effective analogies and metaphors, as well as literary techniques such as repetition and rhetorical questions.

Flawed opinion pieces, on the other hand, share some common weaknesses: They pose questions rather than present answers. They oversimplify complex issues or fail to get beyond burdensome details. They present opinions weakly and present facts without drawing logical conclusions. They attack opponents unfairly. Any of these practices are defects in the process of persuasive communication, and they are likely to meet with little long-term success. Regardless of their depth, position statements generally follow a similar pattern: background on the issue, justification for the position, and conclusions. Let's look at each part of a position statement.

Issue Background

Begin the position statement with a thorough background on the issue. Such a background includes several elements: a clear identification of the issue, an explanation of its significance to the key publics, relevant history, an indication of the current situation, and a projection of likely developments.

Issue Topic. The first part of every position statement should clearly identify the issue being addressed. Don't side-step controversy or embarrassment, but rather identify and deal with the issue head on. Failure to address the significant issue can render the statement useless. It even could become counterproductive if an ambiguous statement allows for an interpretation that the organization is unclear about the issues or is unwilling to deal with them.

A word of caution: When selecting topics for position statements, make sure the issue is a matter of public interest that is open to persuasion, rather than a matter of policy or procedure for your organization or something over which the organization has control. For example, a school district announcing a new dress code would not write a position statement, because the policy is a matter of regulation; it can be enforced by the school district. The district would explain reasons for the new guidelines, but this would be a policy statement rather than a position statement because it doesn't require outside endorsement or public approval. Instead, it simply is a matter of presenting, explaining, and then enforcing the new policy. As an organization's attempt to seek agreement and cooperative action, a position statement is appropriate only when persuasion, not force or enforcement, is called for.

Also, the topic of a position statement should have more than one side, thus giving it the potential to be controversial. A school district isn't likely to issue a position statement in favor of education because that issue doesn't draw any opposition. But homework might be a two-sided issue, and thus one appropriate for a position statement. The school district also might state its position on truancy, alternative bases for school taxes—all positions that some critics might argue with and thus appropriate fodder for position statements.

Significance. Explain the importance of the issue, being very careful to indicate how it affects both your organization and your target public. Even more important than the significance to your organization is the significance to the target publics. A good public relations writer will be very clear about the impact on readers. What does this mean to them? What are the consequences? How will it affect them? Why should they care about the issue?

History. Present background information on the issue being addressed. This section will vary from a few sentences to several pages, depending on the complexity and importance of the issue. For a familiar issue, the background section may be unnecessary. Regardless of the depth to which you present the background information, it should be clear to the audience how the issue has developed to its present point. Present this information in a clear and simple manner, and present it honestly. If you distort the background facts in any way, you are building your case on a weak foundation, and the entire position statement may be rendered useless.

Exhibit 10.1—POSITION STATEMENT   This opinion piece by a fictitious college has all the elements of an effective position statement.

Finnegan State College Position Paper #17

College Rankings

For several decades, respected directories have published factual and comparable information about colleges and universities that students have found useful as they decide where to advance their education. But in a new commercial twist, some non-academic publishers have begun trying to judge the relative merits of institutions of higher education. Magazines such as Business Week, Kiplinger's, Money, Time, and U.S. News & World Report publish "best college" rankings that purport to advise students on which colleges offer the highest quality.

Our Observations About "Best College" Rankings ...

Finnegan State notes that "best college" rankings are increasingly being criticized and questioned by educators across the nation. We find these rankings fundamentally flawed because they use criteria inappropriate to the needs of our students and the mission of our College. We further point out that such rankings are of dubious practical value to either students or institutions of higher education.

...increasingly questioned

Magazine rankings are being criticized more and more, even by schools that rank high in the listings.

▫ Some colleges recently have begun refusing to provide data to the magazines. At least 20 independent liberal arts institutions have organized a boycott.

▫ Other institutions circumvent the rankings by providing their own objective data on Web sites and other locations accessible to prospective students.

▫ Student governments are many colleges and universities have asked magazines to stop the numerical rankings. Additionally, students from 40 schools have formed a pressure group to oppose the rankings.

▫ A new research study points out that rankings based on reputation reflect only past achievements, often underestimating the quality of some schools while overestimating others.

... inappropriate criteria

These rankings feature some criteria biased against institutions such as Finnegan State. More importantly, the criteria are of questionable value to prospective students.

Here are some criteria the rankings use a priority points.

▫ High faculty salaries

▫ Low default rate on student loans

▫ High alumni contributions

▫ Number of faculty research reports and publications

▫ Number of faculty, but not the number of teaching assistants

▫ Number of library books, but not the number of periodicals or electronic resources

▫ Number of graduates who eventually earn doctorates

▫ High acceptance standards and low acceptance rates

Position Paper #17
College Rankings

Promulgated January 2007
by Emmanuel K. Enterline, President of Finnegan State College

Other position papers are available at the Finnegan State Web site:
www.finnegan.edu

...of dubious value

"Best" rankings earn millions of dollars for magazines. The U.S. News rankings issue, for example, is that magazine's annual best seller. But its value to students is questionable.

▫ A student survey shows the rankings to have little impact on college choice. Of much more importance are personal sources (other students, college representatives, parents, counselors, and alumni) and printed materials (brochures published by the colleges, guidebooks without competitive ranking, and Web sites).

▫ In another survey, only six percent of college public information officers found the rankings very helpful to the college-selection process. Most reported the rankings as having only minor impact on recruitment or fund raising.

The Council for Advancement and Support of Education has additional information on college rankings at its Web site:
www.case.org.

Our Response ...

Finnegan State does not believe there is a "best college" or a "worse college" – only a college that provides the best choice and the best fit for an individual student.

We believe that Finnegan State *is* the best college choice for many students.

Given the way magazines rank colleges, frankly we don't expect to find Finnegan State at the top of those commercial listings.

Why?

Because Finnegan State values factors the magazines don't emphasize in their criteria, and because we don't particularly stress some of the criteria the magazines do favor.

For example, instead of trying to be exclusive by having low acceptance rates based on unrealistically high entrance requirements, we want to keep Finnegan State's doors open to as many students as possible. We will continue to risk our reputation with the magazines by giving qualified students a chance to succeed, including those promising students who haven't had the same educational opportunities as others.

Or another example: Our professors are exceptionally well qualified, academically and professionally. They teach because they love to teach, and you are more likely to find them in the classroom or an office meeting with students than holed up doing obscure research. An often-heard tribute is that professors at Finnegan State are both accessible and encouraging.

Our Recommendations ...

Instead of worrying about dubious "best college" rankings, we offer the following practical advice for potential students.

▫ Think about what you seek in a college. Set your own criteria based on what's important to you.

▫ Use an objective non-ranking directory such as Barron's or Peterson's to identify colleges and universities that meet your individual needs.

▫ Look at majors as well as college-wide generalities. Your college experience will be determined mainly by the courses, teachers, resources and opportunities associated with your specific major.

▫ Make decisions only after you have visited several colleges and talked with teachers and students there.

Finnegan State College

And Our Commitment ...

On Reputation... We believe Finnegan State's solid record of success is the surest foundation for its reputation. We also realize that a reputation grows through good performance and accurate information, and we pledge both to rise to the challenges facing higher education and to keep our students and supporters informed about our progress and our plans.

On Student Selectivity... Finnegan State welcomes top high school students, and we offer challenging courses of study. But we do not close the door after the proven achievers have come in. Finnegan State pledges to remain open to students of average achievement as well. Many of our greatest success stories are students who "just got by" in high school and then blossomed here at Finnegan State, paving the way for high achievements in graduate school and in their careers.

On Teaching... Finnegan State pledges to remain committed to quality teaching. We aim for small classes and a low student-faculty ratio that encourages student success. We further pledge that all of our classes will continue to be taught by teaching faculty rather than by graduate teaching assistants.

On Student Achievement... Finnegan State will continue to give students the assistance and encouragement they need to succeed in college. Still, we know that some will opt to leave before they graduate. Recognizing students' right to change their plans, we nevertheless pledge to help every student persevere and graduate in a time that is reasonable for his or her personal, financial and academic circumstances.

Current Status. Note the current situation and bring the background up to date. A factual analysis—free of bias and advocacy—is needed in this section. Because of the evolving nature of most issues, this section of a position statement may need to be updated frequently.

Projection. It may be appropriate to note the issue's trend, projecting for readers how the issue is likely to develop.

Position

Following the background, provide a clear statement of the organization's official position, along with a justification for this position. The justification should include supporting arguments, and it should refute any arguments that opponents are likely to make.

Opinion. This is the heart of the position statement. Here, public relations writers should be at their communicative best. Clearly and explicitly state the organization's point of view. Keep the focus on a clear statement of what the organization feels and why. Beware of allowing this to sound stilted or bureaucratic.

Businesses and nonprofit organizations usually take positions on issues that affect them directly or at least generically. For example, for many years Mobil Oil Corporation engaged in advocacy advertising, publishing a series of position statements on a variety of issues related to business and the economy; the postion statements take the form of advertisements in magazines. The American Federation of Teachers publishes position statements on a variety of issues related to public education.

Some advocacy groups regularly take positions on issues that may not affect them directly but affect their constituent publics (or even unrelated groups they consider to be without the ability to advocate for themselves). This is the case, for example, when religious organizations express positions on issues ranging from apartheid to capital punishment, from abortion to homelessness. Politicians, too, often are expected to have clearly defined position statements on a wide range of issues of interest to their constituents.

Supporting Arguments. Well-stated positions provide a vigorous argument for the stated point of view. A writer preparing a position statement needs to understand the issue well enough to argue for it with credibility and apparent conviction. State reasons that support your opinion. Report facts that bolster your argument, but do so without getting bogged down in detailed statistics that cause readers to lose interest. Recall some of the lessons about persuasive communication, especially those dealing with credible sources, conclusions and appeals to both logic and sentiment.

Refuting Opposing Statements. Every issue has at least two sides, and it is important for a writer to anticipate opposing viewpoints and alternative solutions. These generally are addressed in a position statement. This may be optional if there is no significant opposition, but any organization trying to present its opinion on a controversial topic in an effort to persuade its publics would be foolhardy to ignore opposing sides of the argument. Research into persuasion consistently shows that an argument is most effective when it refutes rather than ignores opposing claims. It is most important to deal honestly and fairly with opposing viewpoints. If you distort opposing claims, you risk being labeled misinformed and illogical—or worse, dishonest.

Conclusion

The position statement ends with recommendations, and sometimes with formal citations that document information included in the statement.

Recommendations. If an organization is going to take a public position on a matter of importance, it owes its publics some reasonable suggestions. End your position statement with recommendations flowing from your stated opinion. Here, the writer should deal with preferred or possible solutions to problems involved in the issue. Or the writer simply may recommend various ways in which the reader might get involved in support of its position.

Citations. The position statement may end with a list of formal citations, identifying reports, articles, books and other sources of the data included in the statement. This allows serious-minded readers of the position statement to find the explicit documentation and references for the information presented.

Writing Elements

The effective writer will study the structure and content of position statements from other organizations and the pattern of editorial opinion in various relevant publications, and learn from the examples.

Exhibit 10.2 shows a graphic organizer for a typical position statement. You might find it helpful to follow this example in your writing, though position statements allow for some

Exhibit 10.2—POSITION STATEMENT GRAPHIC ORGANIZER

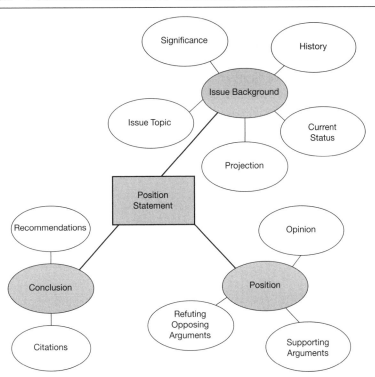

flexibility in format. For example, you may find it helpful to begin with the opinion statement, or to deal with the significance of the issue after you have provided its background and current status, or to combine the arguments and refutation of opposing arguments with the section dealing with the background or significance.

Writing a position statement requires careful research. The public relations writer must know the issue and how it affects the organization. The writer also needs to understand how the issue affects the various publics, and whether they are likely to support or oppose the position being taken by the organization. Such understanding can maximize benefits and minimize risks to the organization concerned about maintaining the support of its publics. Recall that public communication is better at reinforcing attitudes than in changing them. Regardless of the situation, one of your major concerns should be to maintain the support you already have among sympathetic publics.

An organization sometimes takes a position contrary to that of some or even most members of key publics. For example, a journalism school might defend the First Amendment rights of an unpopular extremist group, or a religious organization might support a protest against prayer in public school assemblies. To do this knowingly can be risky, but perhaps it is necessary on occasion for the integrity of organizational leadership. To do this unknowingly is a blunder that can be disastrous to the organization.

A good public relations writer will write with both conviction about the topic and respect for opposing points of view. Remember that people may sincerely arrive at different points of view when they consider the same set of facts. Don't be zealous when you deal with opponents, and don't let your own passion for the topic cause you to risk losing the respect or even the attention of people who differ with your organization's position.

Design Elements

Effective position statements feature clear writing that is enhanced by design elements that aid the reader in absorbing the message. An effective technique is to use subheads to clearly identify the various elements of the position statement. Some statements use bold and/or italic type to highlight key elements such as the opinion or the action statement. Virtually any position statement can be strengthened with such design elements. Also consider the use of boxes such as summaries, step-by-step instructions, pulled quotes, charts, information graphics, people to contact and so on. Such design aids contribute much to overall effectiveness in terms of communicating messages.

For practical reasons, position statements should be clearly labeled as such. They also should feature the date when the statement is adopted or endorsed. It sometimes becomes necessary for an organization to change its position. This can be done with little embarrassment when it is clear that the new position is the result of updated information or events that have occurred since the previous position was taken.

Exercise 10.2—Writing Position Statements

Select one of the following scenarios of issues appropriate for a position statement:

- Your college's or student organization's position on the issue of reactivating the military draft for male citizens between the ages of 18 and 22

- The position of an ethnic, cultural, social or religious minority on the issue of teaching about that group's history in local schools

- A politician's position on a matter of interest to his or her constituents

- A relevant issue of public interest of another organization that interests you. Make sure this issue deals with persuasion; that is, that it is one for which the organization can state an opinion but cannot solve by itself or require others to follow

Prepare a planning sheet, with careful attention to identifying and analyzing key publics and setting public relations objectives. In preparing your message, consider the impact of the position on the publics and whether they are likely to support or oppose the organization's position. Then research the issue and write the position statement. Use word-processing or desktop publishing software to enhance the design of the final writing.   ■

Organizational Statements

Two other types of writing are related to position statements—official statements and contingency statements. These are examples of position paragraphs.

Official statements are generally brief proclamations by an organization's leadership about timely issues that involve the organization. They are much simpler than formal position statements. Often, official statements are prepared when the organization is facing a controversy. The official statement serves as an opportunity for the organization to speak with one voice on a matter in which it has an interest or on an issue in which its response is being sought. Such statements often are used with external publics such as reporters and consumers, and they also can be circulated and published for internal publics within an organization.

Contingency statements, also called *standby statements*, may be written to prepare the organization for various potential situations. A contingency statement is a brief position statement written to deal with different pending scenarios facing the organization. Because it is written before the fact, a contingency statement must be held in strict confidence, because the organization could be embarrassed by its premature use.

For example, one resourceful public relations practitioner went to court to hear the verdict of an officer in her organization charged with a financial crime. In her briefcase were two statements. Anticipating that the media would want an official comment from her organization, she was prepared to distribute whichever statement was appropriate following the verdict. One statement expressed regret the officer had been found guilty and respect for the judicial system. The other expressed pleasure at his acquittal and appreciation for the judicial process. The public relations practitioner was happy to distribute the latter statement.

Exercise 10.3—Writing Contingency Statements

Prepare two contingency statements based on the following scenario: The chief financial officer of your college or university has been on trial for illegally diverting academic scholarship funds for the personal use of varsity athletes.

Write one statement that could be issued if the CFO is found innocent. Write another statement to be used if the CFO is found guilty.   ■

Letters to the Editor

Most publications—newspapers, magazines, journals and an increasing number of news-letters—take seriously their responsibility to provide a forum for their readers. One of the mainstays of this commitment to reader access is a *letters to the editor* column in the publication. These columns provide an excellent opportunity for your organization to present its publicity and advocacy message in its own words.

Newspapers and other publications are not legally required to publish letters from readers, but most do so because the letters column often is one of the most popular features in a publication. Some smaller publications promise to publish all letters that meet stated requirements concerning length, signature and so on. Larger publications print a sampling of the many letters they receive.

You will increase the chances that your letter is published if you model your writing on effective letters. These are short pieces, generally 200 words or less. They feature tight writing, usually addressing only one issue. Despite their brevity, they provide or at least allude to all of the elements identified for position statements. For both ethical and practical considerations, public relations practitioners should identify their relationship to the organization on whose behalf they are writing the letter to the editor. However, public relations practitioners seldom write letters over their own name. More often, they draft letters to be signed by their clients or bosses.

The key to effectively using a letters column for public relations purposes is to exercise discretion. Public relations writers should be careful not to overuse this avenue. Too much visibility can be a problem in letters columns, as it is in virtually every other media opportunity. Organizations should carefully pace their presence in the media so they do not reduce their credibility with overexposure.

"FYI: Audience Commentary and the Law" discusses the legal requirements for the news media to provide a forum for reader comments and organizational replies.

FYI *Audience Commentary and the Law*

Legal requirements vary concerning whether news media need to provide an outlet for audience opinions. In general, newspapers are under no legal obligation to publish letters to the editor and reader commentaries, while broadcast media have some parallel requirements to provide a forum for the opinions of their audience members.

Newspapers. There is no legal requirement that newspapers or other publications must publish any or all readers' letters. Publications that print letters to the editor do so because they find this to be good journalistic practice, not because it is required by law. Nor is there any requirement for editors to be even-handed in their selection of letters to be published.

In *Miami Herald v. Tornillo*, the Supreme Court ruled in 1974 that the law provides no right of reply to published commentaries, even to persons who feel they have been unfairly criticized by the publication itself. The Court said that the law generally cannot interfere with a newspaper's content, presumably including news copy or advertising, as well as commentary.

While press responsibility suggests that a newspaper serves its readers best when all sides of an issue are aired, and while journalistic practice generally is to fulfill this responsibility, it is not required by law.

Broadcast Media. Similar opportunities for responsive commentary exists with some radio and television stations that present their own editorial comments. Many stations that present editorials invite public comment. The Federal Communications Commission requires that radio and television stations provide free rebuttal time to persons whose character has been attacked on the air, either by the station itself or by other commentators. This requirement, one of the few remaining elements of the Fairness Doctrine that was FCC policy from 1949 to 1987, was endorsed by the Supreme Court in *Red Lion Broadcasting Co. v. FCC* (1969).

However, neither the FCC nor the courts have ruled that broadcasters must provide air time to individuals or groups who simply want to present their point of view on matters of public interest. In *CBS v. Democratic National Committee*, the Supreme Court ruled in 1973 that broadcasters do not have to sell advertising time. Policies such as these have frustrated some organizations trying to advocate for their positions on various controversial issues. Occasionally, public relations practitioners are faced with broadcast media that arbitrarily refuse to provide them with air time to present their positions. Generally, stations that refuse to air one side of an issue also refuse to air any point of view on the subject.

That was the situation until recently with topics such as birth control, sexually transmitted disease, pregnancy, abortion and related issues. Many stations refused to provide any air time to either side, whether that involved public service or paid placement. In recent years, however, as it has become more socially acceptable to discuss such issues, many radio and television stations have become more willing to allow such topics to be addressed in a balanced and sensitive fashion on their airwaves.

Letters Generating Publicity

Organizations sometimes use letters columns to call attention to activities that did not attract the attention of news reporters or did not result in what the organization considers adequate coverage for an event.

These letters usually have a positive tone. Some may take the strategy of offering congratulations for an accomplishment. For example, a company may congratulate its employees for achieving a certain business success, or a school district may applaud its students on reversing an escalating dropout rate. Other such letters may simply present information, without noting that the publication declined to report it in the first place. Rather then criticizing the publication, the public relations writer may simply present the information that the organization feels is of interest to readers. Occasionall, the publication may respond with an editor's note that it regrets the omission.

Sometimes, letters can be written to note that an organization was not included in a publication's prior coverage. An effective response may be to express interest and encouragement in the topic and then to provide the relevant information. For example:

> LMNOP Corporation is pleased to see the Review-Journal taking a lead in reporting on the problem of water pollution in the Caterwallerby River, and we applaud the measures taken by the companies noted in the news report. LMNOP has a major commitment to eliminate pollutants from our water discharges . . .

Letters Correcting Errors

Newspapers and magazines occasionally publish incorrect information. Reporters are human. They can make mistakes. When mistakes happen, organizations sometimes look to the letters column to redress errors in the way a publication reported about the organization. The letters column allows an organization to vindicate itself and set the record straight. But assess this option with great care. Ask yourself: Does the reported error warrant the attention of a letter? Is reopening the issue beneficial to the organization or is it better to simply let it fade away?

If the reported error is of minor consequence, it may be best to overlook it. Perhaps there is another avenue, such as the *corrections column*, which corrects factual misstatements. These generally are written at the discretion of an editor, who often provides a sentence correcting a factual error, without context. Here's an example of such as correction statement:

> The provost at Bison State University is Dr. Howard Marion, not Dr. Marion Howard as stated in a recent news article.

It is the lack of context in a corrections column that often moves a public relations practitioner to consider the regular letters-to-the-editor column. When a correction is warranted, writers preparing letters reacting to published error most often prudently decide not to attack the reporter's ethics or ability. For example, the following is not a very good way to begin such a letter:

> The simpleton on your staff obviously can't take accurate notes, so it's no wonder he mistakenly reported that . . .

Rather the effective public relations writer might begin:

> We appreciate the coverage you provided, and we have heard from many people who have told us that they read your report. One point that needs to be clarified is that . . .

The letter might proceed to offer the correction, perhaps under the guise of an information update.

> Readers may be interested to know that the latest figures show . . .

Writers who understand that their effectiveness lies in cultivating long-term relationships with reporters are willing to give the reporter the benefit of the doubt, at least in public. Effective public relations writers also know that the publication has the last word, and a corrections letter stands a possibility of being followed by an editorial response that all but negates the letter's value. Be wary about claiming your company was misquoted unless you are certain—a good reason to tape record every news conference or interview.

As a practical matter, when offering a correction or update to a published article, writers should provide a clear reference—for example, the date, page, and headline—to an article that is the basis for a letter to the editor.

Letters Advocating a Cause

Public relations writers often use letters to the editor to present their opinion on matters of importance to a publication's readers. To be effective with this type of letter, try to link your cause to an issue already on the public agenda. For example, when a man was arrested for killing people while he was drunk, an agency that focuses on alcoholism used the case as an opportunity to present its message. The Research Institute on Addictions, a New York State agency, knew that the drugs-and-violence issue was of interest throughout the state. So when a particularly gruesome and heavily reported incident of drug-induced violence occurred in one community, the institute addressed the news event in the lead of a letter to the editor and then provided information about its findings linking drug or alcohol abuse with violence. Later, when a similar incident occurred in another part of the state, the institute simply rewrote the lead of its letter to focus on the new incident and used the rest of the letter from the earlier version.

Another more generic lead dealt not with local crime but rather with scientific research that had been reported by the newspaper:

> Does violence have a genetic basis? A recent story in The News described research findings which suggest that abnormal brain chemistry helps to cause aggression. While this research adds an important piece to our understanding of violence, we must also recognize the other factors that contribute to aggression, especially alcohol and drug use. Studies conducted at the Research Institute on Addictions and elsewhere have shown that . . .

Exercise 10.4—Developing a Journal of Professional Observations

Using the organization and position statement from Exercise 10.2, identify a plausible news story that the local newspaper could have written yesterday about an issue related to the topic of the position statement.

Then prepare a letter to the editor (maximum 200 words) from the CEO of the organization in question that uses this event as the news peg for the organization to seek support from the newspaper's readers. ■

Commentary

In addition to letters, most publications also provide space for longer and more prominent opinion pieces that present the viewpoint of a person or organization not affiliated with the publication on issues of particular interest to readers. This space is known as *op-ed commentary* (so named because of its traditional location opposite the editorial page). Some publications offer space for *guest editorials*, which are editorials written by invited members of the community instead of members of the editorial board. Others publish bylined commentaries contributed by special-interest organizations. Regardless of how they feature the viewpoints, op-ed commentary gives public relations writers an important vehicle for presenting their organization's position. As with letters, op-ed writers find much competition for space on larger publications. But writers can increase the chances that their editorials will be accepted by carefully preparing their submissions to a publication.

No publication would seriously consider using an op-ed piece on an irrelevant topic. The writer's task is to think like an editor, selecting a topic of interest to the publication and its readers. Use the SiLoBaTi criteria for news (significant, local, balanced, timely) as an indicator of a relevant topic. The guest editorial might not be on a topic that the readers are yet talking about, but it should be on a topic that they will care about when it is presented to them.

The writing itself should be crisp and concise. The public relations practitioner preparing an op-ed piece will review what the publication usually publishes, writing the position statement accordingly. The writer also will consider who might be a credible source to carry the organization's message. Seldom is a guest editorial signed by a public relations writer. Instead, the public relations person acts as ghostwriter who researches and writes the guest editorial, which is then signed by someone else—usually an organizational leader such as the president, CEO or executive director. The format itself for a guest editorial generally includes all of the elements suggested in the earlier section in this chapter for position papers.

Issue Advisory

A different kind of opinion piece—one that may emerge in a crisis situation—is similar to a position statement. But the *issue advisory* deals with emerging topics of immediate concern to various publics. Often, issue advisories are written for internal publics. Because they focus on an emergency in progress, they offer less preparation time than a position statement. Nevertheless, issue advisories call for some planning if they are to be effective vehicles for public relations communication. The short preparation time does not justify carelessness.

When an organization finds itself in the midst of a public relations crisis, it should adopt the *one-voice principle.* This generally means designating one organizational representative to serve as the public spokesperson. While public relations directors may draft the public statement, they seldom are the spokespersons. That role usually goes to someone else in the organization's leadership, freeing the public relations person to coordinate the response behind the scenes.

The spirit of the one-voice principle is preserved when an organization uses the coordinated voices of more than one spokesperson, which is useful when an organization must communicate simultaneously with different publics. The key in either case is that a consistent message is presented. The one-voice principle is reinforced by communicating with employees, volunteers, board members and other internal publics—reminding them of the background of the issue, apprising them of the significance of the issue, informing them of the organization's position, and equipping them with information that will reinforce the public position.

Issue advisories have many applications within organizations. If a school district bans the captain of the football team from playing in the homecoming game because of underage drinking, it can explain the policy to its teachers and staff so they, in turn, can explain it to students and parents.

Consider the following example: A routine blood-screening test at an American Red Cross center inaccurately labeled a donor as being infected with a hepatitis virus. Because of government regulations at the time, the organization was prohibited from notifying the donor. He continued to give blood 28 times over the next 3½ years, and each time the blood had to be thrown out.

When he inadvertently learned of the situation, the donor was confused and angered. He talked with the Red Cross, wrote to local legislators, and finally contacted the newspaper, which published a lengthy report (Sunday edition, Page One: "Faithful donor learns his effort was all in vain; Red Cross kept drawing blood, then disposing of it").

The community relations department prepared an issue advisory for the many Red Cross employees and volunteers to help them deal with questions from blood donors. The advisory addressed questions people were asking and the organization's response.

> *Question: How could you throw the blood away?*
> Response: Our mission is to provide the safest possible blood to those in need. The procedures may be cumbersome, but they are designed to ensure the safety of the blood supply.
>
> *Question: Why wasn't he notified not to continue donating?*
> Response: Government regulations at the time prevented us from doing so.
>
> *Question: Could this happen again?*
> Response: No, because new procedures are in place.

Some organizations call issue advisories *talk papers* or *talking points*. These are similar to position statements, though generally less interested in providing a balanced background on an issue and instead written for the purpose of persuasion and advocacy. The Association of American Universities published talking points about federal student financial aid, one of many topics posted on its Web site: aau.edu. Many government agencies also prepare talking points for both their staff and public consumption. The National Aeronautics and Space Administration posts a series of talking points on its Web site: nasa.gov. The Food and Drug Administration publishes talk papers at fda.gov. Similarly, the Log Cabin Republicans, a gay group within the GOP, publishes a series of talking points on its Web site: online.logcabin.org.

Proclamation

Occasionally, public relations writers are asked to prepare a formal statement commemorating an event or issue to be published over the signature of a governmental or other official. These statements are called *proclamations* or *resolutions*. Mayors and county executives often sign proclamations commemorating an event of local significance. Governors and presidents issue proclamations on issues of wider importance. In matters outside the governmental arenas, proclamations sometimes are issued by officials such as union leaders, religious prelates and organizational executives. Sometimes, such resolutions are initiated by the signers, who ask their public relations people to draft the appropriate proclamations. Others may be initiated by public relations people working in particular organizations or for certain causes, who then will take the proclamation to the appropriate official for its promulgation.

As formal declarations of an organization's opinion, proclamations follow a strict format. Background of the issue is presented by a series of "whereas" paragraphs that build the case, providing a logical base from which to launch toward a conclusion, and a "therefore" or "be it resolved" paragraph that makes the official statement. Alternatively, some proclamations read more like a testimonial letter, with several paragraphs recounting the background of an event or the contributions of an individual or group, followed by a formal declaration: "Now, there, I . . . by virtue of the authority vested in my be . . . do hereby proclaim that . . ."

Some organizations use the Internet to promote widespread use of proclamations. The National Women's History Project (see Exhibit 10.3) provides an online template on its Web site (nwhp.org) as a guide for city councils and school districts in issuing similar proclamations.

Exhibit 10.3—PROCLAMATION   A form of this proclamation was first passed by Congress in 1987 and each year since, designating March as Women's History Money. The White House and many state and local entities issue similar proclamations, thanks in part to the National Women's History Project which posts this online template on its Web site: nwhp.org.

Proclamation: Women's History Month

Whereas American women of every race, class, and ethnic background have made historic contributions to the growth and strength of our Nation in countless recorded and unrecorded ways;

Whereas American women have played and continue to play a critical economic, cultural, and social role in every sphere of the life of the Nation by constituting a significant portion of the labor force working inside and outside of the home;

Whereas American women have played a unique role throughout the history of the Nation by providing the majority of the volunteer labor force of the Nation;

Whereas American women were particularly important in the establishment of early charitable, philanthropic, and cultural institutions in our Nation;

Whereas American women of every race, class, and ethnic background served as early leaders in the forefront of every major progressive social change movement;

Whereas American women have been leaders, not only in securing their own rights of suffrage and equal opportunity, but also in the abolitionist movement, the emancipation movement, the industrial labor movement, the civil rights movement, and other movements, especially the peace movement, which create a more fair and just society for all; and

Whereas despite these contributions, the role of American women in history has been consistently overlooked and undervalued, in the literature, teaching and study of American history:

Now, therefore, be it resolved by the Senate and House of Representatives of the United States of America in Congress assembled, that March is designated as "Women's History Month." The President is authorized and requested to issue a proclamation for each of these months, calling upon the people of the United States to observe those months with appropriate programs, ceremonies, and activities.

Petition

Petitions are a hybrid of advocacy letters and proclamations, prepared for many people to sign. The intent of petition writers is to draft a resolute statement—often a request or demand –that will accomplish several purposes: (1) to educate people about a cause and generate interest, (2) to gain the support of people who will sign their name to the petition, and (3) to ultimately be accepted by the person or organization receiving the petition. As a vehicle of advocacy public relations, petitions often are used to exert a degree of public pressure on the recipient and may be accompanied by news releases, news conferences and other publicity vehicles.

Traditionally, petitions have been circulated person to person, often by volunteers who gather signatures. Many candidates for political offices have used such petitions, as have grassroots movements seeking to impact on government in some way.

Increasingly, petitions are being promoted over the Internet, with invitations being made to potential signers throughout the world. Topics often deal with politics or government as well as civil rights, human rights and consumer rights and advocacy for environmental, religious and other causes. Online petitions call for the impeachment of the president (at least the last three administrations) and support for the president. They ask readers to sign on to protect wildlife, free prisoners, and support political candidates.

Some petitions are sponsored by advocates associated with a particular cause, such as Reporters without Borders (rsf.org), Amnesty International (amnesty.org), the civic action group MoveOn.org, and Act for Change (workingforchange.com/activism). The American Civil Liberties Union (aclu.org) sponsored an online petition directed to the Bush White House to allow military chaplains to pray according to their own faith traditions after specifically Christian prayer was banned in public settings. The Internet also provides a forum for individuals with a self-proclaimed cause, such as the animal rights activist who created WhalesRevenge.com to promote a petition calling on the International Whaling Commission to end commercial whaling.

Online petitions also are posted by groups with multiple agenda interests. One such online forum is operated by Project Democracy for what it calls democratic conversation and deliberative discussions. The organization's Web site (e-thepeople.org) provides e-mail addresses and connections to thousands of public officials. It also posts a changing series of online petitions and invites signers for reader-generated topics such as religious freedom, rights of military veterans, educational malpractice, and immigration reform.

Part Three

PUBLIC RELATIONS WRITING FOR ORGANIZATIONAL MEDIA

In today's communications environment, two pivotal changes are taking place in the way public relations writers approach their work. The first change is that both the reach and the impact of the journalistic media are declining. Newspaper readership has been dropping for decades, and the decline has not been offset by any increase in audience size for radio or television news. As a result, newspaper readers and television news viewers are more heavily representative of older age groups.

In addition, newspaper stories are becoming shorter and more feature oriented, and television news is taking on many of the characteristics of entertainment, even of so-called tabloid journalism. Once, an article in the local newspaper and a mention on the six o'clock news was a surefire way to reach most of the local audience. Today, media attention alone is not sufficient to measure public relations success.

Meanwhile, polls indicate that news reporters have lessening credibility with audiences in both the print and electronic media. The irony is that, while many Americans devour information presented on 24-hour-a-day cable news channels, the credibility of these very new sources is low. The Pew Research Center for People and the Press reported in 2006 that 46 percent of people surveyed said the media gets the facts straight, up from 35 percent a week before the 9/11 attacks. CNN topped the list with 28 percent credibility, Fox News with 25 percent. Local TV news also garners a 25 percent rating for credibility. Meanwhile, the credibility of network news was even lower: 23 percent for NBC, 22 percent each for ABC, CBS and NPR. Among print publications, the Wall Street Journal led the pack with 26 percent credibility. Following in the survey were U.S. News and Time magazine with 21 percent, New York Times with 20 percent, local daily newspapers collectively with 19 percent, Newsweek magazine and USA Today newspaper with 18 percent, and the Associated Press with 17 percent.

Such findings, which have been slowly and steadily dropping for the last decade or more, present an interesting question for public relations writer: If the news media have such low credibility rates, how useful are they for public relations purposes? The major change in the communication environment is that new opportunities are presenting themselves for public relations people to circumvent the news media and take their messages directly to their publics. Advances in technologies such as computers, video, self-publishing, electronic mail and blogs have made it easier for organizations to develop direct communication links with their publics, without the go-between of reporters and editors. What this means for public relations writers is that renewed attention is warranted for the various kinds of organizational media.

Fliers, brochures and Web sites, newsletters and annual reports, and direct mail all have become increasingly important to practitioners. Public relations advertising relies on the public media to carry the message, but unlike other journalism-based activities, it allows organizations to manage the content, presentation and timing of their messages. Likewise, the interpersonal arena of public speaking sometimes involves organizational spokespeople with the news media, but it also provides opportunities in nonjournalistic situations in which the organization manages elements of its message related to content, presentation and timing. And the most important development involves computer-oriented tools: accessible computers and printers, desktop publishing software programs that make it easy to crop photos and produce camera-ready layouts. The Internet especially has opened new communication possibilities.

This shift away from reliance on the journalistic media and toward a newer reliance on more direct communication is having a profound impact on the practice of public relations. Historically, writers have been rooted in journalism and news writing. Today, writing disciplines imported from journalism are essential, but successful public relations writers also need a competence with organizational media. Part 3 of this book deals with ways in which an organization can manage its communication with its publics by using direct channels of communication.

Part 3 includes:

- Chapter 11: Fliers, Brochures and Web Sites
- Chapter 12: Newsletters and Corporate Reports
- Chapter 13: Direct-Mail Appeals
- Chapter 14: Public Relations Advertising
- Chapter 15: Speeches and Interviews.

11

Fliers, Brochures and Web Sites

By some accounts, fliers and brochures were the first written materials used for public relations purposes. Thirty-eight centuries ago, the Babylonians in Mesopotamia prepared fliers (carved on stone tablets) as part of a public education campaign to increase agricultural efficiency and thus shore up the foundations of the empire. The Reformation and the American Revolution, the opening of the American frontier, the abolition of slavery, women's suffrage—each owes a measure of success to the distribution of fliers. Brochures, meanwhile, are an American contribution to the field. The first was a fundraising brochure for Harvard College in 1641.

Fast-forward to the beginning of the third millennium, when every company, cause and nonprofit organization seems to have its own Web site, when electronic distribution of information to both internal and external audiences is a key part of every organization's communication plan, when blogs and other forms of self-publishing are affecting consumer, political and cultural choices.

This chapter will look at fliers and brochures, Web sites and e-mail which, taken together, are among the most direct kinds of organizational media that allow public relations writers to take their messages directly to their publics. Here are your objectives for Chapter 11:

- To write and design a flier
- To understand the role of planning in the development of brochures
- To develop a brochure
- To develop a Web site.

Fliers

Fliers are frequently used public relations tools with several pseudonyms: circulars, broadsides, handbills and fact sheets (though the latter term can be confused with the fact sheets for media use). Whatever you call them, fliers are perhaps the easiest type of public relations writing, because the writer presents a few bits of information. Gather the relevant data, present it clearly and succinctly, and you've done most of the work.

Fliers also offer great flexibility for the writer. It is not uncommon for organizations to distribute many fliers in their efforts to present information about events and activities of interest both to the organization and to its various publics. Fliers generally are used to announce specific events such as meetings, new products such as books or new programs such as college courses.

All fliers share some common attributes that distinguish them from other forms of public relations writing. A flier can be defined as an unfolded sheet meant to be read as a single unit and providing time-specific information that increases the reader's awareness about a topic. Let's look at each of these points individually.

Fliers are unfolded sheets designed to be posted on bulletin boards, delivered by mail or distributed by hand. If they are folded, it is only for the convenience of distributing them; they are meant to be opened up.

Fliers are meant to be read as single units. They are designed to present a single message rather than a series of separate message units. Some fliers are poster-style sheets dominated by artwork or graphic designs. Others are editorial-style sheets with prominent textual information. The latter style sometimes takes the form of a letter written directly to the strategic public, often a folksy or rousing pitch for them to participate in an upcoming activity such as an open house or product demonstration.

Fliers are time specific, and they address a particular event, often with the objective of promoting attendance or participation. A high school band may distribute a circular among the student body to announce auditions. A manufacturing plant may post a flier about a change in employee benefits. A public utility may include a flier in its bills to announce a proposed rate increase.

Fliers serve awareness objectives by presenting information. Whereas other public relations tools seek to motivate, inspire and lead readers to action, fliers more often are informational tools that seek to create awareness about upcoming events and activities. Occasionally, however, fliers have an action component, such as when police departments post fliers with information about a missing child. Primarily, this is based on the information model, though the police are hoping that a citizenry attuned to this information will help them locate the missing child.

Visual Design for Fliers

The key to effective fliers is their visual appeal. Type should be pleasingly placed on the page. For example, use type within the same family; for emphasis, use different type sizes, or use variations within that family of type, such as roman, italic, boldface, lightface, condensed, extended and so on. Times Roman is a popular font with *serifs*, short lines capping the top and bottom strokes of each letter. Helvetica is a popular *sans serif* font, without those capping lines. Two other type-related features are available with some printing systems: changing the *leading*, spacing between lines, and changing the *kerning*, the space between letters.

Also consider the alignment of characters. Fliers often use centered type, sometimes with boxes or text passages set for justified left and right margins, called *full justification.* Other type characteristics are possible. *Flush left* alignment, with a straight left margin and ragged right margin, looks more informal than fully justified columns. *Flush right* copy, with a ragged left column, generally is avoided because it is difficult to read. *Centered* type also is difficult to read in paragraphs, though centering often works well for one or only a few lines such as in headlines or subheads. Additionally, too much centering of type offers little or no impact.

Reverse type (white lettering on a dark background) is difficult to read for body copy, though it can be effective for display or headline type. Fliers can be visually enhanced by discrete use of lines, borders, tints and boxes, and by the use of logos, sketches, clip art and photographs. Most font software also includes typographic elements known as *dingbats*, decorative features that include bullets, boxes, arrows, and other icons such as these:

〄 ⊘⤸☺📃❄☑♫ (). Wingdings and Webdings are two common dingbat fonts copyrighted by Microsoft. One thing to keep in mind when designing a flier is to work with a visually dominant item: a headline, graphic or piece of art. Elements should not compete for the reader's attention. Design the flier so that the most important or useful element draws the eye, with other elements gracefully flowing one to another.

Many computer software programs include a wide variety of display fonts for titles and other special uses. Additionally, some computer programs make it easy to give special design treatments to titles and headlines. Don't overdo the special typographical effects, though, because too much of a good thing is not a good thing. Remember: Give readers a single focal point with dominant visual attraction.

Exercise 11.1—Developing a Flier

Prepare a flier based on the following information. You have more information than you can possibly use in a single flier, so make some choices about what to include and what to leave out. Use the desktop publishing capabilities of your computer to prepare a camera-ready flier.

- Your client is City-County Library, located at 1234 Main Street, Middletown. The telephone number is 123–4567. Jana O'Sullivan is executive director of the library; Paul Eric Jones is director of children's services.

- Your public is parents of children of ages 2 to 6.

- The library will begin its series of children's story hours on the first Wednesday in June; provide the specific date. The sessions are held from 4 to 5 p.m. each Wednesday during June and July, with a new program each week. The sessions also are repeated each Saturday morning from 9 to 10 a.m. The story hours will be held in the Children's Suite of the library.

- The series is entitled "Yarns and Legends." Each week a different children's story will be presented by volunteers from throughout the community. The presentation will include readings and paraphrases from children's stories.

- Some of the stories are children's classics; others are contemporary pieces.

- The stories are designed to appeal to children between the ages of 2 and 6.

- Admission is free.

- The hour-long presentation will include a get-acquainted time, the story presentation, discussion about the story, and refreshments of juice and cookies. Following the story hour, librarians will be available to help children and parents select age-appropriate books to take home.

- Parents may remain with their children, or they may browse elsewhere in the library.

- The program is funded by grants from the United Way and is assisted by the Early Childhood Education Program at your college or university. ∎

Brochures

When a message must last longer than it can with a flier, public relations writers often turn to brochures. These publications serve many purposes and offer many opportunities for presenting an organization's message to its various publics. Some distinctions exist among the various types of publications that an organization may produce. *Leaflet* and *folder* refer to a folded single-sheeted publication. Multipage publications are called, according to their increasing size, *pamphlets*, *brochures* or *booklets*. Other names for multipage publications are *tracts*, *bulletins* and *packets*. All of these publications are known generically as brochures.

A *brochure* can be defined as a controlled, nonpublic medium presenting information of more than transitory interest and published as a stand-alone piece rather than as a part of a series. It is a folded sheet meant to be read as a booklet and providing information meant to be relevant over an extended period of time. The key points in this definition are expanded upon below.

Brochures are a controlled medium. They allow the organization to determine not only the message content but also the presentation of that message, with its timing, duration and repetition. Brochures also allow for controlled distribution as self-mailers, envelope inserts, rack items, or as handouts or pickups.

Brochures are a nonpublic medium. They fall midway between interpersonal communication channels (speeches and open houses) and the public media (newspapers, radio and television). As such, they enjoy two advantages: they can be better directed than public media vehicles such as news releases, and they can reach wider audiences than interpersonal channels.

Brochures are published once rather than as part of a series. To be most effective, brochure topics should be of long-term interest, with writing that serves the needs of various readers over several months, perhaps several years. While a brochure may be revised and updated, it must be complete unto itself (unlike serialized publications such as newsletters, which can develop a topic over several editions).

Brochures are stand-alone pieces that deal with all aspects of a topic. Some organizations publish a series of brochures on related topics, but each of these must stand on its own to provide complete information on its particular topic. For example, an environmental organization may write several brochures, each addressing a different environmental issue. A bank might produce a series of brochures about its different savings and investment options. A local chapter of the Public Relations Society of America may develop a series of brochures, each about individual programs such as accreditation, professional development, community service and so on.

Beyond the basics, the most effective brochures share some additional characteristics that are worth consideration by public relations writers. For one, effective brochures feature two-way communication. The writer may provide a tear-out or clip-out response card, perhaps as an offer for a product sample, a token gift or an opportunity to request additional information. The writer also may invite the reader to call a telephone hotline or otherwise make contact with the organization.

In addition, effective brochures reflect the organization. An investment company would want a brochure that alludes to its success, and a photography studio would want a brochure that showcases its best work. Both probably would opt for a four-color publication with special paper and sophisticated printing techniques. On the other hand, a soup kitchen probably would prefer a humbler look in keeping with its limited financial resources. It might even refuse the offer of a benefactor willing to foot the bill for an elaborate brochure. Some nonprofit organizations have had to apologize to donors and clients because of extravagant promotional materials.

A useful way of categorizing brochures is according to their objectives: awareness, acceptance and action. Here is an overview of each type:

Information (Awareness) Brochures. Some brochures present basic facts about the organization. These informational brochures seek to affect the level of awareness about some aspect of the organization. For example, a fitness organization might prepare a brochure about its history and its success stories, while a historical site could print a visitors' brochure with a self-guided tour of the premises and an introduction to the artifacts on display. Informational brochures also present basic information about issues important to the organization. This, too, focuses on awareness objectives. A credit union might print a brochure that serves as a loan-amortization guide or a medical society might produce a brochure outlining the various specialties within the field of nursing.

Interest (Acceptance) Brochures. Some brochures seek to make an impact on the interests and attitudes of readers. These brochures carry a persuasive message that is intended to gain the interest and acceptance of readers. For example, an environmental organization might produce a brochure about the health hazards of second-hand smoke.

Action Brochures. Finally, some brochures feature a direct call to action or sales pitch. Their objective is to affect the behavior of the reader. One of the environmental organization's brochures might want the reader to send a financial contribution; another offers how-to advice about recycling.

Planning Brochures

You've heard it before; you'll hear it again: All effective public relations writing begins with a plan. Brochures are no exception. In fact, because brochures offer so many different possibilities in both content and writing style, planning is especially important. So you don't get off track, follow this step-by-step outline for preparing brochures.

Planning Sheet. Complete a planning sheet for the brochure, giving particular attention to identifying the specific publics. Some brochures try to do too much. This is understandable, because brochures can be expensive. But remember: It is seldom a wise decision to try to shape one brochure to accomplish the work of two or three. "What Would You Do?: Writing for Different Publics" offers just such a dilemma. Continue the planning process with the usual attention to the key publics: their wants, interests and needs; credible sources; and benefits. Identify the tone you desire for your brochure. Clearly articulate your objectives. Consider the life span you envision for the brochure and the way it will be distributed.

Topical Divisions. Before you begin writing a brochure, subdivide the topic into various categories, like chapters in a book. For example, a brochure by a county agency advocating recycling might include the following sections: benefits of recycling, items to recycle, ways to prepare recyclables for pickup, the local law about recycling, penalties for violating the law, contacts for additional information and other communities' experience with recycling. Your intention here is to identify various facets of your topic and then to deal with each of them in some way. You may decide that some of the sections you identify can be eliminated

---

What Would You Do?   *Writing for Different Publics*

Put yourself in the shoes of a public relations writer preparing a brochure for an organization that provided temporary shelter for homeless women and children. The shelter had a very small budget for public relations materials. It needed to increase volunteers and to obtain contributions of money, food and clothing.

The writer faced a problem: Research identified two different publics with little overlap, but she could afford only one brochure. One public consisted of Evangelical Christian churches, a minority within the community but a group that provided most of the shelter's volunteers and frequent donations of clothing and food. This public expected to hear a religious message about the shelter and its purpose. The second public included businesses and private donors who provided most of the money the shelter used to pay its staff and purchase supplies. This public was aware of the religious mission of the shelter's sponsors, but it gave support because of the shelter's reputation for providing a needed community service.

What is your ethical responsibility to each public? Can you withhold or downplay the religious aspect of the shelter for the business community without betraying the trust of your religious supporters? Are you willing to jeopardize funding for the shelter by emphasizing the religious aspect of the shelter? How can you serve the needs of each on such a limited budget, when your boss has told you categorically that you simply do not have the funds to produce two separate brochures?

(See the note at the end of this chapter for an explanation of how the writer handled this actual case.)

---

and that others can be combined or reorganized. At this stage, your intention is simply to list the various areas of information you want to provide.

First Draft. Based on the sections you have identified, gather the necessary information and write a first draft to address each of them. Remember to write from the perspective of reader interests rather than organizational priorities. Only if the brochure serves the needs of your readers can it be of any use to your organization. "Tips for Better Writing: Writing Brochure Copy" lists additional guidelines.

Copy Revision. After you have written the first draft, review your planning sheet. Pay particular attention to the wants, interests and needs of the target public; the benefits your organization can offer them through this brochure; and your public relations objectives. Also review the way you have segmented the topic. Compare your plan to what you have written, and revise your draft accordingly. If your planning suggests more attention or different treatment of some aspects of the topic, now is the time for revision.

Graphic Elements. You probably will have begun thinking about the design of the brochure as you were writing the first draft. In fact, you probably should begin giving some early thought to the look. But don't let design run the show. Only after the first draft of the brochure has been completed should you seriously deal with design considerations. Effective brochures use illustrations to reinforce the message. While a paragraph provides information to the reader, a chart can present the same data in a visual form, or a photograph may reinforce the message.

The first design decision is to determine how many panels the brochure will have and how these will be folded. The most common format is an 8½-by-11-inch sheet of paper, with two folds into the center. This creates six panels, as shown in Exhibit 11.1. In this format,

---

Tips for Better Writing *Writing Brochure Copy*

The following guidelines may be helpful in writing copy for brochures:

1. *Make the cover interesting.* There's a lot of competition to the reader's time, so you've got to appear to offer something worth the effort of opening the brochure and reading it. A big question mark just won't do it. Use a headline and/or artwork that pulls the reader into the topic.

2. *Highlight the benefit to readers.* Place this on the front cover. The headline doesn't have to be clever and it shouldn't be cute. Instead, it should be an accurate indication of the advantage the reader will find inside. If you have planned well and clearly addressed a specific public, your headline will be most effective when it simply indicates a topic of interest to the reader.

3. *Make the copy easy to read.* Use short sentences and short paragraphs. Highlight important facts. Consider using lists instead of narrative paragraphs. Keep the writing clear and simple. Use language with a readability level appropriate to your intended readers.

4. *Write in personal terms.* Don't hesitate to use "you" words that help readers identify with the topic.

5. *Write on a friendly level.* Consider the appropriateness of keeping your message lighthearted. Even serious topics can be presented in ways that are not ponderous. Write as if you were discussing the topic with a friend.

6. *Write in positive terms.* Even situations with serious consequences can be presented without resort to pessimism or scare tactics.

7. *Don't make information so specific and time bound that it quickly becomes obsolete.* Brochures are meant to last for a period of time. Many have been forced into a reprinting because a price was raised or a director was replaced. Avoid writing about details that change frequently.

8. *Make sure the writing is direct.* Don't make readers guess, but lead them to the desired conclusion or behavior.

9. *Increase reader interest* by providing tips or useful advice. Give readers concrete suggestions rather than abstract ideas.

10. *Highlight headlines and subheads.* These should be more than mere labels. Question heads can be useful. When you use them, make sure the questions are logical and honest. Readers will spot loaded or leading questions and lose respect for the brochure. Readers also are unlikely to tolerate dumb or meaningless questions.

---

the inside cover (Panel E) has importance second only to the front cover, because it is the first panel the reader sees upon opening the brochure. The inside cover serves as a continuation of the front cover and a bridge to the three inside message panels (B, C and D). The back panel (F) can be used either as a message panel or as a self-mailer.

Brochures can be vertical (folded on the side like a greeting card) or horizontal (folded on the top). Most brochures use a vertical design because they are easier to read. But be consistent. Avoid designing a brochure with a horizontal-style cover and with vertical inside panels. "Tips for Better Writing: Designing a Brochure" offers additional suggestions. As you consider the design of the brochure, take into account the method of dissemination. For instance, if the piece will be a self-mailer, you need to reserve a panel for this purpose. If it is supposed to fit into a business envelope, size will become important. Postal criteria also must be considered in design. The "Business Center/Postal Explorer" link on the U.S. Postal Service

Exhibit 11.1—SIX-PANEL BROCHURE   The six-panel fold is the most popular format for brochures—a front cover (Panel A), three inside message panels (B, C and D), an inside focal panel (E) and a back panel (F).

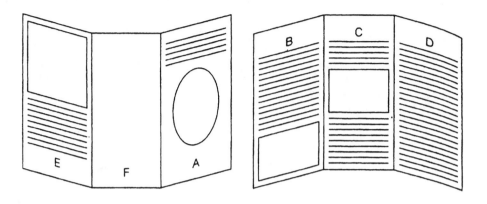

Tips for Better Writing   *Design a Brochure*

Following are some guidelines related to brochure design:

1. *Emphasize the upper third of the front cover* because brochures often are used in display racks. Use a design that makes effective use of this space.

2. *Use type fonts and sizes that are reader friendly.* Type for brochures should be at least 10 point. Serif type is easier to read in paragraphs; sans serif type may be more appropriate for bulleted information. Alternatives to paragraph form include lists, often introduced by dingbats, bullets, hyphens, squares, asterisks and so on.

3. *Text should be set flush left*, with a solid left margin and a ragged right margin. This not only is easier to read but it also provides a relaxed feel. Use boldface and/or italic type for emphasis. Avoid using all caps, which is the print equivalent of shouting. Use large initial capital letters sparingly.

4. *Don't be afraid of white space.* Crowded brochures give the impression of being ponderous, which signals that reading this will be a chore.

5. *Strive for short blocks of type.* Lengthy sections of text can be shortened, or they can be broken up by subheads, artwork, design elements such as lines and boxes, and white space.

6. *Spot color can be effective.* This can be accomplished graphically, using tints or colored heads. Or it can be accomplished artistically, such as with washes of color underneath the text.

7. *Colored paper can enhance a brochure inexpensively.* A low-cost way of adding color is to use paper manufactured in a light or pastel color.

8. *Photographs don't reproduce well in other-than-black ink.* If you are using a color with photos, make sure the ink is a dark shade.

9. *Balance graphic elements on the inside panels.* Spot photos or graphic devices at different locations in each panel. Avoid top-heavy or bottom-heavy layouts.

10. *Don't exaggerate the role of graphics.* Brochures are vehicles primarily for the written word. Don't fall into the trap of having a brochure that is over-designed but underwritten.

Web site (usps.com) has instructions on designing publications for mailing, postage rate calculators and other useful information.

Another piece of advice about graphic design: If you are using an outside printing firm, make contact early. It saves time and energy to have the printer go over his or her needs, such as loading the fonts on the zip disk, making certain the font you choose exists in a format that the printer can use, checking to make certain you have the original art loaded on the zip disk, and so on. If a printer has to substitute a font for one you have chosen, often the type no longer fits.

Polished, Edited Copy. The final stages of preparing a brochure are the same as for any kind of writing: Polish your language. Aim for a unity between the headlines and artwork or other graphic elements. Read the copy out loud and listen to the flow of your words. Edit your copy for style, spelling, punctuation and other mechanics of acceptable writing.

Copyfitting. When you are preparing copy for a brochure, you will need to *copyfit*. This involves the manipulation of type to fit within the design specifications. Complicated mathematical formulas can help writers calculate how typewritten copy will transform into typeset text of various sizes, styles and widths. Happily, there are two alternatives to mathematical madness. One is to ask your printer for help. Many printers are convinced that public relations writers are waifs needing a guiding hand, so they often are happy to oblige requests for direction. The second alternative is to let your computer do the work. With a computer, you can experiment with fonts, type sizes, column widths and line spacing. You can write and rewrite heads and paragraphs so they fit a particular space.

Copy Testing. Pretesting messages is a vital part of effective public relations. With a brochure that will be used for a long time, it is especially important to test it before hundreds, perhaps thousands, are printed. This can be done informally, by showing samples to people representative of your intended audience. For example, if the brochure is to encourage attendance at a senior citizen center, ask some people already attending what they think of it.

Approvals. Brochures may require the approval of one or several organizational executives. After the brochure has been pretested and found appropriate, the writer may need to obtain approval from organizational leaders to publish and distribute the brochure.

Production Schedules

Each of the steps described above takes time. The actual time needed for each step will vary depending on a lot of individual circumstances, but consider the following hypothetical case: You have been asked to produce a brochure for use by transfer students coming into your college. The academic dean who has commissioned this project wants to distribute the brochures at the beginning of the two-week registration period for transfer students, which begins on Monday, August 13. Working backwards, such as X minus three days, you could develop the following schedule.

	X	Distribute to transfer students
3 days	X–3	Pick up from printer; distribution to admissions staff
10 days	X–13	Deliver to printer
5 days	X–18	Get final approvals from Director of Admissions; revise as needed

5 days	X–23	Show samples of the brochure to two seven-person groups of students who transferred into the college last year; these students were contacted in May and were selected because they would be on campus during the summer months
2 days	X–25	Produce a mock-up of the finished brochure; proofread it
5 days	X–30	Vacation week
10 days	X–40	Revise the draft; polish and edit the copy; select the design and graphic elements; obtain needed illustrations
5 days	X–45	Research the subject; identify sections within the copy; write the first draft
5 days	X–50	Develop a budget; obtain budget approval
5 days	X–55	Obtain concept approval from the Director of Admissions
5 days	X–60	Begin the planning; develop strategy and concept for the project

You have determined you will need 60 working days, nearly three months, to complete the project. This schedule is a reasonable projection of the time that could be needed to produce the brochure, though it also offers many opportunities to shorten the time span.

Exercise 11.2—Developing a Brochure

You are a public relations writer preparing a brochure for one of the following organizations:

- County General Hospital: Brochure for children preparing to be admitted for surgical and medical care.
- Jenny's Jazz Club: Brochure supporting the organization's mission to promote interest in various forms of jazz.
- Suburban Shade Nursing Home: Brochure for families considering placing a loved one in the facility.
- An organization in which you are interested: Brochure for one of the organization's programs or services.

Part 1: Develop a planning sheet. Sketch out three different cover designs for this brochure. Discuss your concepts with another student or a colleague, then determine which cover design to use.

Part 2: Identify six to eight possible sections that would be appropriate for a brochure. Then research the topics and write brief paragraphs for each section. Then review the planning sheet and revise the copy as needed.

Part 3: Sketch out the visual elements of the brochure. Produce a final layout or mock-up of the brochure.

Part 4: Create a rough schedule for this project. ∎

Web Sites

Of all the opportunities that computers offer public relations writers, none has more far-reaching consequences than the World Wide Web. The Internet Web is an amazing tool for public relations communication. Today, the Web is one of the most commonly used media. With the cost-effectiveness of both computer hardware and programs, and with the placement of computers in libraries, copy centers and other public places, the Web is increasingly available to individuals and organizations of virtually every economic means. The Web is rapidly changing the way organizations communicate with their publics, just as it is changing the way people gather information about products, services and ideas.

Most organizations today have an Internet presence via a *Web site,* a series of Internet-based screens or pages constructed to allow the user to move through them easily and in an organized manner. But as a public relations writer, you should be concerned with more than mere presence.

First, you should be aware of the relationship among the three major elements of a Web site: graphics, organization and writing. Web pages often are designed with elegant and catchy graphics; this is what wins awards and grabs the attention of clients and readers alike. Good Web managers also pay careful attention to how information flows, the ease and efficiency with which readers can navigate through all the information at the site. And as important as graphics and information flow are, writing is even more important. Too often, not enough attention is given to writing for Web pages.

Second, you should be particularly knowledgeable about how readers use the Web, and thus how you can write effectively for them. The Web is not a linear medium, moving from Point A to Point B. Rather, it is an interactive and interlinking medium. Online readers are used to finding their own way through the information, and your writing should make their journey easier and more effective.

Web designers, especially those in organizations developing their own Web pages, sometimes simply drop in existing text and focus most of their attention on the look and flow of the site. In doing so, they miss the point completely. It's one thing to attract a user to a Web site with engaging graphics, but readers will return to a site only when the written information gives them solid reason to return. Web writers know they can't simply use existing text, such as what they might draw from a brochure, report, news release or some other available written document. That's because Web writers must be translators of the written word, transposing it into an Internet format.

How can you accomplish this? Like any good public relations writing, Web writing begins with a planning sheet. Be clear with yourself about who your key publics are, what they are interested in and what they need to know. Also be clear about what they *don't* need to know. In the planning sheet, articulate your organization's objectives in developing the Web site; consider the effects you hope to achieve in awareness, acceptance and action. Particularly important in planning a Web site is to consider the reading level of your key publics, as well as their fluency and familiarity with the Internet.

Jakob Nielsen, a leading researcher on writing for the Web, recommends that Web writing should be concise, scannable and objective. Each of these elements is described in the following sections. "Tips for Better Writing: Measuring the Effect of Web Writing" describes one of Nielsen's research projects. As you look through various Web sites, pay attention to how the points discussed below are exhibited in these pages.

Tips for Better Writing   *Measuring the Effects of Web Writing*

Jakob Nielsen, a prolific researcher and recognized expert on Web usability, advises that Web users detest promotional writing, "marketese," with its boastful subjective claims. He and research partner John Morkes tested five different versions of the same message about Nebraska tourism, using four performance measures (time, errors, memory and site structure). Here are the test messages and their results:

Promotional writing, which the researchers calculated with a base of 0 percent of reading effectiveness: Nebraska is filled with internationally recognized attractions that draw large crowds of people every year, without fail. In 1996, some of the most popular places were Fort Robinson State Park (355,000 visitors), Scotts Bluff National Monument (132,166), Arbor Lodge State Historical Park & Museum (100,000), Carhenge (86,598), Stuhr Museum of the Prairie Pioneer (60,002), and Buffalo Bill Ranch State Historical park (28,446).

Concise (nonpromotional) text, which was calculated as 58 percent better writing: In 1996, six of the best-attended attractions in Nebraska were Fort Robinson State Park, Scotts Bluff National Monument, Arbor Lodge State Historical Park & Museum, Carhenge, Stuhr Museum of the Prairie Pioneer, and Buffalo Bill Ranch State Historical Park.

Scannable layout, 47 percent better writing: Nebraska is filled with internationally recognized attractions that draw large crowds of people every year, without fail. In 1996, some of the most popular places were:

- Fort Robinson State Park (355,000 visitors)
- Scotts Bluff National Monument (132,166)
- Arbor Lodge State Historical Park & Museum (100,000)
- Carhenge (86,598)
- Stuhr Museum of the Prairie Pioneer (60,002)
- Buffalo Bill Ranch State Historical Park (28,446).

Objective language, 27 percent better writing: Nebraska has several attractions. In 1996, some of the most-visited places were Fort Robinson State Park (355,000 visitors), Scotts Bluff National Monument (132,166), Arbor Lodge State Historical Park & Museum (100,000), Carhenge (86,598), Stuhr Museum of the Prairie Pioneer (60,002), and Buffalo Bill Ranch State Historical park (28,446).

Combined improved version (concise, scannable and objective), calculated as 124 percent better writing: In 1996, six of the most-visited places in Nebraska were:

- Fort Robinson State Park
- Scotts Bluff National Monument
- Arbor Lodge State Historical Park & Museum
- Carhenge
- Stuhr Museum of the Prairie Pioneer
- Buffalo Bill Ranch State Historical Park.

In reporting his test, Nielsen said he expected the performance outcome to be similar for promotional and objective writing. Instead, he found that the more objective the writing, the more usable and preferable it was for the readers. Why? Nielsen suggested that the finding can be explained by his observation that promotional language imposes a *cognitive burden* on users, who must expend mental energy to filter out the hype from the facts, which in turn slows them down and distracts them from gaining usable, memorable information.

Nielsen's Web research and advice are available at his Web site: useit.com.

Nielsen's recent studies have looked at how different groups of Web users read online material. He has noted that low-literacy readers are less likely to scan text. Instead they often focus on each word with a narrow field of vision, ignoring objects outside the main flow of the text. Alternatively, when things become complicated, they skip over whole chunks of text. In addition, they easily lose their place when they have to scroll down pages. Their spelling deficiencies, meanwhile, often diminish the usefulness of a Web site's internal search features. Similar difficulties have been studied involving people with disabilities as well as with teenagers, who often have both low reading abilities and little patience for dealing with nonuserfriendly Web texts. All of these can cause problems for a Web writer, but the difficulties can be minimized with a few writing practices: Write to a 6th-grade reading level, prioritize information, avoid animated text, streamline page design, and simplify navigation.

Concise Web Writing

The same rules and recommendations that guide other types of public relations writing are important in writing for the Web. Effective writing is short, active and clear. It also should be accurate and stylistically consistent. Presume that Web readers will scan and peruse Web pages rather than read the content word for word. An obvious exception to this is the presentation of the full text of a piece of writing, such as magazine articles and teaching materials. These your readers will follow using scrolling pages. But try to make the full text an option for the reader rather than the only choice. Further, assist readers by making it easy for them to download longer documents to disk and print full texts for easier reading on paper. Following is a look at each of the various characteristics of effective writing for the Web.

Short. Keep Web writing short. Computer screens are harder on the eye than printed pages in magazines or newspapers. A survey by Sun Microsystems found that 70 percent of people who visit Web sites scan the material rather than read it word for word.

Single Screen. Studies also have found that most readers do not scroll; they read the information available on the opening screen and then generally move on. Try to limit your Web information to a single screen, two at the most.

Active Voice. Just as with other media, Web writers should use active voice because it is clear, more direct and more powerful.

Clear. Studies show that generous use of subheads helps the reader flow through the text. Make sure subheads are meaningful rather than cute. Headlines should be self-explanatory, and their context should be self-evident. Web pages are not a good place for feature or teaser heads; stick with the conventional summary news headlines or with plain titles.

Accurate. Correct grammar and spelling are important in any medium, but errors seem to leap from a video monitor. Proofread carefully. Use the spellcheck and grammar check, but don't rely solely on your computer to make everything right. The ultimate responsibility for accurate writing lies with the writer, ideally with the assistance of an editor.

Style Guide. Just as with any other writing medium, Web writing calls for consistency. Some organizations adopt a standard style guide—the widely used Associated Press Style or the more formal Chicago Style, for example. Others modify these or develop their own Web style guide. Such style guides often include not only assistance in writing, spelling, capitalization, and usage, but also standards for the type font and size, bullets, colors and templates. As an example, look at the online style guide adopted by the Environmental Protection Agency (epa.gov/productreview/guide/app3.html).

   Style guides also often identify specific dictionaries and other printed or online reference works as the final word; they also may identify how the organization uses its own trademark and other references to patents or copyrighted information. The Web Style Guide (Webstyle guide.com) developed by writer Patrick Lynch and technology specialist Sarah Horton is a helpful resource for online writers.

Scannable Web Writing

Writing for the Web should be *scannable*. That is, it should feature information that is chunked into segments, making it easy for the reader to move through it. Physiologically, it is more difficult to read from a computer monitor than it is from a printed sheet of paper.

Remember the nature of Web reading when you are developing your site. In particular, pay attention to how the text is displayed. Present information according to the inverted pyramid model, and use user-friendly writing elements such as summaries and tables of contents. Additionally, use simple background designs, make sure the page loads quickly, and don't use photographs and other demanding graphics unless they are necessary.

Chunked Text. Avoid long paragraphs and lengthy passages of unrelieved text, which are most difficult to read on a monitor. If lengthy passages are necessary, break them down into several shorter sections that are easier to comprehend.

Links and Navigation Tools. The ease of using Web sites is increased when the site has well-placed links to help users navigate around the site. Links need to be clear so the user is not left wondering where to go next for wanted information. Likewise, good Web sites have clear navigation tools, forward and back arrows, returns to home pages, and other aids to help users find their way around the site.

Display. Accent the text with a variety of visual elements to emphasize key words or concepts. Consider typographical devices such as bullets, indents, italics, boldface, underlines and colored text, but don't overdo these to the point of distraction. Also, be generous in your use of headlines, titles and subheads.

Table of Contents. Consider adding a table of contents to your Web pages so the reader can easily navigate throughout your site. When providing a table of contents, make it easy for a reader to find a particular page. For example, it may be easy for a public relations office to arrange news releases in an archive by release date, but that doesn't necessarily help a reader find a particular release. Consider arranging them topically rather than chronologically. Another helpful feature is a site map that presents an outline of how your site is put together.

Inverted Pyramid. The standard journalistic format is a good one to use in Web writing. Begin with the conclusion or summary, then follow with supporting information and finally with background information.

Summary. Many Web users read only the first sentence of a paragraph, and effective Web pages often include carefully crafted topic sentences for each paragraph. Some sites providing news-based information have found it useful to begin with a summary paragraph set apart from a following news article. A good way to accommodate readers is to provide a summary and a hypertext link to the longer story or the full text. That way, readers can read or print only the summary without wasting time on the longer text if it isn't relevant.

Legible Text. Use a simple type font, preferably a serif font with both capital and lowercase letters for easiest reading. Use black lettering on a white or light background, or use dark-colored text that contrasts highly with a light background. Use text large enough for your readers. In general, avoid text that is moving, blinking or zooming. Remember also that color blindness is fairly common; an estimated 8 percent of Caucasian males—one in 12—are unable to distinguish between reds and greens.

Simple Background. Don't overload your pages with fancy designs or graphics. A simple background color is preferable to a background pattern, which not only can get in the way of reading but also can make printing difficult and loading times long. If you choose to use photos or graphics, make certain they are relevant to the text. Don't include graphics just for show. When they are integral to your story or report, consider including them as hypertext links rather than fixing them within the text. That will make it easier for users to read and print the text only, the graphic only, or both, depending on the reader's interest. Also, when using photos, always include a caption.

Objective Web Writing

Nielsen's research shows that unexaggerated, nonpromotional Web writing is measurably more effective than hype, or "marketese," because the latter is often associated with advertising and other marketing communication (see "Tips for Better Writing: Measuring the Effect of Web Writing"). As such, it is important that Web writing be journalistic and balanced in nature and contain links to other sites.

Journalistic. Avoid promotional writing associated with advertising and other aspects of marketing. Web writing needs to be more journalistic—objective, neutral, professional and unexaggerated. Let the information stand on its own.

Balance. It often is difficult to find just the right balance between the public relations and marketing needs of an organizational Web site. Remember, however, that research on reader usability is on the side of unexaggerated, nonpromotional writing.

Outbound Links. Inviting your reader to visit other sites is good business. It enhances your credibility much the same as citations enhance an academic report. In both cases, the author is helping readers compare information and ideas with those of other sources. Make sure to check these often, and purge or update any dead links pointing to nonexistent sites.

Interactive Web Sites

An advantage of Web sites is that they can be made interactive, with opportunities for the user to communicate with the organization, and vice versa. This provides a great benefit to public relations practitioners trying to connect their organizations and publics in meaningful ways. Here are some of the ways in which an organization's Web site can engage users:

E-Mail Link. Among the simplest ways to accomplish this is to include a "mailto" hot link back to the organization or to a menu of key staff within the organization. This lets the user click on the appropriate icon and be offered the opportunity to write, edit and send an e-mail message to the organization. It is good to supplement this with a listing of traditional contacts, such as telephone numbers, fax numbers and postal addresses.

Electronic Forms. E-mail responses can be structured so the user provides asked-for information that can be edited and then submitted to the host Web site. Such information can deal with online scheduling, applications, order forms, surveys and a range of other uses.

Search Features. A feature that can greatly enhance the interactive aspect of a Web site is an internal search function, such as a pull-down menu that allows the user to click onto various pages or to link to a certain topic. Other search tools allow users to type in a word or phrase and be directed to the appropriate Web page. A study on Internet usability by Jakob Nielsen found that half of all Web users depend on a site's search function rather than do their own navigating.

Audio Options. New technology makes it easier to include in a Web site options for voice, music, audio news clips and sound effects. Because of the unevenness of user capabilities, it is best to offer these as options rather than trying to imbed them in a basic Web site.

Video Options. Web designers can use video for purposes similar to audio, and it can be useful in product or service demonstrations, news clips, artistic performances, and so on. For audiences used to television, computer-based video options can provide valuable information in an agreeable format. But remember that standard production values should be maintained. Dull, corporate talking heads are no more exciting on the computer screen than they are on the television screen. Technological developments offer new ways to deliver video over a Web site, such as streaming video or downloads.

Animation. Technology also offers possibilities for including animation, such as three-dimensional views of models and graphics, virtual tours, transitions, and so on. Keep animation to a minimum, because many users find it more annoying than helpful. Use it with a strategic purpose rather than simply for effect.

Cookie Technology. Another aspect of interactivity is the ability of Web technology to help the organization anticipate the interest of individual visitors to the Web site. *Cookies* are information that becomes active whenever the user connects to a particular Web site. They enable the site to "remember" information about the user—name, previous connections, stated interests, and so on. Thus the organization can deliver messages of particular interest to the user. A Web site that is designed by an organization committed to ethical communication will tell visitors about its use of cookies, offer users the opportunity to disengage the technology, and explain how the cookie-gathered information will be used or shared.

E-Commerce. Nonprofit and political fundraising organizations can use e-commerce technology to receive online contributions from donors. Common e-commerce features are online applications, order forms, order tracking, and requests for information.

Pop-Up Window. Using Java programming, Web sites can feature pop-up windows (also called interstitials) that can enhance user interaction. This feature could provide users with a variety of public relations messages or opportunities to contact the organization or obtain information on demand. Sometimes, pop-up windows can include streaming audio or streaming video, which immediately engages the visitor.

News Groups and Listservs. Some organizations create special-interest forums to make it easier for their publics to communicate both with the organization and with each other. News groups, listservs and electronic bulletin boards are common elements of the overall communication program of some organizations.

Evaluating Web Sites

Web sites can provide top-quality information or plain old garbage, and it's important to be able to determine the difference. Remember that anybody with Internet access and minimal computer skills can put together a Web page. If you are developing a Web site for your organization, keep in mind some of the objective criteria for evaluating Web-based information, so you can build into your site the necessary ingredients that will identify your site as one of excellence. The following sections describe some objective criteria for evaluating Web sites.

Recognized Sponsor. A quality Web site is one that is hosted by a legitimate and recognized organization or individual. The domain name of most Web sites reflects the name of the sponsoring organization. For example, the domain name for most college or university Web sites will feature some variation of the institution's name, followed by .edu (dot edu). A university name followed by .com (dot com) might indicate a rogue site set up by someone wishing to embarrass the institution or to mislead Internet visitors. The user should readily be able to determine the difference. Sometimes, spyware and other intruders hijack legitimate Web sites and divert visitors to rival, commercial or even fake sites.

Verifiable Information. Quality Web sites provide documentation about the source of their information. The source could be an individual, an organization or a document such as a research report, but the user should be able to easily identify where the information originally came from. An e-mail contact should be provided for the author or webmaster.

Authoritative Information. Information at Web sites should be attributable to an expert authority, perhaps the site host, perhaps some other expert. The site should include information about the qualifications and credentials of the author of the Web page. It should be clear whether information reflects the official organizational information or the opinion of one person.

Objective Information. It should be clear to the user whether a Web site is advocating a cause, selling a product or service, soliciting support, or offering objective information.

Up-to-Date Information. Web sites should be kept current. Quality sites will note revision dates not only for the home page but for substantive inside pages. Pay particular attention to sites that provide information based on annual statistics; these should be no more than a year old. Check the site frequently to make sure links are not broken or inactive.

Comprehensive Information. The best Web sites provide a range of information about topics relevant to the sponsoring organization and potential users.

Quick Loading. Downloads for Web pages should be quick, ideally no more than a second. Studies show that users often abort downloads that take too long to load. Images, charts, and unnecessary coding and META tags can slow download time. Make sure the text loads before the graphics. If you wish to use a photo, keep it small, perhaps with a link to a larger version at a separate page. Remember that while the site may load easily on *your* computer, some people may not have access to state-of-the-art hardware or software. Make sure your site is accessible to average users. Consider offering a flexible menu of download options, such as both a flash version and a simpler loading format.

Easy-to-Navigate Site. Web sites should be well designed, with the user in mind. It should be easy for users to locate information. Site maps, menus and internal search tools can be particularly helpful to a visitor who may be unfamiliar with the structure of the Web site or the organization sponsoring it. Easy-to-navigate sites also feature both quick-loading pages and single-screen pages, as well as "Back," "Next" and "Menu" buttons.

Accessibility. Web sites should be accessible to anyone who might be counted as the audience. For sites with an international focus, this may mean that they should offer multilingual sites or translations into various languages. An Internet marketing firm, Internet World Stats, reported in 2006 that 36 percent of Internet users are in Asia, 28 percent in Europe, 21 percent in North America, 8 percent in Latin America and the Caribbean, 3 percent in Africa, 2 percent in the Middle East, and 2 percent in Oceania and Australia. Despite the low percentages, Africa, the Middle East and Latin America represent the highest rate of growth in Internet use.

The report also focused on Internet penetration—the percentage of a population with access to the Internet. World-wide, the penetration is only 16 percent, but this is steadily growing. Top-ranked countries are the United States (where 69 percent of the population has access to the Internet), Canada and Japan (68 percent each), and South Korea (67 percent). Countries with the most Internet users are the United States (205.5 million users), China (123 million) and Japan (86 million). English is the most common Internet language (30 percent), followed by Chinese (14 percent), Japanese (8 percent) and Spanish (7.5 percent). All in all, a lot of statistics—but they point to the advisability for public relations writers to be aware of this diversity and perhaps to be accessible to a wide variety of potential readers and Web users.

Web sites also might need to be made accessible to persons with visual, hearing or motor handicaps. Some organizations are required to make their Web sites conform to guidelines of the Americans with Disabilities Act or to similar laws and regulations in other countries.

Cultural Consideration. In addition to the above general criteria, some Web sites call for special consideration, often based on cultural factors. For example, in evaluating a Web site dealing with American Indian issues, here are some additional questions to ask about the site: Is it authentic? Is a specific tribal affiliation noted (a common practice among most Native peoples), and is the tribal name accurate (for example, Lenape instead of Delaware)? If the site claims to present a tribal view, is it authorized by the tribal government, and does it include the presence of the president or chairman? Does the site feature images that are contemporary and respectful? Is cultural and historic information authoritative and verified?

Tips for Better Writing   *Evaluating Web Sites*

Here is a checklist of things to look for in evaluating any Web site, your own or someone else's.

- Concise writing
- Pages viewable on one or two screens
- Chunked text
- Easy-to-follow navigation links
- Legible text
- Simple background
- Objective, journalistic writing style
- Recognized sponsor
- Verifiable and documented information

- Authoritative information
- Objective information
- Up-to-date information, with appropriate updates
- Comprehensive information
- Outbound links
- Quick loading
- Ease of navigation within site
- Logical flow of pages
- Quick loading
- Appropriately interactive
- Appropriately accessible, accountability for language use and disability

What Would You Do?   *Writing for Different Publics*

The young woman who faced the problem outlined in "What Would You Do" earlier in this chapter was an actual student in a public relations writing class, working part time for the shelter. Her first thought was to seek additional funds to prepare two separate brochures, but no money was available. So she developed a brochure that could be used in two different ways.

First, she prepared a single two-fold brochure that featured the human service aspects of the shelter: the social problem within the community, the shelter's record of success and the need for community support. The brochure invited contributions of food and clothing as well as money. The writer used this brochure in her appeals to the businesses and secular supporters.

Then, for the religious supporters, the writer provided an insert in the form of a prayer card that was the same dimensions as the brochure. The insert featured a religious design, Bible quotes and a spiritual appeal in the style that the religious supporters would find appropriate. The insert was included within the brochure when the shelter presented its message to its religious supporters.

Exercise 11.3—Developing a Web Page

Your academic department at your college or university has decided to develop a Web page for each major, minor and sequence it offers. You have been selected to develop the Web page for your particular academic program.

Part 1: Prepare a planning sheet. Pay particular attention to analyzing your key public(s) for this project, as well as the objectives.

Part 2: Write a welcome or introduction page. Include on this page an indication of the purpose of the academic program and a menu or table of contents for hypertext links to secondary pages, each representing one of the various elements of the information that you think is appropriate for this Web site. Briefly indicate how you would use graphics on this opening page.

Part 3: Write the text for one of the sample linked pages.

Part 4: Write a brief explanation of how you would evaluate the effectiveness of this Web page after it has been in place for one semester.

12

Newsletters and Corporate Reports

Newsletters are important public relations tools for organizations seeking a communication link with key publics. Many public relations graduates find entry-level public relations positions that involve working on employee newsletters, and many seasoned practitioners find that special-interest newsletters offer lucrative career options. This is a field that will draw on your writing abilities, training in news writing and editing, and skill in organization and planning.

Some organizations are expanding their print repertoire beyond simple newsletters. They are publishing internal magazines and organizational newspapers, as well as hybrids with names like *magapapers*, *minimags* and *maganews*. Essentially, all of these are variations on the same theme, different formats for what traditionally has been considered a house organ. For the writer, all of these publications allow a flexibility of writing styles.

This chapter will refer primarily to *newsletters* as an umbrella term for the various kinds of organizational publications. But the student is advised to consider that the same guidelines and observations that are applied here to newsletters may also apply to organizational magazines, newspapers and similar print vehicles for the organization's message. Here are your objectives for Chapter 12:

- To distinguish among the various types of newsletters
- To recognize what makes a newsletter effective
- To write an effective newsletter article based on information recycled from a news release
- To write an effective headline for a newsletter article
- To understand the purpose and importance of corporate reports
- To edit and proofread documents carefully and effectively
- To show an understanding of laws related to copyright and trademark.

Newsletters

Newsletters seem to be everywhere. Newsletters in Print lists more than 12,000 public newsletters in the United States and Canada; the Oxbridge Directory of Newsletters lists more than 13,500. While print publications decrease in number, rapid growth has been seen among online newsletters, which doubled in number between 2005 and 2006. But these are just whispers of the total number of newsletters. Such reports don't include innumerable local newsletters and perhaps as many as 50,000 internal corporate newsletters not generally available to the public, as well as hundreds of thousands of newsletters published by organizations such as churches, schools, community singing groups, bridge clubs, sports organizations, fan clubs and many other such groups.

Newsletters are among the most ancient public relations tools. Herodotus of Thurii, the first Greek historian, is credited with publishing a trade newsletter in 425 B.C.E., and Julius Caesar published a daily handwritten newsletter in Rome during the first century B.C.E. called *Acta Diurna* (Daily Events). The Tang dynasty in 11th-century China circulated a newsletter, as did the financial leaders of many European cities during the Middle Ages and the Renaissance. *Publick Occurrences Both Forreign and Domestick*, the recognized forerunner of American newspapers, was a multipage newsletter published in Massachusetts in 1690; it was intended as a monthly publication but shut down by the colonial government after its first issue. Many of the other early colonial publications were social and political advocacy newsletters that eventually took up the cause of issues related to American independence from Britain.

Newsletter Purpose and Objectives

What, exactly, is a newsletter? Simply said, a *newsletter* is a printed periodic publication distributed by an organization to a particular information-seeking audience. It is part news, part letter. As a provider of news, a newsletter should focus on information relevant to its audience, which mirrors the key publics of the organization that produces the newsletter. The wants, interests and needs of the key public should determine the news value of information for newsletters, and the focus of this news value is the reader rather than the organization that publishes the newsletter.

In addition to being news based, the content of newsletters is presented in a writing style that is less formal—more letterlike, more featurish—than is common with many other public relations media. The basic similarity between the publisher and the reader lends itself to the use of jargon and to the presumption of common and often personal interests that are shared by all. Like other practical public relations activities, newsletters are most effective when they build on the mutual interests of both the organization and its publics and when they foster the mutual benefit of both. They serve several different objectives within an organization's public relations plan. Consider the following objectives for an organization publishing a newsletter:

- To maintain a relationship with a public
- To reinforce attitudes and actions beneficial to an organization
- To create and then maintain a dialogue between the organization and its publics, or among members of the audience
- To increase or maintain a level of awareness by a public about issues important to an organization
- To increase or maintain a level of interest and/or positive attitudes for an active public about an issue.

Note that these objectives deal with enhancing an organization's relationship with publics that are already interested in the organization's message. An organization has several vehicles available to it to communicate with disinterested or latent publics; newsletters are not among these media. Rather, newsletters generally are published for active information-seeking publics. It is a distinction worth remembering, because you don't want to waste time and money by preparing communication tools that are likely to be inappropriate for your key public.

Another consideration is that newsletters need not look like miniature newspapers or little magazines with columns, photos, traditional headlines, and other elements associated with these publications. Some effective newsletters are more like a letter—a string of paragraphs, each with a different topic, sometimes with bold or underlined type to emphasize the topic words and phrases. The value of newsletters is their frequency, consistency, and easy readability, as well as the authority and currency of the information they provide. In short, newsletters need not be fancy; they just need to meet the needs of their audiences.

Exercise 12.1—Freewriting on Newsletters

Freewrite for five minutes on the following topic: *How effective have been recent newsletters I have seen?* Then discuss this with your classmates. ∎

Types of Newsletters

Organizations occasionally publish a single newsletter, thinking it will serve their need to communicate with various publics. Usually, they are mistaken, because information that serves one public may be of little value or interest to another. Organizations that communicate effectively have learned that newsletters should be directed to particular audiences. Some of the categories of newsletter audiences are members, general external publics, special-interest publics, subscribers, consumers and cause-related readers.

Member Newsletters. Member newsletters are aimed at internal publics—employees, volunteers, retirees and other groups of people generically classified as members—as well as consumer groups who identify closely with the organization, such as students or alumni. For many organizations, these are the most important publics, and such newsletters often provide the most important communication tool that exists. For examples of member newsletters, download the PDF of the House Call newsletter in the member section of mcare.org, the Flukeprints newsletters of the Whale Center of New England in the member news section at whalecenter.org, or the Gamofite newsletter for members of Gay Mormon Fathers at gamofites.org.

External Newsletters. Not surprisingly, external newsletters are aimed at nonmembers—customers, consumers, electoral constituents, distributors, suppliers, fans and so on. Like internal newsletters, these external publications are focused on a single organization. An example of this is the Community Newsletter published by Santa Clara University (available online at scu.edu/visitors/newsletter.cfm) or Footy News, the online newsletter of the Australian Football Association of North America (downloadable in the newsletter section at afana.com/drupal).

Special-Interest Newsletters. Special-interest newsletters deal with a particular profession or industry, or with a particular topic or issue. Professional newsletters for public relations practitioners are examples of this, as are publications directed to owners of a particular class of racing sailboat, people interested in making financial investments, nuns, stamp collectors or distributors of imported Norwegian lace. In addition to professions and hobbies, special-interest newsletters may also be based on common concerns about politics, economics, religion, hobbies, social issues, lifestyle and any other issue that provides a common bond among people. The Society of Financial Service Providers publishes a series of newsletters at financialpro.org for people who are professional financial advisers. The National Coalition of American Nuns' newsletter archives at ncan.us deal with social justice issues in church and society.

Subscription Newsletters. Subscription newsletters provide inside information and expert advice to paying subscribers. They offer a particular challenge to writers because of the high demands by subscribers, who may be paying several hundred dollars a year for valuable information in an easy-to-use format. The most popular topics deal with business, communications, computers, health, investments, and international and legal issues. Because of their high pricing, subscription newsletters are especially concerned with providing information of interest to readers, who generally are specialists seeking a level of detail not found in mass media coverage. For example, a network news story about congressional debates over health care reform might focus on the legislative battle, scope of reforms or consequences for the consumers. But a newsletter aimed at insurance agents who market health care policies might give details about specific provisions of the bill relating to licensure of agents, their education requirements and commission controls. The Kiplinger Letter (kiplinger.com), one of the oldest and most respected subscription newsletters, has a circulation of 275,000 subscribers interested in its insight into government and business. Jack O'Dwyer's Newsletter, which specializes in news about public relations and marketing communication, is available in print or online at odwyerpr.com.

Consumer Newsletters. Consumer newsletters provide how-to information for readers interested in a particular topic, such as hydroponic gardening, line dancing and beekeeping. Many of the consumer publications are produced by government agencies as part of their mission to increase understanding and acceptance. For example, the Better Business Bureau archives its Wise Consumer Newsletter at its Web site, bbb.org.

Advocacy Newsletters. Advocacy newsletters attempt to persuade readers by providing a consistent point of view and supportive information about a particular issue. Organizations that produce advocacy newsletters are likely to be focused on politics, the environment, health and safety and other topics in which persuasion plays a key role. Amnesty International publishes News Amnesty, an online advocacy newsletter at news.amnesty.org.

Newsletter Writing

The planning process for newsletters involves attention to the wants, interests and needs of key publics and to the objectives of the organization. This planning often leads organizations to develop a *mission statement* that sets out in writing the philosophy and commitment of the organization that publishes the newsletter. For example, the Latino Community Newsletter of the Southern Tier, published in Binghamton, New York, presents this simple mission statement:

Our purpose is to disseminate information and knowledge for and about the Latino Community. We want to enrich, challenge and uphold our traditions with a vision toward the future. The Latino Community Newsletter features news articles, community resources, cultural items, editorials, interviews and updates on local businesses and community events.

Editorial statements, meanwhile, may be more comprehensive. They often include information on acceptance policies, publication criteria, reprint guidelines, distribution schedules, and other practical information.

A Nose for News

Just as with news releases, public relations writers working on organizational newsletters need to generate interesting and relevant ideas. Often you will be aided by a close collaboration with the human resources department, as well as with various department heads and other employees.

A good public relations writer needs to access many different resources and to develop a nose for news within the organization so that the articles, especially features, can be of interest to the newsletter's audiences. Review the section on "Generating News" in Chapter 5. And remember that, even though you may be writing for an internal audience, you must satisfy your readers' news interests.

Audience Focus

The interests of the intended audience, defined in terms of key publics, will determine the content and writing style of the newsletter. Internal newsletters, for example, often are informal, while external newsletters may be much more businesslike. Special-interest newsletters show a variety of approaches, each reflecting the nature of a particular readership. Most newsletters take on the tone of the leadership of the organization that publishes them. Newsletters often suggest the personality of an organization: formal and distant, open and communicative, issue oriented, growing, familial.

What can you write about in a newsletter? Whatever interests your readers. One way to identify those interests is to ask. Focus groups and readership surveys can be effective ways of learning about reader interests.

The writing process begins with the planning sheet. It is here that the writer carefully considers both the reader's interests and the organization's purpose for writing for this reader. The writing is made much easier when you visualize readers or, better yet, one individual— a typical reader who has the characteristics of your key public. It might be Aunt Bertha or Cousin Arlo or the brother-in-law of your next-door neighbor. Maybe it's an old friend from high school. Whoever it is, conjure up an image and write to this person.

Exercise 12.2—Analyzing Newsletter Articles

Part 1: Obtain a copy of an organizational newsletter, perhaps one produced by your college or university. Check with your college/university relations department or with a specific group such as the alumni association, sports information department, or international exchange program. Identify the category of this newsletter: member, external, special-interest,

subscription, consumer or advocacy. Write a brief explanation to justify why you identified this category.

Part 2: List each article in the newsletter. Identify the apparent key public, and rate each on how interesting you think it is to that public (using a scale of 1 = little or no apparent interest, 2 = some interest, 3 = much interest).

Part 3: Identify at least three other story ideas that you think would be of interest to the readers of this newsletter.

Part 4: Evaluate the overall effectiveness of this newsletter, based on your presumption of the intended key public. ∎

Writing Style

Writing in effective newsletters often displays the following characteristics:

- Informal, but not chatty
- Businesslike language
- Strong verbs
- Few adverbs and adjectives
- Short sentences
- Quotes to personalize and brighten a story.

Newsletter writing generally is concise and crisp. Articles are often packaged in four-to-six paragraphs, and the average length for articles in most newsletters and organizational newspapers is between 300 and 500 words. Organizational magazines, meanwhile, generally feature much longer articles.

Newsletters generally include free use of jargon appropriate to the audience, but they should avoid clichés. They usually are supportive of the sponsoring organization without being overly promotional. They frequently present a respectful tone toward the sponsoring organization, for example, by using capital initial letters for departments and job titles that would be typed in lowercase for external release. Appendix A: "Common Sense Stylebook for Public Relations Writers" notes how the standard Associated Press Stylebook might be modified for organizational newsletters.

Good newsletters also attempt to humanize the message by focusing on people, especially when the message deals with concepts and products. Remember that newsletter readers often share a closer relationship than readers of most other publications. They work for the same company, went to the same university, support the same zoo. They may know each other; they may share many of the same experiences and perspectives.

A good public relations writer should be flexible about various kinds of writing. Sometimes this means news-based writing that is appropriate for news releases. Other times, it may involve more of an opinion or feature approach. The newsletter mission statement will determine the appropriate style, the objectives for a particular writing assignment, and the needs of the key public. Nevertheless, editors of internal newsletters, especially those published by corporations for their employees, are sometimes faced with the task of writing about corporate policies and regulations. This challenges the writer and editor to find an appropriate balance between policy detail and reader interest.

Exercise 12.3—Writing a Newsletter Article

Retrieve a copy of a news release you prepared in Exercise 6.7 about the Happy Pup Company's grant to Dr. Aaron M. Jones. Rewrite this as an article for HP Bulletin, the monthly employee newsletter of the Happy Pup Company. Here is some additional information, to which you may add appropriate quotes and other relevant information:

- Company president Charles Emerson is preparing an extensive public relations campaign for next year, in which the company will aggressively seek out new clients. Part of this campaign will be an attempt to encourage people who do not currently have a pet to consider getting one. Thus, he sees the grant as helping to build a larger potential customer base for the company.

- The company public relations director, Tomiko Sagimoto, believes the grant complements the company's mission statement, which pledges Happy Pup to promote responsible pet ownership that benefits both animals and humans. She has said on several occasions that the company should do more to be seen as an industry leader in enhancing human–animal relationships.

- Major competitors for Happy Pup include other premium-quality dog goods, including Iams and Science Diet, which together control approximately 60 percent of the premium dog food market in North America. HP now accounts for about 18 percent of sales of premium dog food.

- The Happy Pup marketing director, Candace Calloway, reports that the sale of HP dog food has stabilized after moderate decline, from a high three years ago of 22 percent of the market. She attributes the stabilization to a renewed advertising program, which last year cost $1.3 million. By contrast, the public relations budget is about $250,000. Ms. Calloway's current marketing plan calls for a greater use of public relations tactics to increase brand recognition among breeders, veterinarians and pet owners.

- Happy Pup has 250 employees and distributes its products through pet shows, veterinarians and grocery stores in every U.S. state and Canadian province.

Include a planning sheet with information that focuses on the key publics and their wants, interests and needs.

Exercise 12.4—Writing Policy Articles

You are public relations director with the Bagowind Corporation. One of your tasks is to write and edit the newsletter that is distributed to 1,350 employees who work in the corporate headquarters complex. The two following memos arrived in your morning mail. Rewrite each of the memos for your newsletter. (These samples were provided by Professor Richard Fischer at the University of Memphis.)

From: Director of Safety
To: Public Relations Director
Subj: Input for monthly newsletter

Here's our input for the month.

This is a very important policy directive. I know you will want to run it as is on the front page. I ran this by Legal and he thought it was fine.

My point of contact for this matter is C. J. Merryweather, ext. 339.

In accordance with Standard Policy Procedure S0001763 (amended April 7, 1997), henceforth all hourly and/or salaried personnel who for any reason whatsoever must traverse the plant floor during any shift (i.e., 8 a.m. to 4 p.m., 4 p.m. to 12 midnight, or 12 midnight to 8 a.m.) shall wear ear protectors which meet or exceed the O.S.H.A. Spec. 5 guidelines. They shall also have in their possession Type D safety spectacles either with or without protective cowls.

Hourly or salaried personnel who violate this policy will be cited for a safety infraction and processed under Section III.F.1.(c) of the contract of employment.

Industrial equipment (room 113) currently has no remaining stocks of either the ear protectors or safety spectacles in any size, including the extra large size. Until further notice, this provision will be held in abeyance until suitable stocks are available.

For further information, contact the safety foreperson, Ms. Irene Perkins, at extension 318, during the day.

From: Security Director
To: All Personnel
Subj: Security Emblems

In accordance with Corporate Directives 6315.9M, all employees will wear Security Emblems when inside company buildings. Security Emblems shall be worn on the upper torso, above the waist, in plain view, with the picture of the employee facing outward. Emblems may be clipped to clothing or a Security Emblem Chain (with clasp), available in the Security Office (Bldg. B-1, Room 102).

Personnel arriving at work without an Emblem shall request a temporary Emblem at the Guard Office at the main entrance. Employees arriving late to their work areas because of the delay in obtaining an Emblem may lose pay commensurate with their tardiness.

Personnel losing their Security Emblems should report the loss to the Security Office (555–1234) immediately, and not more than 24 hours after the loss. Replacement Emblems may be obtained after paying a $16 Replacement Emblem fee.

Please distribute widely.

Newsletter Headlines

Headlines are both an information component and a design element of newsletters, and the effective writer will consider both of these aspects. As an information component, the headline is meant to summarize the article's contents and/or to attract reader interest. As design elements, headlines play a role in attracting a reader to a particular article and provide a graphical signal to the reader: This is where you should begin. For example, headlines at the top or center of a page, especially those with few words set in large type, will easily attract the reader's eye. Smaller and less imposing headlines, especially those in the bottom half of a page, suggest to the reader that these articles are of lesser importance.

For the writer, headlines pose a particular challenge: How to use just a few words to summarize an entire article or to intrigue a reader. Following are some guidelines for writing headlines, drawn from the disciplines of magazine and newspaper editing.

- Keep headlines short.
- Use short, easy-to-understand words.
- Whenever possible, use active voice.
- Use present or future tense.
- Use nouns and verbs but not complete sentences.
- Use strong words and phrases, each word packed with meaning.
- Do not allow words to break over to a new line.
- Keep prepositional phrases and verb phrases together rather than separating them onto two lines.
- Avoid all-cap headlines, which are difficult to read. Instead, use boldface type to attract reader attention to headlines or italic heads for features or softer news or to provide a visual contrast with other nearby headlines.
- Adopt a capitalization style. *Up style* calls for the capitalization of every word except short conjunctions and prepositions (such as *and*, *to* and *of*). The more contemporary *down style* calls for the use of lowercase letters for everything except the first word of a headline and for proper nouns or proper adjectives. A newsletter may use either style, as long as the style is consistently applied.

Headline Styles

Newsletters lend themselves to a variety of presentation formats for headlines. Some of the most common are main news headlines, kickers, standing headlines and feature headlines.

Main News Headlines. We are most familiar with main news headlines, which capsulize the information in the article. News headlines should include a verb so as not to become a mere label. Notice how the subject, verb and object in the following example provides a sentencelike summary:

Faculty senate seeks more evening classes

Kickers. Typographic devices such as *kickers*, also called *overlines*, are introductory sections set in smaller type above the main news headline. They usually are short labels, though sometimes they can be written as longer explanations. Kickers can set the stage for the main headline or round it out to provide additional information for the reader. Kickers should be independent of the main head and should not read into it.

Dean opposed
Faculty senate seeks more evening classes

Dean calls plan "wasteful, needless"
Faculty senate seeks more evening classes

Standing Heads. Another typographic device known as *standing heads* or *column heads* are labels for frequently used columns in newsletters. The best advice is to avoid them, because they can be pretty dull. Rather than writing headlines such as "President's Remarks" or "New Employees," try using these as kickers for a headline that captures the essence of the article.

Feature Heads. While news heads summarize the contents of an article, *feature heads* or *titles* are meant to entice the reader, often with a playful approach to language. Some feature headlines ask a question. Others promise that the reader will learn something new and of interest. Often this is written as a "how to." They often focus on the "selling point" of the article.

Fourteen Ways to Extend Your Gardening Season (Mother Earth News)

Yes, you can create your own job (Public Relations Journal)

How getting engaged will change your relationship (Brides)

How to teach ancient history: A multicultural model (American Educator)

Deckheads. A design element of many headlines is the use of a *deckhead* or *underline* following the main feature headline. In this style, the feature headline consists of a few powerful words, and the deckhead provides the context and substance of the accompanying article. The following headlines are from magazines, an excellent source of models for headline writers in newsletters.

Olé! Olé!
José María Olazábal of Spain reigned at the Masters to become the sixth European winner in seven years (Sports Illustrated)

Mama's WHITE
In two probing personal essays, a Black daughter and her White mother explore their love, their relationship and the sting of America's reaction (Essence)

The Family
Canadians see tradition in crisis even as a new poll uncovers enduring strength (MacLean's)

When Bad Dates Happen to Good People . . .
12 Real-Life Dating Disasters (and How to Avoid Them) (Seventeen)

The Neighbors from Hell
Their kids are loud and unruly, their dog barks all night and their house is an eyesore. If you complain, it only makes matters worse. But there is hope for this all-too-common problem. (Ladies' Home Journal)

Exercise 12.5—Writing Headlines

Write the following types of headlines for the newsletter article you wrote in Exercise 12.3 about the Happy Pup Company's grant:

- Main news headline
- Kicker with main news headline
- Feature headline with deckhead
- Title headline.

Corporate Reports

The federal Securities and Exchange Commission requires companies that issue stock to publish *corporate reports* each year to their stockholders that discuss the company's financial activity and overall progress. This information is important to investors, financial analysts and business reporters. The two most common forms of corporate reports are annual reports and quarterly reports.

Annual Reports

Annual reports are formal corporate progress reports issued by companies. The first corporate report was issued either by the Borden Company in 1854 or by Baltimore Gas and Electric in 1924, depending on the definition of annual report. In 1899, the New York Stock Exchange began requiring companies to make public financial statements.

Annual reports issued by many organizations go far beyond what the government requires. Many corporations develop elaborate magazinelike publications with high-quality graphics and well-written feature stories about the year's successes, new products, industry future and so on.

Some corporate reports now cost millions of dollars, taking the form of a booklet or a magazine, often with elaborate artwork and photography. Some organizations have experimented with newspaper or video formats, and some have made their annual reports available through online computer networks. A few are published in different languages, even in Braille.

Meanwhile, many nonprofit organizations voluntarily publish annual reports because they find it to be in their best interests to report to their key publics: employees, volunteers, donors, funding sources, government supporters and others. Three-quarters of all annual reports are written in-house by company employees, according to a survey by the National Investor Relations Institute.

Though annual reports may differ in style and design, they often include the following elements:

- Distinctive cover and consistent design theme that reflect the organization's character
- Letter from the organization's CEO or chairman of the board
- Listing of directors and officers of the company

- Financial highlights of the previous year, and often a 10-year financial/management history, with plain-English text along with charts and graphs to explain the financial aspects of the company
- Description of the organization's products or services and the markets where they are sold, with an emphasis on new elements during the previous year
- Discussion of the industry or environment within which the organization operates
- Discussion of key issues facing the organization, perhaps with the organization's approach to those issues
- Audited financial statements, especially those required by the Securities and Exchange Commission, which are usually prepared by the company's financial staff
- An *opinion letter*, the official statement by an outside auditor attesting to the accuracy of the financial information
- Social-responsibility report on corporate philanthropy and other benefits the organization brought to its community.

Planning the annual report begins like any other public relations tool: Identify and analyze the wants, interests and needs of the key publics; indicate benefits for the publics; set public relations objectives; make decisions about the tone or the theme of the report; and consider how the effectiveness of the report will be evaluated.

Writing for annual reports calls for accuracy above all else. This means both technical accuracy in reporting numbers as well as an honest telling of the organization's story. Overly enthusiastic predictions and self-congratulation have no place in annual reports. Good narrative writing can personalize the numbers being reported.

Annual reports fit each category of public relations objectives: awareness, acceptance and action. They mainly have an effect on awareness by providing information that allows key publics to better understand the organization. Beyond basic awareness, annual reports seek a deeper understanding of the organization. They also seek to create a favorable impression and foster a positive attitude toward the organization, but effective writers of annual reports make sure that their writing, though perhaps enthusiastic, is honest and not simply corporate or organizational propaganda. They know that the most expensive annual report is the one that is not read. Ultimately, they seek to have an effect on behavior, whether the purchasing of stock or other demonstrations of support.

Writers interested in working on corporate reports need to have a good understanding of three things: effective writing, public relations strategy and corporate finance. Professional resources for this specialty include the National Investor Relations Institute at niri.org and a private Web site by Cato Communications (sidcato.com) that bills itself as the Official Annual Report Web site.

Effective annual reports also should be readable. Be particularly careful about using company jargon and bureaucratic language. Apply the Fog Index from Chapter 2 to the written draft of text for annual reports. See "FYI: Readability of Annual Reports" for a recent study.

Graphically, annual reports should be reader friendly. Use clear headlines or section titles, with enough subheads to help the reader stay focused. Make sure that all pictures have informative captions. Use charts and graphs to give meaning to financial statistics. Sidebars and boxes also can be helpful for readers.

Quarterly reports and other organizational variations are much less regulated than annual reports. Many organizations use these as a kind of newsletter, brochure, or Web posting to keep their publics, particularly potential clients, informed about their activities.

FYI   *Readability of Annual Reports*

A 2006 study by Professor Feng Li at the University of Michigan found that, overall, annual reports are difficult to read. A Fog Index of 12–14 is considered ideal in this type of writing; higher than 18 is considered unreadable for most audiences: Li found that annual reports in his study earned a rating 19.4, meaning they require about 19 years of education (doctoral level) to be read easily.

Li also found that, for a few years following the SEC's plain-English requirement in 1998, readership levels of annual reports temporarily improved. But in recent years, it has become even more difficult for readers than before the SEC requirement.

In a more troubling finding, Li reported that annual reports of poorly performing companies are more difficult to read than those of companies that are doing well financially. This suggests an attempt on the part of corporate decision makers and their annual report writers to deliberately obscure bad information by burying it in a sea of spin, jargon, vagueness, and excess verbiage.

Copy Editing

Publications produced by organizations require careful editing, because they carry the name of the organization and thus impact its reputation. Sloppy editing suggests either that the organization does not place a high priority on communicating with the reader or that professional standards are low.

Today's effective newsletter is a well-edited communication tool that enjoys the support and involvement of the organization's management without heavy-handed control. The newsletter addresses the mutual interest of both the organization and its readers, doing so in a way that is both professional and polished. Good editing is at the heart of such a publication. Newsletter editors can take a good story and make it better. They also may make it shorter, because lack of space is one of the most persistent restrictions about writing for newsletters.

Annual reports call for a special responsibility, because they are heavily regulated by the Securities and Exchange Commission. Typographical errors that involve statistics or financial projections are not only mistakes, they are violations of the law requiring a company to be absolutely accurate when communicating officially with its stockholders. Writing and editing the annual report often involves working in close collaboration with the legal department. Financial relations experts tell of the need to have every page read and signed off on before the publication can be printed.

Public relations writers pay attention both to copy editing and proofreading. *Copy editing* is the process of reviewing the draft of a piece of writing to make it better. It involves fact checking, revising for style, correcting grammar, rewriting for smoother and more easily understandable language, and so on. *Proofreading* is a follow-up, often final, stage of the editing process. It involves identifying format problems and correcting major errors. Following are some guidelines to follow carefully while copy editing an organizational publication such as a newsletter or an annual report. "Tips for Better Writing: Proverbs for Proofreaders" offers additional suggestions for effective proofreading.

Check the facts. Make sure that names, statistics and other information are accurate. Verify historical references. Be vigilant for information that raises ethical questions or that could lead to lawsuits against the publication.

Tips for Better Writing   *Proverbs for Proofreading*

1. *Love is nearsighted.* When you are the writer, editor, typist, or typesetter proofreading your own work, you will almost certainly suffer from myopia. You are too close to see all the errors. Get help.

2. *Familiarity breeds content.* When you see the same copy over and over again through the different stages of production and revision, you may well miss new errors. Fresh eyes are needed.

3. *If it's as plain as the nose on your face, everybody can see it but you.* Where is the reader most likely to notice errors? In a headline, in a title, in the first line, first paragraph, or first page of copy; and in the top lines of a new page. These are precisely the places where editors and proofreaders are most likely to miss errors. Take extra care at every beginning.

4. *When you change horses in midstream, you can get wet.* It's easy to overlook an error set in type that is different from the text face you are reading. Watch out when type changes to all caps, italics, boldface, small sizes, and large sizes. Watch out when underscores appear in typewritten copy.

5. *Don't fall off the horse in the home stretch.* Errors often slip by at the ends of tables, chapters, sections, and unusually long lines.

6. *Mistakery loves company.* Errors often cluster. When you find one, look hard for others nearby.

7. *The more, the messier.* Be careful when errors are frequent; the greater the number of errors, the greater the number of opportunities to miss them.

8. *Glass houses invite stones.* Beware of copy that discusses errors. When the subject is typographical quality, the copy must be typographically perfect. When the topic is errors in grammar or spelling, the copy must be error-free. Keep alert for words like *typographical* or *proofreading.*

9. *The footbone conneckit to the kneebone?* Numerical and alphabetical sequences often go awry. Check for omissions and duplications in page numbers, footnote numbers, or notations in outlines and lists.

Check any numeration, anything in alphabetical order, and anything sequential (such as the path of arrows in a flowchart).

10. *It takes two to boogie.* An opening parenthesis needs a closing parenthesis. Brackets, quotation marks, and sometimes dashes belong in pairs. Catch the bachelors.

11. *Every yoohoo deserves a yoohoo back.* A footnote reference calls out for its footnote; a first reference to a table or an illustration calls out for the table or the illustration. Be sure a footnote begins on the same page or column as its callout. Be sure a table or illustration follows its callout as soon as possible.

12. *Figures can speak louder than words.* Misprints in figures (numerals) can be catastrophic. Take extraordinary care with dollar figures and dates and with figures in statistics, tables, or technical text. Read all numerals character by character; for example, read "1987" as "one nine eight seven." Be sure any figures in your handwriting are unmistakable.

13. *Two plus two is twenty-two.* The simplest math can go wrong. Do not trust percentages or fractions or the "total" lines in tables. Watch for misplaced decimal points. Use your calculator.

14. *Don't use buckshot when one bullet will do.* Recurring errors may need only one instruction instead of a mark at each instance.

15. *Sweat the small stuff.* A simple transposition turns *marital strife* into *martial strife*, *board room* into *broad room*. One missing character turns *he'll* into *hell*, *public* into *pubic*.

16. *Above all, never assume that all is well.* As the saying goes, "ass-u-me makes an ass out of u and me."

Used with permission. *Mark My Words: Instruction and Practice in Proofreading,* by Peggy Smith, published by EEI, 66 Canal Center Place, Suite 200, Alexandria, VA 22314.

Edit out wordiness and redundancies. Crisply edited newsletters avoid overwritten prose and wordiness, as well as unnecessary and belabored detail. Strive for clear and readable copy.

Use quotes with impact. Make sure that material set off in quotation marks warrants the attention. Too often internal newsletters fall into the trap of presenting puff and fluff. Avoid this by scrutinizing every quote. If the information provided in the quotation is merely factual data, drop the quotation marks. If it is overtly promotional or self-congratulatory, edit this out. On the other hand, keep the quotation that provides an insightful understanding or an effective explanation.

Use pull quotes to highlight important information. A typographic and editorial device that originated with magazines, *pull quotes* are highlighted excerpts from an article that are used both as graphic elements to relieve columns of text and as ways to draw the reader's attention to particularly significant quotes. Pull quotes may be actual short quotes drawn from the article, or they may be edited quotes or even careful paraphrases.

Follow a stylebook. Readers may not pay attention to editing details, but they will notice inconsistency of style. Some publications adopt a particular standard, notably The Associated Press Stylebook. Others create their own *house style*, modifying a style to their own editorial taste. Following the accepted stylebook can prevent unnecessary difficulties for editors, such as the embarrassment of capitalizing one person's title but not another's. Appendix A, "Common Sense Stylebook for Public Relations Writers," is an example of house style. While consistent with The Associated Press Stylebook, this guide offers additional writing and editing principles for internal publications such as newsletters as well as for broadcast copy.

Use accepted copyediting symbols. Because more than one person is involved in the process of preparing copy for publication, writers and editors have developed a standard set of symbols and notations. Anyone involved in editing should use these symbols. Appendix B, "Copy Editing," provides examples of standard copyediting symbols.

Exercise 12.6—Copy Editing (a)

You are editor of The Student Writer, a newsletter aimed at college and university students. Edit the following newsletter article written by one of your staff reporters. Your aim is to make the article stylistically correct. Use the copyediting symbols in Appendix B, "Copy Editing."

"Trust Your Instincts" is the advice that Dr. Scholastica Penner often gives to her students at Outpost State Univ. "Effective writers are those who have learned when and how to following their intuition," I tell my students.

Dr. Penner believes there are three steps that writers can take in learning to trust rely on their instincts.

First, know yor writing preferences and predispositions in writing. For sample, do you naturally write wordy passages with alot of description and examples, or do you get to the point quick. In per suasive writing, do you typical present facts or do you weave a story to personalize the situation? Analyze your writing to identify your prefferences.

Two, determine what is needed by your audience or your medium. A newsletter, for example, may have only limited space, or raeders of a consumer magazine may expect fact's and comparisons. Third, compare your writing predispositions with this analysis of the audience and the medium. That will tell you if you can trust your instincts or if you need to intentionally write different.

"Either way you can be an effective writer," says Doctor penner. "This really is an example of when insight leads to effectivness." ∎

Exercise 12.7—Copy Editing (b)

You are editor of the newsletter of Aardvark State College, writing for alumni, community leaders and other external audiences. Copy edit the following newsletter article written by one of your staff reporters. Your aim is to make the article stylistically correct. Use the copyediting symbols in Appendix B, "Copy Editing."

FOR IMMEDEATE RELEASE
Mar. 15, 2007

AARDVARK STATE NAMES COMMUNICATION DIRECTOR Aardvark N.M.— Aardvark Sate Col. in Aardvark, New Mexico, today (July 6, 2007) announced that they has appointed a former newspaper editor and public relations practicioner, as the colleges new director of communication.

Roger Writesright will begin his new positon on August 1, 2007.

The Aardvark State President, Dr. Mariah Murphy said the new director of communications will oversee the work of the Colleges' advertising, marketing, and media relatiations directors, as well as the publications editor and web editor. He also will be part ofthe presdient's Council to advice on issues managementment, college reputation and crises communications

She proclaimed this new position was created so that the College it can integreat it's various communications activities.

Mr. Writesright said: "The consensus of opinion among large college presidents is that strategic communication plays a very unique role in todays management. I plan to bring my knowlidge of the new media and publec relations to help Aard vark Sate tell its' story more effectivly.

Wrightsright, is a former graduate of AArdvark state with a BS in journalism, 1985, and once was editor at the "Daily Times and Express" in Saint Louis, Mossouri. He also was a managing partner in Writesright and Spellsgood an award winning public relations agency from Seattle. ∎

Intellectual Property Laws

As we discussed in Chapter 5, issues of privacy and libel should be matters of concern to all public relations writers, but another area of law is especially significant for people writing for internal publications. This is the issue of intellectual property, including the legal concepts of copyright, trademark and service mark.

Copyright

Copyright is the legal designation of ownership for original written and other artistic creations. When material is copyrighted, this means that in most circumstances it may not be used without permission. The U.S. Copyright Act was revised in 1976. Copyright law protects articles, stories and opinion pieces, newsletters, brochures, videos, public service advertisements, commercial advertisements, advertising copy, software, TV broadcasts, musical works and lyrics, artistic works (such as sculpture, paintings and photographs) and artistic performances (such as choreographs and dances).

Print news releases and other public relations materials aimed at the news media generally are not copyrighted because they are meant to be used without restriction by the media. However, some practitioners and communication attorneys suggest that some time and use restrictions may be appropriate for video news releases.

Copyright protection extends only to the fixed form of artistic works. It does not cover ideas themselves but rather the expression that a writer or artist has given to those ideas. Thus copyright law does not protect themes, plots, processes, formulas, or titles of books or plays. Nor does copyright law protect basic information such as calendars, measurement charts and government documents. Likewise, it does not prohibit another writer from paraphrasing and referencing an original document.

Copyright Claims.   The person who creates an artistic work can claim copyright in one of two ways. A *copyright notice* is claimed when the creator uses the word "Copyright," the abbreviation "Copr.," and/or the letter C inside a circle (©), that is, the international copyright symbol, along with the year and the name of the person or organization owning the copyright. Here are some examples of how noticed copyright is referenced:

> Copyright, 2007, Smith Communication Counsel
> © 2007, Ronald D. Smith
> © Copyright 2007, Smith Communication Counsel

The Berne Convention for the Protection of Literary and Artistic Works presumes automatic copyright to the creator of artistic works, even if the copyright notice is not displayed. In 1989, the United States became one of the last of the 162 signer countries to adopt the Berne Convention. However, enforcement of copyright protection is easier when the copyright is registered. In the United States, the copyright owner may register the copyright with the federal government (Copyright Office, Library of Congress, Washington, DC, 20559–6000; (202) 707–3000; loc.gov/copyright). Currently this requires a $45 fee for basic registration and file copies (two for published works, one for unpublished works).

Fair Use of Copyrighted Materials. Copyright generally is meant to prevent others from using the copyrighted material, except with permission. Often, this permission is granted only by payment of a fee or royalty. However, there are certain *fair-use* conditions under which copyrighted information may be used without permission:

- One fair use involves *nonprofit* or *noncommercial* purposes. For example, teachers and others involved in advancing knowledge or the public interest may use some copyrighted material with classroom students, giving proper credit to the copyright holder. Such fair use also includes news and commentary, satire, parody and non-commercial research. Courts have extended this use to cover videotaping of television documentaries and news programs. Small numbers of newspaper or magazine reprints for internal use are considered fair use, but large numbers of reprints require permission; note that courts have not definitively established the exact number of reprints allowed. Using copyrighted material for advertising or entertainment purposes generally is not covered by fair-use provisions. In 2003, federal courts ruled that fair-use provisions permit thumbnail photos on the Internet.

- Additionally, *comment* fair use extends to brief reviews or excerpts. Some courts have interpreted this as involving quotations of up to 400 words from a full-length book or up to 50 words for a periodical, though these limits are not defined by law. In working with reviews or excerpts, public relations writers always should give proper credit to the copyright holder.

- Another exemption is given for purposes of *research*. Generally, library users have been free to make copies of copyrighted material, both for personal use and for professional noncommercial research use. However, in the case of *American Geophysical Union v. Texaco*, a federal district court ruled that the fair-use provision of the copyright law does not allow corporate researchers to copy articles from library journals for use in their work with eventual profit potential.

Newsletter editors and other public relations practitioners need to recognize the distinction the Copyright Act makes between *original works* owned by an individual author or artist and *works for hire* owned by an organization that pays the author or artist, either as a salary or as a commission. The law presumes that an employer owns the copyright to artistic or creative works produced as part of the employee's job performance. This presumption affects people who work in public relations, either for an organization or an agency. However, freelancers are not considered employees unless a contract specifically identifies their creations as "works for hire." Otherwise, it is presumed that freelancers give a publisher only one-time rights and retain copyright ownership in their own name.

Public relations practitioners should give special attention to copyright issues involved in their work with freelance writers, photographers and similar artists. In a 1989 case (*Community for Creative Non-Violence v. Reid*), the Supreme Court declared that a sculptor who used his own tools and studio, even though on commission to an organization, was not an employee and therefore retained ownership of his artistic creation. "FYI: Sample Copyright Agreements" offers a sample work-for-hire agreement that may be used when engaging with freelancers.

FYI   *Sample Copyright Agreements*

Copyright Retention

Here is a simple agreement stipulating that a copyright is owned by an employee rather than by the employer. For more formal agreements, consult an attorney familiar with copyright law.

Name and description of artistic work:
Copyright owner:
Basis of copyright ownership:
Work-for-hire created as a commissioned piece for _____ [organization] by _____ [creator]. The creator retains ownership of the copyright for this artistic work.

[Signed by both parties]

Work for Hire

Here is a simple work-for-hire agreement stipulating that the copyright is owned by the employer rather than the employee who created the artistic work as part of the job performance. For more formal agreements, consult an attorney familiar with copyright law.

Name and description of artistic work:
Copyright owner:
Basis of copyright ownership:
☐ Work for hire created by employee: [Name]
☐ Work for hire created as a commissioned piece according to a signed contract or agreement with the creator: [Name]

[Signed by both parties]

Trademark

A *trademark* is a legal tool offering protection to distinctive names, logos, words, symbols and other unique identifications of companies and their products. It can be a word or phrase, or it can be a symbol or design. In many ways, trademarks serve like the cattle brands of the Old West by identifying products as the property of particular companies or organizations. Even today, *brand name* is the common (though nonlegal) term for a trademark or a service mark.

Unlike copyrights that are meant to prevent use by others, trademarks are intended only to protect the relationship between a product name and the company that makes that product. Others may use the name, as long as it is identified with the company that holds the trademark.

Registration of Trademarks. Trademarks are administered by the federal government through the U.S. Patent and Trademark Office of the Department of Commerce (uspto.gov). Canadian trademarks and copyrights both are administered by the Canadian Intellectual Property Office (opic.gc.ca). Filing for U.S. trademarks costs $100 or more, depending on type of registration needed. Additionally, international assistance with trademarks is available from the International Trademark Association (inta.org).

The law makes a distinction between a *common trademark* indicated by the small capital letters TM set in superscript (™) and a *registered trademark*, designated by a capital R in a circle (®). All trademarks are protected by law, but those registered with the Patent and Trademark Office and identified by the trademark symbol are provided worldwide protection guaranteed by international treaties, enjoy more publicity, and generally are easier to enforce.

Trademark Protection. Companies go to great lengths to protect their trademarks because if the names slip into generic use, the companies no longer can maintain the link with their product. In effect, the company loses its distinctive name. Zipper, aspirin, mimeograph, escalator, yo-yo and cellophane once were trademarks that lost their unique association with a particular company's product. Now any company may manufacture products under those names. This is why today, companies like Xerox worry about writers who incorrectly refer to "xeroxing" as a generic verb. Other companies work hard to protect the uniqueness of trademarks such as Coke, Kleenex, Plexiglas, Velcro, Walkman and Scotch Tape. "FYI: Trademarks: Treat 'Em with Respect" lists some common terms that are protected as trademarks.

FYI   *Trademarks: Treat 'Em with Respect*

Below are some common terms that are protected as trademarks. Writers should capitalize these terms when they are used in print. They also may be used with or replaced by their generic equivalents, noted here in parentheses.

Astroturf (artificial grass)
BandAid (adhesive bandage)
Chap Stick (lip balm)
Jell-O (gelatin dessert)
Jockey (underwear)
Kleenex (facial tissue)
Nautilus (exercise machine)
Novocaine (anesthetic)

Nutrasweet (sugar substitute)
Ping-Pong (table tennis)
Pyrex (heat-resistant glassware)
Q-Tip (cotton swab)
Rolodex (card file)
ScotchTape (plastic tape)
Scrabble (crossword game)
Stetson (hat)
Styrofoam (plastic foam)
Teflon (nonstick coating)
Vaseline (petroleum jelly)
Walkman (portable cassette player)
Weight Watchers (diet program)
Xerox (photocopier)

Trademarks also protect phrases associated with companies and their products. "Reach Out and Touch Someone" belongs to AT&T. "This Bud's for You" is only for Budweiser. "We bring good things to life" is a claim only General Electric may make, and only Clairol may ask, "Does she or doesn't she?" Burger King is the only restaurant that may claim to be the "Home of the Whopper" and The New York Times is the only paper that has "All the News That's Fit to Print."

Corporate lawyers are vigilant in monitoring the use of trademarks, which extend beyond product names and slogans. Creations such as the Disney and the Peanuts characters, Barbie and Ken dolls, Superman, even college and sports mascots also are protected by trademarks. Trademark protection can extend even to faces and voices, and companies have been sued for using look-alike or sound-alike actors. For example, Bette Midler received a $400,000 jury award against an advertising agency that used a sound-alike in a car commercial, and Vanna White successfully sued a company for using a Vanna-like robot in an advertisement. A trademark protects not only Tarzan but also his yell, and Vogue magazine was sued for trademark infringement for a fashion feature entitled "Tarzan, Meet Jane."

Designs and packaging also are matters for trademark protection, and some companies have trademarked distinctive typographical treatments of their names, such as the interlocking X's of Exxon and the backward R of Toys R Us. Other examples are the McDonald golden arches and the Apple apple. Even the classic shape of a Coca-Cola bottle, the front grill of a Rolls Royce, and the goldfish shape of Pepperidge Farm snack crackers can be protected as trademarks known as *trade dress*. Color is another element of trade dress, and protection has been extended to Owens-Corning for the use of pink color of its insulation and the black-

and-yellow packaging of Kodak film. Trade dress often carries the same legal protections as unregistered trademarks.

Meanwhile, corporate attorneys and public relations practitioners sometimes turn their attention to other legal issues surrounding trademark. For example, trademarks are not permitted for names that are deceptive or immoral. On the latter point, morality groups in both England and America challenged the right of UK-based clothing company French Connection to trademark its acronym, fcuk™, saying it was a thinly veiled allusion to an obscenity, especially when used with its products such as its "fcuk him™" and "fcuk her™" fragrances and T-shirts with "fcuk me™" and "fcuk football™." The company had to go to court to retain the right to use its acronym as a trademark.

Although companies are vigilant in protecting their trademarks, courts have been reluctant to require journalists and other writers to likewise protect companies. Ted Davis, a specialist in intellectual property law, said courts put the pressure on people who use a company's trademark as if it were their own. But there's not much legal action against writers. Writing in Editor and Publisher (Dec. 3, 2001), Davis said there isn't much a company can do other than send an intimidating letter to a writer who has used a trademarked name generically.

Writing about Trademarks. At the very least, public relations writers should capitalize trademarked names in print. Trademarked names also may be followed by the word "brand" and/or by an appropriate generic noun, such as Kleenex tissues or Jell-O brand gelatin. For internal publications such as newsletters, public relations writers often treat trademarked words distinctively, such as by printing them in all-capital letters, using boldface or italic type, setting them in quotation marks, even printing them in color. Internal publications often feature the trademark symbol as well.

In line with journalistic stylebooks, writers generally do not do this for news releases but rather would capitalize the first letter of the trademarked word and perhaps follow it with the trademark symbol and the word "brand." Often they include a reminder, frequently as a final paragraph of a news release or note to editors, pointing out that a particular term is a registered trademark that must not be used generically.

When public relations writers refer to the trademarked product of companies other than their own, they may determine that the actual trademarked name is not essential to meaning. If this is the case, the trademarked name can be eliminated completely, leaving only a generic reference, for example to tissues or gelatin.

Service Mark

A *service mark* is similar to a trademark, except that it protects symbols and words associated with services and programs rather than product names. Service marks enjoy the same legal protections as trademarks and also are protected by the U.S. Patent and Trademark Office. Examples of service marks are names such as Maid Brigade for the cleaning service and the Hugo Award of the World Science Fiction Society. Both the Better Business Bureau name and the torch logo are service marks of the Council of Better Business Bureaus, Inc. Only Huntington Beach, Calif., can claim to be Surf City USA℠, and only the U.S. Army Reserve can legally use the slogans "Be All That You Can Be."

When organizations wish to point out that their phrase is a service mark, they may follow it with small capital letters SM set in superscript (℠). The letters are in a circle if the service mark is registered with the Patent Office.

13

Direct-Mail Appeals

From events surrounding the Magna Carta through the American Revolution to today's political and social issues, writers often have found themselves facing the task of writing convincing letters to appeal for support for an organization or its cause. The type of support may vary. It may deal with internal relations by seeking new members or soliciting renewals. It may focus on philanthropic public relations by asking for financial contributions. Or it may involve advocacy, such as seeking signatures to a petition or asking people to write letters or contact legislators on behalf of your cause.

As public relations writers consider their alternatives in delivering organizational messages, they increasingly are taking those messages directly to their publics. Their increasing use of direct mail has been one of the major changes taking place within the practice of public relations. In using direct mail, regardless of the type of support needed, your writing will be successful only to the extent that it effectively engages readers and leads them to the anticipated action.

This chapter will focus on writing and packaging appeals for various purposes, both in print and online. Your objectives for Chapter 13 are:

- To write an effective appeal letter
- To demonstrate an understanding of persuasive techniques for written communicatio
- To apply the concepts of writing for both the head and the heart.

Making Appeals

The Independent Sector, a coalition of more than 500 corporations, foundations and charities, reports that 89 percent of American households make charitable contributions each year, an average of $1,620 per household. *Giving USA*, an annual report by the American Association of Fundraising Council and Indiana University, tallies such charitable contributions as more than $260 billion a year in 2005.

Nonprofit organizations frequently use direct appeal mailings for various reasons. Examples of these are in the box, "FYI: Direct Appeal Letters." Some direct-mail pieces such as Congressman Barney Frank's letter to constituents are intended to raise funds. Others such as the National Museum of the American Indian seek to increase membership. Still others are focused on advocacy, such as the letter to senate leaders from Parent Project for Muscular Dystrophy. Some groups appeal to members for action, such as the National Rifle Association's membership alerts asking for letters to Congress. Amnesty International's Urgent Action Network generates letters, e-mails and faxes from its 80,000 volunteers in 80 nations on behalf of what AI calls "prisoners of conscience" or in support of its human rights causes. We'll take a look at each type of appeal in this chapter. Large international organizations may mail millions of such letters each month, while local groups may use direct appeal letters infrequently.

FYI   *Direct Appeal Letters*

Following are excerpts from successful direct mail appeals from various organizations. Emphasis has been added to help readers note some of the key sections.

Fundraising. Congressman Barney Frank (D.-Mass.) used a touch of "us verses them" and a charge of dirty politics in this letter to constituents to solicit political funds:

Having grown up in New York in the fifties, during the heyday of Broadway theater, I have always had a soft spot for twofers—the offering by show producers of two tickets for the price of one . . . What I'm asking you to do is *help finance the opening* of not exactly a new show, but a revival of an old favorite: the return of a Democratic majority to the U.S. House of Representatives.

It's a twofer because by contributing in response to this letter you can do two things at once. First, *you can help the Democrats win back control of the House* and for the first time in too many years put a check on George Bush's arrogant, abusive, plebiscitary presidency . . .

Secondly, and less importantly to the nation but of some relevance to my own ego, you could help me win a bet I made with a reporter. He had called to ask me my reaction to the fundraising letter recently sent by House Speaker Dennis Hastert, the relevant part of which read as follows: "You can be sure that under a Pelosi-led Congress, the conservative ideals of family values and an unwavering commitment to our troops will be ignored, while the interests of San Francisco liberals and trial lawyers will be heard loud and clear by Nancy Pelosi and her liberal friends. Our country can't afford to let Nancy Pelosi, John Murtha, and Barney Frank reverse the progress we've made."

The reference—entirely gratuitous—to San Francisco and the selection of me as one of the three major reasons not to allow the Democrats to take back the House obviously is meant to *appeal in part to anti-gay prejudice* . . .

My bet was that I could raise more money from people who objected to Speaker Hastert's appeal to prejudice than he could raise by making it.. . . My decision to send this unusual extra solicitation this year is motivated mostly by my eagerness to *turn the right wing's bashing to our advantage*, but also a little bit by my ego.. . . So my request to you is for a contribution which I will be using as part of our effort to keep the playing field sufficiently close to even so that the desire of the majority of Americans to put an end to this assault on our values can be made effective in the Congressional elections in November.

Membership. The National Museum of the American Indian evoked a sense of commitment and appreciation of native culture with this membership letter:

At Thanksgiving, most of us look forward to a delicious meal of turkey, dressing, corn, cranberry sauce, pumpkin pie, and other traditional holiday foods. Yet how many of us know why we eat these particular foods when we give thanks each November? In fact, do most of us know what we commemorate at Thanksgiving?

As a Member of the National Museum of the American Indian, *you are committed to the first national museum* dedicated to the histories, cultures, and arts of Native Americans with a collection of more than 817,000 extraordinary Native American objects. You can visit any of our three separate facilities—the Museum on the National Mall in Washington D.C., the George Gustav Heye Center in lower Manhattan, and the Cultural Resources Center in Suitland, Maryland.

In all of our locations, we seek to *convey the vitality and adaptability* of the Native American cultures of this hemisphere.

You see, the native people throughout the Americas developed cultures uniquely suited to the environments in which they lived—*cultures that survived over time and which still thrive today*—despite every attempt to eradicate them.

As you know, the purpose of the National Museum of the American Indian goes beyond maintaining a great collection. The true goal of the Museum is to *change forever the way the native peoples of this hemisphere are viewed*—to correct the misconceptions and to demonstrate how native cultures are enriching this world . . .

I hope that you will make a special gift today—in honor of all those who participated in the First Thanksgiving—as we celebrate the history and cultures of Native Americans. *Your gift will attest to your extraordinary commitment* and will truly have an impact for many generations to come.

Government Support. The Parent Project for Muscular Dystrophy advocacy letter to Senate leaders noted progress already achieved as it urged Congress to address the organization's cause:

On behalf of all patients and families who have been affected by Duchene and Becker Muscular Dystrophy, *we are writing to thank you* and the Committee for the strong support you have provided in recent years, and *to urge continued assistance* as you work toward preparing the FY 2007 Labor, HHS, and Education spending bill.

. . . *We are making progress*, however, thanks to support from your Committee and the Congress. Just a few months ago, a clinical trial began on a treatment that could positively impact the lives of many DBMD patients. Last year, the National Institutes of Health approved three additional Muscular Dystrophy Cooperative Research Centers, further helping to target resources toward efforts aimed at developing successful and safe cures and treatments.

. . .With so many exciting developments in recent years, we hope that you and your colleagues will *help spur additional advances* by continuing to fund DBMD-specific activities adequately in FY 2007. Specifically, we would like to see the following:

- Increase MD funding at the CDC by $2 million, for a total of about $8.5 million in Fiscal Year 2007.
- Increase overall funding at the National Institutes of Health to help ensure adequate funding is provided for MD research at all six MD Centers of Excellence . . .
- Urge CDC and the Agency for Healthcare Research and Quality to complete an ongoing initiative that would establish evidence-driven treatment guidelines for clinicians treating people with Duchene and Becker Muscular Dystrophy.

Political Action. The National Rifle Association wrote with a sense of urgency and challenge in this grassroots alert urging members to contact their senators (though ultimately the Senate failed to consider the bill before it adjourned):

The 109th Congress *has provided gun owners with some tremendous victories*, including passage of the "Protection of Lawful Commerce in Arms Act" in 2005, and in October, legislation to prohibit the confiscation of lawfully owned firearms during states of emergency—to name just a few.

However, in January 2007, control of Congress will change hands, and *anti-gun leaders will be in near full control*. With the 109th Congress winding down and adjourning by year's end, *it is critical that we pull out all the stops* to try to pass one of NRA-ILA's top legislative priorities—H.R. 5092, the NRA-backed "Bureau of Alcohol, Tobacco, Firearms, and Explosives Modernization and Reform Act" . . . This measure will help curb BATFE's efforts to revoke dealers' licenses for minor paperwork errors, establish new guidelines for BATFE investigations, and improve the appeals process for dealers. It will also *provide more accountability and much-needed reform* to this federal law enforcement agency.

. . . *Please contact your U.S. Senators* and urge them to bring H.R. 5092 up for a vote before the 10–9th Congress adjourns. You may call your U.S. Senators at (202) 224–3121.

Volunteer Action. Amnesty International's Urgent Action Network sent this appeal to mobilize about 80,000 volunteers in 90 countries to send letters, e-mails, and telegrams on behalf of one of its causes:

Father Marco Arana and Dr. Mirtha Vasquez Chuquilin have *received repeated death threats* and have been followed and filmed both at work and at home. The threats and harassment appear to be directly linked to their work for the Comprehensive Training for Sustainable Development Group (GRUFIDES), a human rights and environmental organization. GRUFIDES members have been the *target of threats and intimidation* in recent months. All of these incidents have been reported to the authorities but *no action has been taken to investigate them*, or to offer protection to those at risk.

Dr. Vasquez Chuquilin received an anonymous telephone call in which she was told "Te vamos a violar y luego te vamos a matar" (*We will rape you and then we will kill you*). Father Arana received anonymous death threats by telephone. His niece received a telephone call in which she was told: "Dile a tu tio que no se meta, le vamos a disparar un balazo en la cabeza" (*Tell your uncle not to get involved, we will put a bullet through his head*) . . .

GRUFIDES is a non-governmental organization that focuses on sustainable development and environmental issues based in the city of Cajamarca, in Cajamarca Province. It is actively supporting communities opposing the Yanacocha gold mining project led by a US corporation.. . . .

GRUFIDES works closely with campesino (peasant) communities, providing them with training and legal advice. It has recently become involved in supporting the cases of two campesino activists who were allegedly assassinated . . . apparently as a result of their opposition to the expansion of the Yanacocha mining project . . .

Write today to Peru's Attorney General urging him to take steps to guarantee the safety of GRUFIDES staff. We have provided a sample letter, but please be encouraged to add your own thoughts.

Direct mail is also an effective way for public relations writers to appeal to key publics for support that goes beyond the donor generosity. For example, direct mail can be useful in political campaigns and other governmental activities that rest on voter support. Members of Congress and many state legislatures have free *franking privileges*, permission for free mailing to constituents. This allows them to implement ambitious direct-mail campaigns with the voters in their home districts. What are they appealing for? Grassroots support and votes.

Direct mail also has a role in community relations situations in which an organization takes its message directly to the local residents. Corporations and other large organizations often use direct mail to promote employee morale and shareholder awareness. Meanwhile, marketing campaigns often rely on direct mail as a key selling tool, taking the message (and often a sample of the product) directly to the would-be consumer.

Are such mail appeals effective? They seem to be. Some research claims that direct mail draws 10 times as many responses as newspaper ads and 100 times as many as TV ads. E-mail appeals are said to be even more effective. Meanwhile, the use of direct mail has increased at a higher pace than newspaper or magazine advertising; by some estimates as much as a two-to-one growth rate. But much of the research associated with direct mail is proprietary, sometimes contradictory, and still emerging. So the numbers are uncertain. What can be said with certainty is that direct mail is effective and growing. It also is expensive, so the public relations practitioners involved with direct mail will use the technique carefully.

Effective direct appeal promotions have several key ingredients. They must target the right audience and employ the appropriate mailing list. They need to include the right message, based on the self-interest of the readers and tested in pilot studies to make sure it resonates with readers. Effective promotions are packaged so they are visually pleasing. Finally, they must involve strong writing that helps cut through the clutter of so many competing messages.

Before dealing further with appeal letters, it may be helpful to consider your personal experience with such letters.

Exercise 13.1—Freewriting on Direct Mail

Freewrite for five minutes on the following topic: *What has been your personal experience with receiving appeal letters?* Then discuss this with your classmates. ■

Reader Interest

You probably have found that some appeal letters are interesting while others are not. Consider the following proposition: *The only difference between effective appeal letters and junk mail is the recipient's interest in the topic.* What one person finds compelling, another may judge to be of no personal interest. If it is true that communication is a receiver phenomenon, this principle is most apparent with direct-mail appeals. The best writing will still be labeled as junk mail if the topic fails to interest the reader. The real value of a direct-mail appeal is its ability to provide personalized messages of interest to particular readers.

Each year Americans generously support charitable organizations that ask for help, giving hundreds of billions of dollars. We naturally think of donations by philanthropic foundations and corporations, but more than 80 percent of the donations came from individuals—not the wealthy few, but mostly from people of average or below-average financial means. "FYI: Charitable Giving" explains further.

FYI *Charitable Giving*

More than $260 billion was contributed to American charities in 2005, according to the American Association of Fund-Raising Counsel's Trust for Philanthropy, which produces an annual report, *Giving USA*. That represented a 6.1 percent increase over the previous year. Natural disasters in the United States and abroad accounted for about half of the $15 billion increase from the previous year; the other half reflected donor's commitments to other causes that interested them. Some of the contributions for disaster relief were funneled through religious, health and educational organizations.

Where do the contributions come from? The AAFRC report noted the following sources:

- Individual contributors, 77 percent ($199.07 billion)
- Individual bequests, 7 percent ($17.44 billion)
- Foundations, 12 percent ($30 billion)
- Corporations, 5 percent ($13.77 billion).

Where do the contributions go? The report noted that the donations (which are rounded here) went to the following causes:

- Religion and religious charities, 36 percent ($93 billion)
- Education, 15 percent ($39 billion)
- Human services, 10 percent ($25 billion)
- Health, 9 percent ($23 billion)
- Foundations, 8 percent ($22 billion)
- Public/Society benefit, 5 percent ($14 billion)
- Arts, culture & humanities, 5 percent ($14 billion)
- Environment & animals, 3 percent ($8 billion)
- International affairs, 3 percent ($6 billion)
- Unallocated giving, 6 percent ($16 billion).

Additional information is available at the association's Web site: aafrc.org.

Effective appeal letters are based on the reader's self-interest, not on the need of the organization or even the need of the beneficiaries. People don't give money just because an organization asks for it. They don't even give because a child is hungry. They give because they care that the child is hungry and want to help.

People give money (as well as their time, talent, vote or whatever else is of value to them) for self-serving reasons—noble, perhaps; compassionate and beneficial, certainly; but nonetheless reasons that satisfy their own personal wants, interests and needs. Some people give to fulfill a desire to help, because they think they can make a difference in someone's life or because they hope to make a contribution to their community or to humanity at large. They want to provide an education for poor students. Other people give because giving makes them feel good. They contribute because a disease has no cure and they want to be part of its cure. Or perhaps they give because of a moral or religious commitment, fulfilling their accepted duty to give alms and help the needy. Still other people may give because they want to look good in the eyes of others, create a memorial in their name or that of a loved one, or simply to obtain a tax deduction.

Your task as a writer is to first identify the wants, interests and needs of the key public and then to respond to those through your writing. Start by thinking about your own reasons for giving.

Exercise 13.2—Freewriting on Giving

 Freewrite for five minutes on the following topic: *When was the last time I gave money to a nonprofit organization? What motivated me to contribute?* Then discuss this with your classmates.

To ensure reader interest, public relations practitioners give very careful attention to developing targeted mailing lists. Large organizations may have marketing teams that develop and maintain mailing lists, but smaller organizations may expect the writer to oversee the lists. The writer should be able to presume that an appropriate mailing list exists for the writing project at hand. With this in mind, we can proceed to the writing task of preparing an effective appeal letter for the key public represented by the list.

Another key to direct-mail appeals is that they provide for some kind of reader response. Most media communication allows for only modest and delayed audience feedback. But direct mail has refined reader response. Through the use of response cards, stamped self-addressed envelopes, interactive Web sites and toll-free telephone numbers, direct mail provides opportunities that make it easy for the reader to say, "Yes, I want to help!"

Direct mail provides for continual copy testing of a message. This first happens even before the message is presented to a large-scale audience, when the public relations writer tests the message with a focus group or a small mail sample. But a valuable aspect of direct mail is that copy testing continues throughout the life of the campaign.

Some campaigns feature *split runs*, in which different versions of the same message are distributed to different segments of the key public. The versions may vary in their headlines or their photographs or other artwork. Perhaps they will have different writing strategies and persuasive techniques. Implementing a split run is an excellent way for a writer to determine which version of the message is more successful. Eventually, the most successful version is likely to be adopted for the entire key public.

Writing the Appeal

As the heart of the appeal package, the letter requires top-quality writing. The letter needs a personal tone and all the persuasive effectiveness you can pull together. Following are suggestions about the standard elements found in most successful appeal letters.

Plan carefully. It is most important to work from a planning sheet that guides you through the crucial planning stages of focusing your attention on the key public (in this case, the persons receiving the letter); their wants, interests and needs; the benefits you can provide; your writing objectives, and finally the tone of your message.

Use a salutation. Junk mail is defined by the recipient, and a letter that appears to have been sent to thousands of other people hardly qualifies as personal correspondence. Mail that addresses the recipient personally is likely to be read. If individual letters can be generated— and computers often make this possible, even on a large scale—address the reader by name. Be careful not to use gender-specific titles such as Mr., Ms. or Mrs. unless you know for sure that these are accurate. Imagine how many annoying letters have been misaddressed to Mr. Glenn Close or Ms. Marion Barry. In the case of women, make sure you are using the preferred title.

A personalized salutation on the letter increases readership. The Digital Printing Council reports that personalized letters draw five times the response than generic letters. But research shows that there is no particular benefit in carrying the use of the name further within the text of the letter. If a small budget, large mailing list or limited time cause you to use form letters instead, choose an appropriate salutation: Dear Fellow Midstate Graduate, Dear Public Relations Colleague, Dear Lover of Apple Dumplings, Dear Friend of the Environment. Regardless of the salutation, effective appeal letters make frequent use of second person, "you" and "your."

Use simple, direct language. Your writing should be correct, appropriate to your reader and consistent in style. It should be simple, natural, concise, clear and powerful. It should be full of meaning and easy for the reader to identify with.

Start with a powerful lead. The beginning of the letter must create interest. Quickly. Lose the reader here, and the dance is over before it's begun. Introduce a provocative fact. Ask a pertinent question. Give a poignant example. Use a cogent anecdote. Report a paradox.

Ask, ask and ask again. You are writing an appeal letter; this is no time to be subtle or shy. If you want a contribution, request it. If you are seeking new members, invite them. If you want people to write letters to the White House, ask. Experience with direct mail has shown that it is important to ask for help early and often. The first paragraphs should request or suggest some action, at least indirectly. This is one of those situations in which repetition is a good thing.

Use an appropriate tone. It is important that every appeal letter should have its own feel or attitude, appropriate to the cause and the recipient. Some direct-mail appeals are folksy, others are frenzied. Some are friendly invitations. Each letter should be consistent in its approach, and it should be suitable for the reader, the sending organization, and the person signing the letter.

Generate reader interest. As with position papers and speeches, appeal letters will be successful only to the extent that they can interest the reader. The task of the writer is to explain the significance of the topic and gain the reader's interest in it.

Clearly state the benefit. It is important to let the reader know how a contribution will help the organization and its cause. But even more important is to note how a contribution will help the reader who is, after all, a donor-in-waiting. And you, meanwhile, are not a beggar on a street corner. You are an agent of an organization that presumably (because you successfully identified key publics) is of interest to this reader. You have something valuable to offer the reader. Maybe it is an opportunity to help treat an illness that has affected someone in her family. Perhaps it is a way to support a social cause close to his heart. Whatever the benefit, try to awaken the reader's interest. Give the reader a personal, even selfish, reason for supporting your organization. Write so the reader wants to contribute.

Tell a human story. William Shakespeare gave Miranda good words in "The Tempest": "Your tale, sir, would cure deafness." Our stories, if they are poignant and well told, can cure the deafness of an apathetic audience. Use a sort of poster-child approach to humanize the organization. Put a face on your message. Give a personal example. Sketch an actual or a composite portrait of a person who benefits through the organization. Present a vignette about the program. This can bring the appeal to life and make it more compelling for the reader. Even organizations not working with people can "humanize" their messages, such as the SPCA does in "Tip for Better Writing: Personalize the Message."

Write with passion. Write as if you were excited and enthusiastic about the cause you are writing about. If you don't seem to really care, why should the recipient of the appeal letter? Try to make the reader *want* to contribute.

Tips for Better Writing   *Personalize the Message*

Fundraising experts have found great success by personalizing their message, giving it a face and a name. Instead of writing about the statistical thousands or millions, they tell about one or two in ways that engage the reader. Even organizations not dealing with people can use this technique. Here is copy from an actual holiday mailing sent by an SPCA chapter:

Although we have provided shelter and care for 14,000 animals so far this year, we never look at them as a statistic. To us, each is an individual, each has a pair of hopeful eyes and a wagging tail. Each has a unique personality and a unique set of needs. But they all have one need in common—the need for a place to call home, a family to call their own.

There's Santini who spent over a month in our care at the SPCA. This great little terrier mix was turned over to us by his family because they were moving to a place with a no-pets policy. Rather than looking for pet-friendly accommodations, they chose to relinquish their best friend to our shelter.

Shy at first, Santini needed a little coaxing out of his shell. He waited patiently for just the right human to come along and adopt him. Now the two are inseparable. Santini's new "Dad" says it's great to have a best friend who is ALWAYS glad to see him!

And little Clara, the beautiful orange tabby, was brought to the shelter because she kept having kittens. Instead of providing the simple, low-cost spay surgery needed to solve their "problem," her owners decided to leave Clara with us. We matched her up with a wonderful lady who had just lost her husband. Now, the two of them are practically joined at the hip. They share all sorts of quality time with one another. Clara is the queen of the house!

Be positive. Of course, you are dealing with a serious situation. You wouldn't be asking for help if it weren't serious. But don't paint the picture with too many somber tones. Recall what we know from persuasion theory about fear appeals and guilt appeals: A little bit goes a very long way. Certainly, you want to point out the seriousness and perhaps forecast the consequences of inaction. But offer your reader hope. Don't simply say, "This is an awful situation." Continue on: ". . . but you can help make it better." The objective is to motivate would-be donors, not demoralize them.

Understate rather than overstate. Understatement is more effective than hyperbole. If the situation is urgent, say so. But not every appeal is a life-and-death matter or one of critical timeliness. Remember the story of the boy who cried, "Wolf!" Don't risk your long-term credibility on a short-term ploy. Additionally, don't exaggerate the role your organization is playing in the situation being addressed. Any mishandling of facts is likely to come back to haunt you. Be persuasive, but keep things in honest proportion.

Appeal to the head and the heart. People have different psychological make-ups. Current research suggests that some people are more likely to persuaded by factual and logical explanations while others are more influenced by emotional appeals. In the appeal letter, you have the luxury of space to provide both approaches. By all means use the facts, provide statistics, quote authoritative sources. They give credibility to the appeal, and they will be compelling for many readers. But also make the appeal personal, tell a story, humanize the cause. "Tips for Better Writing: Psychological Type and Public Relations Writing" delves further into the subject.

Tips for Better Writing *Psychological Type and Public Relations Writing*

The theory of psychological type identifies four sets of inborn preferences in each person that combine to form basic personality patterns. Two of those patterns have particularly significance for public relations because they deal with persuasive communication.

How can this help you as a public relations writer? It can take you beyond a gut-level impulse and give you a firmer basis for designing messages that are likely to be received and acted upon by particular target publics. In short, it can make your communication more effective.

The author has conducted research based on the Myers-Briggs Type Indicator. One of the MBTI preference areas deals with how people gather information, factually or intuitively. Another is associated with how people make decisions and act on information they have gathered, logically or emotionally. Findings from the study offer three suggestions for using the Myers-Briggs personality typing system for public relations writing:

Guideline 1: Whenever possible, use messages with the same psychological type as their target public.

Guideline 2: When the psychological type of the public is unknown, assume a preference for the Sensing process (factual, literal, reality based) for information-gathering purposes.

Guideline 3: Use both Thinking (writing for the head, logical, analytical) and Feeling (writing for the heart, sentimental, sympathetic) approaches for decision-making purposes.

For a fuller explanation of this, see the published research: Smith, R.D. (1993). "Psychological type and public relations: theory, research, and applications." Journal of Public Relations Research 5, no. 3: 177–99.)

Get the reader involved. Once you have roused a passion in the reader, getting him or her to the point of wanting to help, keep things moving along. Discuss the benefits. Show how the reader can participate in this worthy cause. Don't simply ask for money; ask also for participation. Sure, money is part of it. But this reader can become an ambassador for the cause, an advocate among friends and colleagues, and a petitioner to governments and other authorities on behalf of your organization. At the very least, the donor can tell others about this cause. Ultimately, these are at least as valuable to the organization as a financial contribution.

Offer testimony. Effective appeal letters often include statements of support from people who have benefited from the organization. Appeal programs often link with well-known entertainers, athletes or community figures, both as people who will speak on behalf of the organization and as honorary directors. Often these people will lend their names as signers of appeal letters.

End with a postscript. Restate your most compelling reason for supporting the organization—the need, the benefit to the would-be donor, and the potential for achieving success. Some studies indicate that the postscript receives greater attention than many parts of the body of the letter; often it is read before the letter itself. Readers may skip around the letter, but they almost always pay attention to the P.S. But don't waste the P.S. by noting that the contribution is tax deductible or that a brochure is enclosed. Use it effectively and strategically to restate your key benefit and repeat your request.

Consider the gimmick. You gotta' have a gimmick—that's the advice of many direct appeal experts. Outrage from a political fundraiser because the other side is about to ruin the country. Weeping and wailing over an atrocity caused by evil or reprehensible people. Irony, such as the persistence of hunger in a world spotted with grain-filled silos. Fear and despair that a cure won't be found in time. A guilty conscience for not contributing after receiving a calendar, address labels, or some other unsolicited "gift."

Sometimes, the best gimmick is no gimmick at all. Heifer Project International used to send an appeal to lapsed donors, noting appreciation for the past contribution, admitting that there are many other worthy causes, and gently inviting future support for the anti-hunger organization. Oxfam America eschews emotional photos and guilt-tripping gifts and instead makes the straightforward appeal: You don't need to go to Senegal to help farmers dig a well or to Kosovo to help teachers rebuild their schools. All you need to do is join Oxfam America. Pay your dues, and we'll do the work in your name.

Exercise 13.3—Writing an Appeal Letter

Select a nonprofit organization of personal interest. Prepare a planning sheet for a fundraising letter aimed at a key public of your choosing. Work with other students as an editing team for this exercise. After you have written each part of this exercise, show the other members of your team what you have written, and together discuss the strengths and limitations of each piece of writing.

Part 1: The strength of an appeal letter lies in the impact of its opening. Write three different beginnings for your letter, and discuss these with others in your editing team.

Part 2: Using the best of the three leads, write a complete letter. Make sure your letter includes each of the following elements:

- An opening section with reader impact
- A sentence or paragraph that points out the benefit to the reader
- A paragraph that puts a human face on your appeal with a story or vignette
- A paragraph that presents factual and logical information
- A conclusion to your letter that clearly asks for a contribution
- A celebrity signer, and use of this celebrity throughout the letter
- A postscript.

Putting It Together

Effective direct-mail appeals have various components: envelope, appeal letter, response devise and acknowledgment. Each presents an opportunity for the public relations writer.

Envelope

The purpose of the envelope is to get the letter delivered and opened. An envelope with an address and a stamp is all that is needed to ensure delivery. But dissemination does not equal communication, and the envelope's job is not over when the letter carrier drops it in the mail box. Once the letter arrives at its destination, the envelope has another function: to entice the recipient to read the contents within. Studies indicate that half to three-fourths of unsolicited letters are thrown away unopened. Following are some suggestions for increasing the effectiveness of your direct mail.

Address. Hand-addressed envelopes are likely to get opened. They suggest a personal letter inside, and few people fail to open such an envelope. Nonprofit organizations sometimes find volunteers willing to write addresses on envelopes for appeal letters; some computer type fonts mimic the look of handwriting. Individually typed addresses also are effective, whether they are prepared on a typewriter or computer generated. Least effective are address labels, which have an impersonal, one-of-thousands feel.

Envelope. Professional-looking envelopes are most effective. Most successful appeal envelopes are No. 9 (letter size, approximately 4 by 7 inches) or No.10 (legal size, roughly 4 by 9½ inches). Solid-faced envelopes are more personal than window envelopes, which often have the look of a bill. However, window envelopes require only a personalized letter inside the envelope without the extra administrative fuss of preparing a separate mailing address.

Teaser Copy. Direct mailers take different approaches to teaser copy on the outside of the envelope. Many avoid it because personal letters don't have teasers, and they want an appeal letter to seem as personal as possible. Others believe that teasers can be effective if they involve a celebrity signer, powerful artwork or some other device to entice the recipient inside. For example, envelopes sometimes appeal to a sense of urgency. A pro-choice organization uses a red banner above the address with the notice "Urgent Membership Renewal." The envelope also features a sticker "WARNING: Federal election law prohibits NARAL Pro-Choice America from sending inside political communications to inactive members" (but of course, folks who renew active membership will be able to receive the tantalizing inside information). Mailers should be aware of the Deceptive Mailings Prevention Act of 1990, a federal provision that prohibits the use of mail solicitations that look like government notices such as IRS refund checks.

Postage. First-class postage stamps provide the most effective way to get an appeal letter opened, because they enhance the personal tone of the letter. But first-class postage is expensive for large mailings. An effective alternative is to use a bulk-rate postage stamp available to nonprofit organizations. This costs much less than first-class stamps but carries the same personal touch. Metered mail loses some of the personal tone. Least personal of all is the pre-printed postage block.

Appeal Letter

The appeal letter should be both attractive and easy to understand. Concerning the mechanical elements of the appeal letter, consider the following suggestions.

Letter Length. Longer letters are more effective than shorter ones. This goes against the common wisdom, which supposed that less is better. But psychological studies show that, when people care about the cause or issue, they want to know as much as possible. Optimum length varies according to the topic, the sender, the recipient and the situation. In general, though, the longer the better. Many effective appeal letters are three or more pages long. Make sure the letter goes to people who care about the issue (as it will if you have carefully targeted your publics); then trust that the recipient will want to read your letter and will appreciate the information in it. Generally, people who have willingly involved themselves with organizations that focus on human rights, political issues, medical research and such genuinely want to receive detailed progress reports and other information about the cause.

Appeal Packet. Let the letter dominate the appeal packet. Direct-mail letters may stand alone, or they may be supplemented by brochures or other inserts. If you use more than a letter, don't allow the supplemental materials to take the focus away from the main selling letter, and don't pack the envelope so the reader sees the tangential material before the letter itself.

Letterhead. Use professional-looking paper. Put the appeal letter on organizational letterhead that is attractive. Use either white or off-white, quality-bond paper. Some studies suggest that soft-toned paper enhances response. Use standard black ink, perhaps with a second color for effect.

Format. Appeal letters should look like letters. Type them with a ragged right margin and single spacing, with extra spacing between paragraphs. A more formal printed look destroys the illusion that the letter has been written for the individual reader.

Type Font. Choose a type font that is reader friendly. Generally that means a serif font such as Times, Caslon, or a related font seen most often in books, magazines and newspapers. Fonts with serifs are easier to read in paragraph-length passages. Avoid sans serif text and decorative fonts such as script and gothic. Also avoid Courier fonts that have an amateurish typewriter look. In particular, resist any urge to use cute fonts best suited for birthday invitations, Halloween greetings, and cowboy theme parties.

Graphic Appeal. Use typographical devices to give your letter visual appeal and to increase legibility and readability. These are especially helpful for readers who scan the text quickly, providing them with occasional pause points in their quick trip through the letter. Such typographical devices include all-capital letters, bullets, boldface type, extra spacing between paragraphs, indented paragraphs, italic fonts, subheads and underlines. Also consider using text boxes and/or color highlights for key words or phrases. Use such graphic devices carefully. They should call attention to pertinent words, phrases or sentences. Studies show that typographical devices can enhance readability when they call the reader's attention to a few items on each page. Too much can look like a circus poster.

Photographs. Photographs, charts, graphs and other artwork enhance the written communication. Such art attracts the reader's interest, drawing the eye to an engaging selling point. The figures should enhance the story and be of high technical quality. Make sure the topic is appropriate to your appeal. Humorous photos rarely work. Effective direct-mail pieces generally include captions with each piece of art, both to explain the visual element and to take advantage of heightened reader interest to repeat the central message or appeal.

Margin Notes. Handwritten margin notations can be effective. If the subject involves apparently personal topics, such as membership, children's causes or animals, they can add a personal touch. But again, don't overuse this device.

Exercise 13.4—Designing an Appeal Letter

In addition to strong writing, the public relations person must develop a pleasing look for the appeal letter. Revise the following text of an actual fundraising letter (with only the names changed). Prepare the letter for publication, noting appropriate paragraphing and highlight the text with graphic devices such as bullets, dashes, boldface type, italic type, underlines, and other features. Print your revised letter in its finished form.

Ezekiel Smith
15 Farnham Drive
Someplace, N.Y. 12345

Dear Mr. Smith:

One of the fondest memories of my youth is the warm, relaxed, safe feeling of visiting the public library. Merely by opening a book and turning its pages, I could raft down the Mississippi or learn that stars weren't found just in Hollywood but also in the heavens. Each trip to the Library was like visiting my best friend. If you're like me, you probably still recall the title of your favorite childhood book. As an adult, you know this feeling still exists; the library is the most interesting, most inviting place in town. Whether you want to find a best seller for poolside summer reading or sheet music for a sing-along at the family reunion, whether you're leaning to "surf the Net" at "Technology Tuesdays" or bringing your children or grandchildren to summer reading programs, whether you're looking for information on recent health care issues or upcoming cultural events, the Library is your best option. And that's the reason I am writing you today, to ask you, as one of the thousands of Iroquois County residents whose lives are enriched by the books, facilities and services of our outstanding Library System, to return something to the Library by making a contribution toward its sustenance and growth. A tax-deductible contribution or pledge to the Library is, in reality, a gift to yourself, your family, and to people of all ages in virtually every part of Iroquois County. I hope you will consider making a contribution or pledge of $75, $200 or more to keep our local libraries among the best in the nation. Of course, any amount you can afford will be appreciated. If you make a pledge, you will be billed quarterly. Our 52 branches and member libraries have always been an important source of information, education and recreation. More recently, however, the Iroquois County Public Library has become home to an international celebrity, Huckleberry Finn. Visitors can actually see the original handwritten manuscript of what has been called the greatest American novel on permanent display in the Central Library's new Mark Twain Room. And if you can't visit the Mark Twain Room in person, you can still find all of Twain's works (and all of the other authors in the Library) on our new electronic catalog, Beacon. The Mark Twain Room and Beacon are two of the many projects made possible by generous donations of people like you to The Library Foundation. The days are gone when tax dollars alone can sustain all the unique and special library services our community needs, expects and deserves. That's why it is so important for people like you to take action to preserve all that our libraries offer. Help to ensure that the programs which mean so much are always there to keep our community strong. Please, act now to support the full spectrum of library resources and services that enrich so many lives and promote a brighter future for all of Western New York. Make a generous contribution or pledge to The Library Foundation. Tomorrow's library relies on the generosity you demonstrate today. (signed) Samuel R. Coltrane, President of The Library Foundation of Iroquois County, Inc. ∎

Response Device

The response device should make it easy for the reader to offer support. This is the card or envelope flap that the reader is expected to fill out.

Donor Intention. The most important element of the response device is the statement of support. YES, I want to help save the whales (or feed the orphans, or find a cure, or get him elected or impeached). That YES is crucial. When the reader checks the box, the commitment has been made. All that remains is the follow-up: writing the check, filling out the membership application, signing the petition. But the reader has already taken the pledge, and follow-through is virtually assured.

Donor Information. Include space for the needed details from the reader. In addition to items such as name, postal address, e-mail contact information, perhaps a telephone number, that space also may include practical information for the reader: where to respond, tax deductibility and so on. The reply card should not introduce any new information not previously included in the letter, but the card can restate the main benefits or summarize the appeal.

Suggested Contributions. Include suggested contributions if the appeal is for funds. Give a range of appropriate contribution levels. Studies show it makes little difference if the amounts are listed in ascending or descending order. Giving several amounts is important so the would-be donor has an idea of what would be helpful to the organization. A give-all-you-can or a give-until-it-hurts message does not work well for an appeal letter. Instead, suggest some reasonably painless amounts.

If possible, either the letter or the response device should indicate what various levels of contribution can achieve. Studies suggest the effectiveness of highlighting the preferred contribution: listing it first, using boldface or some other typographical device such as encircling it. Always leave a space for "other." This space will be used either by people who want to be particularly generous or by those who care about the cause even if right now they cannot contribute as much as you have suggested.

A relatively new aspect to fundraising is the option for recipients to defer on giving but to request information or remain connected. "I can't contribute now, but I'd like more information." This gives reason for the organization to consider the recipient a potential future donor and to continue providing information about the organization and its cause.

For organizations operating close to home (a church building project, for example), the option of a monthly contribution is something to consider. For example, a pledge of $10 a month is a rather painless way for a donor to provide the organization with $120 for the year. This is more effective when the donor has continuing involvement with the organization soliciting the donation.

Return Envelope. The return envelope should make it easy for the donor to support the organization. It should be addressed back to the organization. Traditional wisdom is that it should include postage so the donor does not have to scrounge for a stamp. The poster service provides the option for a pre-paid return envelope that costs the organization only for those envelopes actually returned. Studies have found that actual stamps gain a higher return rate than such postage-paid labels. Stamps are more effective than metered postage labels, because stamps are more personal. Some people simply don't want to waste a stamp on the return envelope, so they make at least a small contribution when they otherwise would not.

Another new development is for nonprofit organizations to note in their appeal that the recipient is helping the organization by providing his or her own stamp. There certainly is a logic to this, though to some it seems a bit cheesy to expect the donor both to make the contribution and then to pay for the contribution to be delivered.

Acknowledgment

When someone gives you a gift or helps you in some way, you should say thanks. You learned that in kindergarten. The same thing is appropriate in philanthropic public relations. It also is practical. Following receipt of a contribution or some other type of support, an organization should send a personalized letter of acknowledgment. This letter should be as timely as possible. There is something disingenuous in a letter that thanks you for a contribution you gave 10 months ago and goes on to ask for another as part of this year's campaign.

Specifically, the acknowledgment should thank the donor. It also should reinforce the sentiment that led to the gift: for example, by pointing out how helpful the contribution is, how it will be used or how it benefits the reader or the cause. This is an underlying purpose of the acknowledgment: to lay the groundwork for continued participation and support by the donor.

A residential treatment center for people living with AIDS found an elegant way to express appreciation to donors: "On behalf of the residents at Benedict House, I would like to thank you for your generous and continued support of our work, especially your recent gift of $300. As you are aware, Benedict House exists almost solely through private contributions from supporters such as you. Consequently, your gift was indeed cause for celebrating." The image of people with AIDS *celebrating* because of a donor's gift is an inspiring one indeed.

Exercise 13.5—Writing a Follow-Up Letter

Prepare a follow-up letter thanking your instructor for making a $30 contribution to the project you wrote about in Exercise 13.3. ∎

Fundraising and the Web

A growing phenomenon is the use of the Internet in fundraising. An estimated 69 percent of people living in North America are online, and many nonprofit organizations as well as businesses are finding the Web to be a lucrative new tool to reach them. It's cost effective, with little overhead or promotional expenses.

Nonprofit Organizations

Americans and Canadians respond generally to disasters. Usually we send checks. But philanthropy saw a major change when Internet-based giving became a viable option.

Hurricane Mitch in 1998, one of the worst storms in 50 years, was the first occasion in which a substantial amount of money came through the Internet. Web users visited the sites of relief agencies to learn about the crisis and the humanitarian response to it, and they offered to help. For example, visitors to the CARE-USA Web site doubled, with donors giving $10,000 a day during the first week of the crisis. Meanwhile, the American Red Cross received $450,000 in Internet contributions. And at CARE Canada, with a brand new e-commerce capacity at its Web site, contributions jumped from $180 a month before Mitch to $14,000 the following month.

Other relief situations yielded similar online results. Following a 1999 earthquake in Turkey, for example, the American Red Cross raised $140,000 in one day at its Web site. During the height of the humanitarian crisis in Kosovo, the ARC online giving page recorded $1 million in one month. Meanwhile, Catholic Relief Services raised $700,000 online during the Kosovo crisis. That amount was only 10 percent of the $7 million CRS raised through a more traditional direct-mail solicitation, but it was a significant impact for a new technique that wasn't even active until the Kosovo crisis was easing up.

But it was the September 11 attacks on New York City and Washington in 2001 that caused Internet-based giving to mushroom—more than $1.3 billion in donations within the first several weeks alone, about 20 percent of that from online donors. A survey by the Independent Sector reported that 70 percent of adults in the United States had contributed either money or blood. Online giving surged again following Hurricane Katrina, which hit New Orleans and other cities in August 2005. Within a month, the American Red Cross reported that a third of the $891 million in relief donations was raised over the Internet. Groups as diverse as the American Humane Society, Paralyzed Veterans of America, Catholic Charities-

USA and the American Diabetes Association reported as much as half of their Katrina relief was from online donors.

The Network for Good was established in 2001 as an e-philanthropy portal site where people can donate to various causes, volunteer, or otherwise get involved in issues they care about. It was founded by Time Warner, Yahoo, AOL, Google and dozens of other corporate sponsors representing a partnership of technology companies, media organizations and foundations. The site (networkforgood.org) capitalizes on the instant gratification that online donors want and provides access to 850,000 nonprofit organizations registered with the Internal Revenue Service, allowing donors to channel their contributions through the network to any recipient they wish.

Political Fundraising

Web-based fundraising also has been a significant tool in the political arena. In the 2004 presidential campaign, more than $100 million was raised online. Online contributions averaged $111, compared to $35 for donations sent through the mail, according to a report by the George Washington Graduate School of Political Management. Donations were made online by 80 percent of donors aged 18 to 34 and by 67 percent of those aged 35 to 50. This represented about half of all Democratic donors and a quarter of Republican donors, though political observers said there is little inherent difference because of party affiliation; rather, the Republicans raised more money through traditional means and the Democrats had to work harder to obtain funds from new sources.

The Institute for Politics, Democracy and the Internet at George Washington University concluded that the Internet has transformed how political campaigns communicate with their supporters and has become a tool to organize as well as raise money. The institute also developed a comprehensive profile of the online political donor:

- Most younger donors give online
- Unsolicited contributions have increased because of the Internet
- Internet users are more likely to be asked to contribute and are more likely to be politically active
- And finally, online small donors (less than $200) are no more partisan than other political donors.

Most charitable Web-based fundraising is passive; the organization provides information at its Web site for would-be donors who seek it out. Some political fundraising has taken a more direct route, using e-mail to solicit donors, and political machines often have sophisticated resources to target and track contributions. However, nearly half of the 2004 donors said their contribution was unsolicited and not based on mail, phone or e-mail requests. Because they don't represent potentially large gifts, most individuals are not on the mailing or call lists of most political organizations, and in previous campaigns, the small giver often had to search for ways to contribute.

Another study by professors at Yale, Syracuse and SUNY Albany reported that four times as many people contributed to the 2004 campaign as to the 2000 campaign, most of the increase due to small Internet donors. The researchers also observed that the Internet is leveling the playing field and giving small donors more voice in the political process. Indeed, some observers say this surge in small online contributions is changing the character of American politics by shifting the base away from the wealthy few and into the hands of the average citizens of moderate financial means.

The Power of the Web

Internet-based fundraising offers some real benefits for organizations seeking donor support. Overhead costs are lower. Contributions are higher. And as an added bonus, online donations make it easy for the organization to expand its donor base, yielding new names for future fundraising efforts.

Faster and More Generous. Contributions made via credit card or systems such as PayPal® tend to be higher than donations made by check. They also can provide a very quick response. In late 2005 and early 2006, charitable organizations reported record donations for the tsunami relief effort in Southeastern Asia. Online donations to the Red Cross yielded twice as much in contributions than the traditional phone banks, $18 million in two days following the disaster. Catholic Relief Services was so overwhelmed by donors that its Web site crashed, though the organization went on to post its largest relief effort ever, $190 million.

Most relief agencies reported that between a quarter and a half of their donors gave online: the American Red Cross received $84 million in online donations alone; UNICEF, $35 million online; World Vision, $13 million; Catholic Relief Services, $12 million; Save the Children, $11 million; Salvation Army, $8 million; CARE, $7 million; American Jewish World Services, $3.5 million; Islamic Relief USA, $1 million—all online donations within less than a month of the earthquake and tsunami. Most of those donations were unsolicited by the relief agency and based rather on the donor's self-initiated response to media coverage of the disaster.

A study by the Network for Good reported that online giving had collectively passed $2 billion. The network itself has raised $90 million online directly. It also uses its Web site to help would-be donors channel their contributions to a wide range of individual charities, including the American Red Cross, Catholic Charities, Human Society, Veterans of Foreign Wars, Baptist World Alliance, Doctors with Borders, Islamic Relief, and thousands more.

Wider Pull. Another benefit of Web-based fundraising is that it is not bound by the geographic boundaries of many organizations. For example, CARE Canada receives contributions from throughout the world, though its traditional direct-mail fundraising activities are focused on the Canadian provinces. The agency said its new international donors are younger and more high tech than the agency's usual donor base, a hopeful demographic shift introducing a new group of potential donors that the philanthropic organization undoubtedly will pursue.

New Donor Base. The Internet also can pull in new names to expand the donor base of an organization. One study by Epsilon, a national fundraising company, found that 88 percent of online donors were new contributors to the organization. Essentially, these were people who came to the organization, waiving their money and asking for the privilege of helping out. That's a real turnaround from the traditional direct-mail route of buying or renting names from database organizations.

Younger Donor Base. As the George Washington University study pointed out, more than 80 percent of Americans aged 18 to 34 who contributed to political candidates or causes in 2004 did so online. Such reports offer enormous hope to political and other fundraisers as the Internet solidifies its role as a major means of communication, particularly among younger and more educated people.

The Cost of E-Mail Fundraising

Many experts find e-mail more cost effective than postal mail appeals. For one thing, purchasing postal mail lists often is more expensive than buying e-mail lists. And while e-mail appeals cost little to disseminate, large-scale appeals using postal mail incur heavy costs because of printing and packaging, and testing with a pilot mailing, as well as the postage cost itself.

Additionally, experts who favor e-mail appeals report that they show results within seven to 10 days, compared to four to six weeks needed for response from postal appeals. Thus, e-mail provides a higher return-on-investment for the organization making the appeal.

Another advantage is that e-mail can be "pushed" to its audience like print mail, rather than being posted as a Web site where readers have to "pull" it out. Plus, it is easy to track even those recipients who do not open their e-mail appeals.

Is there a down-side to e-mail appeals? Sure. Like most options, there are minuses as well as plusses. Spam traps on most computers, especially business systems, can filter our unsolicited bulk e-mails, so the message may never get to the reader. And older persons, often more generous in their giving habits, are less likely to be represented among e-mail users. Meanwhile, all e-mail solicitors should be aware of the legal provisions of the CAN-SPAM Act (which stands for Controlling the Assault of Non-Solicited Pornography and Marketing Act of 2003) and the European Privacy and Electronic Communications Regulations, as well as the policies of various Internet providers.

14

Public Relations Advertising

Advertising is a clear example of persuasive communication. Its purpose is obvious: to influence the attitudes, opinions and actions of the audience. All advertising is not the same, however. Consumer advertising, also called product advertising, seeks to sell products or services; it is a tool of sales, merchandising and marketing with little overlap into public relations. Public relations advertising, on the other hand, seeks to "sell" the organization, its ideas, its causes, and other noncommercial messages. Public relations advertising uses the tools and techniques of advertising to help an organization communicate with its publics. It can be paid, as in advocacy advertising, or unpaid, as in public service advertising.

This chapter will first explore the issue of creativity, so vital to public relations advertising. It then will look at the various types of advertising, focusing in on its use for public relations purposes. The chapter then will look at various writing techniques, and finally will address the issue of public service advertising. Here are your objectives for Chapter 14:

- To identify the differences between consumer advertising and public relations advertising
- To explain the concept of advocacy advertising
- To demonstrate an understanding of the concept of public service advertising
- To develop an advertising strategy for a nonprofit organization
- To describe the activities of the Advertising Council
- To write effective copy for a public relations advertisement.

Creativity

Let's begin by acknowledging that everyone is creative to a greater or lesser degree. Each of us holds a place on the creativity scale, somewhere between Steven Spielberg and a tree stump. The consideration is not: Am I creative? Rather the questions should be: In what ways am I creative? How can I become more creative? How can I use my creativity in presenting public relations messages?

What is *creativity*? It's the ability to develop an original solution to a problem, giving it a fresh look or a new angle. Let's call it a blend of imagination and innovation, perhaps with a touch of weirdness. Some people say that creativity is an in-born capability, a gift, a knack. Either you have it or you don't, so they say. But those people are wrong. Imagination can be nurtured, and innovative ability can be learned. As for the weirdness, most people have enough of that already, so all we have to do is acknowledge this and get comfortable with it.

Rather than being an inevitable natural trait, creativity is more like the talent of a musician or the skill of an athlete. It is a seed, present to a degree in everyone, which must be nourished for it to flower. Creativity develops through practice, patience and perseverance. That's not simply a hope. Rather research has shown that (1) everyone has creative capacity, (2) creativity can be learned, and (3) some techniques for building creativity are more effective than others. Actually, we should talk about creativity being relearned. Social scientists note that children are naturally creative, but we lose much of that natural creativity as we grow up and conform to the conventions of school and society.

Professional creativity in public relations is a product of strategic planning—the result of careful analysis of the idea or object being promoted, the public being addressed, and the organization's objectives. This creativity is the result of a person's ability to prepare an effective and imaginative response to resolve a particular problem.

Consider various traits that have been associated with creative people. Some are rooted in natural proclivities and preferences. But all are within the control of any individual, and all can be cultivated and enhanced. Creative people are:

- Able to see the big picture
- Aesthetically interested and artistically inclined
- Curious and inquisitive
- Disciplined and tenacious
- Eclectic and varied in their tastes
- Independent thinkers
- Intelligent and capable
- Intuitive and spontaneous
- Nonconformist and rebellious
- Open to new experiences
- Original and inventive
- Self-confident and resolute
- Visual thinkers
- Voracious readers.

Let's discuss two different types of creativity techniques: free association and forced association. In addition, "FYI: The Creative Environment" speaks to potential creative blocks and what they mean for public relations writers.

FYI   *The Creative Environment*

At Buffalo State College of the State University of New York, the Center for Studies in Creativity offers the only graduate degree program in creativity in the United States. Experts in creativity and innovation have identified several blocks to creativity that can be helpful in understanding and building a creative environment.

Personal blocks to creativity include lack of self-confidence, tendency to conform, need for the familiar, emotional numbness, saturation, excessive enthusiasm, and lack of imaginative control.

Problem-solving blocks to creativity include premature judgments, use of poor problem-solving approaches, lack of disciplined effort, poor language skills, and rigidity.

Situational blocks to creativity include isolation, the belief that only one type of thinking is appropriate, resistance to new ideas, and reliance on experts.

What does this mean to public relations writers? The more we understand about the creative environment, the more we can try to build an environment that is likely to support our efforts to be creative.

Exercise 14.1—Freewriting on Creativity

Freewrite for five minutes on the following topic: *In what ways am I a creative person?* Then discuss this with your classmates. ∎

Free Association Techniques

The mind, when freed of various restraints, can be prompted to generate creative ideas by using undefined connections. The methods for achieving this are called *free association techniques*. They include freewriting, brainstorming, buzz groups and brainwriting. Each is described briefly below. In addition, "Tips for Better Writing: Limbering Up Mentally" offers some advice for pre-writing creative warm-ups.

Tips for Better Writing *Limbering Up Mentally*

Calisthenics and stretching exercises can limber up your body before you jog or work out. Similarly, creativity exercises can limber up your mind before you begin writing. One of the hallmarks of a good writer is a person who can take an ordinary item or action and look at it in a fresh new way. It's also known as thinking outside the box.

The purpose of this exercise is not necessarily to get the right answer but rather to grapple with a problem and approach it from various perspectives. Following are several exercises to limber your creative mind. Answers are located at the end of this chapter.

1. Give at least three answers to the question: What is half of 13?

2. What is the logical pattern for arranging these numbers in the following order: 8, 5, 4, 9, 1, 7, 6, 3, 2, 0?

3. You leave home, take three left turns, and meet two men in masks. Where are you, and who are the masked men?

4. What is the shortest day of the year?

5. A businessman preparing to travel to Tokyo asks an adult Japanese friend, who is from Tokyo, to teach him Japanese. He learns to speak just as his teacher does. When he gets to Tokyo and begins speaking, his business colleagues laugh at him. Why?

6. Look at each of the following words, arranged alphabetically, for 15 seconds. Then, within 90 seconds, arrange them in one complete and logical sentence: always an and at both calm each early emotionally exercising felt has he him hour least made morning physically that.

7. Mary goes to school every day, but seldom does homework. Of the 25 students in Mary's class, 24 are good students. Mary often is called into the principal's office, but never gets into trouble. Why?

8. What English word has six i's?

9. A window washer was cleaning the 25th-floor windows on a skyscraper. He was not protected by a harness or any other kind of safety device, yet when he slipped and fell he was not injured. Why?

10. What can be seen and has no weight, but the more that are put in an empty tin can, the lighter the can becomes?

Freewriting. You're already familiar with *freewriting* through the exercises in this book designed to help you develop some insight and creative approaches to your writing. Freewriting is a creativity technique because it helps you overcome the restrictions of grammar and style as well as the need for logic and coherency in an effort to begin writing. In freewriting, ideas should flow freely; refinements come later.

Brainstorming. You also may be familiar with *brainstorming*. A technique that can be used by one person or a small group, brainstorming calls for participants to set the goal of generating a large quantity of ideas around a particular issue, problem or approach. One of the "rules" of brainstorming is to be open to consider far out and seemingly unworkable ideas. Participants are not permitted to make any judgments about the quality of ideas being generated, and they are encouraged to piggyback on each other's ideas.

Buzz Group. Another method of brainstorming involves the *buzz group*, a method particularly effective with large numbers of people. This involves reorganizing into a series of small subgroups to brainstorm ideas and then reporting them back to the larger group.

Brainwriting. A related activity, *brainwriting*, has participants circulating among a series of poster sheets on various topics, writing at least one idea on each sheet. Participants write a new idea or develop one written by someone else. A variation of this is the *idea card*, in which the people remain in place and the cards circulate among them.

Forced Association Techniques

Another group of activities that stimulate creative ideas deal with forced relationships. Rather than wide-open connections used with free association techniques, *forced association techniques* prompt the mind to generate ideas by using defined connections, relying on some gentle coercion to draw out innovative thinking. These forced relationship techniques for creativity include visual relationships, personification, similes, explained similes, and future statements.

Visual Relationship. The *visual relationship* technique uses photographs or other visual representations to nurture creativity. One implementation of this technique is to select a photograph and then ask a group to associate thoughts as they relate to a topic. For example, public relations writers seeking to promote community interest in a summer camp for children with physical limitations might use a photo of a clown to nurture their thoughts about the camp: fun, happy, frivolous, cheerful, light-hearted, foolish, optimistic, no time for sadness. Or perhaps the picture of a tree: strong, growing, spreading, developing, hardy. Almost any kind of visual stimulus will do, if the participants let their imaginations roam uninhibited.

Personification. Using the technique of *personification,* you get personal with an object, treating it as you would a person. Using the technique of freewriting, this time in a forced association context, write about the object you are seeking to be creative with. Better yet, write *to* the object. For example, if you are seeking to be creative about perfume, write to the bottle of perfume. "When I see your shape, it reminds me of . . ." "When I see your color, it reminds me of . . ." "When I smell you, I think about . . ." "When I dab you on my arm, it makes me remember the time when . . ."

Simile. Another technique, the *simile*, is a verbal method that can accomplish much the same as the visual relationship tool. For example, completing similes such as "Camp is like . . ." can generate a lot of mental images about the camp: paradise, a fun house, a playground, a gym floor for wheelchairs.

Explained Simile. A related forced association technique carries the simile through to explanation. An *explained simile* can lead to some interesting insights: "Our campers are like puppies because. . .": they are inquisitive, they need some attention, they want to be part of everything, they don't know the meaning of "no," their curiosity knows no bounds.

Future Statement. Statements that focus on benefits or potential solutions also can be helpful. One commonly used *future statement* is called a WIBNI (Wouldn't it be nice if . . .?). This can be a powerful formula for freeing your imagination to think of possibilities. "WIBNI our campers could . . ." "WIBNI people in town thought our camp was . . ."

Exercise 14.2—Using the Freewriting Technique

In this exercise and the one following, you will prepare to create an advertisement using creative techniques. In so doing, you are moving beyond the traditional approach to public relations planning, a logical approach through which you have learned to develop planning sheets. Creative approaches can help you accomplish the same thing. In these exercises, you will use different ways to identify some of the wants, interests and needs of your key public. You can focus on the benefits available to this public and gain insight into the position of your school in relation to its competition. Using creative techniques, you also will note some factual information that may become part of the eventual message.

Here's the scenario: You are a public relations writer for your school, and your task is to develop an advertisement to recruit students. But first you need to warm up your creativity muscles. Imagine yourself in the following situation: You are in a hot-air balloon floating above your campus. You can see the entire campus below.

Part 1: Use the freewriting technique to stretch your creativity. In this freewrite, look down on the campus and describe what you see.

Part 2: Go a step beyond the physical campus. Write about what you think about your school. What do you like about it? What makes this a good example of higher education? What academic programs are particularly strong? What do the students you see walking below you think about your school? Why did they come here? Why do they remain?

Part 3: In the balloon with you now is a younger friend who is in 11th grade at the high school you attended. Freewrite about your conversation with this friend. What does he or she think about attending college? What does your friend think about your school?

Part 4: Your hot-air balloon is beginning to drift away from its position above your campus. A strong wind takes it all the way to the campus of a neighboring college. Then the wind dies down, and you and your high-school friend look down on that campus. What do you see? How is it different from your own campus? Go beyond the physical appearance. What do you tell your friend about how this institution compares with your school? ∎

Exercise 14.3—Using the Personification Technique

This exercise will help you understand the technique of personification and how to use it in your own writing. Select a small candy bar. Pick one that isn't currently being heavily advertised, so you can approach this exercise with originality rather than being biased by existing ad campaigns.

Here is the scenario: You are developing an advertising campaign for a candy bar. Your key public is children between the ages of 8 and 14, but you may narrow this a bit, for example by selecting boys or girls only.

Part 1: Freewrite a brief analysis of the wants, interests and needs of this public.

Part 2: Unwrap the candy bar, and look at it for a short time. Then write: "When I see your shape, it reminds me of . . ."

Part 3: Look at the candy bar again, then write: "When I see your color, it makes me think about . . ."

Part 4: Now smell the candy and take a small bite. Then write: "When I smell you and taste you, I think about . . ."

Part 5: Review what you have written, then develop a magazine-type or billboard-type advertisement for this candy. Focus on three elements of the ad: a dominant picture, a headline and a memorable tag line.   ∎

Public Relations and Advertising

Public relations and advertising often have had a love–hate relationship. They are related disciplines, but the question is: How closely related? Some colleges and universities teach public relations and advertising in the same department, sometimes even as a combined major; others separate them. In some organizations, one department may handle both disciplines; in others they are kept apart. Some agencies provide services in both areas; others specialize. This textbook isn't going to resolve the issue of the appropriate relationship between advertising and public relations, but it can look at that relationship.

First, a definition. *Advertising* is the nonpersonal paid communication through various media by an identified organization (either for-profit or nonprofit) for the purpose of informing and influencing a particular audience. Advertising can be classified into two major categories: product advertising and public relations advertising. Let's take a look at each, along with their various subcategories.

Product Advertising

The most common use of advertising is *product advertising*, which is marketing oriented. That is, the ad is intended to sell a product or service. Product advertising types include retail, general and business-to-business.

Retail Advertising. Most of the advertising for local companies and organizations is retail oriented. *Retail advertising* seeks to promote a sale, encourage use of a product or service, or otherwise sell something. Because it is local, retail advertising can be specific, including dates, locations, prices, and information on brands and various models.

General Advertising. The category of *general advertising*, also known as *national advertising*, does not provide specific information about sales dates, store locations, and so on (though sometimes this is possible through Web sites identified in general advertising). In promoting a new automobile, general advertising would tell consumers about a model of car, its quality and its features. Or it might focus on an entire brand of car, rather than a specific model.

Business-to-Business Advertising. Most consumers never see *business-to-business advertising*, in which companies promote themselves in professional, trade or industrial publications read by other businesspeople. For example, a public relations firm might advertise in a magazine for managers of auto dealerships, highlighting its experience and its record of generating community goodwill and support for dealerships.

Public Relations Advertising

Of more immediate interest to public relations practitioners is the category of *public relations advertising*, through which an organization promotes its nonmarketing messages related to the public image of an organization and community support. Public relations advertising includes four subcategories: institutional advertising, advocacy advertising, political advertising and public service advertising. We'll look at each in more depth.

Institutional Advertising. When an ad promotes the merits of a new automobile, that's product advertising. When an ad promotes the name and reputation of the company that manufactures the car, that's *institutional advertising*. It sometimes is called *image advertising* or *corporate advertising* and sometimes is disparaged as *feel-good advertising*. During football season, the NFL uses institutional advertising to enhance its reputation by promoting its charities. Other organizations use this type of advertising for other public relations purposes, such as an educational union's efforts to support an employee relations program by publicly congratulating teachers on the success of their students in a statewide test.

Budweiser is engaging in institutional advertising when it pulls out the Clydesdales for its jingle bells and snowy woods holiday ads that simply say, "Season's Greetings." Polls shows that viewers of Super Bowl XXXIX in 2005 particularly liked an Budweiser image ad depicting soldiers heading off to war, presumably in Iraq, amid smiles and applause through the airport, with a voice-over saying "Thank you."

Sometimes institutional advertising is linked with crisis communications. For example, in the wake of multimillion-dollar legal judgments against them, tobacco companies began using institutional advertising to brag about their community assistance.

Advocacy Advertising. A similar public relations use of advertising tools and techniques is *advocacy advertising* (sometimes called *issue advertising*), which focuses less on an organization and more on a cause or goal important to it. Advocacy advertising is advertising paid for by organizations to communicate their position on public issues related to their mission or business; usually, the issues deal with political, social or economic topics. Utilities use advocacy advertising to explain their position on energy sources or pending legislation. Unions use it to address issues of importance to them. Cause-related organizations use advocacy advertising to explain and justify their positions and to challenge the public to act in what they consider a responsible manner. Nonprofit organizations sometimes use advocacy advertising to speak out on issues that cannot be addressed through public service advertising.

Increasingly, companies are using some of the advertising space for articlelike institutional ads that present what appear to be feature articles, often about celebrities. The boost for the company is the community relations value of being associated with a popular person and a worthwhile project.

Political Advertising. Closely related to advocacy advertising is *political advertising*, in which the focus is not so much on educating the public about important issues or presenting an organization's viewpoint on them, but rather on partisan political gain. Political advertising can deal with encouraging the support (or rejection) of specific candidates or particular pieces of legislation.

Political advertising has become an important weapon in the political arsenal, and many political interest groups are using it to promote causes rather than specific candidates. Sometimes the line gets blurred between addressing issues and influencing voters for or against candidates, and legal questions have been raised about the role of issue advertising in the political process. The Annenberg Public Policy Center at the University of Pennsylvania estimated that special interest groups spent more than $400 million to influence Congress during 2005 both for and against a variety of policy issues such as oil drilling in Alaska, importing prescription drugs from Canada, and tax-cut plans.

In addition to individual candidate ads, topics for issue ads ranged from abortion, gun control and animal rights through campaign reform, health care, education, Social Security, and the environment. The Annenberg Center identified hundreds of organizations sponsoring issue ads, not only Democratic and Republican political groups but also other organizations ranging from American Medical Association to the National Smokers Alliance, and from the United Bowhunters of Pennsylvania to the Coalition for Asbestos Resolution.

Public Service Advertising. Who says the media don't have a heart? Each year television and radio stations, magazines and newspapers give away about several billion dollars worth of free advertising time through *public service advertisements*—promotional and advocacy advertisements for both print and broadcast media in which no placement costs are charged by the medium using the advertising.

Sometimes the line blurs between editorial and advertising, and between product advertising and public relations advertising. Cigna Insurance, for example, produces an advertising series called "The Power of Caring" that runs in magazines such as Time, Fortune, People and Sports Illustrated. The ads present features about celebrities and their charitable causes—Daisy Fuentes and the March of Dimes, Jimmy Smits and the National Hispanic Foundation for the Arts, Faith Hill and her Family Literacy Project, and Lance Armstrong and the Life After Cancer program.

Public Relations Advertising

The late David Ogilvy, one of the pacesetters of advertising, once observed that "you cannot save souls in an empty church." In other words, to engage audiences, advertisers need to take the message to the people. We need to capture first their attention and then their imagination, and we eventually need to summon forth a commitment and action. "FYI: Cost versus Creativity" summarizes another of Ogilvy's statements and the implication for advertisers.

FYI *Cost versus Creativity*

In his seminal book *Ogilvy on Advertising*, David Ogilvy stated a suspicion, unsupported by research. He speculated that there is a "negative correlation between the money spent on producing commercials and their power to sell products."

Research Systems Corp., of Evanston, Ill., took up the challenge. It reported scientific findings that support Ogilvy's hunch. Research Systems found that the most effective advertising cost 40 percent less than less successful ads. Some of the high costs were the result of creative decisions to use expensive celebrity spokespersons or extravagant special effects which, while gaining audience attention, did little to sell the product.

What does this mean for the public relations writer? Don't let yourself be tempted by a desire for bigger promotional budgets. Some top-quality advertisements are simple visual productions, but they are based on effective and insightful messages. Develop a strategy rooted in research about your intended audience and focus on quality writing.

Society today is increasingly complex, and just keeping pace has become a chore. New countries on the map. New chemical elements on the periodic chart. A never-ending parade of newness. *Information overload* is the term social scientists give to this growing complexity. And it is a real burden, because the average person cannot even hope to keep up with new and more readily available information. More organizations are communicating, and organizations are communicating more.

Amid this abundance of public relations messages, we hope that one message—ours—will be heard above the din of the crowd. How can we shine brighter and sing louder? Certainly, we need effective creativity, nurtured through the planning process that you have been practicing throughout this course. We also can learn from the experience of others.

Developing the Message

The public relations writer sometimes uses tools drawn from the field of advertising. When we enter this field, we should learn the successful recipes that have been developed by our advertising colleagues. In particular, we should learn that effective advertisers pay careful attention to each of the various parts of the advertising package. A standard method of evaluating the effectiveness of a print ad is to focus on five specific elements: visual, headline, copy, closing message, and layout. Let's look at each area.

Visual Message. The *visual message*, artwork, presents the concept underlying the advertisement. Some advertisements use studio photographs or computer-enhanced imagery. Others use snapshots or news-type photos. Sketches, diagrams, blueprints, maps, graphs and charts also figure in the visual message. The following four guidelines may be helpful as you begin to develop the visual message for various kinds of public relations advertising.

Use simple images. The illustration is the first thing a reader looks at in an advertisement. If it seems interesting, the reader then will move on to the headline and eventually, perhaps, to the body copy. Advertising art is likely to be more effective when it is uncomplicated. A photograph of one person will attract more readers than a crowd scene. Too much background detail can distract the reader away from the main element.

Make instant connections. The combination of artwork and headline provides the immediate impression for the reader. Most artwork—such as photos, sketches and diagrams—carries a message that can be instantly absorbed and understood. This works for groups of people with various backgrounds, interests and demographic traits. Therefore, select artwork that offers instant connections linking the message with the audience. Sometimes this leads to the use of stereotyped images that, while perhaps not always fully accurate, are usually effective. For example, grandmothers come in all shapes, sizes and ages: 35-year-old dancers, 55-year-old business executives, 75-year-old globe-trotting retirees. But for instant connections, you might go for the stereotype: dowdy, gray-haired, wearing an apron and baking cookies. Just be careful that, in using easy stereotypes, you don't demean the people you are portraying or depict them unfairly.

Show the product. Effective advertising finds a way to display the focus of the advertising message: the service, idea, or product being promoted. Products are easy to display; people can see them. Intangibles that public relations advertisers deal with—organizations, services, ideas, attitudes and values—are more of a challenge. When we can't show a photo or footage of something, we often display it by showing its results. Sometimes it can be "seen" through its absence, or perhaps in comparison with a competitive or alternative image. Often, we rely on symbols to give form to our message.

Promote benefits, not ingredients. The grandmother doesn't buy the chocolate fudge sundae because of its riboflavin content. No, she buys it to help her grandson forget his humiliation on the soccer field or to celebrate his success. An experienced advertiser isn't going to pitch the sundae with a list of nutritional traits, but perhaps rather as pick-me-up food, the soother of a wounded ego, a snack to be shared in good times or bad. The same advice holds for public relations advertising: Promote the benefit, not the ingredients. At University A, professors have written 276 books and published 1,435 research papers. University B has professors who will help you get a good education and a satisfying job? Which message provides the better reason to enroll?

Exercise 14.4—Developing a Visual Strategy

You are public relations writer for your college or university, preparing an advertisement that will be used in high school newspapers in a 100-mile geographic area. Your objective is to interest students in attending your institution. Review the freewriting you did in Exercise 14.2. Then describe the *visual* strategy you might take for the advertisement. ■

Verbal Message. The *verbal message* includes the headlines, body copy and closing message, which together complement and carry on where the visual message leaves off. The public relations writer is on home turf in preparing copy for advertising. This is your area of expertise, and virtually all of the work you have done in this course will come into play as you take on the role of copywriter. Consider the following additional guidelines for writing advertising copy, as well.

Write headlines that focus readers. While artwork attracts attention, headlines provide readers with needed information and strategically redirect the reader to both the message of the ad and the organization sponsoring it. Advertising guru David Ogilvy once pronounced that the headline is the most important element of an ad's effectiveness. In addition, headlines are read at least five-to-10 times more often than body copy. The headline itself can be presented in various ways. From a strategic point of view, consider the following types and examples of headlines:

- *News*: "Introducing a new way to learn Spanish." This type of headline is remembered more than any other.
- *Emotion*: "Little Maria and her brothers go to bed hungry almost every night."
- *How-to*: "Three easy ways to get a great-paying job."
- *Pun*: "A waist is a terrible thing to mind."
- *Question*: "Ever wonder why Hudson-Wallaby employees always seem so happy?"

Beware of asking dumb questions that open themselves to sarcastic answers: "Would you like to get straight A's the easy way?" (Who wouldn't?) Avoid other types of problem headlines: the too-long head, mere labels, heads awash with hype, cute or tricky headlines that fail to reveal the topic, and headlines that don't indicate any benefit.

Brief is best. Most advertising is based on concise copy, and professional copywriters pride themselves on their ability to pack a lot of meaning into a few words. Generally, this is the approach to aim for. It offers the greatest potential for the largest number of readers. But don't sacrifice understanding just to be terse. Research shows that people will read lengthy copy under two conditions: (1) if they are particularly interested in a topic, and (2) if they want more information about that topic.

One thought per ad. Good ads focus on just one idea. Even advertisements of large dimensions don't have the luxury of wandering from one theme to another. For the copywriter the rules are simple: Know your point, make it and don't stray.

Make it memorable. All writers strive to have their words stick in the reader's mind, like a haunting melody that doesn't quite go away. Because advertising copy must be brief, we need to also make it memorable. A good copywriter will work through many drafts, seeking the precise word and creating just the right phrases and sentences. The two parts of an ad where you should strive for memorable phrasing are the headline and the *tag line* (the slogan or parting message). Often the memorable phrases are those that, in their simplicity, are brimming with potential and meaning. "Coke Is It!" isn't the most profound corporate statement ever made, but it is memorable. So is the "Just Do It!" slogan by Nike, the California Milk Processor Board's "Got Milk?" and Wonderbra's "Hello, boys" as well as public relations slogans such as "I love New York" and "The few. The proud. The Marines." Think of some of the memorable messages of public service advertising. "Friends Don't Let Friends Drive Drunk" is wisdom packaged for a bumper sticker. "Give a hoot, don't pollute" has been helping the U.S. Forest Service for years, following a successful long-time run of "Only *you* can prevent forest fires."

Use strong narration. Storytelling is an ancient and very effective form of communication. Good advertising copywriting features well-told stories. Anecdotes, metaphors and parables can be more forceful than mere definitions. Dialogue that is natural and realistic can bring a narrative to life.

Use description. Details and particulars also are the stuff of good advertising writing. In preparing to compose an advertisement, copywriters should know the characteristics of people and places being referred to. Study the technicalities and trivia about the subject of your writing. Picture imaginary scenes in exquisite detail. You will not use every detail, but well-chosen bits of information will flavor your writing and appeal to the audience's senses.

Be specific. Any organization can make claims and assertions, especially when its writers use general terms. But provable reality and unquestioned facts are needed to "sell" the message to the reader. Consider two universities that offer professional-training programs in public relations. University A claims to have "an excellent placement record." University B reports that "80 percent of our graduates get jobs in the public relations field." Which is more convincing? Generalities are easy to hide behind. Facts are more demanding of the writer, requiring careful research and precise use. But facts convince readers far more effectively than vague claims.

Give a strong closing. Readers should come away from the ad with a clear invitation or directive to do something. Vote for Candidate Jones. Visit our Web site. Ask for a free sample. Visit your pharmacist today. Come in for a test drive. Whatever the product, service or cause being promoted, give the reader something to do. Like the P.S. in an appeal letter, the closing message is one of the most important and potentially most useful parts of the ad.

Exercise 14.5—Developing a Verbal Strategy

Using the information you developed in Exercises 14.3 and 14.4, develop the verbal strategy for two different approaches to the advertisement you plan to run in local high school newspapers about your college or university. ■

Advertising Layout. Think artwork. Think copy. Then think of them together. Most ads are a combination of both visual and verbal elements, which work together to determine the effectiveness of the advertising message. Often, the layout style will be suggested by the product itself. For example, an ad for a new computer may need to provide many technical details; thus the ad will rely heavily on copy. On the other hand, an ad for a new shampoo may be all about a strong visual that shows the happy results of using the shampoo. Three common styles of advertising layouts that vary in their balance between visual and verbal messages are standard, poster-style, and editorial-style layouts.

Standard advertising layouts feature both visual and textual messages: a prominent photo or other piece of artwork, along with a substantial written message. These are the advertising messages we see most often in magazines.

Some ads are *poster-style advertising*, heavy on art with very little textual information. You see poster-style layouts in most billboards and often in magazine ads.

Some ads include mainly a headline and a lot of body copy. You find this kind of *editorial-style advertising* layout in advocacy advertising in newspapers and magazines, by which an organization wants to present a detailed point of view. This style also shows up occasionally in publications in which the advertising mimics the look of an article.

Exercise 14.6—Developing an Advertisement

 Using the visual and verbal messages you have put together thus far, draft two different approaches to a display advertisement 8 inches wide by 10 inches high. Both of these designs should include sketched visual elements along with headlines and copy. Working with other students in your class, compare the two approaches, select the one you consider the best and justify your choice.   ■

Advertising Media

Consider the different categories of media for your public relations advertising: print, poster, broadcast and digital. Each category offers its own set of strengths and limitations.

Print Media. Print media advertising combines visual and textual messages, but there are some important differences. Newspaper advertising, for example, generally is implemented in black and white, while magazines regularly feature color advertising. Newspaper ads are sized in various dimensions, whereas magazines most often have full-page ads. Newspapers also place several ads on the same page, so artwork, headlines and text need to work together to attract reader attention away from competing advertisements.

Increasingly, magazines are featuring special advertising features. This is a typical pattern for such advertising features—an ad presented in editorial layout that is strong on the textual message, and a complementary one presented in poster-style layout with emphasis on art and a simple headline.

Poster Media. Poster media such as transit, outdoor and placard advertising highlight the visual messages because viewing time usually is brief. *Transit advertising* is located on buses and subways, either inside or on the outside of the vehicles. *Outdoor advertising* is carried on billboards that may offer the reader only a couple of seconds to grasp the message. *Placard advertising* may complement the outdoor and transit media, sometimes appearing in bus terminals and airports, sometimes in store windows or hanging in hallways and lunchrooms. All forms of poster media emphasize the visual message: a strong illustration, a meaningful headline.

The strategy underlying most poster communication is *reminder advertising*. It reinforces already-known images and ideas. It works best with a well-known and identifiable logo, symbol, or product that provides instant recognition. It often reinforces messages developed more fully in broadcast media. Writers for poster media need to remember that their audiences will have very little time to see and understand the messages. For example, billboards along a highway provide the viewer with less than six seconds of viewing time. Messages on transmit media may literally be moving in the opposite direction.

Broadcast Media. Broadcast and cable television advertising features images that are active and dynamic. Newspapers, magazines and billboards are static media, with images that don't move and visuals that don't make a sound. But broadcast and cable offer possibilities for movement and sound that allow the writer to be creatively effective in presenting the organization's message. Following are some guidelines for writing advertising copy for broadcast media.

- Write conversationally. Make dialogue natural. Use contractions and colloquial language.
- Use short sentences, with active voice and simple words.
- Be careful with pronunciation. Avoid unintended alliteration and unanticipated rhymes.
- Make a place in your script for music and sound effects.

Digital Media. The Internet and other new media increasingly can enhance both the visual and the verbal message. They offer opportunities for animation, movement, color and similar techniques that impact the visual tone of the advertisement. Likewise, the verbal message can be accented by various types of primary and secondary sound, often in an interactive environment. For example, the advertisement can allow each viewer to select the language of the written or spoken message: English, Japanese, Arabic, Spanish, and so on. Advertisers also can control the look of an ad in digital media. *Fixed layouts* maintain the specific size and layout created by the designer that will carry across all different sizes of monitors by various users. *Liquid layouts* allow text and graphic components to be positioned relative to the size of the viewer's browser and monitor.

Writing Public Relations Ads

Writing a public relations advertisement is generally a wide-open field, with few stylistic restrictions. This type of writing observes some of the guidelines associated with broadcast writing, especially the need for natural-sounding dialog and simple words. It is rooted in conversational English, which allows the use of contractions, sentence fragments and colloquialisms and other regional or nonstandard speech. It generally relies on active voice and strong verbs. Repetition, restatement and reinforcement are common techniques. Following are a few of the particular approaches that can be used for public relations ads being prepared for radio and television.

Testimonials. Straightforward, sales-type appeals called *testimonials* provide a platform for someone who has used the product or service, either an expert or an average person. This first-person endorsement can have a powerful influence over the audience; review the information on persuasive message sources in Chapter 3. Public relations writers should be careful about ethical matters related to testimonials. The PRSA Member Code of Ethics and other codes require honesty in word and spirit. The Federal Communications Commission has standards that can affect testimonials and other types of advertising (for example, restrictions on an actor dressing like a doctor).

Celebrity Endorsements. Similar to the testimonial is the *celebrity endorsement*, testimony that comes from a well-known person. Organizations selecting celebrity spokespeople should follow two guidelines: First, choose people who are admired by the public rather than those who simply are favorites of the organization and/or the ad writers. Second, select spokespeople whose professional and personal lives will reflect favorably on the organization and its cause. Many organizations, commercial as well as nonprofit, have been embarrassed by off-camera antics and offenses of celebrity spokespeople. Nonprofit organizations in particular cannot afford to waste production money or risk their reputations by putting their fate into the hands of the wrong spokesperson. Also remember that celebrities may be good at attracting attention for the organization but not particularly effective in creating interest in the issue or generating support for the cause.

Product Demonstrations. Though they are used more often in consumer advertising, *product demonstrations* have a place in the world of public relations advertising. For example, a service agency can take the here-we-are-and-here's-what-we-do approach, providing viewers an overview of its programs and briefly presenting the personal and community benefits it offers. Some demonstration-oriented advertising messages use parallel structure such as a before-and-after approach.

Drama. The technique of *drama* often is useful in public service advertising. Despite the brevity, accomplished writers can present a powerful message in 30 seconds. The secret for writing dramatic scripts for such short time frames is to confine the action: few characters, a single location, a simple plot that is easily set up and just as easily resolved. As with other advertising situations, these mini-dramas often rely on stereotyping and the use of clothing, setting and other nonverbal cues to convey important information to the audience. The dramatic format itself has a variety of categories.

- *Problem-solution ads* set up an obstacle with which the audience can easily identify and then resolve it, often by a hero figure.
- The *fantasy format* may rely on make-believe characters or real (perhaps historical) persons in unreal situations.
- *Animation* sometimes finds its way into public relations advertising, especially some of the high-tech spots aimed at audiences of children, teens and young adults.
- *Humor* is another type of advertising format that can be useful, though often public relations topics do not lend themselves to levity and comedy.

Reflective Pieces. Public services advertising sometimes makes effective use of *reflective pieces*, also known as *mood pieces*. These involve an almost meditative use of music, poetry, scenery and other nonverbal sensory elements that are designed to put the viewer or listener in a favorable frame of mind. This approach echoes the words of Martin Luther King, who observed that "Occasionally in life there are moments which cannot be explained by words. Their meaning can only be articulated by the inaudible language of the heart."

Symbols. Visual *symbols* can be very effective for public service advertising. Nonprofit organizations may have low budgets to produce broadcast spots, but high-impact visual symbols often are enough to carry the message. Think of the symbols in the advertising spot developed by the Partnership for a Drug-Free America: a frying pan, an egg, and a short message about your brain on drugs. That frying egg was a powerful symbol, a visual analogy. Or think of the simple visual metaphors used in the forest fire-prevention campaigns: some dry grass, a flame and a bear cub.

Sound. *Sound* can enhance a radio or television advertisement. Sound effects can be especially useful. Background music easily sets an emotional tone. Studies also have shown that dialogue or narration by on-screen characters is more effective than off-screen voice-overs. If you plan to use music in your advertisement, make sure you do it legally. Use original music, or obtain permission to use recorded music. U.S. Copyright law protects public performances of music, even by nonprofit organizations and even for uses such as nonbroadcast and educational video and telephone music-on-hold. The American Society of Composers, Authors and Publishers (ascap.com) provides information and licensing permission.

Writers do not have the final say on how a scene will be executed. That usually is in the domain of the art director or the video director. However, the writer often includes visual cues in the script as a way of signaling to the director the intended impact of the visual element. For that reason, it is important for writers to understand some of the terms, such as those dealing with broadcasts scripts.

FYI *Video Terms for Broadcast Scripts and Storyboards*

Fixed Camera Shots

(ES) Establishing Shot: Opening shot of a program, spot or scene; often an LS; also called a cover shot

(ECU) Extreme Close Up, (TCU) Tight Close Up: Tight shot of character's face or other scene details

(CU) Close Up: Shot of character to the armpits; used for showing dialogue or registering emotion

(CS) Close Shot: Longer than a CU, this is a shot of the character to the mid-chest level; used most often for "talking heads"; also called a bust shot or a head-and-shoulders shot

(MS) Medium Shot: Shot of character to mid-thigh; provides for some background detail and limited movement of character within the shot

(FS) Full Shot: Shot of character head-to-feet

(LS) Long Shot, (WS) Wide Shot: Any shot longer than FS

Camera Movement

Panning: Horizontal scanning of a scene, or following a moving subject with a stationary camera

Tilt: Vertical scanning of a scene

Travelling: Horizontal or vertical movement of the camera relative to a subject

Zoom: Movement of a scene between the range of ECU and WS; accomplished optically without change in camera position

Transition Between Shots

Cut, Hard Edit: Most common edit between shots, with one shot beginning at frame following the end of a previous shot

Dissolve: Replacement of one scene with another by superimposing a fade-in of the latter over a fade-out of the former; indicates passage or time or change of scene

Fade-In: Transition into a scene from a blank screen (black or color)

Fade-Out: Transition out of a scene into a blank screen (black or color)

Wipe: Change of scenes vertically, horizontally, diagonally or (with advancing technology) using any number of geometrical and other special shapes and effects

Cutaway: Cut, dissolve or wipe to a transitional shot, then on to the next scene (such as a dissolve from a scene to a clock, showing passage of time, then on to the next scene)

Audio Effects

Environmental Sound: Natural sound appropriate to the scene, such as birds and animals in a wilderness scene or traffic sounds in a street scene

(SFX) Sound Effect: Enhanced special sounds beyond environmental ones, such as a telephone tone, the sizzle of frying food, or footsteps

(SOF) Sound-on-Film, (SOT) Sound-on-Tape: Natural sound that is linked with the action seen in the film/tape, such as dialogue between characters

(VO) Voice Over: Narration read over a shot

Production Procedures

(CG) Character Generator: Computer that produces lines, letters, and other graphics for onscreen use; graphics may be moved in and out of position as cuts, fades, dissolves, crawls across the screen, and roll-ups or roll-downs into the screen

Chroma-Key: Process of inserting background from video footage, slide or still photo behind a character who is shot against a solid-colored in-studio wall

Exercise 14.7—Writing a Public Relations Ad

Alone or with a partner, prepare a series of public relations advertisements for your college or university health center (Public: students. Objectives: to promote awareness, interest and action regarding self-examination for breast cancer or testicular cancer), or select an organization of your choice for this exercise and note the publics and objectives.

Prepare a planning sheet and the script for a 30-second television message in each of the following versions:

- Version 1: A testimonial format (celebrity or noncelebrity) with a single voice. Script the narrative and include suggestions for sound effects and/or specific music.

- Version 2: A demonstration or drama format with multiple voices and a narrator. Script the dialogue and narrative, and include suggestions for sound effects and/or specific music.

- Version 3: A reflective format or symbol format. Script the narrative, describe the visuals, and include specific suggestions for sound effects and/or specific music. ∎

Public Service Advertising

Until 1989, television stations were required by federal law to provide public service programming under the mandate to operate in the public interest. That changed with the Reagan administration's deregulation, when the Federal Communications Commission eased its requirements for stations to provide public-interest programming. Most stations now provide significantly less free broadcast time to nonprofit organizations than they once did. However, television stations still are required to operate in the public interest, and stations can cite their broadcast of public service ads to demonstrate service to the local community when they seek license renewal from the FCC. PSAs serve another practical benefit to television stations. They generally are timeless spots that can be dropped in on short notice, such as when a scheduled advertiser withdraws a commercial at the last minute. If no other paying advertisers are available, stations often turn to public service ads as last-minute fill-ins.

Because print media are not regulated by the government, they never developed a strong tradition of publishing public service advertising. However, the Advertising Council and other groups regularly provide newspapers and magazines with various sizes of public service ads. Some of these are published, especially in magazines and smaller nondaily newspapers.

Exercise 14.8—Freewriting on PSAs

Freewrite for five minutes on the following topic: *What do you think about the themes and the writing in public service advertisements with which you are familiar?* Then discuss this with your classmates. ∎

Public-Interest Topics

The point to remember about public service advertisements is that they are gifts, and you can't demand a gift. PSAs are given free air time by television and radio stations and free space in publications that judge the topics to be interesting and fair comments on timely topics in the public interest. This is a call that can be made only by the media. The public relations practitioner may think the topic deals with public interest and can make a case for it. But the decision on whether to provide air time or space for a particular advertising message will be made by the station.

Television programmers who make the decisions about PSAs offer three criteria for a spot to be accepted: local angle, appropriate topic and creative presentation.

Local Angle. Many national organizations provide regional versions of their ads instead of generic national spots. Such spots have a greater chance of being accepted by local broadcasters, who naturally resent being asked for free air time that doesn't appear to serve the interest and needs of their particular audiences. Localizing an advertising spot can be as simple as ending the spot with a three-second local tag, either provided by the national organization or added by the local station. Or it may be as sophisticated as a specially edited version of the spot with local information, images and/or speakers woven into the central message.

Many stations prefer to co-sponsor a public service message with a nonprofit organization rather than simply give the organization free air time. They may add a tag such as "This is a reminder from Channel 7 and the local Girl Scout Council." The result is a closer identification of the station with the public service message, and an ally for the organization that may have spin-off benefits such as promotions, public affairs programming or news coverage.

Appropriate Topic. Each station and publication develops its own guidelines for what topics are appropriate materials for public service advertising, and proposed PSAs must heed these guidelines. Acceptable topics are those dealing with nonpolitical, noncommercial, nonsectarian and socially acceptable themes. Most television and radio stations, for example, would allow for general get-out-the-vote spots, but they would not provide free air time for partisan political advertising. Similarly, a nonpartisan group such as the League of Women Voters may receive free air time, but the local Democratic Party probably would be not, even with the same get-out-the-vote message, because of its vested interest in the outcome of the voting.

Some stations allow nonprofit organizations to ask for support in PSAs but not for financial contributions. However, the station or publication may allow the nonprofit group to purchase commercial time at a discounted rate for its fundraising activities. Stations often provide free air time for the charitable, educational and community service activities of religious organizations, but not for denominational religious messages. Additionally, national projects like the Advertising Council's Religion in American Life campaign and local inter-religious groups have been successful in obtaining PSA status for nondenominational messages on religious, moral or spiritual themes.

Some of the most interesting topics of the day are the controversial ones. Issues that stir the hearts and minds of people are those that are contentious, multifaceted and disputed. Police brutality, euthanasia, international warfare, medical use of marijuana, human rights, pro-life/pro-choice, tax reform—these are the stuff of great and wonderful controversies. As such, they often are off-limits for PSAs.

Why? Think about it. Why would a broadcaster give time to an organization presenting a message that would cause many of its audience members to complain? It is difficult enough for a station to defend its own news coverage and network presentations, without also having to defend free air time for groups with which many viewers or listeners might disagree. So it makes sense that a broadcaster would refuse PSAs on controversial topics. This also causes frustration for public relations practitioners working with organizations that deal with controversial issues, because in some ways it makes their successful advocacy of a point of view dependent on the charity of a broadcaster. That's one of the problems with charity: We can't demand it; we can only request it, and then be thankful when it is given.

Creative Presentation. Interesting and lively writing is essential for public service advertising. There are so many good causes, so many important messages, that a radio or television station cannot hope to provide a voice for each one. Often, a determinant is writing quality. Most television stations, for example, would refuse to accept spots that feature slides or still photographs with off-screen narration. Such an approach is a terrible waste of the impact of television.

Consider this scenario. Organization A and Organization B both have something important to say to the public. Organization A provides a bland, uninteresting script that merely repeats a time-worn message. Organization B deals with the same topic, but does so with a vigor and finesse that creates an interesting new approach. Most likely, Organization B will get the PSA time before Organization A does.

Often the best writing for public service advertising has a conversational tone. Consider the three radio spots in Exhibits 14.1 written by the National Institute on Alcohol Abuse and Alcoholism. One is a simple dialogue, one is an announcer monologue, and the third is a hybrid format. Each is effective in its simplicity.

Eligibility Requirements

A quick call to the media will give you information on what topics are considered for public service time and the details associated with requests for public service advertising. Contact the program director or public service manager at a television or radio station, or the advertising director of a magazine or newspaper. Acceptable topics generally include health and safety issues: seat belts, safe driving, child abuse, disease detection, alcohol and other drug abuse, handicap awareness and medical research. Other topics that often find their way into PSA spots include education, the environment and family life, as long as the presentation isn't partisan or controversial.

Only nonprofit organizations can qualify for PSA time. Sometimes, however, corporations work in partnership with nonprofits, producing their public service spots that are distributed nationally and locally. This is part of the community relations program of some corporations. For example, Ashland Oil developed a multimillion-dollar corporate advertising campaign to support education following a critical report by the National Commission on Excellence in Education. The Kentucky-based global oil company focused ads on how teachers affect individual students and society in general. It sponsored student visits to colleges and universities, and it developed an audiovisual program to encourage students to think about their future. Ashland also sponsored a stay-in-school project by the Advertising Council. Admitting that part of its motivation was to improve its image and support its sales, the company said it sponsored the ads also because "it is the right thing to do, and we are in a position to do it."

Exhibit 14.1—RADIO SCRIPT   Here are 3 scripts written as 30-second radio spots by the National Institute on Alcohol Abuse and Alcoholism, as part of the agency's campaign against teen drinking.

Parent PSA—"It Never Hurts"

SFX: Telephone Ring

Parent 1: Hello?

Parent 2: (Cheery w/ Phone Effect) Hello, Jane? It's Julie. I just wanted to ask about the party your son Tom is having tomorrow? Our daughter, Megan, is coming and I just want to be sure there won't be any alcohol there. I hope you don't mind.

[Beat]

Parent 1: (A bit shocked) My husband and I had planned to be out of town this weekend, Julie—we didn't know anything about a party.

Parent 2: (Suddenly understands) Oh <u>no</u>!

ANNCR: If you're a parent, it never hurts to ask. For more information on talking with your kids about alcohol, visit niaaa.hih.gov.

Brought to you by the Department of Health and Human Services, the National Institutes of Health, and the National Institute on Alcohol Abuse and Alcoholism.

Teen PSA—"So Cool"

Boy 1: So you're at a party, just hanging out, having a great time. When someone goes. . .

Boy 2: "Hey, I know where we can get some beer."

Boy 1: . . .like you're not already having fun. So you say. . . "No Thanks" . . . to let them know you're not interested—and they go. . .

Boy 2: "What's with you? You scared?"

Boy 1: So, you look at all the others, who also aren't drinking, and you go. . . "Yeah—scared of being like you!"

[Natural Laughter]

ANNCR: Thecoolspot.gov. Check it out!

Brought to you by the Department of Health and Human Services, the National Institutes of Health, and the National Institute on Alcohol Abuse and Alcoholism.

Parent PSA—"Who's Talking"

ANNCR: Here's something to think about. . .

    Do you know who's talking to your kids about alcohol?

    Is it the kids with fake IDs?

    Or friends drinking at parties?

    Or maybe someone offering to buy them beer from the local convenience store. . .

    Who <u>is</u> talking to your kids about alcohol?

    Shouldn't it be you?

For more information on how to talk with your kids about underage drinking, visit niaaa.nih.gov.

Brought to you by the Department of Health and Human Services, the National Institutes of Health, and the National Institute on Alcohol Abuse and Alcoholism.

Broadcast stations have varying requirements for how organizations may submit materials for public service use. Radio stations, for example, often will accept scripts that can be read by reporters and on-air personalities. Some radio stations accept brief postcard announcements for upcoming events. Others encourage organizations to record brief announcements over the telephone. Most radio stations can use audiotaped announcements prepared by the organization or by professional production companies.

For television, the requirements are usually higher. Most stations use only professionally prepared videotaped spots. Some stations will provide in-studio production services to organizations that have scripted simple public service advertisements. Sometimes the station will provide the organization with extra copies of the finished PSA tape for other television stations in the area. Additionally, most video production companies can make PSA tapes, either from an organization's script or from a script they prepare for the organization. Both of these services can be expensive. Alternatively, some nonprofit organizations assist each other with scripting and production services, and others find inexpensive help from colleges or universities, public access cable television studios and in-house corporate video facilities.

The actual presentation of a script for a television PSA also can take several forms. Exhibit 14.2 presents a United Negro College Fund ad in a traditional script format. The same PSA is presented in storyboard format in Exhibit 14.3.

The Advertising Council

Loose lips sink . . .
A mind is a terrible thing . . .
Friends don't let friends . . .
Take a bite out of . . .
Only you can prevent . . .

You can probably fill in the blanks for each advertising message. That's a mark of the effectiveness of the Advertising Council, which developed each of these and thousands of other public service messages.

The *Advertising Council* (adcouncil.org) is a joint venture among the sponsor organizations, volunteer advertising agencies, media companies, and industry organizations such as the American Association of Advertising Agencies, the American Advertising Federation, the Advertising Research Foundation and a variety of media organizations representing newspaper, magazine, radio, television, outdoor, direct marketing, and other types of media. It also works with the United Way. Through such partnerships, the council brings together advertising professionals who create and deliver public service messages for various worthy causes. For example, the Ad Council has introduced us to Smokey Bear, the Crash Test Dummies, and McGruff, the crime-fighting dog. To meet the council's selection criteria, a campaign must be noncommercial, nondenominational and nonpolitical, and it must be significant to all Americans.

The council provides public service advertising to newspapers, consumer magazines and the business and medical press as well as to radio, broadcast and cable television, both transit and outdoor advertising companies, and Internet and other new media. The council estimates that its annual campaigns for 2005 were worth more than $1.7 billion of donated media.

Exhibit 14.2—TELEVISION SCRIPT   Concepts for public service advertising can be presented in storyboard format, such as in this outline format, which describes the same ad as seen on the storyboard.

"Portraits"

60-second public service advertisement for United Negro College Fund campaign
Video: Main characters are two African-American girls, depicted at various ages from 6 to 19
Audio 1: Announcer voice-over
Audio 2: Original Music: "Save a place for me. Save a space for me."

		Video	*Audio 1*	*Audio 2*
:05	:05	(MS) Two African-American girls on a sliding board (age 6)	xx	Save a place for me. Save a space for me
:05	:10	(MS) Same girls on swings	xx	in your heart. In your heart.
:05	:15	(ECU) Same girls	xx	Save a place for me.
:05	:20	(ECU) Same girls (age 10)	xx	Save a space for me
:05	:25	(MS) Same girls in school cafeteria	xx	in your heart.
:05	:30	(LS) Same girls sitting and studying on apartment balcony (age 16)	xx	In your heart.
:05	:35	(MS) Same girls still on balcony, studying together	xx	xx
:05	:40	(CU) One girl sitting in college class, looking pensive (age 19)	Every year, the United Negro College Fund	xx
:05	:45	(MS) Same girl in large college class, with other black students	helps thousands of students go to college.	Save a place for me.
:05	:50	(MS) Same girl sitting in college class, looking pensive (empty seat in row behind her)	But for everyone we help	xx
:05	:55	(CU) Empty college desk	there's one we can't.	xx
:05	:60	"The United Negro College Fund. A mind is a terrible thing to waste. 1 800 322-UNCF (with logos of Ad Council and UNCF)	Please support the United Negro College Fund. A mind is a terrible thing to waste.	xx

Exhibit 14.3—UNCF STORYBOARD   Young & Rubicam advertising developed three different versions (60, 30 and 15 seconds) of this spot for the United Negro College Fund, one of the offerings of the Advertising Council.

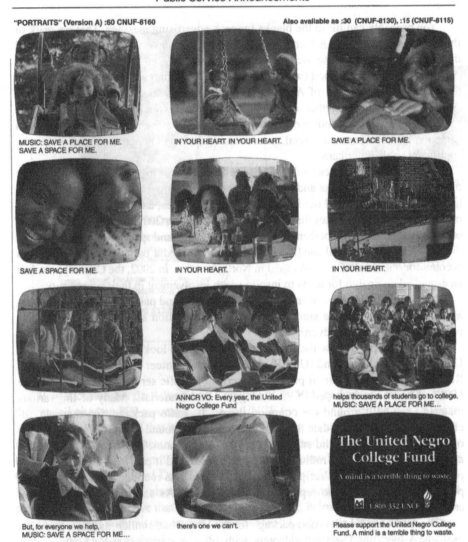

Eighty percent of the advertising time and space is contributed not by the networks but by local media, 22,000 different media outlets. Those campaigns account for one-third of all PSAs used in North America.

In addition to the Advertising Council, advertising and public relations professionals in many cities provide similar creative and production services to organizations preparing public service advertising.

How successful is the Advertising Council? It has raised $1.4 billion for the United Negro College Fund in the past 34 years. The council also reported that its teen-runaway campaign resulted in more than one million telephone calls from teens wishing to return home, and its campaign to recruit new teachers generated half-a-million calls in six years.

Meanwhile, its campaign for the Council on Alcoholism and Drug Dependence generates 3,000 phone calls each week. Smokey Bear is recognized by 95 percent of adults and 77 percent of children. And a survey showed that 93 percent of children believe that McGruff, the crime dog, helps make their communities safe. In line with the message of "Friends Don't Let Friends Drive Drunk," 70 percent of Americans said they have tried to stop someone from driving drunk. And since Vince and Larry, the Crash Test Dummies, were introduced in 1985, seat-belt use has increased from 21 to 70 percent.

"FYI: Public Service Campaigns of the Advertising Council" lists several more of the Council's recent projects.

FYI   *Public Service Campaigns of the Advertising Council*

You've probably seen dozens of messages sponsored by the Advertising Council. Here is a listing of the 2005 campaigns provided to television and radio stations, newspapers and magazines, and billboard companies throughout the United States.

Community
Adoption
Community Drug Prevention
Energy Efficiency
Environmental Conservation
Environmental Giving
Father Involvement
Global Warming
Housing Discrimination
Mentoring
Predatory Lending
Troop Support
Youth Civic Engagement/Youth Voter Participation
Youth Volunteerism

Education
Afterschool Programs
American History Resource
Arts Education
College Access
Credit Scores Education
Early Childhood Development
Family Literacy
Financial Education—Hispanic
Financial Literacy
High School Dropout Prevention
Lewis & Clark Bicentennial
Math/Science for Girls
Parental Involvement in Schools
Supporting Minority Education
Teacher Recruitment—NYC

Health & Safety
Autism Awareness
Blood Donation
Booster Seat Education
Breastfeeding Awareness

Bullying Prevention	National Mental Health Anti-Stigma
Childhood Asthma	Nutrition Education
Childhood Cancer Resource	Online Sexual Exploitation
Childhood Obesity Prevention	Patient Empowerment
Crime Prevention	Reducing Gun Violence
Disease Prevention	Secondhand Smoke & Kids
Domestic Violence Prevention	Skin Cancer Prevention
Drunk Driving Prevention	Stroke Awareness
Emergency Preparedness	Underage Drinking Prevention
Emergency Preparedness—Business	Wildfire Prevention
Flu Vaccination	Youth Reckless Driving Prevention/SUN Safety
Hispanic Underage Drinking Prevention	The Advertising Council Inc.
HIV Detection	261 Madison Avenue
Hurricane Mental Health Awareness	New York NY 10016–2303
Infant & Child Nutrition	(212) 922–1500
Modeling Non-violent Behavior	adcouncil.org

Tips for Better Writing *Limbering Up Mentally*

Answers:

1. Half of 13 could be 6.5 or 6½. Or it could be 1 or 3. Or perhaps "thir" and "teen." Or xi and ii.

2. They are the single-digit numbers arranged alphabetically.

3. Home plate on a baseball diamond, and the men in masks are the catcher and the umpire.

4. On the day Daylight Savings Time begins, the clock is set ahead by one hour, resulting in a 23-hour day.

5. The man's friend was a woman. He imitated the Japanese as she spoke it, which is different from that spoken by men.

6. He has always felt that exercising at least an hour early each morning made him feel more calm, both physically and emotionally.

7. Mary is the teacher.

8. Indivisibility.

9. He was washing windows on the inside.

10. Holes.

15

Speeches and Interviews

Grandpa said it well: "Better you should keep your mouth closed if you can't say it right." Talking isn't the same as speaking, certainly not speaking professionally. That takes skill and practice. It takes even more skill to plan and write or ghostwrite a decent speech or article, or to coach your boss or client in how to effectively handle an interview.

Classical rhetoric, the study of speechmaking, goes back about 3,000 years to the Mediterranean world of Egypt, Greece and Rome. The formal study of rhetoric continued through the ages, particularly in medieval Europe, as well as in the classical eras in China and Japan. More recently, it is studied in universities throughout the world. Most academic work related to public speaking has centered around content, while much of the applied or professional focus has been on delivery. What hasn't been studied as much is the writing of speeches and the role of the speechwriter as a person separate from a speech giver. That is the focus of this chapter.

Here is one central thought for this chapter: Oral communication (such as making speeches or giving interviews) is more about making an impression than imparting information. Good speakers exhort. They entreat and admonish. Good interviewees use their time in front of the microphones to give audiences a feeling about an organization, such as the passion with which it pursues its deal, the depth of its commitment to customer service, and so on. Such impressions don't deal as much with what information is presented as they do with how the speaker relates to his or her audience.

This chapter will focus on planning and writing speeches, as well a evaluating them. It also will look at ways to prepare for and conduct effective interviews. Here are your objectives for Chapter 14:

- To show an understanding of the planning process of speechwriting
- To prepare and write an effective speech
- To plan audiovisual presentation aids to enhance a speech
- To demonstrate an understanding of how to prepare for an interview or news conference.

Speeches

Many are the benefits of a good speech. A *speech* is the primary example of face-to-face communication, the most effective kind of communication. Speeches before a live audience (as compared to televised speeches) provide an environment for two-way communication. Both live and televised speeches can give a human face to organizations.

There is a big difference between talking at an audience and communicating with one. Perhaps you have sat through a bad speech, a dull sermon, or a boring lecture. If so, you know that every speaker isn't necessarily a communicator. That's where the public relations writer can help. Often our behind-the-scenes roles as researcher and counselor equip us well for the task of writing speeches to be delivered by organizational leaders.

Savvy audiences realize that most speakers don't write their own speeches. Few political candidates, government officials and corporate executives have the time needed to plan, research and write a good speech. Even fewer have the writing ability to be particularly effective. So they often turn to public relations writers or to speechwriting specialists, people who are good at taking the would-be speaker's own ideas and weaving them into a personalized speech. Likewise, some executives ask public relations writers to research and write an article for a newspaper, magazine or trade publication that will carry the name not of the actual writer but of the executive who has commissioned it.

Both of these are examples of the functions of a *ghostwriter,* a writer who prepares an article, speech, op-ed commentary or some other piece of writing that will carry the name of someone else. Ghostwriting is an extension of what many public relations writers do in their news releases when they craft a quote for the company CEO or the agency director. "What Would You Do?: Ghostwriting Ethics" explores this position a bit further.

What Would You Do?   *Ghostwriting Ethics*

David Finn of Ruder Finn Public Relations believes business executives cheat their audiences if they rely on others to pen their words. In an article "Exorcise the Executive Ghostwriter," published in Fortune magazine, Finn observes that most executives simply give their name to texts prepared by ghostwriters who write what they think the executive should be saying.

Finn reports a conversation with Sir John Harvey-Jones, chairman of ICI, one of England's largest corpora-

tions, who said, "It would be incredibly rude if people came to hear what I had to say on an important subject and heard someone else's views."

What do you think is the appropriate role of a ghostwriter? Is there any difference between a speech written by a member of an executive's public relations staff and one crafted by an outside professional speech-writer? Does a speaker owe the audience an explanation of who actually wrote the speech?

Companies and nonprofit groups sometimes organize teams of presenters to spread the group's message. These *speakers' bureaus* send organizational representatives to give talks and to invite questions, and public relations officers often have a role in training the speakers, doing background research and providing them with up-to-date information, promoting their availability, scheduling their presentations, and evaluating their effectiveness.

Exercise 15.1—Freewriting on Speech

Part 2: Freewrite for five minutes on the following topic: *How does persuasion fit into the activities of a public relations writer?* Then discuss this with your classmates. ∎

Planning the Speech

For speechwriters, having a good outline or script is important. Ad-libbing is not a safe venture for the organizational executive. And the more nervous or inexperienced the speaker, the greater the need for careful preparation. Following is a step-by-step plan to help you prepare a speech for someone else to deliver. For more information, you can consult speechwriting resources online at such sites as ragan.com, speechwriting.com or executive-speaker.com.

Learn about the Speaker. Unlike a document meant to be read, the text of a speech does not go directly from the writer to the audience. In theoretical terms, the speech is doubly encoded. First, the writer provides the words that encode the meaning to be shared with the receiver. A second encoding is provided by the speaker, who gives a tone and temper to the text. The speaker brings to it a verbal interpretation, an attitude. The text of a speech may provide the words for a moving political rouser or an impassioned homily. But when it is presented by someone not familiar with the text or by a person unskilled in public speaking, the words may be flat and lifeless. That's because a speech has two presenters—the writer who provides the text and the speaker who gives a voice to that text.

Suppose you are asked to draft a speech for your company's president. As the president's speechwriter, you must know how she can handle various kinds of material. What words and phrases sound natural coming from her lips? How does she deliver a speech before an audience? Can she tell a joke? Use an inspiring quotation? Share a personal story? One way to find this out is to listen. Meet with the speaker. Tape record the conversation, so you can later review how the speaker uses language. Does she always speak in complete sentences or does she use exclamatory phrases and sentence fragments. Does she pepper conversation with anecdotes and personal stories? Does the speaker naturally use humor? Passion? Charm?

Know What Needs to Be Said. Besides knowing the speaker's style of speaking, a speechwriter also needs to know what should be said. What is the topic of the speech? Is the purpose to entertain or motivate? How will the speech further organizational objectives? Public relations writers may know what needs to be said because they have been part of the strategic planning that leads to the speech. Or they can ask others within the organization to provide information "for the boss' speech."

Perhaps the best way to know what the speaker wants to say is to ask the speaker. While recording the introductory conversation, ask the speaker to talk about the topic. Even if you already know something about this topic, you need to get the speaker's thoughts on it, as well as phrasing natural to the speaker. Ask the speaker to summarize the issue and identify some key points to be made. Ask about personal experiences on the issue. Ask if there are any points on which the speaker might disagree with mainstream thought on the issue. "Tips for Better Writing: How *Not* to Write a Speech" offers an argument for getting to know your speaker and topic firsthand.

Know the Audience. Go back to one of the basic principles of public relations communication: As a speechwriter, you must be firmly rooted in an understanding of who will be hearing the speech, therefore, you must identify your public. Knowing your audience also means knowing the context in which your audience finds itself. Give thought to the background and circumstances of the proposed speech. Is it part of a wider event? Does the occasion have a theme? Is it an opening keynote, a closing reflection, or something in between? How long is the audience expecting the speech to last?

Tips for Better Writing   *How* Not *to Write a Speech*

Consider this experience of the author, an experience shared by many other public relations people who have worked in military or other governmental agencies.

As a Navy journalist, I was assigned to write a speech for an admiral to deliver to a group of visiting dignitaries. The information came third-hand. I got directives from the public affairs officer, who had heard from the executive officer, who presumably had met with the admiral. The directions were a classic example of communication degradation, the loss of information as a message is transferred from one person to another.

Logic suggested that I walk down the hall and interview the admiral. But military protocol did not facilitate such a face-to-face discussion between the admiral/speaker and the non-officer/speechwriter, so the message was watered down by the time it got to me. In the end, I was frustrated because I knew the speech was not a good one. The admiral was displeased because he had to rewrite it. And the officers in the middle were embarrassed and annoyed.

There's a lesson to be learned: Establish a relationship between the speechwriter and the speech giver.

Sketch Out a Plan. Before you begin writing the speech, prepare a planning sheet. Build on what you know about the public and its wants, interests and needs. Identify the benefits you can offer. Be clear about the objectives you have for your intended audience. Give thought to the best tone for delivering the message. Finally, consider how you will judge the success of this presentation after it has been given.

Give particular attention to how you can make an impact on the audience. Let's say, for example, that you are drafting a speech for a new county executive who ran his campaign on a platform of city-suburban cooperation. It is his first speech before a group of business leaders whom you know to be skeptical about the notion of "big government." Rather than jump right into a controversial idea of consolidation of services, you might decide first to address issues they are likely to support such as low taxes, sharing resources and cost-effectiveness. Next, appealing to their experience as managers, you might note that leadership sometimes means having to make the tough and unpopular decisions. Finally, you could back into the conclusion that consolidation of services, though perhaps unpopular, is nevertheless the right approach because it will serve the long-term interests of the people and businesses of both the city and the suburban areas.

Research the Topic. Launch a more formal gathering of information related to the topic of the speech. Make sure you include recent information available from periodicals, as well as organization-based information that can be obtained from the speaker. Using the example noted above, you might find out how other metropolitan areas have handled consolidation of services. Check with government-reform organizations. Investigate information on Web sites of comparably sized metropolitan areas. Check out positions of organizations such as police and firefighting agencies, and compare the duplication of parallel services in the various municipalities in your region. Interview some people involved in the issue.

Writing the Speech

With your planning and research completed, you now are ready to write the speech. The best way to begin is to provide yourself with a conventional outline that includes the major elements: introduction, proposition, subordinate points and supporting information, and conclusion. Once you've got the outline, the writing itself should come fairly quickly. "Advice from a Pro: Fred Willman on Speechwriting" offers additional suggestions.

Advice from a Pro *Fred Willman on Speechwriting*

Engage your audience, says Fred Willman, a freelance speechwriter who has written for presidential candidates and corporate executives.

Don't just talk at your audience, he suggests. Involve it with questions at the beginning of the speech. That way, says Willman, you will build into the speech a give-and-take relationship between speaker and listeners.

Willman also advises speechwriters and speakers to read the newspapers and magazines to keep abreast of current events. Also read books on current ideas, history, science and literature. Then incorporate appropriate references into the speech.

Introduction. The *introduction* of the speech is like the lead of a feature release. It introduces the topic and sets the tone for what will follow. It establishes a rapport between the speaker and the audience, letting the audience glimpse how the speaker feels about the topic. The introduction also establishes the speaker's credibility as this relates to the subject. In Exhibit 15.1, for example, the speaker is addressing a hearing of the Federal Communications Commission. Note that the first thing he does is introduce himself, then state his credentials.

Exhibit 15.1—FEDERAL COMMUNICATIONS COMMISSION TESTIMONY OPEN HEARING ON MEDIA OWNERSHIP

Chairman Martin, Commissioners Adelstein, Copps, McDowell, and Tat. Thank you for the opportunity to speak at this public hearing on media consolidation and its effect on recording artists, songwriters, and the radio listening public.

My name is Mike Mills. I am the bassist for the band R.E.M., and a member of the Recording Artists' Coalition. I'm also a proud AFTRA member. I have been a recording artist and songwriter for over 25 years. R.E.M. started out as a local band in the college town of Athens, Georgia. Since R.E.M. released our first EP, "Chronic Town," in 1982, we have recorded 13 original studio albums. I have worked with members of the Commission before on this very issue through my work with the Future of Music Coalition.

Ten years ago, Congress passed the 1996 Telecommunications Act, opening the floodgates of almost unlimited media consolidation in the radio industry. On this important 10-year anniversary, we should all ask the question, "Is American radio better today than it was ten years ago?" The answer, in my estimation, is an emphatic "No."

Media consolidation has, without question, harmed localism in radio. It has harmed new and emerging recording artists, as well as local music communities. But most of all, it has harmed the American listening public. The bond between a local station and its local listening audience has largely evaporated. Radio conglomerates have taken the "local" out of local radio to such a degree that, by and large, radio in Atlanta sounds like radio in Denver, Los Angeles, Nashville, or Washington, D.C. Playlists have been corporatized, nationalized, and sanitized. Airplay for local and new artists is a virtual impossibility.

Pre-1996, local radio stations had always enjoyed a special relationship with the local community and especially the local music establishment. Each city or geographic area has its own unique cultural and musical heritage. Many of these local genres are uniquely American—Texas swing, Appalachian bluegrass, zydeco, Tejano, blues and jazz. Local radio outlets that supported these genres contributed to the vitality of music and radio not just on a local level, but on a national level as well. Due to radio consolidation, these distinctly American musical formats have suffered immeasurably. Where are the local radio outlets for these styles of music in an era of nationalized playlists?

Radio consolidation has visited similar hardships on new artists as well. Back when R.E.M. started, many young artists found that one "breakout" song on a local radio station could get them started on the road to national success. Strong support from local DJs and program directors dramatically enhanced the development of up and coming artists and entire local music communities. The harm to localism from development of uniform national playlists most certainly impacts the chances for established artists to prosper, new artists to emerge, and local music communities to remain economically viable.

R.E.M. owes much of its early success to local stations throughout the country. We grew organically through word of mouth, local buzz, and incessant touring. With each record and accompanying tour, we grew increasingly popular. We didn't achieve our first Gold record until our fourth studio album.

It was very difficult as it was for bands to get commercial radio airplay, and a journey like ours would be virtually impossible in today's era of consolidated radio conglomerates and concentrated mega-labels. If a band doesn't have a hit on their first record, they often find themselves dropped.

The FCC has a mandate to consider the goals of localism, diversity, and free competition when contemplating changes in radio ownership rules. However, changes in radio ownership rules since 1996—most notably the increase in station ownership caps—have only had a negative effect on localism, diversity, and competition. As you undertake your review of whether to revise the media ownership rules, the FCC should heed the Hippocratic Oath—first do no harm.

In other words, the Commission should not make the problem of radio consolidation worse by increasing the number of stations that a single company can own in a given market. Ideally, the FCC should lower the station ownership caps back to pre-1996 levels. Absent that, however, the FCC could take intermediate steps to restore some level of competition, diversity of viewpoints, and localism that has been lost as a result of unprecedented radio consolidation over the last 10 years.

Specifically, the Commission could mandate that as part of its public interest obligations, a radio licensee must play a minimum number of hours per week of music by local artists—and not just in the middle of the night. This is done in the television context, wherein broadcasters are required to provide a designated amount of children's programming each week. Radio licensees should have an analogous requirement for local artists.

By all economic accounts, the music industry is in trouble. While piracy is clearly the major reason for the downturn in the music business over the last several years, many believe media consolidation is also a significant factor. As it moves forward with its review of broadcast rules, the FCC should take into consideration the impact of media consolidation on music performers and music listeners.

For instance, the FCC should better understand and take into consideration how media consolidation affects the problem of payola. While payola is an insidious practice, media consolidation has arguably made it worse. Retaliation against recording artists can now take place on a national scale, if, for example, an artist does not concede to unreasonable demands of a radio network or station to play a radio-sponsored concert.

And as the FCC's recently discovered studies of some years ago show, localism in broadcasting has suffered as a result of media consolidation. A proper examination of localism, diversity, and fair competition must include consideration of these issues. This is about more than just some scruffy musicians getting their songs on the radio. This is about the control and flow of information on the public's airwaves—and information is the lifeblood of democracy.

In conclusion, we hope the FCC will not prematurely issue radio ownership rules without fully examining how media consolidation impacts recording artists, the music industry, and the listening public on a local and national scale. We at the Recording Artists' Coalition look forward to working with you on these important matters. Thank you again for the opportunity to appear at this public hearing.

Testimony of Mike Mills on behalf of Recording Artists' Coalition
October 3, 2006. University of Southern California, Los Angeles, Calif.

Proposition. The *proposition* (also called a *thesis*) is the main idea you want to leave with the audience. Speechwriters note three kinds of proposition: factual, value and policy.

- A *factual proposition* asserts the existence of something (for example, an increase in acid rain pollution in the Eastern forests, or a plan to change your college's foreign language requirements). A factual proposition often is linked with public relations objectives focused on awareness, such as increasing attention or building greater understanding.
- A *value proposition* argues the worthiness or virtue of something (the joy of writing, the merits of welfare reform). This relates to public relations objectives dealing with acceptance, such as increasing interest or building more positive attitudes.
- A *policy proposition* identifies a course of action and encourages its adoption (advocacy for requiring a license to practice public relations, or a proposal to make parent-education classes a requirement for a high school diploma, for example). This parallels public relations objectives associated with opinion and action.

Note that Mike Mills' testimony in Exhibit 15.1 involves all three types of propositions: factual propositions (provisions and consequences of the Telecommunications Act), value propositions (the undesirability of losing localness in radio music programming), and policy propositions (his recommendation for a reduction in station ownership caps to pre-1996 levels and minimum requirements for airplay of local musicians).

Arguments. Propositions must be supported with strong *arguments*, also called *subordinate points* or *supporting information*. Propositions are only as good as their arguments. Unsupported propositions come from poor planning or inadequate research. Not only are they weak, they also can be counterproductive because they are easy for audiences to dismiss and because they hurt your speaker's credibility. Consider the following arguments related to Exhibit 15.1:

- Proposition: Almost unlimited media consolidation has harmed localism in radio
- Argument: Media consolidation has broken the prior strong relationship with the local music establishment
- Argument: Media consolidation has made it difficult for new artists to obtain commercial radio airplay
- Argument: Media consolidation has harmed the American listening public by limiting choices
- Argument: The FCC has a mandate to factor localism, diversity and free competition into decisions about radio ownership.

Conclusion. An effective *conclusion* is often a summary that pulls together the major recommendations of the entire speech. In Exhibit 15.1, for example, the speaker ends his FCC testimony with a carefully phrased call for full examination of the effect of media consolidation on recording artists, the music industry, and the listening public.

Tips for Effective Speechwriting

A speech can be structured many ways. Some speechwriters use a pattern similar to that for a position statement, since the same elements should be evident in the text of any speech that seeks to persuade. In many ways, public relations practitioners use a speech to verbally present an organization's position on an issue to both the organization and its publics.

Following are some of the elements of speechwriting. "Advice from a Pro: Matt Hughes on Speechwriting" also offers additional suggestions.

Advice from a Pro *Matt Hughes on Speechwriting*

Matt Hughes is a speechwriter and novelist in British Columbia. A former newspaper editor, he was staff speechwriter to Canada's ministers of justice, environment and small business in the 1970s. Matt is proud of the fact that he is the only speechwriter to have written convention addresses for winning candidates in leadership races in the British Columbia Social Credit, Liberal and New Democratic parties (something like writing for both the Democratic and Republican National Committees).

Here is Hughes' advice on speechwriting:

Make an Impression
Nobody remembers speeches. No one sitting through a 20-minute monologue recalls what was actually said. An audience retains no more than two or three new facts from a speech. Crowd the text with data and the listeners will remember only how boring you were. Ruthlessly pare down to the essential facts.

Get Organized
The easiest and best way to organize a speech is the "three times" approach. Announce very early in the text—the first page is good—what your speech is about and why it is important to the audience. Next, give them your message, with the basic facts or examples or anecdotes. Then close by restating the theme. Your speech will have a definite beginning, middle and end, and the audience will not be confused.

Use Plain English
Plain Anglo-Saxon English is better than a string of jargon and 10-dollar words. It is also the language of emotion. "I'm mad as hell and I'm not going to take it any more" has way more impact than "I am extremely choleric and I encompass no intention of enduring any supplemental experience." Using Anglo-Saxon puts you in good company. From Lincoln's "government of the people, by the people and for the people," to Churchill's "we shall fight on the beaches," to Kennedy's "ask not what your country can do for you," the best speech is plain English.

Get Active
The rules of English grammar allow for an active or a passive voice. In the active, you might say "we have decided"; in the passive, it comes out as "a decision has been reached." Bureaucrats love the passive voice. Totally neutral, it lets them say without having to take responsibility for saying. But it puts audiences to sleep. To fill your speech text with life and emotion, use the active voice.

Don't Tell Them, Show Them
We all have screens inside our heads where we look at pictures that come to us as spoken or written words. Keep your audience's screens full of images. Make your points and deliver your information in word pictures. If you're warning of difficulties ahead, say something like "We're climbing a hill that's getting steeper, and there are rocks and potholes in the road." Word pictures need only a few broad strokes. Don't specify the kind of road or the species of trees in the wood. Your audience's brains will fill in the details without being asked.

Can We Talk?
When writing it, a speech is words on paper. When given, it's one human being speaking live to others. If you're more used to drafting reports or memos, don't let their usually impersonal tone creep into your text. Use "I" and "you" and "we" and "us," and strive for the comfortably informal tone of a network news anchor.

Say It Again, Sam
In reports, letters and memos, repetition is a poor writer's vice; but in speeches, it's a virtue. Your audience can't stop tape and press replay. They hear it live, and if they miss a key point, the rest of your speech may make no sense to them. So, if a thing is worth saying, it's worth saying again for clarity and emphasis. But don't just repeat the same words verbatim. Rephrase the point, giving two or three examples that leave your listeners in no doubt about what you're saying.

Adjust the Facts, Ma'am

What's a speech without statistics? A better speech. Figures are great in a report, but unless each member of your audience has total recall, your stats will mostly pass right through their heads. Always simplify, always round off. Replace "68.2 percent" with "over two-thirds," and "a 112 percent rise in production" with "our output more than doubled." With big numbers, look for word pictures that convey size, but avoid the hackneyed "this many football fields," or "that many times around the world." Reach for your calculator and work out that you produced enough widgets to cover Rhode Island twice. The more novel and arresting the image, the more memorable. Nobody knows how many billions of burgers McDonald's has sold, but if it were enough to make a cow five miles high, people would surely remember that cow.

Make 'Em Laugh

People also remember jokes. Find a way to make a point with humor and your message will stick. If you're expecting a tax increase, you might say, "Well, Congress has finally decided how to divide up the pie; trouble is, we're the pie." Humor relaxes an audience, helping to create the human bond that is crucial to making a memorable impression. But you don't have to open with one of those hoary chestnuts cribbed from a handbook. Try to make the joke fit the substance and the circumstances of your remarks.

The Ins and Outs

The best and simplest way to open a speech is just to tell the audience that you are glad to be there. You may open with "I am pleased to have this opportunity," or "when [whoever] invited me to be your guest speaker, I was delighted," or just "I am very glad to be here tonight." Let the audience know that this is a good experience for you; nobody likes to watch a fellow human being in pain.

After you tell them how glad you are to see them, go on to tell them why: because they are good people and worth talking to. When addressing the chamber of commerce, mention the chamber's community role and good works. If you're addressing the bar association, try to find something nice to say about lawyers. Once you have shown the strange tribe that you are friendly and respect their totems, you may tell them what you're going to tell them, and get on with the job.

The end of a speech is the part most likely to be remembered by your listeners. Put your best writing here—active voice, Anglo-Saxon, word pictures and all—and lead the audience into your vision of the future, as it develops from the message in your speech. If you have hard news to announce, save it till the end. If you have a slogan or catch-phrase you want remembered, use it in the wind-up and repeat it a few times. Got a joke that encapsulates your message? Make it the finale and leave them laughing.

She Sells Seashells

You've followed all the above advice, and now you have a neatly typed speech, ready for delivery. But there's still one job left: Read the thing out loud. Don't trust that silent reading voice in your head, because it won't be there to help you when you are speaking out loud. That little voice can easily read "the Leeth police dismisseth us" in black and white, but try to get it past your lips and teeth, and you've got trouble. Find the hidden verbal potholes in your text, and fill them in with a rewrite.

Additional information is available at Hughes' Web site: mars.ark.com/~mhughes.

Stick to the Topic. Some speeches wander from Boston to Albuquerque and back again. Bad move. Too many speeches don't seem to have a theme—and the audience is left confused and probably bored. The problem is that often you (or your speaker) will have a lot of ideas. But instead of a speech, you can end up with an inventory of thoughts or a laundry list of recommendations. Resist the urge to throw every idea at the audience. Rather, choose one idea and develop it with a series of secondary points and examples. Try to leave the audience with only one main idea. That's probably all anyone will remember anyway. Work with that central thought. State it clearly. Shape it. Repeat it. Express it with examples. Say it again in the conclusion.

Write for the Ear. A speech should not necessarily be written to look good. Rather, it should be written to *sound* good. There is big difference. Look at "Tips for Better Writing: The Well-Tempered (Speech) Sentence." In print, this passage looks choppy and awkward. But read it out loud, and notice how the words work when you hear them. A good speech is written in the tone of conversational English, which is less rigid than more formal styles of literary, commercial or academic English.

People writing for oral presentations strive for a conversational tone that is rooted in the natural rhythms appropriate to the individual speaker. Generally, this involves the use of simple words, personal pronouns, active voice and subject/predicate/object sentence structures. It also frequently involves the use of contractions and sentence fragments.

Tips for Better Writing   *The Well-Tempered (Speech) Sentence*

A paragraph may look good on a page—with a minimum of punctuation marks and short sentences—but it may not really sound good. Funny thing about speeches. They have to play on the ear . . . just so. People who write speeches—the good writers, that is—know this. They use dashes and ellipses and parentheses to provide side comments . . . just the way many people speak. The good writers aren't hung up on the formalities of grammar and syntax, because they know that many of the formalities are more for writing than speaking. The good speech-writers know that run-on sentences can be OK—as long as they sound OK to the audience, and as long as the audience can understand them . . . and audiences can easily understand lengthy passages, when (and this is the key), when the long sentences are broken up by pauses. The same with sentence fragments. The best advice, then, for the speechwriter is this: <u>Write for the ear</u>. Trust your ear to let you know when you've done a good job. Thank you, and have a pleasant afternoon.

Get a Good Start. As with any other type of public relations writing, the beginning of a speech is perhaps the most crucial. The introduction either will signal to the audience that this is a speech worth listening to, or it will signal the start of a boring discourse. Speechwriters have found that the lead can be written in a variety of formats: a compelling question, a shocking statement, an engaging anecdote, an appropriate quotation, a humorous observation or simply a summary of the speaker's proposition.

Use a Variety of Structural Elements. No single structural element is required of speeches; they lend themselves to many features. Consider the role that each of the following could play in a speech you might prepare: analogies, anecdotes and stories, enumeration, examples and explanations, hypothetical situations, illustration, repetition, rhetorical questions, statistics, suspense.

Use Quotations Sparingly. Testimony from authority and attributions to experts can be persuasive features in a speech. But use them only if they are central to your message, and only if they come from people well enough known to impress your audience in the first place. Don't allow quotations to draw your audiences away from your message.

Allude to Relevant Events. The speaker may be presenting information that has been given before, but one way to keep the text relevant is to update it with references to current events. Research shows that current happenings are much more meaningful to audiences than historical allusions. As with quotations, however, make sure the allusions do not distract your audiences from the heart of your message.

Avoid Clichés. Language that is trite diminishes a speech. So do stereotypes. It doesn't matter if such language is the writer's own or if it comes from quotations from others. Avoid clichés from any source, because they make the speech predictable, thus uninteresting and unmemorable.

Use Literary Gimmicks. Games and strategies can help an audience remember a speech. Some speechwriters have used what they call the B list: Be alert. Be prepared. Be resourceful. Others have used what they call Be-attitudes to present a similar list. The object of both approaches is related: to give the listener an easy-to-remember listing of actions, traits and so on. Other speechwriters rely on repetition of ideas and themes.

Avoid Common Errors in Logic. Effective speeches display a soundness of thinking. Ineffective speeches have easy-to-recognize flaws in their reasoning. Here are some of the common errors to avoid:

Overgeneralized arguments fail to persuade because they use limited information to make presumptions that are unsubstantiated. This is a case of leaping to an inexact conclusion.

Drawing *unwarranted conclusions* is a similar error in logical presentation of information. This can happen when the writer begins with the conclusion and then goes searching for data to back it up.

Building on *false facts* that present inaccurate or dishonest information is like erecting a house on sand: Neither will last. You can't make a credible case using incorrect or uncertain data.

Arguing in a circle is an attempt to prove a proposition by restating it. When A equals B, we know also that B equals A. That may mean something in algebra, but in language it's called a *tautology*. It is a "proof" that relies on itself, and therefore isn't much of a proof at all. Arguing in circles is like a hamster on a treadmill—it doesn't get you very far.

Personal criticism is another logical flaw. Criticize the issue being addressed rather than the person addressing it. Intelligent and fair-minded audiences are insulted when they realize they are being manipulated by irrelevant arguments, and personal insults or verbal abuse of opponents can be counterproductive.

An *appeal to tradition* is a common persuasive technique. The we've-always-done-it-this-way argument is an invitation to trouble because it often fails to hold up under close examination. Speeches can safely appeal to tradition only if the audience unconditionally accepts the substance and source of that tradition.

Similarly, *authority appeals* also can be unsupportive of a speaker's claims. Eventually, the argument must stand on its own strength, apart from the star quality of its supporters.

Test the Speech Out Loud. The first step after writing the draft of a speech is to read it out loud. Notice if you get tongue-tied or run out of breath. Observe if the natural cadence becomes awkward or out of rhythm. If necessary, rewrite the draft to eliminate any of these problems. The second step comes when the speaker tries out the speech. The writer should be present during the rehearsal, prepared either to coach the speaker toward a smoother presentation of the words or to rewrite the speech to accommodate the speaker's style.

Prepare a Clean Transcript. The speech text is meant to be read aloud, and speechwriters prepare their final draft in the same style they would prepare a broadcast release. This involves writing out words and providing a pronunciation guide. The text itself should be typed with margins of at least one inch and with double spacing. Use both capital and lowercase letters for easy reading, rather than all-capital letters. Underline any words that require particular emphasis by the speaker, or use boldface type or perhaps a larger font. Break pages only at the end of sentences. Use the same kind of pronouncers that were introduced for broadcast writing in Chapter 8.

Some speechwriters suggest marking sections of the text that can be eliminated if the speaker finds there is less time than planned to deliver the speech. This allows the speaker to present a carefully crafted message. Without this assistance, the speaker might simply present only the first half of the speech, delivering an incomplete message.

Maximize Impact. The speech has been researched and written. It's been rehearsed and presented. End of speech? Not necessarily. An insightful speechwriter can suggest ways to recycle the speech, attracting additional attention to the speaker and spreading the message more widely.

There are many ways to magnify the reach of a speech, including handing out typed copies to interested listeners, distributing reprints to important internal and external publics, posting the text on your Web site, highlighting the speech in the organization's newsletter, and offering formal transcripts to publications that serve as historical records of important speeches.

When a speech is particularly significant beyond the organization, the news media might be included in the dissemination program. For example, you might send out news releases or media advisories about the speech, such as companies like Hewlett Packard did when its CEO Mark Hurd testified about the company's ethics violations and like AT&T did when its chairman testified before a Senate subcommittee. You might provide radio and television stations with audiotapes or video clips respectively, with some of the best sound bites from the speech.

Additionally, organizations can use the Internet to further disseminate the speech. You can post the text of the speech on your Web site for on-demand access by interested readers; you might even include an audio clip that can be downloaded so the Web user can hear all or key parts of the speech.

For major speeches of public interest, you might contact a member of Congress to see about placing the speech in the Congressional Record. You can also submit the speech for possible inclusion in Vital Speeches of the Day, ERIC/Educational Resources Information Center (accesseric.org) for documents dealing with education, or other full-text document resources.

Exercise 15.2—Writing a Speech

You are a public relations writer who has been asked to prepare a speech dealing with one of the following scenarios:

*   The question-and-answer piece you drafted in Exercise 9.6
*   The position statement you drafted in Exercise 10.2.

Part 1: Define an appropriate target public and prepare a planning sheet. Since you already know your instructor's speaking style, presume that he or she is the organizational spokesperson who will give the speech.

Part 2: Write an introduction for the speech.

Part 3: Write the proposition statement.

Part 4: Outline the subordinate points and supporting information. This section may be in bullet form rather than in complete narrative paragraphs.

Part 5: Write a conclusion for the speech.   ■

What Would You Do? *Putting Words in Someone's Mouth*

You are public relations writer for a major bank with branches in most states and Canadian provinces and several major foreign cities. You are preparing a speech to be delivered in three days by your CEO, announcing that the bank commission in your headquarters state has just approved the merger of your bank and a small regional bank. This is part of an ongoing series of mergers that your company has undertaken in recent years. The approval was expected, and there is nothing unusual about the situation.

Your CEO is traveling on banking business and his whereabouts are not to be divulged at this time. You know that the CEO is involved in a series of high-level meetings, scheduled first in Quito, Ecuador and following in Osaka, Japan. The vice president who handled the merger negotiations wants you to write a

speech for the CEO to deliver at an employee meeting of the small bank that is becoming part of your banking system. The vice president suggests a congratulatory statement to the staffs of the acquired bank and a promise to customers that service will not be disrupted and in fact will improve.

You can use information from the vice president, but you are told that the quote should be in the name of your CEO. You also have some corporate reports from recent weeks in which the CEO has enthusiastically discussed the merger.

What should you do? Are there any ethical issues in ghostwriting a speech? Does it matter that you are not able to meet with the CEO prior to submitting the final draft?

Audiovisual Aids

Visual aids can greatly enhance speeches and other oral presentations. Some studies have found that audiences learn between two and 10 times as much when they have visual aids such as charts and photos to supplement what they hear than when they simply hear it.

The value of visual aids is backed up by research. A study from the University of California at Los Angeles reported that more than 90 percent of what an audience understands comes from a combination of visual messages (55 percent) and spoken messages (38 percent), compared with only 7 percent for written messages. A study by the University of Pennsylvania found that audiences remember 50 percent of what they see and hear in presentations, compared to only 10 percent of what they merely hear. A study by the University of Minnesota concluded that presenters who used overhead transparencies and computer-generated slides were 43 percent more persuasive than presenters who used no visuals. The Minnesota study also found that using visuals cuts the length of the speech by 28 percent.

At the beginning of this chapter, it was noted that most speeches can do more to make an impression than to impart information. Especially for workshops, classes, persuasive talks and other information-sharing presentations, visual aids are crucial. What are some of the other benefits of presentation aids? Besides greater understanding, audio and visual aids make speeches and presentations more memorable. They also can lessen the likelihood that an audience will become bored or distracted. Finally, they can save time by eliminating the need for lengthy explanations. A picture not only is worth a thousand words, it communicates a lot quicker.

There are myriad presentation aid options. Some of these include: printed handouts, chalkboards, dry-erase whiteboards, electronic whiteboards, overhead transparencies, computer presentations, slides, audio- and videotapes. Each of these presentation media offers opportunities for several different types of content: graphs and charts, schematic drawings, diagrams, key words and text, maps, photos, models and objects.

Having good visual aids is one thing. Using them well in a presentation is something else. Here are a few guidelines for effective use of presentation aids, whether you are personally delivering a speech or prepping your CEO to present a speech you researched, drafted and/or are staging.

- *Plan for the visual aids.* Include them in your planning right from the start so they form an integral part of the presentation rather than an afterthought.
- *Keep visual aids simple.* Don't crowd too much detail into photos, charts, graphs and other aids. Use each visual aid to make a single point.
- *Make sure everyone can see the visual aid.* Use props and materials of appropriate size. Instead of one television monitor, consider using two or several hooked up to the same video playback system.
- *Know how to use the visual aids.* Both the audience and the speaker can be embarrassed when a computerized presentation won't work. Make sure you practice with the equipment and know how to use it.
- *Have a backup plan.* If you are using any kind of equipment, be prepared for problems. Have an extra overhead presenter or laptop computer in case the one you are using fails to work. Have extra paper for a flip chart, and have handouts available in case the transparencies or computer presentation can't be used.

Exercise 15.4—Planning Presentation Aids

Select one of the following scenarios:

- You are preparing a 10-minute presentation explaining your academic department to potential students for a college or university open house
- You are preparing a 10-minute presentation to generate support for the position you outlined in Exercise 10.2
- You are preparing a 10-minute presentation on behalf of the organization for which you developed a brochure in Exercise 11.2

- You are assisting your CEO in developing a 10-minute presentation to company employees to explain the same information as you wrote for the newsletter article in Exercise 12.3
- You are making a 10-minute speech on behalf of the organization for which you wrote the fundraising appeal letter in Exercise 13.3.

Identify and roughly sketch out at least 10 different specific presentation aids that could be used during your presentation. You may use more than one of the same kind of aid, such as several overhead transparencies.   ■

Tips for Better Writing   *Visual Aids to Support Your Speech*

As we have seen, visual aids can enhance the effectiveness of speeches. Here are a few tips for using visual aids.

PowerPoint. Use no more than seven lines per slide. Use text at least 24 points or larger. Use a single font for all headlines. Use the same or compatible font for all text. Use key words and phrases, not complete sentences. Avoid moving text to keep the audience focus on the speaker, not the screen. Use bullets to outline information. Use slides with simple backgrounds. Avoid garish colors. Use contrasting colors, and avoid red-green, blue-black, and blue-purple combinations.

Whiteboard and Flip Charts. Print legibly. Use different colored markets. Consider having an associate write while the speaker presents information.

Overhead Transparencies. Number transparencies so they can be presented in sequence. Create information large enough for the audience to read. Stand off to one side when using an overhead projector. Face your audience rather than the screen. Use the progressive disclosure technique or overlays to reveal one point at a time rather than an entire transparency.

Evaluating the Speech

Speechwriting and speech giving don't often go through a formal evaluation process, but you can be creative in measuring, both objectively and subjectively, the effects and outcomes of your speeches. Keep a record of various speeches you write for use within your organization. Note the number and tone of comments the speaker receives; note particularly the compliments and criticisms, any feedback that shows a real interest—positive or negative—in the speech. Also keep a record of the number and kind of questions that the speech generates. Likewise, note the instances when the speech finds its way into media use, perhaps as a sound bite or a quote. Finally, note the number of speaking invitations that are generated, and try to find out if these resulted because someone was impressed with previous speeches given on behalf of your organization or client.

Exercise 15.4—Analyzing a Speech

Obtain the text of a speech from a source such as Vital Speeches of the Day. (Note: Contact your academic library for online resources of Vital Speeches.) You can also go to the History Channel Web site (historychannel.com) for the text of many significant historical speeches or contact the Web sites of individual businesses, nonprofit organizations or governmental agencies, many of which post their own important speeches.

Part 1: With a double underline, mark the speaker's proposition. In a margin note, indicate if this is a factual, value or policy proposition.

Part 2: With a single underline, mark each of the subordinate points.

Part 3: Draw a box around the sentence(s) or paragraph(s) that comprise the conclusion.

Part 4: Briefly analyze and evaluate the writing style of the speech.

Part 5: Write a brief analysis and evaluation of the logic used within the speech. ∎

Interviews

Giving a speech is just part of many face-to-face communication situations. Often, the speech is followed by a question-and-answer session, an encounter that can really test a communicator's stamina. Speakers' bureaus organize public presentations and invite questions. Some public relations vehicles change the emphasis—a brief oral presentation followed by an extended question-and-answer session. Town meetings use this approach. So do news conferences that feature a brief statement followed by a volley of questions from reporters.

Each of these situations has one thing in common: The speaker is giving interviews. While question-and-answer sessions take place after the speaker has presented the message, basic interviews seldom have this preparation tool. They get right to the information exchange without much build-up. Giving an interview is one of the best ways of telling your story. Through the questions of a reporter and your response to them, you can present a message and perspective of your organization to a wide and diverse audience. Organizations vary in their ease of dealing with interview situations. In general, the more open an organization is and the more it interacts with its publics, the more successful it will be with creating a favorable public opinion.

Any person who gives an interview should be accurate, fair and professional. Without betraying confidences, the interview giver should provide honest and complete information. If one is to err, let it be on the side of openness, honesty and confidence in the informed opinion of the people who make up our publics.

Interview Requests

If you are asked for an interview, consider the following questions. Your response to these questions will help your decide whether to give an interview.

- Do I understand the topic?
- Do I have the basic information, or can I get needed additional information?
- Am I authorized to be a spokesperson for my organization?
- If not, can I suggest a more appropriate or more knowledgeable spokesperson?

If you answer yes to the first three questions, you may proceed to give an interview. If you answer no, try to get more information, or try to suggest another person to give the interview.

Interview Preparation

If you decide you can give an interview, the following questions will help you prepare for your meeting with the reporter.

- What is the source of the reporter's information? If it is a written source that you haven't seen, ask the reporter for a copy as you prepare for the interview.
- What is the purpose of the interview? The reporter should be able to tell you the nature, likely length and intended use of the interview.
- Who are the publics that are most affected by the topic of this interview? Present your information with them in mind.
- Am I prepared to speak knowledgeably on this topic? Never try to play it by ear, unless you are very familiar with the issue. Even then, you may need to brush up on recent developments and concerns. In addition, put your thoughts on paper and organize them. Write a summary of two or three sentences and memorize it. Find different ways to say the same thing.
- What questions might a reporter ask? This can be one of your best preparation tools, because it may prevent you from having to field unexpected questions that can lead to embarrassing answers. You may also want to use a tape recorder to practice answering questions that a reporter is likely to ask.

Exercise 15.5—Preparing for an Interview

You are public relations director for LakeLand Chemicals, a company that uses chemicals in the manufacturing of paint.

The first thing this morning, you learned that the state Environmental Protection Agency is listing LakeLand as a "borderline violator" for discharging a toxic chemical through its smokestack. The chemical is called tri-chlorofluoromethane, CFM-3; it is in the family of chlorofluorocarbons known as CFCs, which have received considerable media attention in your area because of their negative environmental consequences. The chemical is harmless when used as a liquid, which is how it is used by LakeLand. But it can destroy ozone in the upper atmosphere when it is released as a gas, and the production process at LakeLand transforms some CFM-3 into gas, which escapes through smokestacks.

LakeLand's current emissions of CFM-3 are 91 percent clean; the government requires them to be 92 percent clean. Because of the borderline levels, the EPA will give LakeLand six months to improve emissions before any penalties might be levied.

You learned the information the first thing this morning. You know that the EPA will release the information to reporters by noon today.

You also know that LakeLand has been discussing the purchase of an expensive new high-tech smokestack filter that could significantly decrease the toxic emissions, but you are not yet at liberty to announce this.

Prepare for interviews with reporters with the following activities:

Part 1: Prepare a brief planning sheet indicating your company's key publics; an analysis of their wants, interests and needs; and your main objectives in dealing with reporters.

Part 2: Anticipate questions reporters might ask. Make notes of appropriate responses to these questions.

Part 3: Summarize the main point or points you want to communicate to your key publics. Sketch out anecdotes or examples that might convey that point. ∎

Conducting the Interview

Just shortly before the interview time arrives, take a few minutes to quiet yourself. Focus, center, pray, meditate or do whatever you do to relax and become balanced. Approach the interview as an opportunity to say something positive and be grateful to give public witness, even on controversial subjects. Also, don't feel obliged to respond in depth, especially if you are questioned unexpectedly and don't have time to prepare for the interview. Say: "I just can't talk about that right now, but as soon as the contract is negotiated [or whatever the holdup is] I will be happy to answer all of your questions." Or use the occasion to announce that you will make a statement at some specific later time: "I'll be addressing that at my meeting tomorrow with the stockholders."

The setting for the interview can vary. A news conference can be bustling, with lights, microphones and reporters moving around. It's not uncommon for a television crew to turn off its lights and put its camera away midway through a news conference because the camera operator has gathered enough footage. A one-on-one interview has a much different feel. With a print reporter especially, it probably will take place on home turf, such as your office or a conference room in your building. Be careful not to relax too much, however; you may be in familiar surroundings, but keep a keen awareness that you are being interviewed. For a television interview, you may find that the reporter or camera operator asks you to answer questions in a livelier setting, perhaps outside your building, on the floor of your manufacturing plant or in front of the construction site for your new office complex.

Tips for Better Writing *Effective Interview Techniques*

During an interview, you may find the following recommendations helpful.

- *Be confident.* You are not an uninformed nobody with irrelevant opinions. You are the expert the reporter has sought out. Take confidence in that fact.

- *Be honest.* Answer as fully and as sincerely as you can. The impression you make as a professional representative of your organization will last far longer than the particular facts you convey.

- *Be accurate.* There is nothing worse than an error of fact (except a deliberate error of fact). Don't guess. Say, "I don't know" or "I'll find out for you," but try not to appear ill-prepared or uninformed.

- *Be brief.* For radio and television, think in terms of headlines and sound bites. You'll probably have two or three sentences to tell your story, and perhaps time for a couple of quick answers to questions. For print media, you can expand on that capsule.

- *Stay on topic.* The more you talk, the more opportunity you give a reporter to use peripheral comments instead of central information. Stick to the topic. State the key message in different ways.

- *Be interesting.* Use colorful and pithy language. Use brief anecdotes. Speak directly to the audience. Imagine one individual out there (other than the reporter) and speak to him or her.

- *Be motivated.* Display your motivation and your enthusiasm. The impression you leave with your audience will linger far after they have forgotten your words.

- *Restate your key point.* If you are amid a controversy and are pressed for a comment, use the occasion to reiterate your intended message instead of responding to the detail of the controversy. Question: "Mr. Jones says you environmentalists are trying to impose your beliefs on others." Answer: "We all favor individual freedoms, but the issue here is whether one person's privilege to smoke is more important than everybody's right to clean air in a public restaurant. We believe a public right is more important than a private privilege."

- *Hold your tongue.* Don't comment if you cannot. But give a reason for your inability to answer: "Our policy is not to discuss former employees." Don't say "No comment" when you mean "I can't address that topic now" or "I don't know."

- *Help the reporter.* Insist that your opponent be heard. You can never go wrong by being an advocate of getting both sides out. It's even better if you actually help the news media get in touch with someone from the "other" side. Reporters will find the opposition anyway, and you might be able to steer them toward moderate critics (or perhaps to more extreme rivals who betray a zealotry that actually helps your position). Your insistence that there are various perspectives can only enhance your credibility and integrity.

- *Signal your message.* "The most important thing about this point is . . ." Or "Three things stand out here. One. . . Two. . . And finally . . ." This will make your message clearer, and it will decrease the likelihood that you are quoted out of context.

Exercise 15.6—Conducting an Interview/News Conference

Select two members of your class to act as the organizational spokesperson and public relations counsel for LakeLand Chemicals. The rest of the class will play the role of reporters asking questions about the industrial emissions outlined in Exercise 15.5; these reporters should be interested in the topic but not particularly hostile to the speaker. Conduct a question-and-answer session based on this scenario.

When the question-and-answer session is ended, critique the responses given by the spokesperson. ∎

Handling Hostility

Seldom will reporters be hostile in an interview. They are professionals doing a job that requires an unbiased and objective approach. This does not necessarily mean they won't pursue a line of questioning aggressively. But a professional reporter will do so fairly.

Occasionally, though, you may encounter real hostility in an interview. This might happen because the reporter is seeking a particular angle on the story, or it may be linked with a bad experience the reporter had with your organization in the past. Inevitably, it means that the relationship between your organization and this particular reporter needs mending. Make that your long-term goal.

In the meantime, if you need to deal with hostility, the No. 1 rule is to concentrate and listen carefully to the questions being asked. Also, don't aggravate the situation by sounding arrogant. Instead, maintain an even, professional tone. Remember that audiences won't see the reporter. Any hostility you may feel toward the reporter will seem like hostility toward the audience.

Identify any inaccurate statements, unsound conclusions, unacceptable paraphrases, or false implications. Don't let a reporter put words into your mouth. If confronted with a loaded question, call it for what it is, then restate the question and answer in terms you are comfortable with. Try not to repeat the charge in your response. "No, it's unfair to say that. What we really are doing is . . ." Refute incorrect statements or prejudiced questions. Correct the reporter who misinterprets what you have said or done: "Actually, that's not what quite right. What we are doing is . . ."

Don't tolerate continual interruptions by a reporter. Tell the reporter he or she is interrupting you and not giving you the opportunity to answer the question. Keeping your answers short should prevent interruptions.

Ask where a reporter heard critical information on which questions are being raised. You have a right to know your critics. Respond or don't respond based on the credibility of the critical source.

You are in an interview, not a witness under subpoena. You have the right to say no if a reporter insists on pursuing a line of questioning after you have answered it as far as you can or will. You also have the right to maintain that certain topics are off limits.

Above all, never lose your cool! Don't be drawn into an angry exchange. Don't get so emotional that you can no longer think clearly. The words that come out of your mouth are your responsibility and must always be under your control.

Part Four

PULLING IT ALL TOGETHER

In the time you have spent with this book, you have discovered many possibilities. You have learned planning processes and writing formats that offer many options to help an organization communicate with its publics. Much of what you have found in this book has been based on single formats. But in the real world of public relations, the day's work consists of more than isolated news releases, position statements and speeches. As a professional public relations writer, you will need more than familiarity with various formats. You also should understand what communication tool to use to achieve a particular objective and to address the circumstances facing the organization.

Awareness objectives are furthered by some writing formats: news briefs and news releases for general and local print media; broadcast releases, actualities and video news releases; fact sheets and event listings, and photo captions. Other writing formats that aim for deeper understanding and interest are associated with acceptance objectives. These include biographical narratives, profiles and interviews; organizational histories and backgrounders; Q&As, case histories, service articles and digests. Still other formats seek to present opinions, such as position statements, letters to the editor, guest editorials and issue advisories. Additionally, you have looked at writing for internal media such as newsletters and brochures, speeches and appeal letters, and various types of public relations advertising. And throughout this book you have considered the range of Internet applications, particularly through an organization's Web site, for the various information formats.

News conferences can be an important tool for public relations writers, a tool that involves many of the different writing formats you have worked on previously. Writers preparing for a news conference will draw on their experience in planning, writing news releases and fact sheets, writing feature releases, speechwriting, and preparing for interviews. Part 4 of this book deals with your decisions about how to pull together your writing skills into effective packages and with preparing for news conferences. This section includes two chapters:

- Chapter 16: Information Kits
- Chapter 17: Writing for News Conferences.

16

Information Kits

As a public relations writer, you can use many different writing formats to provide information for particular publics, depending on the various needs and resources of your organization.

In this chapter, you will look at ways to develop a consistent message by packaging several different formats into a single information kit. You also will see how some organizations amplify their impact by recycling various types of public relations writing. Here are your objectives for Chapter 16:

- To show an understanding of how various writing formats complement each other
- To develop complete information kits for various situations
- To modify written public relations pieces for use in other ways.

Information Kits

One of the most useful tools for public relations practitioners is an *information kit*—a folder containing a variety of information written and assembled for a specific public. One of the most common forms of information kit is a *media kit*, which is prepared for reporters and handed out at interviews and news conferences, and perhaps posted to a Web site. Another type is a *user kit* or *consumer packet*, which can be given to people who may use a service or implement an idea.

Contents

Contents of information kits vary depending on the nature of their use. They are assembled with a particular purpose in mind, and their content reflects your strategic decisions about what materials are likely to serve your public relations objectives. Information kits are used to provide information that reporters can use in presenting the story. Do not include in media kits planning materials such as advisories, statements of objectives, budgets, planning sheets or other behind-the-scenes materials.

Common elements are news releases, fact sheets, news statements, auxiliary materials and visual elements.

News Release. Your information kit will always include a news release that presents the primary information you wish to convey. If the kit is meant to accompany a news conference, the news release presents essentially the same information as the news statement. Early in the release, though probably not in the lead, identify the information as the announcement at the news conference.

Fact Sheet. Public relations writers often include in an information kit a fact sheet with the same information as in the news release. This is useful for reporters, especially broadcast journalists, because it gives them ready access to important information about a situation or news event.

News Statement. A transcript of the opening news statement may be included in the information kit. This allows print journalists to concentrate on the announcement rather than writing down quotes, and it assures the accuracy of those quotes. However, do this only if the spokesperson has been trained and coached to follow the script while presenting a polished delivery for the cameras and tape recorders.

Auxiliary Materials. Secondary materials may be part of the information kit. These include auxiliary news releases and fact sheets as well as sidebar stories, biographies and histories. Some news conference topics lend themselves to position papers, backgrounders or consumer-oriented reports. Some media kits include documentation about the topic such as reprints of relevant articles from newspapers and magazines. If you wish to use reprints, obtain permission from the publisher.

Visual Elements. Information kits generally include visual elements such as photographs with captions, charts, graphs, logos and floor plans for use in print publications. Keep in mind the needs of the electronic media, as well. Television stations may be able to use videotapes, just as radio reporters might appreciate audiocassettes to enhance the report.

CDs and Disks. In addition to photos, consider providing a CD or computer disk with photos converted into JPEG or GIF format. You might even include streaming audio and video if the situation warrants, along with the necessary playback software, which generally is available without charge on the Internet. It also can help the reporters by providing electronic copies of every document in the media kit, preferably in Microsoft Word or ASCII formats, sometimes in both PC and Mac versions.

Sample. It may be appropriate to provide a sample in the information kit that can demonstrate a relevant product for reporters. For example, a band announcing an international tour might include a CD with some of its music, or an encyclopedia publisher presenting a new edition might include a sample disk of new entries.

Public Relations Objectives

Effective public relations practitioners select the contents of information packets by their usefulness to the organization. Include materials that serve the relevant levels of your public relations objectives.

Awareness Objectives. Some information kits address awareness-level objectives. They are produced to have an effect on the attention and understanding of reporters, consumers, employees or other publics. They seek to increase awareness about projects, programs and products. A manufacturing company, for example, might prepare a media kit that features factual information on a new product, including a history of the development process, test results and a specification sheet with technical data. The same company also may give a separate information packet to stockholders, with additional information about the development costs, marketing strategy and financial projections.

Acceptance Objectives. Advocacy groups and other organizations promoting a particular point of view may move beyond the information level. They seek to make an impact on the degree of acceptance of an idea. Often, these kits include reprints of articles, speeches and commentaries that public relations practitioners hope will persuade readers about the rightness of their cause. An animal-rights organization, for example, may produce an information packet for high-school students in an effort to persuade readers to support its cause.

Action Objectives. Information packets also may have action-level objectives. Consumer-oriented kits often seek a behavioral effect, while government and other nonprofit agencies may prepare user kits with specific how-to information. The animal-rights organization mentioned above, for example, may prepare a kit to make it easy for teachers to use its materials in the classroom. A state agricultural department, meanwhile, may produce a user kit to help homeowners to turn their back yards into minisanctuaries for birds.

Preparation of an information kit does not require you to select only one level of objectives. A packet may include materials that serve various objectives, as long as they are relevant to the target public receiving the information packet.

Efficient public relations practitioners can produce different versions of the information kits on relatively short notice. Most practitioners have learned to keep basic information on file. News releases and fact sheets may be prepared in response to particular situations, but organizational backgrounders, biographies and issue factoids should be readily available at all times. Consider the many writing formats you have learned throughout this course. Most have a potential place in an information kit.

Materials to be used in an information packet are often gathered into a two-pocket folder. Frequently, these are stock folders printed with the name or logo of the organization. Take a look at the following inventories of the contents of some actual information kits for a corporate project, a special-event promotion, a university, and a fan-based Web site. Most have been developed for distribution to reporters as media kits, though they also could be useful for other publics. Note the range of materials that public relations practitioners selected to include in these kits.

Corporate Project. AT&T prepared a media kit for the launch of a new family of communications satellites. The media kit included the following pieces:

- Main news release: Sections on technology, launch vehicles, positioning, applications and consumer base (3 pages)
- News release: Satellite services (2 pages)
- News release: The AT&T Hawley satellite command center (3 pages)
- News release: Satellite-based educational programming (2 pages) programs (1 page)
- Fact sheet: Telstar 401 (1 page)
- "Telstar Factoids": Multiple-choice test with answers (2 pages)
- Listing: Colleges and universities using satellite-focused "distance learning"
- Historical piece: AT&T communications satellites (4 pages)
- Interview: Transcript of question-and-answer interview with project manager who is a former NASA astronaut (4 pages)

- Biography: General manager of satellite services (1 page)
- Testimonials: Customer comments about satellite services (3 pages)
- Glossary of terms (2 pages)
- Chart: Satellite inventions, milestones and innovations (1 page)
- Technical specification sheets: Satellites and related services (9 pages)
- Color photo with caption: Artist's rendition of the satellite (1)
- Color photo with caption: Classroom use of satellite-based education (1)
- Color photos with caption: Hawley command center (2)
- Black-and-white photo with caption: Project manager (1)
- Black-and-white photo with caption: General manager (1).

Special Event Promotion. Four ethnic-based tobacco-control groups in California sponsored a two-day statewide tobacco education conference. The media kit prepared with assistance from Durazo Communications included the following items:

- News release: English-language announcement of opening event of the conference (2 pages)
- News release: Spanish-language announcement of the opening event of the conference (2 pages)
- Itinerary: Program schedule of events during the two-day conference (3 pages)
- Information digest: Summary of eight relevant and recent research studies about tobacco use among California's diverse ethnic populations, with citation of research source (1 page)
- Research report: Summary of ethnic findings on a four-year study of tobacco use in California, with tables and charts (6 pages)
- Fact sheet on the African American Tobacco Education Network: Member agencies, mission, purpose, services (1 page)
- Fact sheet on the American Indian Tobacco Control Network: Member agencies, objectives, activities (1 page)
- Fact sheet on the Asian-Pacific Islander Tobacco Education Network: Member organizations, activities (1 page)
- Fact sheet on Hispanic-Latino Tobacco Control Network: English-language version with background and listing of services (1 page)
- Fact sheet on La Red Latina Para el Control del Tabaco: Spanish-language version of the previous item with background and listing of services (1 page)
- Program overview: Listing of programs and contacts providing tobacco-control educational programs in each of the four ethnic communities (1 page)
- Program summary: Background information on three programs in each of the four ethnic communities, with details about program content and structure (4 pages).

Educational Program. The online press kit of the Culinary Institute of America (ciachef.edu/media) features 18 high-resolution downloadable photos, a variety of media relations contacts, information about the main campus at Hyde Park, N.Y. (history, academic programs, faculty, facilities, alumni, and accreditation details), information about the satellite campus at St. Helena, Calif. (overview, courses, facilities), plus a variety of quick facts, biography and career overview of the president, and a virtual tour of both campuses.

Fan-Based Web Sites. Meanwhile, many fan-oriented Web sites and associated blogs function like online media kits. Such sites can be found across the spectrum of topics: entertainment, sports, even politics. Look at jackjohnsonmusic.com and you'll find the kind of information on Jack Johnson's music and professional career, his background, photos, and current events paralleling what you would find at many corporate online media sites. Likewise, many of the team sites associated with the National Hockey League (mapleleafs.com, sabers.com, floridapanthers.com, philadelphiafliers.com, calgaryflames.com) offer stats, news, feature stories, photos, audio and video clips, injury reports, player bios—all accessible not only to reporters but also to interested fans. Do an Internet search for fan clubs or supporters for some of the candidates currently running for office, and you'll find many sites—for and against the candidates—with a variety of information on issues, records, testimonials, schedules, and related subtopics.

Exercise 16.1—Preparing an Information Kit

As public relations director for your college or university, you have been informed that the president will retire in three months. The new president will be the person who teaches the public relations writing class at your school. A convocation will be held one month following the retirement date, during which the new president will be installed. Develop a list of materials you will prepare for use in a media kit for the installation ceremony. ■

Recycling Information

The creative public relations practitioner finds ways to reuse the various writing formats. What you prepare for one situation, you can modify for use elsewhere. Usually this does not require a significant time commitment, because much of the work has already been done. For example, as the head of a major public relations agency in Toronto, David Eisenstadt frequently speaks about public relations. He often recycles these speeches as articles for business and professional publication. Eisenstadt prepared the article in Exhibit 16.1 for a national business publication, then reprinted it to explain public relations to other interested people. The reprint is part of a packet The Communications Group sent to Canadian college libraries. It remains solid material for future speeches as well as an impressive "calling card" for potential clients.

Following are suggestions for recycling various types of public relations writing:

- *Actuality.* Organizational video. Web site.
- *Biographical narrative.* Biographical profile. Media kit. Newsletter article. News release. Information packet. Web site.
- *Biographical profile.* Biographical narrative. Media kits. Newsletter article. News release. Information packet. Web site
- *Brochure.* Service article. Newsletter. Direct mail. Information packet. Web site.
- *Case study.* Newsletter article. Media kit. Information packet. News release. Reprint. Direct mail. Web site.
- *Corporate report.* News release. Information kit. Media kit. Brochure. Web site.
- *Direct-mail appeal.* Newsletter.

Exhibit 16.1—MEDIA REPRINT   The Communications Group Inc. uses reprints of articles and speeches as part of an effort to be recognized as a leader in Canadian public relations. Reprinted with permission from The Financial Post.

REPRINTED FROM

The Financial Post

Canada's National Business Newspaper

PR industry could use a little PR

There's plenty of room for the professional

By David Eisenstadt

For The Financial Post

SINCE 1923, when E.L. Bernays published Crystalizing Public Opinion, the volume of literature on public relations has grown rapidly. Students of the business can now gather information in libraries and bookstores, from handbooks on PR and memoirs of its practitioners.

But what the PR person actually does is still misunderstood by many.

In 1976, I made some notes. It was close to my 32nd birthday and I was experiencing the usual agonizing about my age and questioning my career. Fifteen years later, I find my views have stood the test of time.

The list includes the good and bad points about the PR business, which should be considered by anyone thinking about a career in it. And yes — I still like what I'm doing.

The good points:

● PR people have the opportunity to do a variety of tasks. Writing articles, news releases and speeches, preparing brochures, slide presentations and newsletters, contacting the media, management and clients — all these help to create a stimulating work environment, although this may be a mixed blessing.

Doing many things and learning all the while is a big plus. But it's not for the 9-to-5er or someone who enjoys repetitive tasks.

● Everyone likes to see the signs of accomplishment in business and PR provides them. Maybe it's a small thing like a client calling to say thank you for a job well done or, at the other

end of the spectrum, the results of a full-fledged market research project. Evidence of success vindicates one's judgment and provides the catalyst needed to keep going. PR can be a frustrating vocation.

● Working in a business that demands imagination and intelligence, you are surrounded by people with these attributes.

● Believe it or not, PR people, whether in a company's PR department or as independent consultants, have an exceptional opportunity to help their fellow human beings. Most PR decisions have human consequences whether the organizations making them are companies, consultants or not-for-profit operations. In the same vein, defining and conveying the social responsibility of business and industry is a terrific challenge.

● Contact with top management. Meeting decision-makers and being part of a management team (on a par with financial and legal consultants) has been a definite plus in my decision to keep doing what I'm doing.

Along with the likes there are a few dislikes and it would be unfair not to list them.

One of the problems of the PR business is the continuing lack of understanding of just what it is I do. I thought since many of my contemporaries had grown up and been educated at a time when PR's role was expanding and influencing their lives, they'd have gleaned a better understanding of it. Many, however, still offer blank stares and strange definitions — such as "You must be in PR because you like people."

I'm also troubled by the apparent lack of professionalism of some colleagues. Many say, "PR is not a profession so let's stop kidding ourselves."

The Canadian Public Relations Society has about 1,500 members; yet only about 40% of those have taken their accreditation exams. That's not enough.

Perhaps the only true road to professional status is that of licensing PR practitioners and maybe that will happen in my lifetime. If it does, the blank stares might vanish.

Rounding out my list of dislikes is the fact that some PR people still fill the role of being prostitutes for management.

Also, the few flacks in the business still make it difficult to eliminate the press-agentry (slap 'em on the back, buy 'em a beer) heritage. These irritations are now more frustrating to endure than that of the mailman trying to get past the snarling dog.

There are still two overriding problems.

First, PR people must "fess up" and do a better job of communicating what they do and how they do it. Cut the magic act and keep it simple.

Second, there is the continuing problem of doing combat with the inaccurate impression of PR people created by those in the industry and by journalists who have dealt with amateurs.

DAVID EISENSTADT, *partner and president of Toronto-based The Communications Group Inc., is an accredited member of the Canadian Public Relations Society and the Public Relations Society of America.*

THE COMMUNICATIONS GROUP INC.

65 Overlea Blvd., Fourth Floor • Toronto, Canada M4H 1P1 • (416) 696-9900 • Fax (416) 696-9897

Partner PINNACLE WORLDWIDE

- *Event listing.* Newsletter. Bulletin board. Web site.
- *Fact sheet.* Different interest versions. Different educational levels. Information packets. Media kits. Web site.
- *Factoid.* Information packet. Media kit. Newsletter.
- *Flier.* News release. Newsletter. Direct mail. Web site.
- *Guest editorial.* News release. Newsletter. Direct mail. Reprint. Web site.
- *Information digest.* News release. Information packet. Media kit.
- *Interview.* News release. Newsletter article. Interview notes. Reprint.
- *Interview notes.* News release. Newsletter.
- *Issue advisory.* News release. Position statement. Newsletter.
- *Letter to the editor.* Newsletter. Reprint. Public relations advertising.
- *News advisory.* News release. News brief.
- *News brief.* News release. Newsletter.
- *News release.* Separate localized versions. Broadcast version. Newsletter. Release for newsletters of other organizations. Media kit. Web site.
- *Newsletter.* Guest editorial. Letter to the editor. Reprint. Direct mail. Web site. E-mail.
- *Organizational history.* News release. Sidebar. Newsletter article. Media kit. Annual report. Web site.
- *Photo caption.* News release. Newsletter. Information packet.
- *Pitch letter.* Direct mail. Newsletter. News release.
- *Position statement.* Letter to the editor. News release. Issue advisory. Guest editorial. Public relations advertising. Web site.
- *Public relations advertising.* Reprint. Newsletter. Direct mail.
- *Q&A.* Service article. Brochure. Web site.
- *Reprint.* Direct mail.
- *Service article.* Newsletter article. Media kit. Consumer information packet. Web site.
- *Speech.* Brochure. News release. Newsletter article. Booklet. Letter to the editor. Archival transcript. Web site.
- *Story idea memo.* News release. Newsletter. Pitch letter.

A reminder: Whenever you recycle any information to your Web site, be sure to rewrite and revise it. Seldom is it appropriate just to take a brochure or position statement, for example, and simply load it to the Web site. Rather, recycled material should be rewritten to accommodate Web technology and to fit with the interactive features of the site. Review the information in Chapter 11 of this book for suggestions about writing for the Web.

Exercise 16.2—Recycling Previously Written Information

Review the writing that you did in three previous exercises, such as the news release (Exercise 6.11), Q&A feature release (Exercise 9.6), position statement (Exercise 10.2), brochure (Exercise 11.2), or fundraising letter (Exercise 13.3). For each of the three, identify as many different ways as you can think of to recycle this information by packaging it for different writing formats. ■

17

Writing for News Conferences

News conferences often are treated merely as exercises in spoken communication, performance rather than writing. But consider this: Effective performance at a news conference is enhanced by a thorough preparation rooted in the writing process. In the previous chapter, we discussed one of the major preparatory tasks, developing information kits. In this chapter, you will be guided through a step-by-step process and given the opportunity to develop your expertise through various scenarios and exercises. Here are your objectives for Chapter 17:

- To understand the role of writing in preparing news conferences
- To use writing skills to implement effective news conferences
- To write an invitation for a news conference
- To write a statement for a news conference.

News Conference

A *news conference* is an announcement and group interview staged by public relations practitioners to provide an organizational message simultaneously to a large group of reporters. It can be one of the most interesting and rewarding activities a public relations practitioner can undertake. It also can be one of the most risky. The outcome depends on how prepared you are and how much you can control the situation.

News conferences are occasions when you put your professional credibility on the line. You tell reporters that your organization has something of interest to their audiences. And you tell spokespersons and managers that it is in the organization's best interests to hold the news conference. In short, you go out of your way to call attention to your client, business or organization.

With a news conference, you select the topic and present information, but you have no control over the questions reporters will ask, or how or even whether they will use the information you provide. And there is no guarantee the reporters' questions will remain within your selected topic.

Some public relations practitioners like news conferences and use them as often as possible. Some fear them and avoid them. Some find alternative ways to communicate, or they decide not to communicate publicly at all. But news conferences should be determined not merely on personal preferences. Rather, they should be based on a strategic decision that a news conference will be effective in helping an organization communicate in a given situation. Keep in mind that news conferences are not favorites of most reporters, who prefer to get their information and do their interviews one on one rather than in a group with their professional rivals. Because of this, the wise public relations practitioner is selective about using the news conference format.

When it does seem appropriate to call a news conference, give some thought to timing. Consider media deadlines. Select a time most convenient for reporters. For example, 7 p.m. may be too late for all editions of a morning newspaper, and a late-afternoon paper may have a noon deadline. An evening television news show may need information before 4 p.m., while a radio station may be able to take stories up to about 10 minutes before each hourly report. If you aren't certain, ask reporters how much time they need to prepare a story and what they consider the best times for a news conference.

You won't be able to accommodate everyone's schedule each time, especially reporters on competing morning and evening newspapers. Just make sure you don't continually favor one deadline over another. Keep a record in case you are accused of favoritism. Also realize that, while a news conference requires solid news, it's also a bit of a theatrical event. If the subject can be demonstrated, demonstrate it. If it can be shown in a model, as a new building or construction project could be, use a model. To succeed with the electronic media especially, the news conference must be carefully staged to take advantage of every potential for visual impact.

Following the logical steps in preparing for a news conference presented below can make you a more effective public relations practitioner. Note that each of these steps is closely linked with writing skills. "FYI: News Conference Checklist" presents a handy tool for looking at all aspects of the news conference.

FYI   *News Conference Checklist*

Decision to Hold a News Conference
- ❏ Fosters public relations objectives
- ❏ Strong news value
  - ❏ Public interest
  - ❏ Emergency situation
- ❏ More than news release
- ❏ More than a photo opportunity
- ❏ More than a special event
- ❏ More than open house or media tour
- ❏ More than individual interview(s)
- ❏ Appropriate for program or product demonstration
- ❏ Appropriate for commentary by speaker(s)
- ❏ Appropriate for question-and-answer interchange with media
- ❏ Visual element or setting

Writing Preparation
- ❏ Planning sheet
  - ❏ Target publics
  - ❏ Analysis of target publics
  - ❏ Benefit statement
  - ❏ Tone of message
  - ❏ Public relations objectives
- ❏ Invitation
  - ❏ General topic
  - ❏ Logistics: when, where, who
  - ❏ No detailed information
  - ❏ Travel directions (if needed)
  - ❏ Entrance clearance/permission (if needed)
- ❏ News conference statement
- ❏ Anticipated questions and responses

- ❏ Primary news release
- ❏ Secondary information for media kit (bios, backgrounders, reports, etc.)
- ❏ Visual elements for media kit (logos, maps, charts, graphics, etc.)
- ❏ Participants ready
- ❏ Review anticipated questions & appropriate answers
- ❏ Research issues
- ❏ Time for news conference
  - ❏ Aware of media deadlines
  - ❏ Aware of previous news conference vis- à-vis media deadlines
  - ❏ Aware of competition for media attention (especially with popular mid-morning time)
  - ❏ Aware of media availability re: time and date
- ❏ Location for news conference
  - ❏ Conference room versus office
  - ❏ Appropriate to story
  - ❏ Accessible for media
  - ❏ Appropriate logistics to news conference
  - ❏ If outdoor location is selection, indoor backup site
- ❏ Appropriate mailing list
- ❏ Appropriate number of copies of media kit
- ❏ Invitations mailed a week to 10 days in advance
- ❏ Follow-up telephone reminders made one day in advance
- ❏ Physical arrangements
  - ❏ Lectern or table
  - ❏ Microphone feed
  - ❏ Appropriate lighting

- ❏ Know location of main electrical service box
- ❏ Grounded adapter plugs (if needed)
- ❏ Access for media
  - ❏ Parking
  - ❏ Security clearance (if needed)
  - ❏ Alert receptionist
- ❏ Professional hospitality
  - ❏ Coffee or beverages
  - ❏ Telephones
  - ❏ Computers with e-mail
  - ❏ Extra pens and paper
  - ❏ Fax machines
  - ❏ Rest rooms
- ❏ Internal coverage of news conference
  - ❏ Organizational video
  - ❏ Audio recording
  - ❏ Still photography
  - ❏ Organizational newsletter reporter
- ❏ Room
  - ❏ Seating of reporters
  - ❏ Space for television equipment
  - ❏ Lectern/Table for microphones

Following the News Conference
- ❏ Information to invited media that did not attend
  - ❏ News release
  - ❏ Media kit
  - ❏ Audio actualities for radio
  - ❏ Videotaped segments for television
- ❏ Debriefing report

Planning Sheet

A news conference is an occasion for dealing with important news, and it deserves careful planning. A good public relations practitioner will take the necessary time to design a news conference that will serve the interests of the sponsoring company or organization. The standard planning sheet saves you time and will keep you focused on your goals and objectives. This planning effort also will give you more control over the impact your news conference can make on your target publics. Exhibit 17.1 is an example of how the planning might look on paper.

Exhibit 17.1—NEWS CONFERENCE PLANNING SHEET This sample planning sheet helps the public relations practitioner prepare for an effective news conference.

Background: Employees at the LakeLand Chemicals plant in Middletown have been working without a pay increase for 29 months, since the Union of Chemical Workers of America and plant management worked out a mutual wage and hiring freeze for both union and management employees. Negotiations are nearing completion to provide an immediate 7 percent salary increase for all employees and a second-stage increase in six months of 3 to 5 percent. There are two reasons for the increase. One, sales are up, including a $7.3 million two-year export agreement with Guatemala. Two, a six-month-old electronic smokestack filter is unexpectedly efficient in recovering the chemical tri-chlorofluoromethane, thus saving the plant $12,000 a month.

Focus: Announcement of salary increase.

Publics:
- *Public A, reporters* (reporters for county weekly and daily newspapers, radio and television; print photographers and television camera operators): News including financial projections, photo opportunities
- *Public B, employees:* Salary raise, gratitude for sacrifice
- *Public C, union:* Recognized union role in plant recovery
- *Public D, business leaders:* Financial benefit for community
- *Public E, environmentalists:* Affirmation of company's concerns about air pollution and ozone.

Benefit: Company will give salary increase, recognize union-management cooperation, help community with cleaner air.

Tone: Positive, appreciative of worker sacrifices, optimistic re: impact on community.

Common objectives for all publics:
- To have an effect on awareness; specifically to increase understanding about the increase and recovery
- To have an effect on acceptance; specifically to create positive attitudes about the recovery.

Specific objectives for reporters:
- To have an affect on awareness; specifically to create understanding about the increase and recovery
- To have an effect on action; specifically to have them accurately report on the increase and recovery
- To have an effect on action; specifically to have them write favorable editorials on the increase and recovery.

Specific objectives for employees:
- To have an effect on acceptance; specifically to increase morale and positive feedback
- To have an effect on action; specifically to increase productivity by 15 percent.

Specific objectives for union:
- To have an effect on action; specifically to maintain cooperation between union and management.

Specific objectives for business leaders:
- To have an effect on action; specifically to increase positive feedback about the company.

Specific objectives for environmentalists:
- To have an effect on awareness; specifically to create understanding about the firm's environmental practices
- To have an affect on action; specifically to decrease criticism of the company on environmental issues.

Exercise 17.1—Writing a Planning Sheet for a News Conference

You are public relations director for Memorial Hospital. Interview your teacher or another student in your class who will assume the role of hospital administrator. This administrator will provide needed additional information for this and succeeding exercises in this chapter. Use the following background information:

- Memorial Hospital is preparing to build a new wing, which will expand the pediatrics unit and provide high-level neonatal care.

- Part of the renovation will include the purchase and razing of a low-income apartment building and several privately owned houses adjacent to the hospital parking lot. Residents in 23 households, most of them senior citizens, will be displaced.

- The hospital will make a $4 million public appeal to area businesses, organizations and individuals. This fund will be added to a gift of $2 million already received from the estate of a prominent area physician; this bequest has not been announced. The hospital also expects about $4 million from a series of state and federal grants.

Write a planning sheet for an upcoming news conference at which the hospital administrator will make the first public announcement of the new expansion project. Identify each of the following:

- Media publics
- Target publics
- Analysis of publics
- Tone of message
- Objectives
- Evaluation methods.

Also write the key message, the one sentence you want to make sure is presented and repeated during the news conference. ∎

Invitations

The public relations practitioner must invite many media representatives, generally through a written invitation. Invitations essentially are media advisories that provide information of interest to city editors and assignment editors: the general topic; date, time and location; the name of the speaker; information on the availability of photographs for both print and broadcast photographers; and the contact name.

Remember the difference between a news release and a media advisory. For the invitational advisory, provide only a general topic and logistical information. Do not give too much advance information. You don't want to read an article in the morning newspaper that reports the substance of your news conference scheduled for later that day. That not only would put a damper on your news conference, it could also injure your reputation as a fair information source for all the media.

Exhibit 17.2 is a sample of how you might invite reporters to a news conference for your organization. This usually would be sent to news directors for radio and television and to editors for newspapers and magazines. However, if you already have a working relationship with a reporter or if your pending news conference falls within the "beat" of a particular reporter, you may decide to send the invitation to that person. Distribution may be by mail, hand delivery, or faxing.

Occasionally, you may find yourself in the situation of knowing that a news conference will be held, pending some other activity. For example, you may know that a vote on a strike settlement is near, and you may wish to send an advisory to the media, telling them that a news conference will be called on short notice as soon as the vote is decisive. This allows reporters to prepare for the news conference by doing background research and formulating questions, yet it gives you flexibility about the timing.

At other times, you will be dealing with an emergency or unexpected situation. In such cases, you will need to hold a news conference fast, using the telephone or e-mail to contact

Exhibit 17.2—NEWS CONFERENCE INVITATION   This sample invitation tells reporters about the news conference without leaking advance details about the story.

LakeLand Chemicals

13 Short Street • Middletown Xx 12345 • Juan Garcia, Public Relations Manager • (123) 555–1234

To: Editors and news directors
From: Juan Garcia
Date: April 27, 2007
Re: News Conference

Employees of LakeLand Chemicals' Middletown plant have been working without a pay increase for 29 months, since the Union of Chemical Workers of America and plant management agreed to a mutual wage and hiring freeze for both union and management employees. In recent months, the union and management have been renegotiating the issue. A union-management committee is preparing a report with recommendations. This report will be finalized this week. Provisions of the report will be announced at a news conference:

> Thursday, May 3
> 10 a.m.
> LakeLand Chemicals Plant, Building G, 13 Short Street, Middletown
> Speaker: O. Sidney Morris, plant superintendent
> LakeLand Chemicals of Middletown

Following the announcement, Morris will answer questions. Background materials will be available.

YOU ARE INVITED to have reporters and/or photographers cover this news conference.

Contact: Juan Garcia, 555–1234

editors and news directors. Be careful! Journalists are competitive people. They are keenly aware that others are receiving the same invitation. They often use a phone call as an opportunity to begin their news gathering, probing for details you want to hold until the conference itself.

Writing can come to your rescue. Prepare yourself a script for the phone invitation. This will help you give each journalist exactly the same information. If you are asked for more information, politely but firmly say that this will be discussed at the news conference because right now, in fairness to all, you won't provide any more information. Of course, journalists will ask for more information—that's their job. But reporters appreciate a public relations person who is fair, who doesn't play favorites, and who shows an understanding of deadlines and the competitive nature of the news media.

A news conference invitation is a business announcement, not a social invitation, so don't expect a reporter to RSVP. It is your job to follow up, if this is necessary. Public relations practitioners often make follow-up telephone calls or send e-mails after they have invited reporters in writing to attend a news conference. This can be an effective reminder and a good remedy for the occasionally lost notice. If you do telephone your media contacts, don't ask for a guarantee that they will be at your news conference. Instead, simply ask if they have received the invitation and express a polite verbal invitation. Don't expect a commitment, because your news conference will have to stand on its own merits against fires, accidents, trials, visiting celebrities and other news conferences happening at the same time.

Exercise 17.2—Writing an Invitation for a News Conference

 Write an invitation to the news media for a news conference with the hospital administrator to announce the expansion. Be careful not to include too much information about the news that will be announced at the conference. ∎

News Statement

A *news statement* is a combination of a news release, a position paper and a speech. Writing an effective, newsworthy statement for the news conference is imperative. Journalists can tell you far too many stories about the many non-news releases they have encountered, submissions from well-meaning public relations people using poor judgment about the quality of information in their releases. Journalists usually can quickly deal with non-news, but non-news in a news conference wastes reporters' time. It also cheapens your reputation as a reliable ally of the media, for you betray to journalists that you don't know what is news and what isn't, or worse, you know this isn't news but you don't care.

As with a news release, a news statement must present information of high news value. Consider the SiLoBaTi elements of news: significant, local, balanced and timely. A news conference is no place for gimmicks. As with a position paper, the statement must present your organization's opinion and reasons for it. As with a speech, it must be written for the ear, considering delivery as well as content. Exhibit 17.3 is an example of a news conference statement. Include the following elements in your opening statement:

- Introduction of the speaker(s)
- Background information as necessary
- The news announcement
- Personal comments.

What if you don't have solid news and need to rely on a created situation to generate media interest? There is nothing necessarily wrong with this, but understand that this is not a news conference. Consider two alternatives to a news conference when you're light on the news: special events and photo opportunities. A *special event* is an activity created and/or sponsored by an organization for the purpose of attracting attention of the public and the media. A *photo opportunity* is an occasion, likewise created or sponsored by the organization, which offers something of particular interest to photographers with print or television media. "What Would You Do?: Fake News Conferences" raises the issue of holding a news conference when no real news exists.

Exhibit 17.3—NEWS CONFERENCE STATEMENT   This sample statement for a news conference provides important information for reporters.

NEWS CONFERENCE STATEMENT

Public relations director
Thank you for coming today. After our announcement we will respond to your questions. I am pleased to present our speaker, O. Sidney Morris. Mr. Morris is plant superintendent of LakeLand Chemicals here in Middletown.

O. Sidney Morris
As you know, for the last 29 months, employees of LakeLand Chemicals have been working without a pay increase. This salary freeze affected plant managers and members of the United Chemical Workers of America local 312, more than 400 employees in all.

It was a painful but necessary step to prevent layoffs while we tried to become more productive.

I am pleased to announce the following news: Beginning next month, our employees will receive a 7 percent salary increase. We expect to follow this in six months with a second-stage increase of between 3 and 5 percent.

Two factors make the increase possible. First, business is beginning to improve for us. Sales are up, and we have just signed a two-year export agreement with Guatemala worth $7.3 million. Second, an unexpected benefit of our environmental commitment is saving us substantial money. The new electronic smokestack filter which we installed six months ago reduces air pollution to below federal and state levels. It also makes it possible for us to recover a rather expensive chemical called tri-chlorofluoromethane. We can reuse this chemical in the production of paints. Because the filter is more efficient than we had anticipated, we find that it is saving us $12,000 a month.

These last 29 months have been difficult for both LakeLand Chemicals and all the people of Middletown. The union has been understanding of the financial problem and committed to the long-term welfare of union members. After weeks of negotiating, we have come up with an arrangement I believe we all can live with.

What Would You Do? *Fake News Conferences*

While investigating the disappearance of a child, a sheriff's department in New York State gave out false information during a news conference to confuse a suspected killer. This deception led to the eventual confession by the child's mother that the reported disappearance was a cover-up for domestic violence. Was the deception justified?

During wartime, the military sometimes has given out false information during news conferences to confuse the enemy and to protect American soldiers. Are these deceptions justified?

- What do you think are the ethical considerations of such deceptions?

- Should information or misinformation be used as an instrument of war or law enforcement?

- Should public relations practitioners disseminate false or misleading information in an effort to achieve a good result?

Exercise 17.3—Writing a News Conference Statement

Write an introduction for yourself as public relations director and a news statement for the administrator of Memorial Hospital. Give attention to providing both the news announcement and appropriate background information.   ■

Media Kit

The better reporters understand your organization's message, the more accurately they can present it to their audiences who comprise your target publics. Much background and detail may to be given to reporters in the form of an information kit, as discussed in the previous chapter.

Plan on presenting a media kit for every news conference, with one exception: When you are dealing with a crisis situation, especially if you are having frequent news conferences to update the media on emergency developments, you may have neither the time nor the need to prepare a full media kit. But each time you meet with the media, you should have at least an updated fact sheet or news release.

Usually, you will distribute the media kit at the beginning of the news conference. After the conference, provide the media kits to the no-shows. Even reporters who did not attend the news conference may be interested in reporting on your activity. Exhibit 17.4 is an example of a news release to be featured in the media kit for a news conference.

Exhibit 17.4—NEWS CONFERENCE NEWS RELEASE   This sample news release covers the same material as is contained in the news conference statement, Figure 17.3.

LakeLand Chemicals

13 Short Street • Middletown Xx 12345 • Juan Garcia, Public Relations Manager • (123) 555–1234

May 3, 2007
FOR IMMEDIATE RELEASE

MIDDLETOWN—Following a 29-month wage and hiring freeze, LakeLand Chemicals will provide its 408 employees with an immediate 7 percent salary increase. O. Sidney Morris, superintendent of the Middletown plant, said an additional increase of between 3 and 5 percent will be offered in six months. At a Thursday morning news conference, Morris cited two reasons for the salary hike.

"Business is beginning to improve for us," he said. The plant recently signed a two-year export agreement with Guatemala worth $7.3 million.

The second reason for the increase, said Morris, is "an unexpected benefit of our environmental commitment."

An electronic smokestack filter installed six months ago has been "more efficient than we had anticipated," he said. The filter recovers an expensive chemical, tri-chlorofluoromethane, which the company can reuse in manufacturing its paints. This recovery saves LakeLand Chemicals $12,000 a month.

"These last 29 months have been difficult for LakeLand Chemicals and a hardship for all the people of Middletown," said the plant superintendent. He thanked Local 312 of the United Chemical Workers of America for its "understanding of the company's financial problem" and its commitment to the "long-term welfare of union members."

#####

Exercise 17.4—Writing a News Release for a News Conference

Write a one-page news release reporting the hospital administrator's announcement. Date the release for today and mention the news conference. The release will be given to reporters at the news conference and will be delivered or sent to invited media that did not send reporters.

Q&A Responses

You have made a statement and have given reporters written information. But your news conference isn't over yet. You still have to respond to questions. This is another opportunity to present information you feel is significant and newsworthy and which serves your organizational objectives. But to do this well, you must be prepared.

Reporters will be looking for information not included in your original statement, reasons behind the information that are not apparent, and implications for their audiences. They may also probe for a hidden agenda or for information they think you may be reluctant to give them.

Exhibit 17.5 is an example of a public relations writer's anticipated questions and answers to help coach a spokesperson for a news conference. Notice how this example includes guidance for providing additional information, giving forecasts and projections, and handling potentially embarrassing questions.

Exhibit 17.5—SUGGESTED NEWS CONFERENCE Q&A RESPONSES

This sample memo from the public relations practitioner contains suggested Q&A responses for an upcoming news conference.

To:	O. Sidney Morris	Date:	April 27, 2007
From:	Juan Garcia	Re:	News conference

Following are some questions that I anticipate might be asked by reporters during the question-and-answer portion of next Thursday's news conference. Along with the questions are some possible answers you may wish to consider.

How many employees do you have?
Current personnel records: 56 managers, 352 union members. Total 408.

How much will the salary increases cost?
Almost $20,000 a month with the 7 percent increase.

When will you know the extent of the second increase?
Probably within the next quarter when we see exactly how strong our recovery is.

What does the chemical do?
Tri-chlorofluoromethane is a CFC, which is under government regulation because it can destroy ozone in the upper atmosphere. LakeLand Chemicals uses it in the manufacture of paint, where it is safe as a liquid. The environmental risk occurs when it is released as a gas.

How was the export agreement reached?
With help from the U.S. Agency for International Development, as well as local and state Chambers of Commerce.

There are reports that the union was strong-armed to accept the wage freeze.
Talk to the union. I assure you, no coercion was made by company management. We all were being "strong-armed" by a poor economy and the very real threat that the plant might have to be closed. But we sacrificed together, and now we can share in the benefits.

Are any CFCs being released despite the filter?
This filter is the result of the best technology we know of to prevent CFC release into the atmosphere. Government tests show that our emissions are 94 percent free of CFC—2 percent cleaner than the government requires.

Exercise 17.5—Anticipating Questions for a News Conference

Write eight to 10 questions that reporters might ask following your statement from the previous exercise. Then prepare answers or give guidance for responding to these questions. Make sure the questions deal with additional information, forecasts and projections, and embarrassing questions.

∎

Follow-Up

Immediately after the news conference, it usually is a good idea to contact reporters who did not attend but who were expected, especially reporters in key media. There are many reasons why a reporter can't cover a news conference, and often these reasons have little to do with the value of the information being provided. News teams are short-staffed, breaking news usually takes precedence over a scheduled news conference, or perhaps your organization has been in the news too much recently and reporters are reluctant to overplay another story from you.

FYI *Online Interviews and News Conferences*

Gather public relations practitioners, and they will talk knowingly about the dwindling interest in the traditional news conference. Reporters are too busy or not particularly interested in traveling to the organization's location to obtain information, especially to cover a "talking heads" event that deals with good news rather than crises and emergency activities.

So the practitioner needs to deal with the question: Is there an alternative to the traditional news conference? Yes, there is. It's found in the growing use of live online news conferences and interviews. All of the content prepared for reporters can be posted online also. In today's 24-hour news cycles and fast-paced newsrooms, these Internet-based alternatives are sometimes more successful than a traditional on-site news conference.

Another advantage is that online interviews and news conferences often can be accessed not only by reporters but also by other interested and credentialed people, allowing organizations to communicate directly with their key publics. For example, politicians have held online news conferences to announce their legislative agendas,

and business leaders use them to introduce new products. Bill Clinton made media history in 2000 when he became the first sitting president to hold an online interview, with CNN correspondent Wolf Blitzer posing his own questions and facilitating others via e-mail from viewers throughout the world. To commemorate the 34th anniversary of the martial law in the Philippines, organizers provided an online platform for a former journalist and political detainee with journalists and bloggers from the United States, Hong Kong and Australia as well as the Philippines; participants hailed it as an example of technology serving an anti-establishment cause.

Live online interviews and news conferences also allow for the material to be archived. National Public Radio and most commercial news organizations provide podcasts, audio and video news feeds, Web extras, and other online services as well as printed transcripts for both journalists and regular audience members. Television stations provide full coverage of news conferences on their Web sites, in addition to a few seconds of highlights during their regular broadcast news programming.

When you contact missing reporters, don't make them feel guilty. Simply let the reporter know that the information is available; better yet, deliver the information to the reporter. And be available for follow-up questions just as you would with reporters who attended the event.

At a minimum, arrange for all news conference materials to be uploaded to the organization's Web site during the course of the news conference so that reporters who cannot be there nevertheless will have access to everything they need to prepare a story. "FYI: Online Interviews and News Conferences" further explores ways to use the Internet to your organization's advantage.

Evaluation

During the news conference, take careful notes of what media attended, the questions reporters asked, and any follow-up you need to do based on those questions. Exhibit 17.6 shows a summary sheet that can be useful for recording this information.

When the last reporter has left the news conference, you still have some writing to do as you review and debrief the event. This will happen in three stages.

First, immediately after the conference, write a brief report and personal evaluation. Who attended? Who was invited but did not attend? Did reporters seem to understand the statement,

Exhibit 17.6—NEWS CONFERENCE SUMMARY   This sample news conference summary allows the public relations practitioner to keep a careful record of questions asked during a news conference.

News Conference Summary

Date:

Topic:

Speakers:

News Media	Reporter	Questions Asked	Follow-Up Required

or did they need a lot of clarification? What was the tone and substance of questions? How well did the speaker(s) respond? What kind of coverage do you expect?

Second, as the information becomes available, report on the nature of the coverage. Include clippings of print reports and synopses of broadcast reports (or, if the issue is an important one that might affect you in the future, use your cassette and VCR to generate a transcript of the coverage).

Finally, write a brief conclusive evaluation of the news conference. Go back and review your objectives, and consider how successful the conference was in meeting those objectives. Indicate any lessons you learned which can help you in the future.

Such a written evaluation will help you become more effective in preparing news conferences because it leads you to analyze and understand each of your encounters with the media. Just as important, an evaluation report shared with your supervisor or client will enhance the perception of you as a manager and strategist, rather than a mere technician. Exhibit 17.7 is an example of an evaluation report for a news conference.

Exhibit 17.7—NEWS CONFERENCE EVALUATION REPORT   This sample evaluation report allows the public relations practitioner to assess and learn from the news conference.

To: File
From: Juan Garcia
Date: Friday, May 4, 2007
Re: <u>News conference evaluation</u>

<u>Immediate report</u>
Morris made announcement. Spoke well. Handled questions well. Poor eye contact with camera.

<u>Media attending</u>
  – Middletown Daily News   No-Shows:
  – WAAB TV   – WKBE TV
  – WBLN TV   – Centerville Gazette
  – WKMD Radio   – Midstate Business Magazine.
  – WXPT Public Radio
  – The Painter (industry newsletter).

7 questions (2 about environment by WKMD biased against LC; Morris responded well with positive info).

<u>Coverage</u>
  – P1 story in Daily News. Thorough, balanced
  – WAAB :45 at 6p.m., :20 at 11p.m. Balanced
  – WBLN 1:10 at 6p.m. Favorable report
  – WKMD Radio. Lead story at noon; featured in hourly reports. Balanced. 6p.m. included negative accusations by environmental activist re: accuracy of emission reports
  – WXPT Public Radio. 3 reports, 3–4 minutes each, with interview of union head & wife of 20-year employee. Favorable comments. Interview with state Chamber of Commerce, favorable.

Evaluation
Generally favorable coverage.

Meeting objectives (scale 1–5)
- Awareness, 4
- Comprehension, 3
- Employee acceptance, 4
- Employee action, NA/too soon
- Environment awareness, 2
- Environmental action, NA/too soon
- Union, NA/too soon
- Business leaders, 4.

Overall
News conference seems to have been effective. Will monitor continuing coverage & results, especially re: future interaction w/ union and environmentalists.

Lessons
- Remind Morris of need for more eye contact with camera; schedule refresher workshop w/ in-plant TV studio
- Exterior photo opportunity (perhaps Morris and smokestack) could have improved visual impact and coverage.

Exercise 17.6—Evaluating a News Conference

View a television news conference on a cable news or sports channel or on your local broadcast station. Write your evaluation of the following aspects of the news conference: setting, lighting, microphone placement, space for reporters and camera operators, news statement, response to questions, apparent preparation of speaker(s) and overall public relations effectiveness of the news conference.

Appendix A

Common Sense Stylebook
for Public Relations Writers

A stylebook should help writers use the language in a way that is natural, smooth and consistent. Following are guidelines for various public relations writing purposes. They deal with aspects of language that students have identified as needing clarification and order. The style suggestions here are consistent with The Associated Press Stylebook, the most widely used stylebook for journalistic writing. Thus public relations writers will find this Common Sense Stylebook useful in preparing news releases and other writing for newspapers and magazines.

Writing for organizational media such as newsletters and brochures sometimes calls for a stylistic practice that may be different from that used for public media. Nevertheless, writers need to be consistent in style. This Common Sense Stylebook therefore includes guidelines about stylistic options appropriate for organizational media. Though optional, they should be consistently used, according to the organization's internal stylebook.

For more complete references, consult authoritative guides such as The Associated Press Stylebook, Webster's New World Dictionary Fourth Edition, Webster's Third New International Dictionary, and National Geographic Atlas of the World.

Abbreviation

Avoid abbreviations except in situations of common usage. See the following entries in this stylebook: Academic Degree, Address, Date, Dateline, Military, Organizational Name, Period, State Name, Title of People (Courtesy) and Title of People (Formal).

In general, when writing for print media, use capital letters without periods for abbreviations of organizations or terms in which the letters are pronounced separately: *CIA, IBM, CEO, UCLA, TV, VCR, ABC News* (but *Fox News*). Exception: Abbreviate *U.S.* and *U.N.* when these are used as adjectives but do not abbreviate *United States* or *United Nations* when these terms are used as nouns. For broadcast media, use a hyphen between letters to indicate that they are to be pronounced separately: *C-I-A, Y-M-C-A, U-C-L-A*.

Academic Degree

In general, avoid abbreviations for academic degrees. Write out the names of college or university degrees, using lowercase letters except for proper nouns or proper adjectives: *obtained an associate's degree in masonry . . ., received a bachelor's from Central State . . ., obtained a master's degree in business administration . . ., holds a doctorate in French literature* (not *holds a doctor's degree . . .*). Use capital letters but no apostrophe when citing the formal name of a degree: *Bachelor of Arts degree, Master of Science program.*

Do not use abbreviations for academic degrees for public media. Use of academic abbreviations is an option for organizational media if readers are likely to be familiar with the abbreviation: *M.S., Ph.D., M.F.A.* Place these after the name, set off by commas. See Professional Credentials.

Address

When referring to a street without a specific address, spell out *Street, Avenue*, etc.: *Ransom Road, Madison Avenue.*

When referring to a specific address, abbreviate *Ave., Blvd.* and *St.* Use numerals for an address number: *27 Anderson Blvd., 1356 Linwood Ave.* Exception: *One North St.* Write out related words: *Alley, Court, Drive, Parkway, Place, Road, Terrace*, etc.: *20 Mango Lane, 8033 Thyme Circle.*

Write out compass points when only the street name is used without a specific address: *West Main Street.* Abbreviate compass points within a complete address: *15 W. Main St.* For numbered streets, spell out and capitalize *first* through *ninth*; use ordinals for *10th* and above.

Age

Use numerals for all ages: *The child, 5, was . . . At age 15, he went . . .* Use a numeral with a hyphen when the age is used as part of a compound modifier before the noun: *2-year warranty, 5-year-old girl.* Do not use hyphens when using age as a noun: *A 5 year old was rescued . . .*

Bracket the numeral with commas when the age is used parenthetically: *Johnson, 37, was appointed . . .*

Ampersand

Use the ampersand (&) only when it is part of an organization's formal name: *J & R Rentals, Inc., Johnson & Johnson.*

Apostrophe

Do not use an apostrophe to designate the plural of numbers: *in her 30s, during the 1980s, size 8s.* However, do use an apostrophe to indicate omitted numbers: *in the '60s, class of '02.* Do not use an apostrophe with multiple letter designations: *RBIs, WMDs.*

Do not use an apostrophe to designate the plural of words: *dos and don'ts, IOUs.* However, do use an apostrophe to indicate the plural of stand-alone letters: *A's and B's, the Oakland A's.*

Use *'s* with words ending in the letter *s* or the sound of *s*: *Arkansas' capital, Descartes' theories, Marx' biography, the actress's role.*

Brand Name

Capitalize trademarks and brand names: *Xerox, Toyota, Calvin Klein Obsession.* For public media, use lowercase for generic terms: *Lee jeans, Corolla sedan, LexisNexis database, GarageBand music application program.* For organizational media, capitalization of generic terms is optional. Also optional for organizational media is the use of trademark indicators: *LexisNexis®, GarageBand™*.

Capitalize brand names and trademark with food items: *Tobasco sauce*. In general, capitalize proper adjectives when they are part of food names: *Boston baked beans, Swiss cheese, Waldorf salad, Russian dressing.*

Capitalization

For public media, avoid unneeded use of capitalization. Use capital letters for proper nouns, full names and formal titles. Do not capitalize planets, academic or organizational departments, or job titles. Do not capitalize seasons and their derivatives: *spring, wintertime*. Capitalize proper nouns, including brand names, awards and holidays. See the following entries for specific guidelines on capitalization: Academic Degree; Race, Ethnicity and Nationality; Geographic Region; Government; Organizational Name; Politics; State Name; Title of Composition; and Title of People (Formal).

For organizational media, the writer may choose to use capital letters more freely to indicate importance or prestige within the organization.

Use capitals for adjectives derived from proper nouns: *Boston crème pie, German shepherd*. However, some such words have become generic and do not require capitalization: *french fry, siamese cat*.

Collective Noun

Nouns that refer to a grouping of people or things are singular: *committee, board, company, management, team, family, class*. When referring to such a grouping, use a singular pronoun and a singular verb: *The company will build its office* (not *their*). *The board of trustees wants to vote* (not *want*).

When referring to all the individuals within the grouping, use a plural noun to make this clear: *The company managers will build their office. The trustees want to vote.*

Colon

Use a colon to designate a sentence within a sentence or an enumeration: *His promise was simple: He would balance the budget. She indicated three favorite authors: Thomas Merton, Shushako Endo, and Thich Nhat Hahn*. Capitalize the first word following a colon only if it is a proper noun or the beginning of a sentence: *He has several pets: a dog, two cats, and a ferret.*

Comma

In general, place a comma between each element in a series: *The book features an overview of European history, a discussion of the influence of religion, and an analysis of the effects of the rise of literacy*. But with a short and simple series, do not use a comma before the conjunction: *The book deals with history, religion and literacy.*

Put a comma before the conjunction when another conjunction is used within one or more elements in the series: *The book deals with European history, the influence of religion and education, and the rise of literacy*. Use a semicolon instead of a comma to separate items in a series if at least one of the items includes material with a comma: *The book deals with*

European history; the influence of religion, both Christianity, Judaism and Islam; and the rise of literacy.

Place commas before and after parenthetical material and nonessential (nonrestrictive) phrases and clauses: *The president, 42, will . . . The visitor, a native of Mexico, was . . . The senator, who is left-handed, wants . . .* Do not use commas with essential (restrictive) phrases and clauses that provide necessary information: *Students who get an F must repeat the course.*

Use a comma before coordinating conjunctions (*and, or, but, for, nor, yet, so*) when they join independent clauses: *Jaleesa wanted to go to the park, but the weather was bad.* Use a comma after an introductory clause beginning with subordinating conjunctions such as *after, although, because, since, when,* etc. *Because the weather was bad, Jaleesa decided to stay home.*

Use a comma after an introductory clause or phrase: *After becoming a student at the University of Albuquerque, she changed her major.* But do not use a comma following a short introductory phrase: *After dinner she changed her sweater.*

Use a comma to separate a quotation from its attribution: *"This is a beautiful day," he said.* Do not use a comma if the quotation ends with a question mark or an exclamation point: *"Do you think this is a beautiful day?" he asked.*

Commas, like periods, always go inside quotation marks.

Countries

Do not abbreviate *United States* when used as a noun. Abbreviate as *U.S.* when used as an adjective. Give similar treatment to *United Nations* and *United Kingdom.*

Use commonly known designations for foreign nations, avoiding formal titles: *Norway* rather than *Kingdom of Norway, San Marino* rather than *Most Serene Republic of San Marino, India* rather than *Union of India, Jordan* rather than *Hashemite Kingdom of Jordan.*

However, on first reference it may be appropriate to use formal titles, for example to distinguish between the *People's Republic of China* (also called *Mainland China*) and the *Republic of China* (also called *Taiwan*), or between the *Republic of Ireland* (with its capital in Dublin) and *Northern Ireland* (with its capital in Belfast). Likewise, distinguish between *England* (a country in Western Europe), *Great Britain* (an island including the countries of England, Scotland and Wales), and the *United Kingdom* (a political union that includes the countries of England, Scotland, Wales and Northern Ireland).

Date

For public media, use Arabic numbers in the traditional month–day–year format: *Jan. 2, 2007; March 15, 1997.* Optional for organizational media is the usage of *15 March 2007.* Do not use ordinal numbers with dates: *May 1* (not *May 1st*); *April 7* (not *April 7th*).

Abbreviate months with more than five letters (*Jan., Feb., Aug., Sept., Oct., Nov., Dec.*) when the specific date is included. Spell out each month when it is used alone or with a year only: *next September, December 2008.* Do not use a comma to separate the year from a month without a date: *January 2007.*

To indicate a span of years, use an *s* without an apostrophe: *throughout the 1990s, founded in the 1800s.* Lowercase *century* in most usages: *21st century, the last century.*

Write out days of the week when used with the date: *Monday, Dec. 16, 2002.*

Presume the reference *A.D.* unless the reader is likely to become confused. Use the *10th century* rather than the *10th century A.D.* The abbreviation refers to the phrase *anno Domini* (Latin = in the year of the Lord) and is computed on the birth of Jesus, though in common usage it does not have a religious connotation. An alternative term is *C.E.*, referring to the *Common Era.*

B.C. is the traditional designation for years and centuries prior to the A.D. era. The term refers to *Before Christ.* This is the common usage for public media. An alternative and more inclusive term is *B.C.E.*, *Before the Common Era.*

A.D. or C.E. time is computed by adding from the zero point, while B.C. or B.C.E. time is computed by subtracting from the zero point.

Dateline

These designations at the beginning of a news release indicate the place of origin for the release. For U.S. datelines, use city (all capital letters), state abbreviation (caps and lowercase), followed by a dash: *MEMPHIS, Tenn.—Police arrested . . .* For Canadian datelines, use city (all capital letters) and province name (caps and lowercase) [but not the country name], dash: *KINGSTON, Ontario—Officials expected . . .* For other foreign datelines, use city (all caps), country (caps and lowercase), dash: *SAN JOSE, Costa Rica—Authorities investigated . . .*

Some cities are well known regionally, nationally or internationally and may stand alone without the state/province/country designation. Consult the AP Stylebook for a listing of these cities. Let common sense prevail. For datelines in regional releases, omit the state if it is not needed for clarity.

Dimension and Size

Use figures for dimensions, but spell out terms such as *inches* and *feet.* Do not use hyphens or commas. *She is 5 feet 7 inches tall. The carpet measures 6 feet by 9 feet.* However, use hyphens when using as compound adjectives before a noun: *the 5-foot-7-inch woman, the 6-by-9 carpet.*

Use technical forms (an apostrophe to indicate feet and quotation mark to indicate inches; *x* to indicate length and width) only in charts or graphs: *10'11½" platform, 6 × 9 carpet.* Use figures for sizes: *a size 7 dress, 10W shoe.*

Enumeration and Sequence

Use capitals and numerals for numbers of rooms, suites and apartments: *Room 7, Apartment 15B, Channel 7, Route 90.* Use capitals and numerals for parts of a whole: *Chapter 6, Page 17, Section B.* Exception: *a Page One story.* Use *Act 2* to refer to the second act. Abbreviate *number* and use a numeral to indicate rank: *No. 1 draft choice.*

Foreign Personal Name

Use spelling according to the individual's preference, if known, or use the nearest English phonetic equivalent: *Alexander Solzhenitsyn*, not *Aleksandr Solzhenitzyn.* If the name has no close equivalent in English, spell it phonetically to approximate the sound in the original language: *Anwar Sadat.*

Follow an individual's preference in using foreign names. Arabs often use two or three names, but on second reference use the final name in the series. *Amed Butros Yamani* on first reference; *Yamani* on subsequent references. Some Arab names include al- or el-. For example, the ruler of Qatar is *Hamad bin Khalifa bin Hamad Al-Thani*. Hamad is his personal name, he is the son of Khalifa who in turn was the son of Hamad. The family name is Al-Thani. In writing, refer to him either as *Sheik Hamad, Prince Hamad* or *Emir Hamad*, or in news-style writing refer to him as *Al-Thani*.

The official Chinese spelling system known as Pinyin eliminates hyphens previously used in many names. *Mao Zedung* rather than *Mao Tse-Tung*. Keep the traditional hyphenated spelling for well-known historical names such as *Sun Yat-sen*.

Chinese and Japanese names traditionally place the family name first, followed by the personal name. Keep this format for Chinese names. However, for Western audiences, Japanese names are usually revised toward the Western style (personal name first, then family name).

Foreign Place Name

Use spelling from Webster's New World Dictionary or National Geographic Atlas of the World.

Foreign Word

Use sparingly. If the meaning is clear and usage is common, write foreign words without explanation in the text: *bon voyage*. If foreign words or phrases are not commonly known, use quotation marks and provide an explanation in parentheses. *"We will soon have peace, insha'Allah (God-willing)," said the ambassador.*

Geographic Region

Capitalize specific regions: *Midwest, Northeast, West Coast, South Atlantic*. Capitalize words derived from geographic regions: *Western decor, Southern politician, Mediterranean climate, an Easterner.*

Capitalize geographic adjectives that are part of a proper noun: *Northern Ireland, West Indies, North Carolina*. Use lowercase to indicate geographic sections within an area: *northern France, central Mississippi*. (Exception: *Southern California* is a widely used designation that is capitalized.)

Use lowercase to indicate direction: *She traveled south. They hiked northwest.*

Both *Middle East* is preferable to *Mideast*, and includes the following countries: Afghanistan, Cyprus, Egypt, Iran, Iraq, Israel, Kuwait, Jordan, Lebanon, Oman, Qatar, Saudi Arabia, South Yemen, Sudan, Syria, Turkey, United Arab Emirates and Yemen.

Government

Capitalize *House of Representatives, Senate, Assembly, Legislature, Parliament, Ministry of Justice, Supreme Court, Board of Supervisors, City Council*, and so on, when the term refers to a specific governmental body.

Retain capitalization when condensed forms of the term clearly refer to a particular governmental body: *the Securities and Exchange Commission* (first reference), *the Commission* (subsequent references).

For public media, use lowercase when these terms stand alone generically: *Many city councils throughout the state . . .* For organizational media, use of capital letters is optional.

Capitalize *City, County, State, National, Provincial, Federal* and so on, when the term is used as part of a formal name: *Federal Communications Commission, St. Louis City Council, the Chamber of Deputies, Ontario Provincial Police.* Use lowercase in other references: *the city official, 25 counties in the state.*

Capitalize *Constitution* when it refers to the U.S. Constitution, regardless of whether the *U.S.* designation is used. For references to constitutions of states and other nations, capitalize only if it is preceded by the name of the state or nation: *the Kansas Constitution, Poland's Constitution* (but *the constitution of Poland*).

Capitalize sections of the U.S. Constitution: *Bill of Rights, Second Amendment, the Preamble.* Capitalize *Congress* when it refers to the U.S. Congress; use lowercase for *congressional.* Capitalize *Capitol* when it refers to the building in the District of Columbia or to state capitols.

Historic Period or Event

Capitalize names of commonly recognized eras such as *Bronze Age* or *Atomic Age.* Capitalize names of events such as the *Boston Tea Party, Great Depression, Prohibition, War of 1812.* But capitalize only proper nouns or adjectives when referring to general descriptions of a period: *classical Greece, ancient Egypt, the Victorian era.* See Date entry.

Holidays and Holy Days

Capitalize the name of holidays and holy days: *Groundhog Day, Christmas Eve, Passover, Ramadan, Memorial Day.* Use an apostrophe for days such as *New Year's Eve, All Saints' Day, April Fool's Day.* Exceptions: *Veterans Day, Presidents Day.*

Home Town

Do not use commas when designating the home town of a person or organization when the word *of* is used: *Lee Chang of Chicago said . . .; Harder Sporting Goods of Williamsport built . . .*

Hyphen

This punctuation indicates a connection between words or parts of words. Use it to prevent confusion. Use a hyphen to connect compound modifiers before a noun: *a first-rate story, a part-time job.* But usually the same word combinations are not hyphenated when they occur after the noun: *The story is first rate. His job is only part time.*

Use a hyphen to connect phrases used as modifiers before a noun: *her don't-give-me-attitude look.*

Use a hyphen in suspended situations, with a space after the hyphen in the suspended usage: *a six- to 10-month waiting period.*

Use a hyphen with the following prefixes: *all-, anti-, ex-, out-, post-, pro-, self-.* Use a hyphen with *co-* when referring to occupation or status. Do not use a hyphen with the following prefixes: *ante, bi, extra, half, in, multi, mini, non, over, pre, re, semi, sub, super, un.* An exception to this is if the prefix creates a double letter, which would be confusing without the hyphen: *re-elect, over-rated, pre-existing.*

Do not use a hyphen with the following suffixes: *like, fold, wide, wise.* An exception to this is if the suffix causes a triple letter, which would be confusing without the hyphen: *shell-like.*

Do not use a hyphen following *very* or following an adverb ending in *ly.*

Inclusive Language

In general, avoid language that unnecessarily excludes groups or is biased about gender, race, religion, age or physical condition. Try to use inclusive words. However, avoid awkward-sounding or unconventional words that draw attention to their inclusiveness. Avoid *he or she, him or her, his or hers.* For public media, avoid *s/he* and *he/she*, although these may be appropriate for internal (especially business) media.

Internet

The *Internet* (capitalized) is a decentralized worldwide network of computers, also known as the *Net*. The *World Wide Web* (capitalized) is a global system linking documents, images and other files using the Internet. The *Web* is an acceptable shorter form. *Web site* is capitalized and used as two words, but derivative words are not capitalized: *webcast, webmaster.*

Observe correct punctuation when using an Internet address: *www.buffalostate.edu, yahoo.com.* Use a period following the address when it ends a sentence. If an Internet address does not fit entirely on a line, break it at a natural point but do not add a hyphen or other punctuation mark.

Use a lowercase prefix for terms such as *e-mail, e-commerce* and *e-philanthropy.* Use *dot-com* as an informal adjective describing a company that does business on the Internet.

Addresses for the Internet follow a protocol of the Uniform Resource Locator (URL). Various categories of Internet addresses have specific suffices: *com* for commercial enterprises, *org* for nonprofit organizations, *edu* for educational institutions, *gov* for government agencies, *mil* for military sites, *net* for network operators, and *int* for international organizations. Other sites use a suffix indicating the country in which they are based. Some of the common national suffixes are *jp* for Japan, *ca* for Canada, *au* for Australia, *fr* for France, *es* for Spain, and *il* for Israel. Some less familiar national suffixes include *az* for Azerbaijan, *va* for Vatican City, *bf* for Burkina Faso, *gl* for Greenland, and *zw* for Zimbabwe. Additionally, there are some special URL suffixes to designate American Indian sites that use the suffix *nsn* (Native sovereign nation) such as *hopi.nsn.us, mohegan.nsn.us* or *rosebudsiouxtribe.nsn.us.*

Military

Capitalize names of military organizations when referring to U.S. forces, regardless of whether the designation U.S. is used: *He served in the Army. She is an ensign in the U.S. Coast Guard. Congress is debating Navy policy.*

Capitalize military titles when they appear as a title before a name; do not capitalize such titles in other situations. For print media, abbreviate most military ranks when used before a name: *Gen., Adm., Cmdr., Maj., Capt., Sgt., Cpl.* Do not abbreviate qualifiers for such terms: *Lance Cpl., Master Sgt.* Exceptions: *Ensign, Seaman, Petty Officer, Airman.* Also, do not abbreviate complex forms of such terms: *Senior Airman, Petty Officer 1st Class.* Do not abbreviate any military titles for broadcast media.

Both *Marines* and *Marine Corps* are appropriate terms. Do not use abbreviations such as *U.S.A.F.* or *U.S.M.C.*

Do not abbreviate titles standing alone without a name.

Use short titles before a name: *Lt. Jones retired . . . Adm. Marvin attended . . .* Use longer titles following the name: *Lewis, a petty officer 2nd class, was . . .*

Money

Use lowercase with names of money, both American and foreign: *dollar, nickel, euro, yen, peso, Canadian dollar.*

In general, round off amounts of money to the nearest dollar without using a decimal: *$25*, not *$25.00*. If it is necessary to designate cents less than a dollar, use numerals and the word *cents: 5 cents*. For amounts more than a dollar, use the dollar sign and decimal: *$1.05*.

For dollar amounts less than $1 million, use the dollar sign and numbers: *$250, $198,750*. For dollar amounts of $1 million or more, use the dollar sign and numerals up to two decimal places with the appropriate word: *$3 million, $5.25 billion*.

Do not use a hyphen when using dollar amounts as nouns: *$10 million*. Do not use a hyphen with *million* or *billion* used as a compound adjective: *the $10 million surplus*.

Do not use the dollar sign for informal expressions: *I feel like a million bucks. She has a million-dollar smile.*

Number

Write out cardinal numbers below 10: *one, five, nine*. Use numerals for cardinal numbers of 10 or above: *15, 103, 5,372*. (For exceptions, see the following entries: Age, Date, Dimension and Size, Enumeration and Sequence, Money, Time, and Weight.)

For print media, use numerals and words without a hyphen for rounded cardinal numbers of 1 million or above: *5 million, 6.5 billion*. For specific cardinal numbers above 1 million when the exact number is important, use numerals only: *a city of 2,378,525*.

For broadcast media, use hyphenated numerals and words as the number should be pronounced for cardinal numbers above 100: *one-hundred-and-three, 86-thousand spectators, 14-thousand dollars*.

Numerals should not begin a sentence. *Fifty-seven people attended.* To prevent an awkward sentence beginning with a long number, rewrite the sentence. *More than 11,000 people attended.*

With ordinal numbers, use numerals: *1st, 115th*. (Exception: Spell out commonly used ordinal numbers: *First Amendment, second base*.)

Use Roman numerals to designate sequences for wars and for people: *World War I, Queen Elizabeth II, Pope Benedict XVI*. In using Roman numerals, I = 1, V = 5, X = 10, L = 50, C = 100, M = 1,000.

For fractions, spell out amounts less than one and use a hyphen: *one-fourth, two-thirds*. Use numerals for fractions greater than one: *1½, 4⅔*. Or translate fractions greater than one into decimals.

Within text, percentages should be written as figures: *0.8 percent, 1 percent, 7.5 percent*. Write out the word *percent* within text. In statistical matter, the percent sign (%) may be used without a space following the number.

Ratios should be used with the word *to*: *student–teacher ratio of 25-to-1*. Odds and election or competition results are used without the word *to*: *3–2 against her*; *vote of 675–346*; *a 27–23 victory*.

Do not use numerals for casual references to numbers: *I've told you a million times*.

Organizational Name

On first reference, spell out the full name of an organization. Do not immediately follow the full name with an abbreviation in parentheses. On subsequent reference, use initials or organizational abbreviations with no periods: *IBM, PTA*.

In unusual situations, follow the organization's preference: *eBay, Toys R Us*.

For public media, abbreviate common terms for business organizations (*Co., Inc., Corp., Bros., Ltd.*) when they are used with a specific name: *Robotron Inc., Boffo Corp.* When they stand alone without an organization's name, do not abbreviate such terms.

Spell out *association* in all instances: *Benjamin County Lung Association*.

For public media, use lower case generic names when designating organizational groupings: *biology department, marketing section, sales division, board of directors*. Capitalize proper names in such a context: *English department, Japan division*. Capitalize organizational groupings if the structure is unusual or unique to the organization: *General Assembly of the United Nations, Standing Council of Canonical Orthodox Bishops*.

For organizational media, capitalization of organizational groupings is optional.

Commonly used alternatives may be used in place of lengthy formal names. *U.S. Department of Defense, Defense Department* and *the Pentagon* all refer to the same government agency.

Period

Do not use periods with the initials of well-known organizations and individuals: *CIA, PRSA, UNESCO, JFK*.

Use periods with abbreviations of states and nations: *W.Va., U.K.* Do not use a space between the letters.

Use periods with *U.S.* and *U.N.* when these are used as adjectives: *U.S. Mint, U.N. secretary-general*. Do not use a space between the letters.

Personal Name

For public print media, use the following order: first name or initial; middle initial(s) or middle name(s); surname; qualifiers such as *Jr.* or *III* with no commas: *Robert L. Marsteen Jr.*; *J. Winston McNamara*; *C.J. Johnson*. Do not use a space between two consecutive initials.

Generally, a woman should be identified by her own first name rather than that of her husband: *Dawn Smith* rather than *Mrs. Ronald Smith*.

For public broadcast media, common practice is to use only the first name and surname. *Robert Marsteen* (instead of *Robert L. Marsteen Jr.*). An exception to this is when the individual is commonly known by a more complete name: *Martin Luther King, Michael J. Fox*.

For all public media, generally use full names, unless people are well known by single names: *Moby, Madonna, Eminem, Ludacris*. Avoid using nicknames unless these are used consistently and professionally by the individual: *Jimmy Carter, 50 Cent, Magic Johnson, Ice*

T, Meat Loaf. For organizational media, the use of middle initials and nicknames is optional. Use quotation marks around a nickname when the full name is given: *Paul "Bear" Bryant, Eric "E-Train" Lindros.*

For foreign names, use the foreign spelling when it is familiar to the reader: *José Canseco.* Otherwise use spelling and pronunciation guides that approximate English usage. If there is no English equivalent, use an English spelling that approximates the pronunciation of the name.

Place Name

For towns and cities, write out terms in place names such as *Point, Fort, Mount.* Abbreviate Saint in place names: *St. Louis, Port St. Lucie, Sault Ste. Marie.* Exception: *Saint John, New Brunswick.*

Politics

Capitalize the names of political parties, whether they are used as a noun or an adjective: *that Republican, this Socialist candidate, the Democratic platform.* Capitalize the word *party* when it used with the specific name: *the Reform Party.*

Use lowercase when the term refers to a political philosophy: *conservative cause, liberal agenda, democratic ideals.*

When political-party affiliation is relevant, use the full party designation before or after the name: *Democratic Assemblyman Kim Chang . . . Assemblyman Kim Chang, a Democrat . . .* Or use abbreviations for the party and the state or district: *Kim Chang (D-Colo.).* (Note the lack of a period with the party affiliation.)

Proper Noun

Capitalize any proper nouns that refer to a specific person, place or thing: *Susquehanna River, Willamette Valley, Pendleton Ballroom.*

For public media, use lowercase when the noun stands alone: *river, valley, ballroom.* For organizational media, use of the lowercase on subsequent reference is optional.

Capitalize the word *church* when it is used in reference to a denomination: *The doctrine of the Episcopal Church includes . . .* Capitalize the word when the proper name is used in reference to a specific congregation or parish: *St. Timothy Episcopal Church is located . . .* But use lowercase when it refers to a building without the proper name: *An Episcopal church is located . . .*

Professional Credentials

Do not use professional credentials for public media. For organizational media, use them sparingly. If they are necessary and recognized by readers, place them after a name, set off by commas and used without periods: *Ronald D. Smith, APR.* See Academic Degree.

Pronoun Agreement

Indefinite pronouns use the form of the verb that agrees with their meaning. Some indefinite pronouns are singular: *each, everyone, nobody,* etc. Singular pronouns take singular verbs: *Nobody is happy about this.*

Other indefinite pronouns are plural: *both, few, many, several.* Plural pronouns take plural verbs: *Few are happy about this.*

Some indefinite pronouns can be either singular or plural: *all, any, most, none, some.* These pronouns take the verb appropriate to the meaning of the prepositional phrase following the pronoun: *Some of the candy was gone. Most of the people were happy to see her.*

Quotation Mark

Place quotation marks before and after all quoted matter. Periods and commas always precede closing quotation marks. Question marks and exclamation points are placed before closing quotation marks if they apply only to the material being quoted. They follow quotation marks if they apply to the entire sentence.

Quotation marks are not needed in formats clearly identified as questions and answers.

For quoted materials that run more than a single paragraph, use open quotation marks at the beginning of each paragraph but use the closing quotation mark only at the end of the final paragraph.

For news release formats, a quotation usually begins a paragraph. Generally, the attribution follows the quoted sentence or is inserted within the quoted sentence(s): *"I hear you," she said. "But I don't like what you are saying."*

Use quotation marks around the names of songs, plays, computer games, television and radio programs, poems, speeches, and works of art. Do not use quotation marks for names of magazines, newspapers or reference materials such as dictionaries, handbooks and encyclopedias. For journalism-orientated materials such as news releases, follow AP Style and use quotation marks for names of books. In more literacy publications such as books, use italics for names of books. For organizational media such as brochures, Web publications, and so on, adopt a cconsistent style. See Title of Composition.

Race, Ethnicity and Nationality

Capitalize proper names (either as nouns or adjectives) of races, nationalities, tribes, peoples, etc.: *Arab, Jewish, Caucasian, Sioux history, Nordic pride.* Lowercase informal terms for race: *black, white, mulatto.* Do not mention race unless it is pertinent to the story; avoid derogatory racial and ethnic terms. When pertinent, use terms of personal heritage that are preferred by members of the group. Avoid terms that are outdated or those that may cause offense.

Both *American Indian* and *Native American* are acceptable umbrella terms, but try to be specific: *Navajo tribal official, Ojibwa writer, Yakama journalist.* Avoid potentially offensive terms such as *squaw* and *warpath.* Capitalize the names of American Indian tribes and nations: *Arawak, Cherokee, Hopi, Seneca Nation of Indians.*

Hispanic and *Latino* are umbrella terms, encompassing specific ethnicities such as *Cuban, Dominican, Puerto Rican* and *Chilean.* Note that people from Portugal and Brazil are Latino but not Hispanic. Avoid *Chicano* as a pejorative term.

State Name

Do not abbreviate the name of one of the 50 United States when is it used without a city name within text, either as a noun or adjective. Within text, use common abbreviations (right columns, below) when the state is used with a city or town or with a military base: *Watertown,*

N.Y., *Patuxent River Naval Air Station*, *Md.* For mailing purposes, use the official two-letter postal abbreviations (left columns, below) for states and U.S. territories.

AL	Ala.	NE	Neb.
AK	Alaska	NV	Nev.
AZ	Ariz.	NH	N.H.
AR	Ark.	NJ	N.J.
CA	Calif.	NM	N.M.
CO	Colo.	NY	N.Y.
CT	Conn.	NC	N.C.
DC	District of Columbia	ND	N.D.
DE	Del.	OH	Ohio
FL	Fla.	OK	Okla.
GA	Ga.	OR	Ore.
GU	Guam	PA	Pa.
HI	Hawaii	PR	Puerto Rico
ID	Idaho	RI	R.I.
IL	Ill.	SC	S.C.
IA	Iowa	SD	S.D.
KS	Kan.	TN	Tenn.
KY	Ky.	TX	Texas
LA	La.	UT	Utah
ME	Maine	VT	Vt.
MD	Md.	VA	Va.
MA	Mass.	VI	Virgin Islands
MI	Mich.	WA	Wash.
MN	Minn.	WV	W.Va.
MS	Miss.	WI	Wis.
MO	Mo.	WY	Wyo.
MT	Mont.		

Use *New York state* to distinguish it from *New York City*, and *Washington state* to distinguish it from *Washington, D.C.* In such uses, the word *state* is not capitalized because it is not part of the formal name. However, use capitals for the names of government agencies, such as *New York State Board of Regents*.

Use the common abbreviation when it intrudes into a proper noun: *The Sacramento (Calif.) Bee, Lock Haven (Pa.) University*.

Time

For print media, use figures with lowercase designations: *7:30 p.m.* Use the simple form for hourly designations: *10 a.m.* rather than *10:00 a.m.* An exception to the use of figures is to write out *noon* rather than *12 a.m.* and *midnight* instead of *12 p.m.*

For broadcast media, use conversational time designations: *10 o'clock this morning, 7:30 every night.*

Title of Composition

Capitalize principal words of composition titles (plays, articles, television programs, movies, songs, computer games, works of art and speeches). Place quotation marks around such composition titles. Do not underline or italicize titles of compositions. For journalism-orientated materials such as news releases, follow AP Style and use quotation marks for names of books. In more literacy publications such as books, usse italics for names of books. For organizational media such as brochures, Web publications, and so on, adopt a consistent style.

Capitalize but do not use quotation marks with reference books such as catalogs, dictionaries, almanacs, encyclopedias and handbooks or with periodicals such as newspapers and magazines. Also, capitalize but do not use quotation marks with religious scriptures such as the Bible or the Quran.

Capitalize the word *the* when it is part of the formal and preferred name of a periodical: *The Wall Street Journal.*

Capitalize the word *magazine* only if it is an official part of the title: *Newsweek magazine, Harper's Magazine.*

Title of People (Courtesy Title)

Courtesy titles are polite designations of personal and marital status. First names and surnames used without courtesy titles are the preferred usage for first reference. Do not indicate marital status unless it is pertinent to the piece being written.

For subsequent references for men, the surname without the courtesy title *Mr.* is preferred. For subsequent references for women, the traditional practice remains common to use the courtesy title—*Mrs., Miss, Ms.*—according to the woman's preference, followed by the surname. For subsequent references to married couples, use courtesy titles for both husband and wife: *Mr. and Mrs. Jones.*

Do not use *Mr.* (except as *Mr. and Mrs. Jones*). Do not indicate marital status unless it is pertinent to the piece being written.

For organizational media, it is common to use the courtesy title with the surname for subsequent references. Use *Mr.* for men, and *Mrs., Miss* or *Ms.* according to the woman's preference. These abbreviations may be used for both print and broadcast media.

Generally, courtesy titles are not used for people under the age of 18. Instead, use the child's first name.

For print media, abbreviate *Junior* and *Senior* after a name and use without commas: *Emmanuel Lee Jr.* Do not abbreviate these titles for broadcast media.

Title of People (Formal Title)

Formal titles are governmental, professional or religious designations that are an integral part of the identity of an individual. In general, capitalize the title when they are used before the name and as part of the name, but use lowercase if titles stand alone or are used after the name.

For both internal and public media, capitalize formal titles when they appear before the name, but use lowercase when the title is used without the name: *President Bush said . . . The president said . . .*

Most titles of government officials are written out rather than abbreviated: *mayor, president, prime minister, king.* A few common governmental titles are abbreviated for print media when they are used before a full name or a surname: *Gov. Anne Crosby-Jones, Sen. Nathaniel Stern, Rep. Seneca.* Do not abbreviate these titles when they are used without the name or in any usages for broadcast media.

Do not abbreviate titles of religion: *bishop, rabbi, monsignor, father, sister, brother, imam, mullah.* An exception to this is *Rev.*, which is abbreviated and used as an adjective with the word *the: the Rev. Lee Breckenridge.*

For print media, abbreviate most military ranks when used with a name: *Gen., Adm., Cmdr., Maj., Capt., Sgt., Cpl.* Exceptions: *ensign, seaman, petty officer, airman.* Do not abbreviate any military titles for broadcast media.

Do not abbreviate academic titles such as *dean, professor* and *chancellor: Professor Marta Borodin.*

Do not abbreviate qualifiers: *Associate Justice Jaime Gonzalez, Assistant Professor Marc Tannenbaum.* Capitalize formal qualified titles before the name, but do not capitalize informal qualifiers: *He met with acting Mayor Jones.*

For all print media, abbreviate *Dr.* Spell out *doctor* as a title with a name when writing for broadcast media. Because readers of general publications will probably presume that the title of doctor refers to someone with a medical degree, be clear if you are referring to someone with an academic degree. Do not use the title of doctor for someone holding an honorary degree.

For organizational media, abbreviations of formal titles and their use on subsequent reference are optional.

For public media, do not repeat a title for a man on subsequent reference: *Mayor Kevin O'Mally said.* . . (first reference). *O'Mally said.* . . (subsequent references). As an exception to this guideline, repeat the title of persons known only by a religious name: *Patriarch Theodosius, Mother Teresa.*

For women, use a courtesy title or a religious title with the surname on subsequent reference, unless the woman prefers not to have the title used: *Mayor Maureen A. O'Mally said* . . . (first reference). *Mrs. O'Mally said.* . . or *O'Mally said.* . . (subsequent references). For organizational media, use of titles on subsequent reference is optional.

Formal titles of honor generally are not used for public media. For organizational media, it is appropriate to use both forms of religious titles such as *Father Joseph Martin* or *Pastor Soo* as well as more formal titles, such as *the Right Rev. Joseph Martin.* It also is appropriate to use titles of nobility and prestige in organizational media: *His Honor, Her Majesty, His Eminence, Her Royal Highness.*

Formal titles sometimes are used following the name. Lengthy titles should follow rather than precede the name.

For public media, do not capitalize formal titles used after the name: *Julio Castaneda, the senator from Texas; Eugenie Buchanan, professor of fine arts.* For organizational media, capitalization of formal titles that follow the name is optional.

Title of People (Functional Title)

Functional titles are descriptions of an individual according to an occupation or a role within an organization. *CEO* is an acceptable title, but spell out similar job titles such as *chief financial officer.*

Short functional titles may be used either before or after the name. Use no commas when they are placed before the name, but use commas when they follow the name: *Newspaper editor Pierre Mercier said* . . . *Pierre Mercier, the newspaper editor, said* . . .

Long functional titles should follow the name and should be set off by commas: *Evelyn Brown, senior director for public affairs, said . . . Mitsuo Ogawa, interim vice president for administration, will begin . . .*

For public media, do not capitalize functional titles preceding or following the name. For organizational media, capitalization of functional titles is optional.

Weight

Use figures for weights, but spell out terms such as *pounds* and *grams*. Do not use hyphens, but use commas to separate categories. *The baby weighs 8 pounds, 11 ounces.* However use hyphens and no comma when using a compound adjective before a noun: *the 8-pound 11-ounce baby.*

Appendix B

Copy Editing

Following are common copyediting symbols. use them during the proofreading stage of writing in preparing copy for it's final, publishable version.

Abbreviate: Draw a circle around the word to be abbreviated: Saint Paul's Church.

Add letters to a word: Write in the miss letters.

Apostrophe: Write in an apostrophe above the line: Editing is a writers tool.

Boldface: Draw a squiggled underline to set in boldface

Capitalize: Draw three lines below the letter(s) or word(s) to indicate capitals: Becoming a public Relations Writer

Center: Indicate brackets on each side:]centre[

Colon: Draw a circle around a colon at the place where it should be inserted, such as before a listing ⊙

Comma: Write in a comma below the line at the place where it should be inserted: Within a sentence add a comma.

Dash: Write a horizontal line with vertical marks on both sides to indicate a dash.

Delete a letter and close up the space: Draw a slash with a bridge to delete a letter

Delete one or more words and close up the space: Draw a horizontal line and a bridge to delete the words that may be unnecessary.

Extensive deletions: Draw horizontal lines through the text to be deleted and draw guidelines from the end of the previous section to the beginning of the subsequent section.

Flush left: [Indicate a bracket with the solid side on the left.

Flush right: Indicate a bracket with the solid side on the right]

Hyphen: Use short double horizontal lines to indicate a hyphen: full service bank.

Insert: Add a mising letter or a/word

Italics: Draw a straight <u>underline</u> to set text in italics.

Lowercase: Draw a slash through the letter to indicate lowercase: Beoming a Public RElations Writer.

Numbers (Change from words to numerals): (fifteen) books.

Numbers (Change from numerals to words): (9) pigeons

Paragraph indent: . . . one sentence ends. | Another paragraph begins.

Paragraph run-in: . . . one sentence ends.⌐
       ⌐Another paragraph begins.

Period: Draw a circle around a period at the place where it should be inserted, such as at the end of a sentence⊙

Question Mark: Draw in a question mark: Why he wanted to know.

Quotation marks: Insert quotation marks, I said.

Semicolon: Write in a semicolon below the line at the place where it should be inserted: . . . so ends the clause a new clause begins

Space (add): Use a vertical line to indicate space: Add a needed space.

Space (close up): Draw a bridge to eliminate a space: Close up an unnecessary space.

Spell out: Draw a circle around a word to spell out an abbreviation; the First (St.) Station.

Transpose: Draw a backward S to transpose lettres or to words transpose.

Undo a change: *stet* (Latin for "let it stand").

Verification (punctuation): Place a check mark above a punctuation mark to verify unusual placement . . . in colours of red, brown, blue and green, and yellow.

Verification (spelling): Draw a circle around the word OK to verify unusual spelling: James R. Smeth

Appendix C

Careers in Public Relations

Public relations is a growing field, ripe with opportunities for employment and advancement. Labor analysts predict that the demand for public relations practitioners will grow at least as fast as the general employment scene, and faster than many jobs. That's good news for the public relations student. The job search may take a while, but it can be successful.

Public relations has a promising future. Most corporations and nonprofit organizations have public relations departments. In smaller organizations, public relations projects may be handled by employees who have more than additional jobs, often involving marketing, human resources, fundraising, recruitment, and other areas of contact with the public. Money magazine rates job opportunities in public relations as likely to increase above average over the next 10 years.

The Bureau of Labor Statistics, part of the U.S. Department of Labor, reported in 2004 that public relations managers have an average salary of $70,000. Money magazine rates public relations in the top 20 best jobs in 2006, with an average salary of $84,600 for all public relations specialists. Communication directors top the list of public relations specialties with a median salary of $127,000. Salary.com says the average annual salaries for public relations directors is $117,300; with $79,300 for public relations managers and $39,800 for entry-level public relations specialists.

The 2006 survey of credentialed public relations professionals in agencies and corporate offices reports a range of salaries: in agencies $50,000 for account executive (an entry-level position in agencies), $79,000 for account supervisor and $146 senior vice president; and in corporations $77,000 for communication specialists, $145,000 for directors and $205,000 for senior vice presidents. Perhaps more relevant for readers of this book, the National Association of Colleges and Employers reported in 2006 that salaries for entry-level jobs in public relations range from $30,300 to $40,000 for agencies and from $34,500 to $48,300 for corporations.

An older but more detailed nationwide survey by PR Week in 2000 reported averages of $76,400 for corporate public relations, $69,800 for public relations agencies, $56,400 for government, and $54,100 for nonprofit organizations. Freelancers in public relations work earned an average of $85,600, according to the survey. Among public relations specialties, crisis communication received the highest average salary of $90,100; investor relations $88,100; marketing communication $82,300; public affairs/government relations $82,200; media relations $62,300; internal communication $60,400; and community relations $54,700.

Employment analysts cite increasing opportunities for women and minorities. The PR Week survey found a proportion of 65 percent female and 35 percent male in the public relations profession. This breaks out as 91 percent white, 3.3 percent black and 2.4 percent Hispanic, low percentages for minorities. However, the PRSA salary study showed African American practitioners earning above the average, probably because they tended to be employed at supervisory positions in corporations. In public relations as in American society, a gender gap still exists in salaries. But among entry-level positions, salaries for women and men are similar, and the gap is narrowing as women build their credentials and advance through management.

Entry-Level Jobs

The PRSA Foundation, the research and education arm of PRSA, looks at five levels of job categories in public relations: technician, supervisor, manager, director and executive.

Students can expect entry-level positions that emphasize technical competence in writing and related areas. Skills typically required for such positions include proficiency in preparing brochures, memos and letters, newsletter articles, news releases, proposals, reports, scripts and speeches. Related skills include conducting research, editing and interviewing. Look for openings with job titles such as public relations writer, public affairs or public relations specialist, media relations assistant, newsletter or publications editor, or account assistant. Also look for generic job titles such as staff associate and associate director.

A career-minded novice in public relations should use an entry-level position as an opportunity to move toward the next level of positions. Cultivate interpersonal and problem-solving skills. Develop an expertise in a particular specialty such as public affairs, publications, research, investor relations or internal relations.

An excellent source of information for anyone seeking a job in public relations is the Public Relations Body of Knowledge, a compendium of articles, books and other published materials that deal with the profession. In its book, *Public Relations Professional Career Guide*, the PRSA Foundation identifies many sources of information related to the skills and knowledge expected of entry-level technicians in public relations writing and related areas. It also identifies articles associated with advanced career levels.

Coursework and Other Educational Avenues

The most useful advice for obtaining a job in public relations is to get the best education possible. The following categories of courses and knowledge/skill areas may help you plan your academic career.

Public Relations. A report by the Commission on Public Relations Education recommended four specific courses for undergraduates in a public relations minor or sequence: introduction to public relations; public relations writing and production; public relations research, measurement and evaluation; and a public relations internship. For students in an undergraduate major in public relations, the report adds the following courses to the above listing: public relations case studies, public relations campaigns, and public relations planning and management. Additionally, electives are recommended in advertising, broadcasting, photography, graphic design, persuasion and advanced media writing.

Writing. Employers consistently seek effective writers. Courses in public relations writing are especially useful, but don't stop there. Look to journalism and broadcast reporting courses. Look to courses in poetry, play writing and other types of creative writing. Investigate courses in professional and technical writing.

Organizational and Business Studies. Increasingly, public relations is seen as a profession rooted not only in the communication arts but also in management science. Business courses enhance your value to an organization, particularly courses focused on marketing, research and management.

Ethics, Problem-Solving and Critical-Thinking Skills. Traditional areas such as philosophy and literature and newer areas such as creative studies offer opportunities to develop your competence in analytical skills sought by employers.

Statistics. Painful as it may be to some creative and literary types, skill in mathematics and statistics is a vital element of the education of a public relations professional. Practitioners often deal with budgets, surveys, evaluation reports, and other topics that require proficiency in mathematics.

Liberal Arts. The Commission on Public Relations Education recommends that 60 to 75 percent of undergraduate coursework be in liberal arts, social sciences, business and language study. The Accreditation Council on Education in Journalism and Mass Communication echoes this expectation for professional programs including undergraduate public relations degrees. Employers prefer candidates who are well rounded. Expand your value to an employer by taking courses in the arts and humanities, natural and social sciences, and applied studies.

Foreign Language and Culture. Increasingly, organizations are finding themselves involved in an environment that is more global and more diverse. Public relations often is expected to lead this change. Job applicants familiar with another culture, conversant in another language, or knowledgeable about social or ethnic pluralism often catch the eye of employers. Study-abroad programs are particularly good ways to develop such cultural proficiency.

Technological Proficiency. Employers often count on the fact that college graduates may have greater computer skills than practitioners working in the field. Expose yourself as much as possible to computer applications for word processing, research, presentation, graphic design, and Internet technology.

Practical Experience. In addition to relevant courses, employers are looking for people with work experience. How do you get that before you have a job? Internships. Part-time jobs. Volunteer work. Student organizations. For example, internships often are available through colleges and universities, and many larger employers offer internships to graduates. Part-time jobs and volunteer service are other ways to gain work experience; try to use these opportunities to show what you can do in public relations projects. Student organizations, especially those related to public relations, provide opportunities for professional training. The Public Relations Student Society of America, which is affiliated with PRSA, has chapters on many campuses. IABC also has established student chapters, and many colleges and universities have independent student public relations groups unrelated to either of the two professional organizations.

Graduate School. The minimum academic qualification for a job in public relations is a bachelor's degree. Increasingly, competition for jobs includes people with master's degrees. Many universities throughout North America offer advanced studies in public relations, organizational communication and related areas. The Commission on Public Relations Education has recommended the following courses for a master's degree: communication theory, communication research, research methodology, communication in society, advanced public relations case studies, public relations management, and a thesis project or comprehensive examinations.

Job Search

There is no easy formula for landing your first job or getting a foothold in the profession of your choice. However, some techniques have been used by many job seekers and found to be effective. Following are several suggestions for breaking into jobs in public relations.

Assess Your Personal Interests. You've heard it before: Life is too short to work at a job you hate, even a well-paying job. Before you plunge into the job search, give some time for a bit of soul searching. Do you like continual change or a routine and stable environment? Do you thrive on pressure, or does it grind you down? Are you willing to relocate for a job with potential? These are questions you should answer before preparing any applications. Many types of personal inventories are available at career development offices in colleges and universities. These can help you assess your personal interests, aspirations and work styles, using the information to direct your career path.

Assess the Employment Scene. Research the field. Learn who is hiring and where the jobs are. Investigate opportunities in other parts of the country, and look into job possibilities in related fields such as marketing, research, advertising and technical writing. Explore possibilities in both corporate and nonprofit organizations, as well as agencies. Don't be afraid to ask for an information interview with a senior person in the public relations profession.

Use Your Contacts. Network. Let everyone know that you are looking for a job. Ask friends to pass along your name to their friends and colleagues who may know someone looking for an eager public relations employee. Join the student chapter of a professional organization such as PRSA or IABC, and transfer your membership to a professional chapter when you graduate. Try to participate in both local chapter meetings and national conferences. Build an expanding network of professional contacts through your internships, through shadowing and mentoring programs with practitioners, through visitors to your campus, and through contacts with alumni of your school who work in your areas of interest.

Tailor Your Cover Letter. A cover letter is your first introduction to a prospective employer. Make a strong first impression.

- *Ensure accuracy and professionalism.* Send an original letter, never a photocopy. Make sure there are no misspellings, smudges or other imperfections. Present a professional tone that reflects you without being humorous, overly confident, curt or avant garde.
- *Address the cover letter to a real person.* This is more effective than sending it to a nameless office holder such as Personnel Director or Public Affairs Manager. A quick

search of the organization's Web site or a telephone call to the receptionist should yield the name you need.

- *Indicate your interest in the position.* State where you heard about the opening. Indicate why you are interested in this job, and express confidence that you can do it effectively. Keep the focus on what you can do for the organization rather than on your need for a job.
- *Briefly describe your philosophical approach.* Indicate what you think about this type of work, its importance, and your commitment to it.
- *Summarize your qualifications.* Tell how they relate to the particular job for which you are applying. Pull out the two or three items from your résumé that highlight your competence for this particular position.
- *Ask for an interview.* End the cover letter with a specific request to obtain a response or to meet with the employer. If it is appropriate, offer to telephone for an appointment, or ask for a formal application.

Build a Portfolio. Every applicant for a public relations job should have a comprehensive portfolio of writing samples, graphic designs and other relevant materials. At a minimum, this should include several news releases. Ideally, it also will include a brochure, direct-mail package, fact sheet, newsletter article, opinion piece, pitch letter and public relations advertisement. Include a planning sheet for each piece of writing to give some context. If possible, also include clippings related to news releases and fact sheets. Display the portfolio in a professional-looking binder, with plastic page sheathes to display your writing and other materials.

Develop a Résumé. Every job seeker needs a quality résumé, a listing of professional credentials and experience. This should be tightly written to highlight your strengths.

- *Keep the résumé to a single page.* This is sufficient for new graduates and other entry-level job seekers. One way of accomplishing this is to use résumé language that features action statements such as "edited newsletter" or "conducted research" rather than complete sentences.
- *Use a summary rather than an objective.* Traditional résumé objectives focus on *what you want*, such as "position in public relations" or "challenging writing position with opportunity for advancement." Instead, consider using a personal summary highlighting *what you have to offer*. For example: "Recent graduate & agency intern familiar with research techniques. Background includes diverse writing skills. Able to clearly present technical material. Experience with PRSSA accounts. Degree in public relations." That would be much more interesting to a potential employer than "College grad seeks entry-level position in public relations."
- *Design the résumé for eye appeal.* Especially in the field of public relations, where appearance is important and where design ability is expected, would-be employers expect résumés that look professional. Use quality paper. Bold or underlined section heads with bullet items can be useful. People read from the left, so use the left side of the sheet for the most important information; save details such as inclusive dates for less-prominent positions.
- *Avoid gimmicks.* Neon-colored paper, personal brochures, techno typeface and bizarre graphics may be attention getters, but they often fail to generate a positive response. Stick with conventional and professional styles.

- *Avoid hype words.* Control the urge to call yourself "a dynamic, self-motivated go-getter" and avoid other such hyperbolic statements. Arrogance, self-praise and inflated ego have no place in a résumé. Instead use objective words, numbers and strong verbs. Give examples of past success.

- *Use buzzwords.* Showing that you know the language can attract the attention of the person initially screening applications. Consider what is expected for the job you are applying for, and then use words to address those expectations. High on the list of most public relations employers are the following words: analyze, design, edit, evaluate, plan, research and write.

- *List professional experience.* Include paid employment, internships, volunteer work and military service. Indicate the company or organizational name, job title, and dates (years, or months and years) of employment. If you have many part-time or summer jobs unrelated to public relations, summarize these under one heading. List your professional experience concisely, using bullets and brief action statements. Don't exaggerate or use minute detail. Focus on tangible tasks rather than broad job categories, and use strong action verbs. Indicate not only your work projects but also their results. For example: "Increased student agency accounts by 35 percent." Many résumés present experience in reverse chronological order focused on jobs. An alternative is to focus on areas of skill or achievement, such as separate sections on writing, editing and research, followed by a brief work history.

- *List educational achievements.* Include the name of your school, major, degree, awards and special concentrations of study. Indicate your grade average if it is noteworthy (3.0 or better on a 4.0 scale). List your most recent education first. Do not list high school unless it adds a particular credential, such as Academy for Visual Arts if you are citing experience in design. If you do not have much work experience, list relevant courses, using generic course titles, and don't overlook nonmajor courses in business, language and other disciplines.

- *List professional affiliations and memberships.* Even in an entry-level job search, you can show involvements with job-relevant organizations.

- *Provide an e-mail contact.* You may have to establish a new e-mail, if you have been relying on one provided by your college or university. Also, be careful about the name you choose. SuperKrak, Btchsbk, LilMama and StudMonkey may be fine for e-mails to friends, but they don't create the professional impression you need for business purposes.

- *Be selective with personal information.* Language fluency, computer skills and other personal capabilities relevant to employment should be listed. List organizational and volunteer activities if they are relevant to public relations or if they show leadership experience. Hobbies, political involvement, religious affiliation, marital status and other such personal information are out of bounds in a job search.

- *Do not list personal references.* Save these for a separate sheet including names, postal addresses, e-mail contacts and telephone numbers for people who have indicated their willingness to give you a good recommendation. Always ask permission to list a reference, and don't be shy about asking if that person feels comfortable about giving you a positive recommendation. Don't waste space on the résumé with the obvious note that references are available on request.

Prepare for Your Interview. Employers tell of hundreds of applications submitted for a single job opening. Obviously, the cover letter and résumé are the initial screening devices. The competition is tough, but a few of the standouts make it through. If you are lucky enough to get an interview, make the most of it.

- *Research your interviewer.* Find out all you can about the organization: its mission, reputation and activities. Investigate its standing within the community, perhaps with a call to the Chamber of Commerce or the Better Business Bureau. Do an online computer search to see if the organization has been in the news lately. Check into biographical materials for information on its leaders.
- *Be an active listener.* During the interview, maintain eye contact, look for nonverbal cues, concentrate on the discussion, and evaluate the significance of questions before your respond.
- *Ask you own questions.* Prepare a list of questions relevant to the prospective position, questions that show you to be a person eager to make a contribution. Indicate that you will work hard, learn fast, and quickly become a contributing member of the organization. Hold questions of salary, benefits, vacations and other personal concerns until you have a job offer.
- *Show your portfolio.* Bring your portfolio to the job interview so you can show your work rather than merely talking about it. Offer it early in the meeting so the interviewer can glance at it during the discussion.
- *Have some leave-behinds.* Bring photocopies of the most appropriate portfolio items to leave with the organization.
- *Expect a writing test.* As part of the interview process, many employers hiring writers want to see how candidates perform under pressure. You may be given a set of facts and asked to prepare a news release. If so, do a brief planning sheet to make sure you are focusing on the appropriate publics and addressing their interests.
- *Adopt an air of confidence and professionalism.* Maintain eye contact with your interviewer, and control any anxiety you may have. After all, this organization thinks you are good enough to consider hiring you. Dressing professionally can be an ego boost, and knowing that you are prepared can go a long way to calm your nervousness.
- *Follow the interview with a thank-you letter.* Immediately following the interview, mail a note or card that expresses appreciation for the opportunity to be considered for the position. Use this as another opportunity to restate your interest in the job and to reiterate your main qualifications.

Appendix D

Professional Organizations

Canadian Public Relations Society (CPRS)
Société Canadienne de Relations Publiques
4195 Dundas Street West, Suite 346, Toronto, Ontario, M8X 1Y4
(416) 259-7034 cprs.ca
> CPRS is a bilingual professional society with more than 1,600 members, with a career center through the national office. Some of the 16 member societies (chapters) offer job placement services.

College Sports Information Directors of America (CoSIDA)
cosida.com
> This organization includes more than 1,800 public relations and public information specialists with college and university athletic departments in the United States and Canada.

Council for the Advancement and Support of Education (CASE)
1307 New York Avenue NW, Suite 1000, Washington DC 20005-4701
(202) 328-2237 case.org
> CASE involves 15,250 people in public relations, fundraising and related activities in 2,900 colleges, universities, and private elementary and secondary schools.

Council of Public Relations Firms
317 Madison Avenue, Suite 2320, New York NY 10017
(877) 773-4767 prfirms.org
> Though primarily an organization of agency executives, CPRF has a career center with useful information for students and interns.

Entertainment Publicists Professional Society
PO Box 5841, Beverly Hills CA 90209-5841
(888) 399-EPPS eppsonline.org
> This organization with networking bases in Los Angeles and New York includes a student-membr section.

International Association of Business Communicators (IABC)

One Hallidie Plaza, Suite 600, San Francisco CA94102

(800) 776-4222 iabc.org

> IABC is an international organizatio nof more than 13,700 communicators in 72 countries, primarily the United States and Canada. Members work in areas such as employee communication, publications, marketing, advertising, community relations and media relations. The organization publishes the monthly magazine Communication World and offers an online job listing. IABC has professional and student chapters.

International Public Relations Association (IPRA)

1 Dunley Hill Court, Ranmore Common, Dorking, Surrey RH5 6SX, UK

44 1483 280 130 ipra.org

> IRPA is an international association of senior-level public relations practitioners in more than 60 countries. IPRA is a consultant organization within UNESCO. It maintains links with national and regional public relations organizations and sponsors delegates to the United Nations and several international organizations.

National Investor Relations Institute (NIRI)

8020 Towers Crescent Drive, Suite 250, Vienna VA 22182

(703) 506-3570 niri.org

> NIRI is an association of managers and investor relations specialists responsible for communicating between their companies and their stockholders, as well as the financial community. The association includes 4,300 members in 34 chapters throughout the United States.

National School Public Relations Association (NSPRA)

15948 Denwood Road, Rockville MD 20855

(301) 519-0496 nspra.org

> NSPRA in an association of practitioners and administrators interested in public relations as practiced by schools and school districts. It is organized into 40 chapters.

Public Relations Society of America (PRSA)

33 Maiden Lane (11th Floor), New York NY 10038-5150

(212) 460-1400 prsa.org

> PRSA is a professional society of 20,000 public relations practitioners, with 16 professional interest sections. The organization publishes the montly magazine Public Relations Review. PRSA has 114 chapters in 10 districts.

Public Relations Student Society of America (PRSSA)

33 Maiden Lane (11th Floor), New York NY 10038-5150

(212) 460-1466 prsa.org

> PRSSA is the association of campus-level chapters affiliated with PRSA. It includes 8,500 members in more than 270 campus chapters.

Religion Communicators Council (RCC)

475 Riverside Drive, Room 1355, New York NY 10155

(212) 870-2985 religioncommunicators.org

RCC (formerly Religious Public Relations Council) is an interfaith association of more than 500 religious communicators and the oldest professional public relations organization in America. RCC has 13 chapters. The organization offers online job postings and student scholarships.

Appendix E

Ethical Standards

Public Relations Society of America

Member Code of Ethics
Approved by the PRSA Assembly. October, 2000

Preamble

- Professional Values
- Principles of Conduct
- Commitment and Compliance.

This Code applies to PRSA members. The Code is designed to be a useful guide for PRSA members as they carry out their ethical responsibilities. This document is designed to anticipate and accommodate, by precedent, ethical challenges that may arise. The scenarios outlined in the Code provision are actual examples of misconduct. More will be added as experience with the Code occurs.

The Public Relations Society of America (PRSA) is committed to ethical practices. The level of public trust PRSA members seek, as we serve the public good, means we have taken on a special obligation to operate ethically.

The value of member reputation depends upon the ethical conduct of everyone affiliated with the Public Relations Society of America. Each of us sets an example for each other—as well as other professionals—by our pursuit of excellence with powerful standards of performance, professionalism, and ethical conduct.

Emphasis on enforcement of the Code has been eliminated. But, the PRSA Board of Directors retains the right to bar from membership or expel from the Society any individual who has been or is sanctioned by a government agency or convicted in a court of law of an action that is in violation of this Code.

Ethical practice is the most important obligation of a PRSA member. We view the Member Code of Ethics as a model for other professions, organizations, and professionals.

PRSA Member Statement of Professional Values
This statement presents the core values of PRSA members and, more broadly, of the public relations profession. These values provide the foundation for the Member Code of Ethics and

set the industry standard for the professional practice of public relations. These values are the fundamental beliefs that guide our behaviors and decision-making process. We believe our professional values are vital to the integrity of the profession as a whole.

Advocacy

- We serve the public interest by acting as responsible advocates for those we represent.
- We provide a voice in the marketplace of ideas, facts, and viewpoints to aid informed public debate.

Honesty

- We adhere to the highest standards of accuracy and truth in advancing the interests of those we represent and in communicating with the public.

Expertise

- We acquire and responsibly use specialized knowledge and experience.
- We advance the profession through continued professional development, research, and education.
- We build mutual understanding, credibility, and relationships among a wide array of institutions and audiences.

Independence

- We provide objective counsel to those we represent.
- We are accountable for our actions.

Loyalty

- We are faithful to those we represent, while honoring our obligation to serve the public interest.

Fairness

- We deal fairly with clients, employers, competitors, peers, vendors, the media, and the general public.
- We respect all opinions and support the right of free expression.

PRSA Code Provisions
Free Flow of Information

Core Principle
Protecting and advancing the free flow of accurate and truthful information is essential to serving the public interest and contributing to informed decision making in a democratic society.

Intent

- To maintain the integrity of relationships with the media, government officials, and the public.
- To aid informed decision making.

Guidelines
A member shall:

- Preserve the integrity of the process of communication.
- Be honest and accurate in all communications.
- Act promptly to correct erroneous communications for which the practitioner is responsible.
- Preserve the free flow of unprejudiced information when giving or receiving gifts by ensuring that gifts are nominal, legal, and infrequent.

Examples of Improper Conduct under this Provision

- A member representing a ski manufacturer gives a pair of expensive racing skis to a sports magazine columnist, to influence the columnist to write favorable articles about the product.
- A member entertains a government official beyond legal limits and/or in violation of government reporting requirements.

Competition

Core Principle
Promoting healthy and fair competition among professionals preserves an ethical climate while fostering a robust business environment.

Intent

- To promote respect and fair competition among public relations professionals.
- To serve the public interest by providing the widest choice of practitioner options.

Guidelines
A member shall:

- Follow ethical hiring practices designed to respect free and open competition without deliberately undermining a competitor.
- Preserve intellectual property rights in the marketplace.

Examples of Improper Conduct under this Provision

- A member employed by a "client organization" shares helpful information with a counseling firm that is competing with others for the organization's business.
- A member spreads malicious and unfounded rumors about a competitor in order to alienate the competitor's clients and employees in a ploy to recruit people and business.

Disclosure of Information

Core Principle
Open communication fosters informed decision making in a democratic society.

Intent

- To build trust with the public by revealing all information needed for responsible decision making.

Guidelines
A member shall:

- Be honest and accurate in all communications.
- Act promptly to correct erroneous communications for which the member is responsible.
- Investigate the truthfulness and accuracy of information released on behalf of those represented.
- Reveal the sponsors for causes and interests represented.
- Disclose financial interest (such as stock ownership) in a client's organization.
- Avoid deceptive practices.

Examples of Improper Conduct under this Provision

- Front groups: A member implements "grassroots" campaigns or letter-writing campaigns to legislators on behalf of undisclosed interest groups.
- Lying by omission: A practitioner for a corporation knowingly fails to release financial information, giving a misleading impression of the corporation's performance.
- A member discovers inaccurate information disseminated via a Web site or media kit and does not correct the information.
- A member deceives the public by employing people to pose as volunteers to speak at public hearings and participate in "grassroots" campaigns.

Safeguarding Confidences

Core Principle
Client trust requires appropriate protection of confidential and private information.

Intent

- To protect the privacy rights of clients, organizations, and individuals by safeguarding confidential information.

Guidelines
A member shall:

- Safeguard the confidences and privacy rights of present, former, and prospective clients and employees.

- Protect privileged, confidential, or insider information gained from a client or organization.
- Immediately advise an appropriate authority if a member discovers that confidential information is being divulged by an employee of a client company or organization.

Examples of Improper Conduct under this Provision

- A member changes jobs, takes confidential information, and uses that information in the new position to the detriment of the former employer.
- A member intentionally leaks proprietary information to the detriment of some other party.

Conflicts of Interest

Core Principle
Avoiding real, potential or perceived conflicts of interest builds the trust of clients, employers, and the publics.

Intent

- To earn trust and mutual respect with clients or employers.
- To build trust with the public by avoiding or ending situations that put one's personal or professional interests in conflict with society's interests.

Guidelines
A member shall:

- Act in the best interests of the client or employer, even subordinating the member's personal interests.
- Avoid actions and circumstances that may appear to compromise good business judgment or create a conflict between personal and professional interests.
- Disclose promptly any existing or potential conflict of interest to affected clients or organizations.
- Encourage clients and customers to determine if a conflict exists after notifying all affected parties.

Examples of Improper Conduct under this Provision

- The member fails to disclose that he or she has a strong financial interest in a client's chief competitor.
- The member represents a "competitor company" or a "conflicting interest" without informing a prospective client.

Enhancing the Profession

Core Principle
Public relations professionals work constantly to strengthen the public's trust in the profession.

Intent

- To build respect and credibility with the public for the profession of public relations.
- To improve, adapt and expand professional practices.

Guidelines

A member shall:

- Acknowledge that there is an obligation to protect and enhance the profession.
- Keep informed and educated about practices in the profession to ensure ethical conduct.
- Actively pursue personal professional development.
- Decline representation of clients or organizations that urge or require actions contrary to this Code.
- Accurately define what public relations activities can accomplish.
- Counsel subordinates in proper ethical decision making.
- Require that subordinates adhere to the ethical requirements of the Code.
- Report ethical violations, whether committed by PRSA members or not, to the appropriate authority.

Examples of Improper Conduct under this Provision

- A PRSA member declares publicly that a product the client sells is safe, without disclosing evidence to the contrary.
- A member initially assigns some questionable client work to a non-member practitioner to avoid the ethical obligation of PRSA membership.

PRSA Member Code of Ethics Pledge

I pledge:

- To conduct myself professionally, with truth, accuracy, fairness, and responsibility to the public;
- To improve my individual competence and advance the knowledge and proficiency of the profession through continuing research and education;
- And to adhere to the articles of the Member Code of Ethics 2000 for the practice of public relations as adopted by the governing Assembly of the Public Relations Society of America.

I understand and accept that there is a consequence for misconduct, up to and including membership revocation.

And, I understand that those who have been or are sanctioned by a government agency or convicted in a court of law of an action that is in violation of this Code may be barred from membership or expelled from the Society.

International Association of Business Communicators

Code of Ethics

Communication and Information Dissemination

1.   Communication professionals will uphold the credibility and dignity of their profession by encouraging the practice of honest, candid and timely communication.

    The highest standards of professionalism will be upheld in all communication. Communicators should encourage frequent communication and messages that are honest in their content, candid, accurate and appropriate to the needs of the organization and its audiences.

2.   Professional communicators will not use any information that has been generated or appropriately acquired by a business for another business without permission. Further, communicators should attempt to identify the source of information to be used.

    When one is changing employers, information developed at the previous position will not be used without permission from that employer. Acts of plagiarism and copyright infringement are illegal acts; material in the public domain should have its source attributed, if possible. If an organization grants permission to use its information and request public acknowledgment, it will be made in a place appropriate to the material used. The material will be used only for the purpose for which permission was granted.

Standards of Conduct

3.   Communication professionals will abide by the spirit and letter of all laws and regulations governing their professional activities.

    All international, national and local laws and regulations must be observed, with particular attention to those pertaining to communication, such as copyright law. Industry and organizational regulations also will be observed.

4.   Communication professionals will not condone any illegal or unethical act related to their professional activity, their organization and its business or the public environment in which it operates.

    It is the personal responsibility of professional communicators to act honestly, fairly and with integrity at all times in all professional activities. Looking the other way while others act illegally tacitly condones such acts whether or not the communicator has committed them. The communicator should speak with the individual involved, his or her supervisor or appropriate authorities—depending on the context of the situation and one's own ethical judgment.

Confidentiality/Disclosure

5.   Communication professionals will respect the confidentiality and right-to-privacy of all individuals, employers, clients and customers.

    Communicators must determine the ethical balance between right-to-privacy and need-to-know. Unless the situation involves illegal or grossly unethical acts, confidences should be maintained. If there is a conflict between right-to-privacy and need-to-know, a communicator should first talk with the source and negotiate the need for the information to be communicated.

6. Communication professionals will not use any confidential information gained as a result of professional activity for personal benefit or that of others.

    Confidential information cannot be used to give inside advantage to stock transactions, gain favors from outsiders, assist a competing company for whom one is going to work, assist companies in developing a marketing advantage, achieve a publishing advantage or otherwise act to the detriment of an organization. Such information must remain confidential during and after one's employment period.

Professionalism

7. Communication professionals should uphold IABC's standards for ethical conduct in all professional activity, and should use IABC and its designation of accreditation (ABC) only for purposes that are authorized and fairly represent the organization and its professional standards.

    IABC recognizes the need for professional integrity within any organization, including the association. Members should acknowledge that their actions reflect on themselves, their organizations and their profession.

Canadian Public Relations Society
Société Canadienne de Relations Publiques

Code of Professional Standards

Members of the Canadian Public Relations Society are pledged to maintain the spirit and ideals of the following stated principles of conduct, and to consider these essential to the practice of public relations.

1. **A member shall practice public relations according to the highest professional standards.**

    Members shall conduct their professional lives in a manner that does not conflict with the public interest and the dignity of the individual, with respect for the rights of the public as contained in the Constitution of Canada and the Charter of Rights and Freedoms.

2. **A member shall deal fairly and honestly with the communications media and the public.**

    Members shall neither propose nor act to improperly influence the communications media, government bodies or the legislative process. Improper influence may include conferring gifts, privileges or benefits to influence decisions

3. **A member shall practice the highest standards of honesty, accuracy, integrity and truth, and shall not knowingly disseminate false or misleading information.**

    Members shall not make extravagant claims or unfair comparisons, nor assume credit for ideas and words not their own.

    Members shall not engage in professional or personal conduct that will bring discredit to themselves, the Society or the practice of public relations.

4. **A member shall deal fairly with past or present employers/clients, fellow practitioners and members of other professions.**
    Members shall not intentionally damage another practitioner's practice or professional reputation. Members shall understand, respect and abide by the ethical codes of other professions with whose members they may work from time to time.

5. **Members shall be prepared to disclose the names of their employers or clients for whom public communications are made and refrain from associating themselves with anyone who would not respect such policy.**
    Members shall be prepared to disclose publicly the names of their employers or clients on whose behalf public communications is made. Members shall not associate themselves with anyone claiming to represent one interest, or professing to be independent or unbiased, but who actually serves another or an undisclosed interest.

6. **A member shall protect the confidences of present, former and prospective employers/clients.**
    Members shall not use or disclose confidential information obtained from past or present employers/clients without the expressed permission of the employers/clients or an order of a court of law.

7. **A member shall not represent conflicting or competing interests without the expressed consent of those concerned, given after a full disclosure of the facts.**
    Members shall not permit personal or other professional interests to conflict with those of an employer/client without fully disclosing such interests to everyone involved.

8. **A member shall not guarantee specified results beyond the member's capacity to achieve.**

9. **Members shall personally accept no fees, commissions, gifts or any other considerations for professional services from anyone except employers or clients for whom the services were specifically performed.**

International Public Relations Association

International Code of Ethics (Code of Athens)
CONSIDERING that all Member countries of the United National Organisation have agreed to abide by its Charter which reaffirm "its faith in fundamental human rights, in the dignity and worth of the human person" and that having regard to the very nature of the profession, Public Relations practitioners in these countries should undertake to ascertain and observe the principles set out in this Charter;

CONSIDERING that, apart from "rights," human beings have not only physical or material needs but also intellectual, moral and social needs, and that their rights are of real benefit to them only in-so-far as these needs are essentially met;

CONSIDERING that, in the course of their professional duties and depending on how these duties are performed, Public Relations practitioners can substantially help to meet these intellectual, moral and social needs;

And lastly, CONSIDERING that the use of the techniques enabling them to come simultaneously into contact with millions of people gives Public Relations practitioners a power that has to be restrained by the observance of a strict moral code.

On all these grounds, all members of the International Public Relations Association agree to abide by this International Code of Ethics, and that if, in the light of evidence submitted to the Council, a member should be found to have infringed this Code in the course of his/her professional duties, he/she will be deemed to be guilty of serious misconduct calling for an appropriate penalty.

Accordingly, each member:

SHALL ENDEAVOR

1. To contribute to the achievement of the moral and cultural conditions enabling human beings to reach their full stature and enjoy the indefeasible rights to which they are entitled under the "Universal Declaration of Human Rights";
2. To establish communications patterns and channels which, by fostering the free flow of essential information, will make each member of the group feel that he/she is being kept informed, and also give him/her an awareness of his/her own personal involvement and responsibility, and of his/her solidarity with other members;
3. To conduct himself/herself always and in all circumstances in such a manner as to deserve and secure the confidence of those with whom he/she comes into contact;
4. To bear in mind that, because of the relationship between his/her profession and the public, his/her conduct—even in private—will have an impact on the way in which the profession as a whole is appraised;

SHALL UNDERTAKE

5. To observe, in the course of his/her professional duties, the moral principles and rules of the "Universal Declaration of Human Rights";
6. To pay due regard to, and uphold, human dignity, and to recognise the right of each individual to judge for himself/herself;
7. To establish the moral, psychological and intellectual conditions for dialogue in its true sense, and to recognise the right of these parties involved to state their case and express their views;
8. To act, in all circumstances, in such a manner as to take account of the respective interests of the parties involved: both the interests of the organisation which he/she serves and the interests of the publics concerned;
9. To carry out his/her undertakings and commitments which shall always be so worded as to avoid any misunderstanding, and to show loyalty and integrity in all circumstances so as to keep the confidence of his/her clients or employers, past or present, and of all the publics that are affected by his/her actions;

SHALL REFRAIN FROM

10. Subordinating the truth to other requirements;
11. Circulating information which is not based on established and ascertainable facts;
12. Taking part in any venture or undertaking which is unethical or dishonest or capable of impairing human dignity and integrity;

13. Using any "manipulative" methods or techniques designed to create subconscious motivations which the individual cannot control of his/her own free will and so cannot be held accountable for the action taken on them.

Code of Conduct (Code of Venice)

   A.   *Personal and Professional Integrity*

   1. It is understood that by personal integrity is meant the maintenance of both high moral standards and a sound reputation. By professional integrity is meant observance of the Constitution rules and, particularly the Code as adopted by IPRA.

   B.   *Conduct towards Clients and Employers.* A member has a general duty of fair dealing towards his/her clients or employers, past and present. A member shall not represent conflicting or competing interests without the express consent of those concerned. A member shall safeguard the confidences of both present and former clients or employers. A member shall not employ methods tending to be derogatory of another member's client or employer. In performing services for a client or employer a member shall not accept fees, commission or any other valuable consideration in connection with those services from anyone other than his/her client or employer without the express consent of his/her client or employee, given after a full disclosure of the facts. A member shall not propose to a prospective client or employer that his/her fee or other compensation be contingent on the achievement of certain results; nor shall he/she enter into any fee agreement to the same effect.

   C.   *Conduct toward the Public and the Media.* A member shall conduct his/her professional activities with respect to the public interest and for the dignity of the individual. A member shall not engage in practice which tends to corrupt the integrity of channels of public communication. A member shall not intentionally disseminate false or misleading information. A member shall at all times seek to give a faithful representation of the organisation which he/she serves. A member shall not create any organisation to serve some announced cause but actually to serve an undisclosed special or private interest of a member or his/her client or employer, nor shall he/she make use of it or any such existing organisation.

   D.   *Conduct towards Colleagues.* A member shall not intentionally injure the professional reputation or practice of another member. However, if a member has evidence that another member has been guilty of unethical, illegal or unfair practices, including practices in violation of this Code, he should present the information to the Council of IPRA. A member shall not seek to supplant another member with his employer or client. A member shall co-operate with fellow members in upholding and enforcing this Code.

Bibliography

Advertising and Copywriting

Blake, G., & Bly, R.W. (1998). *The elements of copywriting: The essential guide to writing copy that gets the results you want*. MacMillan.

Bly, R.W. (2006). *The copywriter's handbook: A step-by-step guide to writing copy that sells* (3rd ed.). Owl Books.

Gabbay, J.J. (2003). *Teach yourself copywriting* (3rd ed.). McGraw-Hill.

Lewis, H.G. (2003). *On the art of writing copy: The best of print, broadcast, Internet and direct mail* (3rd ed.). Racom & Direct Marketing Association.

Sheridan, S. (2000). *Writing great copy*. How To Books.

Sugerman, J. (1998). *Advertising secrets of the written word: The ultimate resource on how to write powerful advertising copy from one of America's top copywriters and mail order entrepreneurs*. DelStar.

Broadcast Writing

Attkisson, S. (2002). *Writing right for broadcast and Internet news*. Allyn & Bacon.

Dotson, B., Lauer, M., & Block, M. (2000). *Make it memorable: Writing and packaging TV news with style*. Bonus.

Mayeau, P. (2000). *Broadcast news writing and reporting*. Waveland.

Rowe, J. (2005). *Broadcast news writing for professionals*. Marion Street.

Thompkins, A. (2002). *Aim for the heart, write for the ear, shoot for the eye: A guide for TV producers and reporters*. Bonus.

White, T. (2005). *Broadcast news writing, reporting, and producing* (4th ed.). Focal.

Brochures and Newsletters

Abbott, R.F. (2001). *A manager's guide to newsletters: Communicating for results*. Word Engines Press.

Beach, M., & Floyd, E. (1997). *Newsletter sourcebook*. F&W.

Brooks, P. (2002). *The easy step-by-step guide to writing newsletters and articles*. Rowmark.

Katz, M.J. (2003). *E-newsletters that work: The small business owner's guide to creating, writing and managing an effective electronic newsletter*. Xlibris.

Woodard, C. (2004). *Starting and running a successful newsletter or magazine* (4th ed.). NOLO.

General Writing

Lederer, R., & Dowis, R. (2001). *Sleeping dogs don't lay: Practical advice for the grammatically challenged*. Griffin.

O'Connor, P.T. (2000). *Words fail me: What everyone who writes should know about writing.* Harvest.

O'Connor, P.T. (2004). *Woe is I: The grammarphobe's guide to better English in plain English* (2nd ed.). Riverheat.

Strunk Jr., W., White, E.B., & Angell, R. (2000). *The elements of style* (4th ed). Allyn & Bacon.

Walsh, B. (2000). *Lapsing into a comma: A curmudgeon's guide to the many things that can go wrong in print—and how to avoid them.* McGraw-Hill.

Fundraising Writing

Kuniholm, R. (1995). *The complete book of model fundraising letters.* Aspen.

Warsick, M. (2001). *How to write successful fundraising letters.* Wiley & Sons.

Journalistic Writing

Hicks, W., Adams, S., & Gilbert, H. (1999). *Writing for journalists.* Routledge.

Kessler, L., & McDonald, D. (2003). *When words collide: A media writer's guide to grammar and style* (6th ed.). Wadsworth.

Mencher, M. (2005). *News reporting and writing* (10th ed.). McGraw-Hill.

Rich, C. (2002). *Writing and reporting news: A coaching method.* Wadsworth.

Stephens, M., & Lanson, G. (1997). *Writing and reporting the news.* International Thompson.

Stovall, J.G. (2005). *Writing for the mass media* (6th ed.). Allyn & Bacon.

Whitaker, W.R., Ramsey, J.E., & Smith, R.D. (in press). *MediaWriting* (3rd ed.). Lawrence Erlbaum.

Magazine Writing

Daugherty, G. (1999). *You can write for magazines.* Writer's Digest.

Jacobi, P. (1997). *The magazine article: How to think it, plan it, write it.* Indiana University Press.

Ruberg, M., & Yagoda, B. (2004). *Writer's Digest handbook of magazine article writing* (2nd ed.). Writer's Digest.

Sloan, C. (2004). *Writing for magazines: A beginner's guide* (2nd ed.). McGraw-Hill.

Online Writing

Bly, R. (2003). *The online copywriter's handbook: Everything you need to know to write electronic copy that sells* (2nd ed.). McGraw-Hill.

Guilford, C. (2006). *Paradigm online writing assistant.* BookSurge.

Hammerich, I., & Harrison, C. (2001). *Developing online content: The principles of writing and editing for the Web.* Wiley & Sons.

Holtz, S. (1999). *Writing for the wired world: The communicator's guide to effective online content.* IABC.

Mill, D. (2005). *Content is king: Writing and editing online*. Butterworth-Heinemann.

Nielsen, J. (2000). *Designing Web usability*. New Riders.

Nielsen, J., & Loranger, H (2006). *Prioritizing Web usability*. New Riders.

Porter, Y., Sullivan, P., & Johnson-Eilola, J. (2003). *Professional writing online* (2nd ed.). Longman.

Persuasion

Barbato, J., & Furlich, D.W. (2000). *Writing for a good cause: The complete guide to crafting proposals and other persuasive pieces for nonprofits*. Fireside.

Carrick, N., & Finsen, L. (1997). *The persuasive pen: Reasoning and writing*. Jones & Bartlett.

Charvet, S.R. (2002). *Words that change minds: Mastering the language of influence* (2nd ed.). Kendall-Hunt.

Howe, M. (2004). *Persuasive writing made easy*. OC Publishing.

Mills, H.A. (2000). *Artful persuasion: How to command attention, change minds and influence people*. AMACOM.

Public Relations (General)

Aronson, E.W., & Pinkleton, B.E. (2001). *Strategic public relations management: Planning and managing effective communication programs*. Lawrence Erlbaum.

Ault, P.H., Agee, W.K., Cameron, G.T., & Wilcox, D.L. (2002). *Public relations: Strategies and tactics* (7th ed.). Allyn & Bacon.

Burnett, J., & Moriarty, S. (1998). *Introduction to marketing communications: An integrated approach*. Prentice Hall.

Caywood, C.L. (1997). *The handbook of strategic public relations and integrated communications*. McGraw-Hill.

Cutlip, S.M., Center, A.H., & Broom, G.M. (2005). *Effective public relations* (9th ed.). Prentice Hall.

Harris, T.L. & Kotler, P. (1999). *Value added public relations: The secret weapon of integrated marketing*. McGraw-Hill.

Harris, T.L., & Whalen, P.T. (2006). *The marketer's guide to public relations in the 21st century*. South-Western.

Kendall, R. (1999). *Public relations campaign strategies: Planning for implementation* (3rd ed.). HarperCollins.

Lewis, J., & Jones, D. (2001). *How to get noticed by the national media*. Trellis.

Levine, M., & Gendron, G. (2001). *Guerrilla PR wired: Waging a successful publicity campaign on-line, offline and anywhere in between*. McGraw-Hill.

Levine, M. (1994). *Guerilla PR: How you can wage an effective publicity campaign . . . without going broke*. HarperBusiness.

Levinson, J.C., Frishman, R., & Lublin, J. (2002). *Guerrilla publicity: Hundreds of sure-fire tactics to get maximum sales for minimum dollars*. Adams.

Newsom, D., Turk, J.V., & Kruckenberg, D. (2006). *This is PR: The realities of public relations* (9th ed.). Wadsworth.

Ries, A., & Roes, L. (2004). *The fall of advertising & the rise of PR*. Collins Reprint.

Seitel, F.P. (2006). *The practice of public relations* (10th ed.). Prentice Hall.

Smith, R.D. (2004). *Strategic planning for public relations* (2nd ed.). Lawrence Erlbaum.

Wilcox, D.L., Cameron, G.T., Ault, P.H., & Agee, W.K. (2003). *Public relations: Strategies and tactics* (7th ed). Allyn & Bacon.

Public Relations Writing

Aronson, M., & Spetner, D. (1998). *The public relations writer's handbook*. Jossey-Bass.

Begovich, R. (2001). *Writing for results: Keys to success for the public relations writer*. Alta Villa.

Bivins, T.H. (2004). *Public relations writing: The essentials of style and format* (5th ed.). McGraw-Hill.

Bordon, K. (1995). *Bulletproof news releases: Help at last for the publicity deficient*. Franklin Sarrett.

Foster, J.L. (2005). *Effective writing skills for public relations* (3rd ed.). Kogan Page.

Newsom, D., & Haynes, J. (2004). *Public relations writing: Form and style* (7th ed.). Wadsworth.

Treadwell, D., & Treadwell, J.B. (2005). *Public relations writing: Principles in practice*. Allyn & Bacon.

Wilcox, D. (2004). *Public relations writing and media techniques* (5th ed.). Allyn & Bacon.

Yale, D., & Carothers, A.J. (2001). *The publicity handbook new edition: The inside scoop from more than 100 journalists and PR pros on how to get great publicity coverage*. McGraw-Hill.

Reference and Style Books

Bass, F. (2002). *The Associated Press guide to Internet research and reporting*. Perseus.

Cappon, R.J. (2003). *The Associated Press guide to punctuation*. Perseus.

Goldstein, N. (2006). *The Associated Press stylebook and briefing on media law*. Perseus.

Horton, B. (2000). *The Associated Press guide to photojournalism*. McGraw-Hill.

Kalbfeld, B. (2001). *Associated Press broadcast news handbook*. McGraw-Hill.

Martin, P.R. (2002). *The Wall Street Journal guide to business style and usage*. Wall Street Journal.

Schwartz, J. (2001). *The Associate Press guide to reporting*. McGraw-Hill.

Siegal, A.M., & Connolly, W.G. (2002). *The New York Times manual of style and usage: The official style guide used by writers and editors of the world's most authoritative newspaper*. Three Rivers Press.

Wilstein, S. (2001). *The Associate Press sports writing handbook*. McGraw-Hill.

Speechwriting

Cook, J.S. (1996). *The elements of speechwriting and public speaking*. Longman.

Carpenter, R.H., & Thompson, W.D. (1998). *Choosing powerful words: Eloquence that works* (part of the *Essence of Public Speaking* series). Allyn & Bacon.

Glossary

acceptance objectives   public relations affective objectives that state expectations about interest or attitude

acknowledgment   thank-you letter prepared as a followup to a direct-mail response

action objectives   public relations conative objectives that state expectations about opinion or behavior

active voice   grammatical term indicating syntax emphasizing the doer of an action; compared with passive voice

actuality   cassette or tape recording accompanying printed release, providing quotations for radio use; see **sound bite**

advertising layout   approach to design of print advertisements; categories include **standard layout**, **poster-style layout**, and **editorial-style layout**

Advertising Council   joint venture of advertising agencies, advertisers and the media to provide persuasive messages of public interest

agenda-setting theory   theory that public media are effective in telling people what to think about

altruism   a person's innate desire to help others; important to public relations writers involved with volunteers and fundraising

analogy   writing technique in which an unfamiliar thing is explained by likening it to something familiar to the audience

annual report   organizational progress report required of stock-issuing companies and voluntarily produced by many others

apologetics   systematic attempt to assert the reasonableness of an idea and to refute opposing arguments

appeal letter   central part of a direct-mail package that presents the persuasive message to the reader

archives   an organization's formal collection of documents, records, photographs, letters and memorabilia; useful for public relations researchers

art   umbrella term for visual design elements such as photographs, computer-generated imagery, sketches, diagrams, maps, charts, etc.

audience   group of people who use a particular medium such as newspaper, radio station or television station; of interest to public relations writers because it includes members of the **strategic public**

audit   see **public relations audit**

awareness objectives   public relations cognitive objectives that state expectations about attention, retention or understanding

B-roll   type of video news release that provides unedited videotaped pieces for reporters' use

background only   see **deep background**

backgrounder   type of public relations release that provides factual information to give a context to an organization or an issue; categories include **corporate backgrounder** focusing on an organization and **issue backgrounder** focusing on a particular issue

balance   element of newsworthiness stressing the fair and accurate reporting of information; see **SiLoBaTi + UnFa**

balance theory   theory suggesting that people seek an attitude similar to that of their communication partners; also called **consonance theory** or **symmetry theory**

behavior   outward physical expression of an internal attitude; compared with **opinion**

benefit statement   part of planning sheet that articulates the benefit or advantage the organization can offer the target public; also part of a news release that articulates this benefit or advantage

biographical information release   record of personal information used by public relations writers; also called **bio sheet**

biographical narrative   factual, usually chronological, presentation of personal information; compare with **personal profile**

brainstorming   creativity technique of free association used to generate a large number of ideas

brainwriting   creativity technique of free association used to generate ideas within a group

broadcast faxing   method of transmitting multiple and simultaneous fax messages

broadcast media   umbrella term for radio and television; cable television is popularly included within this term, though cable is not technically a broadcast medium; usually refers to public media and excludes organizational video and audio services

broadcast news release   version of a news release prepared specifically for radio and television, usually briefer than releases for print media, more conversational in tone, and including **pronouncers**

broadcast television   public media that provides local and network programming

broadside   see **flier**

brochure   printed form of organization media, usually folded sheets meant to be read as a booklet and providing information meant to be relevant over an extended period of time; also called **leaflet**, **folder**, **pamphlet**, **booklet**, **tract** and **bulletin**.

bullet theory   theory based on the **powerful effects model** of communication

bulletin   see **brochure**

buzz group   creativity technique of free association used to generate ideas when working with a large group of people

cable television   nonbroadcast public media that provides local, network and independent television programming

Canadian Public Relations Society   major Canadian professional organization focused on public relations

caption   written information that describes the action and identifies recognizable people and things depicted in a photograph; also called a **cutline**

case study   consumer-interest release that narrates how a particular organization identified and addressed a problem or issue; also called a **case history**

charisma   element of persuasive communication based on how well an audience likes the message source

circular   see **flier**

cliché   expression that is so overused that it is trite and boring

code of ethics   public standards of professional organizations, including those involved in public relations, that articulate ideals for practitioners

cognitive dissonance theory   theory focusing on confusion caused when information is out of step with a person's attitude, with the suggestion that people try to reduce the confusion, usually by ignoring the information or reinterpreting it to fit their attitude

color   rhetorical style of information that makes a story come alive; includes analogies, metaphors, quotes and descriptions

compliance   change in the outward acceptance of an attitude in order to avoid punishment or gain reward

congruity theory   theory that people experience confusion when two attitudes are in conflict and that they attempt to resolve the conflict, usually by adopting the easier attitude or by trying to blend the opposing attitudes

connotation   implicit suggestion or nuance of word meaning that goes beyond the explicit definition; compared with **denotation**

consent   consent verbal or written permission given by a person, used as a legal defense against invasion of privacy

consent release   written permission by a person allowing the use of his/her identity or creative works; may be an **individual consent release** written for a specific purpose or a **blanket consent release** granting general permission

consonance theory   see **balance theory**

consumer-interest release   type of public relations release that provides direct benefits to audiences; examples include **question-and-answer pieces**, **case studies**, **service articles** and **information digests**

consumers   publics comprising customers who use an organization's product or service

content analysis   formal research technique that provides quantitative information about the content of texts such as letters and news reports

contingency statement   type of position statement prepared in different versions to accommodate various potential situations or outcomes; also called a **stand-by statement**

control   element of persuasive communication based on the power or authority the message source has over an audience

controlled media   designation of media that allow the public relations practitioner to control the message content, tone and distribution; compare with **uncontrolled media**

copy editing   process of marking type prior to setting it into its finished design

copyright   legal designation of ownership for written and other artistic creations; the current U.S. Copyright Act was revised in 1976; copyright means material may not be used without permission

corporate speech   designation of comments presented on behalf of an organization as compared with personal comments of individuals; legal distinctions exist between corporate and personal speech

corrections column   feature in many publications that offer public relations writers an opportunity to clarify or correct a misstatement

creative writing   approach to writing that emphasizes imaginative, artistic and sometimes innovative style; coexists in public relations with functional writing

credibility   element of persuasive communication based on the ability of the message source to be believed

credit   caption information indicating the name and affiliation of the photographer

cultivation theory   theory that exposure to public media cultivates a person's perceptions and expectations, with a major difference between heavy and light viewers

cutline   see **caption**

dateline   designation in a news release of the name of the city or town where the release originates; the actual date is not included

deckhead   line(s) of type placed below the main line of a headline; also called an **underline**

deep background   condition under which a news source provides information to a reporter but stipulates that it may be used only without any identification of the source

defamation   communication that harms a person; see **slander** and **libel**

demographics   application of persuasive communication that segments audiences by factors such as age, sex, income, etc.

denotation   dictionary meaning of a word; compared with **connotation**

dependency theory   theory that audiences use media to the extent that the media provide information important to them

desktop publishing   computer programs that combine word processing and graphic design, making it easier for organizations to produce printed materials in-house

doublespeak   language that obviously and sometimes deliberately obscures the real meaning behind the words

down style   approach to writing style that uses capital letters as little as possible; compare with **up style**

draft   version of a piece of writing; from first draft as a rough beginning to final draft as a revised and corrected writing product

editorial statement   type of mission statement indicating the purpose and philosophy of a publication

editorial-style advertising layout   design of print advertisements that emphasize written text, with a minimum of artwork

electronic mail   computer technology that provides opportunities for business communication, research and dissemination of information

embargo   designation that information provided in a news release should not be used before a given hour and day

enablers   publics that make it possible for an organization to operate within its environment

end mark   typographical device indicating the end of a news release or similar written piece; usually a series of hatch marks, the word "end" or the journalistic symbol -30-

environmental audit   type of public relations audit that identifies an organization's publics and issues important to these publics

ethos   rhetorical concept focusing on source credibility; compare with **pathos** and **logos**

event listings   writing format that provides basic information for use in calendars and other listings of upcoming activities

evergreen   type of photograph that can be filed and kept for possible future use

expectancy-value theory   theory that people make media choices based on what they want and expect from the media

explicit permission   written permission, such as a **consent release**

fact sheet   writing format that provides information in outline or bullet form rather than in paragraphs

factoid   type of fact sheet that provides background information rather than details about events and activities

factual proposition   thesis within a speech or written commentary asserting the existence of something; compare with **value proposition** and **policy proposition**

fair comment and criticism   legal defense against defamation based on the right to critique and criticize in matters of public interest

fair use   freedom to use copyrighted material for purposes of education, news, commentary, satire and non-commercial research

fame   element of newsworthiness stressing the prominence of personalities figuring in the report; see **SiLoBaTi+ UnFa**

fax   increasingly common method of distributing news releases, fact sheets and advisories

fear appeals   rhetorical technique of shaping a message to appeal to the fear or insecurity of the audience

feature   type of story that emphasizes personalities and human-interest angles rather than hard news

feedback   theoretical concept referring to the ability of receivers to respond to the sender of a message

flier   printed form of organization media, usually unfolded sheets meant to be read as single units and providing time-specific information; also called **circular**, **broadside** and **handbill**

focus group   research technique that provides in-depth anecdotal information from a small group representative of an organization's public

Fog Index   technique for measuring the level of reading difficulty for any piece of writing; also called **Gunfling readability formula**

folder   see **brochure**

forced association techniques techniques for creativity that prompt the mind to generate ideas by using defined connections; examples include **visual relationships**, **similes**, **explained similes** and **future statements**

framing   theory that news media create a framework for how audiences think about topics

franking privilege   permission given to members of congress for free mailing to their constituents

free association techniques   techniques for creativity that prompt the mind to generate ideas by using widefined connections; examples include **freewriting**, **brainstorming**, **buzz groups** and **brainwriting**

freewriting   technique of writing without stopping and without self-editing for a period of time to get initial thoughts on paper; creativity technique of free association

functional writing   approach to writing that emphasizes purpose, format and objectives; coexists in public relations with creative writing

future statements   creativity technique of forced relationships that elicits ideas through the use of benefit statements and potential solutions

gatekeepers   people who control the flow of information, usually applied to editors, news directors, web masters and others who make decisions about what information will be presented to media audiences

gender bias   language that does not display characteristics of inclusive language because it excludes members of a target public or audience on the basis of sex; sometimes called **sexist language**

geodemographics   application of persuasive communication that segments audiences by geographic and other demographic factors

ghostwriter   unidentified person who assists the signer or speaker by drafting or refining the draft of a column, letter, speech or other commentary

guest editorial   opinion piece presenting the opinion of a person or organization not affiliated with the publication; presented as an editorial of the publication; similar to **op-ed commentary**

guilt appeals   rhetorical technique of shaping a message in a way to make the audience feel guilty if a course of action is not followed

handbill   see **flier**

handout   inappropriate term for **news release**

headline   approach to article identification in newspapers, magazines and newsletters that focuses on summaries rather than labels; compare with **title**

hierarchy of needs   listing of levels of personal need that motivate and interest people

how-to article   see **service article**

human interest   see **unusual**

hypodermic needle theory   theory based on the **powerful effects model** of communication

identification   change in acceptance in imitation of an admired person or group

identification paragraph   optional concluding paragraph of a news release providing information about an organization; also called **organizational ID**

implicit permission   legal concept based on the notion that a reasonable observer would see that a person is willingly participating in a situation, such as an interview or a posed photograph; compared by **explicit permission**

inclusive language   language that is neutral in its application to all members of a target public or audience

info/action statement   part of a news release that clearly presents information on how audiences can take action

information digest   consumer-interest approach that presents information based on technical reports in language accessible for nontechnical or lay readers

information kit   variety of public relations written pieces assembled for a particular public; categories include **media kit** and **user kit**

information overload   sociological term indicating the growing quantity and complexity of information

information-on-demand   method of disseminating information in which consumers request information via telephone or computer systems; also called **release-on-demand**

intellectual property   body of law associated with issues of copyright and trademark

internalization   adoption of an attitude because it is understood to be consistent with a person's beliefs or values

International Association of Business Communicators   large professional organization focused on public relations

interview   (1) method of research to gather information from knowledgeable persons; (2) type of feature article based on an interview with a knowledgeable person

interview notes   type of public relations release that provides reporters with an unedited transcript of an interview that they can use to develop a story

intrusion   legal term related to privacy referring to information gathered secretly or surreptitiously

inverted pyramid   pattern of news-style writing that presents the most important information first

issue advisory   type of position statement prepared for internal audiences

issues management   category of public relations that predicts and tracks public issues that accept an organization and its mission

jargon   technical language; words and phrases that have a particular meaning within a limited environment

kerning   horizontal spacing between the letters in any printed material

kicker   introductory line of type placed above the main line of a headline; also called an **overline**

lead   beginning paragraph of a news release, written to gain the attention of the audience

lead time   amount of time needed by reporters and editors between receiving or gathering information and final publication or presentation of the resulting news report

leading   vertical spacing between the lines in any printed material

leaflet   see **brochure**

legend   headline-like title in a caption; also called an **overline**

letter to the editor   column in many publications that offers public relations writers publicity and advocacy opportunities

libel   written **defamation**; compare with **slander**

limited effects model   approach to communication theory that concludes the media exert a weak influence over people

limiters   publics that oppose an organization or weaken its ability to operate within its environment

linkage   concept from systems theory that helps identify an organization's publics by focusing on consumers, producers, enablers and limiters

literature review   research technique that provides current information about an issue or a topic

local   element of newsworthiness stressing the proximity of the audience to events or issues being reported; see **SiLoBaTi + UnFa**

logos   rhetorical concept focusing on appeals to logic or reason; compare with **ethos** and **pathos**

media advisory   memo notifying reporters about an upcoming activity; also called **media alert**

media directory   collection of data related to newspapers and magazines, radio and television, telecommunications, advertising and other media-related areas

media kit   information packet for reporters, including fact sheets, news releases, photos and captions, biographies and related material; inappropriately called a **press kit**

misappropriation   legal term related to privacy referring to the unauthorized use of a person's name, image or voice

mission statement   written statement of the purpose and philosophy of an organization or a program; similar to **editorial statement**

moderate-to-powerful effects model approach to communication theory that concludes the media exert a significant, complex and long-time influence over people

more line   designation at the bottom of a news release page to indicate a continuation to a following page

news   information of interest to media and their audiences

news brief   opening paragraphs of a news release including the summary lead and the benefit statement, written either to stand alone or to provide the beginning of a lengthier release

news conference   announcement and group interview staged by public relations practitioners to provide an organizational message simultaneously to a large group of reporters

news flag   designation on a news release heading emphasizing the term "news" or "news release"

news release   common format used by organizations to provide information to the news media; types include **announcement releases** and r**esponse releases**

newsletters   printed form of organizational media, usually multipage serialized publications prepared for particular publics; categories include **member newsletters, external newsletters, special-interest newsletters, subscription newsletters, consumer newsletters** and **advocacy newsletters**

noise   theoretical concept referring to anything that interferes with the clarity of a message

non sequitur   conclusion or inference that does not logically follow from the arguments or premises

not for attribution   condition under which a news source provides information to a reporter but stipulates that it may not be linked with the news source by name

noticed copyright   explicit use of the word "copyright" by the creator of an artistic piece

objectives   clear statements of the expected or intended result of a public relations activity and its effect on a target public; levels of objectives are **awareness, acceptance** and **action**

odious labels   legal term referring to defamatory words that portray people in a negative light

off the record   condition under which a news source provides information to a reporter but stipulates that it may not be reported

official statement   type of position statement that focuses on brief proclamation of timely issue

one-step library resources   materials that provide information directly, such as encyclopedias; compare with **two-step resources**

one-voice principle   practice of designating a single organizational spokesperson or a coordinated team of spokespersons to provide a consistent message from an organization, especially in a crisis situation

online data network   computer-based sources of information

op-ed commentary   opinion piece presenting the opinion of a person or organization not affiliated with the publication; presented as a column; similar to **guest editorial**

operational English   common form of English most often used in business, communication, education and other settings where geographic and cultural variations are inappropriate; also called **standard English** or **network English**

opinion   outward vocal expression of an internal attitude; compared with **behavior**

organizational history   type of public relations release that provides a feature article based on the background of an organization

organizational television   nonbroadcast and nonpublic media that provides programming within an organization

overline   see **kicker** and **legend**

oxymoron   figure of speech in which contradictory terms are used together, rendering a confused meaning

pamphlet   see **brochure**

passive voice   grammatical term indicating syntax emphasizing the receiver of an action; compared with active voice

pathos   rhetorical concept focusing on appeals to emotion or sentiment; compare with **ethos** and **logos**

performance/perception audit   type of public relations audit that tracks an organization's performance, visibility and reputation

personal profile   feature article presenting personal information; compare with **biographical narrative**

persuasion   process of communication that intends to influence through ethical means that enhance a democratic society

phonetic guide   method used within **pronouncers**

photo caption   see **caption**

photo opportunity   activity created and/or sponsored by an organization to create something of visual interest to media photographers; also called a **photo op**

pitch letter   promotional letter to media gatekeepers to persuade them to report on some aspect or activity of an organization

planning sheet   outline to guide a writer toward preparing effective pieces of writing; focuses attention on **target publics**, **benefits**, **objectives** and **tone**

policy proposition   thesis within a speech or written commentary advocating a course of action; compare with **factual proposition** and **value proposition**

polishing   process of revising a written draft by considering and refining the flow of language

position statement   public relations format presenting the formal and public position of an organization on a particular topic; categories include **position paper** and **position paragraph**, depending upon the length of the statement; compare with **official statement** and **contingency statement**

poster-style advertising layout   design of print advertisements that emphasize artwork and headline, with a minimum of written text

powerful effects model   approach to communication theory which concludes that media exert a direct and predictable influence over people's attitudes, opinions and behavior; associated with **bullet theory** or **hypodermic needle theory**

press kit   see **media kit**

press release   inappropriate term for **news release**

priming   theory that news media remind audiences of previous information on a topic

print media   umbrella term for newspapers and magazines; usually refers to public media and excludes newsletters, brochures and other internal printed media

private facts   legal term referring to personal information that is intrusive and not of legitimate public concern

privilege   legal term referring to situations in which a writer is exempt from prosecution for defamation, such as when reporting court or legislative testimony

proclamation   formal statement issues by an organizational or public authority commemorating an event; also called a **resolution**

producers   publics that provide an organization's product or service

pronouncers   phonetic tips included in news release, scripts and other public relations vehicles to help readers correctly pronounce unfamiliar words, usually names of people and places; also called a **pronunciation guide**

proofreading   process of revising a written draft by considering and correcting errors of style, spelling, punctuation, etc.

propaganda   persuasive communication that is deceptive about the source of the message or that presents misinformation to audiences; draws on some acceptable rhetoric techniques

proposition central message of a speech or written commentary; also called a **thesis**

pseudoevent newsworthy event created by public relations practitioner to attract media attention; compare with **publicity stunt**

psychographics application of **psychological type theory** to marketing aspects of persuasive communication that segments audiences by personality and lifestyle factors rather than demographic ones

psychological type theory theory that innate personality factors give each person a predisposition toward particular persuasive techniques, with some people more influenced by emotional appeals and others by logical appeals

public group of people sharing a common bond or relationship with an organization; see **target public**

public advisory announcement notifying media audiences about an important matter, usually one with potential harm

public relations advertising term involving commercial and noncommercial advertising focusing on advocacy and image rather than on the marketing of products and services

public relations audit systematic analysis of an organization, its communication practices and its relationship with its publics; categories include **environmental audit** and **performance/perception audit**

Public Relations Association of America largest of several professional organizations focused on public relations

public service advertising promotional and advocacy advertisements for both print and broadcast media in which no placement costs are charged by the

medium using the advertising; also called **PSAs**

publicity function of public relations focused on using the news media to present an organization's message

publicity stunt gimmick used mainly to attract media attention to event with little inherent news value; compare with **pseudoevent**

query letter see **story idea memo**

question-and-answer piece consumer-interest release that uses a format of brief questions posed directly to readers and responses to each **question**

quotes statements within news releases and similar types of public relations writing that provide comments and opinions, presented with attribution to the source; more formally called **quotations**

radio news release public relations information packaged as a completed broadcast report for radio

readability range part of planning sheet that identifies the educational range of the target public; the written message eventually will be measured using a readability formula such as the **Fog Index**

receiver phenomenon theoretical concept suggesting that the ability to communicate is controlled by the receiver of a message, who has the power of choosing whether to receive a message and how to interpret and act upon it

redundancy use of words that repeat a meaning already existing

registered copyright type of **copyright** registered with the Copyright Office of the Library of Congress

release-on-demand see information-on-demand

reminder advertising strategy that reinforces already known images and ideas

research systematic way of gathering information about a topic

resolution see **proclamation**

response device   card or envelope flap within a directmail package that the reader is expected to fill out

rhetoric   art of persuasive communication, with ancient origins and contemporary insights

RNR   see **radio news release**

selectivity theory   family of theories related to the observation that people expose themselves to messages they think they will like and avoid what they expect not to like; related concepts are **selective exposure, selective attention, selective retention, selective perception** and **selective recall**

service article   consumer-interest release that provides step-by-step instructions in addressing a problem or issue; also called a **how-to article**

service mark   legal designation of ownership of a name, logo, symbol or other identification of a service or program; compare with **trademark**

significance   element of newsworthiness stressing the importance of information; see **SiLoBaTi + UnFa**

SiLoBaTi + UnFa   mnemonic device referring to ingredients of news value— significance, localness, balance, timeliness, plus unusualness and fame

similes   creativity technique of forced relationships that elicits ideas through verbal techniques

slander   oral **defamation**; compare with **libel**

sleeper effect   hypothesis that, over time, people forget the source of a message but remember the message itself, weakening the effect of source credibility or non-credibility

slug line   designation within a news release of topic and number of pages following the first page

social judgment theory   theory that attitude change is more a change in a person's perception than a change in belief

soft lead   type of lead for broadcast media that is an attention-getter rather than a summary; also called **throw-away lead, tune-in lead** and **warm-up lead**

sound bite   brief, memorable quote used by a news source, especially for radio and television reports; see **actuality**

source credibility   factor in message persuasiveness that deals with the believability of a message source; factors include expertise and sincerity

special event   activity created and/or sponsored by an organization to attraction attention of the media and their audiences

speech tag   phrase such as "she said" used to attribute information in a news release and similar types of writing; used for both direct quotes and paraphrases

spiral of silence theory   theory that public media may hinder communication by giving people a sense of isolation and reluctance if their opinions differ from the majority opinion presented through the media

split run   technique in direct-mail campaigns in which different versions of the same message are distributed to different target publics

stand-by statement   see **contingency statement**

standard advertising layout   design of print advertisements that blend artwork, headline and written message

story idea memo   memo to interest the media in reporting on a person or program, usually involving soft news or feature possibilities; similar to a **query letter**

strategic public   public identified as particularly important to an organization in a particular situation; compare with **audience**

stylebook   listing of preferences for spelling, word usage, punctuation and other elements of writing; adopted by a publication or organization to maintain writing consistency

summary news lead   most common beginning for news releases, providing a succinct overview of the report

survey   formal research technique that provides quantitative information from a sample representative of an organization's public

symbiosis   mutually beneficial relationship, as between public relations writers and journalists

symmetry theory   see **balance theory**

syntax   aspect of grammar that deals with orderly arrangement of words into sentences

temperament theory   modification of **psychological type theory**

textual advertising message   body copy within an advertisement; compare with **visual advertising message**

thesis   see **proposition**

throw-away lead   see **soft lead**

timely   element of newsworthiness stressing the recency of information; see **SILoBaTI + UnFa**

title   approach to article identification in newspapers, magazines and newsletters that focuses on labels rather than summaries; compare with **headline**

tone   part of planning sheet that articulates the ambiance sought for the message

tract   see **brochure**

trade dress   trademark-like protection of distinctive shapes and packaging; compare with **trademark**

trademark   legal designation of ownership of a name, logo, symbol or other identification of a company or product; also called **brand name**; trademark means

materials may not be used without identification of the trademark holder; compare with **service mark**

tune-in lead   see **soft lead**

two-step flow of communication theory observation that the media influence opinion leaders, who in turn influence others through interpersonal means; later extended into the **multistep flow of communication theory**

two-step library resources   materials that direct researchers to information in other sources, such as indexes; compare with **one-step resources**

uncontrolled media   designation of media opportunities such as news releases, interviews and news conferences that do not allow the public relations practitioner to control the message content, tone and distribution;. compare with **controlled media**

underline   see **deckhead**

unusual   aspect of newsworthiness that focuses on unusual or touching information; see **SiLoBaTi + UnFa**

up style   approach to writing style that uses capital letters as much as possible; compare with **down style**

uses-and-gratifications theory   theory that people make active choices in selecting media for particular purposes

value proposition   thesis within a speech or written commentary asserting the worthiness or virtue of something; compare with **factual proposition** and **policy proposition**

video news release   public relations information packaged as a partial or completed broadcast report for television; see **B-roll**

video teleconferencing   method of distributing live or prerecorded television programming from an organization to multiple sites simultaneously

visual advertising message   headline and artwork within an advertisement; compare with **textual advertising message**

visual relationships   creativity technique of forced relationships that elicits ideas through the use of photographs or other visual props

VNR   see **video news release**

warm-up lead   see **soft lead**

WIN (wants, interests and needs)   basis for analyzing strategic publics

work for hire   legal designation of an artistic copyright owned by the organization because it paid a salary or commission to the creator

Index